Frommer's®

San Antonio & Austin

8th Edition

by David Baird

Here's what the critics say about Frommer's:

"Amazingly easy to use. Very portable, very complete."
—BOOKLIST

"Detailed, accurate, and easy-to-read information for all price ranges."
—GLAMOUR MAGAZINE

"Hotel information is close to encyclopedic."
—DES MOINES SUNDAY REGISTER

"Frommer's Guides have a way of giving you a real feel for a place."
—KNIGHT RIDDER NEWSPAPERS

Wiley Publishing, Inc.

ABOUT THE AUTHOR

When not traveling, **David Baird** hangs his hat in Austin. Upon leaving college he took a vow of poverty and has faithfully kept it through a variety of pursuits, including anthropology and travel writing. He's something of a homebody but will occasionally rouse himself for an evening out, always for the selfless purposes of research.

Published by:

WILEY PUBLISHING, INC.

111 River St.
Hoboken, NJ 07030-5774

ISBN: 978-0-470-43789-6

Editor: Christina Summers, with Cate Latting
Production Editor: Jonathan Scott
Cartographer: Roberta Stockwell
Production by Wiley Indianapolis Composition Services

Front cover photo: Mission San Jose exterior, doorway
Back cover photo: Austin's South Congress Avenue (SoCo) landmark, Allens Boots

For information on our other products and services or to obtain technical support, please contact our Customer Care Department within the U.S. at 877/762-2974, outside the U.S. at 317/572-3993 or fax 317/572-4002.

Wiley also publishes its books in a variety of electronic formats. Some content that appears in print may not be available in electronic formats.

Manufactured in the United States of America

5 4 3 2 1

CONTENTS

4 SUGGESTED SAN ANTONIO ITINERARIES 60

5 WHERE TO STAY IN SAN ANTONIO 70

6 WHERE TO DINE IN SAN ANTONIO 91

7 EXPLORING SAN ANTONIO 111

8 SHOPPING IN SAN ANTONIO 139

9 SAN ANTONIO AFTER DARK 150

10 SIDE TRIPS FROM SAN ANTONIO 159

11 SUGGESTED AUSTIN ITINERARIES 169

12 WHERE TO STAY IN AUSTIN 178

13 WHERE TO DINE IN AUSTIN 196

14 EXPLORING AUSTIN 219

15 SHOPPING IN AUSTIN 249

16 AUSTIN AFTER DARK 264

17 SIDE TRIPS FROM AUSTIN 278

18 TOURING THE TEXAS HILL COUNTRY 286

FAST FACTS, TOLL-FREE NUMBERS & WEBSITES 312

INDEX 322

LIST OF MAPS

AN INVITATION TO THE READER

In researching this book, we discovered many wonderful places—hotels, restaurants, shops, and more. We're sure you'll find others. Please tell us about them, so we can share the information with your fellow travelers in upcoming editions. If you were disappointed with a recommendation, we'd love to know that, too. Please write to:

Frommer's San Antonio & Austin, 8th Edition
Wiley Publishing, Inc. • 111 River St. • Hoboken, NJ 07030-5774

AN ADDITIONAL NOTE

Please be advised that travel information is subject to change at any time—and this is especially true of prices. We therefore suggest that you write or call ahead for confirmation when making your travel plans. The authors, editors, and publisher cannot be held responsible for the experiences of readers while traveling. Your safety is important to us, however, so we encourage you to stay alert and be aware of your surroundings. Keep a close eye on cameras, purses, and wallets, all favorite targets of thieves and pickpockets.

Other Great Guides for Your Trip:

Frommer's Texas

Frommer's USA

Frommer's National Parks of the American West

FROMMER'S STAR RATINGS, ICONS & ABBREVIATIONS

Every hotel, restaurant, and attraction listing in this guide has been ranked for quality, value, service, amenities, and special features using a **star-rating system.** In country, state, and regional guides, we also rate towns and regions to help you narrow down your choices and budget your time accordingly. Hotels and restaurants are rated on a scale of zero (recommended) to three stars (exceptional). Attractions, shopping, nightlife, towns, and regions are rated according to the following scale: zero stars (recommended), one star (highly recommended), two stars (very highly recommended), and three stars (must-see).

In addition to the star-rating system, we also use **seven feature icons** that point you to the great deals, in-the-know advice, and unique experiences that separate travelers from tourists. Throughout the book, look for:

Finds	Special finds—those places only insiders know about
Fun Facts	Fun facts—details that make travelers more informed and their trips more fun
Kids	Best bets for kids, and advice for the whole family
Moments	Special moments—those experiences that memories are made of
Overrated	Places or experiences not worth your time or money
Tips	Insider tips—great ways to save time and money
Value	Great values—where to get the best deals

The following **abbreviations** are used for credit cards:

AE	American Express	DISC	Discover	V	Visa
DC	Diners Club	MC	MasterCard		

FROMMERS.COM

Now that you have this guidebook to help you plan a great trip, visit our website at **www.frommers.com** for additional travel information on more than 4,000 destinations. We update features regularly to give you instant access to the most current trip-planning information available. At Frommers.com, you'll find scoops on the best airfares, lodging rates, and car rental bargains. You can even book your travel online through our reliable travel booking partners. Other popular features include:

- Online updates of our most popular guidebooks
- Vacation sweepstakes and contest giveaways
- Newsletters highlighting the hottest travel trends
- Podcasts, interactive maps, and up-to-the-minute events listings
- Opinionated blog entries by Arthur Frommer himself
- Online travel message boards with featured travel discussions

What's New in San Antonio & Austin

Though San Antonio has weathered the economic downturn fairly well, there has been a drop in commercial construction and a halt to new hotel development. In 2008, San Antonio lost its largest corporate citizen when AT&T opted to move its corporate headquarters to Dallas, citing better airline connections. This was a big blow to the city, which had hoped to persuade AT&T to stay with changes it had made to the airport. The economic impact of AT&T's relocation has been partially ameliorated by the construction of a massive data center by the Microsoft Corporation in north San Antonio.

The city continues to lengthen the River Walk in both directions from its center. You can now walk the river all the way to the King William District, which adds greatly to the attraction of staying in a bed-and-breakfast in this neighborhood.

In early 2008, Austin had eight hotel projects planned for downtown, but the banking crisis froze lending, and seven have been postponed or cancelled. One of those projects, a Marriott, caused the demise of a local favorite restaurant, Las Manitas.

Traffic in Austin continues to be a problem, but new road construction and a new light-rail project may alleviate some of the congestion. A new toll road, Hwy. 130, now connects to I-35 north and south of the city, allowing truck traffic from the border to by-pass Austin. In spring of 2009, a commuter train will start running between downtown and the northern suburbs. Meanwhile, ridership on the city's buses has increased despite the fact that fares recently rose from 50¢ to 75¢, with talk that they will go up again in 2010.

More of an impact for Austin visitors are the changes to the 'Dillos—the buses that circulated through the downtown and university campus area and were free of charge. Now there are only two routes: one runs north–south from the Capitol to South Congress, and the other runs east–west along Sixth and Fifth streets. The charge for both is 50¢.

SAN ANTONIO ACCOMMODATIONS The owners of hotel property Radisson Hill Country Resort & Spa have hired Hilton Hotels to takeover the management of the property. It's now been renamed the **Hilton San Antonio Hill Country Hotel & Spa** (© **800/774-1500**). Much will be the same, including the rates, but guest room interiors will undergo a makeover.

AUSTIN ACCOMMODATIONS A remarkable new property, which opened in December 2008, is **Hotel Saint Cecilia** (© **512/852-2400**), with its 14 large, ultra-plush rooms, featuring stereos with turntables (and a large vinyl collection in reception) and hand-made Swedish mattresses. It's located on a large property just off Austin's hip South Congress Avenue.

Lake Austin Spa Resort (© **800/847-5637**) performed quite a coup, winning top honors on *Condé Nast's* list of favorite spa resorts for 2008. It is indeed a beautiful property and is not only a favorite with visitors, but with locals, as well. Also recognized in 2008, luxury hotels The Driskill (© **800/252-9367**), and the Four Seasons.

SAN ANTONIO DINING The well-known chef Andrew Weissman, owner of Le Rêve, opened a small restaurant around the corner from his first restaurant. It's called **Sandbar** (© **210/222-2426**), and it serves the freshest seafood you're going to get anywhere. The restaurant is small and open only for dinner.

San Antonio lost a couple of restaurants in 2008, including a favorite for interior Mexican cuisine called La Calesa.

AUSTIN DINING An iconic Mexican food cafe, **Las Manitas,** and its day-care school were closed in late 2008 to make way for a hotel construction project on the 200 block of Congress Avenue, in Austin's downtown. Public opposition was vociferous but ineffectual. In an ironic twist, shortly after the cafe's closing the hotel project collapsed from lack of financing. There has been no announcement yet by the sisters who owned the restaurant about when they might reopen.

Another well-known cafe, **Mother's Café** (© **512/451-3994**), a vegetarian restaurant in the old Hyde Park neighborhood, has reopened. It suffered heavy fire damage in 2007, from a fire started by a homeless man who was attempting to cook a bit of steak (there's that irony again). It has come back strong, with a more attractive dining area. The food is good, and the dining experience is calmer than in most of Austin's popular eateries.

Another big change to Austin's dining scene is **Cipollina** (© **512/477-5211**), in the Clarksville neighborhood. It has reinvented itself and is no longer the Italian deli that it once was. The owners have brought in a chef who's offering fine dining in a bistro setting that emphasizes local ingredients and great attention to details. The chef likes to do his own butchering and curing. The same great pizzas are still there, with some great additions.

SAN ANTONIO ATTRACTIONS The **Marion Koogler McNay Art Museum,** 6000 N. New Braunfels Ave. (© **210/824-5368**), has just completed an ambitious expansion that nearly doubles its gallery space. The new addition is modern and airy, yet somehow it doesn't detract from this museum's intimate feel. It was designed by French architect Paul Villa and makes use of natural light, filtered and adjusted to match the needs of any particular exhibition, to illuminate the art.

AUSTIN ATTRACTIONS The **Blanton Museum of Art** (© **512/471-7324**) opened a new building that holds a museum cafe and lecture space. The lecture space will allow it to hold more public events to explore diverse aspects of the art world.

But the big news is the fire at the **Governor's Mansion** (© **512/463-5516**), which was deliberately set by unknown delinquents. At the time of the fire, the mansion was closed for remodeling, and the governor and his wife were living elsewhere. It was later established that some of the security measures (the responsibility of the Dept. of Public Safety) were nonfunctional. The fire caused extensive damage to the structure of this magnificent old house, but the furnishings were largely spared because they had been moved off-site for the renovation. So far, authorities have not given a target date for reopening the mansion.

AUSTIN SHOPPING **Tesoros Trading Co.** (© **512/477-7500**), the large and entertaining import store next to Las Manitas, was also forced to move. It relocated to South Austin, at 1500 South Congress, where it now forms part of the engaging restaurant and shopping area that has grown up on this stretch of the avenue.

1

The Best of San Antonio & Austin

Drawing up best-of lists (and reading those of others) has become a favorite pastime in the U.S. these days. Almost every national magazine or Podunk weekly newspaper has its yearly best-of list. Sometimes it's given a little extra dressing up and called "awards." In this game, anybody can play (and the Internet seems to be the favorite playground), so don't let me have all the fun. Make your own lists. There are a lot of things in San Antonio and Austin that lend themselves to such lists: best walks through downtown, best margarita, best puffy taco, best way to work off the aftereffects of too many margaritas and puffy tacos. Make your lists, but let me help with the research.

1 MOST UNFORGETTABLE EXPERIENCES

- **Strolling the Grounds of the Alamo:** In the middle of this bustling city, the grounds of the Alamo (holy grounds, if you consider yourself a Texan) can seem curiously quiet on some days, when the crowds have abated—so quiet you can hear the wind blowing through the oak trees. Perhaps it was that quiet in the moments before the final siege. Perhaps it was that quiet when days earlier William Travis purportedly drew his famous line in the sand. See p. 111.
- **Walking the River in Downtown San Antonio:** The first planned urban green space in Texas, the River Walk, is still the best. Follow the original course of the river as it meanders through this old city, a city that owes to this river its origin, its layout, and, now, even its prosperity. Old bridges, some quite low, span the river at varying angles. Here and there you glimpse between buildings a distant view of something such as an old skyscraper, but mostly it's the feel of an urban canyon, with buildings rising up along both banks. See it both at daytime and at nighttime as you get two different views. See p. 116.
- **Lazing in the Courtyard at the Marion Koogler McNay Art Museum:** As fine as many of the paintings here are, when it comes to transcendent experiences, you can't beat sitting out on the lovely tree-shaded patio of the McNay. See p. 117.
- **Riding a bike through the King William District and Upper Southside:** Riding through this area just south of downtown is a trip through time and across cultures, from the opulent mansions built here by German merchants in the 19th century to the artsy and ethnic Hispanic areas south and east. See chapter 7.
- **Splashing around Barton Springs Pool:** The bracing waters of this natural pool have been drawing Austinites to its banks for more than 100 years. If there's one thing that everyone in town can agree on, it's that there's no better plunge pond on a hot day than this one. See p. 224.
- **Joining the Healthy Hordes on Austin's Hike-and-Bike Trails:** Head over to the shores of Town Lake to see why *Walking* magazine chose Austin as

America's "Most Fit" city. Walkers and runners share the path with cyclists and strollers. You get good vistas of the city and the lake and see quite a bit of local society, too. See p. 245.

- **Sipping a Margarita While Watching the Sun Set over Lake Travis:** Relax at the Oasis on one of the many decks that stretch across a hillside high above Lake Travis, order a large margarita, and begin congratulating yourself on living the high life. Laid out before you are miles of watery landscape. If conditions are right, a soft redness will tint the view and create a warm, fuzzy feeling of oneness with the world. See p. 216.
- **Attending a Taping of Austin City Limits:** This will be a matter of luck, but if you come to town at the right time, and the show that will be taped happens to be music you like, then there's nothing better than getting tickets to be part of the show. And then, sometime later, when the show airs, you can relive the experience. See p. 265.
- **Checking Out Who Is Playing at the Continental Club:** While you're in town, there will be some act playing at the Continental Club that you positively can't miss. It might be a happy hour show; it might be an evening show; it might be somebody you haven't even heard of yet. But take my word for it, with the variety and quality of acts that perform at this famous little club on South Congress Avenue, there's no better place to expand your musical tastes. See p. 272.

2 BEST SPLURGE HOTELS

- **Omni La Mansión del Río** (San Antonio): There's no hotel more San Antonio than this luxurious palace on the River Walk. Graceful buildings and courtyards, balconies overlooking the river amid tall cypress trees, handsome rooms decorated in traditional San Antonio style—La Mansión has it all. See p. 75.
- **The Watermark Hotel & Spa** (San Antonio): Also on the river, this hotel, sister to La Mansión, specializes in pampering with style. A spa takes care of the details. See p. 75.
- **Hyatt Regency Hill Country Resort & Spa** (San Antonio): Visiting San Antonio with the family? Hole up in this place and the kids will forever be in your debt. With tubing and many other outdoor activities on the property and SeaWorld in the neighborhood, there's plenty to keep them busy while you enjoy your own relaxing activities or sneak off to the more urbane pleasures of the city. See p. 88.
- **Hotel Contessa** (San Antonio): With its great location on the river and its bold design, this hotel offers a promising setting for an enjoyable stay. The guest rooms offer comfort and great views of either the River Walk or the skyline. See p. 72.
- **Four Seasons Austin** (Austin): Settle into one of the large guest rooms overlooking the lake, have the front desk schedule a massage at the highly regarded spa, get the concierge to line up dinner reservations at your favorite restaurant, and then pinch yourself to make sure you're not dreaming. The only thing that could make a stay at this hotel any more special would be billing someone else for it. See p. 180.
- **The Driskill** (Austin): This hotel is Austin's jewel. It's got all the history, all the character, and now, all the comfort that you could want. In the original building, where big cattle baron Jesse Driskill still surveys the scene (in stone effigy), you'll find suites with the most character. See p. 180.

- **The Mansion at Judges Hill** (Austin): Splurge and reserve one of the large signature rooms on the second floor of the original mansion. These have access to the sweeping upper porch, which is one of the mansion's best features and a great place to relax and have a cocktail. Lots of amenities and personal service make this place perfect for any kind of visit to Austin, but especially a pleasure trip. See p. 187.
- **Lake Austin Spa Resort** (Austin): This spa resort gets more write-ups by the national press than any other lodging in town. Most of the articles do a good job conveying how relaxing and serene the place is, but not many do justice to its beauty. It's a rare combination of all these things. See p. 193.
- **Hotel Saint Cecilia** (Austin): This new hotel captures a good bit of the feel for what's fun about the South Congress scene but takes the comfort to an entirely new level. Sleep deeply on a handmade Swedish mattress, greet the morning with whatever your favorite crepe is. Lounge on the private deck or patio of your room, or spin some vinyl on your in-room turntable. The only inherent problem with this arrangement is getting the motivation to leave the hotel. See p. 185.

3 BEST MODERATELY PRICED HOTELS

- **Riverwalk Vista** (San Antonio): Lots of character, space, and amenities are what this independent, moderately priced hotel is known for. And the downtown location is central for those wanting to enjoy all the city has to offer. See p. 80.
- **O'Brien Historic Hotel** (San Antonio): Near La Villita and the River Walk, the location is great. Rooms are attractive and contain extras, such as robes and good-quality linens not usually seen at this price level. See p. 80.
- **Beckmann Inn and Carriage House** (San Antonio): Get the full bed-and-breakfast experience in the beautiful Victorian-era neighborhood of the King William District. Built in 1886, in Queen Anne style, the house features a lovely wraparound porch, perfect for enjoying the afternoon in this quiet spot near the San Antonio River. Rooms and common areas are set off with lots of antiques. See p. 81.
- **Bonner Garden** (San Antonio): In an Italianate Villa with a rooftop deck and panoramic views, you can find lovely rooms that steer clear of the cluttered look. You'll also find that rarest of features in a bed-and-breakfast—a large pool. Just north of downtown, the location is central and convenient. See p. 83.
- **Austin Motel** (Austin): In Austin's cool SoCo district is this hip, funky, completely remodeled old motel. The place keeps an air of the past about it, but the rooms have been individually furnished, many with fun and flair. See p. 186.
- **Austin Folk House** (Austin): This bed-and-breakfast, with a great location on the west side of the university campus, offers rooms with plenty of character. Check out the artwork and enjoy some of the uncommon architectural features of this house. You're close to both downtown and the shops and restaurants on or just off of Lamar Boulevard. See p. 187.
- **Habitat Suites** (Austin): Several hotels in Austin take ecoconsciousness beyond the old "we won't wash your towels" option, but no one takes it nearly as far as Habitat Suites. Almost everything here is ecofriendly. It's also guest friendly, with quality linens and amenities, and lots of extras you don't see in other hotels. See p. 188.

- **Holiday Inn Austin Town Lake** (Austin): Okay, it's a freeway hotel, but you're also on the lake. And by the time this book hits the shelves the hotel will have gone through a major remodeling. Get a room facing the lake and you'll have gorgeous views. The location is close to all the central Austin attractions. See p. 184.

4 BEST DINING EXPERIENCES

- **Le Rêve** (San Antonio): Generally acknowledged as the best French food in Texas and one of the top restaurants in the country, this small restaurant on the river offers the ultimate dining experience, where every detail has been thought through. Choose between a three-, four-, or five-course menu or, better still, opt for the tasting menu and have a sampling of several different sensations. See p. 96.
- **Las Canarias** (San Antonio): For a romantic dinner for two, dine either along the River Walk or inside one of the cozy, softly lit dining rooms, accompanied by the soft music of a guitar or piano. Start off with one of the aperitifs, for which the bar has a good reputation. Then move on to a meal that, like San Antonio, represents the melding of unlikely cultural influences. See p. 94.
- **Silo** (San Antonio): This place serves new American cooking exactly the way it should be done—with much art and little fuss. The surroundings are spacious, low-key, and comfortable. And the service is attentive and knowledgeable, but without attitude. See p. 105.
- **Liberty Bar** (San Antonio): This is the place for letting your hair down and enjoying a little local society. There are few other places in San Antonio that so effortlessly reflect the culture of their town, especially in matters of eating and drinking. Periodically, the managements tries to fancy things up, but it meets more than a little resistance from the regulars. See p. 102.
- **Uchi** (Austin): Don't think of Uchi as just a great place for sushi and Japanese cuisine. It's a great restaurant, period, with creative cooking that transcends its humble roots. The setting, in a beautifully revamped 1930s house, is transcendent too. See p. 205.
- **Threadgill's** (Austin): As the locals say about this place, "It's world famous, at least in Austin." What's so famous about it is the honest, old-style cooking that Austinites have been praising for years: the chicken-fried steak with cream gravy, the fried okra, and the ham steak with Jezebel sauce. Local musicians love playing here; the owner is one of the city's biggest supporters of live music. There is no restaurant more Austin than this one. See p. 212.
- **Kreuz Market** (Lockhart): It's a short, pleasant drive to Lockhart and to this pilgrimage site for the barbecue faithful. Kreuz has the best sausage and ribs I've ever tasted. But don't expect to be putting any sauce on your meat. That would be an insult to the cook, and they take these things personally down here. If you positively must have that rich and tangy Texas barbecue sauce, then steer your car toward Black's, also in Lockhart, and held in high esteem by the must-have-sauce crowd. See p. 279.
- **Curra's Grill** (Austin): It's not the decor (or maybe it's the absence of decor) that brings people from all walks of life to this homey eatery in South Austin. It's for Curra's particular style of Mexican cooking that is, for locals, a delicious departure from standard Tex-Mex, without

getting too far away from Tex-Mex's comfort food aspect. Not that the visitor would recognized them, but the place gets a lot of local celebrities. See p. 207.

5 BEST THINGS TO DO FOR (ALMOST) FREE

- **Scouting the Alamo and the River Walk:** How many other cities have freebies as their two major attractions? All the more reason for seeing the Alamo—and for seeing it more than once—until you find just the right moment to savor within its ancient walls. It's hard to say whether the River Walk is better at night or during the day, so see it both ways and make up your own mind. See chapter 7.
- **Visiting San Antonio Missions National Historic Park/Attending Mariachi Mass at San José:** See these as a day trip or break it up into a couple of visits. Now with the hike and bike path completed, you can see them as part of a 12-mile physical and religious exercise. On Sundays at noon, a mass is held by the community of San José to the accompaniment of a mariachi band. Now that's pure San Antonio. See chapter 7.
- **Exposing Yourself to Art at the Blue Star Arts Complex:** Enter this huge warehouse at the south end of San Antonio's downtown area, and you'll find thousands of square feet of studio and gallery space. In the thick of it all is the artist-run Contemporary Arts Center—a fertile home for whatever's new in the local art scene. See chapter 7.
- **Taking Austin's Visitor Center Walking Tour:** These history excursions are provided free by the city and are superb. See chapter 14.
- **Visiting the LBJ Library** (Austin): There's a lot to interest the visitor here, including an animatronic replica of the former President. LBJ was often very quotable, as the exhibits make clear. See chapter 14.
- **Touring Central Market or Whole Foods** (Austin): Those who track this kind of information tell me that these two supermarkets are among the top five most popular attractions in Austin. While you're there, take a break and have lunch or dinner. Dining in grocery stores has become de rigueur in Austin. See chapter 15.
- **Touring the Capitol** (Austin): Definitely take the free tour rather than the self-guided tour. You'll have an easy time remembering you're in Texas; the place is loaded with state icons, and the size—bigger than all other state capitols—says it all. See chapter 14.
- **Enjoying Free Outdoor Concerts** (Austin): There are so many free outdoor concerts in Austin sponsored by both public and private money that you will probably have a chance to catch one. Check the local papers for info. See chapter 16.

6 BEST SAN ANTONIO SHOPPING

- **Buying Day of the Dead Souvenirs in Southtown:** The Day of the Dead (actually 2 days, Nov 1–2) is commemorated throughout the largely Hispanic Southtown, but you can buy T-shirts with dancing skeletons and folk-art tableau typical of the holiday at Tienda Guadalupe year-round. See p. 145.
- **Checking out the Headgear at Paris Hatters:** Even if you're not in the market for a Stetson, you should at least wander over to this San Antonio

institution that has sold hats to everyone from Pope John Paul II and Queen Elizabeth to lesser lights such as TV's Jimmy Smits. See how big your head is compared to those of the stars. See p. 148.

- **Shopping for Handmade Boots at Lucchese:** For the adult male Texan of a certain class, and especially for the San Antonian, getting fitted for Lucchese (pronounced Loo-*kaiz*-ee) boots is a sign that one has made it in the world. For establishment Texas, these boots are a symbol of Texas roots and should be worn both with suits and jeans. See p. 148.
- **Buying "Easy-Life" Potion from a Neighborhood Botanica:** Okay, you might prefer the standard love potion, but for my money, getting the easy-life mojo up and running is far more important. Truth be told, there is a lot more to explore in these places than simple potions. Stores like Papa Jim's are fertile grounds for the amateur urban anthropologist. Check them out. See p. 146.

7 BEST HOUR IN AUSTIN

- **Enjoying a Massage:** With a little planning ahead for that idle hour, you can change the whole complexion of the rest of your day. This is very much a common practice here, and when in Rome (er, Austin) . . . Most independent hotels can arrange an appointment with a massage therapist. See chapter 12.
- **Strolling up South Congress:** You never know what you're going to find when walking along this row of shops, eateries, and galleries. It's the best window shopping in Austin. You'll be hard pressed to keep it to just an hour. See chapter 15.
- **Browsing through Tesoros:** This store is one of a kind, but, as it deals in imports, has nothing in the way of local goods. Still, visitors and locals are fascinated by the variety of crafts and folk art for sale. There's plenty to capture the eye across a wide range of prices. See chapter 15.

8 BEST AUSTIN OUTDOOR ACTIVITIES

- **Feasting the Eyes on the Colorful Gardens at the Lady Bird Johnson Wildflower Center:** Spring is prime viewing time for the flowers, but Austin's mild winters ensure that there will always be bursts of color at Lady Bird Johnson's pet project. See p. 225.
- **Playing in the Water at Lake Travis:** The longest of the seven Highland Lakes, Travis offers the most opportunities for watersports, including jet-skiing, snorkeling, and angling. See p. 233.
- **Going Batty:** From late March through November, thousands of bats emerge in smokelike clouds from under the Congress Avenue Bridge, heading out for dinner. It's an intriguing sight, and you can thank each of the little mammals for keeping the air pest free—a single bat can eat as many as 600 mosquitoes in an hour. See p. 220.
- **Having Coffee at Mozart's:** Picture a deck overlooking Lake Austin. Add to the picture the delights of coffee and baked goods, and perhaps a good book, and you have nature and civilization in perfect balance. See p. 218.

9 BEST PLACES TO HANG WITH AUSTINITES

- **The B Scene at the Blanton Museum:** On the first Friday of every month, local art lovers socialize over wine and finger food at the new Blanton Museum. Music, too, is provided, but not so much that it puts a damper on the conversation. See p. 219.
- **Early Evenings at Scholz Garten:** At Austin's oldest drinking establishment, you can buy a pint of draft beer and claim your spot at one of the large picnic tables that fill the outdoor patio. People show up after work to slow down and enjoy some casual conversation. On Thursday evenings in cool weather, a brass band will play for beer, and they're not bad. See p. 275.
- **First Thursdays in SoCo:** The first Thursday of every month is a lively time on South Congress. Crowds show up to hear the free music, look over the goods at the street stalls, and enter the shops that stay open late for the occasion. You never know who or what will show up, and everyone is in the mood to have a good time. See p. 250.
- **The Broken Spoke:** There are a lot of dance halls in central Texas, but you would be hard pressed to find a better, more fun place to go than this one. You'll see lots of local color and enjoy the easy-going society that Austin is known for. Everybody has a good time. See p. 270.

10 BEST PLUNGES INTO EXCESS

The following is not for everyone. To enjoy these experiences for what they are requires a certain appreciation for irony and absurdity.

- **Best Stereotype Wrapped Up in a Caricature** (San Antonio): A visit to the Buckhorn Saloon and Museum makes you ponder some of the deeper questions, such as "Why don't more museums sell beer?" There are no easy answers. Yes, much is made of the Old West's culture of violence. You can see gunfights enacted and exhibits on blood-thirsty desperadoes. It's all good family fun. But to those who would still cock an eyebrow at this place, I have one thing to say: costumed fleas. They must be seen (barely) to be believed. See p. 121.
- **Best Sensory Overload** (San Antonio): Excess, thy name is mariachi. To set the scene perfectly you need a table by the river, a rather large platter of Tex-Mex food in front of you, a frozen margarita at your right hand, and the aforesaid mariachis, belting out some standard, such as "Guadalajara, no te rajes," with great bravado. They must of course be topped with their large sombreros and one of them plucking the strings of one of those large bass guitars. Lesser mortals might well recoil from the stimulation of so many nerve cell receptors. But you can placidly take it all in, comfortable in the knowledge that you have reached the promised land of travel brochures. Congratulations. Fortunately for you, San Antonio can provide all these ingredients without much effort.
- **Best Way to Take the "Walk" out of River Walk** (San Antonio): Big boats on a small river—there's something very Texas about this, as there is with the boat captain's monologue. See p. 116.
- **Best White Elephant Souvenirs** (San Antonio): Are you in the market for a souvenir with no redeeming aesthetic value? Are you looking for that perfect

something to quiet forever those pesky requests to bring something back from your trips? Souvenir stores can be found scattered throughout the touristy areas of downtown, but there is an especially fertile hunting ground along the west side of Alamo Plaza. Take your pick of such gems as an Alamo ashtray, a beer can wind chime, or a barbed wire candle, just to name a few.

2

San Antonio & Austin in Depth

Though only 80 miles apart and sharing the same climate, soil, and natural resources, San Antonio and Austin grew into very different cities. San Antonio is older, both historically and culturally. It's organized around communities that provide strong social structures. Firstly, there's San Antonio society, some members of which trace their heritage back to the original Canary Islanders who settled here in the early 18th century. Others have family going back to the days of the empresarios of the early 19th century, who contracted with the Mexican government to bring settlers to Texas from the United States. This deeply rooted society is unknown elsewhere in Texas. Dallas and Houston have relatively old families, but money is the main factor in establishing social status.

Strong neighborhood identity is another element of central San Antonio, where many neighborhoods have families that go back for generations. This is especially the case on the south side but is true of neighborhoods on the north and east sides, too. These neighborhoods have forged tight-knit networks of social connections and lend strong neighborhood identities to their members. Information about local happenings gets circulated through these networks without need for a neighborhood list server. Finally, there is the vast military society of active and retired officers. This, too, is a highly structured organization with plenty of communications networks.

With these structures in place, San Antonio has a placid air about it, which masks the city's economic dynamism. It doesn't feel at all like the boom town that it is. Much of the change of the last 20 years has been growth at the city's periphery. At its core San Antonio still feels like a small town. The neighborhoods and communities that make up the city are largely responsible for lending it its equable, unhurried air. Moving through neighborhoods in Central San Antonio, one gets the impression that nothing of much importance has happened since 1960.

Austin produces the opposite impression on the visitor—that nothing of real importance occurred before 1960. There is a fluidity in Austin society and lack of structure. Austinites do not have a strong sense of identity as members of a community within the city. They are primarily Austinites. Longtime residents most often have lived in various parts of the city. The growth of social structures can't keep up with the pace of change, as Austin has completely reinvented itself in the last 50 years. And the effects of this rapid transformation is the object of much lamentation.

Mobility is a key factor in Austin's identity. It's the seat of the state government, so it sees politicians, lobbyists, and functionaries come and go as their careers take them to larger or smaller political stages. Austin is also a university town with a large and mobile student body. And Austin is also a center for the tech industry, which itself is very fluid and has successes and failures at a rapid rate. All of this gives the city a more wide open feel than San Antonio.

SAN ANTONIO

San Antonio, home to the Alamo and the River Walk, has more character than any other big city in Texas. Indeed, it is often lumped together with New Orleans, Boston, and San Francisco as one of America's most distinctive cities. And, if you're looking for a destination for the whole family, you can't go wrong with San Antonio. It has a downtown area that is attractive and comfortable, a couple of large theme parks—SeaWorld and Fiesta Texas—and resorts that cater specifically to families.

There is a richness in San Antonio that goes beyond the images often seen in posters and brochures. Visitors today will encounter a city with a strong sense of community, a city whose downtown shows its age and its respect for the past despite the number of new hotels that have sprouted up in the last 20 years.

The eighth largest city in the United States (its population is approximately 1.2 million), and one of the oldest, is undergoing a metamorphosis. For a good part of the past century, San Antonio was a military town that happened to have a nice river promenade running through its decaying downtown area. Now, with the continuing growth in tourism, San Antonio's number two industry—it has an annual economic impact of approximately $7.2 billion—the city is increasingly perceived by outsiders as a place with a terrific river walk.

Although the city's outlying theme parks and central area attractions are also benefiting from increased visitation, and work continues on the redevelopment of the River Walk for 13 miles from Brackenridge Park to Mission Espada, downtown is by far the most affected section. The city's Henry B. Gonzalez Convention Center doubled in size at the end of the 1990s, and its $187-million expansion was completed in the beginning of the new century. And, as though the Alamodome, the state-of-the-arts sports arena built in the last decade of the 20th century, wasn't high-tech enough for the Spurs, the huge new AT&T Center opened nearby in 2002. But the biggest trend in the last decade or so has been recovering the past: historic became hot. It started a bit earlier, with the renovation of the Majestic Theatre, which was reopened in the late 1980s after many years of neglect. This proved a great success and a point of civic pride, and resulted in the birth of several projects. The Empire Theatre came back in the late 1990s, and several hotels were restored to their former grandeur. And now, every time you turn around, some reclamation project is in the works.

Residential development in the suburbs was, until the bursting of the bubble, running at a fast pace. But construction was not based on speculation, and the city's growth has kept the excess of housing stock to a manageable level. The local economy relies on much more than just tourism and the convention business. In fact, the city's number one industry, healthcare and bioscience, has a total economic impact of at least $12.9 billion, including medical conferences and the many people who travel to San Antonio for medical treatment. Boeing and Lockheed Martin are among the aviation companies that have been attracted to the former Kelly Air Force Base, now KellyUSA. And an $800-million Toyota truck manufacturing plant brought more than 2,000 jobs into the area when it began producing full-size pick-ups in November of 2006. The effects of the economic downturn have also been felt here, but the city has been cushioned by its diversity. Some of that diversity is unraveling. In 2008, AT&T, the giant telecommunications company, announced that it would move its corporate

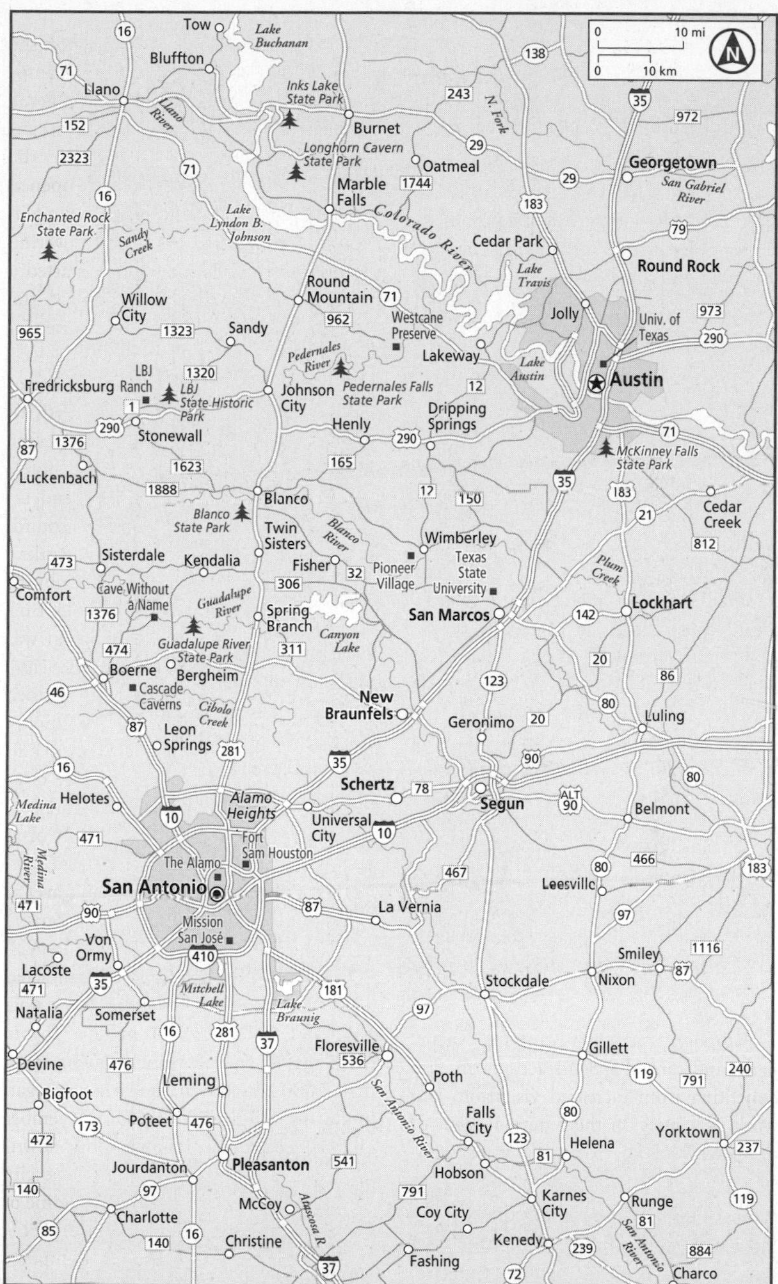
0 10 mi
0 10 km
N
Tow
Lake Buchanan
Bluffton
Llano
Llano River
Inks Lake State Park
Burnet
Longhorn Cavern State Park
Oatmeal
Marble Falls
Georgetown
San Gabriel River
Lake Lyndon B. Johnson
Colorado River
Enchanted Rock State Park
Sandy Creek
Cedar Park
Round Rock
Lake Travis
Round Mountain
Willow City
Jolly
Univ. of Texas
Westcane Preserve
Sandy
Lakeway
Pedernales River
Lake Austin
Austin
LBJ Ranch
LBJ State Historic Park
Fredricksburg
Johnson City
Pedernales Falls State Park
Dripping Springs
Stonewall
Henly
McKinney Falls State Park
Luckenbach
Blanco
Cedar Creek
Blanco State Park
Twin Sisters
Blanco River
Wimberley
Sisterdale
Kendalia
Plum Creek
Fisher
Pioneer Village
Texas State University
Comfort
Cave Without a Name
Guadalupe River
Spring Branch
San Marcos
Lockhart
Canyon Lake
Guadalupe River State Park
Boerne
Bergheim
Cascade Caverns
Cibolo Creek
New Braunfels
Geronimo
Luling
Leon Springs
Schertz
Segun
Belmont
Medina Lake
Helotes
Alamo Heights
Universal City
Fort Sam Houston
Medina River
The Alamo
San Antonio
Leesville
La Vernia
Mission San José
Von Ormy
Lacoste
Smiley
Nixon
Stockdale
Mitchell Lake
Natalia
Somerset
Lake Braunig
Floresville
Gillett
Devine
Poth
San Antonio River
Leming
Bigfoot
Falls City
Yorktown
Poteet
Helena
Jourdanton
Pleasanton
Hobson
Karnes City
Runge
McCoy
Atascosa R.
Coy City
Charlotte
Christine
Kenedy
San Antonio River
Fashing
Charco
N. Fork

Fun Facts **Did You Know?**

- More jars of salsa than ketchup are consumed in the United States today.
- The first military flight by an American took place at Fort Sam Houston in 1910; in 1915, the entire U.S. Air Force—six reconnaissance planes—resided at the fort.
- Barbed wire was first demonstrated in San Antonio's Military Plaza.

headquarters to Dallas, where it could take advantage of Dallas's larger, better-connected airport.

The North American Free Trade Agreement (NAFTA), signed in 1994, has been a boon for the city, which hosts the North American Development Bank—the financial arm of NAFTA—in its downtown International Center. Representatives from the various states of Mexico are housed in the same building as part of the "Casas" program. With its large Hispanic population, regular flights to Mexico City, cultural attractions such as the Latin American wing of the San Antonio Museum of Art, and the Centro Alameda project—the first cornerstone of which, Museo Alameda, opened in 2007—and a history of strong business relations with Mexico, San Antonio is ideally positioned to take advantage of the economic reciprocity between the two nations. And the fact that Meximerica Media, which is starting a chain of Spanish-language newspapers, established its headquarters in San Antonio in 2004 strengthens the city's status as a major center for marketing and media aimed at the U.S. Hispanic population, including some of the country's top Hispanic advertising firms.

Even with its rosy outlook, the city is facing some major problems, ones it shares with other rapidly growing Southwest urban centers. San Antonio and Austin are 80 miles and political light-years apart, but the two cities are growing ever closer. Although they haven't yet melded to form the single, huge metropolis that futurists predict, the increasing suburban sprawl and the growth of New Braunfels and San Marcos, two small cities that lie between San Antonio and Austin, are causing a great deal of congestion on I-35, which connects all four cities.

An even more serious concern is the city's water supply. Currently, the Edwards Aquifer is the city's only source of water, and ominously, no one knows exactly how many years' worth of water it contains. San Antonio is the largest city in the country that is totally dependent on ground water. A proposal is in the works to bring surface water from the lower Colorado River or from neighboring water districts, and these could work to ensure plenty of water for the city's long-term growth.

AUSTIN

In almost anything you read or hear about Austin, you will be told that it is a laid-back city. "Laid-back" has become Austin's defining trait. First-time visitors get here and expect to find a city whose denizens all move about and express themselves in the unhurried manner of Willie Nelson. They must feel a little put upon when they drive into town only to find bearish traffic and pushy drivers and a downtown that is looking uncomfortably similar to Houston or Dallas.

Over the years, Austin has gotten bigger and busier, but it hasn't lost its essential nature. Stay here for a couple of days and you'll feel the laid-back quality you've heard about. Austinites are personable, gracious, and open, and for them the enjoyment of the simple pleasures of life holds a great deal more attraction than the rat race. At times it seems that everyone you meet is either a musician, a massage therapist, or has some other sort of alternative career.

Austinites of all walks of life enjoy the outdoors. Barton Springs is the preferred spot for a swim; the popular hike-and-bike trail that encircles Town Lake is a favorite place for either a leisurely walk or a serious run. The city streets and bike lanes are filled with Austin's many cyclists. Just outside of town are several parks and nature preserves and rivers and lakes that can be enjoyed. Hand in hand with this love of the outdoors is a strong environmental consciousness, which is reflected in the local government. Austin leads the nation in green energy production, has the most aggressive recycling and energy conservation programs in the state, and, though starting late, it has instituted programs to reduce traffic and urban sprawl.

One can't talk about Austin for very long without mentioning the rather large university at its center. The University of Texas feeds the Austin scene. It has brought thousands of bright, young students here, some of which, once they get their degrees, decide that they don't want to leave. They stay and add to a large pool of educated people looking for a livelihood. This has attracted large high-tech companies who seek a large educated work force. Austin has also been fertile grounds for a lot of native start-up companies in all kinds of fields.

During the 1990s, Austin's population increased by 41% (from 465,600 to 656,600). Many of the new residents moved to the suburban west and northwest, but the economic expansion also fueled a resurgence in the older central city.

Downtown projects of the last 15 years include the restoration of the capitol and its grounds; the refurbishing of the State Theatre; the renovation of the Driskill Hotel and the reopening of the Stephen F. Austin Hotel, two grand historic properties. The convention center doubled in size and the Bob Bullock Texas History Center, a major tourist attraction, opened in 2001. And downtown's skyline has been changing, too. In early 2004, both the high-rise Hilton Austin Convention Center Hotel and the chic Art Deco–style Frost Bank Tower, the city's tallest building, were completed.

The downtown area has become popular as residential space, too. It began with a move to convert former warehouses and commercial lofts into residential housing. Then townhouse projects on the edge of downtown picked up, which was then followed by expensive multistory condominium projects. A popular farmers' market has sprouted up Saturday mornings on Republic Square, and, with the flagship store (and corporate headquarters) of the Austin-based Whole Foods Markets at Sixth and Lamar, living downtown is easy and convenient, if not cheap.

Just across the river, South Congress Street (aka SoCo, of course) continues to see the development of a hip retail and restaurant district with one-of-a-kind galleries and boutiques, which stay open late once a month to take part in the First Thursdays block party. The popularity of SoCo has altered the rest of South Austin, sending house prices up and increasing the number of apartments and townhouses under construction.

This boom in real estate sits uneasily on the minds of many Austinites. There's now a gated residential complex right down the street from the famed Continental Club, and, with the rise in rents, many of the struggling musicians who gave Austin's music scene its vitality can no longer afford to live here. Many of Austin's new restaurants are owned by groups of outside investors, and some funky midtown eateries, such as Kerbey Lane, have spun characterless counterparts in the city's soulless northwest. And although the new airport prides itself on its use of local concessionaires, the restaurants and hotels that are springing up alongside the facility are chains. Indeed, locals are sufficiently worried about the city's evolving character that they've spawned a small industry of bumper stickers and T-shirts pleading KEEP AUSTIN WEIRD.

One of the most pressing problems is out-of-control traffic. Streets are filling with cars, and the freeways, especially I-35, are seeing frequent jams and delays. Some of the traffic is created by trucks running from the Mexico border up to Dallas and various points north. Until recently, all this traffic was forced to pass through central Austin for lack of an alternative route. A new toll road (Hwy. 130) has been built to the east of town. It seems to be siphoning off some of the traffic. Officials hope more will follow when another 40-mile segment is completed in 2012.

Another solution to the traffic is a commuter rail service that will run from the northern satellite of Cedar Park to downtown. It was built using an existing railway and entered into service in 2009. It will certainly ease some of the traffic that clogs the northern freeways during rush hour, but how much relief is in question. Plans are currently on the table for an electric street car system to circulate through downtown and connect it to the university, Zilker Park, Austin-Bergstrom airport, and some of the central neighborhoods on the eastside.

The burst in the housing bubble has made for a glut of condos in the downtown market. Several planned developments, including a few hotel/condo towers, have been postponed or cancelled. But the downturn has not stopped the construction of new housing in other areas in the central city. A major mixed-use project at the site of the old inner-city Robert Mueller airport is continuing with construction of single- and multifamily housing, and these units are continuing to sell so far. But most observers predict that pressure on the state government's budget will reduce employment in the public sector and eventually lead to a slow down in demand for all forms of housing.

2 LOOKING BACK

SAN ANTONIO

San Antonio's past is the stuff of legend, the Alamo being but the most famous episode. If it were a movie, the story of the city would be an epic with an improbable plot, encompassing the end of a great empire, the rise of a republic, and the rescue of the river with which the story began.

For most of its history, San Antonio was the largest city in Texas and the "cosmopolitan" center, where multiple cultures came together and coexisted. At the time of the arrival of the Spanish, the land was inhabited by native Indians called Coahuiltecans, who eventually populated the first Franciscan missions. Also settling into the area were 15 families from the Canary Islands, sent there by order of the King of Spain, and a small garrison of soldiers. The settlement prospered. The church eventually built five missions. Later, during the fight for Mexican Independence and then Texan Independence (1821 and 1836, respectively), San Antonio saw several hard-fought battles, including the famous siege of the Alamo. This greatly reduced the population for more than a decade until it began to attract thousands of German settlers fleeing the revolutions in Europe. So many came that, by 1860, German speakers in the city outnumbered both Spanish

Impressions

From all manner of people, business men, consumptive men, curious men, and wealthy men, there came an exhibition of profound affection for San Antonio. It seemed to symbolize for them the poetry of life in Texas.

—Stephen Crane, *Patriot Shrine of Texas*, 1895

or English speakers. Through the following decades, these different immigrant groups would accommodate each other and forge a unique local culture.

Mission San Antonio

At the time of the first mission's founding, the Spanish Empire in America stretched from Texas to Tierra del Fuego. Administering such a vast territory was difficult. Spain divided the continent into viceroyalties. The viceroyalty of New Spain included all of Mexico, Guatemala, and large stretches of the southwestern United States, where it had a minimum presence.

In 1691, an early reconnaissance party passed through what is now San Antonio and found a wooded plain watered by a clear river, called Yanaguana by the native Coahuiltecan Indians. They named it San Antonio de Padua, after the saint's day on which they arrived. The Coahuiltecans, by that time, were suffering the depredations of the Apaches and looked to the Spaniards for protection. They asked to be converted to Christianity and invited the Spanish to establish missions there.

And so it was that in 1718, Mission San Antonio de Valero—later known as the Alamo—was founded. To protect the religious complex from Apache attack, the presidio (fortress) of San Antonio de Béxar went up a few days later. In 1719, a second mission was built nearby, and in 1731, three ill-fated missions in East Texas, which were nearly destroyed by French and Indian attacks, were moved hundreds of miles to the safer banks of the San Antonio River. In March of that same year, the Canary Island settlers arrived and established the village of San Fernando de Béxar close by the garrison.

Thus, within little more than a decade, what is now downtown San Antonio became home to three distinct, though related, settlements: a mission complex, the military garrison designed to protect it, and the civilian town known as Béxar, which was officially renamed San Antonio in 1837. To irrigate their crops, the early settlers were given narrow strips of land stretching back from the river and from the nearby San Pedro Creek, and centuries later, the paths connecting these strips, which followed the winding waterways, were paved and became the city's streets.

Remember the Alamo

As the 18th century wore on, bands of Apache Indians would frequently attack the village, but these attacks killed fewer of the native population than did the diseases brought from Europe, for which the Coahuiltecans had little resistance. By the beginning of the 19th century, the Spanish missions were sorely depopulated. In 1794, Mission San Antonio de Valero was secularized, its farmlands redistributed. In 1810, recognizing the military potential of the thick walls of the complex, the Spanish authorities turned the former mission into a garrison. The men recruited to serve here all hailed from the Mexican town of San José y Santiago del Alamo de Parras. The name of their station was soon shortened to the Alamo (Spanish for "cottonwood tree").

By 1824, all five missions had been secularized and Mexico had gained its independence from Spain. Apache and Comanche roamed the territory freely, and it was next to impossible to persuade more Spaniards to live there. Although the political leaders of Mexico were rightly suspicious of Anglo-American designs on their land, they entered into an agreement with Moses Austin to settle some 300 Anglo-American families in the region to the east of San Antonio. Austin died before he could carry out his plan, and it was left to his son Stephen to bring the settlers into Texas. Shortly afterwards, others (now called empresarios) made similar agreements with the Mexican government.

The Mexicans wanted a buffer between the Indians and their settlements in northern Mexico, but eventually grew nervous about the large numbers of Anglos entering their country from the north. Having already repealed many of the tax breaks they had initially granted the settlers, they now prohibited all further U.S. immigration to the territory. When, in 1835, General Antonio López de Santa Anna abolished Mexico's democratic 1824 constitution, Tejanos (Mexican Texans) and Anglos alike balked at his dictatorship, and a cry rose up for a separate republic.

One of the first battles for Texas independence was fought in San Antonio when the insurgents attacked the garrison there. The battle was intensely fought, much of it door-to-door combat. Eventually Mexican general Martín Perfecto de Cós surrendered on December 9, 1835. Under terms of the surrender, the Mexicans were allowed to leave, as no one had food for so many prisoners.

But the Mexican army, under General Santa Anna, would return in force the next year to retake the Alamo, in a lopsided battle against the Texan forces that would capture the American imagination. The siege lasted from February 23 through March 6, 1836. Some 180 volunteers—among them Davy Crockett and Jim Bowie—serving under the command of William Travis, died in the final attack, defending the Alamo against a force that was 10 times their number. The delay allowed Sam Houston to muster his forces and eventually defeat the Mexican army at San Jacinto with the battle cry "Remember the Alamo!"

After the Fall

Ironically, few Americans came to live in San Antonio during Texas's stint as a republic (1836–45), but settlers came from overseas in droves: By 1850, 5 years after Texas joined the United States, Tejanos (Mexican Texans) and Americans were outnumbered by European, mostly German, immigrants. The Civil War put a temporary halt to the city's growth—in part because Texas joined the Confederacy

SAN ANTONIO: DATELINE

- **1691** On June 13, feast day of St. Anthony of Padua, San Antonio River was discovered and named by the Spanish; governor of Spanish colonial province of Texas makes contact with Coahuiltecan Indians.
- **1718** Mission San Antonio de Valero (later nicknamed the Alamo) founded; presidio San Antonio de Béxar established to protect it and other missions to be built nearby.
- **1720** Mission San José founded.
- **1731** Missions Concepción, San Juan Capistrano, and Espada relocated from East Texas to San Antonio area; 15 Canary Island families, sent by Spain to help populate Texas, establish the first civil settlement in San Antonio.
- **1793–94** The missions are secularized by order of the Spanish crown.
- **1820** Moses Austin petitions Spanish governor in San Antonio for permission to settle Americans in Texas.
- **1821** Mexico wins independence from Spain.
- **1835** Siege of Béxar: first battle in San Antonio for Texas independence from Mexico.

Fun Facts The Lay of the Land

Frederick Law Olmsted's description in his 1853 *A Journey Through Texas* is poetic. San Antonio, he writes, "lies basking on the edge of a vast plain, through which the river winds slowly off beyond where the eye can reach. To the east are gentle slopes toward it; to the north a long gradual sweep upward to the mountain country, which comes down within five or six miles; to the south and west, the open prairies, extending almost level to the coast, a hundred and fifty miles away."

and most of the new settlers were Union sympathizers—but expansion picked up again soon afterward. As elsewhere in the West, the coming of the railroad in 1877 set off a new wave of immigration. Riding hard on its crest, the King William district of the city, a residential suburb named for Kaiser Wilhelm, was developed by prosperous German merchants.

Some of the immigrants set up Southern-style plantations, others opened factories and shops, and more and more who arrived after the Civil War earned their keep by driving cattle. The Spanish had brought Longhorn cattle and *vaqueros* (cowboys) from Mexico into the area, and now Texas cowboys drove herds north on the Chisholm Trail from San Antonio to Kansas City, where they were shipped east. Others moved cattle west, for use as seed stock in the fledgling ranching industry.

Over the years, San Antonio had never abandoned its role as a military stronghold. As early as 1849, the Alamo was designated a quartermaster depot for the U.S. Army, and in 1876 the much larger Fort Sam Houston was built to take over those duties. Apache chief Geronimo was held at the clock tower in the fort's Quadrangle for 40 days in 1886, en route to exile in Florida, and Teddy Roosevelt outfitted his Rough Riders—some of whom he recruited in San Antonio bars—at Fort Sam 12 years later.

As the city marched into the 20th century, Fort Sam Houston continued to expand. In 1910, it witnessed the first military flight by an American, and early aviation stars such as Charles Lindbergh honed their flying skills here. From 1917 to 1941, four Army air bases—Kelly Field, Brooks Field, Randolph Field, and Lackland Army Air Base—shot up, making San Antonio the largest military complex in the United States outside the Washington, D.C., area. Although Kelly was downsized

- **1836** The Alamo falls after 13-day siege by Mexican general Santa Anna; using "Remember the Alamo!" as a rallying cry, Sam Houston defeats Santa Anna at San Jacinto. Republic of Texas established.
- **1845** Texas annexed to the United States.
- **1861** Texas secedes from the Union.
- **1876** Fort Sam Houston established as new quartermaster depot.
- **1877** The railroad arrives in San Antonio, precipitating new waves of immigration.
- **1880s** King William, first residential suburb, begins to be developed by German immigrants.
- **1939–40** Works Project Administration builds River Walk, based on plans drawn up in 1929 by architect Robert H. H. Hugman.
- **1968** HemisFair exposition—River Walk extension, Convention Center, Mansión del Rio, and Hilton Palacio del Rio completed for the occasion, along with Tower of the Americas and other fair structures.
- **1988** Rivercenter Mall opens.

continues

and privatized, the military remains the city's major employer today.

A River Runs Through It

The city continued to grow. In the early 1900s it showcased the first skyscraper in Texas. But San Antonio wasn't growing fast enough to keep up with Houston or Dallas. By the 1920s, it had become Texas's third-largest city and had arrived at a crossroads. Was it to follow Houston and Dallas in their bull-rush towards growth and modernism? Or was it to go its own way, preserving what it thought most valuable? This crossroads took the form of a political dispute over the meandering San Antonio River. In 1921, during a violent storm, the river overflowed its banks and flooded the downtown area, killing 50 people and destroying many businesses. A city commission recommended draining the riverbed and channeling the water through underground culverts to remove the threat of flooding and free up space for more downtown buildings. This outraged many locals. A group of women's clubs formed to save the river and create an urban green space along its banks. (And this was decades before anyone in Texas had ever heard of urban planning.) The women's campaign was multipronged and even included a puppet-show dramatization. They won the battle, and the rest, as they say, is history.

In 1927, Robert H. H. Hugman, an architect who had lived in New Orleans and studied that city's Vieux Carré district, came up with a detailed design for improving the waterway. His proposed River Walk, with shops, restaurants, and entertainment areas buttressed by a series of floodgates, would render the river profitable as well as safe, and also preserve its natural beauty. The Depression intervened, but in 1941, with the help of a federal Works Project Administration (WPA) grant, Hugman's vision became a reality.

Still, for some decades more, the River Walk remained just another pretty space and it was not until the 1968 HemisFair exposition drew record crowds to the rescued waterway that the city really began banking on its banks.

AUSTIN

A vast territory that threw off foreign rule to become an independent nation, Texas has always played a starring role in the romance of the American West. So it's only fitting that Texas's capital should spring, full-blown, from the imagination of a man on a buffalo hunt.

A Capital Dilemma

The man was Mirabeau Buonaparte Lamar, who had earned a reputation for bravery in Texas's struggle for independence from Mexico. In 1838, when our

- **1989** Premier of the newly refurbished Majestic Theatre.
- **1993** Alamodome, huge new sports complex, completed.
- **1995** Southbank and Presidio complexes open on the river.
- **1998** Opening of the Nelson A. Rockefeller Center for Latin American Art, a three-story, $11-million addition to the San Antonio Museum of Art; reopening of the Empire Theatre.
- **1999** San Antonio Spurs outgrow the Alamodome; funding approved for the new SBC Center. Spurs win the NBA championship.
- **2001** Completion of Convention Center expansion.
- **2002** Opening of SBC Center, new home to the Spurs, the rodeo, and more; now called AT&T center.
- **2003** Spurs win the NBA championship.
- **2005** Spurs win the NBA championship again.
- **2006** Large Toyota plant opens. First pick-up truck rolls off the line.
- **2008** AT&T moves corporate headquarters from San Antonio to Dallas.

story begins, Lamar was vice-president of the 2-year-old Republic of Texas, and Sam Houston, the even more renowned hero of the Battle of San Jacinto, was president. Although they shared a strong will, the two men had very different ideas about the future of the republic. Houston tended to look eastward, toward union with the United States, while Lamar saw independence as the first step to establishing an empire that would stretch to the Pacific.

That year, an adventurer named Jacob Harrell set up a camp called Waterloo at the western edge of the frontier. Lying on the northern banks of Texas's Colorado River (not to be confused with the larger waterway up north), it was nestled against a series of gentle hills. Some 100 years earlier, the Franciscans had established a temporary mission here. In the 1820s, Stephen F. Austin, Texas's earliest and greatest land developer, had the area surveyed for the smaller of the two colonies he was to establish on Mexican territory.

But the place had otherwise seen few Anglos before Harrell arrived, though for thousands of years, mainly nomadic Indian tribes, including the Comanches, Lipan Apaches, and Tonkawas, had visited it. Thus, it was to a rather pristine spot that, in the autumn of 1838, Harrell invited his friend Mirabeau Lamar to take part in a shooting expedition. The buffalo hunt proved extremely successful, and when Lamar gazed at the rolling, wooded land surrounding Waterloo, he saw that it was good.

In December of the same year, Lamar became president of the Republic. He ordered the congressional commission that had been charged with the task of selecting a site for a permanent capital, to be named after Stephen F. Austin, to check out Waterloo. Much to the dismay of residents of Houston—home to the temporary capital—who considered Waterloo a dangerous wilderness outpost, the commission recommended Lamar's pet site.

In early 1839, Lamar's friend Edwin Waller was dispatched to plan a city—the only one in the United States besides Washington, D.C., designed to be an independent nation's capital. The first public lots went on sale on August 1, 1839, and by November of that year, Austin was ready to host its first session of Congress.

Austin's position as capital was far from entrenched, however. Attacks on the republic by Mexico in 1842 gave Sam Houston, now president again, sufficient excuse to order the national archives to be relocated out of remote Austin. Resistant Austinites greeted the 26 armed men who came to repossess the historic papers with a cannon. After a struggle, the men returned empty-handed, and Houston abandoned his plan, thus ceding to Austin

AUSTIN: DATELINE

- **1730** Franciscans build a mission at Barton Springs, but abandon it within a year.
- **1836** Texas wins independence from Mexico; Republic of Texas established.
- **1838** Jacob Harrell sets up camp on the Colorado River, calling the settlement Waterloo; Mirabeau B. Lamar succeeds Sam Houston as president of Texas.
- **1839** Congressional commission recommends Waterloo as site for new capital of the republic. Waterloo's name changes to Austin.
- **1842** Sam Houston succeeds Lamar as president, reestablishes Houston as Texas's capital, and orders nation's archives moved there. Austinites resist.
- **1844** Anson Jones succeeds Houston as president and returns capital to Austin.
- **1845** Constitutional convention in Austin approves annexation of Texas by the United States.
- **1850s** Austin undergoes a building boom; construction of the capitol (1853), Governor's Mansion (1856), and General Land Office (1857).
- **1861** Texas votes to secede from the Union (Travis County, which includes Austin, votes against secession).

continues

Impressions

Like the ancient city of Rome, Austin is built upon seven hills, and it is impossible to conceive of a more beautiful and lovely situation.

—George W. Bonnell, Commissioner of Indian Affairs of the Republic of Texas, 1840

the victory in what came to be called the Archive War.

Although Austin won this skirmish, it was losing a larger battle for existence. Houston refused to convene Congress in Austin. By 1843, Austin's population had dropped down to 200 and its buildings lay in disrepair. Help came in the person of Anson Jones, who succeeded to the presidency in 1844. The constitutional convention he called in 1845 not only approved Texas's annexation to the United States, but also named Austin the capital until 1850, when voters of what was now the state of Texas would choose their governmental seat for the next 20 years. In 1850, Austin campaigned hard for the position and won by a landslide.

A Capital Solution

Austin thrived under the protection of the U.S. Army. The first permanent buildings to go up during the 1850s construction boom following statehood included an impressive limestone capitol. Two of the buildings in its complex, the General Land Office and the Governor's Mansion, are still in use today.

The boom was short-lived, however. Although Austin's Travis County voted against secession, Texas decided to join the Confederacy in 1861. By 1865, Union army units—including one led by General George Armstrong Custer—were sent to restore order in a defeated and looted Austin.

But once again Austin rebounded. With the arrival of the railroad in 1871, the city's recovery was secured. The following year Austin won election as state capital.

Still, there were more battles for status to be fought. Back in 1839, the Republic of Texas had declared its intention to build a "university of the first class," and in 1876, a new state constitution mandated its establishment. Through yet another bout of heavy electioneering, Austin won the right to establish the flagship of Texas's higher educational system on its soil. In 1883, the

- **1865** General Custer is among those who come to restore order in Austin during Reconstruction.
- **1871** First rail line to Austin completed.
- **1883** University of Texas opens.
- **1923** Santa Rita No. 1, an oil well on University of Texas land, strikes a gusher.
- **1937** Lyndon Johnson elected U.S. representative from 10th Congressional District, which includes Austin.
- **Late 1930–early 1950s** Six dams built on the Colorado River by the Lower Colorado River Authority, resulting in formation of the Highland Lakes chain.
- **1960s** High-tech firms, including IBM, move to Austin.
- **1972** Willie Nelson moves back to Texas from Nashville; helps spur live-music scene on Sixth Street.
- **1976** PBS's *Austin City Limits* airs for the first time.
- **1980s** Booming real-estate market goes bust, but South by Southwest (SXSW) Music Festival debuts (1987).
- **1993** SXSW adds interactive (tech) and film components to its festival.

classrooms not yet completed, the first 221 members of what is now a student body of more than 50,000 met the eight instructors of the University of Texas.

The university wasn't the only Austin institution without permanent quarters that year. The old limestone capitol had burned in 1881, and a new, much larger home for the legislature was being built. In 1888, after a series of mishaps—the need to construct a railroad branch to transport the donated building materials, among them—the current capitol was completed. The grand red-granite edifice looking down upon the city symbolized Austin's arrival.

Dams, Oil & Microchips

The new capitol notwithstanding, the city was once again in a slump. Although some believed that quality of life would be sacrificed to growth—a view still strongly argued today—most townspeople embraced the idea of harnessing the fast-flowing waters of the Colorado River as the solution to Austin's economic woes. A dam, they thought, would not only provide a cheap source of electricity for residents, but also supply power for irrigation and new factories. Dedicated in 1893, the Austin Dam did indeed fulfill these goals—but only temporarily. The energy source proved to be limited, and when torrential rains pelted the city in April 1900, Austin's dreams came crashing down with its dam.

Another dam, attempted in 1915, was never finished. It wasn't until the late 1930s that a permanent solution to the water power problem was found. The successful plea to President Roosevelt for federal funds on the part of young Lyndon Johnson, the newly elected representative from Austin's 10th Congressional District, was crucial to the construction of six dams along the lower Colorado River. These dams not only afforded Austin and central Texas all the hydroelectric power and drinking water they needed, but also created the seven Highland Lakes—aesthetically appealing and a great source of recreational revenue.

Still, Austin might have remained a backwater capital seat abutting a beautiful lake had it not been for the discovery of oil on University of Texas (UT) land in 1923. The huge amounts of money that subsequently flowed into the Permanent University Fund—worth some $4 billion today—enabled Austin's campus to become truly first-class. While most of the country was cutting back during the Depression, UT went on a building binge and began hiring a faculty as impressive as the new halls in which they were to hold forth.

The indirect effects of the oil bonus reached far beyond College Hill. In 1955,

- **1995** Capitol, including new annex, reopens after massive refurbishing.
- **1997** Completion of the refurbishing of the capitol's grounds and of the Texas State Cemetery.
- **1999** Opening of Austin-Bergstrom International Airport.
- **2000** The Driskill revamp completed, and the Stephen F. Austin Hotel reopens.
- **2001** The Bob Bullock Texas State History Museum opens.
- **2002** The tech recession hits, but Austin's still partying like it's 2000, as the Austin City Limits Music Festival debuts.
- **2003** Samsung announces major 3-year expansion.
- **2004** Debut of Austin's tallest building, the Frost Bank Tower, on Congress Avenue. Austin City Limits celebrates 30 years on-air as the longest running music program in American TV history.
- **2006** The new Blanton Museum of Art is inaugurated with a weekend-long celebration.
- **2008** Completion of Hwy. 130 bypass for Austin, intended to reduce the volume of traffic on I-35, the main transit route between the Mexico–U.S. border and central United States.

UT scientists and engineers founded Tracor, the first of Austin's more than 250 high-tech companies. Lured by the city's natural attractions and its access to a growing bank of young brainpower, many outside companies soon arrived: IBM (1967), Texas Instruments (1968), and Motorola's Semiconductor Products Section (1974). In the 1980s, two huge computer consortiums, MCC and SEMATECH, opted to make Austin their home. And wunderkind Michael Dell, who started out selling computers from his dorm room at UT in 1984 and is now the CEO of the hugely successful Austin-based Dell Computer Corporation, spawned a new breed of local "Dellionaires" by rewarding his employees with company stock.

Willie Nelson's return to Austin from Nashville in 1972 didn't have quite as profound an effect on the economy, but it certainly had one on the city's live-music scene. Hippies and country-and-western fans could now find common ground at the many clubs that began to sprout up along downtown's Sixth Street, which had largely been abandoned. These music venues, combined with the construction that followed in the wake of the city's high-tech success, helped spur a general downtown resurgence.

3 LAY OF THE LAND

San Antonio and Austin lie on the boundary between two distinct geographical regions of Texas: the coastal prairies and the Hill Country. The coastal prairies extend from the Gulf Coast all the way into Central Texas. They are mostly flat, with gentle undulations as they stretch inland. In the descriptions of early settlers this prairie land was metaphorically described as a sea of grass, for its vastness, uniformity, and lack of natural features. When the wind would blow, the metaphor was even more striking, as the tall grass would bend to and fro in waves that rolled across the landscape.

The Hill Country is situated on a large limestone shelf that has been pushed up over 1,000 feet by volcanic uplifting. The entire raised area is known as the Edwards Plateau. And it is the eastern side of this plateau that is labeled the Texas Hill Country, where the warping of the Earth's crust produced the hilly terrain.

The boundary between the coastal prairie and Hill Country is the Balcones Fault, which crosses central Texas in a diagonal line from southwest to northeast, roughly paralleling the interstate highway I-35. In this fault zone the limestone shelf is fractured, and the water pouring off the plateau on its way to the Gulf seeps into the fissures and returns to the surface in the form of natural springs, which are abundant in this region. Water coursing through the limestone has also carved out caverns and formed stalactites and other mineral formations. Most of these caverns are not far from the interstate highway, and can make for enjoyable breaks from driving.

The higher altitude of the Hill Country makes for slightly milder, less humid summer weather. Whereas San Antonio and Austin are roughly 600 feet above sea level, Kerrville and Fredericksburg, the two largest towns of the Hill Country, are at an altitude of more than 1,700 feet. The soil is generally thin and more appropriate for ranching than farming, but certain areas, especially the land around the German farming community of Fredericksburg, are rich enough to sustain intensive agriculture. Indeed, Fredericksburg peaches, harvested from May to July, are famous in Texas for their quality. But the real agricultural boom these days is in grapes for wine-making. Several vineyards are now well established in the Hill Country, and their number increases annually.

4 SAN ANTONIO & AUSTIN IN POPULAR CULTURE

SAN ANTONIO

For a quick and easy look at what Texas is all about, try *All Hat & No Cattle,* a collection of somewhat irreverent observations on Texas fashions, cuisine, music, animals, and the like by humorist Anne Dingus. Before Frederick Law Olmsted became a landscape architect—New York's Central Park is among his famous creations—he was a successful journalist, and his 1853 *A Journey Through Texas* includes a delightful section on his impressions of early San Antonio. William Sidney Porter, better known as O. Henry, had a newspaper office in San Antonio for a while. Two collections of his short stories, *Texas Stories* and *Time to Write,* include a number of pieces set in the city, among them "A Fog in Santone," "The Higher Abdication," "Hygeia at the Solito," "Seats of the Haughty," and "The Missing Chord."

O. Henry wasn't very successful at selling his newspaper *Rolling Stone* (no, not *that* one) in San Antonio during the 1890s, but there's a lively literary scene in town today. Resident writers include Sandra Cisneros, whose powerful, critically acclaimed short stories in *Women Hollering Creek* are often set in the city; and mystery writer Jay Brandon, whose excellent *Loose Among the Lambs* kept San Antonians busy trying to guess the identities of the local figures they (erroneously) thought had been fictionalized therein. Rick Riordan, whose hard-boiled detective novels such as *Tequila Red* and *Southtown* take place in an appropriately seamy San Antonio, is also a resident.

Two Austin writers use San Antonio settings: Novelist Sarah Bird's humorous *The Mommy Club* pokes fun at the yuppies of the King William district, while Stephen Harrigan's *The Gates of the Alamo* is a gripping, fictionalized version of Texas's most famous battle.

AUSTIN

The foibles of the Texas "lege"—along with those of Congress and the rest of Washington—are hilariously pilloried by Molly Ivins, who, until she died in 2007, was Austin's resident scourge. Her syndicated newspaper columns have been published in two collections: *Molly Ivins Can't Say That, Can She?* and *Nothin' But Good Times Ahead.* George W. Bush was a more recent target in Ivins's *Shrub: The Short but Happy Political Life of George W. Bush.* Austinite Lou Dubose and Jan Reid give more insight into the inner workings of Texas (and national) politics with *The Hammer:* Tom DeLay, God, Money, and the Rise of the Republican Congress. Serious history buffs might want to dip into Robert Caro's excellent multivolume biography of Lyndon B. Johnson, the consummate Texas politician, who had a profound effect on the Austin area.

For background into the city's unique music scene, try Jan Reid's *The Improbable Rise of Redneck Rock.* Barry Shank's *Dissonant Identities: The Rock 'n' Roll Scene in Austin, Texas,* does a more scholarly take on the same topic.

William Sydney Porter, better known as O. Henry, published a satirical newspaper in Austin in the late 19th century. Among the many short tales he wrote about the area—collected in *O. Henry's Texas Stories*—are four inspired by his stint as a draftsman in the General Land Office. Set largely in Austin, Billy Lee Brammer's *The Gay Place* is a fictional portrait of a political figure loosely based on LBJ.

Sarah Bird has published a new novel that pokes light fun at what passes for society in Austin. It's called *How Perfect is That.* She uses her insider knowledge and a novelist's eye to explore the values and contradictions of Austin's Terrytown set.

Fun Facts And the Beat Goes On . . .

Both Janis Joplin, who attended the University of Texas for a short time, and Stevie Ray Vaughan, enshrined in a statue overlooking Town Lake, got their starts in Austin clubs in the 1960s. During the 1970s, the area was a hotbed for "outlaw" country singers Willie Nelson, Waylon Jennings, and Jerry Jeff Walker. During the 1980s, there was a national surge of interest in local country-folk artists Lyle Lovett, Eric Taylor, Townes Van Zandt, Darden Smith, Robert Earl Keen, and Nanci Griffith. And the tradition continues with Austin's current musical residents including Grammy Award winners Shawn Colvin and the Dixie Chicks, among others.

The city's most famous resident scribe, the late James Michener, placed his historical epic *Texas* in the frame of a governor's task force operating out of Austin. The city is also the locus of several of Austin resident Mary Willis Walker's mysteries, including *Zero at the Bone* and *All the Dead Lie Down;* it is also the setting for *The Boyfriend School,* a humorous novel by San Antonian Sarah Bird. Shelby Hearon, who attended the University of Texas, lovingly and humorously contrasts old and new Austin in *Ella in Bloom.* Her novel *Armadillo in the Grass* is also set in Austin.

It's only logical that the king of cyberpunk writers, Bruce Sterling, should live in Austin; he gets megabytes of fan mail each week for such books as *Islands in the Net, The Difference Engine* (with William Gibson), and *Holy Fire.* His nonfiction work, *The Hacker Crackdown,* details a failed antihacker raid in Austin. His latest, *Tomorrow Now: Envisioning the Next 50 Years,* moves him from cyberpunk to prognostication. For a unique take on Austin, check out *The Great Psychedelic Armadillo Picnic: A "Walk" in Austin,* a travel guide and music history of the city where the writer grew up, by Kinky Friedman—a mystery writer, musician (his most famous band was Kinky Friedman and the Texas Jewboys), aspiring politician (he ran for governor of Texas in 2006) and all-around curmudgeon.

3

Planning Your Trip to San Antonio & Austin

For additional help in planning your trip and for more on-the-ground resources in San Antonio and Austin, please turn to the "Fast Facts, Toll-Free Numbers & Websites" appendix on p. 312.

1 VISITOR INFORMATION

Phone or fill out an online form on the website of the **Texas Department of Tourism** (© **800/8888-TEX;** www.traveltex.com) to receive the *Texas State Travel Guide,* a glossy book full of information about the state, along with a statewide accommodations booklet and map. The Travel Guide is a good companion when driving through the state. Most of the small towns that you're apt to pass through are described briefly, with some amusing, sometimes intriguing, local color for each.

The **Texas Travel Information Center** has a toll-free number (© **800/452-9292**) to call for the latest on road conditions, special events, and general attractions in the areas you're interested in visiting. Traveler counselors will even advise you on the quickest or most scenic route to your intended destination. *Texas Monthly* magazine, another good source of information, can be accessed at **www.texasmonthly.com**.

In planning your trip, you might want to consult some maps. Of course, the online interactive maps at **MapQuest** (www.mapquest.com) or **Google Maps** (http://maps.google.com) will work for this, and, if you want an actual map of the city to have in hand when you get to town, you can order them online from **Rand McNally** (www.randmcnally.com), which offers a good variety of maps of San Antonio, Austin, and the region.

SAN ANTONIO For a useful pretrip information packet, including a visitors' guide and map, lodging guide, detailed calendar of events, arts brochure, and *SAVE San Antonio* booklet with discount coupons for a number of hotels and attractions, call © **800/252-6609.** You can also get pretrip information, without discount coupons, online at the San Antonio Convention and Visitor's Bureau website, **www.sanantoniovisit.com**.

AUSTIN This is one of the country's most wired cities, and I'm not talking caffeine. If you're not e-oriented, call the **Austin Visitor Center,** 209 E. Sixth St., Austin, TX 78701 (© **866/GO-AUSTIN**), to receive a general information packet in the mail; otherwise, log on to www.austintexas.org. Austin City Connection, the city's municipal site, www.ci.austin.tx.us, is a good source for learning about several aspects of the city, not just the airport, roads, police, and the like; you'd be surprised how many attractions fall under the aegis of the Department of Parks and Recreation. The site also provides several useful links, for example to the University of Texas. To read the entertainment listings and reviews in *The Austin-American Statesman,* the city's mainstream newspaper, log on to www.austin360.com. You'll find the ***Austin Chronicle,*** the city's alternative newspaper, at www.auschron.com.

2 ENTRY REQUIREMENTS

PASSPORTS

New regulations issued by the Department of Homeland Security now require virtually every air traveler entering the U.S. to show a passport. As of January 23, 2007, all persons, including U.S. citizens, traveling by air between the United States and Canada, Mexico, Central and South America, the Caribbean, and Bermuda are required to present a valid passport. As of January 31, 2008, U.S. and Canadian citizens entering the U.S. at land and sea ports of entry from within the western hemisphere will need to present government-issued proof of citizenship, such as a birth certificate, along with a government-issued photo ID, such as a driver's license. A passport is not required for U.S. or Canadian citizens entering by land or sea, but it is highly encouraged to carry one.

For information on how to obtain a passport, go to "**Passports**" in the "**Fast Facts**" appendix (p. 315).

VISAS

The U.S. State Department has a **Visa Waiver Program (VWP)** allowing citizens of the following countries to enter the United States without a visa for stays of up to 90 days: Andorra, Australia, Austria, Belgium, Brunei, Denmark, Finland, France, Germany, Iceland, Ireland, Italy, Japan, Liechtenstein, Luxembourg, Monaco, the Netherlands, New Zealand, Norway, Portugal, San Marino, Singapore, Slovenia, Spain, Sweden, Switzerland, and the United Kingdom. (***Note:*** This list was accurate at press time; for the most up-to-date list of countries in the VWP, consult www.travel.state.gov/visa.). Even though a visa isn't necessary, in an effort to help U.S. officials check travelers against terror watch lists before they arrive at U.S. borders, as of January 12, 2009, visitors from VWP countries must register online before boarding a plane or a boat to the U.S. Travelers will complete an electronic application providing basic personal and travel eligibility information. The Department of Homeland Security recommends filling out the form at least 3 days before traveling. Authorizations will be valid for up to 2 years or until the traveler's passport expires, whichever comes first. Currently, there is no fee for the online application. Canadian citizens may enter the United States without visas; they will need to show passports (if traveling by air) and proof of residence, however. ***Note:*** Any passport issued on or after October 26, 2006, by a VWP country must be an **e-Passport** for VWP travelers to be eligible to enter the U.S. without a visa. Citizens of these nations also need to present a round-trip air or cruise ticket upon arrival. E-Passports contain computer chips capable of storing biometric information, such as the required digital photograph of the holder. (You can identify an e-Passport by the symbol on the bottom center cover of your passport.) If your passport doesn't have this feature, you can still travel without a visa if it is a valid passport issued before October 26, 2005, and includes a machine-readable zone, or between October 26, 2005, and October 25, 2006, and includes a digital photograph. For more information, go to **www.travel.state.gov/visa**.

Citizens of all other countries must have (1) a valid passport that expires at least 6 months later than the scheduled end of their visit to the U.S., and (2) a tourist visa. To obtain a visa, applicants must schedule an appointment with a U.S. consulate or embassy, fill out the application forms (available from www.travel.state.gov/visa), and pay a $131 fee. Wait times can be lengthy, so it's best to initiate the process as soon as possible.

As of January 2004, many international visitors traveling on visas to the United States will be photographed and fingerprinted on arrival at Customs in airports

Cut to the Front of the Airport Security Line as a Registered Traveler

In 2003, the **Transportation Security Administration** (**TSA;** www.tsa.gov) approved a pilot program to help ease the time spent in line for airport security screenings. In exchange for information and a fee, persons can be prescreened as registered travelers, granting them a front-of-the-line position when they fly. The program is run through private firms—the largest and most well-known is Steven Brill's **Clear** (www.flyclear.com), and it works like this: travelers complete an online application providing specific points of personal information, including name, addresses for the previous 5 years, birth date, social security number, driver's license number, and a valid credit card (you're not charged the $99 fee until your application is approved). Print out the completed form and take it, along with proper ID, with you to an "enrollment station" (this can be found in over 20 participating airports and in a growing number of American Express offices around the country, for example). It's at this point where it gets seemingly sci-fi. At the enrollment station, a Clear representative will record your biometrics necessary for clearance; in this case, your fingerprints and your irises will be digitally recorded.

Once your application has been screened against no-fly lists, outstanding warrants, and other security measures, you'll be issued a clear plastic card that holds a chip containing your information. Each time you fly through participating airports (and the numbers are steadily growing), go to the Clear Pass station located next to the standard TSA screening line. Here you'll insert your card into a slot and place your finger on a scanner to read your print—when the information matches up, you're cleared to cut to the front of the security line. You'll still have to follow all the procedures of the day, such as removing your shoes and walking through the X-ray machine, but Clear promises to cut 30 minutes off your wait time at the airport.

On a personal note: Each time I've used my Clear Pass, my travel companions are still waiting to go through security while I'm already sitting down, reading the paper, and sipping my overpriced smoothie. Granted, registered traveler programs are not for the infrequent traveler, but for those of us who fly on a regular basis, it's a perk I'm willing to pay for.

—David A. Lytle

and on cruise ships in a program created by the Department of Homeland Security called **US-VISIT.** Exempt from the extra scrutiny are visitors entering by land or those (mostly in Europe; see p. 316) that don't require a visa for short-term visits. For more information, go to the Homeland Security website at **www.dhs.gov/dhspublic**.

For specifics on how to get a visa, go to **"Visas"** in the **"Fast Facts"** appendix (p. 316).

MEDICAL REQUIREMENTS

Unless you're arriving from an area known to be suffering from an epidemic (particularly cholera or yellow fever), inoculations or vaccinations are not required for entry into the United States.

CUSTOMS

What You Can Bring Into the U.S.

Every visitor more than 21 years of age may bring in, free of duty, the following: (1) 1 liter of wine or hard liquor; (2) 200 cigarettes, 100 cigars (but not from Cuba), or 3 pounds of smoking tobacco; and (3) $100 worth of gifts. These exemptions are offered to travelers who spend at least 72 hours in the United States and who have not claimed them within the preceding 6 months. It is forbidden to bring into the country almost any meat products (including canned, fresh, and dried meat products such as bullions, soup mixes, and so on). Generally, condiments including vinegars, oils, spices, coffee, tea, and some cheeses and baked goods are permitted. Avoid rice products, as rice can often harbor insects. Bringing fruits and vegetables is not advised, though not prohibited. Customs will allow produce depending on where you got it and where you're going after you arrive in the U.S. Foreign tourists may carry in or out up to $10,000 in U.S. or foreign currency with no formalities; larger sums must be declared to U.S. Customs on entering or leaving, which includes filing form CM 4790. For details regarding U.S. Customs and Border Protection, consult your nearest U.S. embassy or consulate, or **U.S. Customs** (www.customs.ustreas.gov).

What You Can Take Home from Texas

U.S. Citizens: For specifics on what you can bring back and the corresponding fees, download the invaluable free pamphlet *Know Before You Go* online at www.cbp.gov. (Click on "Travel," and then click on "Know Before You Go! Online Brochure.") Or contact the U.S. Customs & Border Protection (CBP), 1300 Pennsylvania Ave., NW, Washington, DC 20229 (© **877/287-8667**), and request the pamphlet.

Canadian Citizens: For a clear summary of Canadian rules, write for the booklet *I Declare,* issued by the Canada Border Services Agency (© **800/461-9999** in Canada, or 204/983-3500; www.cbsa-asfc.gc.ca).

U.K. Citizens: For information, contact **HM Customs & Excise** at © **0845/010-9000** (from outside the U.K., 020/8929-0152), or consult their website at **www.hmce.gov.uk**.

Australian Citizens: A helpful brochure available from Australian consulates or Customs offices is *Know Before You Go.* For more information, call the **Australian Customs Service** at © **1300/363-263,** or log on to **www.customs.gov.au**.

New Zealand Citizens: Most questions are answered in a free pamphlet available at New Zealand consulates and Customs offices: *New Zealand Customs Guide for Travellers, Notice no. 4.* For more information, contact **New Zealand Customs,** The Customhouse, 17–21 Whitmore St., Box 2218, Wellington (© **04/473-6099** or 0800/428-786; **www.customs.govt.nz**).

3 WHEN TO GO

Most tourists visit San Antonio and Austin in summer, though it's not the ideal season. The weather is hot, and restaurants and attractions tend to be crowded. That said, there are plenty of places to cool off around town, and hotel rates are slightly lower (conventioneers come in the fall, winter, and spring). Also consider that some of the most popular outdoor attractions, such as SeaWorld and Six Flags Fiesta Texas, either open only in summer or keep far longer opening hours in summer.

In fall and spring, temperatures are comfortable for exploring. If there's a large convention in **San Antonio,** downtown hotels will have high occupancy rates and, consequently, higher prices. ***Tip:*** If you have some flexibility, check hotel rates for different weeks or go online to the San Antonio CVB website (www.visit sanantonio.com) and click on "Meeting Professionals," then go to the calendar. By entering dates you can see the meetings planned for that time period and just how many hotel rooms each meeting is projected to fill. Winter is a slow season for San Antonio hotels, and good deals can be had. December, in particular, is a great time to see San Antonio, if you don't mind running the risk of cold weather (see below). The River Walk is all lit up with lights, and piñatas can be seen everywhere.

San Antonio is the most popular in-state destination for Texans, many of whom come for the weekend. This, too, can raise room rates for hotels on the River Walk, but not necessarily for the pure business hotel, such as those that are downtown, but not on the river, and those just north of downtown, in the vicinity of the airport. Try these options on weekends for discount rates.

Try to avoid coming to **Austin** in March unless you're planning to come to the SXSW Music Festival. This is the busiest month of the year, and rooms are expensive and hard to come by. Summer season is typically busy, and legislative sessions (the first half of odd-numbered years) and University of Texas events (graduation, say, or home football games) can also fill up the town's lodgings.

CLIMATE

From late May through September, expect regular high temperatures and often high humidity.

Fall and spring are prime times to visit; the days are pleasantly warm and, if you come in late March or early April, the wildflowers in the nearby Hill Country will be in glorious bloom. Temperate weather combined with the lively celebrations surrounding Christmas also makes November and December good months to visit. Sometimes a "Norther" wind blows in, dropping daytime temperatures to between 40 and 50 degrees Fahrenheit (4–10 degrees Celsius). January and February can be colder, but not necessarily—it's a matter of luck.

San Antonio/Austin's Average Daytime Temperature (°F & °C) & Monthly Rainfall (Inches)

	Jan	Feb	Mar	Apr	May	June	July	Aug	Sept	Oct	Nov	Dec
Avg. Temp. (°F)	51	55	62	70	76	82	85	85	80	71	60	53
Avg. Temp. (°C)	11	13	17	21	24	28	29	29	27	22	16	12
Rainfall (in.)	1.7	1.9	1.6	2.6	4.2	3.6	1.9	2.5	3.2	3.2	2.1	1.7

SAN ANTONIO CALENDAR OF EVENTS

Please note that the information contained below is always subject to change. For the most up-to-date information on these events, call the number provided, or check with the **Convention and Visitors Bureau** (© **800/447-3372,** ext. 4; www.sanantoniovisit.com).

For an exhaustive list of events beyond those listed here, check http://events.frommers.com, where you'll find a searchable, up-to-the-minute roster of what's happening in cities all over the world.

January

Michelob ULTRA Riverwalk Mud Festival, River Walk. Every year, when the horseshoe bend of the San Antonio River Walk is drained for maintenance purposes, San Antonians cheer themselves up by electing a king and queen to reign over such events as Mud Stunts Day and the Mud Pie Ball (✆ **210/227-4262;** www.thesanantonioriverwalk.com). Mid-January.

February

Stock Show and Rodeo, AT&T Center. In early February, San Antonio hosts more than 2 weeks of rodeo events, livestock judging, country-and-western bands, and carnivals. It's been going (and growing) since 1949 (✆ **210/225-5851;** www.sarodeo.com). Early February.

San Antonio CineFestival, Guadalupe Cultural Arts Center. The nation's oldest and largest Chicano/Latino film festival screens more than 70 films and videos (✆ **210/271-3151;** www.guadalupeculturalarts.org). Mid- to late February.

March

Dyeing O' the River Green Parade. Are leprechauns responsible for turning the San Antonio River into the green River Shannon? Irish dance and music fill the Arneson River Theatre from the afternoon on (✆ **210/227-4262;** www.thesanantonioriverwalk.com). St. Patrick's Day weekend.

April

Starving Artist Show, River Walk and La Villita. Part of the proceeds from the works, sold by nearly 900 local artists, goes to benefit the Little Church of La Villita's program to feed the hungry (✆ **210/226-3593;** www.lavillita.com). First weekend of the month.

Fiesta San Antonio. What started as a modest marking of Texas's independence in 1891 is now a huge event, with an elaborately costumed royal court presiding for 9 or 10 days of revelry: parades, balls, foodfests, sporting events, concerts, and art shows all over town. Call ✆ **877/723-4378** or 210/227-5191 for details on tickets and events, or log on to www.fiesta-sa.org. Late April (always includes Apr 21, San Jacinto Day).

May

Tejano Conjunto Festival, Rosedale Park and Guadalupe Theater. This annual festival, sponsored by the Guadalupe Cultural Arts Center, celebrates the lively and unique blend of Mexican and German music born in south Texas. The best *conjunto* musicians perform at the largest event of its kind in the world. Call ✆ **210/271-3151** for schedules and ticket information, or check the website, www.guadalupeculturalarts.org. Early May.

Return of the Chili Queens, Market Square. An annual tribute to chili, which originated in San Antonio, with music, dancing, crafts demonstrations, and (of course) chili aplenty. Bring the Tums (✆ **210/207-8600;** jessemo@sanantonio.gov). Memorial Day weekend.

June

Texas Folklife Festival, Institute of Texas Cultures. Ethnic foods, dances, crafts demonstrations, and games celebrate the diversity of Texas's heritage (✆ **210/458-2224;** www.texancultures.utsa.edu). Four days in early June. In 2009, June 12 through June 14.

Juneteenth, various venues. The anniversary of the announcement of the Emancipation Proclamation in Texas in 1865 is the occasion for a series of African-American celebrations, including an outdoor jazz concert, gospelfest, parade, picnic, and more. Call the San Antonio Convention and Visitors Bureau for details at ✆ **800/447-3372.** June 19.

Fun Facts **The Fiesta City**

San Antonio's nickname refers to its huge April bash, but it also touches on the city's tendency to party at the drop of a sombrero. It's only natural that a place with strong Southern, Western, and Hispanic roots would know how to have a good time. Elaborately costumed festival queens, wild-and-woolly rodeos, and parades and mariachis are rolled out year-round.

July

Contemporary Art Month, various venues. More than 400 exhibitions at more than 50 venues make this month a contemporary art lover's heaven (especially inside the air-conditioned galleries). To find out what's showing where, call ✆ **210/212-7082** or log on to www.camsanantonio.org.

September

Diez y Seis, various venues. Mexican independence from Spain is feted at several different downtown venues, including La Villita, the Arneson River Theatre, and Guadalupe Plaza. Music and dance, a parade, and a *charreada* (rodeo) are part of the fun (✆ **210/223-3151;** www.agatx.org). Weekend nearest September 16.

Jazz'SAlive, Travis Park. Bands from New Orleans and San Antonio come together for a weekend of hot jazz (✆ **210/212-8423;** www.saparksfoundation.org). Third weekend in September.

October

Oktoberfest, Beethoven Halle and Garten. San Antonio's German roots show at this festival with food, dance, oompah bands, and beer (✆ **210/222-1521;** www.beethovenmaennerchor.com/oktoberfest.htm). Early October.

International Accordion Festival, La Villita. Inaugurated in 2001, this squeezebox fest was such a success that it became an annual event. More than a dozen ensembles play music from around the globe, from Cajun, merengue, zydeco, and conjunto to klezmer, Basque, and Irish music. There are also dancing and workshops for all ages (✆ **210/865-8578;** www.internationalaccordionfestival.org). Mid-October.

November

New World Wine and Food Festival, various venues. Celebrity chefs from around Texas help celebrate San Antonio's culinary roots with everything from tequila tastings and chocolate seminars to cooking classes. It's a taste treat, and it's all for charity (✆ **210/930-3232;** www.newworldwinefood.org). First weekend in November.

Ford Holiday River Parade and Lighting Ceremony. Trees and bridges along the river are illuminated by some 122,000 lights. Celebrities, duded-up locals, and lots of bands participate in this floating river parade, which kicks off the Paseo del Rio Holiday Festival (✆ **210/227-4262;** www.thesanantonioriverwalk.com). Friday following Thanksgiving.

December

Fiestas Navideñas, Market Square. The Mexican market hosts piñata parties, a blessing of the animals, and surprise visits from Pancho Claus (✆ **210/207-8600;** www.sanantonio.gov/sapar). First 3 weekends in December.

La Gran Posada, Milam Park to San Fernando Cathedral. Dating back to the 1800s, when it was staged in the same area, this candlelit procession reenacts Mary and Joseph's search for shelter in a moving rendition of the Christmas story (✆ **210/227-1297;** www.sanantonio.gov/sapar). Third Sunday in December.

AUSTIN CALENDAR OF EVENTS

Many of Austin's festivals capitalize on the city's large community of local musicians and/or on the great outdoors. The major annual events are listed here. See also chapter 16 for information on the various free concerts and other cultural events held every summer. Additional local events may also be found by logging on to www.austintexas.org, www.austin360.com, and www.auschron.com, detailed in this chapter's first section.

For an exhaustive list of events beyond those listed here, check http://events.frommers.com, where you'll find a searchable, up-to-the-minute roster of what's happening in cities all over the world.

JANUARY

Red Eye Regatta, Austin Yacht Club, Lake Travis. The bracing lake air at this keelboat race should help cure what ails you from the night before (✆ **512/266-1336;** www.austinyachtclub.net). New Year's Day.

FEBRUARY

Carnival Brasileiro, Palmer Events Center. Conga lines, elaborate costumes, samba bands, and confetti are all part of this sizzling Carnavale-style event, started in 1975 by homesick Brazilian students at the University of Texas (✆ **512/452-6832;** www.sambaparty.com). First or second Saturday of February.

MARCH

Kite Festival, Zilker Park. Colorful handmade kites fill the sky during this popular annual contest, one of the oldest of its kind in the country (✆ **512/647-7488;** www.zilkerkitefestival.com). First Sunday in March.

South by Southwest (SXSW) Music and Media Conference & Festival, various venues. The Austin Music Awards kick off this huge conference, which organizes hundreds of concerts at more than two dozen city venues. Aspiring music-industry and high-tech professionals sign up months in advance (✆ **512/467-7979;** www.sxsw.com). Usually around third week in March (during University of Texas's spring break).

Star of Texas Fair and Rodeo, Travis County Exposition Center. This 2-week Wild West extravaganza features rodeos, cattle auctions, a youth fair, a parade down Congress Avenue, and lots of live country music (✆ **512/919-3000;** www.staroftexas.org). Mid- to late March.

Jerry Jeff Walker's Birthday Weekend, various locations. Each year, singer/songwriter Walker performs at such venues as the Broken Spoke and the Paramount Theatre; proceeds of related events—perhaps a silent auction or golf tournament—benefit a foundation to establish a music school for at-risk youth. It's a good cause—and the man knows how to throw a party (✆ **512/477-0036;** www.jerryjeff.com). Late March, early April.

Statesman Capitol 10,000, downtown. Texas's largest 10K race winds its way from the state capitol through West Austin, ending up at Town Lake (✆ **512/445-3598;** www.statesman.com/cap10k). Late March, early April.

APRIL

Austin Fine Arts Festival, Republic Square. The major fundraiser for the

Austin Museum of Art, this show features a large juried art show, local musicians, and lots of kids' activities (✆ **512/458-6073;** www.austinfineartsfestival.org). First weekend in April.

Saveur Texas Hill Country Wine and Food Festival, most events at the Four Seasons Hotel. Book a month in advance for the cooking demonstrations, beer, wine, and food tasting, and celebrity chef dinners. For the food fair, just turn up with an appetite (✆ **512/542-WINE;** www.texaswineandfood.org). Third or fourth weekend in April.

Old Settlers Music Festival, Salt Lick BBQ Pavilion. More than two dozen bluegrass bands descend on nearby Driftwood to take part in this Americana roots music fest, which also includes songwriter workshops, arts and crafts booths, and children's entertainment (✆ **512/346-0999,** ext. 3; www.oldsettlersmusicfest.org). Mid- to late April.

May

Old Pecan Street Spring Arts and Crafts Festival, Sixth Street. Eat and shop your way along Austin's restored Victorian main street while bands play in the background (✆ **512/441-9015;** www.roadstarproductions.com). First weekend in May.

Cinco de Mayo Music Festival, Fiesta Gardens and other locations. Norteño, Tejano, and other rousing music, as well as food, arts and crafts, and competitions—for example, a jalapeño-eating contest—are all part of this 4-day family-friendly event to celebrate Latin American culture (✆ **512/867-1999;** www.austin-cincodemayo.com). Around May 5.

O. Henry Museum Pun-Off, O. Henry Museum. One of the "punniest" events around, this annual battle of the wits is for a wordy cause—the upkeep of the O. Henry Museum (✆ **512/472-1903;** www.punpunpun.com). Mid-May.

June

Republic of Texas Biker Rally, Sixth Street and Congress. The city fills with the sound of rolling thunder as hordes of bikers descend on Austin for a weekend of partying. The rally provides an opportunity for enthusiasts to off their rides. Famous custom bike makers from around the country bring their newest creations to be put on display and admired. Sixth Street becomes a giant parking lot of choppers and hogs, each one fancier than the next (www.rotrally.com). Usually the second weekend of the month.

Juneteenth, various venues, mostly in East Austin. The celebration of African-American emancipation, which became a Texas state holiday in 1980, generally includes a parade, gospel singing, and many children's events. The best source of information is the George Washington Carver Museum and Cultural Center (✆ **512/472-4809;** www.ci.austin.tx.us/carver). June 19.

July

Austin Symphony Orchestra, Auditorium Shores. Cannons, fireworks, and of course a rousing rendition of the "1812 Overture" contribute to the fun at this noisy freedom celebration (✆ **888/4-MAESTRO** or 512/476-6064; www.austinsymphony.org). July 4th.

August

***Austin Chronicle* Hot Sauce Festival,** Waterloo Park. The largest hot-sauce contest in the world features more than 300 salsa entries, judged by celebrity chefs and food editors. The bands that play this super party are *muy caliente,* too (✆ **512/454-5766;** www.austinchronicle.com). Last Sunday in August.

SEPTEMBER

Fall Jazz Festival, Zilker Hillside Theater. Zilker Park swings with 2 days of free concerts by top local jazz acts (✆ **512/442-2263**). Second weekend of September.

Diez y Seis, Plaza Saltillo and other sites. Mariachis and folk dancers, conjunto and Tejano music, as well as fajitas, piñatas, and clowns, help celebrate Mexico's independence from Spain. The highlight is the crowning of the Fiestas Patrias Queen (✆ **512/974-2264** for Plaza Saltillo events; **512/476-7502** for other events). Four days usually starting around September 16.

Austin City Limits Music Festival, Zilker Park. Yet more evidence of Austin's devotion to live music, this 3-day music extravaganza kicked off in 2002 and has grown exponentially every year since. Expect a superb lineup of musical talent (✆ **866/GO-AUSTIN** [462-8784]; www.aclfestival.com). Late September.

OCTOBER

Austin Film Festival, Paramount Theatre and other venues. If you like the idea of sitting in the dark and watching 80 films in 8 days—everything from restored classics to new indie releases—or are an aspiring screenwriter or filmmaker, this one's for you (✆ **800/310-FEST** [3378] or 512/478-4795; www.austinfilmfestival.com). Eight days in mid-October.

Texas Book Festival, State Capitol. One of the largest literary events in the Southwest, this 2-day fundraiser for Texas public libraries draws literati from all over the U.S., though Texas authors rule the roost (✆ **512/477-4055;** www.texasbookfestival.org). Late October.

Halloween, Sixth Street. Nearly 100,000 costumed revelers take over 7 blocks of historic Sixth Street (✆ **866/GO-AUSTIN** [462-8784]). October 31.

NOVEMBER

Chuy's Christmas Parade, Congress Avenue. With giant balloons, marching bands, floats, and gifts for needy kids, what better way is there to ring in the season (✆ **888/439-2489;** www.chuysparade.com)? Saturday after Thanksgiving.

DECEMBER

Zilker Park Tree Lighting. The lighting of a magnificent 165-foot tree is followed by the Trail of Lights, a mile-long display of life-size holiday scenes. This being Austin, a 5K run is also involved (✆ **512/974-6700;** www.cityofaustin.org/tol). First Sunday of the month (tree lighting); second Sunday through December 23 (Trail of Lights).

Armadillo Christmas Bazaar, Austin Music Hall. Revel in Tex-Mex food, live music, and a full bar at this high-quality art, craft, and gift show (✆ **512/447-1605;** www.armadillobazaar.com). Begins approximately 2 weeks before Christmas.

4 SAN ANTONIO: GETTING THERE & GETTING AROUND

GETTING TO SAN ANTONIO

By Plane

The **San Antonio International Airport** (airport code SAT; ✆ **210/207-3411;** www.ci.sat.tx.us/aviation) is 7 miles north of downtown. It is compact, well marked, and has two terminals. Among its various amenities are a postal center, ATM, foreign-currency exchange, game room, and well-stocked gift shops. Advantage, Alamo, Avis, Budget, Dollar, Enterprise, Hertz,

National, and Thrifty all have rental car desks at both of the airport terminals.

Arriving at the Airport

IMMIGRATION & CUSTOMS CLEARANCE International visitors arriving by air, no matter what the port of entry, should cultivate patience and resignation before setting foot on U.S. soil. U.S. airports have considerably beefed up security clearances in the years since the terrorist attacks of September 11, and clearing Customs and Immigration can take as long as 2 hours.

Getting into Town from the Airport

Loop 410 and U.S. 281 south intersect just outside the airport. If you're renting a car here (see "By Car," in "Getting Around," later in this chapter), it should take about 15 to 20 minutes to drive downtown via U.S. 281 south.

Most of the hotels within a radius of a mile or two offer **free shuttle service** to and from the airport (be sure to check when you make your reservation). If you're staying downtown, you'll most likely have to pay your own way.

VIA Metropolitan Transit's bus no. 5 is the cheapest ($1.10) way to get downtown. The trip should take from 40 to 50 minutes. You need exact change.

SATRANS (✆ **800/868-7707** or 210/281-9900; www.saairportshuttle.com), with a booth outside each of the terminals, offers shared van service from the airport to the downtown hotels for $18 per person one-way, $32 round-trip. Prices to other destinations vary; call or check the website for specifics. Vans run from about 7am until 1am; phone 24 hours in advance for van pickup from your hotel.

There's a **taxi** queue in front of each terminal. Airport taxis will cost about $30 for downtown destinations.

Long-Haul Flights: How to Stay Comfortable

- Your choice of airline and airplane will definitely affect your leg room. Find more details about U.S. airlines at **www.seatguru.com**. For international airlines, the research firm Skytrax has posted a list of average seat pitches at **www.airlinequality.com**.
- Emergency exit seats and bulkhead seats typically have the most legroom. Emergency exit seats are usually left unassigned until the day of a flight (to ensure that someone able-bodied fills the seats); it's worth checking in online at home (if the airline offers that option) or getting to the ticket counter early to snag one of these spots for a long flight. Many passengers find that bulkhead seating offers more legroom, but keep in mind that bulkhead seats have no storage space on the floor in front of you.
- To have two seats for yourself in a three-seat row, try for an aisle seat in a center section toward the back of coach. If you're traveling with a companion, book an aisle and a window seat. Middle seats are usually booked last, so chances are good you'll end up with three seats to yourselves. And in the event that a third passenger is assigned the middle seat, he or she will probably be more than happy to trade for a window or an aisle.
- To sleep, avoid the last row of any section or the row in front of an emergency exit, as these seats are the least likely to recline. Avoid seats near highly trafficked toilet areas. Avoid seats in the back of many jets—these can be narrower than those in the rest of coach. Or reserve a window seat so you can rest your head and avoid being bumped in the aisle.
- Get up, walk around, and stretch every 60 to 90 minutes to keep your blood flowing. This helps avoid **deep vein**

thrombosis, or "economy-class syndrome." See the box "Avoiding 'Economy-Class Syndrome,'" p. 49.

- Drink water before, during, and after your flight to combat the lack of humidity in airplane cabins. Avoid caffeine and alcohol, which will dehydrate you.

By Car

For listings of the major car-rental agencies in San Antonio, please see the "Fast Facts" appendix (p. 312).

If you're visiting from abroad and plan to rent a car in the United States, keep in mind that foreign driver's licenses are usually recognized in the U.S., but you should get an international one if your home license is not in English.

If you plan to rent a car in the United States, you probably won't need the services of an additional automobile organization. If you're planning to buy or borrow a car, automobile-association membership is recommended. **AAA (American Automobile Association; © 800/222-4357;** www.aaa.com) is the country's largest auto club and supplies its members with maps, insurance, and, most important, emergency road service. The cost of joining runs from $71 to $124 for singles and from $97 to $178 for two members, but if you're a member of a foreign auto club with reciprocal arrangements, you can enjoy free AAA service in America.

San Antonio is fed by four interstates (I-35, I-10, I-37, and I-410), three U.S. highways (U.S. 281, U.S. 90, and U.S. 87), four state highways (Tex. 16, Tex. 211, Tex. 151, and Tex. 1604), and several Farm-to-Market (FM) roads. In San Antonio, I-410 and Highway 1604, which circle the city, are referred to as Loop 410 and Loop 1604. All freeways lead into the central business district; U.S. 281 and Loop 410 are closest to the airport.

San Antonio is 975 miles from Atlanta; 1,979 miles from Boston; 1,187 miles from Chicago; 1,342 miles from Los Angeles; 1,360 miles from Miami; 527 miles from New Orleans; 1,781 miles from New York; 1,724 miles from San Francisco; and 2,149 miles from Seattle. The distance to Dallas is 282 miles, to Houston 199 miles, and to Austin 80 miles.

The most cost-effective, convenient, and comfortable way to travel around the United States is by car. The interstate highway system connects cities and towns all over the country; in addition to these high-speed, limited-access roadways, there's an extensive network of federal, state, and local highways and roads. The Texas state highway system is one of the best in the U.S., as it is funded with oil revenues.

By Train

Amtrak provides service three times a week, going east to Orlando (via Houston, Lafayette, and New Orleans), and west to Los Angeles (via El Paso and Tucson). Trains leave from the depot at 350 Hoefden St. (**© 210/223-3226**). There is also daily service between San Antonio and Chicago via Austin, Dallas, Forth Worth, Little Rock, and St. Louis. Call **© 800/USA-RAIL,** or log on to www.amtrak.com for current fares, schedules, and reservations.

GETTING AROUND

Like other Sunbelt cities, San Antonio has a relatively compact downtown nucleus, encircled by old neighborhoods and commercial areas, which then give way to wide stretches of suburbia. Most visitors will have an easy time finding their way around the downtown area. For the rest of the city, they need only a general understanding of the freeway system and the locations of the major attractions that lie outside the center of town. The rest can be gleaned upon arrival. North of downtown, and not very far away, are the airport, several museums, and many of the best dining spots. To the southeast are the old Spanish missions. SeaWorld is on the far west side, and Six

Flags Fiesta Texas theme park is in the far northwest.

I find that the freeways are laid out in a fairly reasonable pattern, and they're easy to use so long as you have a map. But you can also avoid the freeways by using the main avenues and streets that crisscross the area. A map would be absolutely essential for this, and you should be aware that there are a few large, enclosed areas of town occupied by military installations, which you have to drive around. San Antonio and the military have a long relationship. Among members of the Army and Air Force, San Antonio is often referred to as Military City, and it is a favorite location for retired military personnel.

By Car

Unless you're planning to stay within the confines of San Antonio, having a car is the easiest and most time-saving method of travel.

RENTING San Antonio is a convention town. You need to reserve a rental car ahead of your visit. Nothing really above the usual requirements is necessary. When choosing a rental that fits your budget, don't forget to take taxes into account. In San Antonio the tax for rentals at the airport is 16%, elsewhere in town 11%.

Here's a quick list of the rental agencies in San Antonio: **Advantage** (✆ 800/777-5500; www.advantagerentacar.com), **Alamo** (✆ 800/327-9633; www.alamo.com), **Avis** (✆ 800/331-1212; www.avis.com), **Budget** (✆ 800/527-0700; www.budget.com), **Dollar** (✆ 800/800-4000; www.dollarcar.com), **Enterprise** (✆ 800/325-8007; www.enterprise.com), **Hertz** (✆ 800/654-3131; www.hertz.com), **National** (✆ 800/CAR-RENT; www.nationalcar.com), and **Thrifty** (✆ 800/367-2277; www.thrifty.com) all have desks at both of the airport terminals. **Hertz** is also represented downtown at the Marriott Rivercenter at Bowie and Commerce (✆ 210/225-3676).

Almost all the major car-rental companies have their own discount programs. Your rate will often depend on the organizations to which you belong, the dates of travel, and the length of your stay. Some companies give discounts to AAA members, for example, and some have special deals in conjunction with various airlines or telephone companies. Prices are sometimes reduced on weekends (or midweek). Call as far in advance as possible to book a car, and always ask about specials.

The basic insurance coverage offered by most car-rental companies, known as the **Loss/Damage Waiver (LDW)** or **Collision Damage Waiver (CDW),** can cost as much as $20 per day. It usually covers the full value of the vehicle with no deductible if an outside party causes an accident or other damage to the rental car. You will probably be covered in case of theft as well. If you are at fault in an accident, however, you will be covered for the full replacement value of the car but not for liability. Most rental companies will require a police report in order to process any claims you file, but your private insurer will not be notified of the accident.

The car-rental companies also offer additional liability insurance (if you harm others in an accident), personal accident insurance (if you harm yourself or your passengers), and personal effects insurance (if your luggage is stolen from your car). If you have insurance on your car at home, you are probably covered for most of these "unlikelihoods." If your own insurance doesn't cover rentals, or if you don't have auto insurance, you should consider the additional coverage (keeping in mind that the car-rental companies are liable for certain base amounts).

Check out **Breezenet.com,** which offers domestic car-rental discounts with some of the most competitive rates around. Also worth visiting are **Orbitz.com, Hotwire.com, Travelocity.com,** and **Priceline.com,** all of which offer competitive online car-rental rates. For additional car-rental agencies, see the "Fast Facts, Toll-Free Numbers & Websites" appendix, p. 312.

Most rental agencies will give you a small map of San Antonio that's good only for general orientation. For anything more than that, you'll need to get a city map. Both **Rand McNally** and **Gousha's** maps of San Antonio are reliable; you'll find one or the other at most gas stations, convenience stores, drugstores, bookstores, and newsstands.

San Antonio lies at the southern edge of the Texas Hill Country and is mostly flat. Streets, especially those in the old parts of town, are jumbled, while a number of the thoroughfares leading in and out of town follow old Spanish trails or 19th-century wagon trails.

MAIN ARTERIES & STREETS Most of the major roads in Texas meet in San Antonio, where they form a rough wheel-and-spoke pattern. There are two loops: I-410 circles around the city, coming to within 6 to 7 miles of downtown in the north and east, and as far out as 10 miles in the west and south; and Highway 1604, which forms an even larger circle with a 13-mile radius. The spokes of the wheel are formed by highways I-35, I-10, I-37, U.S. 281, U.S. 90, and U.S. 87. Occasionally two or three highways will merge onto the same freeway, which will then carry the various designations. For example, U.S. 90, U.S. 87, and I-10 converge for a while in an east–west direction just south of downtown, while U.S. 281, I-35, and I-37 run together on a north–south route to the east; I-10, I-35, and U.S. 87 bond for a bit going north–south to the west of downtown.

Among the most major of the minor spokes are Broadway, McCullough, San Pedro, and Blanco, all of which lead north from the city center into the most popular shopping and restaurant areas of town. Fredericksburg goes out to the Medical Center from just northwest of downtown. You may hear locals referring to something as being "in the Loop." That doesn't mean it's privy to insider information, but rather, that it lies within the circumference of I-410. True, this covers a pretty large area, but with the spreading of the city north and west, it's come to mean central.

Downtown is bounded by I-37 to the east, I-35 to the north and west, and U.S. 90 (which merges with I-10) to the south. Within this area, Durango, Commerce, Market, and Houston are the important east–west streets. Alamo on the east side and Santa Rosa (which turns into South Laredo) on the west side are the major north–south streets. ***Note:*** A lot of the north–south streets change names midstream (or, I should say, mid-macadam). That's another reason, besides the confusing one-way streets, to consult a map carefully before attempting to steer your way around downtown.

LOCATING AN ADDRESS Few locals are aware that there's any method to the madness of finding downtown addresses, but in fact directions are based on the layout of the first Spanish settlements—back when the San Fernando cathedral was at the center of town. Market Street is the north–south divider, and Flores separates east from west. Thus, South St. Mary's becomes North St. Mary's when it crosses Market, with addresses starting from zero at Market going in both directions. North of downtown, San Pedro is the east–west dividing line, although not every street sign reflects this fact.

There are few clear-cut rules like this in Loop land, but on its northernmost stretch, Loop 410 divides into east and west at Broadway, and at Bandera Road, it splits into Loop 410 north and south. Keep going far enough south, and I-35 marks yet another boundary between east and west. Knowing this will help you a little in locating an address, and explains why, when you go in a circle around town, you'll notice that the directions marked on overhead signs have suddenly completely shifted.

DRIVING In downtown San Antonio, the pattern of one-way streets is a bit confusing and slow going. It's more enjoyable to park your car and walk or take the bus, which is easy to use in the downtown area.

As for highway driving, pay attention. Because of the many convergences of major freeways in the area—described in the "Main Arteries & Streets" section, above—you can find yourself in an express lane headed somewhere you really don't want to go. Don't let your mind wander; watch signs carefully, and be prepared to make quick lane changes.

Rush hour lasts from about 7:30 to 9am and 4:30 to 6pm Monday through Friday. The crush may not be bad compared with that of Houston or Dallas, but it's getting worse all the time. Because of San Antonio's rapid growth, you can also expect to find major highway construction or repairs going on somewhere in the city at any given time. For more info, log on to the Texas Department of Transportation's website at **www.dot.state.tx.us**.

PARKING San Antonio is one of those rare cities that has plenty of parking, even downtown. Within a few blocks of all sites of interest, you'll find open air parking lots. Most of these work by the hour and the day. There's usually no attendant. You pay at a kiosk (keep on hand plenty of bills of lower denominations and make sure you put your money into the slot that corresponds to your parking space). Rates run from $5 to $10 per day, though the closer you get to the Alamo and the River Walk, the more expensive they become. Prices tend to go up during special events and summer weekends, so a parking lot that ordinarily charges $6 a day is likely to charge $9 or more. Out in suburbia all parking is free and usually plentiful.

By Bus

San Antonio's public transportation system is visitor-friendly and fares are inexpensive. **VIA Metropolitan Transit Service** offers regular bus service for $1.10, with an additional 15¢ charge for transfers. You'll need exact change. Call ✆ **210/362-2020** for transit information, check the website at **www.viainfo.net**, or stop in one of VIA's many service centers, which you can find by checking the website. The most convenient for visitors is the downtown center, 260 E. Houston St. (✆ **210/475-9008**), open Monday to Friday 7am to 6pm, Saturday 9am to 2pm. A helpful bus route is the no. 7, which travels from downtown to the San Antonio Museum of Art, Japanese Tea Garden, San Antonio Zoo, Witte Museum, Brackenridge Park, and the Botanical Garden. It is particularly geared toward tourists. ***Tip:*** During large festivals, such as Fiesta and the Texas Folklife Festival, VIA offers many Park & Ride lots that allow you to leave your car and bus it downtown.

In addition to its bus lines, VIA offers four convenient downtown streetcar routes that cover all the most popular tourist stops and run with great frequency. Designed to look like the turn-of-the-century trolleys used in San Antonio until 1933, the streetcars cost the same as buses (exact change required; drivers carry none). The trolleys, which have signs color-coded by route, display their destinations.

If you're planning to spend most of the day exploring downtown and other parts of the city, your best option is to buy a day pass for $4. You can by them at the service centers, such as the one mentioned above.

By Taxi

Cabs are available outside the airport, near the Greyhound and Amtrak terminals (only when a train is due, however), and at most major downtown hotels, but they're next to impossible to hail on the street; most of the time, you'll need to phone for one in advance. The best of the taxi companies in town (and also the largest, as it represents the consolidation of two of the majors) is **Yellow-Checker Cab** (✆ **210/222-2222**), which has an excellent record of turning up when promised. The base charge on a taxi is $2; add $2.15 for each mile (plus a fuel charge if gasoline is over $3 per gallon).

On Foot

Downtown San Antonio is a treat for walkers, who can perambulate from one tourist attraction to another or stroll along a beautifully landscaped river. Traffic lights even have buttons to push to make sure the lights stay green long enough for pedestrians to cross without putting their lives in peril. Jaywalking is a ticketable offense, but it's rarely enforced.

5 AUSTIN: GETTING THERE & GETTING AROUND

GETTING TO AUSTIN

By Plane

Austin-Bergstrom International Airport (✆ **512/530-ABIA;** airport code **AUS**) opened in 1999 on the site of the former Bergstrom Air Force Base, just off Highway 71 (Ben White Blvd.) and only 8 miles southwest of the capitol. For more information about the airport, go to www.ci.austin.tx.us/austinairport.

THE MAJOR AIRLINES **America West** (✆ 800/235-9292; www.americawest.com), **American** (✆ 800/433-7300; www.aa.com), **Continental** (✆ 800/525-0280; www.continental.com), **Delta** (✆ 800/221-1212; www.delta.com), **Frontier** (✆ 800/432-1359; www.frontierairlines.com), **JetBlue** (✆ 800/538-2583; www.jetblue.com), **Northwest** (✆ 800/225-2525; www.nwa.com), **Southwest** (✆ 800/435-9792; www.southwest.com), and **United** (✆ 800/241-6522; www.united.com) all fly into Austin. There are currently nonstop flights from the following U.S. cities (outside of Texas): Atlanta; Baltimore; Chicago; Cincinnati; Cleveland; Denver; Detroit; Las Vegas; Los Angeles; Memphis; Minneapolis/St. Paul; Nashville; New York; Orlando; Phoenix; Raleigh-Durham; St. Louis; San Diego; San Francisco; Tampa; and Washington, D.C.

FINDING THE BEST AIRFARE All the airlines run seasonal specials that can lower fares considerably. If your dates of travel don't coincide with these promotions, however, the least expensive way to travel is to purchase tickets 21 days in advance, stay over Saturday night, and travel during the week.

Arriving at the Airport

IMMIGRATION & CUSTOMS CLEARANCE International visitors arriving by air, no matter what the port of entry, should cultivate patience and resignation before setting foot on U.S. soil. U.S. airports have considerably beefed up security clearances in the years since the terrorist attacks of September 11, and clearing Customs and Immigration can take as long as 2 hours.

Getting into Town from the Airport

Taxis from the major companies in town usually form a line outside the terminal, though occasionally you won't find any waiting. To ensure off-hour pickup in advance, phone **American Yellow Checker Cab** (✆ **512/452-9999**) before you leave home. The ride between the airport and downtown costs around $25.

If you're not in a huge rush to get to your hotel, **SuperShuttle** (✆ **800/BLUE-VAN** [258-3826] or 512/258-3826; www.supershuttle.com) is a less expensive alternative to cabs, offering comfortable minivan service to hotels and residences. Prices range from $12 one-way ($22 round-trip), for trips to a downtown hotel, to $14 ($24 round-trip), for trips to a central hotel, to $18 ($26 round-trip) for trips to a hotel in the northwestern part of town. The drawback is that you often must share your ride with several others, who may be dropped off first. You don't have to book in advance for pickups at the airport, but you do need to phone 24 hours ahead of time to arrange for a pickup when you're leaving town.

For 75¢, you can go from the airport to downtown or the university area on a city bus called the **Airport Flyer** (Rte. 100). It runs until about midnight. The passenger pickup is outside the arrival gates, close to the end of the concourse. Busses depart about every 40 minutes. You can grab a route schedule from the city's visitor information office, by the baggage carrousels. Or you can download it from the website **Capital Metro Transit** (✆ **512/474-1200** or TTY 512/385-5872; www.capmetro.org). It's also available ABIA's website (http://www.ci.austin.tx.us/austinairport), just click on "Ground Transportation." See also the "By Bus" section, below, and "By Public Transportation" in "Getting Around," later in this chapter, for additional information.

Most of the major car-rental companies—Advantage, Alamo, Avis, Budget, Dollar, Hertz, National, and Thrifty—have outlets at the airport; see "Car Rentals" in the "Getting Around" section, later in this chapter, for details. The trip from the airport to downtown by car or taxi takes about 20 minutes, much more if you're headed to north Austin. During rush hour, there are often backups all along Highway 71. Be sure to allow extra time when you need to catch a flight.

By Car

I-35 is the north–south approach to Austin; it intersects with **Highway 290,** a major east–west thoroughfare, and **Highway 183,** which also runs roughly north–south through town. If you're staying on the west side of Austin, hook up with **Loop 1,** almost always called Mo-Pac by locals.

Stay on I-35 north and you'll get to Dallas/Fort Worth in about 3 to 4 hours. Highway 290 leads east to Houston, approximately 2½ hours away, and west, via a scenic Hill Country route, to I-10, the main east–west thoroughfare. I-10 can also be picked up by heading south to San Antonio, some 80 miles away, on I-35.

For listings of the major car-rental agencies in Austin, please see the "Fast Facts" appendix (p. 320).

By Train

To get to points east or west of Austin on the Sunset Limited by **Amtrak,** 250 N. Lamar Blvd. (✆ **800/872-7245** or 512/476-5684; www.amtrak.com), you'll have to pass through San Antonio (see "By Train," earlier in this chapter). Trains depart from Austin to San Antonio nightly. The Texas Eagle runs from Austin to Chicago daily.

By Bus

You'll also be going through San Antonio if you're traveling east or west to Austin via **Greyhound,** 916 E. Koenig Lane (✆ **800/231-2222** or 512/458-4463; www.greyhound.com). There are approximately seven buses between the two cities each day, with one-way fares running around $15.

GETTING AROUND

In 1839, Austin was laid out in a grid on the northern shore of the Colorado River, bounded by Shoal Creek to the west and Waller Creek to the east. The section of the river abutting the original settlement is now known as Town Lake, and the city has spread far beyond its original borders in all directions. The land to the east is flat Texas prairie; the rolling Hill Country begins on the west side of town.

MAIN ARTERIES & STREETS I-35, forming the border between central and east Austin (and straddling the Balcones Fault Line), is the main north–south thoroughfare; Loop 1, usually called Mo-Pac (it follows the course of the Missouri-Pacific railroad, although some people like to say it got its name because it's "mo' packed"), is the westside equivalent. Highway 290, running east–west, merges with I-35 where it comes in on the north side of town, briefly reestablishing its separate identity on the south side of town before merging with Highway 71 (which is called Ben White Blvd. btw. 183 and Lamar Blvd.). Highway 290 and Highway 71 split up again in Oak Hill, on the west side of town. Not confused enough yet? Highway 2222 changes its name from Koenig to Northland and, west of Loop 360, to Bullcreek, while, in the north, Highway 183 is called Research Boulevard. (Looking at a map should make all this clear as mud.) Important north–south city streets include Lamar, Guadalupe, and Burnet. If you want to get across town north of the river, use Cesar Chavez (once known as First St.), 15th Street (which turns into Enfield west of Lamar), Martin Luther King, Jr. Boulevard (the equivalent of 19th St., and often just called MLK), 38th Street, or 45th Street.

FINDING AN ADDRESS Congress Avenue was the earliest dividing line between east and west, while the Colorado River marked the north and south border of the city. Addresses were designed to move in increments of 100 per block, so that 1500 N. Guadalupe, say, would be 15 blocks north of the river. This system still works reasonably well in the older sections of town, but breaks down where the neat street grid does (look at a street map to see where the right angles end). All the east–west streets were originally named after trees native to the city (for example, Sixth St. was once Pecan St.); most that run north and south, such as San Jacinto, Lavaca, and Guadalupe, retain their original Texas river monikers.

STREET MAPS The maps available for no cost at the Austin Convention and Visitors Bureau, as well as at many car-rental companies at the airport, should help you locate major landmarks. For more detail, you can buy street maps at convenience stores, pharmacies, and bookstores.

By Car

With its lack of traffic planning, driving in Austin is a bit of a challenge for visitors. Don't fall into a driver's daze anywhere in town; you need to be as vigilant on the city streets as you are on highways. The former are rife with signs that suddenly insist LEFT LANE MUST TURN LEFT or RIGHT LANE MUST TURN RIGHT—generally positioned so they're noticeable only when it's too late to switch. A number of major downtown streets are one-way; many don't have street signs or have signs so covered with foliage they're impossible to read. Driving is particularly confusing in the university area, where streets like "32½" suddenly turn up. Multiply the difficulties at night, when you need X-ray vision to read the ill-lit street indicators.

The highways are no more pleasant. I-35—nicknamed "the NAFTA highway" because of the big rigs speeding up from Mexico—is mined with tricky on-and-off ramps and, around downtown, a confusing complex of upper and lower levels; it's easy to miss your exit or find yourself exiting when you don't want to. The rapidly developing area to the northwest, where Highway 183 connects I-35 with Mo-Pac and the Capital of Texas Highway, requires particular vigilance, as the connections occur very rapidly. There are regular lane mergers and sudden, precipitous turnoffs.

Nervous? Good. Better you're a bit edgy than lost or injured. Consult maps in advance and, when driving around the university or downtown, try to gauge the number of blocks before turns so you won't have to be completely dependent on street signs. You can also check the Texas Department of Transportation's (TxDOT) website, www.dot.state.tx.us, for the latest information on road conditions, including highway diversions, construction, and closures.

CAR RENTALS If you're planning to travel at a popular time, it's a good idea to book as far in advance as you can, both to secure the quoted rates and to ensure that you get a car.

Advantage (© 800/777-5500; www.arac.com), **Alamo** (© 800/327-9633; www.alamo.com), **Avis** (© 800/831-2847; www.avis.com), **Budget** (© 800/527-0700; www.budget.com), **Dollar** (© 800/800-4000; www.dollarcar.com), **Hertz** (© 800/654-3131; www.hertz.com), **National** (© 800/227-7368; www.nationalcar.com), and **Thrifty** (© 800/367-2277; www.thrifty.com) all have representatives at the Austin airport.

Lower prices are usually available for those who are flexible about dates of travel or who are members of frequent-flyer or frequent-hotel-stay programs or of organizations such as AAA or AARP. Car-rental companies are eager to get your business, so they're as likely as not to ask whether you belong to any group that will snag you a discount, but if the clerk doesn't inquire, it can't hurt to mention every travel-related program you're a member of—you'd be surprised at the bargains you might turn up.

Try checking out **Breezenet.com,** which offers domestic car-rental discounts with some of the most competitive rates around. Also worth visiting are **Orbitz.com, Hotwire.com, Travelocity.com,** and **Priceline.com,** all of which offer competitive online car-rental rates. For additional car-rental agencies, see the "Toll-Free Numbers & Websites Appendix," p. 319.

PARKING Unless you have congressional plates, you're likely to find the selection of parking spots downtown extremely limited during the week (construction isn't making the situation any better); as a result, lots of downtown restaurants offer valet parking (with hourly rates ranging $4–$6). There are a number of lots around the area, costing anywhere from $5 to $7 per hour, but the most convenient ones tend to fill up quickly. If you're lucky enough to find a metered spot, it'll run you 75¢ per hour, with a 2-hour limit, so bring change. Although there's virtually no street parking available near the capitol before 5pm during the week, there is a free visitor garage on 15th and San Jacinto (2-hr. time limit).

In the university area, trying to find a spot near the shopping strip known as "the Drag" can be just that. However, cruise the side streets and you're eventually bound to find a pay lot that's not filled. The two most convenient on-campus parking garages are located near San Jacinto and East 26th streets and off 25th Street between San Antonio and Nueces. There's also a (free!) parking lot near the LBJ Library, but it's far from the central campus. Log on to **www.utexas.edu/parking** for additional places to drop off your car.

DRIVING RULES Unless indicated, right turns are permitted on red after coming to a full stop. Seat belts and child-restraint seats are mandatory in Texas (http://www.txdps.state.tx.us/director_staff/public_information/carseat.htm).

By Bus

Austin's public transportation system, **Capital Metropolitan Transportation Authority** (www.capmetro.org), operates more than 50 bus lines and features low fares. New fares were established in late 2008. A single fare on a Cap Metro bus is 75¢. A day pass costs $1.50; an express day pass to/from various Park & Ride lots costs $3. (Though nothing definite has been stated, it looks like fares will rise again in early 2010: $1 for single fares, $2 for a day pass.) You'll need exact change or fare tickets to board the bus. Day passes are a good option because they're more flexible. It costs the same as a roundtrip and allows you to ride as many buses or 'Dillos (see below) as you want for that day. Tell the bus driver you're buying a day pass before you insert your money in the machine.

Call © **800/474-1201** or 512/474-1200 from local phones for point-to-point routing information. You can also pick up a schedule booklet at any H-E-B, Fiesta, or Albertsons grocery store; at stores and hotels throughout the downtown area; or at the Cap Metro Transit Store, 323 Congress Ave., first floor.

When moving around downtown and the South Congress area, you can make use of the handy "'Dillo" routes. (This is short for armadillo, which was a symbol of Austin weirdness in the 1970s, before being appropriated by mainstream culture.) These are the buses that look like trolley cars, which are seen in several other cities. Until late 2008, they were free of charge but now cost 50¢ for a 2-hour pass (no charge with a day pass). The routes were reduced to two. One moves north and south along Congress Avenue from the state capitol across the bridge to Riverside Drive, at the beginning of SoCo district. The other circulates along Sixth Street (west) and Fifth Street (east) for several blocks on either side of Congress Avenue. They run at a frequency of every 5 to 10 minutes, depending on the time of day. They stop running around 6 or 7pm.

By Train

In spring of 2009, Cap Metro began light rail service between downtown and the bedroom communities in the north. This was a relatively inexpensive way to introduce light rail to the city by using existing train track. The downside is that the train doesn't follow the preferred routes. This will be of interest to Austin visitors only if they are staying in hotels in north central Austin. The train will travel 32 miles, from downtown Austin to the town of Leander. Along the way it will stop in seven stations. The first two are in east Austin, far from any attractions or hotels. The third station is close to Highland Mall and a couple of hotels in that area. It would be the only station of interest to visitors. On its way north, the train will not pass by the Arboretum or any center for shops, hotels, or restaurants. This is just the beginning. Future plans are to open a line that will do more to connect central and east Austin.

6 MONEY & COSTS

The disparity between prices inside and outside the tourism zones is greater in **San Antonio** than in other U.S. cities. Prices for goods and services are noticeably higher in areas around the River Walk, the theme parks, and other attractions. In the city's neighborhoods and in parts of the downtown not visited by tourists, you can find cheap *taquerías* and other restaurants, discount stores, and so on. The average San Antonio salary is not terribly high, and the cost of living is about 10% lower than the country's average, and much lower than in cities such as New York and Los Angeles.

Prices in **Austin** are roughly the same as for the largest Texas cities. Restaurants tend to be a little cheaper than those of Houston and Dallas, and roughly on a par with those of San Antonio. Rents, on the other hand, are higher. (So are property values.) This isn't good for people, like students in this university town, but that hasn't stopped young people from coming here anyway to study and work in some of the low-wage service-industry jobs to cover

What Things Cost in San Antonio	US$
Taxi from the airport to the city center	30.00
Streetcar ride between any two downtown points	1.10
Local telephone call	0.50
Long-neck beer	4.00
Double at Westin Riverwalk Inn (very expensive)	360.00
Double at Drury Inn & Suites Riverwalk (moderate)	150.00
Double at Best Western Sunset Suites (inexpensive)	135.00
Lunch for one at Rosario's (moderate)	12.00
Lunch for one at Twin Sisters (inexpensive)	7.00
Dinner for one, without wine, at Las Canarias (very expensive)	60.00
Dinner for one, without beer, at La Fonda on Main (moderate)	16.00
Dinner for one, without beer, at Schilo's (inexpensive)	10.00
Adult admission to the Witte Museum	7.00
Ticket to the San Antonio Symphony	20.00–80.00
Ticket to a Spurs game	50.00–100.00

the extra expense. Of course, the real bargains are in the nightlife and live music venues. I don't know of another city where going to hear music is this economical.

If you compare the cost of living in Austin to that of California or New York, you'll see why there's been such a large influx of people from both these places in recent years. Long-time locals do a little good-natured grousing about the run-up in real estate prices, but it stops there.

ATMS

Credit cards are accepted nearly universally and automated teller machines (ATMs) linked to national networks are strewn around tourist destinations and, increasingly, within hotels. **Cirrus** (✆ **800/424-7787;** www.mastercard.com) and **PLUS** (✆ **800/843-7587;** www.visa.com) are the two most popular networks. Call or check online for ATM locations in San Antonio.

Be sure you know your personal identification number (PIN) and daily withdrawal limit before you depart. ***Note:*** Remember that many banks impose a fee every time you use a card at another bank's ATM, and that fee can be higher for international transactions (up to $5 or more) than for domestic ones (where they're rarely more than $2). In addition, the bank from which you withdraw cash may charge its own fee. To compare banks' ATM fees within the U.S., use **www.bankrate.com**. For international withdrawal fees, ask your bank.

CREDIT CARDS & DEBIT CARDS

Credit cards are the most widely used form of payment in the United States: **Visa** (Barclaycard in Britain), **MasterCard** (EuroCard in Europe, Access in Britain, Chargex in Canada), **American Express, Diners Club,** and **Discover.** They also provide a convenient record of all your expenses, and they generally offer relatively good exchange rates. You can withdraw cash advances from your credit cards at banks or ATMs, provided you know your PIN.

What Things Cost in Austin	US$
Taxi from the airport to downtown	20.00
Double at the Four Seasons (very expensive)	380.00
Double at the Holiday Inn Austin Town Lake (moderate)	159.00
Double at the Austin Motel (inexpensive)	90.00
Lunch for one at the Roaring Fork (expensive)	17.00
Lunch for one at Shady Grove (inexpensive)	8.00
Dinner for one, without drinks, at Jeffrey's (very expensive)	72.00
Dinner for one, without drinks, at Vivo (moderate)	18.00
Dinner for one, without drinks, at The Iron Works (inexpensive)	9.00
Soft drink at restaurant	1.50
Cup of espresso	3.50
Admission to Texas State History Museum	5.00
Roll of ASA 100 Kodacolor film, 36 exposures	7.50
Movie ticket	9.00
Austin Symphony ticket	30.00

Visitors from outside the U.S. should inquire whether their bank assesses a 1% to 3% fee on charges incurred in foreign currency.

It's highly recommended that you travel with at least one major credit card. You must have one to rent a car, and hotels and airlines usually require a credit card imprint as a deposit against expenses.

If coming from abroad, it's better to have more than one card in case, for some reason, the card is declined. The security departments of some credit card issuers are on the look out for surges in expenses, especially when done in a different country. It's a good idea to give advance notice of your travel plans to your credit card issuers, if you're coming from abroad, but bring extra cards, too, just in case.

ATM cards with major credit card backing, known as **"debit cards,"** are now a commonly acceptable form of payment in most stores and restaurants. Debit cards draw money directly from your checking account. Some stores enable you to receive "cash back" on your debit-card purchases as well. The same is true at most U.S. post offices.

Tips Pocket Change

If you're visiting San Antonio and/or Austin from another country, you'll avoid lines at airport ATMs by exchanging at least some money—just enough to cover airport incidentals and transportation to your hotel—before you leave home.

When you change money, ask for some small bills or loose change. Petty cash will come in handy for tipping, parking, and public transportation. Consider keeping the change separate from your larger bills, so that it's readily accessible and you'll be less of a target for theft.

TRAVELER'S CHECKS

Traveler's checks are widely accepted in San Antonio, but foreign visitors should make sure that they're denominated in U.S. dollars; foreign-currency checks are often difficult to exchange.

You can buy traveler's checks at most banks. Most are offered in denominations of $20, $50, $100, $500, and sometimes $1,000. Generally, you'll pay a service charge ranging from 1% to 4%.

The most popular traveler's checks are offered by **American Express** (✆ **800/807-6233,** or 800/221-7282 for card holders—this number accepts collect calls, offers service in several foreign languages, and exempts Amex gold and platinum cardholders from the 1% fee); **Visa** (✆ **800/732-1322**)—AAA members can obtain Visa checks for a $9.95 fee (for checks up to $1,500) at most AAA offices or by calling ✆ **866/339-3378;** and **MasterCard** (✆ **800/223-9920**).

If you do choose to carry traveler's checks, keep a record of their serial numbers separate from your checks, in the event that they are stolen or lost. You'll get a refund faster if you know the numbers.

CURRENCY The most common bills are the $1 (a "buck"), $5, $10, and $20 denominations. There are also $2 bills (seldom encountered), $50 bills, and $100 bills (the last two are usually not welcome as payment for small purchases).

Coins come in seven denominations: 1¢ (1 cent, or a penny); 5¢ (5 cents, or a nickel); 10¢ (10 cents, or a dime); 25¢ (25 cents, or a quarter); 50¢ (50 cents, or a half dollar); the gold-colored Sacagawea coin, worth $1; and the rare silver dollar.

7 HEALTH

Contact the **International Association for Medical Assistance to Travelers** (**IAMAT;** ✆ **716/754-4883** or, in Canada, 416/652-0137; www.iamat.org) for tips on travel and health concerns. The **United States Centers for Disease Control and Prevention** (✆ **800/311-3435;** www.cdc.gov) provides up-to-date information on health hazards by region or country and offers tips on food safety. The website **www.tripprep.com**, sponsored by a consortium of travel medicine practitioners, may also offer helpful advice on traveling abroad.

Avoiding "Economy-Class Syndrome"

Deep vein thrombosis, or as it's know in the world of flying, "economy-class syndrome," is a blood clot that develops in a deep vein. It's a potentially deadly condition that can be caused by sitting in cramped conditions—such as an airplane cabin—for too long. During a flight (especially a long-haul flight), get up, walk around, and stretch your legs every 60 to 90 minutes to keep your blood flowing. Other preventative measures include frequent flexing of the legs while sitting, drinking lots of water, and avoiding alcohol and sleeping pills. If you have a history of deep vein thrombosis, heart disease, or another condition that puts you at high risk, some experts recommend wearing compression stockings or taking anticoagulants when you fly; always ask your physician about the best course for you. Symptoms of deep vein thrombosis include leg pain or swelling, or even shortness of breath.

COMMON AILMENTS

HEAT STROKE The most common ailment for visitors to San Antonio and Austin, especially in the summer, is heat exhaustion and dehydration. If care is not exercised, the more serious condition known as heat stroke can develop. The Texas sun can be surprisingly hot for visitors from the north and can dehydrate a person quickly. Drink plenty of liquids. How much water is needed varies depending on individual metabolism, but the easiest thing to do is pay attention to signs of thirst. Also, plan your day so that the hottest part is spent indoors, or in an activity requiring little physical exertion. Be especially cautious with the young and old. And remember not to drink much alcohol the night before an active day. Symptoms of dehydration and heat exhaustion are weakness, dizziness, dry skin that doesn't sweat, and dry mouth. If these symptoms appear, get the person indoors, give liquids, and apply cool water to the body. Use a fan to cool and stimulate the sweat glands.

BUGS, BITES & OTHER WILDLIFE CONCERNS San Antonio, Austin, and the Hill Country are home to the scorpion, whose sting is not as venomous as desert scorpions, and rarely leads to complications. In the countryside, rattlesnakes and water moccasins are not commonly encountered, but their bites can be fatal. Contact a medical professional should you run into any of the above.

WHAT TO DO IF YOU GET SICK AWAY FROM HOME

For medical emergencies, dial ✆ **911.** The main downtown hospital in San Antonio is **Baptist Medical Center,** 111 Dallas St. (✆ **210/297-7000**). **Christus Santa Rosa Health Care Corp.,** 333 N. Santa Rosa St. (✆ **210/704-2011**), is also downtown. Contact the **San Antonio Medical Foundation** (✆ **210/614-3724**) for information about other medical facilities in the city.

The closest emergency rooms in Austin are at Brackenridge and Seton hospitals: **Seton Medical Center,** 1201 W. 38th St. (✆ **512/324-1000**) and **Brackenridge Hospital,** 601 E. 15th St. (✆ **512/324-7000**).

If there is urgency, consider going to a minor emergency clinic. One that is close to central Austin is **Pro Med,** at 2000 W. Anderson Lane (✆ **512/459-4367**). This place is open until 9 or 10pm.

In the downtown San Antonio area the closest urgent care facility is **Downtown Minor Emergency Center** (✆ **210/224-4661**) at 343 W. Houston St., #151. You can contact the **Bexar County Medical Society** at 6243 W. IH 10, Ste. 600 (✆ **210/301-4368;** www.bcms.org), Monday through Friday from 8am to 5pm. We list **additional emergency numbers** in the "Fast Facts" appendix, p. 312.

If you suffer from a chronic illness, consult your doctor before your departure. Pack **prescription medications** in your carry-on luggage, and carry them in their original containers, with pharmacy labels—otherwise they won't make it through airport security. Visitors from outside the U.S. should carry generic names of prescription drugs. For U.S. travelers, most reliable health-care plans provide coverage if you get sick away from home. Foreign visitors may have to pay all medical costs up front and be reimbursed later.

8 SAFETY

Central Texas is a safe city for visitors as compared with other cities of similar size in the U.S. Travelers shouldn't have any problems so long as they practice all the normal precautions—locking car doors, keeping valuables in a safe place, avoiding poorly lit areas at night.

A lot has been said about the love affair between Texans and their guns. In places unaccustomed to the wide availability of firearms, the image of the gun-toting Texan has reached the level of caricature. It's an issue that always comes up when I'm traveling abroad, and many people I talk to express concern over the issue. Yes, a large number of households possess guns. And yes, many Texans carry concealed firearms. But the lack of gun control isn't much of a threat to visitors. Not nearly so much as it is to Texans, at least. Statistics show that gun violence is more likely to strike in the household or the work place or out in the woods during hunting season, not in hotels, restaurants, theme parks, museums, or most public places.

9 SPECIALIZED TRAVEL RESOURCES

TRAVELERS WITH DISABILITIES

Most disabilities shouldn't stop anyone from traveling in the U.S. Thanks to provisions in the Americans with Disabilities Act, most public places are required to comply with disability-friendly regulations. Almost all public establishments (including hotels, restaurants, museums, and so on, but not including certain National Historic Landmarks), and at least some modes of public transportation provide accessible entrances and other facilities for those with disabilities.

Lots of work has been done in recent years to make San Antonio friendlier to those who use wheelchairs. The Riverwalk Trolley Station, for example, was built with a large elevator to transport people down to the water. Contact the **San Antonio Planning Department** (✆ **210/207-7245,** voice and TTY) for additional information (including a map of River Walk access), or log on to the disability access section of the department's website (www.sanantonio.gov/planning/disability_access.asp). Several taxis have also been equipped with lifts and ramps; **Yellow-Checker** (✆ **210/222-2222**) has most of them. And two downtown trolleys and about 85% of the public buses are now accessible. For **VIA Trans Disabled Accessibility Information,** phone ✆ **210/362-2140** (voice) or 210/362-2217 (TTY), or click on the "Accessible Service" section of **www.viainfo.net**. In addition, the Weekender section of the *San Antonio Express-News* includes accessibility symbols for restaurants, theaters, galleries, and other venues.

There's an active **Americans with Disabilities Act (ADA)** office in Austin. Its website, www.ci.austin.tx.us/ada, has lots of useful links. You can also call ✆ **512/974-3256** or 512/974-1897 if you have questions about whether any of the hotels or other facilities you're curious about is in compliance with the Act.

Many travel agencies offer customized tours and itineraries for travelers with disabilities. Among them are **Flying Wheels Travel** (✆ **507/451-5005;** www.flyingwheelstravel.com), **Access-Able Travel Source** (✆ **303/232-2979;** www.access-able.com), and **Accessible Journeys** (✆ **800/846-4537** or 610/521-0339; www.disabilitytravel.com). **Avis Rent a Car** has an "Avis

Access" program that offers such services as a dedicated 24-hour toll-free number (✆ **888/879-4273**) for customers with special travel needs; special car features, such as swivel seats, spinner knobs, and hand controls; and accessible bus service.

Organizations that offer assistance to travelers with disabilities include **MossRehab** (www.mossresourcenet.org), the **American Foundation for the Blind** (**AFB;** ✆ **800/232-5463;** www.afb.org), and **SATH** (**Society for Accessible Travel & Hospitality;** ✆ **212/447-7284;** www.sath.org). **AirAmbulanceCard.com** is now partnered with SATH and allows you to preselect top-notch hospitals in case of an emergency.

The community website **iCan** (www.icanonline.net/channels/travel) has destination guides and several regular columns on accessible travel. Also check out the quarterly magazine ***Emerging Horizons*** (www.emerginghorizons.com) and ***Open World*** magazine, published by SATH.

GAY & LESBIAN TRAVELERS

San Antonio has a fairly large, but not exceedingly visible, gay and lesbian population. To get info about activities, check out the website **www.outinsanantonio.com**. It has columns, blogs, and a calendar of events. If you stay at the **Painted Lady Inn,** a lesbian-owned bed-and-breakfast at 620 Broadway (✆ **210/220-1092;** www.thepaintedladyinn.com), you can also find out all you want to know about the local scene. In addition, the **Esperanza Peace & Justice Center,** 922 San Pedro (✆ **210/228-0201;** www.esperanzacenter.org), often screens films or has lectures on topics of interest to gay, lesbian, and transgender travelers. See also chapter 9 for information about gay bars.

A university town and the most left-leaning enclave in Texas, Austin is generally gay-, lesbian-, bisexual-, and transgender-friendly. To find out about clubs in addition to those listed in chapter 16 (Oilcan Harry's and Rainbow Cattle Co.), log on to http://austin.gaycities.com. **Book Woman,** 918 W. 12th St., at Lamar (✆ **512/472-2785;** www.ebookwoman.com), and **Lobo,** 3204-A Guadalupe St. (✆ **512/454-5406**), are the best places to find gay and lesbian books and magazines, as well as the Austin Gay and Lesbian Yellow Pages and the statewide *Texas Triangle* weekly newspaper.

Established in 1987, the annual **Austin Gay and Lesbian International Film Festival,** held in late August/early September, debuts works by gay, lesbian, bisexual, and transgender filmmakers across the world. The festival recently established its headquarters at the refurbished Regal Arbor Cinema at Great Hills. Log on to **www.agliff.org** for additional information, or call ✆ **512/302-9889.**

The International Gay and Lesbian Travel Association (**IGLTA;** ✆ **800/448-8550** or 954/776-2626; www.iglta.org) is the trade association for the gay and lesbian travel industry, and offers an online directory of gay- and lesbian-friendly travel businesses; go to their website and click on "Members."

Many agencies offer tours and travel itineraries specifically for gay and lesbian travelers. Among them are **Above and Beyond Tours** (✆ **800/397-2681;** www.abovebeyondtours.com) and **Now, Voyager** (✆ **800/255-6951;** www.nowvoyager.com).

Gay.com Travel (✆ **800/929-2268** or 415/644-8044; www.gay.com/travel or www.outandabout.com) is an excellent online successor to the popular ***Out & About*** print magazine. It provides regularly updated information about gay-owned, gay-oriented, and gay-friendly lodging, dining, sightseeing, nightlife, and shopping establishments in every important destination worldwide.

The following travel guides are available at many bookstores, or you can order them from any online bookseller: ***Spartacus***

International Gay Guide (Bruno Gmünder Verlag; www.spartacusworld.com/gayguide); ***Odysseus: The International Gay Travel Planner*** (Odysseus Enterprises Ltd.); and the ***Damron*** guides (www.damron.com), with separate, annual books for gay men and lesbians.

For more gay and lesbian travel resources visit www.frommers.com/planning.

SENIOR TRAVEL

Members of **AARP** (formerly known as the American Association of Retired Persons), 601 E St. NW, Washington, DC 20049 (✆ **888/687-2277;** www.aarp.org), get discounts on hotels, airfares, and car rentals. AARP offers members a wide range of benefits, including *AARP: The Magazine* and a monthly newsletter. Anyone over 50 can join.

Museums and attractions in San Antonio usually have discounts for seniors.

Austin's **Old Bakery and Emporium,** 1006 Congress Ave. (✆ **512/477-5961;** www.ci.austin.tx.us/parks/bakery1.htm), not only sells crafts and baked goods made by senior citizens, but also serves as a volunteer center for people over 50. It's a good place to find out about any senior activities in town. Another excellent resource is the monthly ***Senior Advocate*** newspaper, 3710 Cedar St., Box 17, Austin, TX 78705 (✆ **512/451-7433;** www.senioradvocatenews.com), which you can pick up, gratis, at H-E-B supermarkets, libraries, hospitals, and many other places. You can also call or write in advance for a subscription ($15 per year). The online version has links to many other resources for seniors.

Recommended publications offering travel resources and discounts for seniors include: the quarterly magazine ***Travel 50 & Beyond*** (www.travel50andbeyond.com); ***Travel Unlimited: Uncommon Adventures for the Mature Traveler*** (Avalon); ***101 Tips for Mature Travelers,*** available from Grand Circle Travel (✆ **800/221-2610** or 617/350-7500; www.gct.com); and ***Unbelievably Good Deals and Great Adventures That You Absolutely Can't Get Unless You're Over 50*** (McGraw-Hill), by Joann Rattner Heilman.

For more information and resources on travel for seniors, see www.frommers.com/planning.

FAMILY TRAVEL

The family vacation is a rite of passage for many households. As any veteran family vacationer will assure you, a family trip can be among the most pleasurable and rewarding times of your life; it can also quickly devolve into a farce worthy of a *National Lampoon* movie. Good advance travel planning is essential.

The San Antonio edition of the free monthly ***Our Kids*** magazine includes a calendar that lists daily local activities oriented toward children. You can read it online at **http://sanantonio.parenthood.com**; order it in advance from 8400 Blanco, Suite 201, San Antonio, TX 78216 (✆ **210/349-6667**); or find it in San Antonio at H-E-B supermarkets, Wal-Mart stores, Hollywood Video, and most major bookstores.

To locate accommodations, restaurants, and attractions that are particularly kid-friendly, refer to the "Kids" icon throughout this guide.

Recommended family travel websites include **Family Travel Forum** (www.familytravelforum.com), a comprehensive site that offers customized trip planning; **Family Travel Network** (www.familytravelnetwork.com), an award-winning site that offers travel features, deals, and tips; **Traveling Internationally with Your Kids** (www.travelwithyourkids.com), a comprehensive site offering sound advice for long-distance and international travel with children; and **Family Travel Files** (www.thefamilytravelfiles.com), which offers an online magazine and a directory of off-the-beaten-path tours and tour operators for families.

For a list of more family-friendly travel resources, visit www.frommers.com/planning.

STUDENT TRAVEL

Check out the **International Student Travel Confederation** (**ISTC;** www.istc.org) website for comprehensive travel services information and details on how to get an **International Student Identity Card (ISIC),** which qualifies students for substantial savings on rail passes, plane tickets, entrance fees, and more. It also provides students with basic health and life insurance and a 24-hour helpline. The card is valid for a maximum of 18 months. You can apply for the card online or in person at **STA Travel** (✆ **800/781-4040** in North America; ✆ 132-782 in Australia; ✆ 087/1230-0040 in the U.K.; www.statravel.com), the biggest student travel agency in the world; check out the website to locate STA Travel offices worldwide. If you're no longer a student but are still under 26, you can get an **International Youth Travel Card (IYTC)** from the same people, which entitles you to some discounts. **Travel CUTS** (✆ **800/592-2887;** www.travelcuts.com) offers similar services for both Canadians and U.S. residents. Irish students may prefer to turn to **USIT** (✆ **01/602-1904;** www.usit.ie), an Ireland-based specialist in student, youth, and independent travel.

There are endless resources for students in this university town. Just stop by the **University of Texas Student Union Building** (see the map in chapter 14) to check out the scene. Austin's oldest institution of higher learning, **Huston-Tillotson College,** 600 Chicon St. (✆ **512/505-3000;** www.htu.edu), in East Austin, is especially helpful for getting African-American students oriented. **Hostelling International–Austin** (see chapter 12) is another great repository of information for students.

VEGETARIAN TRAVEL

Austin has a large population of vegetarians and vegans. Most restaurants have plenty of vegetarian menu items, and there are several vegan restaurants in town. They can be found in the "Restaurants by Cuisine" list in chapter 13.

For more vegetarian-friendly travel resources, go to www.frommers.com/planning.

10 SUSTAINABLE TOURISM

Sustainable tourism is conscientious travel. It means being careful with the environments you explore, and respecting the communities you visit. Two overlapping components of sustainable travel are **ecotourism** and **ethical tourism.** The **International Ecotourism Society** (TIES) defines ecotourism as responsible travel to natural areas that conserves the environment and improves the well-being of local people. TIES suggests that ecotourists follow these principles:

- Minimize environmental impact.
- Build environmental and cultural awareness and respect.
- Provide positive experiences for both visitors and hosts.
- Provide direct financial benefits for conservation and for local people.
- Raise sensitivity to host countries' political, environmental, and social climates.
- Support international human rights and labor agreements.

You can find some ecofriendly travel tips and statistics, as well as touring companies and associations—listed by destination under "Travel Choice"—at the **TIES** website, www.ecotourism.org. Also check out **Ecotravel.com**, which lets you search for sustainable touring companies in several

It's Easy Being Green

Here are a few simple ways you can help conserve fuel and energy when you travel:

- Each time you take a flight or drive a car greenhouse gases release into the atmosphere. You can help neutralize this danger to the planet through "carbon offsetting"—paying someone to invest your money in programs that reduce your greenhouse gas emissions by the same amount you've added. Before buying carbon offset credits, just make sure that you're using a reputable company, one with a proven program that invests in renewable energy. Reliable carbon offset companies include **Carbonfund** (www.carbonfund.org), **TerraPass** (www.terrapass.org), and **Carbon Neutral** (www.carbonneutral.org).
- Whenever possible, choose nonstop flights; they generally require less fuel than indirect flights that stop and take off again. Try to fly during the day—some scientists estimate that nighttime flights are twice as harmful to the environment. And pack light—each 15 pounds of luggage on a 5,000-mile flight adds up to 50 pounds of carbon dioxide emitted.
- Where you stay during your travels can have a major environmental impact. To determine the green credentials of a property, ask about trash disposal and recycling, water conservation, and energy use; also question if sustainable materials were used in the construction of the property. The website **www.greenhotels.com** recommends green-rated member hotels around the world that fulfill the company's stringent environmental requirements. Also consult **www.environmentallyfriendlyhotels.com** for more green accommodation ratings.
- At hotels, request that your sheets and towels not be changed daily. (Many hotels already have programs like this in place.) Turn off the lights and air-conditioner (or heater) when you leave your room.
- Use public transport where possible—trains, buses, and even taxis are more energy-efficient forms of transport than driving. Even better is to walk or cycle; you'll produce zero emissions and stay fit and healthy on your travels.
- If renting a car is necessary, ask the rental agent for a hybrid, or rent the most fuel-efficient car available. You'll use less gas and save money at the tank.
- Eat at locally owned and operated restaurants that use produce grown in the area. This contributes to the local economy and cuts down on greenhouse gas emissions by supporting restaurants where the food is not flown or trucked in across long distances. Visit **Sustain Lane** (www.sustainlane.org) to find sustainable eating and drinking choices around the U.S.; also check out **www.eatwellguide.org** for tips on eating sustainably in the U.S. and Canada.

categories (water-based, land-based, spiritually oriented, and so on).

While much of the focus of ecotourism is about reducing impacts on the natural environment, ethical tourism concentrates on ways to preserve and enhance local economies and communities, regardless of location. You can embrace ethical tourism by staying at a locally owned hotel or shopping at a store that employs local workers and sells locally produced goods.

Responsible Travel (www.responsibletravel.com) is a great source of sustainable travel ideas; the site is run by a spokesperson for ethical tourism in the travel industry. **Sustainable Travel International** (www.sustainabletravelinternational.org) promotes ethical tourism practices, and manages an extensive directory of sustainable properties and tour operators around the world.

In the U.K., **Tourism Concern** (www.tourismconcern.org.uk) works to reduce social and environmental problems connected to tourism. The **Association of Independent Tour Operators (AITO;** www.aito.co.uk) is a group of specialist operators leading the field in making holidays sustainable.

11 STAYING CONNECTED

TELEPHONES

The telephone system in the United States is run by private corporations, so rates, especially for long-distance service and operator-assisted calls, can vary widely. In central Texas the largest local service provider is AT&T. The area code for **San Antonio** is **210,** in **Austin** it's **512.** To make a local call, dial the 7-digit number without the area code.

For **local directory assistance** ("information"), dial 411; for long-distance information, dial 1, then the appropriate area code and 555-1212.

Most long-distance and international calls can be dialed directly from any phone. **For calls within the United States and to Canada,** dial 1 followed by the area code and the seven-digit number. **For other international calls,** dial 011 followed by the country code, city code, and the telephone number of the person you are calling.

Calls to area codes **800, 888, 877,** and **866** are toll-free. However, calls to numbers in area codes **700** and **900** (chat lines, bulletin boards, "dating" services, and so on) can be very expensive—usually a charge of 95¢ to $3 or more per minute, and they sometimes have minimum charges that can run as high as $15 or more.

For **reversed-charge or collect calls,** and for person-to-person calls, dial 0 (zero, not the letter O) followed by the area code and number you want; an operator will then come on the line, and you should specify that you are calling collect, or person-to-person, or both. If your operator-assisted call is international, ask for the overseas operator.

Large hotels usually have surcharges for local and long-distance calls. Many travelers avoid paying these surcharges by using their cellphones. If you don't have a cellphone, you can use a **public pay telephone,** which can be found in public buildings, hotel lobbies, restaurants, convenience stores, gas stations, and other private establishments, though they are becoming fewer in the age of the cellphone. Local calls cost 50¢. Pay phones do not accept pennies, and few will take anything larger than a quarter. For long distance calls you can use **prepaid calling cards,** which can be purchased in denominations up to $50 from convenience stores, pharmacies, and other retail outlets. These can be the least expensive way to call home. Some public phones accept American Express, MasterCard, and Visa credit cards.

Most hotels have **fax machines** available for guest use (be sure to ask about the charge to use it). Many hotel rooms are even wired for guests' fax machines. A less expensive way to send and receive faxes may be at stores such as **The UPS Store** (formerly Mail Boxes Etc.), a national chain of retail packing service shops. (Look in the Yellow Pages directory under "Packing Services.")

There are two kinds of telephone directories in the United States. The so-called **"White Pages"** list private households and business subscribers in alphabetical order. The inside front cover lists emergency numbers for police, fire, ambulance, the

Tips Hey, Google, did you get my text message?

It's bound to happen: The day you leave this guidebook back at the hotel for an unencumbered stroll through [neighborhood in your destination], you'll forget the address of the lunch spot you had earmarked. If you're traveling with a mobile device, send a text message to ✆ **46645 (GOOGL)** for a lightning-fast response. For instance, type "carnegie deli new york," and within 10 seconds you'll receive a text message with the address and phone number. This nifty trick works in a range of search categories: Look up weather ("weather philadelphia"), language translations ("translate goodbye in Spanish"), currency conversions ("10 usd in pounds"), movie times ("harry potter 60605"), and more. If your search results are off, be more specific ("the abbey gay bar west hollywood"). For more tips and search options, see www.google.com/intl/en_us/mobile/sms/. Regular text message charges apply.

Online Traveler's Toolbox

- **www.mysanantonio.com**. The website of the city's only mainstream newspaper, the *San Antonio Express-News,* is a one-stop e-shop for the city: In addition to providing the daily news, it also links to local businesses such as dry cleaners and florists and to movie, nightlife, and restaurant listings and reviews. A couple of caveats: You have to register to use the site (a one-time annoyance, and no fee is involved) and many of the searches require zip codes, so be sure to know the one you'll be traveling from when you log on.
- **www.sanantonio.gov**. The City of San Antonio's website offers timely information on such topics as traffic and street closures. Most of the other sections that would be of interest to visitors, such as the city-sponsored arts events and public parks, can be found in the "Recreation" section.
- **www.visitsanantonio.com**. You're not going to get honest critiques of hotels and attractions on the San Antonio Convention and Visitors Bureau's website; however, you are going to get useful links to many of them. The "Discounts" section is especially good if you're looking for discounts on everything from accommodations to theme parks. This is not the easiest site to navigate, but once you click on "Visitors," you should be able to find what you need.
- **http://sanantonio.citysearch.com**. I don't always agree with this site's reviews, but it's always good to have a variety of opinions about dining, nightlife, and shopping (even if mine are ultimately right). And there are a few things I can't do—such as provide you with an up-to-date weather report or Yellow Pages information—that this site can.
- **www.texasmonthly.com**. You won't necessarily find San Antonio stories on the *Texas Monthly* site, but the state's best magazine offers in-depth treatments of lots of interesting topics, so you'll be keyed into a Texas mindset. And the site sometimes highlights hot new San Antonio dining spots.

Coast Guard, poison-control center, crime-victims hotline, and so on. The first few pages will tell you how to make long-distance and international calls, complete with country codes and area codes. Government numbers are usually printed on blue paper within the White Pages. Printed on yellow paper, the so-called **Yellow Pages** list all local services, businesses, industries, and houses of worship according to activity with an index at the front or back. (Drugstores/pharmacies and restaurants are also listed by geographic location.) The Yellow Pages also include city plans or detailed area maps, postal zip codes, and public transportation routes.

CELLPHONES

If you're not from the U.S., you'll be appalled at the poor reach of the **GSM (Global System for Mobile Communications) wireless network,** which is used by much of the rest of the world. Your phone will probably work in most major U.S. cities; it definitely won't work in many rural areas. To see where GSM phones work in the U.S., check out www.t-mobile.com/coverage. And you may or may not be able to send SMS (text messaging) home.

To have the use of a cellphone while visiting central Texas, the easiest thing to do is buy a cheap prepaid cellphone. These are for sale in various outlets, but the cheapest deal probably is offered at the local H-E-B grocery stores. This chain has entered into business with an Austin-based company called Fusion Mobil. Locally owned Pocket Communications is also in the prepaid cellphone business, and has kiosks in some H-E-B stores. Go to www.heb.com to use a store locator.

INTERNET & E-MAIL

With Your Own Computer:

Most lodging options in San Antonio or Austin offer high-speed Internet access, often without any fees. If your hotel charges too much, check out this website for free Wi-Fi connections around town: **www.ilovefreewifi.com/sanantonio**.

Without Your Own Computer:

An organization called **Austin Free-Net** works to provide the public with free access to computers and the Internet. They have computers in all the city libraries as well as other community locations. For lists of all locations go to **www.austinfree.net.**

In Austin, you can always use a computer station at any **FedEx Kinko's Copy Print Center.** There's one in the university area that's open 24 hours. It's just north of the main campus at 2901 Medical Arts St. (✆ **512/476-3242**). Another one is downtown at 327 Congress Ave., #100 (✆ **512/472-4448**).

In San Antonio, hit the computer station at the **FedEx Kinko's Copy Print Center's** central location at 4418 Broadway (✆ **210/821-6911**).

Also, you can visit the eye-catching San Antonio Public Library and use its computer station. For location and hours see "More Attractions" in chapter 7.

4 Suggested San Antonio Itineraries

The following itineraries are merely a suggestion for how to see San Antonio if your time is limited. The first itinerary is structured for people with only 1 day. On this tour you'll see all that makes San Antonio unique. Having followed it, you'll leave town understanding what this place is all about. People with more time can tack on the second day's activities. Unlike the first itinerary, this one requires a car, but the driving is easy. By adding on a third day, you can embellish your San Antonio experience with a taste of the Texas Hill Country.

If you're coming with kids (San Antonio is a big family destination), and you're considering one of the theme parks, allow a full day for it and get your money's worth. Most kids won't be able to handle any more excitement in a day than what these parks provide. If old enough, they may enjoy the first itinerary, and, should it be necessary, you can make some substitutions using some of the downtown entries in the "Especially for Kids" section of chapter 7.

But first, I should give a brief description of the different areas of San Antonio where the attractions are located. For information on moving through San Antonio, see the "Getting Around" section of chapter 3.

THE NEIGHBORHOODS IN BRIEF

The older areas described here, from downtown through Alamo Heights, are all "in the Loop" (410). The Medical Center area in the Northwest lies just outside it, but the rest of the Northwest, as well as North Central and the West, are expanding beyond even Loop 1604.

Downtown Site of San Antonio's original Spanish settlements, this area includes the Alamo and other historic sites, along with the River Walk, the Alamodome, the convention center, the Rivercenter Mall, and many high-rise hotels, restaurants, and shops. It's also the center of commerce and government, so many banks and offices, as well as the county courthouse and City Hall buildings, are located here. Downtown is fun and vibrant. The River Walk is the centerpiece, but there's a lot more that can be seen and appreciated that takes a bit of exploring.

King William The city's first suburb, this historic district directly south of downtown was settled in the mid- to late 1800s by wealthy German merchants who built some of the most beautiful mansions in town. It began to be yuppified in the 1970s, and, at this point, you'd never guess it had ever been allowed to deteriorate. Only two of the area's many impeccably restored homes are generally open to the public, but a number have been turned into bed-and-breakfasts. As you might imagine, the location is ideal for those who want to explore the central city.

Southtown Alamo Street marks the border between King William and Southtown, an adjoining commercial district. Long a depressed area, it's slowly becoming trendy thanks to a Main Street refurbishing project and the opening of the Blue Star Arts Complex. You'll find a nice mix of Latin American neighborhood shops and funky coffeehouses and galleries here, but few hotels worth staying in.

South Side The old, largely Latin American southeast section of town that begins where Southtown ends (there's no agreed-upon boundary, but I'd say it lies a few blocks beyond the Blue Star Arts Complex) is home to four of the city's five historic missions. This is one of the many areas of the central part of the city where time seems to have stood still, and the denizens of South Side share a strong communal identity.

Monte Vista Area Immediately north of downtown, Monte Vista was established soon after King William by a conglomeration of wealthy cattlemen, politicos, and generals who moved "on to the hill" at the turn of the century. A number of the area's large houses have been split into apartments for students of nearby Trinity University and San Antonio Community College, but many lovely old homes have been restored in the past 30 years. It hasn't reached King William status, but this is already a highly desirable (read: pricey) place to live. Monte Vista is close to the once thriving, but now less lively, restaurant and entertainment district along North St. Mary's Street between Josephine and Magnolia known locally as **The Strip.**

Fort Sam Houston Built in 1876 to the northeast of downtown, Fort Sam Houston boasts a number of stunning officers' homes. Much of the working-class neighborhood surrounding Fort Sam is now run-down, but renewed interest in restoring San Antonio's older areas is beginning to have some impact here, too.

Alamo Heights Area In the 1890s, when construction in the area began, Alamo Heights was at the far northern reaches of San Antonio. This is now home to San Antonio's well-heeled residents and holds most of the fashionable shops and restaurants. **Terrell Hills** to the east, **Olmos Park** to the west, and **Lincoln Heights** to the north are all offshoots of this area. The latter is home to the Quarry, once just that, but now a ritzy golf course and popular shopping mall. Shops and restaurants are concentrated along two main drags: Broadway and, to a lesser degree, New Braunfels. Most of these neighborhoods share a single zip code ending in the numbers "09"—thus the local term "09ers," referring to the area's affluent residents. The Witte Museum, San Antonio Botanical Gardens, and Brackenridge Park are all in this part of town.

Northwest The mostly characterless neighborhoods surrounding the South Texas Medical Center (a large grouping of healthcare facilities referred to as the **Medical Center**) were built relatively recently. The area includes lots of condominiums and apartments, and much of the shopping and dining is in strip malls (the trendy, still-expanding Heubner Oaks retail center is an exception). The farther north you go, the nicer the housing complexes get. The high-end Westin La Cantera resort, the exclusive La Cantera and Dominion residential enclave, several tony golf courses, and the Shops at La Cantera, San Antonio's fanciest new retail center, mark the direction that development is taking in the far northwest part of town, just beyond Six Flags Fiesta Texas and near the public Friedrich Park. It's becoming

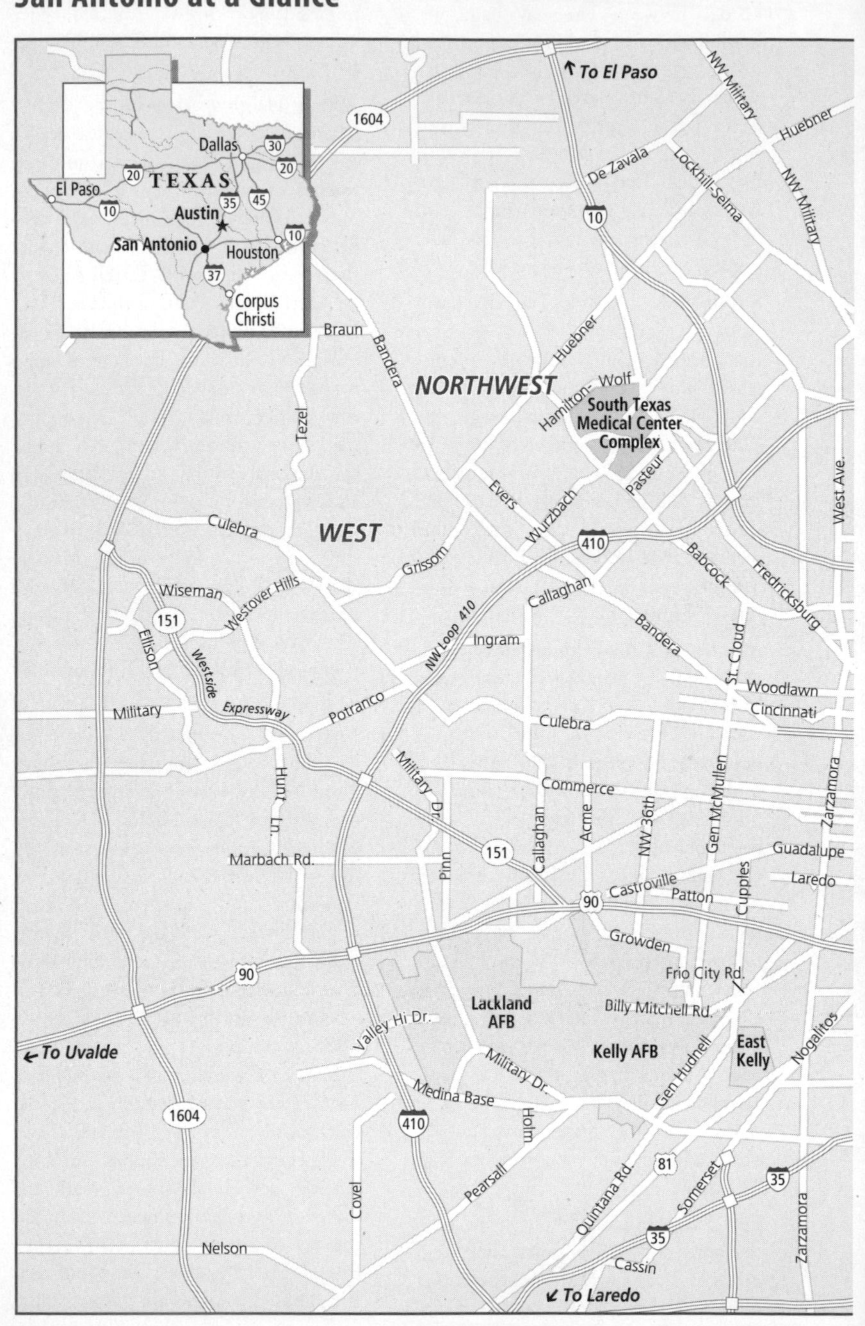

To El Paso
To Uvalde
To Laredo
TEXAS
El Paso
Dallas
Austin
San Antonio
Houston
Corpus Christi
NORTHWEST
WEST
South Texas Medical Center Complex
Lackland AFB
Kelly AFB
East Kelly
1604
410
151
90
10
35
81
NW Military
Huebner
De Zavala
Lockhill-Selma
Braun
Bandera
Tezel
Hamilton-Wolf
Evers
Wurzbach
Pasteur
Culebra
Grissom
Wiseman
Westover Hills
Ellison
Westside Expressway
Military
Potranco
NW Loop 410
Ingram
Callaghan
Babcock
Fredricksburg
West Ave.
St. Cloud
Woodlawn
Cincinnati
Commerce
Military Dr.
Hunt Ln.
Marbach Rd.
Pinn
Acme
NW 36th
Gen McMullen
Zarzamora
Guadalupe
Laredo
Castroville
Patton
Cupples
Growden
Frio City Rd.
Billy Mitchell Rd.
Valley Hi Dr.
Gen Hudnell
Nogalitos
Medina Base
Holm
Pearsall
Covel
Quintana Rd.
Somerset
Cassin
Nelson

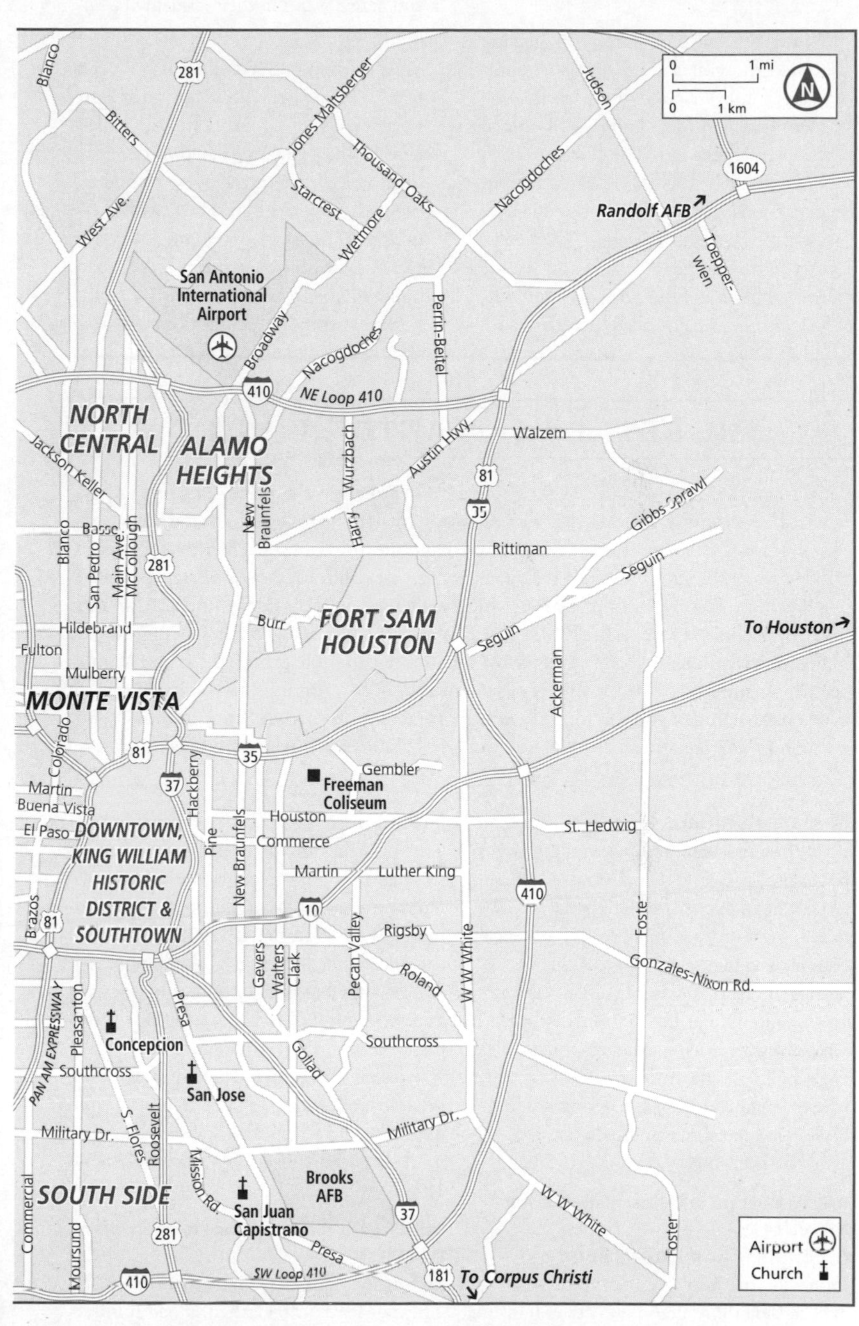
0 1 mi
0 1 km
N
Blanco
281
Bitters
Jones Maltsberger
Thousand Oaks
Judson
1604
Randolf AFB
Toepper-wien
West Ave.
Starcrest
Wetmore
Nacogdoches
San Antonio International Airport
Broadway
Nacogdoches
Perrin-Beitel
410
NE Loop 410
NORTH CENTRAL
ALAMO HEIGHTS
Jackson Keller
Austin Hwy.
Walzem
Wurzbach
81
35
Gibbs Sprawl
Basse
Blanco
San Pedro
Main Ave.
McCollough
281
New Braunfels
Harry
Rittiman
Seguin
Hildebrand
Fulton
Mulberry
Burr
FORT SAM HOUSTON
Seguin
To Houston
Ackerman
MONTE VISTA
Colorado
81
35
37
Hackberry
Martin
Buena Vista
Gembler
Freeman Coliseum
Houston
El Paso
DOWNTOWN, KING WILLIAM HISTORIC DISTRICT & SOUTHTOWN
Pine
Commerce
St. Hedwig
Martin Luther King
New Braunfels
410
Brazos
81
10
Rigsby
Foster
Gonzales-Nixon Rd.
Gevers
Walters
Clark
Pecan Valley
W W White
Roland
PAN AM EXPRESSWAY
Pleasanton
Presa
Concepcion
Goliad
Southcross
Southcross
San Jose
Military Dr.
S. Flores
Roosevelt
Military Dr.
Mission Rd.
Brooks AFB
W W White
Commercial
SOUTH SIDE
San Juan Capistrano
37
Foster
281
Presa
Moursund
410
SW Loop 410
181
To Corpus Christi
Airport
Church

one of San Antonio's prime growth areas.

North Central San Antonio is inching toward Bulverde and other Hill Country towns via this major corridor of development clustered from Loop 410 north to Loop 1604, east of I-10 and west of I-35, and bisected by U.S. 281. The airport and many developed industrial strips line U.S. 281 in the southern section, but the farther north you go, the more you see the natural beauty of this area, hilly and dotted with small canyons. Recent city codes have motivated developers to retain trees and native plants in their residential communities.

West Although SeaWorld has been out here since the late 1980s, and the Hyatt Regency Hill Country Resort settled here in the early 1990s, other development was comparatively slow in coming. Now the West is booming with new midprice housing developments, strip malls, schools, and businesses. Road building hasn't kept pace with growth, however, so traffic can be a bear.

1 THE BEST OF SAN ANTONIO IN 1 DAY

This itinerary is a bit like the walking tour of downtown in chapter 7. The biggest differences between the two are that this one only hits the big attractions and leaves the Alamo for late afternoon (btw. 4:30 and 5pm) and the Tower of the Americas for later in the day when the sun is low and the view is at its best. Both tours were designed so that you'll avoid the crowds at the Alamo, which are largest in the midday hours. Also, this itinerary includes a stop at the IMAX that could not be put in any self-respecting "walking" tour, even though I feel it helps make for a more enjoyable experience at the Alamo. See which one works best for you. It's usually warm in San Antonio, so you may want to take a hat to protect yourself from the sun. Fortunately, downtown San Antonio is compact, and this itinerary isn't taxing. You can stroll along easily, even with kids in tow.

❶ Market Square ★

If you haven't eaten breakfast, you can begin by having a bite at **Mi Tierra** (p. 99), a restaurant in the middle of Market Square that is very much a reflection of the local culture. The same can be said of this market area. It's a blend of Mexican and Texas styles and is enjoyable in the mornings, when it's semi-deserted. Facing Market Square is a large building, the modern and attractive **Museo Alameda** (p. 122), recognizable by its singular metal screen facade bordered by elaborate ironwork.

Walk 1½ blocks east on Commerce Street. On your right will be the:

❷ Spanish Governor's Palace ★

Don't let the word "palace" lead you to expect something grandiose. It's a translation of *palacio,* which in Mexico means any building used as the seat of government. This was the seat of local government in colonial times. It's a handsome adobe-style building that holds a number of period pieces. Look for the keystone above the entrance that bears the double-headed eagle—a symbol of Hapsburg rule—as well as the date of 1749. The palace sits on the old Military Plaza, or Plaza de Armas, which was the center of town after Texas became independent. The famous chili queens would set up their stalls in this plaza until they were moved to Market Square in 1886. See p. 123.

Walk 2½ blocks east. You will come to the city's Main Plaza and the:

❸ San Fernando Cathedral ★

The San Fernando Cathedral had humble beginnings as a parish church. It was commissioned as a simple stone church in 1738. The colonial society of the day was divided into two principal classes: the Canary Islanders, who, having been born in the Old World, were above those of Spanish descent born in the New World, which included most of the garrison and their families. But the project of building a church united them, and in choosing the patron saints, they selected one from each continent—from Europe, Our Lady of Candlemas, and from the Americas, Our Lady of Guadalupe. What you see today mostly dates from the 1870s when the church was elevated to cathedral. Changes continue into the present century. Enter and have a look at the gilt altar piece that was introduced only a few years ago. See p. 123.

Walk a couple of blocks farther east; you will come to the:

❹ River Walk ★★★

The section you see was man made and is the plainest part of the River Walk. Cross the bridge over the river and turn right. Follow the river and you'll soon find an access stairway leading down to the walkway that follows the original river bank. Continue in the same direction and you'll come to the prettiest sections of the River Walk, with tall cypress trees, patches of flowers, ornamental bushes, and bridges crisscrossing the river this way and that. See p. 116.

TAKE A BREAK

Take a breather at this fun and fine old German restaurant, **Schilo's,** where Commerce Street crosses the river. You can fill up on one of their moderately priced sandwiches or a slice of the cheesecake. 424 E. Commerce. ✆ **210/223-6692.** See p. 99.

Head 1 block west on Commerce Street to the Rivercenter Mall.

❺ IMAX Theater Rivercenter ★

The main course of the Rivercenter Mall was built over a section of Blum Street, where the house of a famous desperado and scalp hunter named John Glanton, fictionalized in Cormack McCarthy's novel *Blood Meridian,* once stood. The IMAX theater has multiple show times (almost hourly) of a 45-minute documentary about the siege of the Alamo. This and the diorama in front of the ticket counter give you good context for what you're about to see at the Alamo. The movie schedule is subject to change, so call ahead for times and ticket reservations. Or buy your tickets at the theater and spend time exploring this pleasant, well-lighted mall while you wait. See p. 127.

When you exit the theater, turn right and walk down the main concourse to the door leading to Blum Street. Make another right at the corner. Walk a block and on your right you'll see:

❻ The Alamo ★★

By midafternoon the crowds will have thinned here. The church and long barrack are good examples of frontier colonial Spanish architecture, whose traits were to give shape to the region's architecture. The grounds are lovely and reflect the fact that San Antonio is on the cusp of four different ecological zones: Hill Country, Gulf coast plains, South Texas chaparral, and West Texas desert. Thus you'll find magnificent live oak trees, gnarled mesquites, fronded palms, and prickly cacti and ocotillo, all growing within the walls of the mission. In addition to the native species, here and there grow patches of flowering ornamentals to lend more color and please the eye. What today is Alamo Plaza was the original *atrio* of the church—a walled plaza for celebrating mass when the celebrants numbered too many to fit into the church. It played a prominent part in the battle. See p. 111.

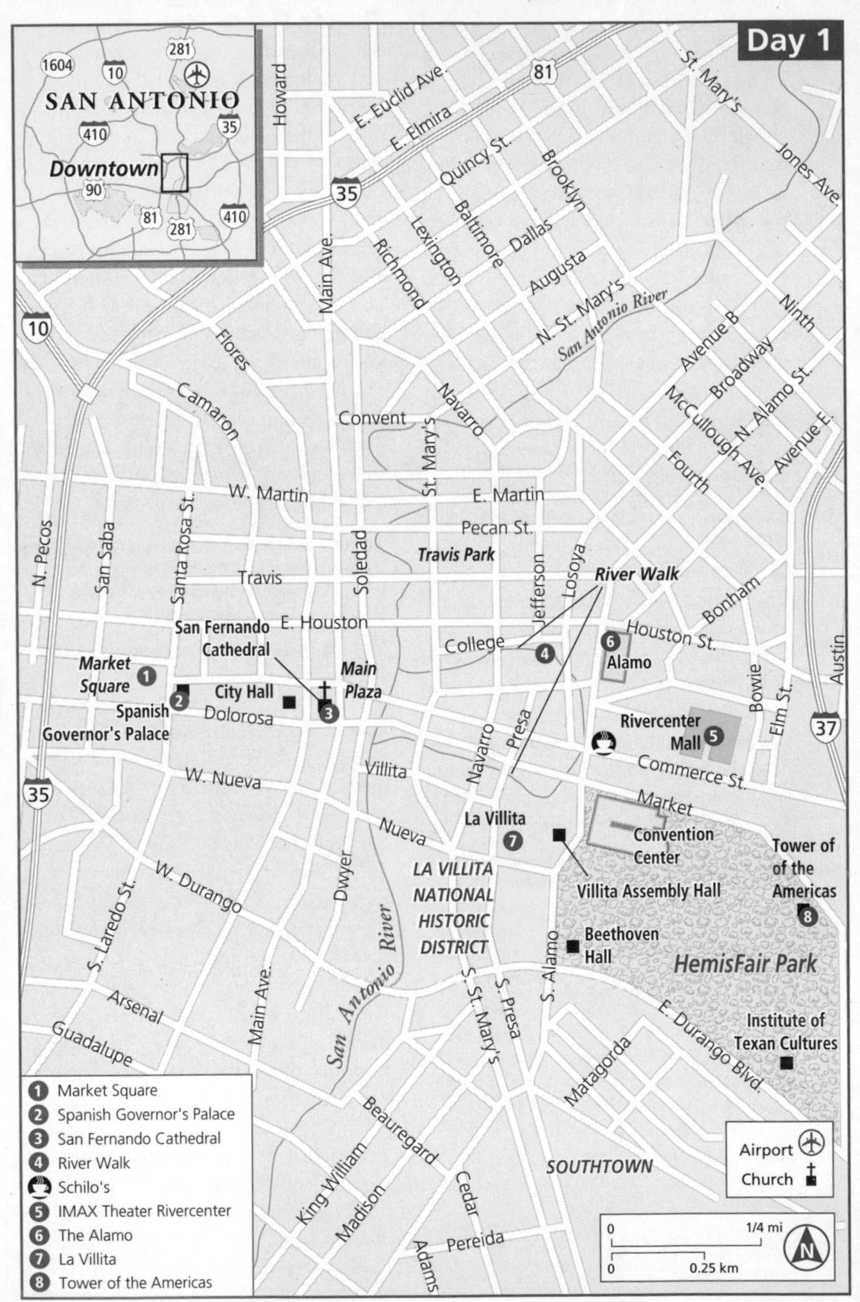
Day 1
SAN ANTONIO
Downtown
1604
10
281
410
35
90
81
Howard
E. Euclid Ave.
E. Elmira
St. Mary's
Jones Ave.
Quincy St.
Brooklyn
Baltimore
Lexington
Richmond
Dallas
Augusta
N. St. Mary's
San Antonio River
Main Ave.
Avenue B
Ninth
Broadway
N. Alamo St.
McCullough Ave.
Avenue E
Fourth
Flores
Camaron
Navarro
Convent
St. Mary's
W. Martin
E. Martin
Pecan St.
Travis Park
N. Pecos
San Saba
Santa Rosa St.
Travis
Soledad
Jefferson
Losoya
River Walk
Bonham
San Fernando Cathedral
E. Houston
College
Houston St.
Alamo
Market Square
City Hall
Main Plaza
Spanish Governor's Palace
Dolorosa
Presa
Rivercenter Mall
Bowie
Elm St.
Austin
37
Villita
Commerce St.
W. Nueva
Market
La Villita
Nueva
Convention Center
Tower of the Americas
LA VILLITA NATIONAL HISTORIC DISTRICT
Villita Assembly Hall
W. Durango
Dwyer
S. Laredo St.
Beethoven Hall
HemisFair Park
S. Alamo
S. St. Mary's
S. Presa
Arsenal
E. Durango Blvd.
Institute of Texan Cultures
Guadalupe
Matagorda
Beauregard
King William
Madison
Cedar
SOUTHTOWN
Pereida
Adams
Airport
Church
0 1/4 mi
0 0.25 km
N
1 Market Square
2 Spanish Governor's Palace
3 San Fernando Cathedral
4 River Walk
Schilo's
5 IMAX Theater Rivercenter
6 The Alamo
7 La Villita
8 Tower of the Americas

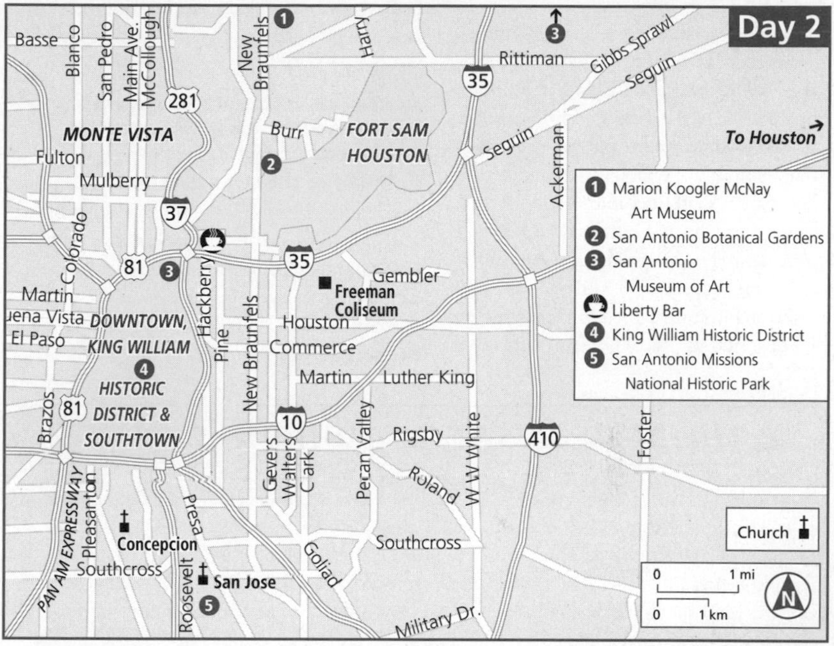

Day 2
Basse
Blanco
San Pedro
Main Ave.
McCollough
New Braunfels
Harry
Rittiman
Gibbs Sprawl
Seguin
281
35
MONTE VISTA
Burr
FORT SAM HOUSTON
Fulton
Mulberry
Seguin
Ackerman
To Houston
37
Colorado
81
Hackberry
35
Gembler
Freeman Coliseum
Martin
Buena Vista
El Paso
DOWNTOWN, KING WILLIAM HISTORIC DISTRICT & SOUTHTOWN
Pine
New Braunfels
Houston
Commerce
Martin Luther King
Brazos
81
10
Pecan Valley
Rigsby
Roland
W W White
410
Foster
Gevers
Walters
Clark
PAN AM EXPRESSWAY
Pleasanton
Concepcion
Southcross
Presa
Roosevelt
San Jose
Goliad
Southcross
Military Dr.
1 Marion Koogler McNay Art Museum
2 San Antonio Botanical Gardens
3 San Antonio Museum of Art
Liberty Bar
4 King William Historic District
5 San Antonio Missions National Historic Park
Church
0 1 mi
0 1 km
N

Day 3
2828
Medina
337
To Vanderpool
Bandera
16
Medina River
Pipe Creek
46
Boerne
Cascade Caverns
Bergheim
46
Bulverde
10
470
1077
Tarpley
1283
87
Leon Springs
Hill Country State Natural Area
16
Lakehills
281
Helotes
173
Medina Lake
Mico
471
462
Rio Medina
1604
San Antonio
1796
471
Castroville
90
410
Medina River
0 10 mi
0 10 km
N
1 Boerne
2 Bandera
3 Castroville

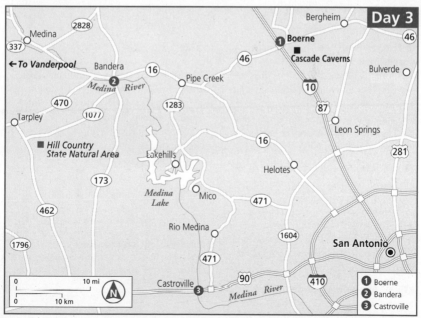

Head south on Alamo Street and in 4 blocks you'll see a group of buildings on your left. This is:

❼ La Villita ★

In colonial society, even on the frontier, society's divisions shaped settlement patterns. While the Canary Islanders settled on the west side of the river, the families of the garrison soldiers settled on the east side in what is now La Villita. In the mid–19th century, La Villita became a popular residential area with the Europeans (Germans, Swiss, and French), giving the Spanish village some European flavor. Its well preserved architecture earned it its designation as a historical district. Though it has been a craft center since the 1930s, my favorite thing about it is the architecture. I like it best when the shops are closing and there's just enough bustle to give it a lived-in feeling. See p. 112.

Across Alamo Street, at about 2 blocks' distance, you'll see the needle that is a distinctive part of San Antonio's skyline.

❽ Tower of the Americas ★

Built for the HemisFair world exposition of 1968, the Tower of the Americas is still the tallest building in San Antonio. The observation deck on top provides a grand view of the city in every direction, and the glass elevators provide the rush. See p. 124.

2 THE BEST OF SAN ANTONIO IN 2 DAYS

This trip makes use of the morning to see the best art museums while the mind and spirit are still fresh. The second half of the day takes the visitor to the residential King William District and then to the outlying missions that dot the Mission Trail. If, by this time of day, it's feeling more like *Mission Impossible,* you can abbreviate the trip by seeing only San José and Espada. Between museum stops, I've sandwiched a visit to the city's impressive botanical garden, where one can replenish one's energies gazing on all varieties of foliage. ***Note:*** This trip is best done with a car.

❶ Marion Koogler McNay Art Museum ★★

I love the building, the landscaping, and the view, but also the collection. It holds works by many of the great artists of the late 19th and early 20th centuries including Cézanne, Matisse, and O'Keeffe. See p. 117.

❷ San Antonio Botanical Garden ★

Here you'll find wonderful gardens, a great variety of habitats, and plenty of literature to help you with your own landscaping. The city of San Antonio faces serious water problems. It's the largest city in America to use an aquifer as its main water source. See p. 126.

❸ San Antonio Museum of Art ★★

Housed in the old Lone Star Beer Brewery, the San Antonio Museum of Art is an excellent recycling of old structures to create a distinctive museum. Concentrate on the Rockefeller Center of Latin American Art, and if you still have energy left, follow your tastes. If you like Asian art, the museum's Brown Collection is rather good; if you prefer antiquities, there's a small but handsome collection of Egyptian and Greek pieces. See p. 116.

TAKE A BREAK

I like mixing up high culture and natural beauty with the down-home and relaxed local experience at **Liberty Bar ★**. The lunch specials in this old saloon are good and reasonably priced. 328 E. Josephine. ✆ **210/227-1187.** See p. 102.

❹ King William District ★

After lunch, stretch your legs in this neighborhood, where there are about 25 blocks of houses. You can do a self-guided tour by picking up a booklet at the offices of the San Antonio Conservation Society, located at 107 King William St., or simply take in the views along King William Street, where you'll see the majority of the grandest houses. See p. 112.

❺ San Antonio Missions National Historical Park ★★

These missions depict the story of an incredible human endeavor—Franciscan friars walking all the way from central Mexico (riding horseback or in carriages was forbidden by their vows of poverty) into the wilds of central Texas, hoping to build here a community of God, free from the corruptions then occurring in the heart of colonial Mexico. The trail starts with Concepción. The missions are within 2 or 3 miles of each other, never very far from the river. In each you will find a park station that provides tourist info and driving directions. Of the four, make sure to see San José, the most historical and architecturally interesting, and Espada, which is interesting from a community perspective. See p. 118.

3 THE BEST OF SAN ANTONIO IN 3 DAYS

Now that you've been cooped up in the city for 2 days it's time to see a bit of the Hill Country. The driving distances in this loop north and west of San Antonio are quite comfortable, which is really saying something in Texas. You can easily see these three towns in a day, do a little strolling around, browse through some antiques stores, and even get in a horseback ride. I like this trip best in the fall and winter months and in the middle of the week, when traffic and crowds are light.

❶ Boerne ★

Take I-10 northwest out of San Antonio. In 30 miles, you arrive at the town of Boerne (pronounced *bur*-nee), a German settlement known for its quaint buildings and antiques stores. It's a good place for walking around, talking to the locals, and enjoying the slow rhythm of life here. See p. 286.

Take Hwy. 46 west to Hwy. 16 west to the town of:

❷ Bandera ★

Bandera is one of the main centers for cowboy culture in Texas, and it holds an important annual rodeo. It's also the dude ranch capital of Texas. But you don't have to stay the night to enjoy a horseback ride. See p. 293.

❸ Castroville

South of Bandera is an oddity for the Texas Hill Country—an old Alsatian settlement from the 1840s. For the first few decades of its existence, it remained an isolated community, with residents not often venturing to neighboring towns. Even today, there remain Alsatian speakers here. See p. 292.

TAKE A BREAK

You've probably already stopped for lunch in Bandera, but you might still want to pass by **Haby's Alsatian Bakery** to pick up some wonderful baked goods for the drive back to San Antonio. 207 U.S. 90 East, Castroville. ✆ **830/931-2118.** See p. 292.

5

Where to Stay in San Antonio

San Antonio has the greatest number of historic hotels of any city in Texas. Those who enjoy staying in hotels that capture the old grandeur will have a lot to choose from. All of these, as well as most of the new luxury hotels, are in the downtown area, which is the most convenient place to stay for getting to know the city. Prices in this prime location tend to be high, especially for hotels on the river. But there are some moderately priced hotels, too.

Near downtown are the King William and Monte Vista historic districts. These have several houses and mansions that have been converted into bed-and-breakfasts. Several are reviewed here. For information about other bed-and-breakfasts in these areas and in other parts of town, check out www.sanantoniobb.org, the website of the **San Antonio Bed & Breakfast Association.** Several of San Antonio's inns can also be booked via **Historic Accommodations of Texas,** P.O. Box 203, Vanderpool, TX 78885 (✆ **800/HAT-0368;** www.hat.org).

On the outskirts of San Antonio are two top-notch destination resorts: the Regency Hill Country Resort & Spa and the Westin La Cantera Resort. Most of their customers are either families or golfers who come here to hole up, relax, and maybe play some golf, with sightseeing as a secondary potential goal.

Expect most downtown hotels to fall into the Very Expensive or Expensive range, especially if they sit right on the river. With a few notable exceptions, detailed below, only chain hotels on the outskirts of downtown tend to be Moderate or Inexpensive. You'll do better to stay in a B&B in a historic area near downtown (the Monte Vista neighborhood gives especially good value), where the rooms are attractive and the service is personal. Although they're not formally called concierges, B&B owners and innkeepers do far more to guide their guests around town than employees given that title in many large city hotels. You can also expect B&Bs to provide fax and other business services, and these days most offer wireless Internet connections.

With a few other exceptions detailed here, the vast majority of the other lodgings around town are low-priced chains. The most convenient are clustered in the northwest, near the Medical Center, and in the north central area, around the airport. For a full alphabetical listing of the accommodations in the city, mapped by area and including rate ranges as well as basic amenities, phone the **San Antonio Convention and Visitors Bureau** (✆ **800/447-3372**) and request a lodging guide. The "Accommodations" section of **www.sanantoniovisit.com** is also a good resource.

Wherever you decide to stay, try to book as far in advance as possible—especially if the property is located downtown. And don't even think about coming to town during Fiesta (the third week in Apr) if you haven't reserved a room 6 months in advance.

In the following reviews, price categories are based on rates for a double room in high season, and they don't factor in the 16.75% room tax. Rates often will be a little higher during Fiesta.

Deal Well, Sleep Well

In large hotels, room rates vary quite a bit based on occupancy, so don't automatically write off hotel choices because of their price category without doing a little checking on prices. The prices listed here are the hotel's "rack rates," the room rate charged without any discount, and you can almost always do better. The San Antonio Convention and Visitors Bureau's annual **SAVE** (San Antonio Vacation Experience) promotion features discounts on hotel rooms (more than 50 properties participate) as well as on dining and entertainment. Some bed-and-breakfasts and hotels offer better rates to those who book for at least 4 days, although a week is usually the minimum. Even though most leisure travelers visit in summer, rooms tend to be less expensive then; in general, rates are highest from November through April, when conventions converge on the town. Rates also are at their highest when the city's festivals cause a run on rooms.

But even during peak times, hotel rates vary widely. Some hotels in San Antonio host business clients during the week, whereas others cater to tourists who come on the weekend, so you never know when a property is not fully booked and willing to give you a good deal. In addition, ask about any discounts you can think of—corporate, senior citizen, military, Internet, AAA, entertainment/hotel coupon books, your Uncle Morty's high-school friendship with the manager—and about packages such as family, romance, or deals that include meals or sightseeing tours. ***Bottom line:*** *Always ask for the lowest-priced room with the most perks available.* Reservation agents are eager to sell rooms, so you shouldn't have a problem getting a good deal.

For more tips on getting the best accommodations and booking rooms online, see also chapter 3.

1 BEST SAN ANTONIO HOTEL BETS

- **Best Place for the Trendy to Be Seen:** The **Hotel Valencia Riverwalk,** 150 E. Houston St. (✆ **866/842-0100** or 210/227-9700), hosts Vbar and Citrus, two of the hottest hangouts in town. And flanking the hotel are Acenar and Sip, two other top stylish spots. See p. 74.
- **Best Value for Business Travelers:** Such features as a location near the convention center and high-speed Internet access in the room make the **O'Brien Historic Hotel,** 116 Navarro St. (✆ **800/257-6058** or 210/527-1111), convenient for all business travelers, while low rates and perks such as free local phone calls make it especially appealing to those whose companies aren't picking up the tab. See p. 80.
- **The Best Place to See (or Feel) a Ghost:** San Antonio's got plenty of historic hotels—the kind where haunts tend to linger—but only **The Menger,** 204 Alamo Plaza (✆ **800/345-9285** or 210/223-4361), claims to have 32 ghosts. You can take your pick of the spirits you want to sleep with—or drink with. The bar where Teddy Roosevelt recruited his Rough Riders is in this hotel, too. See p. 77.

- **Best for Families:** If you can afford it, the **Hyatt Regency Hill Country Resort & Spa,** 9800 Hyatt Resort Dr. (© **800/233-1234** or 210/647-1234), just down the road from SeaWorld, is ideal for a family getaway. Kids get to splash in their own shallow pool, go tubing on a little river, and participate in a kids' camp, and you get to relax in the resort's spa or play a few holes on its expanding golf course. See p. 88.
- **Best Riverside Bargain:** The **Drury Inn & Suites,** 201 N. St. Mary's St. (© **800/DRURY-INN** [378-7946] or 210/212-5200), is a good, economical downtown bet located in a historic building right on the river. Breakfast and afternoon cocktails are included in the room rate, and in-room fridges and microwaves mean you can cut down on food costs in this pricey area even further. See p. 79.
- **Best Budget Lodging:** How do I love the savings at the **Best Western Sunset Suites,** 1103 E. Commerce St. (© **866/560-6000** or 210/223-4400)? Let me count the ways: Low room rates, lots of freebies, and a convenient location near downtown, plus very attractive rooms, make staying here a super deal. See p. 78.
- **Best B&B:** The King William area abounds with B&Bs, but the **Ogé House,** 209 Washington St. (© **800/242-2770** or 210/223-2353), stands out as much for its professionalism as for its gorgeous mansion and lovely rooms. New management has added such modern amenities as Wi-Fi, too. It's hard to beat this mix of the old and the new. See p. 81.
- **Best One-Stop Lodging:** You never have to wander far from the **Marriott Rivercenter,** 101 Bowie St. (© **800/228-9290** or 210/223-1000), with its excellent health club (on the same floor as the hotel's free washers and dryers, no less); its proximity to the Rivercenter Mall and to water taxis that take you along the River Walk; and its abundant on-site eateries. See p. 74.
- **Best Place to Spot Celebrities:** Everyone from Paula Abdul to ZZ Top (hey, they're big in Texas) has stayed at **Omni La Mansión del Río,** 112 College St. (© **800/292-7300** or 210/518-1000); discretion, a willingness to cater to special requests, and a location that's just slightly away from the action might explain why. See p. 75.
- **Best for River Views:** The River Walk is best viewed from a modest height, because you lose something from 12 stories up. At **Omni La Mansión del Río,** 112 College St. (© **800/292-7300** or 210/518-1000), the views from the hotel's balconies are ideal. The hotel is only six stories tall, and this stretch of the river, bordered by tall cypress trees, evokes a sense of calm. See p. 75.

2 DOWNTOWN

VERY EXPENSIVE

Hotel Contessa ★★ This is one of the newest hotels to be built on the river, and its location makes you wonder why someone waited so long to build here. Fronting the property is a massive cypress tree crowning a small circle of land that juts out into the river.

The architecture follows a familiar pattern, with rooms surrounding a soaring atrium. Glass elevators take you up the 12 stories to the rooms, all of them suites. All open to a sitting room of good size. Rooms are furnished in more traditional style than the common areas of the hotel, with Southwestern accents. Both the furniture and the lighting are more comfortable than most of the hotels in this category. The bathroom is attractive and ample, but nothing beyond the norm. The next door leads to the bedroom, which

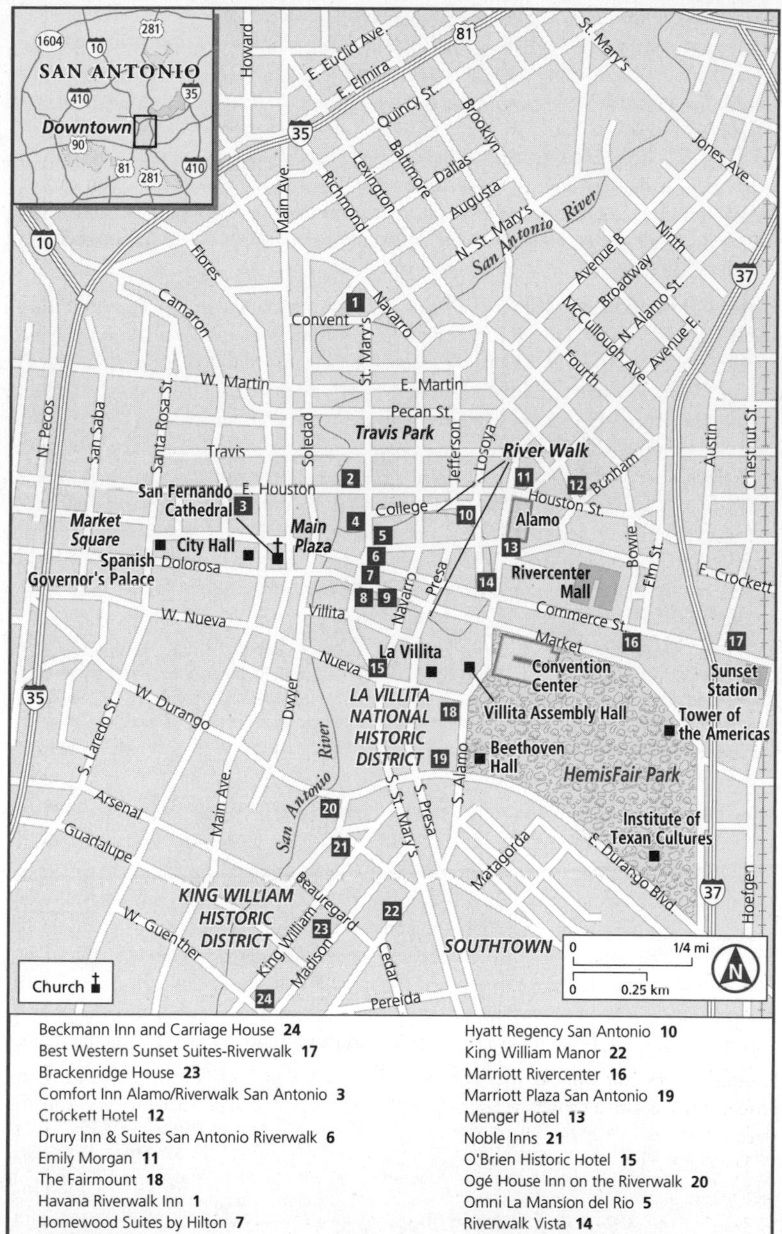
SAN ANTONIO
Downtown
Howard
E. Euclid Ave.
E. Elmira
St. Mary's
Quincy St.
Brooklyn
Main Ave.
Richmond
Lexington
Baltimore
Dallas
Augusta
N. St. Mary's
San Antonio River
Jones Ave.
Ninth
Avenue B
Broadway
N. Alamo St.
McCullough Ave.
Avenue E.
Fourth
Flores
Camaron
Convent
Navarro
St. Mary's
W. Martin
E. Martin
Pecan St.
Travis Park
N. Pecos
San Saba
Santa Rosa St.
Travis
Soledad
Jefferson
Losoya
River Walk
Bonham
Austin
Chestnut St.
San Fernando Cathedral
E. Houston
Houston St.
College
Alamo
Market Square
City Hall
Main Plaza
Spanish Governor's Palace
Dolorosa
Presa
Rivercenter Mall
Bowie
Elm St.
E. Crockett
W. Nueva
Villita
Commerce St.
Market
Nueva
La Villita
Convention Center
Sunset Station
LA VILLITA NATIONAL HISTORIC DISTRICT
Villita Assembly Hall
Tower of the Americas
Beethoven Hall
HemisFair Park
W. Durango
S. Laredo St.
Dwyer
Main Ave.
S. St. Mary's
S. Presa
S. Alamo
Arsenal
Guadalupe
Institute of Texan Cultures
E. Durango Blvd.
Matagorda
Hoefgen
Beauregard
KING WILLIAM HISTORIC DISTRICT
W. Guenther
King William
Madison
Cedar
SOUTHTOWN
Pereida
Church
0 1/4 mi
0 0.25 km
N
Beckmann Inn and Carriage House 24
Best Western Sunset Suites-Riverwalk 17
Brackenridge House 23
Comfort Inn Alamo/Riverwalk San Antonio 3
Crockett Hotel 12
Drury Inn & Suites San Antonio Riverwalk 6
Emily Morgan 11
The Fairmount 18
Havana Riverwalk Inn 1
Homewood Suites by Hilton 7
Hotel Contessa 9
Hotel Valencia Riverwalk 2
Hyatt Regency San Antonio 10
King William Manor 22
Marriott Rivercenter 16
Marriott Plaza San Antonio 19
Menger Hotel 13
Noble Inns 21
O'Brien Historic Hotel 15
Ogé House Inn on the Riverwalk 20
Omni La Mansíon del Rio 5
Riverwalk Vista 14
The Watermark Hotel & Spa 4
Westin Riverwalk Inn 8

comes with either a river or a city view. The best river views are down low, at level with the cypress trees, and the best city views are up high. All rooms are nonsmoking. Each comes with either a king-size or two double beds.

Hotel operations are handled by Benchmark, which, in my experience, does a commendable job at providing services and running properties. All things being equal, I would prefer staying here to staying at the Westin, next door. The matter would depend largely on the rates.

306 W. Market St. (at Navarro), San Antonio, TX 78205. ✆ **866/435-0900** or 210/229-9222. Fax 210/229-9228. www.thehotelcontessa.com. 265 units. $219–$289 suite; executive suites from $339. AE, DC, DISC, MC, V. Valet parking $25. **Amenities:** Restaurant; bar; outdoor heated pool; gym; spa; Jacuzzi; concierge; business center; room service until 10pm; laundry service; dry cleaning. *In room:* A/C, TV, Wi-Fi, minibar, coffeemaker, hair dryer, iron, safe.

Hotel Valencia Riverwalk The Valencia is considered one of the hippest hotels on the River Walk. The rooms are super chic—lots of contrasts, retro lamps, and tongue-in-cheek touches, such as the faux mink throw on the bed—and very techie-friendly. The on-site **Vbar** and **Citrus** restaurant are übertrendy, and the panoply of colors and sounds (a splashing waterfall, music wafting through the halls) that you encounter as you enter the hotel is stimulating. But the entryway, on a busy street with a limited area for luggage (or vehicle) drop-off, is a tad *too* stimulating, whether or not the remote Palm Pilot check-in is in operation. The hallways leading to the guest quarters are narrow and dark, and the rooms themselves have too many individual dimmer switches and lighting devices, and not enough space. The priciest rooms offer river views from narrow balconies. If you're looking for something bold, new, and different, the Valencia is a great choice. But if you're regular folk just seeking a stress-free getaway, look elsewhere.

150 E. Houston St. (at St. Mary's), San Antonio, TX 78205. ✆ **866/842-0100** or 210/227-9700. Fax 210/227-9701. www.hotelvalencia.com. 213 units. $189–$289 double; suites from $450. Leisure, corporate, and Internet rates available. AE, DC, DISC, MC, V. Valet parking $27. **Amenities:** Restaurant; bar; exercise room; spa; concierge; business center; Wi-Fi in public areas; 24-hr room service; laundry service; dry cleaning. *In room:* A/C, TV w/pay movies, high-speed Internet access and Wi-Fi, minibar, hair dryer, iron.

Hyatt Regency San Antonio on the River Walk ★ All that glass and steel rising from this hotel's lobby is impressive. With the Hyatt's signature cage elevators ascending and descending through the sky-lit atrium, the sense of open space and airiness makes the hotel feel bustling rather than overcrowded. The hotel gets business travelers and families alike, who both enjoy its convenience to all the downtown attractions. The Hyatt is on the popular South Bank section, where the river runs closest to the Alamo, and some of that water runs through the lobby, adding to the overall effect. Unlike with many Hyatts, the rooms here have a sense of place thanks to decor and artwork that mark something of a southwest style. These rooms are comfortable, especially the mattresses. Of note, too, is the New Orleans style bar **The Landing,** longtime home to the Dixieland jazz of Jim Cullum and his band (see chapter 9).

123 Losoya St. (at College St.), San Antonio, TX 78205. ✆ **800/233-1234** or 210/222-1234. Fax 210/227-4925. www.sanantonioregency.hyatt.com. 632 units. $269–$349 double; $328–$768 suite. AE, DC, DISC, MC, V. Self-parking $21; valet parking $27. **Amenities:** Restaurant; 2 bars; outdoor heated pool; 24-hr. health club; concierge; business center; Wi-Fi in public areas; shopping arcade; room service; laundry; dry cleaning; club-level rooms. *In room:* A/C, TV w/pay movies, Wi-Fi, minibar, coffeemaker, hair dryer, iron.

Marriott Rivercenter This high-rise hotel connected to the Rivercenter Mall has access to the river and is close to the Alamo, HemisFair Park, and the convention center.

It has a lot of rooms and consequently does a lot of convention business. The location is great for shoppers and sightseers alike.

Guest rooms are attractive and comfortable, and most afford good views of the city. But they aren't readily distinguishable from Marriott hotel rooms anywhere else in the country. Convenience is definitely a plus here; for example, free washers and dryers on the same floor as the health club allow you to bicycle while your clothes cycle. If you find all this convenience and its accompanying bustle a bit overwhelming, an option is to stay at the smaller Marriott Riverwalk across the street. This slightly older and less-expensive sister hotel has comfortable Southwest-style rooms, and its guests have access to all the facilities of the Rivercenter. All rooms are nonsmoking.

101 Bowie St. (at Commerce St.), San Antonio, TX 78205. ✆ **800/228-9290** or 210/223-1000. Fax 210/223-6239. www.marriott.com. 1,001 units. $249–$349 double; suites from $450. AE, DC, DISC, MC, V. Self-parking $21; valet parking $26. Pets under 20 lb. permitted with $25 deposit. **Amenities:** 3 restaurants; indoor pool; outdoor pool; health club; Jacuzzi; sauna; concierge; car-rental desk; business center; Wi-Fi in public areas; 24-hr. room service; babysitting; laundry service; dry cleaning; free use of washers and dryers; club-level rooms; shoeshine stand; ATM. *In room:* A/C, TV/w pay movies, high speed Internet access, Wi-Fi, coffeemaker, hair dryer, iron.

Omni La Mansión del Río ★★ This hotel is pure San Antonio and is the favorite choice of Texan out-of-towners. The core of the building was constructed in 1852 for a seminary, and renovations and expansions have kept the character of the original. Rooms have local flavor, with many featuring Mexican tile floors, beamed ceilings, and wrought-iron balconies. Unlike many of the other big hotels on the river, this six-floor one is not a high-rise. Rooms with a river view are level with the tall cypress trees that line the river bank, and the hotel's location on a central, yet relatively quiet, section of the River Walk is ideal. Interior rooms look out over landscaped courtyards. Since the Omni chain took over management in 2006, all the rooms have been remodeled. Most are large and are decorated with highly textured plush fabrics to set off the rustic elements of the room.

Guests can use the health club and spa at the hotel's sister property, the Watermark (see below), just across the river. The hotel's dining room, **Las Canarias,** serves up its excellent American cuisine accompanied by a terrific view of the river (see chapter 6 for the full review).

112 College St. (between St. Mary's and Navarro), San Antonio, TX 78205. ✆ **800/830-1400** or 210/518-1000. Fax 210/226-0389. www.omnilamansion.com. 337 units. $229–$429 double; suites from $1,039. AE, DC, DISC, MC, V. Valet parking $28. Pets under 20 lb. accepted for $25 per pet per day. **Amenities:** Restaurant; outdoor heated pool; fitness room; concierge; business center; 24-hr. room service; laundry/dry cleaning; complimentary transportation around downtown business district. *In room:* A/C, TV w/pay movies, high-speed Internet access, minibar, coffeemaker, hair dryer, iron.

The Watermark Hotel & Spa ★★★ This is the most luxurious of the River Walk hotel properties. The welcoming Western-style lobby pays tribute to the historic L. Frank Saddlery Building that once occupied this site. The rooms are some of the nicest in San Antonio. Bright, with high ceilings, they have a Texas-meets-Tokyo elegance, their leather and wrought-iron accents balanced by a Zen-like sea-foam green and off-white color scheme; the marble bathrooms offer jetted tubs. Outside of the resorts on the outskirts of town, this hotel has the city's best spa and beauty salon—not to mention **Pesca,** arguably San Antonio's premiere seafood restaurant (see chapter 6 for the full review).

And that's not even getting into the service. Instead of a stressful encounter at the front desk when you arrive, you're escorted to your room—where your minifridge has been stocked with goodies that you requested in advance—to complete the check-in process. With the spa, the soothing guest quarters, and the staff attentiveness, you'd have to have the personality of Woody Allen not to relax in this place. All rooms are nonsmoking.

212 W. Crockett St. (at St. Mary's), San Antonio, TX 78205. ✆ **800/785-1400** or 210/396-5800. Fax 210/226-0389. www.watermarkhotel.com. 99 units. $319–$469 double; $939 suite. AE, DC, DISC, MC, V. Valet parking $28. **Amenities:** Restaurant; cafe; outdoor pool; health club; spa; whirlpool; concierge; business center; salon; 24-hr. room service; dry cleaning. *In room:* A/C, TV w/pay movies, high-speed Internet access, minifridge, coffeemaker, hair dryer, iron, safe.

Westin Riverwalk Inn ★★ (Kids) The recycling of downtown historic buildings into hotels is an admirable trend, but there's also something to be said for new construction—at least when it's done right. Opened at the very end of the last century, this property was designed to blend in architecturally with the older structures that flank it on this (relatively) quiet section of the river bend, but its clean lines are attuned to 21st-century style.

From the lobby to the rooms, varying materials of contrasting textures and Spanish colonial accents create an atmosphere that's soothing without being bland. Of course, the property includes Westin's signature "Heavenly Beds." Perhaps in a nod to its many high-end Latin American business visitors, the hotel has a traditional Merienda Wednesday to Friday evenings, which includes Mexican hot chocolate, sweet bread, cookies, and refreshments (it's free to hotel guests). This Westin has also nicely incorporated several kid-friendly features (see "Family-Friendly Hotels" on p. 82). All rooms are nonsmoking.

420 W. Market St. (at Navarro), San Antonio, TX 78205. ✆ **800/WESTIN-1** [937-8461] or 210/224-6500. Fax 210/444-6000. www.westin.com/riverwalk. 473 units. $339–$419 double; $419–$479 suite. AE, DC, DISC, MC, V. Valet parking $25. **Amenities:** Restaurant; lounge; outdoor heated pool; health club; sauna; concierge; business center; 24-hr. room service; laundry service; dry cleaning. *In room:* A/C, TV w/pay movies, high speed Internet access, Wi-Fi, minibar, coffeemaker, hair dryer, iron, safe.

EXPENSIVE

Emily Morgan ★★ (Value) This hotel is 2 blocks from the River Walk, on the north side of the Alamo. It's in a tall, classic skyscraper built in the 1920s, when architects didn't shy away from exuberance and had large budgets for architectural detail. The style is heavily Gothic, which makes it one of the most easily recognized landmarks in San Antonio. Many rooms have excellent views of the Alamo and its grounds. The furnishings are contemporary, plush, and streamlined; sliding doors to the bathroom add to the uncluttered look. These features lend the rooms a clean, up-to-date look. A nod to romance is provided by votive candles and a CD player. This place is considerably less expensive than many comparable hotels on the river, and its combination of style, luxury, and history is hard to beat. The hotel has a very liberal pet policy and even includes cat and dog treats on the room-service menu. Smoking is not permitted in any of the guest rooms.

705 E. Houston St. (at Ave. E), San Antonio, TX 78205. ✆ **800/824-6674** or 210/225-5100. Fax 210/225-7227. www.emilymorganhotel.com. 177 units. $169–$269 double; $229–$279 suite. Corporate promotional rates available. AE, DC, DISC, MC, V. Valet parking $26. Pets permitted with $75 fee. **Amenities:** Restaurant; outdoor heated pool; exercise room; Jacuzzi; sauna; concierge; Wi-Fi in public areas; 24-hr. room service; laundry service; dry cleaning. *In room:* A/C, TV w/pay movies, Wi-Fi, minifridge, coffeemaker, hair dryer, iron, CD player.

The Fairmount ★★ Not to be confused with the Fairmont luxury hotels, this is a small San Antonio original, independently owned and one of a kind. Built in 1906 for the benefit of railroad passengers, the entire three-story, redbrick Victorian was moved 6 blocks (in one piece) to its present site in 1985. The move made headlines and the *Guinness Book of World Records.* Elaborate decorative details in the hotel's interior were thus preserved and add to the charm of staying here. All the rooms are decorated in period style and furnished with antiques. They vary a great deal, but most are of comfortable size and have lovely marble bathrooms. What doesn't vary is the personal service, which is quite attentive. Staying here, you won't be lost among the masses, as can be the case at larger hotels; and because the rooms are so different, you can come several times and have a different experience on each visit. All rooms are nonsmoking.

401 S. Alamo St. (at E. Nueva), San Antonio, TX 78205. ✆ **877/229-8808** or 210/224-8800. Fax 210/224-2767. www.fairmountsa.com. 37 units. $179–$229 double; suites from $399. AE, DC, DISC, MC, V. Valet parking $25. Pets permitted with no extra charge or deposit. **Amenities:** Restaurant; bar; exercise room; concierge; business center; room service; in-room massage; laundry service; dry cleaning. *In room:* A/C, TV/DVD, Wi-Fi, minibar, minifridge (in half of the rooms), coffeemaker, hair dryer, iron.

Marriott Plaza San Antonio ★ Pheasants and peacocks stroll the beautifully landscaped grounds of this gracious hotel, located across from HemisFair Park, close to La Villita, and just north of the King William district. Four 19th-century buildings that were saved from HemisFair's bulldozer in 1968 were later incorporated into the Plaza complex. Three are used for small conference centers—the initialing ceremony for the North American Free Trade Agreement was held in one of them—and the fourth houses a health club and spa. This is also one of the few hotels in town that has lit tennis courts—not to mention a croquet lawn.

The service is old-world, too. The staff is efficient and friendly, and you're pampered with such touches as a complimentary shoeshine and evening turndowns with bottled water and filled ice buckets. And while the old-world-style facilities had begun to look just plain old in recent years, a $6-million revamp of the public areas and rooms has more than made up for the ravages of time. All rooms are nonsmoking.

555 S. Alamo St. (at Durango), San Antonio, TX 78205. ✆ **800/421-1172** or 210/229-1000. Fax 210/229-1418. www.plazasa.com. 251 units. $169–$274 double; suites from $400. AE, DC, DISC, MC, V. Self-parking $21; valet parking $27. Pets up to 20 lb. accepted with $50 deposit. **Amenities:** Restaurant; bar; outdoor pool; tennis courts; croquet garden; health club; Jacuzzi; bikes (free); concierge; business center; Wi-Fi in public areas; limited room service; massage; babysitting; laundry service; dry cleaning. *In room:* A/C, TV w/pay movies, high-speed Internet access, coffeemaker, hair dryer, iron.

Menger Hotel ★ In the late 19th century, no one who was anyone would consider staying anywhere but the Menger, which opened its doors in 1859 and has never closed them. Ulysses S. Grant, Sarah Bernhardt, and Oscar Wilde were among those who walked—or, rumor has it, in the case of Robert E. Lee, rode a horse—through the halls, ballrooms, and gardens. Successfully combining the original, restored building with myriad additions, the Menger now takes up an entire city block. The hotel's location is terrific—smack between the Alamo and the Rivercenter Mall, a block from the River Walk. And its public areas, particularly the Victorian Lobby, are gorgeous. The **Menger Bar** (see chapter 9) is one of San Antonio's historic taverns, and while nearly every historic hotel in town promotes a ghost, this one claims to have no fewer than 32. The Menger also has a small spa, still a relative rarity in San Antonio hotels.

Ask for one of the recently refurbished rooms, as those that haven't been redone are somewhat tired. Decor ranges from ornate 19th-century to modern. If you want one of the antiques-filled Victorian rooms, be sure to request it when you book. All rooms are nonsmoking.

204 Alamo Plaza (at Crockett St.), San Antonio, TX 78205. ✆ **800/345-9285** or 210/223-4361. Fax 210/228-0022. www.historicmenger.com. 316 units. $159–$229 double; $250–$495 suite. Internet specials sometimes available. AE, DC, DISC, MC, V. Valet parking $25. **Amenities:** Restaurant; bar; outdoor pool; fitness room; spa; Jacuzzi; shopping arcade; limited room service; laundry service; dry cleaning. *In room:* A/C, TV w/pay movies, high-speed Internet access, hair dryer, iron.

MODERATE

Best Western Sunset Suites–Riverwalk ★ Value Don't be put off by the fact that this all-suites hotel is located on the wrong side of the tracks, er, highway. In a converted turn-of-the-century building, you'll find some of the nicest rooms in downtown San Antonio for the price—large, with custom-made Arts and Crafts–style furnishings, including comfy lounge chairs and faux Tiffany lamps. They're well equipped, too. All offer sleeper sofas, microwaves, minifridges, and 27-inch TVs.

1103 E. Commerce St. (at Hwy. 281), San Antonio, TX 78205. ✆ **866/560-6000** or 210/223-4400. Fax 210/223-4402. www.bestwesternsunsetsuites.com. 64 units. $120–$165 double. Internet specials available. AE, DC, DISC, MC, V. Free parking. **Amenities:** Health club; business center. *In room:* A/C, TV w/pay movies, Wi-Fi, kitchenette, coffeemaker, hair dryer, iron.

Comfort Inn Alamo/Riverwalk San Antonio Value I'm no expert on the Comfort Inn chain, but I've been in enough of the lodgings to know that this one is nothing like the rest. First and foremost, it occupies the old Bexar (pronounced *bear*) County Jail and is a regular hotel with indoor corridors and a front desk at the entrance. But what impressed me was the cleanliness and the comfort of the rooms. The bathrooms were also a surprise, a little larger and much more attractive than the usual at this price level, with such touches as polished granite countertops. The largest rooms come with two queen beds and are quite comfortable. Other options are a king bed and the studio king. Service here is friendly and attentive. All rooms are nonsmoking.

In the last couple of years it has become popular with repeat visitors to San Antonio, but you can still occasionally get a deal. Because it is under the Comfort Inn label, you might find this property discounted by some of the hotel room vendors. The location is good, in the western part of downtown San Antonio, about 3 blocks from the River Walk.

120 Camaron St. (btw. Houston and Commerce), San Antonio, TX 78205. ✆ **800/223-4990** or 210/281-1400. Fax 210/228-0007. www.comfortinnsanantonio.com. 82 units. $120–$189 double. Rates include continental breakfast. AE, DC, DISC, MC, V. Off-site parking (1 block away). **Amenities:** Outdoor heated pool; Jacuzzi; business center; laundry service; dry cleaning; coin-op washer/dryer. *In room:* A/C, TV, high-speed Internet access, fridge, microwave, coffeemaker, hair dryer, iron.

Crockett Hotel ★ Value This hotel comes by its name honestly, unlike many of the places that bank on Davy Crockett's moniker. The famed Alamo hero definitely walked the land on which this hotel rose in 1909, as it—the land, that is—served as the Alamo's battleground. The property is a bit of a hybrid, consisting of the original historical landmark building (expanded in 1927) and several low-slung, motel-style units that surround what may be downtown's nicest swimming pool and a tropical landscaped courtyard. Rooms in both sections of the hotel are attractive, with lots of vibrant Southwest colors and allusions to Texas history (regional artwork, pine beds with Lone Star headboards, and the like). Look for deals; rooms here are discounted for every imaginable reason. The location is excellent, by the Alamo and the Rivercenter Mall and close by the river.

320 Bonham St. (at Crockett St.), San Antonio, TX 78205. ✆ **800/292-1050** or 210/225-6500. Fax 210/225-7418. www.crocketthotel.com. 204 units. Rooms $139–$157; suites from $375. Various discounts (including Internet booking and specials). AE, DC, DISC, MC, V. Valet parking $25. Pets accepted; $100 deposit required ($50 refundable). **Amenities:** Restaurant; lounge; unheated outdoor pool and hot

tub; limited room service; coin-op laundry; same day dry cleaning (Mon–Fri). *In room:* A/C, TV w/pay movies, high-speed Internet access, coffeemaker, hair dryer, iron.

Drury Inn & Suites San Antonio Riverwalk (Value) One of San Antonio's most recent River Walk conversions, the one-time Petroleum Commerce Building is now a comfortable modern lodging. The polished marble floors and chandeliers in the lobby and the high ceilings and ornate window treatments in the guest rooms hearken back to a grander era, also evoked in perks such as free hot breakfasts, free evening cocktails and snacks, free local phone calls, and 1 hour of free long distance per day. Guests also appreciate the 24-hour business center. Anyone who wants to economize on meals will also like the fact that many of these attractive Southwest-style rooms are equipped with refrigerators and microwaves.

201 N. St. Mary's St. (at Commerce St.), San Antonio, TX 78205. ✆ **800/DRURY-INN** [378-7946] or 210/212-5200. Fax 210/352-9939. www.druryhotels.com. 150 units. $129–$164 double; $164–$199 suite. AE, DC, DISC, MC, V. Self-parking $14. Small pets accepted. **Amenities:** Restaurant; outdoor pool; exercise room; Jacuzzi; 24-hr. business center; Wi-Fi in public areas; dry cleaning. *In room:* A/C, TV, Wi-Fi, fridge and microwave (in king rooms and suites), coffeemaker, hair dryer, iron.

Havana Riverwalk Inn ★ Decked out to suggest travelers' lodgings from the 1920s, this intimate inn—built in 1914 in Mediterranean Revival style—oozes character. All the guest quarters are delightfully different, with a safari hat covering a temperature control gauge here, an old photograph perched over a toilet paper roll there, gauzy curtains draped on a canopy bed, wooden louvers on the windows, and so on. Such touches as fresh flowers and bottled water add to the charm, and modern amenities, such as irons, have not been ignored. Not all rooms have closets, however, so be prepared to have your clothes (ironed or not) hanging in public view if you plan to invite anyone to your room. Singles will absolutely want to hit the hotel's happening cigar bar, **Club Cohiba.** Rooms are nonsmoking.

1015 Navarro (btw. St. Mary's and Martin sts.), San Antonio, TX 78205. ✆ **888/224-2008** or 210/222-2008. Fax 210/222-2717. www.havanariverwalkinn.com. 28 units. $149–$199 double; $399–$599 suite. AE, DC, DISC, MC, V. Self-parking $10. Only children ages 15 and older accepted. **Amenities:** Restaurant; bar; concierge; business center; secretarial services; limited room service; laundry service; dry cleaning. *In room:* A/C, TV, high-speed Internet access, hair dryer, iron.

Homewood Suites by Hilton ★ (Kids) Occupying the former San Antonio Drug Company building (built in 1919), this all-suites hotel is a good downtown deal. Located on a quiet stretch of the river, it's convenient to west-side attractions, such as Market Square, and located only a few more blocks away from the Alamo. In-room amenities, such as microwave ovens, refrigerators with ice makers, and dishwashers, appeal to business travelers and families alike. The dining area can double as a work space, and there's a sleeper sofa in each suite as well as two TVs with VCRs, which means fewer squabbles over TV shows and movies. The decor is a cut above that of most chains in this price range, with Lone Star–design headboards, wood desks, and bureaus. Suites on the south side have river views.

432 W. Market St. (at St. Mary's St.), San Antonio, TX 78205. ✆ **800/CALL-HOME** [225-5466] or 210/222-1515. Fax 210/222-1575. www.homewood-suites.com. 146 units. $169–$299 suite. Rates include breakfast and (Mon–Fri) afternoon drinks and snacks. AE, DC, DISC, MC, V. Valet parking $24. **Amenities:** Outdoor pool; fitness center; Jacuzzi; concierge; business center; Wi-Fi in public areas; coin-op washer/dryers; dry cleaning. *In room:* A/C, TV/VCR w/pay movies, high-speed Internet access, full kitchens, coffeemaker, hair dryer, iron.

O'Brien Historic Hotel ★ Value This hotel is not all that historic; the 1904 building it occupies was gutted, so only the facade is old. But who cares when you've got attractive rooms with luxury appointments for very reasonable prices? Deep greens and golds, gilt touches, and nice carpeting lend a richness to the guest quarters, as do the upscale bed and bath linens, robes, CD players, and such perks as a free overnight shoeshine. Some rooms offer balconies and/or whirlpool tubs. And the savings afforded by moderate room rates are supplemented by such things as free bottled water and local phone calls. Opened in 2003, this small property became an instant hit with conventioneers who like the in-room business perks and the location, some 4 blocks from the convention center. It's great for leisure travelers, too, as it's right near La Villita and a quiet part of the River Walk, and close to both the heart of downtown and the King William district. This is a totally nonsmoking hotel.

116 Navarro St. (at St. Mary's), San Antonio, TX 78205. ✆ **800/257-6058** or 210/527-1111. Fax 210/527-1112. www.obrienhotel.com. 39 units. $199 double. Rates include continental breakfast. AE, DC, DISC, MC, V. Self-parking $15. **Amenities:** Exercise room; coin-op washer/dryers; dry cleaning. *In room:* A/C, TV w/HBO, high-speed Internet access, coffeemaker, hair dryer, iron.

Riverwalk Vista ★★ Value Intimacy, history, amenities—that's a tough combination to beat. The 17 rooms in the 1883 Dullnig building are extremely attractive, with beautifully finished pine floors, large windows, high ceilings, and elegant reproduction pieces. They come with all the modern fittings, including flatscreen TVs with DVD players, as well as such posh touches as plush robes, makeup mirrors, and umbrellas. The location (near the River Walk, Alamo, and other top downtown sights) and lack of parking make this hotel a good choice for those without a car. In this area, you're far better off without one anyway. Rooms can be a little noisy but come equipped with a white-noise machine. This hotel's location and charm, combined with amenities that you usually get only in pricier spots, make it worth considering. This is a nonsmoking hotel.

262 Losoya (at Commerce St.), San Antonio, TX 78205. ✆ **866/898-4782** or 210/223-3200. www.riverwalkvista.com. 17 units. $120–$210 double; $180–$270 suite; midweek convention discounts often available. Rates include continental breakfast. AE, DC, DISC, MC, V. **Amenities:** Passes to nearby fitness center; business center. *In room:* A/C, TV/DVD player, high-speed Internet access, minifridge, coffeemaker, hair dryer, iron, safe.

3 KING WILLIAM HISTORIC DISTRICT

EXPENSIVE

Noble Inns ★ It's hard to imagine that Donald and Liesl Noble, both descended from King William founding families, grew up in the neighborhood when it was rundown. The area has undergone an amazing metamorphosis in the short span of the young couple's life. Indeed, their gracious lodgings—the 1894 Jackson House, a traditional-style B&B, and, a few blocks away, the 1896 Aaron Pancoast Carriage House, offering three suites with full kitchens—are a tribute to just how far it has come. The decor in both houses hearkens back to the period in which they were built and manages to do so without being overly fussy. Rooms individually decorated with fine antiques are ideal for business and leisure travelers alike. All have gas fireplaces, while three in the Jackson House and one in the Carriage House feature two-person Jacuzzi tubs. Other luxurious touches include Godiva chocolate at turndown and fresh flowers. A silver-gray classic Rolls Royce is available for airport transportation or downtown drop-off.

107 Madison St. (off St. Mary's St.), San Antonio, TX 78204. ✆ **800/221-4045** or 210/225-4045. Fax 210/227-0877. www.nobleinns.com. 9 units. $159–$225 double; $199–$295 suite. Rates at Jackson House include full breakfast, afternoon snacks, and beverages; rates at Carriage House include continental breakfast. Corporate, Mon–Fri discounts available. AE, DC, DISC, MC, V. Free off-street parking. **Amenities:** Outdoor pool; Jacuzzi; Wi-Fi in public areas. *In room:* A/C, TV, high-speed Internet access, kitchen (carriage house suites only), hair dryer, iron.

Ogé House Inn on the River Walk ★★ One of the most glorious of the mansions that grace the King William district, this 1857 Greek revival–style property is more of a boutique inn than a bed-and-breakfast. You'll still get the personalized attention you would expect from a host home, but it's combined here with the luxury of a sophisticated small hotel. All rooms are impeccably decorated in high Victorian style, yet feature modern conveniences such as small refrigerators. Many rooms also have fireplaces and views of the manicured, pecan-shaded grounds, and one looks out on the river from its own balcony. The units downstairs aren't as light as those on the upper two floors, but they're less expensive and offer private entrances.

A bountiful breakfast is served on individual white-clothed tables set with the finest crystal and china. Travelers can also bury themselves in daily newspapers laid out on the bureau just beyond the dining room. In late 2004, the Nobles (see Noble Inns listing, above) acquired the inn and added such modern touches as Wi-Fi throughout and high-speed Internet access in the rooms.

209 Washington St. (at Turner St.), San Antonio, TX 78204. ✆ **800/242-2770** or 210/223-2353. Fax 210/226-5812. www.ogeinn.com. 10 units. $189–$229 double; suites from $269. Rates include full breakfast. Corporate rates available for single business travelers. 2-night minimum stay Sat–Sun; 3 nights during holidays and special events. AE, DC, DISC, MC, V. Free off-street parking. **Amenities:** Wi-Fi in public areas. *In room:* A/C, TV, high-speed Internet access, high-speed Internet access, fridge, hair dryer, iron.

MODERATE

Beckmann Inn and Carriage House Sitting on the lovely wraparound porch of this 1886 Queen Anne home, surrounded by quiet, tree-lined streets on an underdeveloped stretch of the San Antonio River, you can easily imagine yourself in a kinder, gentler era. In fact, you can still see the flour mill on whose property the Beckmann Inn was originally built. The illusion of time travel won't be dispelled when you step through the rare Texas red-pine door into the high-ceilinged parlor.

The house is filled with antique pieces that do justice to the setting, such as the ornately carved Victorian beds in each of the guest rooms. Two of the rooms have private entrances, as does the separate Carriage House, decorated in a somewhat lighter fashion. Smoking is prohibited in the rooms but allowed in outdoor common areas. A full breakfast—perhaps cranberry French toast topped with orange twist—is served in the formal dining room, but you can also enjoy your coffee on a flower-filled sun porch.

222 E. Guenther St. (at Madison St.), San Antonio, TX 78204. ✆ **800/945-1449** or 210/229-1449. Fax 210/229-1061. www.beckmanninn.com. 6 units. $109–$199. Rates include full breakfast. AE, DC, DISC, MC, V. Free off-street parking. **Amenities:** Wi-Fi in public areas. *In room:* A/C, TV, Wi-Fi, fridge, hair dryer, iron.

Brackenridge House (Finds) These days many B&Bs are beginning to resemble boutique hotels, with an almost hands-off approach on the part of the hosts. If you seek out B&Bs because you prefer warmer, more traditional treatment, this King William abode is likely to suit you.

It's not just that the house is homey rather than fancy—although it's got its fair share of antiques, you don't feel as though they're too priceless to approach—but that owners Sue and Bennie (aka the King of King William) Blansett instantly make you feel welcome. They

Family-Friendly Hotels

Homewood Suites (p. 79) This reasonably priced all-suites hotel near the River Walk, with in-room kitchen facilities and two TVs per suite (each with its own VCR)—not to mention a guest laundry—is extremely convenient for families.

Hyatt Regency Hill Country Resort & Spa (p. 88) In addition to its many great play areas (including a beach with a shallow swimming area), and its proximity to SeaWorld, this hotel offers Camp Hyatt—a program of excursions, sports, and social activities for children ages 3 to 12. The program fills up fast during school breaks and other holidays, making reservations mandatory.

O'Casey's Bed & Breakfast (p. 84) Usually B&Bs and family vacations are a contradiction in terms, but O'Casey's is happy to host well-behaved kids. ***Best bet:*** Stay in the separate guesthouse with the fold-out bed, and then join the main-house guests for breakfast in the morning.

Omni San Antonio (p. 88) This hotel's proximity to the theme parks as well as in-room Nintendo and various other Omni Kids features makes the Omni appealing to families.

Hilton San Antonio Hill Country Hotel & Spa (p. 89) Seasonal specials, such as the Ultimate SeaWorld Adventure package, providing passes, transportation, and complimentary souvenirs for both you and the kids, make this an excellent option.

Westin La Cantera (p. 85) It's close to Six Flags Fiesta Texas, it's got two pools just for children, and it offers the Enchanted Rock Kids Club—an activities program for ages 5 through 12—from May through Labor Day.

Westin Riverwalk Inn (p. 76) Though not as family-friendly as the Westin La Cantera, this Westin on the River Walk still offers such amenities as free in-room movies, a kids' treat pack upon check-in, and bedtime stories told over the phone.

also help you find whatever you need and even provide free trolley passes to get you there. But that's not to say you have to be communal constantly. All rooms have TVs with HBO and Showtime, as well as minifridges, microwaves, and coffeemakers. And if you're really antisocial (or traveling with kids and/or a pet), you can always book the separate carriage house, a few doors down from the main house.

230 Madison St. (off Beauregard St.), San Antonio, TX 78204. ✆ **800/221-1412** or 210/271-3442. www.brackenridgehouse.com. 6 units. $120–$250 double; $150–$275 suites and carriage house. Rates include breakfast (full in main house, continental in carriage house). Corporate, state, and federal rates; extended stay plans available for the carriage house. 2-night minimum stay required Sat–Sun. AE, DC, DISC, MC, V. Free off-street parking. Small pets accepted in carriage house. **Amenities:** Outdoor heated pool; hot tub; Wi-Fi in public areas. *In room:* A/C, TV, Wi-Fi, fridge, microwave, coffeemaker, hair dryer, iron.

King William Manor ★ Guests can stay in the 1892 Greek revival mansion or in an adjacent guesthouse built 9 years later. The mansion is the more opulent and offers unusual walk-through windows leading to a veranda and lots of common areas, which are available to all. Most of the guest rooms are in the guesthouse, which affords more variety, including some large rooms. One of the biggest and most private is the cottage attached to the guesthouse.

The new owners, native Texan Tim Sulak and Brian Wollard, live on the property in a separate cottage and go out of their way to make people feel at home. They've made extensive changes to this property, formerly known as The Columns on Alamo. In addition to installing an outdoor pool and landscaping the grounds, they also refurnished the guest rooms to make them lighter and more comfortable. They've been working hard, and it shows. The location in the King William area is excellent. Within a few blocks are several restaurants, and just 2 blocks away is an entrance to the river trail, which you can take all the way to the River Walk.

1037 S. Alamo (at Sheridan, 5 blocks south of Durango), San Antonio, TX 78210. ✆ **800/405-0365** or 210/222-0144. www.kingwilliammanor.com. 12 units. $119–$175 double. Rates include full breakfast. 2-day minimum stay. AE, DISC, MC, V. Free off-street parking. **Amenities:** Outdoor pool; Wi-Fi in public areas. *In room:* A/C, TV, Wi-Fi, fridge, hair dryer, iron.

4 MONTE VISTA HISTORIC DISTRICT

MODERATE

The Inn at Craig Place ★ This 1891 mansion-turned-B&B appeals to history, art, and architecture buffs alike. It was built by one of Texas's most noted architects, Alfred Giles, for H. E. Hildebrand, a major public figure at the time. The living room holds a mural by Julian Onderdonk, an influential Texas landscape artist, who grew up in Monte Vista in the 1880s.

But that's all academic. More to the point, this place is gorgeous, with forests of gleaming wood and clean Arts and Crafts lines, as well as cushy couches and a wraparound porch. Rooms are equipped for modern needs but still very luxurious; all have working fireplaces and hardwood floors, and come with robes, slippers, feather pillows, and down comforters. The inn offers several packages; be sure to check their website.

117 W. Craig Place (off N. Main Ave.), San Antonio, TX 78212. ✆ **877/427-2447** or 210/736-1017. Fax 210/737-1562. www.craigplace.com. 5 units. $125–$199 double; $160–$210. Corporate rates available. Rates include full breakfast. AE, DC, DISC, MC, V. Free off-street parking. No children younger than 12 years old. *In room:* A/C, TVDVD player, Wi-Fi, hair dryer, iron, no phone.

INEXPENSIVE

Bonner Garden ★ Value Those who like the charm of the bed-and-breakfast experience but aren't keen on Victorian froufrou should consider the Bonner Garden, located about a mile north of downtown. Built in 1910 for Louisiana artist Mary Bonner, this large, Italianate villa has elegantly appointed rooms that steer clear of the cluttered look. It also has something not commonly found at B&Bs: a large 45-foot swimming pool.

The Portico Room, in which guests can gaze up at a painted blue sky with billowing clouds, enjoys a private poolside entrance. You don't have to be honeymooners to enjoy the Jacuzzi tub in the pretty Bridal Suite with its blue porcelain fireplace. Most of the rooms feature European-style decor, but Mary Bonner's former studio, separate from the main house, is done in an attractive Santa Fe style. A rooftop deck affords a sparkling nighttime view of downtown. Smoking is permitted in outdoor areas only.

145 E. Agarita (at McCullough), San Antonio, TX 78212. ✆ **800/396-4222** or 210/733-4222. Fax 210/733-6129. www.bonnergarden.com. 6 units. $115–$165 double. Rates include full breakfast. Extended-stay discount (minimum 3 nights) and corporate rates available. 2-night minimum stay Sat–Sun. AE, DISC, MC, V. Free off-street parking. **Amenities:** Outdoor pool; Wi-Fi. *In room:* A/C, TV/VCR, Wi-Fi, hair dryer, iron (in some rooms).

O'Casey's Bed & Breakfast (Kids) (Value) If there's a twinkle in John Casey's eye when he puts on a brogue, it's because he was born on U.S. soil, not the auld sod. But he and his wife Linda Fay exhibit a down-home friendliness that's no blarney. This Irish-themed B&B is one of the few around that welcomes families and is well equipped to handle them. One suite in the main house has a sitting area with a futon large enough for a couple of youngsters; another has a trundle bed for two kids in a separate bedroom. Studio apartments in the carriage house both offer full kitchens. All of this is not to suggest that accommodations are utilitarian—far from it. Rooms in the main house, a gracious structure built in 1904, feature hardwood floors and antiques, and many bathrooms display claw-foot tubs. There's a wraparound balcony upstairs, too. For a treat, ask Linda (a professional pianist) and John (a choir director and singer) to perform a few numbers for you. All guest rooms are nonsmoking; smoking is permitted in outdoor areas.

225 W. Craig Place (btw. San Pedro Ave. and Main St.), San Antonio, TX 78212. ✆ **800/738-1378** or 210/738-1378. www.ocaseybnb.com. 7 units. $89–$110 double (single-night stays Sat–Sun may be slightly higher). Rates include full breakfast. Extended-stay discounts sometimes available. DISC, MC, V. Street parking. Pets allowed in apartments only; $10 for up to a week. **Amenities:** Wi-Fi in public areas. *In room:* A/C, TV, Wi-Fi, kitchen (in apartments).

Ruckman Haus The accommodations in this pretty turn-of-the-century stucco home, just a block from San Pedro Springs Park, are comfy but elegant, with lots of antiques and plenty of light. Two offer showers with three body jets—almost as good as an in-room massage (which is also available). One unit, the Highlands, is large enough to sleep four, should you decide to bring the kids. Breakfasts are generous, and you can bond with fellow guests over afternoon drinks on either the covered deck or the fern-shaded side patio. The in-room refrigerators come stocked with water, soft drinks, and beer. Hey, it can get toasty in San Antonio, and your friendly hosts don't want you to dehydrate! Designated smoking areas are outside.

629 W. French St. (at Breeden, 1 block west of San Pedro Ave.), San Antonio, TX 78212. ✆ **866/736-1468** or 210/736-1468. Fax 210/736-1468. www.ruckmanhaus.com. 5 units. $100–$120 double; $150–$170 suite. Rates include full breakfast. Corporate rates for single travelers. AE, DISC, MC, V. Free off-street parking. Pets accepted (inquire when making reservations). **Amenities:** Wi-Fi in public areas. *In room:* A/C, TV, Wi-Fi, fridge, coffeemaker, hair dryer.

5 FORT SAM HOUSTON AREA

INEXPENSIVE

Bullis House Inn (Value) This graceful neoclassical mansion, just down the street from the Fort Sam Houston quadrangle and easily accessible from the airport and downtown by car, is an excellent bed-and-breakfast bargain, especially for those who don't mind sharing bathrooms. It was built from 1906 to 1909 for General John Lapham Bullis, a frontier Indian fighter who played a key role in capturing Geronimo (some claim the Apache chief's spirit still roams the mansion). More concerned with creature comforts when he retired, the general had oak paneling, parquet floors, crystal chandeliers, and marble fireplaces installed in his home, which is now often used for wedding receptions. Guest rooms all have 14-foot ceilings and are furnished with some period antiques along with good reproductions; three of them feature fireplaces, and one offers a private bathroom. The family room, which sleeps up to six, also has a refrigerator. VCR and video rentals are among the other perks.

621 Pierce St. (at Grayson, directly across from Fort Sam Houston), San Antonio, TX 78208. ✆ **877/477-4100** or 210/223-9426. Fax 210/299-1479. www.bullishouseinn.com. 8 units. $65–$99 double w/shared bathroom; $109 double w/private bathroom. Weekly rates available; rates reduced if you opt out of breakfast. Rates include continental breakfast. AE, MC, V. Free off-street parking. **Amenities:** Outdoor pool. *In room:* A/C, TV, no phone (except 1 room).

San Antonio International Youth Hostel Right next door to the Bullis House Inn (see above), this youth hostel has a reading room, small kitchen, dining area, lockers, and picnic tables, in addition to male and female dorms and three private rooms. Hostellers are welcome at the Bullis House Inn, and the two lodgings share a pool. A continental breakfast, served at the inn, is available for an additional $5.

621 Pierce St. (at Grayson, directly across from Fort Sam Houston), San Antonio, TX 78208. ✆ **210/223-9426.** Fax 210/299-1479. HISanAnton@aol.com. 38 beds. Dorm beds $25; private rooms $69–$99. AE, MC, V. **Amenities:** Outdoor pool. *In room:* A/C, TV (in private rooms), no phone.

6 NORTHWEST

VERY EXPENSIVE

Westin La Cantera ★★★ Kids This resort gives the slightly older Hyatt Regency Hill Country Resort & Spa (see under "West," below) a run for its money with the well-heeled golfing crowd. They're similar in many ways, with great facilities; sprawling, gorgeous grounds; and loads of Texas character. Both are family-friendly, with theme parks in their backyards (here it's Six Flags Fiesta Texas) and excellent children's programs. But the Westin has the edge when it comes to golf, boasting two championship courses (in addition to the much-praised La Cantera, there's a newer Arnold Palmer–designed course) plus a professional golf school. It's a tad more romantic, too, with dramatic rocky outcroppings and gorgeous views from its perch on one of the highest points in San Antonio. And The Shops at La Cantera provides a mall (with the only Neiman Marcus and Nordstrom in San Antonio) close by with lots of stores and boutiques.

The resort is designed around state historical motifs. The Texas colonial architecture is impressive, and the tales and legends detailed in plaques in the various rooms are interesting; but you'll probably be too busy having fun to pay them much mind. Likewise, the casual, conservatively decorated rooms, although equipped with all the business amenities conference attendees need, are likely to be abandoned for the resort's myriad recreational areas, or at least for the balconies that many of the guest quarters offer. Remnants of the limestone quarry on which the resort was built were incorporated into the five swimming pools interconnected with bridges and channels and a dramatic waterfall. Indigenous wildlife, including deer, rabbits, and wild turkeys, make their appearance at dusk, which is a good time to be exploring the resort's grounds. Or you can enjoy the dusk at the resort's restaurant, **Francesca's at Sunset,** which serves Southwestern and American cooking.

Greater San Antonio Accommodations & Dining

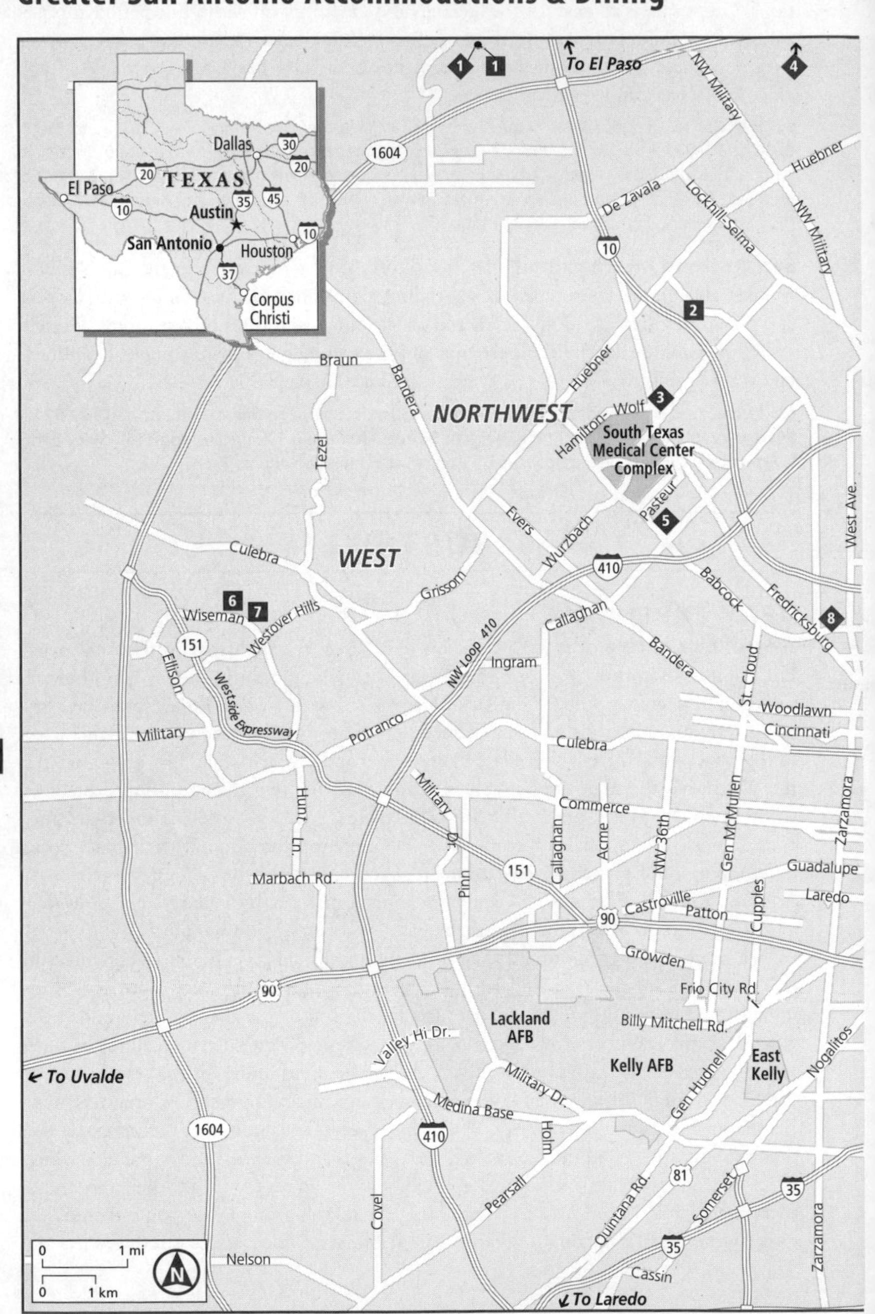

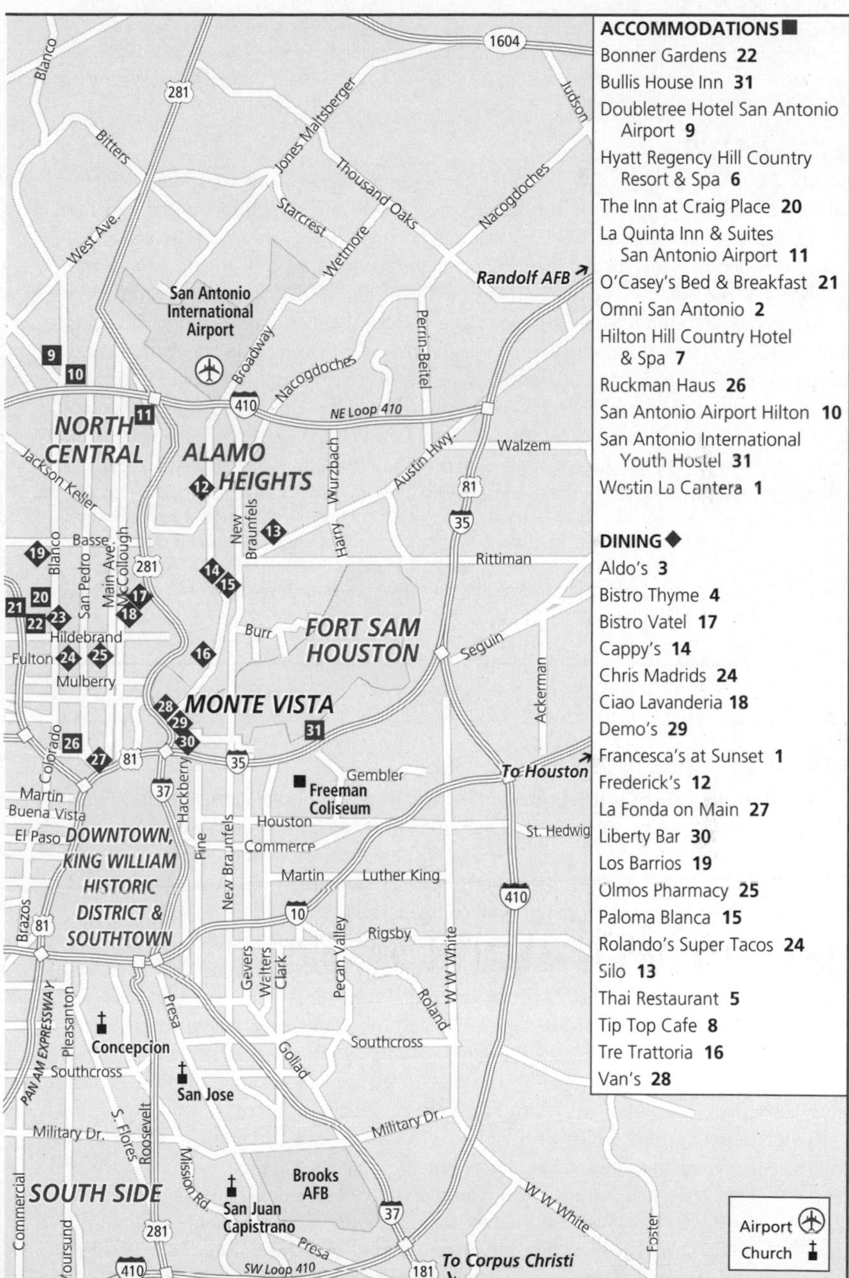
ACCOMMODATIONS
Bonner Gardens 22
Bullis House Inn 31
Doubletree Hotel San Antonio Airport 9
Hyatt Regency Hill Country Resort & Spa 6
The Inn at Craig Place 20
La Quinta Inn & Suites San Antonio Airport 11
O'Casey's Bed & Breakfast 21
Omni San Antonio 2
Hilton Hill Country Hotel & Spa 7
Ruckman Haus 26
San Antonio Airport Hilton 10
San Antonio International Youth Hostel 31
Westin La Cantera 1
DINING
Aldo's 3
Bistro Thyme 4
Bistro Vatel 17
Cappy's 14
Chris Madrids 24
Ciao Lavanderia 18
Demo's 29
Francesca's at Sunset 1
Frederick's 12
La Fonda on Main 27
Liberty Bar 30
Los Barrios 19
Olmos Pharmacy 25
Paloma Blanca 15
Rolando's Super Tacos 24
Silo 13
Thai Restaurant 5
Tip Top Cafe 8
Tre Trattoria 16
Van's 28
Airport
Church
NORTH CENTRAL
ALAMO HEIGHTS
FORT SAM HOUSTON
MONTE VISTA
DOWNTOWN, KING WILLIAM HISTORIC DISTRICT & SOUTHTOWN
SOUTH SIDE
San Antonio International Airport
Freeman Coliseum
Brooks AFB
Concepcion
San Jose
San Juan Capistrano
Randolf AFB
To Houston
To Corpus Christi
NE Loop 410
SW Loop 410
PAN AM EXPRESSWAY

16641 La Cantera Pkwy. (take the La Cantera Pkwy. exit off I-10 and turn left; resort entrance is ¾ mile ahead, on the right), San Antonio, TX 78256. ✆ **800/WESTIN-1** or 210/558-6500. Fax 210/641-0721. www.westinlacantera.com. 508 units. $229–$369 double; suites from $380; casitas from $350. AE, DC, DISC, MC, V. Free self-parking; valet parking $15. **Amenities:** 3 restaurants; 2 bars; outdoor heated pool; 2 golf courses; 2 lit tennis courts; health club; spa; Jacuzzi; children's center; video arcade; concierge; business center; 24-hr. room service; massage; dry cleaning. *In room:* A/C, TV w/pay movies, Wi-Fi, minibar, coffeemaker, hair dryer, iron, safe.

EXPENSIVE

Omni San Antonio ★ Kids This polished granite high-rise off I-10 west is convenient to SeaWorld, Six Flags Fiesta Texas, the airport, and the Hill Country, and the shops and restaurants of the 66-acre Colonnade complex are within easy walking distance. The lobby is soaring and luxurious, and guest rooms are well-appointed in a traditional but cheery style. The proximity to the theme parks, as well as in-room Nintendo and various other Omni Kids features, makes this hotel appealing to families. Business travelers appreciate its exercise facilities, which are better than most in San Antonio and definitely the best in this part of town. Guests can also get treadmills brought into their rooms as part of the Omni "Get Fit" program. Although the hotel sees a lot of tourist and Medical Center traffic, service here is prompt and courteous.

9821 Colonnade Blvd. (at Wurzbach), San Antonio, TX 78230. ✆ **800/843-6664** or 210/691-8888. Fax 210/691-1128. www.omnihotels.com. 326 units. $169 double; suites from $300. A variety of discount packages available. AE, DC, DISC, MC, V. Free self-parking; valet parking $10. Pets 25 lb. or less permitted; $50 nonrefundable fee. **Amenities:** Restaurant; bar; indoor pool; outdoor pool; health club; Jacuzzi; sauna; concierge; free airport shuttle; business center; Wi-Fi in public areas; limited room service; laundry service; dry cleaning; club-level rooms. *In room:* A/C, TV w/pay movies, high-speed Internet access, Wi-Fi, minibar, coffeemaker, hair dryer, iron.

7 WEST

VERY EXPENSIVE

Hyatt Regency Hill Country Resort & Spa ★★★ Kids If I were feeling flush and didn't want to spend a lot of time downtown, this would be my favorite place to settle in for a week. The setting, on 200 acres of former ranch land on the far-west side of San Antonio, is idyllic. The resort's interiors are contemporary and make much use of the native limestone, with Spanish-style wrought iron accents. The on-site activities, ranging from golf to yoga to tubing on the 950-foot-long Ramblin' River, will please a wide range of interests.

And it just keeps getting better. A spa was added with the new millennium. Low-key and relaxing, it boasts all the latest treatments and is one of the best pampering palaces in this part of Texas. The rooms are finished in Southwestern colors and are furnished in a kind of modern version of Spanish colonial. They are large, and many offer French doors that open out onto wood-trimmed porches or balconies.

This resort is the most family-friendly in San Antonio. SeaWorld sits at your doorstep, there are free laundry facilities and a country store for supplies, and every room has a refrigerator (not stocked with goodies). When you're tired of all that family bonding, the Hyatt Kids Club will keep the youngsters happily occupied while you spend some quality time relaxing on "Ramblin' River," which amounts to a kind of re-creation of a central Texas river, of the kind suitable for floating in and letting yourself be carried by the current.

9800 Hyatt Resort Dr. (off Hwy. 151, between Westover Hills Blvd. and Potranco Rd.), San Antonio, TX 78251. ✆ **800/55-HYATT** or 210/647-1234. Fax 210/681-9681. http://hillcountry.hyatt.com. 500 units. $285–$400 double; $450–$2,550 suite. Rates lower late Nov–early Mar; packages available. AE, DC, DISC, MC, V. Free self-parking; valet parking $10. **Amenities:** 6 restaurants; 2 bars; 4 outdoor pools; golf course; 3 tennis courts (1 lit); 24-hr. health club; spa; 5 Jacuzzis; bikes on loan; children's programs; youth spa; game room; concierge; business center; Wi-Fi in public areas; room service; laundry/dry cleaning; free washer/dryer; club-level rooms. *In room:* A/C, TV w/pay movies, Wi-Fi, high-speed Internet access, fridge, hair dryer, iron, safe.

EXPENSIVE

Hilton San Antonio Hill Country Hotel and Spa ★ Kids This hotel went from being a Radisson property to a Hilton property in January of 2009. Not much else changed besides mattresses and linens and a few other guest-room amenities. It continues to be family hotel that represents a less-expensive alternative to the nearby Hyatt Regency Hill Country Resort & Spa (see above). It has some of the same features as the Hyatt, including an understated Texas-themed decor, an on-site ATM, and an upscale convenience store. But it doesn't have all the on-site activities, such as the "Ramblin River," the golf course, and tennis courts. But vacationers will be able to enjoy the spa treatments and products, as well as guest privileges at two nearby golf courses. Rooms are large and traditional in decoration, and the bathrooms are a cut above what's normal for this price range. Suites offer jetted tubs and rainforest shower heads, and all accommodations feature Hilton's "Serenity" bedding. There's plenty to appeal to families: Seasonal specials such as the Ultimate SeaWorld Adventure package provide passes, transportation, and complimentary souvenirs for both you and the kids.

9800 Westover Hills Blvd. (off Hwy. 151), San Antonio, TX 78251. ✆ **800/774-1500** or 210/509-9800. Fax 210/767-5329. www.hilton.com. 227 units. $120–$220 double; $240–$300 suite. Internet rates available. AE, DISC, MC, V. Free parking. **Amenities:** Restaurant; bar; 3 outdoor pools; health club; spa; Jacuzzi; business center; room service; laundry/dry cleaning. *In room:* A/C, TV w/pay movies, high-speed Internet access, fridge (suites only), coffeemaker, hair dryer, iron.

8 NORTH CENTRAL (NEAR THE AIRPORT)

EXPENSIVE

San Antonio Airport Hilton ★ The rooms at this airport Hilton offer a bit of local character, with a few Southwestern decorative touches. They're attractive and spacious. The hotel is straight west of the airport, on the north side of Loop 410, making it easy to get to and easy to find. Of course, it's predominantly a business traveler's hotel, but it doesn't have that feel, thanks to such things as the cheerful lobby with colorful Texas mural, the large outdoor pool, and the family-oriented **Tex's Grill** (p. 157) that serves some mean Texas barbecue. Such nongeneric features as an outdoor putting green also help make your stay enjoyable. But while this hotel may be playful, it also knows how to get down to business.

611 NW Loop 410 (San Pedro exit), San Antonio, TX 78216. ✆ **800/HILTONS** [445-8667] or 210/340-6060. Fax 210/377-4674. www.hilton.com. 386 units. $169–$199 double; suites from $175. Romance and Sat–Sun packages available. AE, DC, DISC, MC, V. Free covered parking. **Amenities:** Restaurant; bar; outdoor pool; putting green; courtesy car; business center; Wi-Fi in public areas; 24-hour room service; same-day dry cleaning; club-level rooms. *In room:* TV w/pay movies, Wi-Fi, high-speed Internet access, coffeemaker, hair dryer, iron.

MODERATE

Doubletree Hotel San Antonio Airport ★ For an airport hotel, the Doubletree is surprisingly serene. The same developer who converted a downtown seminary into the posh La Mansión del Río hotel (see "Downtown," earlier in the chapter) was responsible for this hotel's design. Moorish arches, potted plants, stone fountains, and colorful tile create a Mediterranean mood in the public areas. Intricate wrought-iron elevators descend from the guest floors to the lushly landscaped pool patio, eliminating the need to tromp through the lobby in a swimsuit. Guest rooms are equally appealing, with brick walls, wood-beamed ceilings, draped French doors, and colorful contemporary art. And because this hotel gets a large business clientele from Mexico, most of the staff is bilingual. Guest rooms are nonsmoking.

37 NE Loop 410 (McCullough exit), San Antonio, TX 78216. ✆ **800/535-1980** or 210/366-2424. Fax 210/341-0410. www.doubletree.com. 290 units. $139–$229 double; $250–$350 suite. Packages available. AE, DC, DISC, MC, V. Free self-parking. **Amenities:** Restaurant; 2 bars; outdoor pool; exercise room; spa; Jacuzzi; sauna; concierge; courtesy car; business center; limited room service; dry cleaning; club-level rooms; ATM. *In room:* A/C, TV w/pay movies, high-speed Internet access, coffeemaker, hair dryer, iron, safe.

INEXPENSIVE

La Quinta Inn & Suites San Antonio Airport Bunched up around the intersection of Highway 281 and Loop 410 are a number of airport hotels. Among them is this property, which is nicely located so that it doesn't front either freeway. It's still easy to find, has an airport shuttle that can also take you to any restaurant in a 2-mile radius, and has easy access to Hwy. 281 South, which leads to downtown. The property is only 5 years old and is well maintained. Guest rooms are plain but comfortable and functional. And the bathrooms are a cut above the competition in this category in that they have a little more room and better lighting.

850 Halm Blvd., San Antonio, TX 78216. ✆ **800/753-3757** or 210/342-3738. Fax 210/348-9666. www.lq.com. 276 units. $100–$155 double. Rates include free breakfast buffet. AE, DC, DISC, MC, V. Free parking. Pets accepted for free. **Amenities:** Outdoor pool; airport shuttle; laundry service; dry cleaning. *In room:* A/C, TV, high-speed Internet access, coffeemaker, hair dryer, iron.

6

Where to Dine in San Antonio

When people come to San Antonio, they usually have Tex-Mex food on their minds. But that's hardly all you'll find to eat in town. New American cuisine, emphasizing fresh regional ingredients and spices combined in creative ways, is served in elegant settings, as well as in some unlikely dives. Also, there is haute French, old-fashioned Italian, anything Asian, chicken-fried steak, burgers, barbecue . . . in short, something to satisfy every taste and budget. The national chains are well represented here, naturally—everything from McDonald's to Morton's—but I've concentrated on eateries that are unique to San Antonio, or at least to Texas.

The downtown dining scene, especially that found along the River Walk, sees the most visitors; and because most out-of-towners either stay downtown or spend the day there, I've devoted a good deal of space to restaurants in this area. Keep in mind, however, that many excellent restaurants in other parts of town can offer more serenity and perhaps a little more food and service for the money. (To locate restaurants in Downtown, see the map on p. 95.)

You'll find some good restaurants in Southtown, the aptly named area just below downtown, but most prime places to chow down are scattered throughout the north. By far the most fertile ground for outstanding San Antonio dining is on and around Broadway, starting a few blocks south of Hildebrand, extending north to Loop 410, and comprising much of the posh area known as Alamo Heights. Brackenridge Park, the zoo, the botanical gardens, and the Witte and McNay museums are all situated in this part of town, so you can combine your sightseeing with some serious eating.

Although I've mostly stuck to areas that out-of-towners are likely to visit, I've also included a few restaurants worth driving out of your way to find. (To locate restaurants outside of Downtown, see the map on p. 86.)

RESTAURANT CATEGORIES

Rather than trying to make fine distinctions between overlapping labels such as Regional American, New Southwestern, and American Fusion, which generally identify the kind of cooking that tweaks classic American dishes using out-of-the-ordinary ingredients—roast chicken with tamale stuffing, coffee-crusted tenderloin, blue cheese fritters with pesto dipping sauce—I lump them all under the rubric of **New American.** Tex-Mex is,

Tips **The Early Bird**

If you're budget conscious, consider eating early; some restaurants have early-bird specials. Also, you might sample the expensive restaurants at lunch, when many upscale eateries offer lunch specials.

of course, **Tex-Mex,** and should not be confused with the cooking in the heart of Mexico, which is labeled **Mexican.**

The price categories into which the restaurants have been divided are only rough approximations, based on the average costs of the appetizers and entrees. By ordering carefully or splurging, you can eat more or less expensively at almost any place you choose.

1 BEST SAN ANTONIO DINING BETS

- **Best for a Romantic Dinner:** On a quiet stretch of the River Walk, **Las Canarias,** at La Mansión del Río, 112 College St. (✆ **210/518-1063**), avoids the noise that plagues most water-view restaurants. You'll enjoy candlelight and superb, discreet service. See p. 94.
- **Best Movable Feast:** It used to be that you could dine on the river only if you were with a group, but among the restaurants that now offer reservations on communal tables to individuals and couples, **Boudro's,** 421 E. Commerce St./River Walk (✆ **210/224-8484**), tops the meals-on-river-barge-wheels list. See p. 97.
- **Best for Serious Foodies:** After several years on the fine dining scene, **Le Rêve,** 152 E. Pecan St. (✆ **210/212-2221**), has proved that it's got staying power. It keeps piling up awards from the national food press and has answered the question many were asking: "Is San Antonio ready for formal fine dining, where men have to wear jackets and almost everything is chosen for dinner?" The answer is "yes," so long as the kitchen keeps producing stellar French food. See p. 96.
- **Best Seafood:** Andrew Weissman's small seafood restaurant, **Sandbar,** E. Pecan and N. St. Mary St. (✆ **210/222-2426**), serves the best seafood in town. Like his other restaurant, it's all about the food. But if you want a place that's less cramped, and you want it on the river, then your choice is obvious: **Pesca,** 212 W. Crockett St. (✆ **210/396-5817**). Both places will take a bite out of your dining budget. See p. 97.
- **Best Place to Listen to Music While You Eat:** Enjoy creative South American, Mexican, and Caribbean fare at Southtown's **Azuca,** 713 S. Alamo St. (✆ **210/225-5550**), while listening to salsa, merengue, and other Latin sounds. See p. 100.
- **Best Blast from the Past: Schilo's,** 424 E. Commerce St. (✆ **210/223-6692**), not only serves up German deli in portions that date back to pre-cholesterol-conscious days but also retains prices from that era. See p. 99.
- **Best Fine Dining Kept Simple:** It's a tie: Not only do I like the food at both of these places, but I appreciate the lack of ostentation and the effort to keep things simple. **Silo,** 1133 Austin Hwy. (✆ **210/824-8686**), offers enough variety to please just about anyone, while steering clear of strangely worded descriptions and playing at one-upmanship. At **Ciao Lavanderia,** 226 E. Olmos Dr. (✆ **210/822-3990**), you have simplicity itself in the menus. Everything is in one of three price categories, and there's no mistake about the offerings. See p. 105.
- **Best Place to Rub Elbows with the Locals:** Terrific food, a nice selection of libations, good prices, and a fun, funky atmosphere draw local characters of all kinds to the **Liberty Bar,** 328 E. Josephine St. (✆ **210/227-1187**). See p. 102.

2 RESTAURANTS BY CUISINE

American

Cappy's ★ (Alamo Heights Area, $$$, p. 105)

Guenther House ★ (Southtown, $, p. 101)

Little Rhein Steak House (Downtown, $$$$, p. 96)

Olmos Pharmacy (Alamo Heights Area, $, p. 107)

Pesca on the River ★★ (Downtown, $$$$, p. 96)

Tip Top Cafe (Northwest, $$, p. 109)

Burgers

Chris Madrids (Monte Vista Area, $, p. 103)

Chinese

Van's (Alamo Heights Area, $$, p. 106)

Deli

Madhatters (Southtown, $, p. 101)

Schilo's (Downtown, $, p. 99)

Twin Sisters (Downtown and Alamo Heights Area, $, p. 99)

Eclectic

Madhatters (Southtown, $, p. 101)

French

Bistro Vatel ★★ (Alamo Heights Area, $$$, p. 104)

Frederick's ★★ (Alamo Heights Area, $$$, p. 105)

Le Rêve ★★★ (Downtown, $$$$, p. 96)

German

Schilo's (Downtown, $, p. 99)

Greek

Demo's (Monte Vista Area, $, p. 103)

Health Food

Twin Sisters (Downtown and Alamo Heights Area, $, p. 99)

Italian

Aldo's (Northwest, $$$, p. 107)

Ciao Lavanderia ★ (Alamo Heights Area, $$, p. 105)

Paesano's Riverwalk ★ (Downtown, $$$, p. 97)

Tre Trattoria ★ (Alamo Heights Area, $$, p. 106)

Japanese

Sushi Zushi ★ (Downtown, $$, p. 98)

Van's (Alamo Heights Area, $$, p. 106)

Mexican

Acenar ★ (Downtown, $$, p. 97)

Aldaco's ★ (Downtown, $$, p. 98)

La Fonda on Main (Monte Vista Area, $$, p. 102)

Paloma Blanca ★ (Alamo Heights Area, $$, p. 106)

New American

Biga on the Banks ★★★ (Downtown, $$$$, p. 94)

Bistro Thyme ★ (Northwest, $$$, p. 107)

Boudro's ★ (Downtown, $$$, p. 97)

Las Canarias ★★ (Downtown, $$$$, p. 94)

Liberty Bar ★ (Monte Vista Area, $$, p. 102)

Silo ★★ (Alamo Heights Area, $$$, p. 105)

Nuevo Latino

Azuca ★ (Southtown, $$$, p. 100)

Seafood

Pesca on the River ★★ (Downtown, $$$$, p. 96)

Sandbar ★★ (Downtown, $$$, p. 97)

Sushi Zushi ★ (Downtown, $$, p. 98)

Key to Abbreviations: $$$$ = Very Expensive $$$ = Expensive $$ = Moderate $ = Inexpensive

Southwestern

Francesca's at Sunset ★★ (Northwest, $$$$, p. 107)

Steaks

Little Rhein Steak House (Downtown, $$$$, p. 96)

Tex-Mex

Casa Rio (Downtown, $$, p. 98)
La Fonda on Main (Monte Vista Area, $$, p. 102)
Los Barrios (Monte Vista Area, $$, p. 102)
Mi Tierra (Downtown, $, p. 99)
Rolando's Super Tacos (Monte Vista Area, $, p. 103)
Rosario's ★ (Southtown, $$, p. 101)

Thai

Thai Restaurant ★ (Northwest, $$, p. 108)

Vietnamese

Van's (Alamo Heights Area, $$, p. 106)

3 DOWNTOWN

VERY EXPENSIVE

Biga on the Banks ★★★ NEW AMERICAN Right on the River Walk is one of San Antonio's first establishments to serve innovative haute cuisine. The setting is an improvement over the restaurant's original location, and the design mirrors the cooking—bold and contemporary. Clean lines, high ceilings, and gleaming wood floors find a contrast in the heavy textured draperies that frame views of the river. This is the scene for chef/owner Bruce Auden's intriguing cuisine with a subtle Texas influence. The menu changes daily, but here are some representative offerings. For starters, try Asian spring rolls filled with minced venison, buffalo, ostrich, and pheasant accompanied by two spicy dipping sauces, or Duck confit *bao* buns (those unearthly doughy balls filled with seasoned meat that is usually slightly salty, spicy, and sweet). For the main course, choose a juicy bone-in tenderloin steak with beer-battered onion rings and habanero ketchup or mustard-crusted Australian lamb. For dessert, the Paseo de Chocolate will answer anyone's chocolate craving.

If you're willing to eat before 6:30pm or after 9pm, you can sample a three-course meal for $37 per person or four courses for $43.

International Center, 203 S. St. Mary's St./River Walk. ✆ **210/225-0722.** www.biga.com. Reservations recommended. Main courses $19–$36; brunch $32 adults, $17 ages 12 and younger. AE, DC, DISC, MC, V. Sun–Thurs 5:30–10pm; Fri–Sat 5:30–11pm.

Las Canarias ★★ NEW AMERICAN Dining at La Mansión del Río has a couple of things going for it, namely the setting and the food. Sit outside on a riverside terrace shaded by palm trees or inside in one of the cozy, softly lit dining rooms, enjoying the guitarist or pianist playing in the background.

Menus change seasonally, but such dishes as seared ahi tuna with saffron jasmine rice, pepper-crusted venison loin with sweet potato crisps, and a cream soup of *huitlacoche* (corn truffle), corn, and squash blossoms demonstrate the range of the chef's interests in combining unusual textures and flavors. You can also get a nicely grilled steak, and the brunch offers all the classic breakfast dishes.

La Mansión del Río, 112 College St./River Walk. ✆ **210/518-1063.** Reservations recommended. Main courses $23–$32; champagne Sunday brunch $40 adults, $20 children. AE, DC, DISC, MC, V. Sun–Thurs 6:30am–10pm; Fri–Sat 6:30am–11pm; Sun brunch 10:30am–2:30pm.

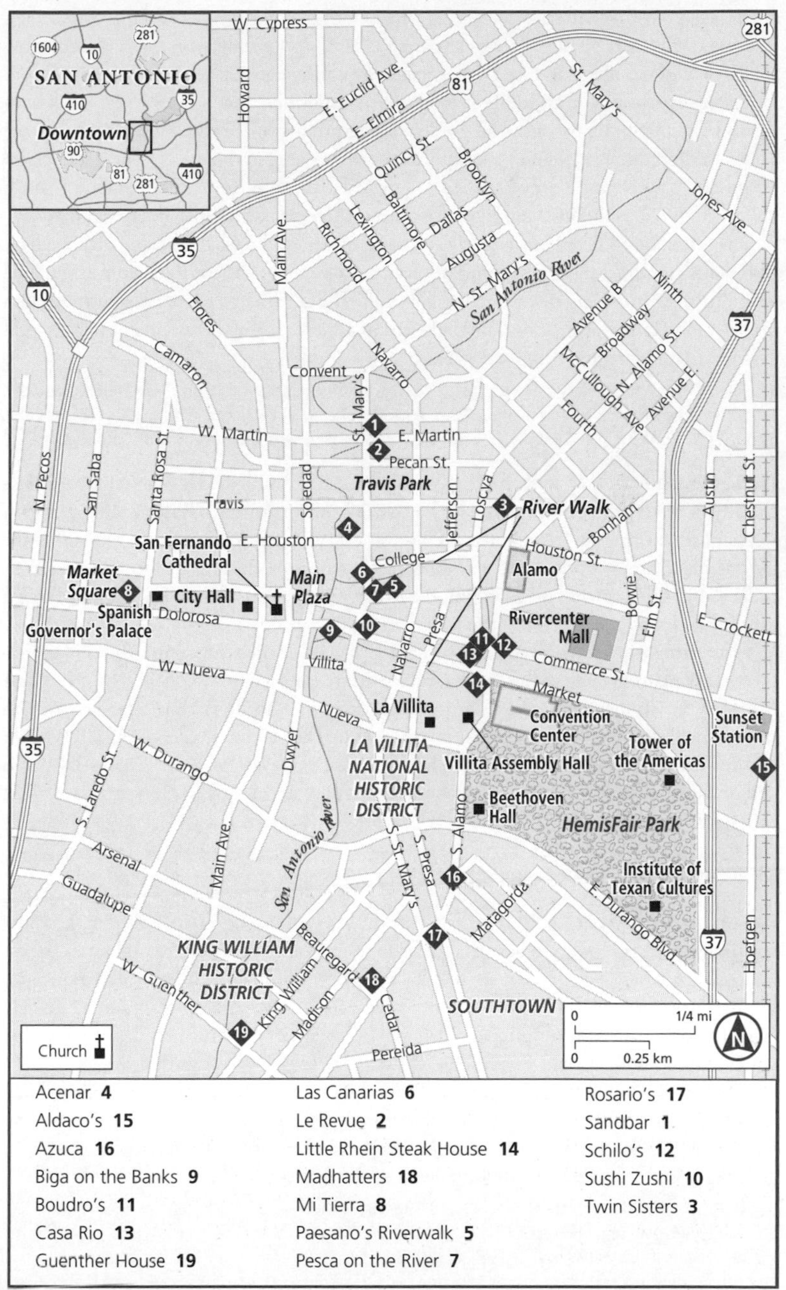

Acenar **4**
Aldaco's **15**
Azuca **16**
Biga on the Banks **9**
Boudro's **11**
Casa Rio **13**
Guenther House **19**
Las Canarias **6**
Le Revue **2**
Little Rhein Steak House **14**
Madhatters **18**
Mi Tierra **8**
Paesano's Riverwalk **5**
Pesca on the River **7**
Rosario's **17**
Sandbar **1**
Schilo's **12**
Sushi Zushi **10**
Twin Sisters **3**

Le Rêve ★★★ FRENCH This restaurant is for serious diners, for whom fine dining is one of the ultimate expressions of civilized life. Chef/owner Andrew Weissman is originally from San Antonio but has spent many years honing his craft in France and elsewhere. His method of cooking has garnered lavish praise and won many awards from the national food press, and Le Rêve is generally considered the best restaurant in Texas. Mr. Weissman aims for an ideal—thoughtful composition that strikes the note of simplicity. The menu items come and go depending upon availability. When they're on the menu, scallop dishes as well as beef tournedos dishes are good choices. The caramelized onion tart is a perennial fave. Nothing can be ordered a la carte. A tasting menu is available with or without wine, and five-, four-, and three-course menus are available, too.

The attention to detail extends to the choice of wines, the small size and arrangement of the dining room, and the manner of service—all is aimed at complementing the food without being imposing or distracting. To enjoy the experience properly, you must allot ample time (2 hrs. at a minimum) and eliminate sources of disturbance such as cellphones. Men are required to wear jackets.

152 E. Pecan St., at St. Mary's. ✆ **210/212-2221.** www.restaurantlereve.com. Reservations required. Jacket required for men. Tasting menu $100, $165 with wine; prix-fixe 3-course meal $80, 4 courses $90, 5 courses $100. AE, DC, DISC, MC, V. Tues–Sat 5:30–11pm (last reservation taken for 8:30pm seating).

Little Rhein Steak House AMERICAN/STEAKS Built in 1847 in what was then the Rhein district, the oldest two-story structure in San Antonio has hosted an elegant steakhouse abutting the river and La Villita since 1967. Antique memorabilia decks the indoor main dining room, and a miniature train surrounded by historic replicas runs overhead. Leafy branches overhanging the River Walk patio—elevated slightly and railed off for privacy—are draped in little sparkling lights.

The setting is pretty as ever, and the choice USDA prime steaks from the restaurant's own meat plant are tasty; but recent competition from chains such as The Palm and Morton's nearby has resulted in a price hike. Now everything here is a la carte, which means you'll shell out $4 for a baked potato and another $7 for creamed spinach (you do still get a loaf of fresh wheat bread). The restaurant can also get noisy. That said, this is still one of the few family-owned steakhouses around, and it offers a unique River Walk dining experience.

231 S. Alamo at Market. ✆ **210/225-2111.** www.littlerheinsteakhouse.com. Reservations recommended. Main courses $21–$42. AE, DC, DISC, MC, V. Daily 5–10pm.

Pesca on the River ★★ AMERICAN/SEAFOOD For terrific fish in a swank nautical setting, it's tough to beat the riverside restaurant at the Watermark Hotel. Except for the oyster bar at the center of the dining room, the marine touches are more subliminal than overt: sea-blue table settings; hardwood floors; smooth glass surfaces; sleek, vaguely boat-shaped water pitchers. But once you tuck into the "catches" of the day, you'll have no doubt about this restaurant's deep devotion to things Piscean.

The creamy, smooth, cool asparagus soup with a mound of crab at the bottom is an excellent choice. The oyster sampler, the seared rare tuna crusted with coriander and fennel seed . . . nothing is disappointing. ***Note:*** Meat eaters and even vegetarians won't go hungry here—but they won't find a vast sea of selections, either.

212 W. Crockett St. (Watermark Hotel). ✆ **210/396-5817.** www.watermarkhotel.com. Reservations recommended on Sat–Sun. Main courses $25–$42. AE, DC, DISC, MC, V. Daily 6:30am–11pm.

EXPENSIVE

Boudro's ★ NEW AMERICAN Locals tend to look down their noses at River Walk restaurants, but Boudro's has long been the exception, and with good reason. The kitchen uses fresh local ingredients—Gulf Coast seafood, Texas beef, Hill Country produce—and the preparations and presentations do them justice. The setting is also out of the ordinary, boasting a turn-of-the-century limestone building with hardwood floors and a handmade mesquite bar.

You might start with the guacamole, prepared tableside and served with tostadas, or the pan-fried Texas crab cakes. The prime rib, blackened on a pecan-wood grill, is deservedly popular, as is the pork chop with sun-dried cherry and chili marmalade. The food may be innovative, but portions are hearty nevertheless. Lighter alternatives include the coconut shrimp with orange horseradish and the rosemary-grilled yellowfin tuna. For dessert, the whisky-soaked bread pudding is fine, and the lime chess pie with a butter pastry crust is divine. Service is very good despite the volume of business and the time the servers spend mixing up guacamole.

421 E. Commerce St./River Walk. ✆ **210/224-8484.** www.boudros.com. Reservations strongly recommended. Main courses $20–$33. AE, DC, DISC, MC, V. Sun–Thurs 11am–11pm; Fri–Sat 11am–midnight.

Paesano's Riverwalk ★ ITALIAN This River Walk incarnation of a longtime San Antonio favorite relinquished its old Chianti bottle–kitsch decor for a soaring ceiling, lots of inscrutable contemporary art, and a more up-to-date menu. But the one thing the restaurant couldn't give up, at the risk of a local insurrection, was the signature shrimp Paesano's. The crispy crustaceans are as good as their devotees claim, as are the reasonably priced pizzas, including the one topped with grilled chicken, artichokes, basil pesto, and feta cheese. Other good values are the hearty southern Italian staples such as lasagna with meat sauce. Standouts among the pricier entrees include the grilled pork chops with potato gnocchi, as well as the veal Francesa. Locals tend to go to the newer—and somewhat quieter—Paesano's, across from the Quarry Golf Club, at 555 Basse Rd., Ste. 100 (✆ **210/828-5191**).

111 W. Crockett, Ste. 101/River Walk. ✆ **210/227-2782.** www.paesanosriverwalk.com. Reservations accepted for 10 or more only. Pizzas $14; pastas $10–$19; main courses $20–$31. AE, DC, DISC, MC, V. Sun–Thurs 11am–10pm; Fri–Sat 11am–11pm.

Sandbar ★★ SEAFOOD Andrew Weissman, the owner of Le Rêve, mentioned above, has opened this restaurant just around the corner from his original place. Look for a blue awning on North St. Mary Street. This is another small restaurant, with only a bar section and around eight tables. It's designed simply in black, white, and stainless steel. Don't expect the formal dining that Le Rêve is famous for; this place is casual, but the attention to the food is serious. Emphasis is on fresh, most evident in the raw oysters (six or seven varieties daily), the sashimi, and ceviche. Sampling these makes you wonder what this restaurant knows that other seafood places don't. The lobster bisque is heavenly.

152 E. Pecan St. (at N. St. Mary) ✆ **210/222-2426.** Reservations accepted. Main courses $20–$40. AE, MC, V. Tue–Sat 5:30–11pm.

MODERATE

Acenar ★ (Value MEXICAN When Lisa Wong (Rosario) and Bruce Auden (Biga), two longtime darlings of the San Antonio dining scene, collaborate on a restaurant, you figure the food and the atmosphere are going to be creative. Their "modern Tex-Mex" fare and the seemingly endless series of wildly colorful dining rooms (one on the river) in which it's served don't disappoint. In fact, both the food and the service exceed expectations, given the (over) size of this place and the crowds that immediately began to throng to it.

It's hard to go wrong with any of the dishes, but standouts include the crepes with duck in a tamarind-cherry-grilled-onion sauce, the *enchiladas verdes,* the tacos filled with crabmeat *tinga* (a kind of stew with onions, tomatoes, and chipotle chilies) served with avocado, and the duck chorizo chalupas with cabbage lime slaw. The specialty dishes, such as garlic and chipotle shrimp with roasted creamed corn hash, are pricier but can be worth the splurge.

146 E. Houston St. (next to the Hotel Valencia). ✆ **210/222-CENA** [222-2362]. www.acenar.com. Reservations not accepted (priority seating for large parties). Lunch $7–$10 (specialties $10–$16); dinner $13–$15 (specialties $16–$30). AE, DC, MC, V. Mon–Thurs 11am–10pm, Fri–Sat 11am–11pm; bar Mon–Wed 4–10pm, Thurs–Sat 4pm–2am.

Aldaco's ★ MEXICAN Yes, this restaurant is in a converted train station–cum–entertainment complex and has been known to host large convention groups, but there's nothing transient or impersonal about either the setting or the food. With its original wood beams, murals of Mexican scenes, wrought-iron room dividers, and large plants, the high-ceiling room feels very festive, and an outdoor patio adds charm. The menu, created by owner Blanca Aldaco and Chef Richard Jiménez, includes several dishes from the western state of Jalisco—for example, tostadas made with shrimp *ceviche,* and *pozole rojo,* a pork and hominy soup. You'll also find some standard Tex-Mex dishes, such as chicken fajitas and nachos. The few vegetarian options include a grilled *chile relleno* stuffed with corn, zucchini, and white cheese. And no one can resist the traditional *tres leches* (three-milk) cake. Aldaco's is located downtown, east of HemisFair Park, on the other side of the freeway, by the Alamodome.

100 Hoefgen St., in Sunset Station. ✆ **210/222-0561.** www.aldacos.net. Reservations accepted. AE, MC, V. Lunch $6–$17; dinner $10–$23. Mon–Thurs 11am–10pm; Fri–Sat 11am–11pm.

Casa Rio TEX-MEX I often hear the question "Where can I eat some Tex-Mex food at a good table by the river?" The answer is that your options are many and few; many bad options and a few passable ones. Of these, my choice would be Casa Rio. When the weather is glorious, few things are more enjoyable than getting a table at the water's edge, ordering a big platter of something spicy, meaty, and crispy, and sipping down a frozen margarita. This place has an excellent location, not as crowded as most, and so long as you stick to the Tex-Mex classics, you'll do fine. Steer clear of the tortilla soup and the tamales (which aren't really a Tex-Mex forte) and go with something like flautas, tacos, or fajitas. Enjoy. This is San Antonio, after all, and you're supposed to do these things.

430 E. Commerce St./River Walk. ✆ **210/225-6718.** www.casa-rio.com. Reservations not accepted. AE, MC, V. Main courses $8–$14. Daily 11am–11pm (weather permitting).

Sushi Zushi ★ Value JAPANESE/SEAFOOD For a Japanese food fix in a congenial atmosphere, you can't beat this clean, well-lit place. You'll find sushi in all its incarnations here, including a My Spurs roll—yellowtail, cilantro, avocado, chives, and *serro* chilies—but far more is on the menu. Choose from rice bowls, soba noodle bowls, soups, teppanyakis, tempuras—a mind-boggling array of food options, not to mention a long list of sakes. The need to make all those decisions notwithstanding, this spot is popular with downtown office workers who know that, in this case, they'll be rewarded for whatever bold initiatives they take.

Three more branches of Sushi Zushi are in the Northwest, at the Colonnade Shopping Center, 9867 W I-10 (✆ **210/691-3332**); in the Northeast, at Stone Oak Plaza II, 18720 Stone Oak Pkwy., at Loop 1604 (✆ **210/545-6100**); and in Lincoln Heights, at 999 E. Bosse, at Broadway (✆ **210/826-8500**).

203 S. St. Mary's St. (The International Center). ✆ **210/472-2900.** www.sushizushi.com. Reservations recommended Sat–Sun. Sushi rolls and sashimi $6–$15; bowls, tempuras, and other hot entrees $8–$17. AE, DISC, MC, V. Mon–Thurs 11:30am–10pm; Fri 11:30am–11pm; Sat 12:30–11pm; Sun 5–9pm.

INEXPENSIVE

Mi Tierra (Moments) TEX-MEX If you've come to San Antonio with the idea of tasting traditional Tex-Mex as it is cooked day in and day out, this is a great place. Sure, you do see out-of-towners finding their way here because the restaurant is so famous, but you see a lot more locals than anybody else—locals who know their city and know their restaurants. The atmosphere is unselfconsciously *so* San Antonio. I love it. Don't order the *mole* or the fine cuts of steak—that's not why you should be here. Order the Tex-Mex and bring your appetite. You can start with the botanas platter, which offers a good smattering of such dishes as flautas and minitostadas. The top-shelf margarita makes a nice accompaniment. Then move on to the classic Tex-Mex enchiladas bathed in chili gravy.

Mi Tierra is also noted for its bakery, which produces all the baked sweet breads of Mexico collectively known as *pan dulce.* Try one, along with a cup of coffee or hot chocolate Mexican-style. The *polvorones,* a kind of sugar cookie, are especially popular with gringos.

You may pay a couple dollars more here than you would at a Tex-Mex joint on San Pedro, but it's well worth it—for the food, for the atmosphere, and for the convenience. The place is open 24/7, so you don't have to check your watch or your calendar before heading on over.

218 Produce Row (Market Sq.). ✆ **210/225-1262.** www.mitierracafe.com. Reservations accepted for large groups only. Breakfast $7–$10; lunch and dinner plates $8–$19. AE, MC, V. Open 24 hrs.

Schilo's (Value) (Kids) GERMAN/DELI This place has been here since they built the Alamo. It makes for a good place to stop, rest your feet, and enjoy a hearty bowl of split-pea soup or a piece of the signature cherry cheesecake. They also make a mean Reuben sandwich. The large, open room with its worn wooden booths is classic. The waitresses—definitely not "servers"—wear dirndl-type outfits, and German live bands play on Saturday from 5 to 8pm. The menu has a large kid-friendly selection and retro low prices. Come Friday or Saturday evening if you want to be serenaded by accordion music.

424 E. Commerce St. ✆ **210/223-6692.** Reservations for large groups for breakfast and dinner only. Sandwiches $4–$6; hot or cold plates $5–$7; main dishes (served after 5pm) $7–$8.95. AE, DC, DISC, MC, V. Mon–Sat 7am–8:30pm.

Twin Sisters (Finds) HEALTH FOOD/DELI If you want to avoid overpriced sandwiches and junk food while sightseeing, join the downtown working crowd at this bakery and health-food cafe just a few blocks from the Alamo. Eggless and meatless doesn't mean tasteless here; you can get great Greek salads, spicy tofu scrambles, and salsa-topped veggie burgers. Carnivores can also indulge in the likes of ham, pastrami, and salami sandwiches on the excellent bread made on the premises.

Tip: This popular place fills up by 11:30am but empties after 12:45pm, so plan your visit accordingly. A branch in Alamo Heights, 6322 N. New Braunfels (✆ **210/822-2265**), has longer hours (Mon–Fri 7am–9pm; Sat 7am–3pm; Sun 9am–2pm) and live music on Friday nights.

It's Always Chili in San Antonio

It ranks up there with apple pie in the American culinary pantheon, but nobody's mom invented chili. The iconic stew of meat, chilies, onions, and a variety of spices was likely conceived around the 1840s by Texas cowboys who needed to make tough meat palatable while covering up the taste as it began to go bad. The name is a Texas corruption of the Spanish *chile* (*chee*-leh), after the peppers—which are not really peppers at all, but that's another story—most conventionally used in the stew.

The appellation chili *con carne* is really redundant in Texas, where chili without meat isn't considered chili at all. Indeed, most Texans think that adding beans is only for wimps. Beef is the most common base, but everything from armadillo to venison is acceptable.

No one really knows exactly where chili originated, but San Antonio is the prime candidate for the distinction. In the mid–19th century, accounts were widespread of the town's "chili queens," women who ladled steaming bowls of the concoction in open-air markets and on street corners. They were dishing out chili in front of the Alamo as late as the 1940s.

William Gebhardt helped strengthen San Antonio's claim to chili fame when he began producing chili powder in the city in 1896. His Original Mexican Dinner package, which came out around 20 years later, included a can each of chili con carne, beans, and tamales, among other things, and fed five for $1. This precursor of the TV dinner proved so popular that it earned San Antonio the nickname "Tamaleville."

Oddly enough, chili isn't generally found on San Antonio restaurant menus. But modern-day chili queens come out in force for special events at Market Square, as well as for Nights in Old San Antonio, one of the most popular bashes of the city's huge Fiesta celebration. And there's not a weekend that goes by without a chili cook-off somewhere in the city.

124 Broadway, at Travis. ✆ **210/354-1559.** www.twinsistersbakeryandcafe.com. Reservations not accepted. Breakfast $3–$6; lunch $5–$9. MC, V. Mon–Fri 8am–3pm.

4 KING WILLIAM/SOUTHTOWN

EXPENSIVE

Azuca ★ NUEVO LATINO Anyone familiar with the late, great Latina singer Celia Cruz knows that her signature shout was "Azuca!" (roughly, "Sweetie!") This Southtown restaurant pays tribute to the Cuban-born salsa star—and not just in the name or the pop images of her that hang in one of the dining rooms. The cooking is strong on Caribbean tastes, using regional spices such as *achiote* and *sofrito,* and such foods as yuca and ripe plantains. South American dishes include delicious Bolivian *empanadas* and Argentine *parrillada.* The menu is large and has something to please just about everyone. Super fresh ingredients often lend color to the dishes.

The setting is as colorful as the food, with contrasting bold tones and modern lines. On weekends, live salsa and merengue is on offer in one of the dining rooms.

713 S. Alamo. ✆ **210/225-5550.** www.azuca.net. Reservations recommended. Lunch (salads and sandwiches) $7–$9.50; dinner main courses $14–$27. AE, DC, DISC, MC, V. Mon–Thurs 11am–9:30pm (bar until 11pm); Fri–Sat 11am–10:30pm (bar until 2am).

MODERATE

Rosario's ★ TEX-MEX This longtime Southtown favorite, one of the first restaurants to establish a hip culinary presence in the area, has toned its menu down a bit; maybe owner Lisa Wong's adventurous urges have found an outlet in Acenar (see "Downtown," earlier in this chapter). But the airy room, with its Frida Kahlo and Botero knockoffs and abundant neon, is as fun as ever. And contemporary Tex-Mex fare, prepared with super-fresh ingredients, makes this a great choice for visitors to San Antonio. You might start with the chicken or chorizo quesadillas with guacamole or the fresh-tasting *ceviche fina* (white fish, onions, and jalapeños marinated in lime juice), and then go on to the delicious *chile relleno,* with raisins and potatoes added to the chopped beef stuffing. The large size of the room means that you generally don't have to wait for a table, but it also means that the noise level can make conversation difficult. I like to go to at midafternoon, when the place is usually empty.

910 S. Alamo. ✆ **210/223-1806.** www.rosariossa.com. Reservations not accepted. Lunch $6–$9; dinner main courses $8–$23. AE, DC, DISC, MC, V. Mon 11am–3pm; Tues–Thurs 11am–10pm; Fri–Sat 11am–11pm (bar until 2am on Fri).

INEXPENSIVE

Guenther House ★ Value AMERICAN If you're not staying in a King William B&B, this is your chance to visit one of the neighborhood's historic homes. And the food is a winner. Hearty breakfasts and light lunches are served both indoors—in a bright, cheerful old-style dining room added on to the Guenther family residence (built in 1860)—and outdoors on a trellised patio. The Guenther family owns the Pioneer Flour Mill, which is right across the river and can be seen from the house, so the restaurant emphasizes baked goods. Breakfast biscuits and gravy, waffles, and pancakes are popular items, but you can also get breakfast tacos. Breakfast is served all day. The lunch menu is on the light side and includes chicken salad (made with black olives) and mild chicken enchiladas made with flour tortillas. Adjoining the restaurant are a small museum, a Victorian parlor, and a mill store featuring baking-related items, including baking mixes, cookbooks, and kitchen gear. The house fronts a lovely stretch of the San Antonio River.

205 E. Guenther St. ✆ **210/227-1061.** www.guentherhouse.com. Reservations not accepted. Breakfast $3.95–$7.50; lunch $6.50–$7.25. AE, DC, DISC, MC, V. Daily 7am–3pm (house and mill store Mon–Sat 8am–4pm; Sun 8am–3pm).

Madhatters Finds Kids DELI/ECLECTIC This colorful, sprawling storefront attracts everyone from nouveau hippies to buttoned-down office workers, to the occasional clutch of housewives out for lunch. They come for Age-of-Aquarius-meets-south-of-the-border food: granola bowls and breakfast burritos in the morning, veggie and deli sandwiches for lunch, and pork tamales in the evening. The rambling house has several indoor and outdoor dining areas, all with a comfortable lived-in feel. The main dining area, where you place your order, has cold cases full of reasonably priced wines and beers. You can also bring the kids to have afternoon tea, which can include peanut-butter-and-jelly sandwiches (crusts cut off, naturally). The NO CELLPHONES sign seems to be taking effect, so you no longer have to retreat from the bustling front room to have a conversation without hearing ringing in your ears (though the back room is pleasant and still considerably quieter).

320 Beauregard St. (at S. Alamo). ✆ **210/212-4832.** www.madhatterstea.com. Reservations not accepted. Breakfast $4–$10; sandwiches and salad plates $5.95–$9.95; high tea for 2 $18. AE, DISC, MC, V. Mon–Thurs 7am–10pm; Fri 7am–11pm; Sat 8am–11pm; Sun 9am–9pm.

5 MONTE VISTA AREA

MODERATE

La Fonda on Main Value Kids MEXICAN/TEX-MEX One of San Antonio's oldest continually operating restaurants, established in 1932, never went the way of most culinary institutions thanks to Cappy Lawton, of Cappy's fame (see "Alamo Heights Area," below), who acquired it and spiffed up both menu and premises in the late 1990s. The red-tile-roof residence is cheerful and bright—almost as inviting as the garden-fringed outdoor patio. The menu is divided between Tex-Mex, featuring giant combination plates such as the La Fonda Special (two cheese enchiladas, a beef taco, a chicken tamale, guacamole, Mexican rice, refried beans), and a "Cuisines of Mexico" section, including such traditional dishes as *mojo de ajo* (Gulf shrimp with garlic butter served with squash). Many celebrities dined here in the old days—including Franklin Roosevelt, John Wayne, and Yul Brynner, among others—and the fresh, tasty, generous specialties dished up here daily still attract power-lunch types and local families alike.

2415 N. Main. ✆ **210/733-0621.** www.lafondaonmain.com. Reservations recommended for 6 or more. Main courses $8–$12. AE, DC, MC, V. Sun–Thurs 11am–3pm and 5–9:30pm; Fri–Sat 11am–3pm and 5–10:30pm; Sun brunch 11am–3pm.

Liberty Bar ★ Moments NEW AMERICAN For years, this place has been an informal hangout spot for locals. A former bar and brothel that dates back to 1890, the two-story building leans a bit. It's definitely noticeable, and the curious effect it produces in most who view it is the desire for a drink. The atmosphere here is quite cheerful and the food is good, too. You'll find comfort food—rib-eye steaks, crab cakes, and the like—and a lot of original dishes as well. Choices abound among the salads and sandwiches—some of these are original, too. The entrees on the daily menu often show a good bit of flare. I've often found things that have grabbed my attention and satisfied my palate: a salad with hazelnuts and prosciutto and pecorino cheese, a grilled sandwich of tomato and gruyere cheese flavored with *chile morita,* or a classic bread pudding with hard sauce. The Liberty Bar is several blocks north of the main downtown area, a couple of blocks off of Broadway.

328 E. Josephine St. ✆ **210/227-1187.** www.liberty-bar.com. Reservations recommended. Main courses $8–$22. AE, DISC, MC, V. Sun–Thurs 11:30am–10:30pm; Fri–Sat 11:30am–midnight; Sun brunch 10:30am–2pm (bar until midnight Sun–Thurs, until 2am Fri–Sat).

Los Barrios TEX-MEX This very popular Tex-Mex joint has been around since the '70s, when it first opened in a former Dairy Queen. Remnants of a big expansion in the '80s can still be in seen in the peach and light-green color combination. All in all, it has the unpretentiousness necessary for popular local restaurants in San Antonio.

The excellent Tex-Mex enchiladas are made of red tortillas and cheese bathed in a hearty chili gravy. Or you could go for the five-enchilada plate, with one of every variety served here. Departures from Tex-Mex include *cabrito* (goat) in salsa and the *milanesa con papas,* described on the menu (accurately) as a Mexican-style chicken-fried steak. If you're really hungry, try the Los Barrios deluxe special platter, which includes two beef tacos, two cheese enchiladas, a strip of steak, rice, beans, and guacamole. Portions are large. If you're watching what you eat, you can easily satisfy hunger pangs with a *chalupa Vallarta* a la carte ($3.50), and you'll get a large red tortilla stacked with chicken, lettuce, tomato, guacamole, carrot strips, jalapeños, cheese, and sour cream. Nothing at Los Barrios is too spicy.

Mondays and Tuesdays are popular for "Fajita Nights," when you can get a pound of fajitas with all the sides for $10 ($16 regular price). Wednesdays are "Margarita Nights," and on Thursdays, there's a special on longnecks.

4223 Blanco Rd. ✆ **210/732-6017.** Reservations accepted for large groups only. Dinners $7–$12. AE, DC, DISC, MC, V. Mon–Thurs 10am–10pm; Fri–Sat 10am–11pm; Sun 9am–10pm.

INEXPENSIVE

Chris Madrids Kids BURGERS It's hard to drop much money at this funky gas-station-turned-burger-joint, but you might lose your shirt; over the years, folks have taken to signing their tees and hanging them on the walls. An even more popular tradition is trying to eat the macho burger, as huge as its name might indicate. Several burgers are made with a Tex-Mex twist, adding refried beans, hot sauce, or jalapeños to the mix. The kid-friendly menu includes burgers, nachos, fries, and various combinations of these. The casual atmosphere and down-home cooking keep the large outdoor patio filled.

1900 Blanco. ✆ **210/735-3552.** www.chrismadrids.com. Reservations not accepted. Main courses $4–$6. AE, DC, DISC, MC, V. Mon–Sat 11am–10pm.

Demo's Value GREEK Demo's is a little bit of Greece in San Antonio. Located across the street from a Greek Orthodox church, it's a favorite among members of the local Greek community here. Occasionally you might see a belly-dancing show (not only here, but in the other two locations as well). You can dine on the airy patio or in the dining room, decorated with murals of Greek island scenes. The menu includes gyros, Greek burgers, dolmas, spanakopita, and other Mediterranean specialties. If you go for the Dieter's Special—a Greek salad with your choice of gyros or souvlaki—you might be able to justify the baklava. In addition to this location, the original (but more characterless) restaurant is at 7115 Blanco Rd. (✆ **210/342-2772**), near Loop 410, across from what used to be Central Park Mall; a third location is farther out at Blanco and Loop 1604 (✆ **210/798-3840**).

2501 N. St. Mary's St. ✆ **210/732-7777.** www.demosgreekfood.com. Reservations accepted for parties of 10 or more only. Main courses $6–$12. AE, DC, DISC, MC, V. Mon–Thurs 11am–9pm; Fri–Sat 11am–midnight.

Rolando's Super Tacos Value TEX-MEX Rolando's, one of the many small businesses that pack both sides of W. Hildebrand between I-10 and Trinity University, offers further proof that once you get out of the downtown tourist zone, you'll find San Antonio a dining bargain. Next door to a Chevron gas station, Rolando's is a rambling shack painted in vivid red and green. It doesn't look that big, especially when you walk through the door into a small room, but the dining room beyond goes way back and turns a corner, running all along the back of the shack. The surroundings aren't spectacular. In fact, this place is a real dive, but it's representative of old San Antonio: a blue-collar, old-time Tejano eatery.

Rolando's is open only for breakfast and lunch and is famous for its extra large "super tacos," which can be had in corn or flour tortillas with a variety of fillings. One makes a

Kids Family-Friendly Restaurants

Chris Madrids (p. 103) The kid-friendly menu includes burgers, nachos, fries, and various combinations thereof; and the casual atmosphere and down-home cooking make it popular with families.

La Fonda on Main (p. 102) With its friendly staff and inexpensive children's plates, this restaurant is a great places to introduce your kids to Mexican food. (Anglo options are available as well.)

Madhatters (p. 101) Even if your kids aren't up for an entire children's tea, they'll be happy to find their faves on the menu, from PB&J to plain turkey or cheese sandwiches. The chocolate-chip cookies and brownies won't be sneezed at, either.

Olmos Pharmacy (p. 107) Bring your kids to this old-time soda fountain and you can relive the pleasures of your childhood vicariously through them. There are a couple of items on the drinks menu and artifacts behind the counter that most kids won't be familiar with. You can tell them about the old days.

Schilo's (p. 99) A high noise level, a convenient location near the River Walk (but with prices far lower than anything else you'll find there), and a wide selection of familiar food make this German deli a good choice for the family.

meal. Also popular are the *carne guisada* (beef stewed in a chili sauce) plate and the puffy tacos.

919 W. Hildebrand (just west of Blanco Rd.) ✆ **210/732-6713.** Reservations not accepted. Super tacos $5.50; plates $7–$10. DC, DISC, MC, V. Mon and Wed–Fri 7am–3pm; Sat 7am–4pm; Sun 8am–3pm.

6 ALAMO HEIGHTS AREA

EXPENSIVE

See also Paesano's, in the "Downtown" section, p. 97.

Bistro Vatel ★★ Value FRENCH Talk about a pressure cooker: In 1671, the great French chef Vatel killed himself out of shame because the fish for a banquet he was preparing for Louis XIV wasn't delivered on time. Fortunately, his descendant, Damian Watel, has less stress to contend with in San Antonio, where diners are very appreciative of the chef's efforts to bring them classic French cooking at comparatively reasonable prices. In fact, despite its strip-mall location, the place is so popular that it had to expand into the store next door. Comfortable furniture, ample space, white tablecloths, and excellent service make for a satisfying dining experience.

You can't go wrong with the rich escallop of veal with foie gras and mushrooms, and fans of sweetbreads will be pleased to find them here beautifully prepared in truffle crème fraîche sauce. Your best bet is the prix-fixe dinner; choose one each from four appetizers (perhaps shrimp *vol au vent*) and entrees such as roasted quail, then enjoy the dessert of the day.

218 E. Olmos Dr. at McCullough. ✆ **210/828-3141.** www.bistrovatel.com. Reservations recommended on weekends. Main courses $15–$27; prix-fixe dinner $35. AE, MC, V. Tues–Sat 11am–9pm; Sun 5–9pm.

Cappy's ★ AMERICAN One of the earliest businesses to open in the now-burgeoning Alamo Heights neighborhood, Cappy's is set in an unusual broken-brick structure dating back to the late 1930s. The cheerful main dining area has lots of windows, high ceilings, hanging plants, and colorful work by local artists. A tree-shaded patio invites diners outside. The smell of a wood-burning grill (not mesquite, but the milder live oak) foreshadows some of the house specialties: the peppercorn-crusted prime tenderloin or the slow-roasted Italian chicken with porcini mushrooms. Lighter fare includes honey-glazed salmon on polenta with sautéed spinach. A chef's prix fixe lets you choose an appetizer, salad, and entree. See chapter 9 for **Cappyccino's ★**, an offshoot of Cappy's down the block with a great by-the-glass wine list and a more casual Southwest menu.

5011 Broadway (behind Twig Book Store). ✆ **210/828-9669.** www.cappysrestaurant.com. Main courses $17–$32. AE, DC, MC, V. Mon–Fri 11am–2:30pm and 5:30–10pm; Sat 11am–3pm and 5:30–11pm; Sun 10:30am–3pm (for brunch) and 5–10pm.

Frederick's ★★ (Finds) FRENCH Not as well-known as many of San Antonio's glitzier culinary stars, this restaurant in the back of a Broadway strip mall has its own body of loyal customers. The setting is nothing special, a sedate dining room with low ceiling, soft lights, and white draperies and tablecloths. But the customers don't come for the setting. No, the customers come for the excellent French food and the nonfussy atmosphere in which it is served. It's a refreshing combination.

For starters, consider caramelized pork ribs with a spicy sauce; the delicate and crispy spring rolls of shrimp, pork, and mushrooms; or a zesty crab salad with avocado. Entrees might include baked sea bass in truffle oil with artichoke hearts, or a duck breast cooked in a sauce of green peppercorns and cognac.

7701 Broadway, Ste. 20 (in the back of Dijon Plaza). ✆ **210/828-9050.** Reservations recommended on weekends. Main courses $17–$33. AE, DC, MC, V. Mon–Thurs 11:30am–2pm and 5:30–10pm; Fri 11:30am–2pm and 5:30–10:30pm; Sat 5:30–10:30pm.

Silo ★★ NEW AMERICAN For my money, this is the best place for fine dining if you want something other than French food. In contrast with many other chic restaurants that try to get attention by creating fanciful sounding dishes with a "cutting-edge" use of ingredients, Silo quietly goes about its business, focusing on creating dishes that satisfy the palate and deliver something new. The last couple of meals I had here were perfect. Memorable dishes included the chipotle marinated pork tenderloin with white cheddar andouille grits and peach chutney, the crab spring rolls with shitake mushrooms and tantalizing dipping sauces, some pan-seared scallops treated very simply, and some wonderful mango-wasabi crab cakes. The attentive waitstaff could answer most of the questions put to them.

1133 Austin Hwy. ✆ **210/824-8686.** www.siloelevatedcuisine.com. Reservations recommended. Main courses $19–$39; prix fixe (salad, entree, dessert) $25 (5:30–6:30pm nightly). AE, DC, DISC, MC, V. Lunch daily 11am–2:30pm; dinner Sun–Thurs 5:30–10pm, Fri–Sat 5:30–10:30pm.

MODERATE

Ciao Lavanderia ★ (Value) ITALIAN When the owner of Bistro Vatel (see above) opened a casual Italian eatery just a few doors down from his French restaurant, he stuck with his winning good-food-at-good-prices formula. In an open, cheery storefront with post-mod tributes to the business that used to reside here (exposed ductwork, an old washing machine), you select from dishes in three price categories. For $6 you can get minestrone, a salad, or sauté; for $12 you can sample one of the pastas, thin-crust pizzas, or lighter seafood and chicken dishes; while for $16 you might enjoy such hearty entrees as a quail and mushroom risotto or pork loin scaloppine parmigiana. Daily specials, such as osso buco, tend to fall into these price categories, too. Everything's fresh and delicious, and the portions are geared toward a normal human appetite, not supersize. A nice selection of (mostly) Italian wines enhances an already optimal experience.

226 E. Olmos Dr. ✆ **210/822-3990.** Reservations accepted for large parties only. Pastas and pizzas $12; main courses $16. AE, DC, DISC, MC, V. Mon–Fri 11:30am–1:30pm and 5:30–10pm; Sat 5:30–10pm.

Paloma Blanca ★ MEXICAN This popular choice for interior Mexican food sports modern, comfortable, and attractive dining areas and an outdoor patio area graced with a fountain and decorative plants. The main dining room is spacious and has an open feel to it thanks to some large glass windows that bring in a lot of natural light. In some ways it reminds one of upscale Mexico City restaurants. On the menu are some great soups, such as the cream soup flavored with *poblano chile* (if you like that combination of cream and poblano but want to forgo a soup course, try the *pollo en crema poblana*). Several mainstays of Mexican cooking are offered: enchiladas in a dark, earthy *mole* sauce, or in a tangy *salsa verde;* steak *a la tampiqueña;* and a Veracruz-style red snapper. Tex-Mex standards include enchiladas in chili gravy and crispy tacos. There are some honest vegetarian dishes such as a great vegetable *chile relleno.* A separate gluten-free menu is available, too (you have to ask for it). The bar is comfortable and has a full margarita menu, which I'm pretty sure is gluten-free as well. Keep this place in mind, too, if you just want to enjoy some savory finger food with drinks in attractive surroundings. The menu has plenty of appetizers and a sampler platter.

5600 Broadway. ✆ **210/822-6151.** www.palomablanca.net. Reservations recommended for large groups only. Main courses $10–$25. AE, MC, V. Tues–Wed 11am–9pm; Thurs–Fri 11am–10pm; Sat 10am–10pm; Sun 10am–9pm.

Tre Trattoria ★ ITALIAN This new restaurant on Broadway is the perfect place to enjoy a leisurely meal. Casual and modern, with a cozy bar/lounge and a good selection of wines, you can get comfortable in the overstuffed chairs while you wait for your table. Sit inside in a well-lit, not-too-noisy dining room or outside on an inviting deck sufficiently distant from the street noise. Among the choices of salads are an interesting grilled radicchio with lemon vinaigrette, and also a butterleaf lettuce salad with a creamy herb dressing. The dinner menu is organized in typical Italian style with first and second courses; the second courses are served family-style, to be shared among up to four people. The grilled rainbow trout with crispy skin is marvelous. Another option is the small pizzas; three or four varieties have out-of-the-ordinary combinations of toppings. Quite good.

4003 Broadway (next to the Witte Museum). ✆ **210/805-0333.** www.tretrattoria.com. Reservations accepted. Main courses $15–$20. AE, MC, V. Mon–Thurs 11am–10pm; Fri–Sat 11am–11pm.

Van's CHINESE/JAPANESE/VIETNAMESE Talk about pan-Asian. The sign outside announces that Van's is a "Chinese Seafood Restaurant and Sushi Bar," but you'll also find Vietnamese dishes on the huge menu. The dining room is low-key but appealing, with crisp green-and-white cloth table coverings. If you like seafood, go for the shrimp in a creamy curry sauce or the fresh crab with black-bean sauce. Alternatively, consider one of the meal-size soups—beef brisket with rice noodles, say, or a vegetable clay pot preparation—or tasty versions of such Szechwan standards as spicy kung pao chicken with carrots and peanuts. Van's also has a surprisingly large wine list, so scour the shelves and cold cases for a bottle.

3214 Broadway. ✆ **210/828-8449.** Reservations for large parties only. Main courses $9–$15. AE, DISC, MC, V. Daily 11am–10pm.

INEXPENSIVE

Olmos Pharmacy Finds Kids AMERICAN When was the last time you drank a rich chocolate malt served in a large metal container—with a glass of whipped cream on the side? Grab a stool at Olmos's Formica counter and reclaim your childhood. Olmos Pharmacy, opened in 1938, also scoops up old-fashioned ice-cream sodas, Coke or root beer floats, sundaes, banana splits . . . if it's cold, sweet, and nostalgia-inducing, they've got it. This is also the place to come for filling American and Mexican breakfasts, a vast array of tacos, and classic burgers and sandwiches, all at seriously retro prices.

3902 McCullough. ✆ **210/822-3361.** Main courses $2–$5.50. AE, MC, V. Mon–Fri 7am–5pm (fountain until 6pm); Sat 8am–4pm (fountain until 5pm).

7 NORTHWEST

VERY EXPENSIVE

Francesca's at Sunset ★★ SOUTHWESTERN A menu created by Chef Mark Miller of the famous Coyote Café, an excellent wine list (about 150 bottles, including some 30 by the glass), fine service, and idyllic Hill Country views from a romantic terrace—what's not to like about Francesca's at Sunset? Starters on the seasonally changing menu might include a jumbo crab cake on spicy slaw or quail on corn basil grits. For entrees, you might find loin of antelope rubbed with *mole* and served with blue corn griddlecakes, or free-range chicken spiced with *pasilla chiles* sided by a piquant squash stew. I haven't tasted anything here that was too hot to handle, but if you're spice intolerant, it might be best to ask about the heat of whatever you're contemplating ordering. Of course, you can always placate your palate with excellent house-made sorbets or a Jack Daniels pecan tart.

Westin La Cantera, 16641 La Cantera Pkwy. ✆ **210/558-6500.** www.westinlacantera.com/francescas.asp. Reservations recommended. Main courses $26–$39. AE, DC, DISC, MC, V. Tues–Sat 6–10pm.

EXPENSIVE

Aldo's ITALIAN A northwest San Antonio favorite, Aldo's offers good, old-fashioned Italian food in a pretty, old-fashioned setting. You can enjoy your meal outside on a tree-shaded patio or inside a 100-year-old former ranch house in one of a series of Victorian dining rooms. The scampi Valentino, sautéed shrimp with a basil cream sauce, is a nice starter, as are the lighter steamed mussels in marinara sauce, available seasonally. A house specialty, sautéed snapper di Aldo, comes topped with fresh lump crabmeat, artichoke hearts, mushrooms, and tomatoes in a white-wine sauce.

8539 Fredericksburg Rd. ✆ **210/696-2536.** Reservations recommended, especially on weekends. Pastas $12–$18; main courses $19–$28. AE, DC, DISC, MC, V. Mon–Thurs 11am–10pm; Fri 11am–11pm; Sat 5–11pm; Sun 5–10pm.

Bistro Thyme ★ Finds NEW AMERICAN You can't leave this bistro without that feeling of utter satisfaction that comes after a meal of well-prepared, delicious comfort food. But this is comfort food that also answers the need for something different. The

Frozen Assets

Austin has long had Amy's ice cream, but when it comes to homegrown frozen desserts, San Antonio has been, well, left out in the cold. But that's all changed with the new century and the introduction of **Brindles Awesome Ice Cream,** 11255 Huebner Rd. (✆ **210/641-5222**). Brindles features more than 200 varieties of creative ice creams, gelati, and sorbets. About 45 to 50 flavors are available on any given day. You might find such unique creations as spice apple brandy or bananas Foster ice cream; white chocolate Frangelico or candied ginger gelato; and champagne or cranberry sorbet—as well as, in every category, far more traditional flavors for ice-cream purists. Among the best-selling ice creams is the signature Brindles, a butterscotch fudge crunch inspired, like the store's name, by the multicolored coat of the owners' pet boxer. And don't miss "The Kick" ice cream whenever it's available. This mixture of pineapple, coconut, mint, and habanero chili doesn't taste hot initially, but it packs a bit of a wallop afterward.

If you don't want to have to trek all the way to Brindles' mother ship, the espresso and ice-cream parlor in the Strand shopping center on San Antonio's northwest side, you can also sample Brindles products at several of San Antonio's finest restaurants, including Acenar, Biga on the Banks, Bistro Vatel, Boudro's, and Ciao Lavanderia, all covered elsewhere in this chapter.

cooking is a hearty version of New American cuisine, which emphasizes meats expertly grilled or seared. When in doubt, you can't go wrong with the signature rack of lamb with blackberry peppercorn sauce. And, although I don't generally like buffets, the one served here (Tues–Fri 11:15am–1:45pm) is a gourmet treat as well as a bargain (it's just $12). This is not a place to watch your weight, however; portions are huge, and rich sauces are a specialty. Desserts are particularly hard to resist; if you're lucky, a supremely chocolaty Sacher torte might be in your stars.

1321 N. Loop 1604 E., Ste. 105. ✆ **210/495-0244.** www.bistrothymesa.com. Reservations accepted. Main courses $17–$30. AE, DC, DISC, MC, V. Mon–Thurs 11am–10pm; Fri–Sat 11am–11pm; Sun 11am–8pm.

MODERATE

See also Sushi Zushi, in the "Downtown" section of this chapter.

Thai Restaurant ★ Value THAI The cooking is marvelous at this small, family-owned restaurant in a small strip center just outside Loop 410. The menu offers many of Thailand's most famous dishes, and these are cooked with great care and fresh ingredients. The pad Thai (not too sweet, noodles cooked to the perfect texture, very fresh bean sprouts), the pad kra pao (generous with the basil leaves), and the panang curry (nicely scented, with just the right hint of lime and shrimp paste) were all hits with me. So, too, were the rolls, and an uncommon appetizer of fried stuffed tofu. The latter was served with a delicious peanut and cilantro dipping sauce. And last but not least is the *yum nua,* a cold beef salad with fresh butter lettuce, red onion, tomato, and cucumber, covered in a citric dressing. The attentive service, the low prices, and the quiet dining room (quiet until 9pm, when music from the bar next door begins to seep through the wall) also make this place an attractive choice.

1709 Babcock Rd. (at Callaghan) ✆ **210/341-0606.** Reservations accepted. Main courses $7–$10. DISC, MC, V. Mon–Fri 11am–3pm, 5–10pm; Sat 11am–10pm.

Tip Top Cafe (Finds) AMERICAN This place is timeless in so many ways. You've got to love the look of the adobe and neon exterior. Inside are wood-paneled walls (both real and imitation) adorned with everything from antlers to letters of recognition, as well as comfortable old-style tables and chairs, classic booths, and a solid wood lunch counter. The staff has been here forever. Example: My waitress mentions that she's the "new kid," having worked here for only 8 years.

Comfort food is the draw here. Favorites include chicken-fried steak (and the chicken-fried steak sandwich), fried shrimp, and onion rings, not to mention the meatloaf on Thursdays, and chicken and dumplings—the ultimate in comfort food—served on Fridays starting at 5pm and ending sometime on Saturday when it runs out. All the pies are made in-house. Among them, there's always an apple and at least one other fruit pie, as well as a cream pie or two, and usually a pecan pie. Note that this isn't the place for people who are in the habit of dining late. The locals come early, and they have a point: Chicken-fried steak requires time to be digested.

2814 Fredericksburg Rd. (btw. Santa Anna and Santa Monica) ✆ **210/735-2222.** Reservations not accepted. Sandwiches $3–$5; main courses $8–$13. No credit cards. Tues–Sat 11am–8pm; Sun 11am–7pm.

8 ONLY IN SAN ANTONIO

Some of San Antonio's best and most popular places to eat have been reviewed in this chapter, but you can be sure you'll run into San Antonians who are passionate about other eateries I haven't covered in detail.

TAQUERIAS

Everyone has a favorite *taquería* (taco joint). A couple of high-ranking ones near downtown are **Estela's,** 2200 W. Martin St. (✆ **210/226-2979**), which has musical (salsa, mariachi) breakfasts on Saturday and Sunday from 10am to noon, as well as a great conjunto/Tejano jukebox; and **Taco Haven,** 1032 S. Presa St. (✆ **210/533-2171**), where the breakfast *migas* (hearty egg and tortilla dish) or *chilaquiles* (tortillas layered with meats, beans, and cheese) will kick-start your day. In Olmos Park, **Panchito's,** 4100 McCullough (✆ **210/821-5338**), has hungry San Antonians lining up on weekend mornings for *barbacoa* (Mexican-style barbecue) plates, heaped with two eggs, potatoes, beans, and homemade tortillas.

BARBECUE

You'll also find emotions rising when the talk runs to barbecue, with many locals insisting that their favorite is the best joint in town. Maybe it's because the meat has been smoked the longest, or because the place uses the best smoking technique, or its sauce is the tangiest—the criteria are endless and often completely arcane to outsiders.

Of San Antonio's more than 90 barbecue joints, a longtime local favorite that's spawned a Texas chain is **Rudy's,** 24152 I-10 West at the Leon Springs/Boerne Stage Road exit (✆ **210/698-2141**). Cowboys, bicyclists, and other city folk come from miles around for what they insist are the best pork ribs, brisket, and turkey legs in town. A newer Rudy's is located near SeaWorld at 10623 Westover Hills, corner of Highway 151 (✆ **210/520-5552**).

County Line, 111 W. Crockett St., Ste. 104 (✆ **210/229-1941**), brings the menu and the signature 1940s Texas decor of a popular Austin-based restaurant to the River Walk, although its smoker is not actually on the premises. Locals liked the brisket, sausage—and sweet ice tea—at the homegrown **Bill Miller Bar-B-Q** so much that it spread to 49 San Antonio locations (Austin and Corpus Christi are the only other two cities where Bill has ventured). To find the one nearest to you, log on to www.billmillerbbq.com.

San Antonians have been coming to **Bun 'N' Barrel,** 1150 Austin Hwy. (✆ **210/828-2829**), since 1950 to chaw barbecue and to check out each other's cool Chevys. Hang around on a Friday night and you might even see the occasional drag race down Austin Highway. This joint is in a featureless area, but it's not far from the McNay Museum and the botanical gardens. ***Note to film buffs:*** If you're short on time, catch shots of this retro classic eatery in the film *Selena.*

Exploring San Antonio

San Antonio has a wide selection of attractions that can satisfy a variety of interests. You could easily fill your time hitting each one on your list, but I would suggest that you set aside at least a little time for aimlessly strolling about the city's downtown. You'll come across unexpected sights such as, for instance, the Bexar (pronounced *bear*) County Court House, which, though not remarkable enough to merit specific listing among the city's attractions, still is quite attractive and lends an appreciation to the city's character. Also, a couple of plazas lie almost forgotten, one of which in the old days was the scene of a running battle with a Comanche raiding party.

Before you visit any of the paid attractions, stop in at the **San Antonio Visitor Information Center,** 317 Alamo Plaza (✆ **210/207-6748**), across the street from the Alamo, and ask for their *SAVE San Antonio* discount book; it includes coupons for everything from the large theme parks to some city tours and museums. Many hotels also have a stash of discount coupons for their guests.

1 THE TOP ATTRACTIONS

DOWNTOWN AREA

The Alamo ★★ When most visitors see the Alamo for the first time, their common reaction is "Hmmm, I thought it would be bigger." Though the shape of the facade of the Alamo is widely recognized by most Americans, most think of it as a large fortress. This only underscores how heroic and desperate were the actions of the Alamo's defenders, who in 1836 held off a siege by a large Mexican army for 13 days. The Alamo today is more a shrine than a museum. It's main purpose is to honor the fallen. The siege played an important role in Texas independence, both strategic and iconic. And the actions of its defenders, whether real or imagined, went a long way toward creating the larger-than-life mystique that Texas was eventually to acquire. Among the defenders were famous men of their day, such as Davy Crockett and Jim Bowie, and the idea of their sacrifice for Texas independence gave added meaning to the struggle almost immediately. "Remember the Alamo!" became the battle cry at San Jacinto, when the Texans finally defeated the Mexican army and captured its general, López de Santa Anna.

The Daughters of the Republic of Texas, who saved the crumbling mission from being turned into a hotel by a New York syndicate in 1905, have long been the Alamo's stewards. They have installed exhibits to display the various roles the mission played, including serving as a Native American burial ground. The Alamo's original name was Mission San Antonio de Valero, and many converted Indians from a variety of tribes lived and died here. The complex was secularized by the end of the 18th century and leased out to a Spanish cavalry unit; however, by the time the famous battle took place, it had been abandoned. **A Wall of History,** erected in the late 1990s, provides a chronology of these events.

The outlying buildings of the original mission are gone. Only the **Long Barrack** (formerly the *convento,* or living quarters for the missionaries) and the much-photographed **mission church** are still here. The former houses a museum detailing the history of Texas in general and the battle in particular, and the latter includes artifacts of the Alamo fighters, along with an information desk and a small gift shop. The exhibit doesn't do the best job of explaining how the battle developed. If you want to understand more, see the IMAX show in the nearby Rivercenter Mall.

A larger **museum** and gift shop are at the back of the complex. A peaceful **garden** and an excellent **research library** (closed Sun) are also on the grounds. All in all, though, the complex is fairly small. You won't need to spend more than an hour here. Interesting historical presentations are given every half-hour by Alamo staffers; for private, after-hour tours, phone © **210/225-1391,** ext. 34.

300 Alamo Plaza. © **210/225-1391.** www.thealamo.org. Free admission (donations welcome). Mon–Sat 9am–5:30pm; Sun 10am–5:30pm. Closed Dec 24–25. Streetcar: Red or Blue lines.

King William Historic District ★ San Antonio's first suburb, King William was settled in the late 19th century by prosperous German merchants who displayed their wealth through extravagant homes and named the 25-block area after Kaiser Wilhelm of Prussia. (The other residents of San Antonio were rather less complimentary about this German area, which they dubbed "Sauerkraut Bend.")

The neighborhood fell into disrepair for a few decades, but you'd never know it from the present condition of most houses here today. The area has become so popular that tour buses have been restricted after certain hours. Anyway, if the weather's agreeable, it's much more pleasant to be on foot here than in a tour bus. You can stroll down tree-shaded King William Street and admire the old houses and their beautifully landscaped yards. Stop at the headquarters of the San Antonio Conservation Society, 107 King William St. (© **210/224-6163;** www.saconservation.org), and pick up a self-guided walking tour booklet outside the gate. If you go at a leisurely pace, the stroll should take about an hour. Only the Steves Homestead Museum (see "More Attractions," later in this chapter) and the **Guenther House** are open to the public; figure 2 more hours if you plan to visit both. If you're staying downtown and are a good walker, you can get to the neighborhood in 15 minutes by following the recently completed extension of the River Walk. It's a pleasant hike. If you're hungry, choose from quite a few options for lunch in the neighborhood and on South Alamo Street (see chapter 6).

East bank of the river, just south of downtown. Streetcar: Blue line.

La Villita National Historic District ★ Developed by European settlers along the east bank of the San Antonio River in the late 18th and early 19th centuries, La Villita (the Little Village) was on the proverbial wrong side of the tracks until natural flooding of the west-bank settlements made it the fashionable place to live. It fell back into poverty by the beginning of the 20th century, only to be revitalized in the late 1930s by artists and craftspeople and the San Antonio Conservation Society. Now boutiques, crafts shops, and restaurants occupy this historic district, which resembles a Spanish/Mexican village, replete with shaded patios, plazas, brick-and-tile streets, and some of the settlement's original adobe structures. You can see (but not enter, unless you rent it for an event) the house of General Cós, the Mexican military leader who surrendered to the Texas revolutionary army in 1835, or attend a performance at the Arneson River Theatre (see "The Performing Arts," chapter 9). Walking tour maps of these and other historical structures are available throughout the site. It'll take you only about 20 minutes to do a quick walk-through, unless you're an inveterate shopper—in which case, all bets are off.

Bounded by Durango, Navarro, and Alamo sts. and the River Walk. © **210/207-8610.** www.lavillita.com. Free admission. Shops daily 10am–6pm. Closed Thanksgiving, Dec 25, and Jan 1. Streetcar: Red, Purple, or Blue lines.

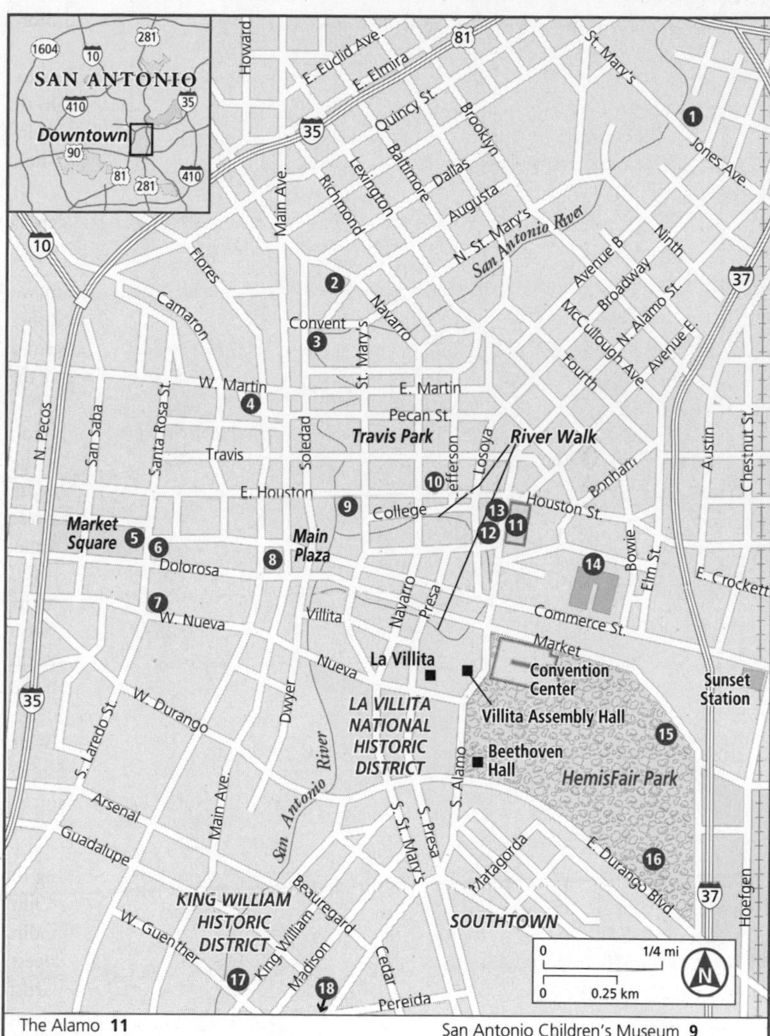

The Alamo **11**
Artpace **4**
Blue Star Arts Contemporary Arts Center **18**
Buckhorn Saloon & Museum **10**
Casa Navarro State Historical Park **7**
Institute of Texan Cultures **16**
Museo Alameda **5**
Plaza Wax Museum & Ripley's Believe It or Not **12**
Ripley's Haunted Adventure, Guinness World Records Museum, and Davy Crockett's Tall Tales Ride **13**
San Antonio Children's Museum **9**
San Antonio Central Library **3**
San Antonio IMAX Theatre Rivercenter **14**
San Antonio Museum of Art **1**
San Fernando Cathedral **8**
Southwest School of Art & Craft **2**
Spanish Governor's Palace **6**
Steves Homestead Museum **17**
Tower of the Americas **15**

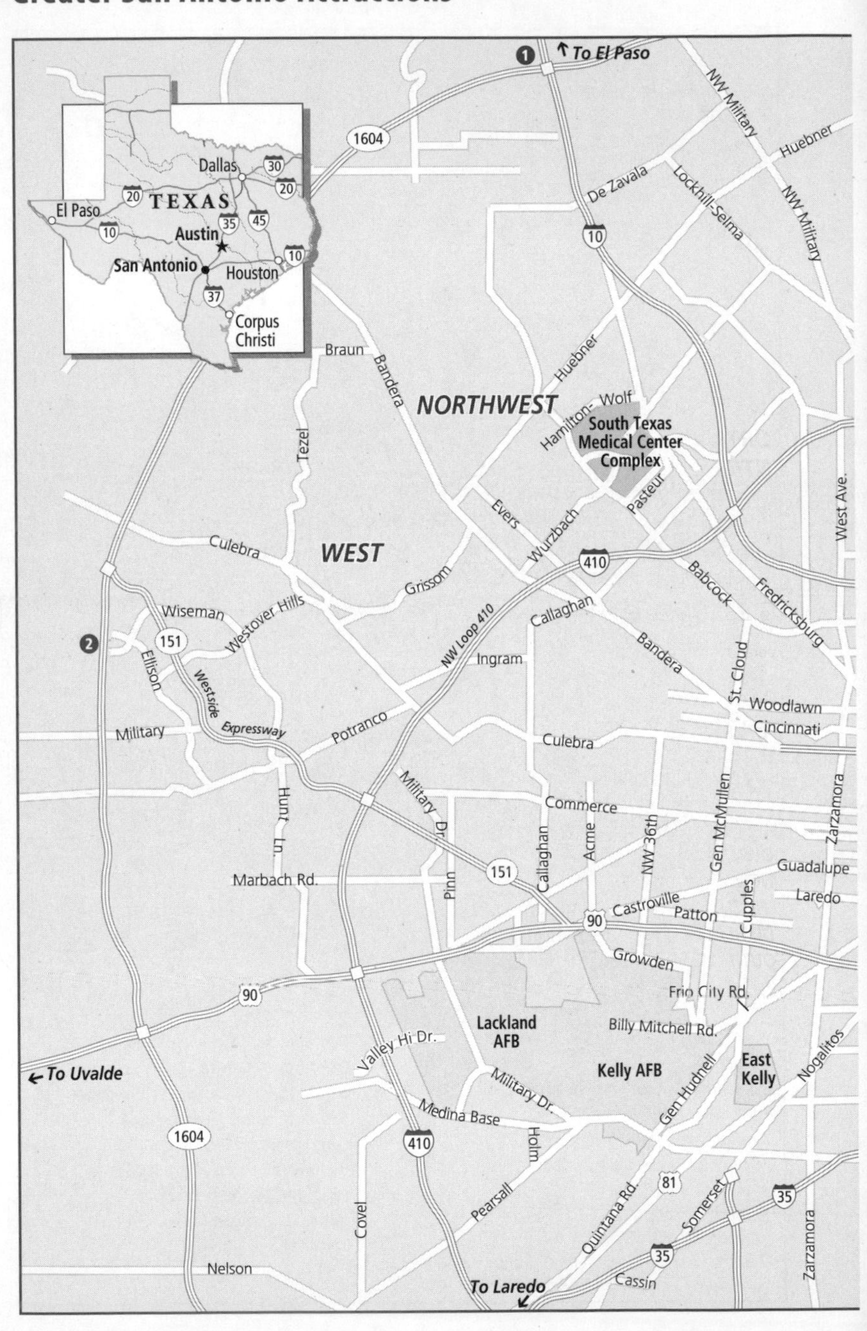
To El Paso
1604
NW Military
Huebner
De Zavala
Lockhill-Selma
NW Military
10
TEXAS
Dallas
El Paso
Austin
San Antonio
Houston
Corpus Christi
Braun
Bandera
NORTHWEST
Huebner
Hamilton- Wolf
South Texas Medical Center Complex
Tezel
Evers
Wurzbach
Pasteur
West Ave.
Culebra
WEST
Grissom
410
Babcock
Fredricksburg
Wiseman
Westover Hills
Callaghan
Bandera
151
Ellison
Westside Expressway
NW Loop 410
Ingram
St. Cloud
Woodlawn
Cincinnati
Military
Potranco
Culebra
Military Dr.
Commerce
Hunt Ln.
Callaghan
Acme
NW 36th
Gen McMullen
Zarzamora
Marbach Rd.
Pinn
Guadalupe
Laredo
Castroville
Patton
Cupples
90
Growden
Frio City Rd.
Lackland AFB
Billy Mitchell Rd.
Valley Hi Dr.
Kelly AFB
East Kelly
Gen Hudnell
Nogalitos
To Uvalde
Military Dr.
Medina Base
Holm
1604
410
81
Quintana Rd.
Somerset
35
Pearsall
Covel
Zarzamora
Nelson
To Laredo
Cassin

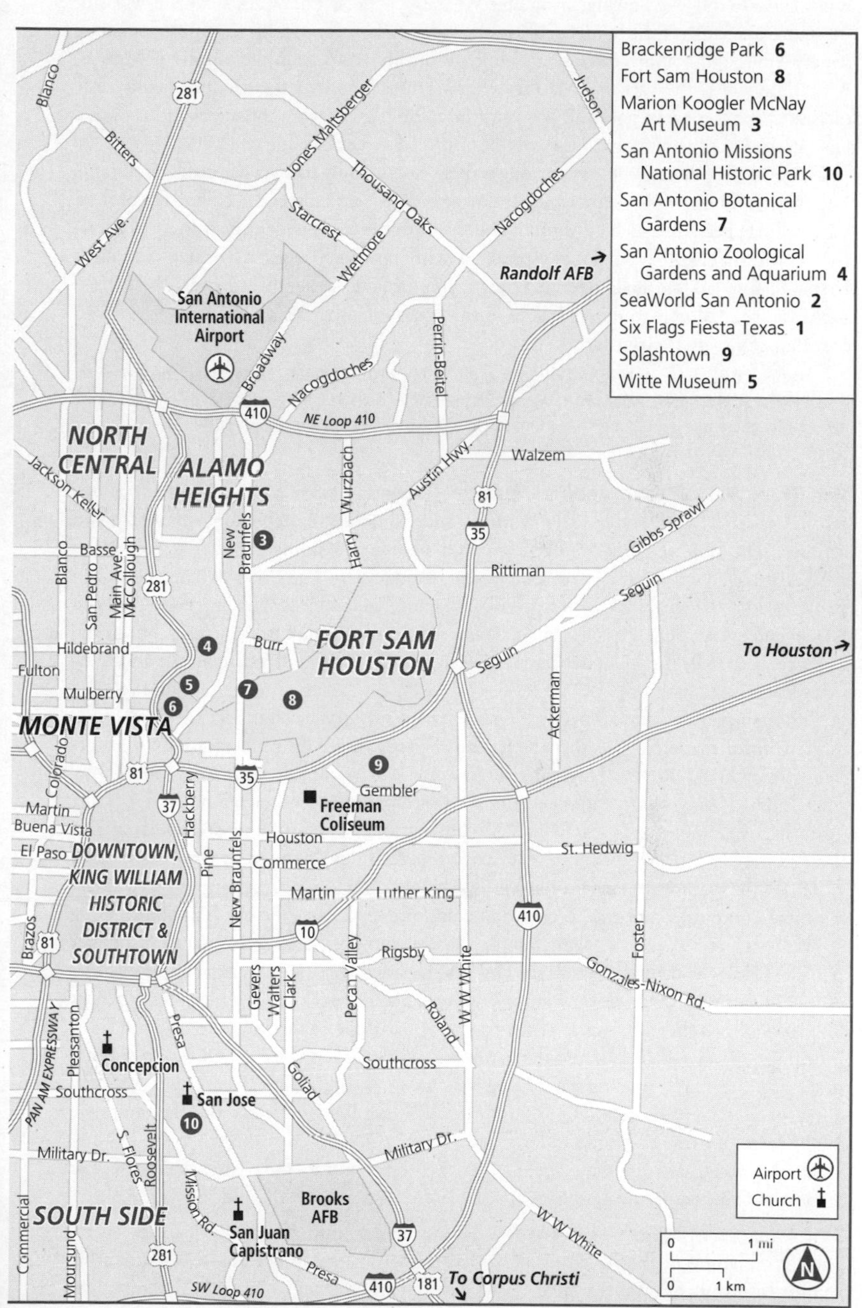

Brackenridge Park 6
Fort Sam Houston 8
Marion Koogler McNay Art Museum 3
San Antonio Missions National Historic Park 10
San Antonio Botanical Gardens 7
San Antonio Zoological Gardens and Aquarium 4
SeaWorld San Antonio 2
Six Flags Fiesta Texas 1
Splashtown 9
Witte Museum 5
San Antonio International Airport
Randolf AFB
NORTH CENTRAL
ALAMO HEIGHTS
FORT SAM HOUSTON
MONTE VISTA
DOWNTOWN, KING WILLIAM HISTORIC DISTRICT & SOUTHTOWN
SOUTH SIDE
Freeman Coliseum
Brooks AFB
Concepcion
San Jose
San Juan Capistrano
To Houston
To Corpus Christi
Airport
Church
1 mi
1 km

Market Square ★ It may not be quite as colorful as it was when live chickens squawked around overflowing, makeshift vegetable stands, but Market Square will still transport you south of the border. Stalls in the indoor El Mercado sell everything from onyx paperweights and manufactured serapes to high-quality crafts from the interior of Mexico. Across the street, the Farmers' Market, which formerly housed the produce market, has carts with more modern goods. If you can tear yourself away from the merchandise, take a look around at the buildings in the complex; some date back to the late 1800s.

Bring your appetite along with your wallet: In addition to two Mexican restaurants (see chapter 6 for the Mi Tierra review), almost every weekend sees the emergence of food stalls selling specialties such as *gorditas* (chubby corn cakes topped with a variety of goodies) or funnel cakes (fried dough sprinkled with powdered sugar). Most of the city's Hispanic festivals are held here, and mariachis usually stroll the square. The Museo Alameda (see "More Attractions," later in this chapter) provides a historic context to an area that can seem pretty touristy.

Bounded by Commerce, Santa Rosa, Dolorosa, and I-35. ✆ **210/207-8600.** www.marketsquaresa.com. Free admission. El Mercado and Farmers' Market Plaza summer daily 10am–8pm; winter daily 10am–6pm; restaurants and some shops open later. Closed Thanksgiving, Dec 25, Jan 1, and Easter. Streetcar: Red, Purple, or Yellow lines.

The River Walk (Paseo del Río) ★★★ Below the streets of downtown San Antonio lies another world, alternately soothing and exhilarating, depending on where you venture. The quieter areas of the $2^{1}/_{2}$ paved miles of winding riverbank, shaded by cypresses, oaks, and willows, exude a tropical, exotic aura. The River Square and South Bank sections, chockablock with sidewalk cafes, tony restaurants, bustling bars, high-rise hotels, and even a huge shopping mall, have a festive, sometimes frenetic feel. Tour boats, water taxis, and floating picnic barges regularly ply the river, and local parades and festivals fill its banks with revelers.

Although plans to cement over the river after a disastrous flood in 1921 were stymied, it wasn't until the late 1930s that the federal Works Project Administration (WPA) carried out architect Robert Hugman's designs for the waterway, installing cobblestone walks, arched bridges, and entrance steps from various street-level locations. And it wasn't until the late 1960s, when the River Walk proved to be one of the most popular attractions of the HemisFair exposition, that its commercial development began in earnest.

The River Walk is in danger of becoming overdeveloped—new restaurants and entertainment complexes continue to open at an alarming pace, and the crush of bodies along the busiest sections can be claustrophobic in the summer heat—but plenty of quieter spots still exist. In the last 3 years, the city has extended the River Walk a couple of miles in each direction so that it's now fairly lengthy. These extensions are quiet places perfect for walking, but they lack some of the features of the core, especially the majestic trees. Mornings are a good time to see the main part of the River Walk, when the crowds are smaller and the light filters softly through the trees. At night the River Walk takes on a different character; if you're caught up in the sparkling lights reflected on the water, you might forget anyone else is around.

All the streetcars stop somewhere along the river's route. The River Walk Streetcar Station at Commerce and Losoya is accessible to travelers with disabilities.

San Antonio Museum of Art ★★ This attraction may not be top-listed by everyone, but I enjoy doable (read: not overwhelmingly large) museums with interesting architecture and collections related to the cities in which they're located. This one definitely fits the bill on all those counts. Several castlelike buildings of the 1904 Lone Star

The Alamo: The Movie(s)

At least one weighty tome, Frank Thompson's *Alamo Movies,* has been devoted to the plethora of films featuring the events that occurred at San Antonio's most famous site. Some outtakes:

Most famous movie about the Alamo not actually shot at the Alamo: *The Alamo* (1959), starring John Wayne as Davy Crockett. Although it has no San Antonio presence, it was shot in Texas. Wayne considered shooting the film in Mexico, but was told it wouldn't be distributed in Texas if he did.

Latest controversy-ridden attempt to tell the story of the Alamo: A 2004 Disney version, also called *The Alamo,* that was originally supposed to be directed by Ron Howard but was eventually only co-produced by him. Directed by John Lee Hancock and starring Dennis Quaid, Billy Bob Thornton, and Jason Patric, among others, it was not a complete success in any shape or form, but it wasn't an embarrassment, either.

Most accurate celluloid depiction of the Alamo story (and also the largest): *Alamo—The Price of Freedom,* showing at the San Antonio IMAX Theater Rivercenter. According to writer and historian Stephen Harrigan in an interview on National Public Radio, it's "90% accurate."

Least controversial film featuring the Alamo: *Miss Congeniality,* starring Sandra Bullock and Benjamin Bratt. A beauty pageant presided over by William Shatner takes place in front of the shrine to the Texas martyrs.

Brewery were gutted, connected, and transformed into a visually exciting exhibition space in 1981, which also offers terrific views of downtown from the multiwindowed crosswalk between the structures. Although holdings range from early Egyptian, Greek, Oceanic, and Asian (see note, below) to 19th- and 20th-century American, it's the Nelson A. Rockefeller Center for Latin American Art, opened in 1998, that is the jewel of the collection. This 30,000-square-foot wing hosts the most comprehensive collection of Latin American art in the United States, with pre-Columbian, folk, Spanish colonial, and contemporary works. You'll see everything here from magnificently ornate altarpieces to a whimsical Day of the Dead tableau. Computer stations add historical perspective to the collection, which is a nationwide resource for Latino culture. If any of this sounds appealing to you, allot at least 2 hours for your visit.

The Lenora and Walter F. Brown Asian Art Wing represents another major collection, the largest Asian art collection in Texas and one of the largest in the Southwest. To see everything, which I don't particularly recommend, would take more than 4 hours.

200 W. Jones Ave. ✆ **210/978-8100.** www.samuseum.org. Admission $8 adults, $7 seniors, $5 students with ID, $3 children 4–11, free for children under 4. Free general admission Tues 4–9pm (fee for some special exhibits). Tues 10am–8pm; Wed–Sat 10am–5pm; Sun noon–6pm. Closed Thanksgiving Day, Dec 25, Jan 1, Easter Sunday, and Fiesta Friday. Bus: 7, 8, 9, or 14.

ALAMO HEIGHTS AREA

Marion Koogler McNay Art Museum ★★★ Well worth a detour from downtown, this museum is one of my favorite spots. A knockout setting on a hill north of

Brackenridge Park with a forever view of the city is home to a sprawling Spanish Mediterranean–style mansion (built in 1929) so picturesque that it's constantly used as a backdrop for weddings and photo shoots. The art collection, though not perhaps the equivalent of collections in bigger cities, is quite good if you enjoy modern art. It has at least one work by most American and European masters of the past 2 centuries, including works by Van Gogh, Manet, Gauguin, Degas, O'Keeffe, Hopper, Matisse, Modigliani, Cézanne, and Picasso, to name just a few of the artists.

Like the San Antonio Art Museum, this museum is not sprawling. The McNay just finished a modern addition that nearly doubles its gallery space, yet the museum manages to retain an intimate feel. The addition, designed by French architect Jean Paul Viguier, is modern and airy and quite enjoyable, adding variety to the original gallery space. It has an innovative roof and ceiling that allows it to filter and adjust the lighting to the needs of a particular exhibit. The McNay occasionally hosts major traveling shows and, with the new addition, will probably host more of these exhibits. It'll take you 2 hours to go through this place at a leisurely pace, longer if it's cool enough for you to stroll the beautiful 23-acre grounds dotted with sculpture and stunning landscaping. You might also enjoy the 15-minute orientation film about oil heiress and artist Marion Koogler McNay, who established the museum. And, of course, there's a gift shop.

6000 N. New Braunfels Ave. ✆ **210/824-5368.** www.mcnayart.org. Admission $13 adults, $10 seniors, $10 students w/ID, free for children 12 and under. Tues–Wed 10am–4pm; Thurs 10am–9pm; Sat 10am–5pm; Sun noon–5pm. Closed Jan 1, July 4th, Thanksgiving, and Dec 25. Bus: 14.

Witte Museum ★ Kids A family museum that adults will enjoy, too, the Witte focuses on Texas history, natural science, and anthropology, with occasional forays as far afield as the Berlin Wall. Your senses will be engaged along with your intellect: You might hear bird calls as you stroll through the Texas Wild exhibits, or feel rough-hewn stone carved with Native American pictographs beneath your feet. Children especially like exhibits devoted to mummies and dinosaurs, as well as the EcoLab, where live Texas critters range from tarantulas to tortoises. But the biggest draw for kids is the terrific H-E-B Science Treehouse, a four-level, 15,000-square-foot science center that sits behind the museum on the banks of the San Antonio River; its hands-on activities are geared to all ages. Also on the grounds are a butterfly and hummingbird garden and three restored historic homes. ***Note:*** Several years ago the museum acquired the wonderful Herzberg Circus Collection, and parts of it are regularly incorporated into the museum's exhibits.

3801 Broadway (adjacent to Brackenridge Park). ✆ **210/357-1900.** www.wittemuseum.org. Admission $7 adults, $6 seniors, $5 children 4–11, free for children under 4. Free Tues 3–8pm. Tues 10am–8pm; Mon and Wed–Sat 10am–5pm; Sun noon–5pm. Closed 3rd Mon in Oct, Thanksgiving, and Dec 24–25. Bus: 7, 9, or 14.

SOUTH SIDE

San Antonio Missions National Historical Park ★★ The Alamo was just the first of five missions established by the Franciscans along the San Antonio River to Christianize the native population. The four other missions, which now fall under the aegis of the National Park Service, are still active parishes, run in cooperation with the Archdiocese of San Antonio. But the missions were more than churches: They were whole communities. The Park Service has assigned each mission an interpretive theme to educate visitors about the roles they played in early San Antonio society. You can visit them separately, but if you have the time, see them all; they were built uncharacteristically close together and—now that you don't have to walk there or ride a horse—it shouldn't take you more than 2 or 3 hours to see them.

The easiest way to see them is to drive. The missions are about 3 miles apart from each other. Each has an information office with free maps and can give you driving instructions to the next mission. New signs make touring the missions easier. If you ever get turned around, remember that all the missions are built along the river. The main information office is at Mission San José. The other option for touring the missions is a 12-mile hike-and-bike trail that for the most part follows the river as it passes close by each mission. If you want to try biking it, see later in this chapter for bike rentals.

The first of the missions you'll come to as you head south, **Concepción,** 807 Mission Rd., at Felisa, was built in 1731. The oldest unrestored Texas mission, Concepción looks much as it did 200 years ago. We tend to think of these old missions as somber and austere places, but traces of color on the facade and restored wall paintings inside show how cheerful this one originally was.

San José ★★, 6701 San José Dr., at Mission Road, established in 1720, was the largest, best known, and most beautiful of the Texas missions. It was reconstructed to give visitors a complete picture of life in a mission community—right down to the granary, mill, and Indian quarters. The beautiful rose window is a big attraction, and popular mariachi masses are held here every Sunday at noon (come early if you want a seat). This is also the site of the missions' excellent visitor center. If you're going to visit only one of the missions, this is it.

Moved from an earlier site in east Texas to its present location in 1731, **San Juan Capistrano,** 9101 Graf, at Ashley, doesn't have the grandeur of the missions to the north—the larger church intended for it was never completed—but the original simple chapel and the wilder setting give it a peaceful, spiritual aura. A short (.3-mile) interpretive trail, with a number of overlook platforms, winds through the woods to the banks of the old river channel.

The southernmost mission in the San Antonio chain, **San Francisco de la Espada ★**, 10040 Espada Rd., also has an ancient, isolated feel, although the beautifully maintained church shows just how vital it still is to the local community. Be sure to visit the Espada Aqueduct, part of the mission's original *acequia* (irrigation ditch) system, about 1 mile north of the mission. Dating from 1740, it's one of the oldest Spanish aqueducts in the United States.

Headquarters: 2202 Roosevelt Ave. Visitors Center: 6701 San José Dr., at Mission Rd. ✆ **210/932-1001.** www.nps.gov/saan. Free admission (donations accepted). All the missions open daily 9am–5pm. Closed Thanksgiving, Dec 25, and Jan 1. National Park Ranger tours daily. Bus: 42 stops at Mission San José (and near Concepción).

FAR NORTHWEST

Six Flags Fiesta Texas ★ Kids Every year brings another thrill ride to this theme park, set on 200 acres in an abandoned limestone quarry and surrounded by 100-foot cliffs. Among the extreme rides are the Tornado, an exhilarating wet and wild tunnel and funnel tubing experience; the Superman Krypton Coaster, nearly a mile of twisted steel with six inversions; the Rattler, one of the world's highest and fastest wooden roller coasters; the 60-mph-plus Poltergeist roller coaster; and Scream!, a 20-story space shot and turbo drop. Laser games and virtual reality simulators complete the technophilia picture. Feeling more primal? Wet 'n' wild attractions include the Lone Star Lagoon, the state's largest wave pool; the Texas Treehouse, a five-story drenchfest whose surprises include a 1,000-gallon cowboy hat that tips over periodically to soak the unsuspecting; and Bugs' White Water Rapids.

If you want to avoid both sogginess and adrenaline overload, check out a vast variety of food booths, shops, crafts demonstrations, and live shows of everything from 1950s musical revues to the laser-fireworks shows (held each summer evening). This theme park still has some local character, dating back to the days when it was plain old Fiesta Texas: Themed areas include a Hispanic village, a western town, and a German town. But when it came under the aegis of Six Flags, a Time Warner company, Looney Tunes cartoon characters such as Tweety Bird became ubiquitous, especially in the endless souvenir shops.

17000 I-10W (corner of I-10W and Loop 1604). ✆ **800/473-4378** or 210/697-5050. www.sixflags.com/parks/fiestatexas. Admission $50 adults, $37 seniors 55 and over, $32 children less than 48 in., free for children under age 3. Discounted 2-day and season passes available. Parking $15 per day. The park opens at 10am; closing times vary depending on the season, as late as 10pm in summer. The park is generally open daily late May to mid-Aug; Sat–Sun Mar–May and Sept–Oct; closed Nov–Feb. Call ahead or visit website for current information. Bus: 94 (summer only). Take exit 555 (La Cantera Pkwy.) on I-10W.

WEST SIDE

SeaWorld San Antonio ★ Kids Leave it to Texas to provide Shamu, the performing killer whale, with his most spacious digs: At 250 acres, this SeaWorld is the largest of the Anheuser-Busch–owned parks, which also makes it the largest marine theme park in the world. Fascinating walk-through habitats house penguins, sea lions, sharks, tropical fish, and flamingos. But if you're a theme park fan, you might find even more fun in the aquatic acrobatics at such stadium shows as Shamu Adventure, combining live action and video close-ups, and Viva, where divers and synchronized swimmers frolic with whales and dolphins.

You needn't get frustrated just looking at all that water because there are loads of places here to get wet. The Lost Lagoon has a huge wave pool and water slides aplenty, and the Texas Splashdown flume ride and the Rio Loco river-rapids ride also offer splashy fun. Younger children can cavort in Shamu's Happy Harbor and the "L'il Gators" section of the Lost Lagoon or take a ride on the Shamu Express kiddie coaster.

Nonaquatic activities abound, too. You can ride the Steel Eel, a huge "hypercoaster" that starts out with a 150-foot dive at 65 mph, followed by several bouts of weightlessness, or Great White, the Southwest's first inverted coaster—which means riders will go head-over-heels during 2,500 feet of loops (don't eat before either of them). It's well worth sticking around for the shows offered in the evening during the peak summer season or for the Halloween activities held on October weekends—if you're not too tuckered from the rides.

10500 SeaWorld Dr., 16 miles northwest of downtown San Antonio at Ellison Dr. and Westover Hills Blvd. ✆ **800/700-7786.** www.seaworld.com. 1-day pass $45 adults, $42 seniors (55 and older), $40 children ages 3–9, free for children under age 3. Discounted 2-day and season passes available. Internet purchase discounts. Parking $12 per day. Open early Mar–late Nov. Days of operation vary. Open at 10am on operating days, closing times vary. Call ahead or check website for current information. Bus: 64. From Loop 410 or from Hwy. 90W, exit Hwy. 151W to the park.

2 MORE ATTRACTIONS

DOWNTOWN AREA

ArtPace San Antonio's contemporary art gallery features rotating shows, displaying the work of artists selected by a guest curator for 2-month residencies at the facility. One artist must be from Texas, one from anywhere else in the United States, and one from

First Fridays

On the first Friday of every month, San Antonio closes off a section of South Alamo Street in the artsy Southtown district and holds something between an "art walk" and a street carnival, which centers around the Blue Star Contemporary Art Center (see below) and extends northward, almost to downtown. It's a popular activity that attracts a lot of people, and with the people come street vendors, sidewalk artists, and street performers. Local merchants and restaurants get involved, too. For the visitor, it can be an entertaining pastime. If you're staying in the King William District, you'll be right next to the action.

anywhere else in the world. The result has been a fascinating melange, including everything from twists on the traditional—such as a monumental drawing of a winter landscape populated by men in black tracksuits and a lenticular print (an image that shows depth and motion when the viewing angle changes) in which the Alamo vanishes before one's eyes—to the more cutting edge: an installation of 5,500 pounds of airplane parts or rooftop speakers that sing until the sun sets. Lecture series by the artists as well as public forums to discuss the work have also helped make this a very stimulating art space.

445 N. Main Ave. ✆ **210/212-4900.** www.artpace.org. Free admission. Wed and Fri–Sun noon–5pm; Thurs noon–8pm. Check local listings or call for lectures and other special events. Bus: 2, 82, or 88.

Blue Star Contemporary Art Center ★ This huge former warehouse in Southtown hosts a collection of working studios and galleries, along with a performance space for the Jump-Start theater company. The 11,000-square-foot artist-run Contemporary Art Center is its anchor. The style of work varies from gallery to gallery—you'll see everything from primitive-style folk art to feminist photography—but the level of professionalism is generally high. One of the most interesting spaces is SAY Si, featuring exhibitions by talented neighborhood high-school students that might include collages or book art. A number of galleries are devoted to (or have sections purveying) arty gift items such as jewelry, picture frames, and crafts.

116 Blue Star (bordered by Probandt, Blue Star, and South Alamo sts. and the San Antonio River). ✆ **210/227-6960.** www.bluestarart.org. Free admission ($2 suggested donation for art center). Hours vary from gallery to gallery; most are open Wed–Sun noon–6pm, with some opening at 10am. Streetcar: Blue line.

Buckhorn Saloon & Museum Overrated If you like your educational experiences accompanied by a tall cold brew, this is the place for you. With its huge stuffed animals, mounted fish, and wax museum version of history, this collection fulfills every out-of-stater's stereotype of what a Texas museum might be like. To enjoy it best, you have to have an appreciation for cheesiness and heavy-handed commercialization of the idea of the Old West. It's not nearly as funky as it was when it was in the old Lone Star brewery (all those dead animals seem out of place in this modern space), but it's still got such exhibits as the church made out of 50,000 matchsticks and pictures designed from rattlesnake rattles. The facility includes a re-creation of the turn-of-the-century Buckhorn saloon, a curio shop, and a transported historic bar. Lots of people like this place, but others think it's a bit pricey for what you get.

318 E. Houston St. © **210/247-4000.** www.buckhornmuseum.com. Admission $10 adults, $9 seniors (55 and older), $7.50 children age 3–11. Labor Day–Memorial Day daily 10am–5pm; rest of year daily 10am–6pm (later hours in summer). Closed Thanksgiving and Dec 25. Streetcar: Red or Blue lines.

Casa Navarro State Historic Site A key player in Texas's transition from Spanish territory to American state, José Antonio Navarro was the Mexican mayor of San Antonio in 1821, a signer of the 1836 Texas Declaration of Independence, and the only native Texan to take part in the convention that ratified the annexation of Texas to the United States in 1845. His former living quarters, built around 1850, are an interesting amalgam of the architectural fashions of his time: The restored office, house, and separate kitchen, constructed of adobe and limestone, blend elements from Mexican, French, German, and pioneer styles. Guided tours and demonstrations are available; call ahead to inquire.

228 S. Laredo St. © **210/226-4801.** Admission $2 adults, $1 children ages 6–12, free for children under age 6. Wed–Sun 10am–4pm. Streetcar: Purple line.

Institute of Texan Cultures (Kids) It's the rare visitor who won't discover here that his or her ethnic group has contributed to the history of Texas: 26 different ethnic and cultural groups are represented in the imaginative, hands-on displays of this educational center, which is one of three campuses of the University of Texas at San Antonio. Outbuildings include a one-room schoolhouse, an adobe home, a windmill, and the multimedia Dome Theater, which presents images of Texas on 36 screens. A variety of heritage festivals and kid-friendly shows and events, such as pioneer life reenactments, holography exhibits, ghost-tale storytellers at Halloween, and the like, are always on tap; phone or check the institute's website for a current schedule. An excellent photo archive here, open to the public by appointment, holds more than 3 million images. Call © **210/458-2298** for information on using it.

801 S. Bowie St. (at Durango St., in HemisFair Park). © **210/458-2300.** www.texancultures.utsa.edu. Admission $7 adults; $4 seniors, military (with ID), and children ages 3–12. Tues–Wed 10am–6pm; Thurs–Sat 10am–8pm; Sun noon–5pm. Dome shows presented at 11am, 12:30, 2, and 4pm (Thurs–Sat 6pm shows also, Sun no 11am show). Closed Thanksgiving, Dec 24–25, Jan 1, and for 3 days during the Texas Folklife Festival (held in June). Streetcar: Yellow or Purple lines.

Museo Alameda Inaugurated in April of 2007, the Museo Alameda is the nation's largest museum celebrating Latino culture. It has 20,000 sq. ft. of exhibition space divided up into 11 galleries. Its location in San Antonio is ideal in that the majority of the city's population is Hispanic. Though the Museo doesn't have a permanent collection, it has many resources to lean on, including a close association with the Smithsonian Institute. The exhibits, each running about 6 months, seek to place in view the Latino experience in America. They are meant to explore themes such as the various things that America represents for Latinos, and what the old homeland, be it Mexico or another country, comes to signify, as well. Such a broad purpose embraces art and artifact, art and history, to piece together its narrative on Latino culture. It necessarily leans heavily on the expertise of the curators who will create these exhibitions. The building proper is an attractive addition to the area around Market Square. It injects color and bold modern lines. The main decorative feature is some elaborate stainless steel panels that variously bring to mind the wrought iron work of colonial Latin America and the humble decorative practice of cutting designs into folded paper (*papel picado*).

101 S. Santa Rosa Blvd. (at Commerce, in Market Square). © **210/299-4300.** www.thealameda.org. Suggested donation adults $4, seniors $3, students with ID $2, families $12. Tues–Sat 10am–6pm, Sun noon–6pm. Streetcar: Red, Purple, or Yellow lines.

San Antonio Central Library San Antonio's main library, opened in the mid-1990s at a cost of $38 million, has a number of important holdings (including part of the Hertzberg Circus Collection, scattered when it lost its museum home in 2001), but it is most notable for its architecture. Ricardo Legorreta, renowned for his buildings throughout Mexico, created a wildly colorful and whimsical public space that people apparently love to enter; by the second month after the library opened, circulation had gone up 95%. The boxy building, painted what has been called "enchilada red," is designed like a hacienda around an internal courtyard. A variety of skylights, windows, and wall colors (including bright purples and yellows) afford a different perspective from each of the six floors. A gallery offers monthly exhibits of paintings, photography, textiles, and more.

600 Soledad. ✆ **210/207-2500.** www.sanantonio.gov/library. Free admission. Mon–Thurs 9am–9pm; Fri–Sat 9am–5pm; Sun 11am–5pm. Bus: 3, 4, 90, 91, or 92.

San Fernando Cathedral ★ Construction of a church on this site, overlooking what was once the town's central plaza, was begun in 1738 by San Antonio's original Canary Island settlers and completed in 1749. Part of the early structure—the oldest cathedral sanctuary in the United States and the oldest parish church in Texas—is incorporated into the magnificent Gothic revival–style cathedral built in 1868. Jim Bowie got married here, and General Santa Anna raised the flag of "no quarter" from the roof during the siege of the Alamo in 1836. The cathedral underwent major interior and exterior renovations in 2002; its most impressive new addition, a 24-foot-high gilded *retablo* (altarpiece), was unveiled in 2003.

115 Main Plaza. ✆ **210/227-1297.** www.sfcathedral.org. Free admission. Daily 6am–7pm; gift shop Mon–Fri 9am–4:30pm, Sat until 5pm. Streetcar: Purple or Yellow lines.

Southwest School of Art and Craft ★ A stroll along the River Walk to the northern corner of downtown will lead you into another world: a rare French-designed cloister where contemporary crafts are now being created. An exhibition gallery and artist studios–cum–classrooms (not open to visitors) occupy the garden-filled grounds of the first girls' school in San Antonio, established by the Ursuline order in the mid–19th century. Learn about both the school and the historic site at the Visitors Center Museum in the First Academy Building. The Ursuline Sales Gallery carries unique crafts items, most made by the school's artists. You can enjoy a nice, light lunch in the Copper Kitchen Restaurant (Mon–Fri 11:30am–2pm, closed national holidays). The adjacent Navarro Campus, built in the late 1990s, is not as architecturally interesting, but it's worth stopping there for its large contemporary art gallery—and for the Art*O*Mat [sic], a converted vending machine selling local artists' work for $5 a pop. What a steal!

300 Augusta. ✆ **210/224-1848.** www.swschool.org. Free admission. Mon–Sat 9am–5pm (galleries on both campuses), Sun 11am–4pm (Navarro Campus gallery only); Mon–Sat 10am–5pm (gift shop); Mon–Sat 10am–5pm, Sun 11am–4pm (museum). Streetcar: Blue line.

Spanish Governor's Palace ★ Finds Never actually a palace, this 1749 adobe structure formerly served as the residence and headquarters for the captain of the Spanish presidio. It became the seat of Texas government in 1772, when San Antonio was made capital of the Spanish province of Texas and, by the time it was purchased by the city in 1928, it had served as a tailor's shop, barroom, and schoolhouse. The building, with high ceilings crossed by protruding viga beams, is beautiful in its simplicity, and the 10 rooms crowded with period furnishings paint a vivid portrait of upper-class life in a rough-hewn society. It's interesting to see how the other half lived in an earlier era, and I love to sit out on the tree-shaded, cobblestone patio, listening to the burbling of the stone fountain.

Impressions

We have no city, except, perhaps, New Orleans, that can vie, in point of picturesque interest that attaches to odd and antiquated foreignness, with San Antonio.

—Frederick Law Olmsted, *A Journey Through Texas,* 1853

Be sure to ask a staff member to explain the symbols carved in the grand wooden entryway to the complex.

105 Plaza de Armas. ✆ **210/224-0601.** www.sanantonio.gov/dtops/SpanGovPal.asp. Admission $2 adults, $1 children ages 7–13, free for children under age 7. Mon–Sat 9am–5pm; Sun 10am–5pm. Closed Jan 1, San Jacinto Day (Apr 21), Thanksgiving, and Dec 25. Streetcar: Purple line.

Steves Homestead Museum Built in 1876 for lumber magnate Edward Steves, this Victorian mansion was restored by the San Antonio Conservation Society, to whom it was willed by Steves's granddaughter. Believed to have been built by prominent San Antonio architect Alfred Giles and one of the only houses in the King William Historic District open to the public, it gives a fascinating glimpse into the lifestyles of the rich and locally famous of the late 19th century. You can't enter without taking a 30- to 45-minute-long docent-led tour; that's no problem, as you don't want to miss the great gossip about the Steves family that the Society's very knowledgeable volunteers pass along.

509 King William St. ✆ **210/225-5924.** www.saconservation.org. Admission $6 adults, $4 seniors, $3 students and active-duty military with ID, free for children under age 12. Daily 10am–4:15pm (last tour at 3:30pm). Closed major holidays. Streetcar: Blue line.

Tower of the Americas ★ For a good take on the lay of the land, just circle the eight panoramic panels on the observation deck of the Tower of the Americas. The 750-foot-high tower was built for the HemisFair in 1968. The deck sits at the equivalent of 59 stories and is lit for spectacular night viewing. The tower also hosts a rotating restaurant with surprisingly decent food (for the revolving genre) as well as a thankfully stationary cocktail lounge.

600 HemisFair Park. ✆ **210/207-8615.** www.toweroftheamericas.com. Admission $11 adults, $10 seniors 55 and older, $9 children ages 4–11, free for children under age 4. Sun–Thurs 10am–10pm; Fri–Sat 10–11pm. Streetcar: Yellow or Purple lines.

ALAMO HEIGHTS AREA

San Antonio Zoological Gardens and Aquarium (Kids) I want to like this zoo, considered one of the top facilities in the country because of its conservation efforts and its successful breeding programs (it produced the first white rhino in the U.S.). Home to more than 700 species, it has one of the largest animal collections in the United States. But, although the zoo has expanded and upgraded its exhibits many times since it opened in 1914, the cages are small, the landscaping looks droopy, and some of the animals seem depressed. Still, kids who haven't recently been to SeaWorld or the San Diego Zoo will get a kick out of many critters (the Lory Encounter is especially popular), and parents will appreciate the fact that they won't run into an expensive gift shop around every corner.

3903 N. St. Mary's St., in Brackenridge Park. ✆ **210/734-7183.** www.sazoo-aq.org. Admission $9 adults, $7 seniors 62 and older and children ages 3–11, free for children under age 3. Daily 9am–5pm (until 6pm in summer). Bus: 7 or 8.

FORT SAM HOUSTON AREA

Fort Sam Houston Since 1718, when the armed Presidio de Béxar was established to defend the Spanish missions, the military has played a key role in San Antonio's development, and it remains one of the largest employers in town today. The 3,434-acre Fort Sam Houston affords visitors an unusual opportunity to view the city's military past (the first military flight in history took off from the fort's spacious parade grounds) in the context of its military present—the fort currently hosts the Army Medical Command and the headquarters of the Fifth Army. Most of its historic buildings are still in use and thus off-limits, but three are open to the public. The **Fort Sam Houston Museum,** 1210 Stanley Rd., Bldg. 123 (© **210/221-1886;** free admission; Wed–Sun 10am–4pm), details the history of the armed forces in Texas, with a special focus on San Antonio. The **U.S. Army Medical Department Museum,** 2310 Stanley Rd., Bldg. 1046 (© **210/221-6277** or 210/221-6358; www.ameddgiftshop.com/museum.htm; free admission; Tues–Sat 10am–4pm), displays army medical equipment and American prisoner-of-war memorabilia. The oldest building on the base, the **Quadrangle ★**, 1400 E. Grayson St. (no phone; free admission; Mon–Fri 8am–5pm, Sat–Sun noon–5pm), an impressive 1876 limestone structure, is centered on a brick clock tower and encloses a grassy square where peacocks and deer roam freely. The Apache chief Geronimo was held captive here for 40 days in 1886. Free self-guided tour maps of the historic sites are available in all three buildings. Anyone wishing to visit the fort must enter through the Walters Gate (take the Walters St. exit off I-35) and present a driver's license.

Grayson St. and New Braunfels Ave., about 2½ miles northeast of downtown. © **210/221-1151** (public affairs). There is no longer public transportation to the Quadrangle.

3 PARKS & GARDENS

Brackenridge Park ★ With its rustic stone bridges and winding walkways, the city's main park has a charming, old-fashioned feel and serves as a popular center for such recreational activities as golf, polo, biking, and picnicking. I especially like the **Japanese Tea Garden ★** (also known as the Japanese Sunken Garden), created in 1917 by prison labor to beautify an abandoned cement quarry, one of the largest in the world in the 1880s and 1890s. (The same quarry furnished cement rock for the state capitol in Austin.) You can still see a brick smokestack and a number of the old lime kilns among the beautiful flower arrangements—lusher than those in most Japanese gardens. After Pearl Harbor, the site was officially renamed the Chinese Sunken Garden, and a Chinese-style entryway was added on. Not until 1983 was the original name restored. Just to the southwest, a bowl of limestone cliffs found to have natural acoustic properties was turned into the **Sunken Garden Theater** (see "The Performing Arts" in chapter 9). A 60-foot-high waterfall and water lily–laced ponds are among its lures. Across from the entrance to the **San Antonio Zoological Gardens** (see above), you can buy tickets for the **Brackenridge Eagle** (© **210/734-7183**), a miniature train that replicates an 1863 model. The pleasant 2-mile ride through the park takes about 20 minutes (tickets $2.50 for adults, $2 for children 3–11; daily 9:30am, weather permitting, to when zoo gate closes).

Main entrance 2800 block of N. Broadway. © **210/207-3000.** www.sanantonio.gov/sapar. Daily dawn–dusk. Bus: 7, 8, or 9.

HemisFair Park Built for the 1968 HemisFair, an exposition celebrating the 250th anniversary of the founding of San Antonio, this urban oasis boasts **water gardens** and

(Fun Facts **Did You Know?**

- Elmer Doolin, the original manufacturer of Fritos corn chips, bought the original recipe from a San Antonio restaurant in 1932 for $100. He sold the first batch from the back of his Model-T Ford.
- *Wings,* a silent World War I epic that won the first Academy Award for best picture in 1927, was filmed in San Antonio. The film marked the debut of Gary Cooper, who was on screen for a total of 102 seconds.
- Lyndon and Lady Bird Johnson were married in San Antonio's St. Mark's Episcopal Church.

a **wood-and-sand playground** constructed for children (near the Alamo St. entrance). Among its indoor diversions are the **Institute of Texan Cultures** and the **Tower of the Americas** (both detailed above). Be sure to walk over to the Henry B. Gonzales Convention Center and take a look at the striking mosaic **mural** by Mexican artist Juan O'Gorman. **The Schultze House Cottage Garden** ★, 514 HemisFair Park (✆ **210/229-9161**), created and maintained by Master Gardeners of Bexar County, is also worth checking out for its heirloom plants, varietals, tropicals, and xeriscape area. Look for it behind the Federal Building.

Bounded by Alamo, Bowie, Market, and Durango sts. No phone. Streetcar: Blue, Yellow, or Purple lines.

San Antonio Botanical Garden ★ Take a horticultural tour of Texas at this gracious 38-acre garden, encompassing everything from south Texas scrub to Hill Country wildflowers. Fountains, pools, paved paths, and examples of Texas architecture provide visual contrast to the flora. The formal gardens include a garden for the blind, a Japanese garden, an herb garden, a biblical garden, and a children's garden. Perhaps most outstanding is the $6.9-million Lucile Halsell Conservatory complex, a series of greenhouses replicating a variety of tropical and desert environments. The 1896 Sullivan Carriage House, built by Alfred Giles and moved stone-by-stone from its original downtown site, serves as the entryway to the gardens. It houses a gift shop (✆ **210/829-1227**) and a restaurant (✆ **210/821-6447**) offering salads, quiches, sandwiches, and outrageously rich desserts, open Tuesday to Sunday from 11am to 2pm.

555 Funston. ✆ **210/207-3250.** www.sabot.org. Admission $7 adults; $5 seniors, students, and military; $4 children 3–13; free for children under 3. Daily 9am–5pm. Closed Dec 25 and Jan 1. Bus: 7, 9, or 14.

4 ESPECIALLY FOR KIDS

Without a doubt, the prime spots for kids in San Antonio are **SeaWorld** and **Six Flags Fiesta Texas.** They'll also like the hands-on, interactive **Witte Museum** and the various ethnic-pride kids' programs at the **Institute of Texas Cultures.** There's a children's area in the **zoo,** which vends food packets so kids can feed the fish and the ducks. The third floor of the main branch of the **San Antonio Public Library** is devoted to children, who get to use their own catalogs and search tools. Story hours are offered regularly, and there are occasional puppet shows.

In addition to these sights, detailed in "The Top Attractions" and "More Attractions" sections, earlier in this chapter, and the **Magik Theatre** (p. 151), the following should also appeal to the sandbox set and up.

Plaza Wax Museum & Ripley's Believe It or Not ★ Adults may get the bigger charge out of the waxy stars—Dustin Hoffman and Dallas Cowboy coach Tom Landry are among the latest to be added to an impressive array—and some of the oddities collected by the globe-trotting Mr. Ripley, but there's plenty for kids to enjoy at this twofer attraction. The walk-through wax Theater of Horrors, although tame compared to *Friday the 13th*–type adventures, usually elicits some shudders. At Believe It or Not, youngsters generally get a kick out of learning about people around the world whose habits—such as sticking nails through their noses—are even weirder than their own.

301 Alamo Plaza. ✆ **210/224-9299.** www.plazawaxmuseum.com. Either attraction $18 adults, $10 children ages 4–12; both attractions $22 adults, $12 children 4–12. Memorial Day–Labor Day daily 9am–10pm; remainder of the year Sun 9am–8pm, Mon–Thurs 9:30am–8pm, Fri–Sat 9am–10pm (ticket office closes 1 hr. before listed closing times). Streetcar: Red or Blue lines.

Ripley's Haunted Adventure, Guinness World Records Museum, and Tomb Rider 3D ★ San Antonio's newest attraction, this multimillion-dollar downtown entertainment complex just keeps growing—and getting better. Ripley's Haunted Adventure, which debuted in 2002, is a 10,000-square-foot, state-of-the-art haunted house (if that's not a contradiction in terms), combining live actors, animatronics, and lots of special effects. The Guinness Museum, opened in 2003, brings the famed record book to life with such hands-on exhibits as a drum set that lets you see how hard it is to best the most-drum-beats-per-minute record and a multiple-choice quiz room where you can guess at the actual world record. Tomb Rider 3D, opened in 2007, combines a theme park–style ride through ancient tombs, with an interactive video game format where you shoot the mummies and spirits you encounter on the trip.

329 Alamo Plaza. ✆ **210/226-2828.** www.alamoplazaattractions.com. Admission $19 for any 1 attraction, $22 for 2, $27 for all 3 for adults; $11 for 1, $14 for 2, $17 for 3 for children ages 4–12; $1 off any rate for seniors. Labor Day–Memorial Day Sun–Thurs 10am–10pm, Fri–Sat 10am–midnight; off-season Sun–Thurs 10am–7pm, Fri–Sat 10am–10pm. Call ahead to verify hours and prices.

San Antonio Children's Museum ★★ San Antonio's children's museum offers a terrific, creative introduction to the city for the pint-sized and grown-up alike. San Antonio history, population, and geography are all explored through such features as a miniature River Walk, a multicultural grocery store, a bank where kids can use their own ATM, and even a miniature dentist's office (more fun than you'd imagine). Activities range from crawl spaces and corn-grinding rocks to a weather station and radar room. Don't miss this place if you're traveling with children younger than age 10.

305 E. Houston St. ✆ **210/21-CHILD** [212-4453]. www.sakids.org. Admission $7, free for children under age 2. Memorial Day–Labor Day Mon–Fri 9am–5pm, Sat 9am–6pm, Sun noon–4pm; rest of the year Tues–Fri 9am–2pm, Sat 9am–6pm, Sun noon–4pm. Bus: 7 or 40. Streetcar: Red line.

San Antonio IMAX Theater Rivercenter ★ Having kids view this theater's main attraction, *Alamo—The Price of Freedom,* on a six-story-high screen with a stereo sound system is a sure-fire way of getting them psyched for the historical battle site (which, although it's just across the street, can't be reached without wending your way past lots and lots of Rivercenter shops). It's a reasonably accurate rendition of the historical events, to boot. The first commercial IMAX venue to double its viewing pleasures by introducing a second megascreen (this one with 3-D capability and a state-of-the-art sound system) at the beginning of the 21st century, this theater also shows thrilling—and educational—nature and scientific adventure movies produced especially for the large screen.

849 E. Commerce St., in the Rivercenter Mall. ✆ **800/354-4629** or 210/247-4629. www.imax-sa.com. You can reserve seats by phone. Admission $10 adults, $9 seniors and youth 12–17, $6.75 children 3–11. Times of daily shows vary, but generally the first show is screened at 8:30 or 9am, the last at 9:45pm. Streetcar: All lines.

Splashtown Cool off at this 20-acre water park, which includes a huge wave pool, hydro tubes nearly 300 feet long, a Texas-size water bobsled ride, more than a dozen water slides, and a two-story playhouse for the smaller children. A variety of concerts, contests, and special events are held here.

3600 N. I-35 (exit 160, Splashtown Dr.). ✆ **210/227-1100** (recorded info) or 210/227-1400. www.splashtownsa.com. Admission $25 adults, $20 children under 48 in. (after 5pm, $15 for any age), free for seniors over 65 and children under 2. Call ahead or check website for exact dates and closing times.

5 SPECIAL-INTEREST SIGHTSEEING

FOR MILITARY HISTORY BUFFS

San Antonio's military installations are crucial to the city's economy, and testaments to their past abound. Those who aren't satisfied with touring Fort Sam Houston (see "More Attractions," earlier in this chapter) can also visit the **Hangar 9/Edward H. White Museum** at Brooks Air Force Base, Southeast Military Drive, at the junction of I-37 (✆ **210/536-2203;** www.brooks.af.mil). The history of flight medicine, among other things, is detailed via exhibits in the oldest aircraft hangar in the Air Force. Admission is free, and it's open Monday to Friday 8am to 3pm, except the last 2 weeks of December. Lackland Air Force Base (12 miles southwest of downtown off U.S. 90, at Southwest Military Dr. exit; www.lackland.af.mil) is home to the **Air Force History and Traditions Museum,** 2051 George Ave., Bldg. 5206 (✆ **210/671-3055**), which hosts a collection of rare aircraft and components dating back to World War II. Admission is free; it's open Monday to Friday 8am to 4:30pm. At the **Security Forces Museum,** about 3 blocks away, at Bldg. 10501 (on Femoyer St., corner of Carswell Ave., ✆ **210/671-2615**), weapons, uniforms, and combat gear dating up to Desert Storm days are among the security police artifacts on display. Admission is free; it's open Monday to Friday 8am to 3pm. Inquire at either museum about the 41 static aircraft on view throughout the base. With current security measures in place, the bases are sometimes restricted to retired military, their families, and those sponsored by someone who works at the base. But you can try phoning the museums or the Public Affairs Office at Brooks (✆ **210/536-3234**) or the visitor center at Lackland (✆ **210/671-6174**) to inquire about visitation status. In any case, phone ahead to find out if anyone is permitted on the base on the day you're planning to visit. As may be expected, the museums are closed all national holidays.

FOR THOSE INTERESTED IN HISPANIC HERITAGE

A Hispanic heritage tour is almost redundant in San Antonio, which is a living testament to the role Hispanics have played in shaping the city. **Casa Navarro State Historic Site, La Villita, Market Square, San Antonio Missions National Historical Park,** and the **Spanish Governor's Palace,** all detailed earlier in this chapter, give visitors a feel for the city's Spanish colonial past, while the Nelson A. Rockefeller wing of the **San Antonio Museum of Art,** also discussed earlier, hosts this country's largest collection of Latin

Old Movie Palaces of San Antonio

In the first half of the 20th century, Old San Antone was a movie-going town, and four grand old movie palaces still survive. Each deserves to be an attraction in its own right. Back then theaters were in the business of selling glamour and fantasy, which they presented with their size, design, and decoration. They were also expressions of local pride, so the fantastical decorations most often had some tie-in with the heritage of the city.

Two of the theaters—the **Empire** and the **Majestic**—have been fully restored to their former glory and function now as venues for a wide range of performances and entertainment. Unfortunately, no one gives tours of them; to see them you would need to attend one of the events, many of which are fun and worth seeing (p. 152). Both theaters were designed and decorated with exuberance. Just to get an idea, visit the website www.majesticempire.com. The Empire is smaller and older (1913) and is on the historic registry of buildings. The walls are thickly textured with molded plaster and gold leaf. The Majestic (1929) is larger and grander. Its decoration is ultrabaroque and presents the audience with an imaginative vision of Moorish and Spanish design. Any performance here will feel like a special occasion owing to the grandness of the auditorium.

The old Aztec Theater was built in 1926 and completely refurbished in 2006; it was renamed **Aztec on the River** (✆ **877/43-AZTEC** [432-9832]; www.aztecontheriver.com) in the process to emphasize that it's on the River Walk (across from the Omni La Mansión del Río Hotel). The theater lobby is a fanciful rendition of an Aztec temple, with pre-Columbian iconography blanketing the columns and walls with great Art Deco touches. Playing on this pagan vision, the restorers installed an elaborate sound and light show that tells the tale of the feathered-serpent god and ends with the god rising up through the floor of the lobby. The museum is closed again and being remodeled as another performance venue.

Finally, there is the **Alameda,** which is not yet open to the public, but might be the most original of the four theaters. It was built much later than the others, in 1949, and was a center for the Latino community. In the late '40s, Mexican cinema was living its heyday, and big stars would come from Mexico to be present for film screenings. The only part of the theater you can see now is the exterior decoration, including a marvelous terrazzo mosaic on the sidewalk that flows into the theater lobby, a beautiful and unique tile facade made here in the city, and a towering marquee decorated with much neon. The neon is working and is a fabulous sight after dark. Inside the auditorium are two black-light murals in need of restoration. Revolutionary for their day, the murals had a deep blue background decorated in Day-Glo paints (p. 130).

American art. The sixth floor of the main branch of the **San Antonio Public Library** (see above) hosts an excellent noncirculating Latino collection, featuring books about the Mexican-American experience in Texas and the rest of the Southwest. It's also the place to come to do genealogical research into your family's Hispanic roots.

The city is in the process of exploring its Hispanic roots and evolving Latino culture. The **Centro Alameda cultural zone** on downtown's west side includes the old **Alameda Theater** at 310 W. Houston St. This theater dates from 1949 and has many great features of the old grand movie palaces. First, there's the spectacular 86-foot-high sign adorning the marquee. Lit by rare cold cathode technology, not neon, it's one of a kind and a spectacular sight at night. Other features include "Deco tropical" tile work hand-created in San Antonio and a mural with phosphorescent paint and black lights. The Alameda was one of the last of its kind and the largest movie palace ever dedicated to Spanish-language entertainment. It has been described as being "to U.S. Latinos what Harlem's Apollo Theater is to African Americans." The theater is being painstakingly refurbished as a performing arts venue. The work is being done by an arts organization called The Alameda National Center of Latino Arts and Culture, which is the only arts complex to be linked to both the Smithsonian and the Kennedy Center, both of whom are helping with this work as well as with opening exhibition space to be dedicated to Mexican and Latino art exhibits. (The Museo Alameda is part of the Alameda National Center of Latino Arts and Culture; the museum has a permanent display called "Palace of Dreams: The Golden Age of the Alameda Theatre." See p. 122.) For additional information and progress reports, log on to **www.thealameda.org** or call ✆ **210/299-4300.**

Cultural events and blowout festivals, many of them held at Market Square, abound. The **Guadalupe Cultural Arts Center,** which organizes many of them, is detailed in chapter 9. In HemisFair Park, the **Instituto Cultural Mexicano/Casa Mexicana,** 600 HemisFair Plaza Way (✆ **210/227-0123**), sponsored by the Mexican Ministry of Foreign Affairs, hosts Latin American film series, concerts, conferences, performances, contests, and workshops—including ones on language, literature, and folklore as well as art. The institute also hosts shifting displays of art and artifacts relating to Mexican history and culture, from pre-Columbian to contemporary (free admission; Tues–Fri 10am–5pm; Sat–Sun noon–5pm).

For information on the various festivals and events, contact the **San Antonio Hispanic Chamber of Commerce** (✆ **210/225-0462;** www.sahcc.org). Another roundup resource for Latin *cultura* is the **"Guide to Puro San Antonio,"** available from the San Antonio Convention and Visitors Bureau (✆ **800/447-3372**).

6 STROLLING DOWNTOWN SAN ANTONIO

One of downtown San Antonio's great gifts to visitors on foot is its wonderfully meandering early pathways—not laid out by drunken cattle drivers as has been wryly suggested, but formed by the course of the San Antonio River and the various settlements that grew up around it. Turn any corner in this area and you'll come across some fascinating testament to the city's historically rich past.

Note: Stops 1, 5, 6, 7, 9, 11, 13, and 14 are described earlier in this chapter. Entrance hours and admission fees (if applicable) are listed there. See chapter 5 for additional information on stop no. 2 and chapter 8 for additional information on stop no. 3.

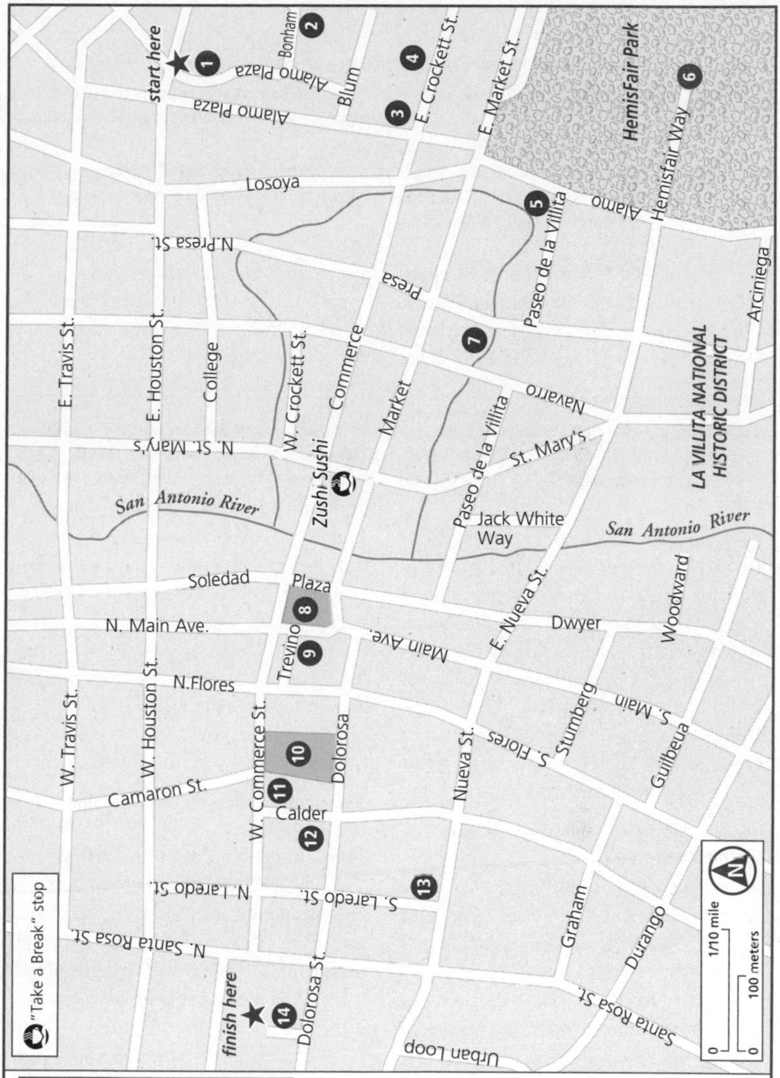

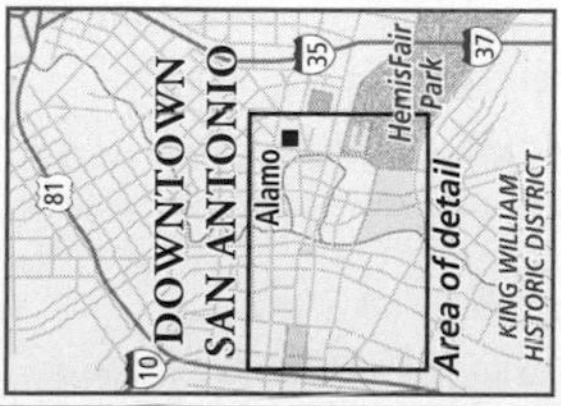

1 The Alamo
2 The Menger Hotel
3 Joske's (Dillard's)
4 St. Joseph's Catholic Church
5 La Villita
6 HemisFair Plaza
7 The River Walk
8 Main Plaza
9 San Fernando Cathedral
10 Military Plaza
11 The Spanish Governor's Palace
12 San Pedro Creek
13 Casa Navarro State Historical Site
14 Market Square

START: The Alamo.

FINISH: Market Square.

TIME: Approximately 1½ hours, not including stops at shops, restaurants, or attractions.

BEST TIMES: Early morning during the week, when the streets and attractions are less crowded. If you're willing to tour the Alamo museums and shrine another time, consider starting out before they open (9am).

WORST TIMES: Weekend afternoons, especially in summer, when the crowds and the heat render this long stroll uncomfortable. (If you do get tired, you can always pick up a streetcar within a block or two of most parts of this route.)

Built to be within easy reach of each other, San Antonio's earliest military, religious, and civil settlements are concentrated in the downtown area. The city spread out quite a bit in the subsequent 2½ centuries, but downtown still functions as the seat of the municipal and county government, as well as the hub of tourist activities.

Start your tour at Alamo Plaza (bounded by E. Houston St. on the north); at the plaza's northeast corner, you'll come to the entrance for:

❶ The Alamo

Originally established in 1718 as the Mission San Antonio de Valero, the first of the city's five missions, the Alamo was moved twice before settling at this site. The heavy limestone walls of the church and its adjacent compound later proved to make an excellent fortress. In 1836, fighters for Texas's independence from Mexico took a heroic, if ultimately unsuccessful, stand against Mexican general Santa Anna here.

When you leave the walled complex, walk south along the plaza to:

❷ The Menger Hotel

German immigrant William Menger built this hotel in 1859 on the site of Texas's first brewery, which he opened with partner Charles Deegan in 1855. Legend has it that Menger wanted a place to lodge hard-drinking friends who used to spend the night sleeping on his long bar. Far more prestigious guests—presidents, Civil War generals, writers, stage actors, you name it—stayed here over the years, and the hotel turns up in several short stories by frequent guest William Sidney Porter (O. Henry). The Menger has been much expanded since it first opened but retains its gorgeous, three-tiered Victorian lobby.

On the south side of the hotel, Alamo Plaza turns back into North Alamo Street. Take it south 1 block until you reach Commerce Street, where you'll spot:

❸ Joske's (now Dillard's)

This is San Antonio's oldest department store. The modest retail emporium, opened by the Joske Brothers in 1889, was swallowed up in 1939 by the large modernist building you see now, distinctive for its intricate Spanish Renaissance–style details; look for the miniaturized versions of Mission San José's sacristy window on the building's ground-floor shadow boxes.

Walk a short way along the Commerce Street side of the building to:

❹ St. Joseph's Catholic Church

This church was built for San Antonio's German community in 1876. The Gothic revival–style house of worship is as notable for the intransigence of its congregation as it is for its beautiful stained-glass windows. The worshipers' refusal to move from the site when Joske's department store was rising up all around it earned the church the affectionate moniker "St. Joske's."

Head back to Alamo Street and continue south 2 blocks past the San Antonio Convention Center to reach:

❺ La Villita

Once the site of a Coahuiltecan Indian village, La Villita was settled over the centuries by Spanish, Germans, and, in the 1930s and '40s, a community of artists. A number of the buildings have been continuously occupied for more than 200 years. The "Little Village" on the river was restored by a joint effort of the city and the San Antonio Conservation Society, and now hosts a number of crafts shops and two upscale restaurants in addition to the historic General Cós House and the Arneson River Theatre.

Just south of La Villita, you'll see HemisFair Way and the large iron gates of:

❻ HemisFair Park

This park was built for the 1968 exposition held to celebrate the 250th anniversary of San Antonio's founding. The expansive former fairgrounds are home to two museums, a German heritage park, and an observation tower—the tallest structure in the city and a great reference point if you get lost downtown. The plaza is too large to explore even superficially on this tour, so come back another time.

Retrace your steps to Paseo de la Villita and walk 1 block west to Presa Street. Take it north for about half a block until you see the Presa Street Bridge, and descend from it to:

❼ The River Walk

You'll find yourself on a quiet section of the 2³/₅-mile paved walkway that lines the banks of the San Antonio River through a large part of downtown and the King William Historic District. The bustling cafe, restaurant, and hotel action is just behind you on the stretch of the river that winds north of La Villita.

Stroll down this tree-shaded thoroughfare until you reach the St. Mary's Street Bridge (you'll pass only one other bridge, the Navarro St. Bridge, along the way) and ascend here. Then walk north half a block until you come to Market Street. Take it west 1 long block, where you'll find:

❽ Main Plaza (Plaza de Las Islas)

This is the heart of the city established in 1731 by 15 Canary Island families sent by King Philip V of Spain to settle his remote New World outpost. Much of the history of San Antonio—and of Texas—unfolded on this modest square. A peace treaty with the Apaches was signed (and later broken) on the plaza in 1749. In 1835, the Texan forces battled Santa Anna's troops here before barricading themselves in the Alamo across the river. Much calmer these days, the plaza still sees some action as home to the Romanesque-style Bexar County Courthouse, built out of native Texas granite and sandstone in 1892.

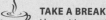

TAKE A BREAK

I know, it's not strictly in keeping with the Hispanic history of this area, but multiculturalism is San Antonio's trademark. And if you like Japanese food as much as I do, you'll enjoy cooling your heels at **Zushi Sushi,** in the International Center, 203 S. St. Mary's St., at Market (✆ **210/472-2900**). You can get a quick raw-fish fix at the sleek sushi bar (they've got lots of cooked and vegetarian rolls, too) or settle in at one of the tables for a bowl of soba noodles or some teppan-grilled beef.

Walk along the south side of Main Plaza to the corner of Main Avenue. Across the street and just to the north you'll encounter:

❾ San Fernando Cathedral

This is the oldest parish church building in Texas and site of the earliest marked graves in San Antonio. Three walls of the original church started by the Canary Island settlers in 1738 can still be seen in the rear of the 1868 Gothic revival cathedral, which recently underwent a massive renovation. Among those buried within the sanctuary walls are Eugenio Navarro, brother of José Antonio Navarro (see stop no. 13, below), and Don Manuel Muñoz, first governor of Texas when it was a province of a newly independent Mexico.

On the north side of the cathedral is Trevino Street; take it west to the next corner and cross the street to reach:

❿ Military Plaza (Plaza de Armas)

This used to be the parade grounds for the Spanish garrison charged with guarding

San Antonio de Béxar. The garrison was stationed here in 1718, the same year the mission San Antonio de Valero (the Alamo) was established. After Texas won its independence, Military Plaza became one of the liveliest spots in Texas, where cowboys, rangers, and anyone passing through would come to obtain local news. In the 1860s, it was the site of vigilante lynchings, and after the Civil War, it hosted a bustling outdoor market. At night, the townsfolk would come to its open-air booths to buy chili con carne from their favorite chili queen. The plaza remained completely open until 1889, when the ornate City Hall was built at its center.

The one-story white building you'll see directly across the street from the west side of the plaza is the:

⓫ Spanish Governor's Palace

This was the former residence and headquarters of the captain of the Presidio de Béxar (but not of any Spanish governors). From here, the commander could watch his troops drilling across the street. The source of the house's misnomer is not entirely clear; as the home of the highest local authority and thus the nicest digs in the area, the "palace" probably hosted important Spanish officials who came through town.

From the front of the Governor's Palace, walk south until you come to the crosswalk; just west across Dolorosa Street is a drainage ditch, the sad remains of:

⓬ San Pedro Creek

The west bank of this body of water—once lovely and flowing, but now usually dry—was the original site of both Mission San Antonio de Valero and the Presidio de Béxar. At the creek's former headwaters, approximately 2 miles north of here, San Pedro Park was established in 1729 by a grant from the king of Spain; it's the second-oldest municipal park in the United States (the oldest being the Boston Common).

Continue west along Dolorosa Street to Laredo Street and take it south about three-quarters of a block until you come to:

⓭ Casa Navarro State Historic Site

The life of José Antonio Navarro, for whom the park is named, traces the history of Texas itself: He was born in Spanish territory, fought for Mexico's independence from Spain, and then worked to achieve Texas's freedom from Mexico. (He was one of only two Texas-born signatories to the 1836 Texas Declaration of Independence.) In 1845, Navarro voted for Texas's annexation to the United States, and a year later, he became a senator in the new Texas State Legislature. He died here in 1871, at the age of 76.

Trace your steps back to Laredo and Dolorosa, and go west on Dolorosa Street; when you reach Santa Rosa, you'll be facing:

⓮ Market Square

This square was home to the city's Market House at the turn of the century. When the low, arcaded structure was converted to El Mercado in 1973, it switched from selling household goods and personal items to crafts, clothing, and other more tourist-oriented Mexican wares. Directly behind and west of this lively square, the former Haymarket Plaza has become the Farmers' Market and now sells souvenirs instead of produce. If you haven't already stopped for sushi, you can enjoy a well-deserved lunch here at Mi Tierra, reviewed in chapter 6. At the entryway to Market Square is the Museo Alameda. The stainless steel screen that fronts it is inspired by the Mexican craft of *hojalatería* (tin work), the 30-foot-high screen consists of a series of panels that incorporate Hispanic cultural symbols, from the Pre-Columbian headdress of the Aztec god Quetzalcoatl to the Smithsonian sun logo.

7 ORGANIZED TOURS

BUS TOURS

San Antonio City Tours This company serves up a large menu of guided bus tours, covering everything from San Antonio's missions and museums to shopping forays south of the border and Hill Country excursions.

1331 N. Pine. ✆ **800/868-7707** or 210/228-9776. www.sacitytours.net. Half-day tours $18 adults, $12 children 4–10, free for children under 4; full-day tours $45 adults, $23 children 4–10. Earliest tours depart at 9am, latest return is 6pm daily (including holidays).

TROLLEY TOURS

Alamo Trolley Tour This is a good way to sightsee without a car. The trolley tour touches on all the downtown highlights, plus two of the missions in the south. If you want to get off at any of these sights, you can pick up another trolley (they run every 45 min.) after you're finished. At the least, you get oriented and learn some of the city's history.

216 Alamo Plaza (next to the Alamo). ✆ **210/228-9776.** www.sacitytours.net. Tickets for 60-min. tour are $17 adults, $20 for "hop" pass (good for 2 days); $7.50 children 3–11, $9 for the pass. Daily 9:30am–4:15pm.

RIVER CRUISES

Rio San Antonio Cruises ★ Maybe you've sat in a River Walk cafe looking out at people riding back and forth in open, flat-bottom barges. Go ahead—give in and join 'em. An amusing, informative tour, lasting from 35 to 40 minutes, will take you more than 2 miles down the most built-up sections of the Paseo del Río, with interesting sights pointed out along the way. You'll learn a lot about the river and find out what all those folks you watched were laughing about. The company also runs a non-narrated shuttle.

Ticket offices: Rivercenter Mall and River Walk, under Market St. Bridge and Alamo St. ✆ **210/244-5700.** www.riosanantonio.com. (Tickets can be purchased online.) Tickets $7.75 adults, $5 seniors and active-duty military with ID, $2 children under 6. Boats depart daily every 15–20 min. Nov to mid-Mar Sun–Thurs 10am–8pm, Fri–Sat 10am–9pm; extended hours rest of the year.

8 STAYING ACTIVE

Most San Antonians head for the hills— that is, nearby Hill Country—for outdoor recreation. Some suggestions of sports in or around town follow; see chapter 18 for more on Hill Country.

BIKING With the creation and continuing improvements of the biking paths along the San Antonio River, part of the larger **Mission Trails** project (see the San Antonio Missions National Historical Park listing earlier in this chapter), local and visiting cyclists will finally have a good place within the city to spin their wheels (it's not quite there yet, but soon . . .). Other options within San Antonio itself include **Brackenridge Park; McAllister Park** on the city's north side, 13102 Jones-Maltsberger (✆ **210/207-PARK** [207-7275] or 207-3120); and around the area near **SeaWorld of Texas.** If you didn't bring your own, **Charles A. James Bicycle Company,** 329 N. Main Ave. (✆ **210/224-8717;** www.charlesajamesbicycle.com), will deliver bikes to your door free if you're staying downtown ($10 extra charge for delivery and pickup to other parts of the city). Rates run up to $30 for 24 hours. Another rental shop is in Southtown, at the **Blue Star Bike Shop,** 1414 S. Alamo (✆ **210/212-5506;** www.bluestarbrewing.com). Perhaps the best resource in town is the website of the San Antonio Wheelmen, **www.sawheelmen.com,** with details on local organized rides, links to bicycle shops in the area, and more (it's even got an essay on the history of bicycling).

FISHING Closest to town for good angling are **Braunig Lake,** a 1,350-acre, city-owned reservoir, a few miles southeast of San Antonio off I-37, and **Calaveras Lake,** one of Texas's great bass lakes, a few miles southeast of San Antonio off U.S. 181 South and Loop 1604. A bit farther afield but still easy to reach from San Antonio are **Canyon Lake,** about 20 miles north of New Braunfels, and **Medina Lake,** just south of Bandera. Fishing licenses—sold at most sporting-goods and tackle stores and sporting-goods departments of large discount stores such as Wal-Mart or Kmart, as well as county courthouses and Parks and Wildlife Department offices—are required for all nonresidents; for current information, call ✆ **512/389-4800,** ext. 3, or go to www.tpwd.state.tx.us/publications/annual/fish/fishlicense.phtml. **Tackle Box Outfitters,** 6330 N. New Braunfels (✆ **210/821-5806;** www.tackleboxoutfitters.com), offers referrals to private guides for fishing trips to area rivers and to the Gulf coast ($250–$400 per person).

GOLF Golf has become a big deal in San Antonio, with more and more visitors coming to town expressly to tee off. Of the city's six municipal golf courses, two of the most notable are **Brackenridge,** 2315 Ave. B (✆ **210/226-5612**), the oldest (1916) public course in Texas, featuring oak- and pecan-shaded fairways; and northwest San Antonio's $4.3-million **Cedar Creek,** 8250 Vista Colina (✆ **210/695-5050**), repeatedly ranked as South Texas's best municipal course in golfing surveys. For details on both and other municipal courses, log on to www.sanantonio.gov/sapar/golf.asp. Other options for unaffiliated golfers include the 200-acre **Pecan Valley,** 4700 Pecan Valley Dr. (✆ **210/333-9018**), which crosses the Salado Creek seven times and has an 800-year-old oak near its 13th hole; the high-end **Quarry,** 444 E. Basse Rd. (✆ **800/347-7759** or 210/824-4500; www.quarrygolf.com), on the site of a former quarry and one of San Antonio's newest public courses; and **Canyon Springs,** 24405 Wilderness Oak Rd. (✆ **888/800-1511** or 210/497-1770; www.canyonspringsgc.com), at the north edge of town in the Texas Hill Country, lush with live oaks and dotted with historic rock formations. There aren't too many resort courses in San Antonio because there aren't too many resorts, but the two at the **Westin La Cantera,** 16401 La Cantera Pkwy. (✆ **800/446-5387** or 210/558-4653; www.lacanteragolfclub.com)—one designed by Jay Morish and Tom Weiskopf, the other by Arnold Palmer—have knockout designs and dramatic hill-and-rock outcroppings to recommend them. Expect to pay $37 to $53 per person for an 18-hole round at a municipal course with a cart, from $70 to as much as $130 (Sat–Sun) per person at a private resort's course. Twilight (afternoon) rates are often cheaper. To get a copy of the free *San Antonio Golfing Guide,* call ✆ **800/447-3372** or log on to www.sanantoniovisit.com/visitors/things_golfhome.asp.

HIKING The 240-acre **Friedrich Wilderness Park,** 21480 Milsa (✆ **210/698-1057;** wildtexas.com/parks/fwp.php), operated by the city of San Antonio as its only nature preserve, is crisscrossed by 5.5 miles of trails that attract bird-watchers as well as hikers; a 2-mile stretch is accessible to people with disabilities. **Enchanted Rock State Natural Area,** near Fredericksburg, is the most popular spot for trekking out of town (see chapter 18).

RIVER SPORTS For tubing, rafting, or canoeing along a cypress-lined river, San Antonio river rats head 35 miles northwest of downtown to the 2,000-acre **Guadalupe River**

State Park, 3350 Park Rd. 31 (✆ **830/438-2656;** www.tpwd.state.tx.us/park/guadalup), near Boerne (see chapter 18 for more details about the town). Five miles north of Highway 46, just outside the park, you can rent tubes, rafts, and canoes at the **Bergheim Campground,** FM 3351 in Bergheim (✆ **830/336-2235**). Standard tubes run $10 per person (but the ones with a bottom, at $12, are better), rafts are $15 per person ($10 for ages 12 and younger), and canoes go for $35. The section of the Guadalupe River near Gruene is also extremely popular; see the "New Braunfels" section of chapter 18 for details.

SWIMMING/WATERPARKS Most hotels have swimming pools, but if yours doesn't, the Parks and Recreation Department (✆ **210/207-3113;** www.sanantonio.gov/sapar/swimming.asp) can direct you to the nearest municipal pool. Both SeaWorld and Six Flags Fiesta Texas, detailed in the section "The Top Attractions," earlier in this chapter, are prime places to get wet (the latter has a pool in the shape of Texas and a waterfall that descends from a cowboy hat). Splashtown water recreation park is described in the "Especially for Kids" section, earlier in this chapter. Many San Antonians head out to New Braunfels to get wet at Schlitterbahn, the largest water park in Texas; see the "New Braunfels" section of chapter 18 for additional information.

TENNIS You can play at the 22 lighted hard courts at the **McFarlin Tennis Center,** 1503 San Pedro Ave. (✆ **210/732-1223**), for the very reasonable fee of $3 per hour per person ($1 for students and seniors), $3.50 per hour ($2) after 5pm. Log on to www.sanantonio.gov/sapar/tennis.asp for additional information about McFarlin, which requires reservations for you to play, and for a list of other city facilities (all operate on a first-come, first-served basis).

9 SPECTATOR SPORTS

BASEBALL From early April through early September, the minor-league **San Antonio Missions** plays at the Nelson Wolff Stadium, 5757 Hwy. 90 W. Most home games for this Seattle Mariners farm club start at 7:05pm, except Sunday games, which start at 4:05pm. Tickets range from $6 for adult general admission to $9 for seats in the lower box. Call ✆ **210/675-7275** for schedules and tickets, or check the website at www.samissions.com.

BASKETBALL Spurs madness hits San Antonio every year from mid-October through May, when the city's only major-league franchise, the **San Antonio Spurs,** shoots hoops. At the end of 2002, the Spurs found a new home at the state-of-the-art SBC Center near downtown. In 2005, the name changed to AT&T Center. Ticket prices range from $10 for nosebleed-level seats to $100 for seats on the corners of the court. Tickets are available at the Spurs Ticket Office in the AT&T Center, which is at One AT&T Center Pkwy. (✆ **210/444-5819**), or via Ticketmaster San Antonio (✆ **210/224-9600;** www.ticketmaster.com). Get schedules, players' stats, and promotional news—everything you might want to know or buy relating to the team—online at www.nba.com/spurs.

GOLF The **AT&T Championship,** an Official Senior PGA Tour Event, is held each October at the Oak Hills Country Club, 5403 Fredericksburg Rd. (✆ **210/698-3582**). One of the oldest professional golf tournaments, now known as the **Valero Texas Open,** showcases the sport in September at the Resort Course at La Cantera Golf Club, 16401

La Cantera Pkwy. (✆ **201/345-3818**). Log on to www.pgatour.com/r/schedule for information about both.

HORSE RACING **Retama Park,** some 15 minutes north of San Antonio, in Selma (✆ **210/651-7000;** www.retamapark.com), is the hottest place to play the ponies; take exit 174-A from I-35, or the Lookout Road exit from Loop 1604. The five-level Spanish-style grandstand is impressive, and the variety of food courts, restaurants, and lounges is almost as diverting as the horses. Live racing is generally from late April through mid-October on Wednesday or Thursday through Sunday. Call or check the website for thoroughbred and quarter horse schedules. Simulcasts from top tracks around the country are shown year-round. General admission for live racing is $2.50 adults, $1.50 seniors; for clubhouse, $3.50 adults, $2.50 seniors; for simulcast, $2. Kids 15 and younger and members of the military, active or retired, can enter gratis.

ICE HOCKEY San Antonio has had professional hockey only since 1994, when the Central Hockey League's San Antonio Iguanas appeared on the scene. Disbanded after the 2001–02 season, they were replaced by the American Hockey League's **San Antonio Rampage,** who dropped their first puck at the AT&T Center (One AT&T Center Pkwy.) in 2002. AHL tickets cost $7 to $55. Try ✆ **210/227-GOAL** [227-4625] or www.sarampage.com for schedules and other information.

RODEO If you're in town in early February, don't miss the chance to see 2 weeks of Wild West events like calf roping, steer wrestling, and bull riding at the annual **San Antonio Stock Show and Rodeo.** You can also hear huge amounts of major live country-and-western talent—Reba McEntire, Alan Jackson, Brooks and Dunn, and Lady Antebellum were on the 2009 roster—and you're likely to find something to add to your luggage at the AT&T Center's exposition hall, packed with Texas handicrafts. Call ✆ **210/225-5851,** or log on to www.sarodeo.com for information on schedules. Smaller rodeos are held throughout the year in nearby **Bandera,** the self-proclaimed "Cowboy Capital of the World." Contact the Bandera County Convention and Visitors Bureau (✆ **800/364-3833** or 830/796-3045; www.banderacowboycapital.com) for more information.

8

Shopping in San Antonio

San Antonio offers the shopper a nice balance of large malls and little enclaves of specialized shops. You'll find everything here from the utilitarian to the unusual: a huge Sears department store, a Saks Fifth Avenue fronted by a 40-foot pair of cowboy boots, a mall with a river running through it, and some lively Mexican markets.

You can count on most shops around town being open from 9 or 10am to 5:30 or 6pm Monday through Saturday, with shorter hours on Sunday. Malls are generally open Monday through Saturday 10am to 9pm and on Sunday noon to 6pm. Sales tax in San Antonio is 8.25%.

1 THE SHOPPING SCENE

Most out-of-town shoppers will find all they need **downtown,** between the large Rivercenter Mall, the boutiques and crafts shops of La Villita, the colorful Mexican wares of Market Square, the Southwest School of Art and Craft, and assorted retailers and galleries on and around Alamo Plaza. More avant-garde boutiques and galleries, including Blue Star, can be found in the adjacent area known as Southtown.

Most mainstream San Antonians prefer to shop in the malls along Loop 410, especially North Star, Heubner Oaks, and Alamo Quarry Market. The city's newest large scale mall is out along the outer loop (Loop 1604), 14 miles northwest of downtown, just west of where the loop intersects I-10. This is now the fanciest mall in town, having secured the city's only Neiman Marcus and only Nordstrom, and it has plenty of smaller retail stores to match the same well-heeled customer base. More up-market retail outlets can be found closer to downtown in the fancy strip centers that line Broadway, where it passes through Alamo Heights (the posh Collection and Lincoln Heights are particularly noteworthy). Weekends might see locals poking around a number of terrific **flea markets.** For bargains on brand labels, they head out to San Marcos, home to two large **factory outlet malls** (see chapter 10 and 17, respectively).

2 SHOPPING A TO Z

ANTIQUES

In addition to the places that follow, a number of antiques shops line Hildebrand between Blanco and San Pedro, and McCullough between Hildebrand and Basse.

Center for Antiques A great place for an antiques forage near the airport, this shop hosts more than 115 vendors with specialties from knickknacks, records, and clothing to high-quality furniture for serious collectors. Be careful not to spend too much time here and miss your flight. 8505 Broadway. ✆ **210/804-6300.** www.centerforantiques.com.

The Land of Was Every inch of space on the two floors of this shop is crammed with stuff—some of it strange and funky, more of it rare and pricey. The store is especially strong on Spanish-colonial and Mexican antiques; if you're seeking an altarpiece or a treasure chest, try here first. 3119 Broadway. ✆ **210/822-5265.**

ART GALLERIES

ArtPace, in the northern part of downtown, and the **Blue Star Arts Complex,** in Southtown (see "More Attractions," in chapter 7, for details on both), are the best venues for cutting-edge art, but **Finesilver Gallery,** 816 Camaron St., Ste. 1–2, just north of downtown (✆ **210/354-3333;** www.finesilver.com), is a good alternative. Downtown is home to several galleries that show more established artists. Two of the top ones are **Galería Ortiz,** 102 Concho (in Market Square, ✆ **210/225-0731**), San Antonio's premier place to buy Southwestern art; and **Nanette Richardson Fine Art,** 555 E. Basse Rd. (✆ **210/930-1343;** www.nanetterichardsonfineart.com), with a wide array of oils, watercolors, bronzes, ceramics, and handcrafted wood furnishings.

For more details on these and other galleries, pick up a copy of the **San Antonio Gallery Guide,** prepared by the San Antonio Art Gallery Association, at the San Antonio Convention and Visitors Bureau, 317 Alamo Plaza (✆ **800/447-3372** or 210/207-6000). You can also check out the art scene online at the Office of Cultural Affairs' website, www.sahearts.com, with links to several local galleries, and schedules for events held during July's Contemporary Art Month (see chapter 3).

CRAFTS

See also Alamo Fiesta, San Angel Folk Art, and Tienda Guadalupe in "Gifts/Souvenirs," below. Another top option is the Ursuline Sales Gallery in the Southwest School of Art and Craft (see chapter 7).

Garcia Art Glass, Inc. If you like to see the creative process in progress, come here to see beautiful glass bowls, wall sconces, mobiles, and more come into being. Not everything is very portable, but the bracelets and other pretty baubles made out of glass beads definitely are. 715 S. Alamo St. ✆ **210/354-4681.** www.garciaartglass.com.

Glassworks (Finds) With Dale Chihuly practically a household name, you know that glass art has come of age. The goal of this Alamo Heights store is to show that, in addition to being gorgeous, blown glass can also be formed into items that are interesting—a golf putter, for example—affordable, and accessible. Everyone who walks into these stores is encouraged to touch the work ("It's all insured," owner/artist Judy Millspaugh declares cheerfully). 6350 N. New Braunfels Ave. ✆ **210/822-0146.**

DEPARTMENT STORES

Dillard's You'll find branches of this Arkansas-based chain in many Southwestern cities and in a number of San Antonio malls (North Star, Ingram, and Rolling Oaks); all offer nice mid- to upper-range clothing and housewares, but the Dillard's in the Rivercenter Mall also has a section specializing in Western fashions. Enter or exit on Alamo Plaza so you can get a look at the historic building's ornate facade (see "Walking Tour: Downtown San Antonio," in chapter 7, for details). 102 Alamo Plaza (Rivercenter Mall). ✆ **210/227-4343.** www.dillards.com.

Saks Fifth Avenue Forget low-key and unobtrusive; this is Texas. Sure, this department store has the high quality, upscale wares, and attentive service one would expect

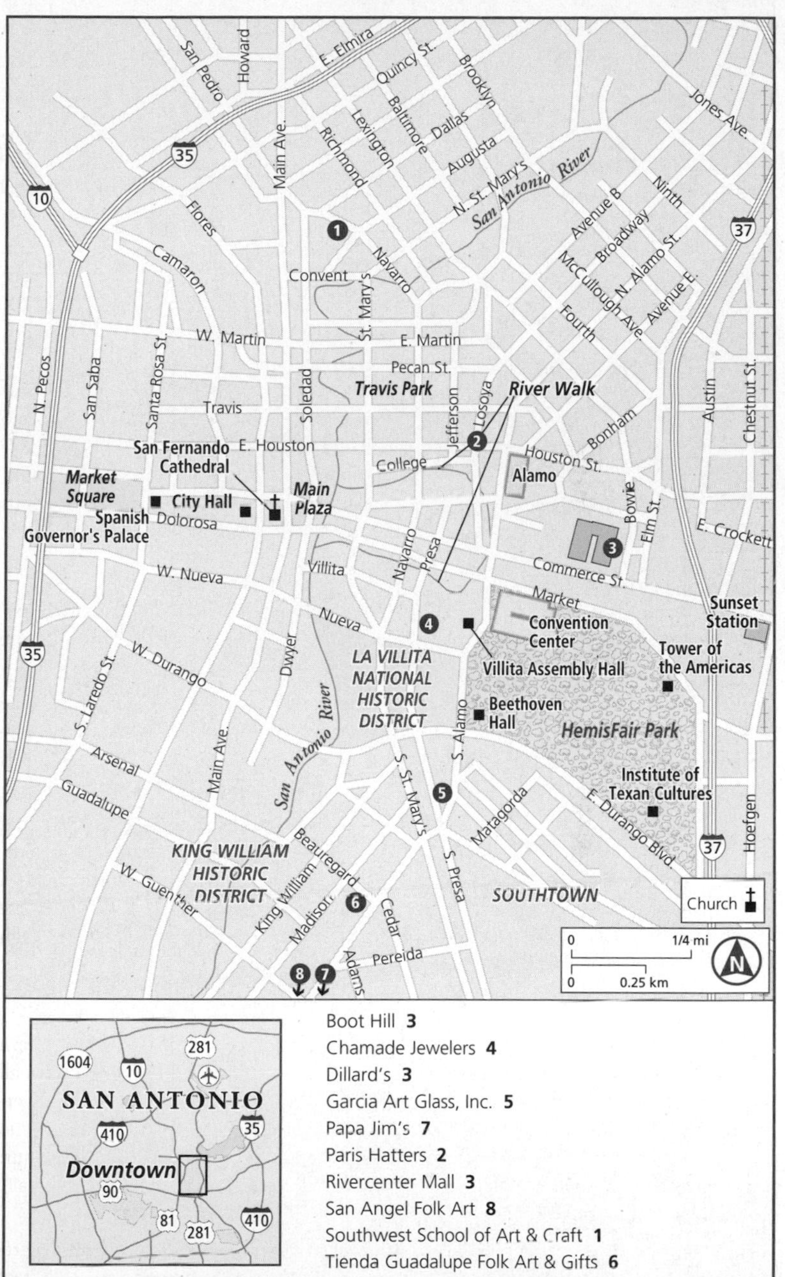
San Pedro
Howard
E. Elmira
Quincy St.
Brooklyn
Baltimore
Lexington
Richmond
Main Ave.
Dallas
Augusta
N. St. Mary's
San Antonio River
Jones Ave.
Ninth
Avenue B
Broadway
N. Alamo St.
McCullough Ave.
Avenue E.
Fourth
Flores
Camaron
Convent
Navarro
St. Mary's
W. Martin
E. Martin
Pecan St.
Travis Park
River Walk
N. Pecos
San Saba
Santa Rosa St.
Travis
Soledad
Jefferson
Losoya
Bonham
Austin
Chestnut St.
San Fernando Cathedral
E. Houston
College
Houston St.
Alamo
Market Square
City Hall
Main Plaza
Spanish Governor's Palace
Dolorosa
Bowie
Elm St.
E. Crockett
Villita
Navarro
Presa
Commerce St.
W. Nueva
Market
Sunset Station
Nueva
Convention Center
Tower of the Americas
W. Durango
Dwyer
LA VILLITA NATIONAL HISTORIC DISTRICT
Villita Assembly Hall
S. Laredo St.
Beethoven Hall
HemisFair Park
Main Ave.
S. Alamo
Arsenal
San Antonio River
S. St. Mary's
Institute of Texan Cultures
Guadalupe
Matagorda
E. Durango Blvd.
Hoefgen
KING WILLIAM HISTORIC DISTRICT
Beauregard
W. Guenther
King William
Madison
Cedar
S. Presa
SOUTHTOWN
Church
Pereida
Adams
0 1/4 mi
0 0.25 km
N
1604
10
281
35
410
90
81
SAN ANTONIO
Downtown
37
Boot Hill 3
Chamade Jewelers 4
Dillard's 3
Garcia Art Glass, Inc. 5
Papa Jim's 7
Paris Hatters 2
Rivercenter Mall 3
San Angel Folk Art 8
Southwest School of Art & Craft 1
Tienda Guadalupe Folk Art & Gifts 6

Greater San Antonio Shopping

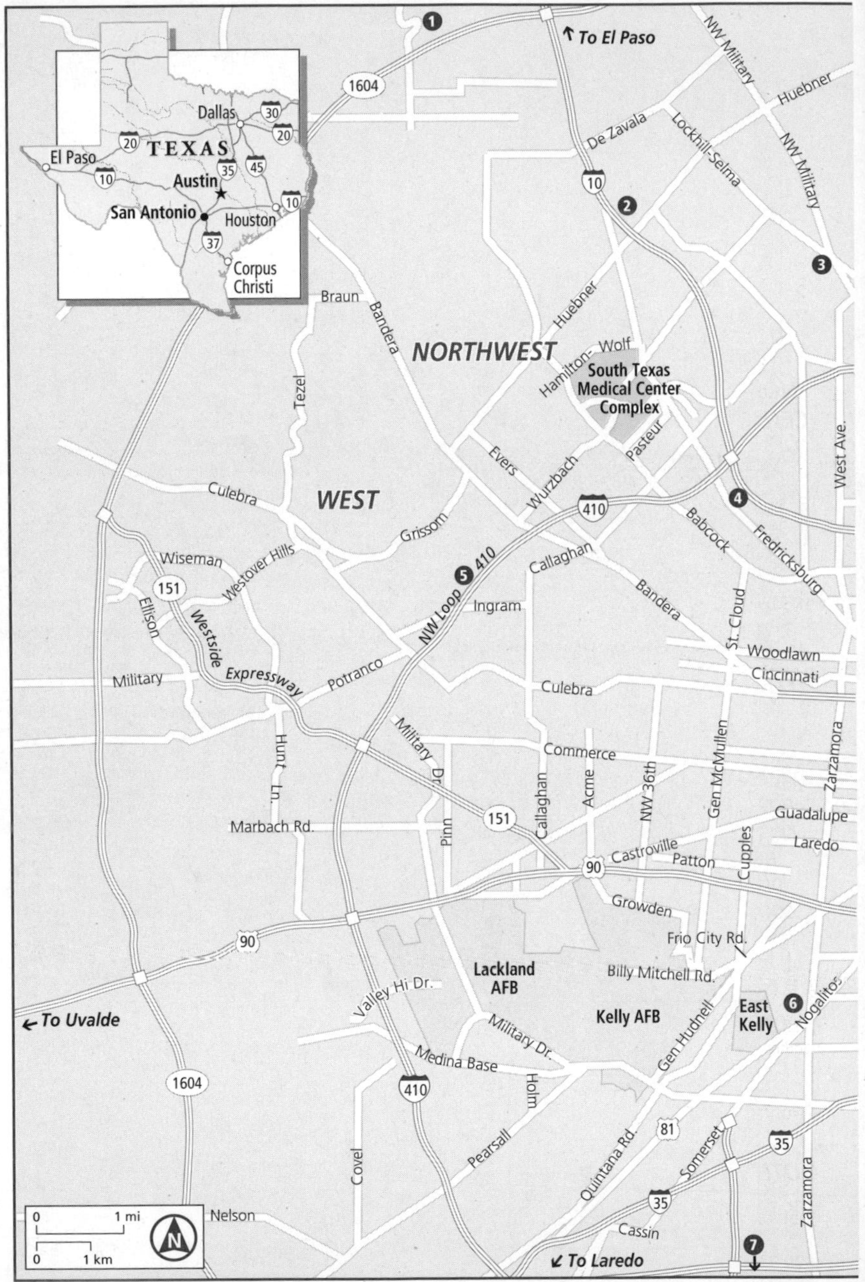

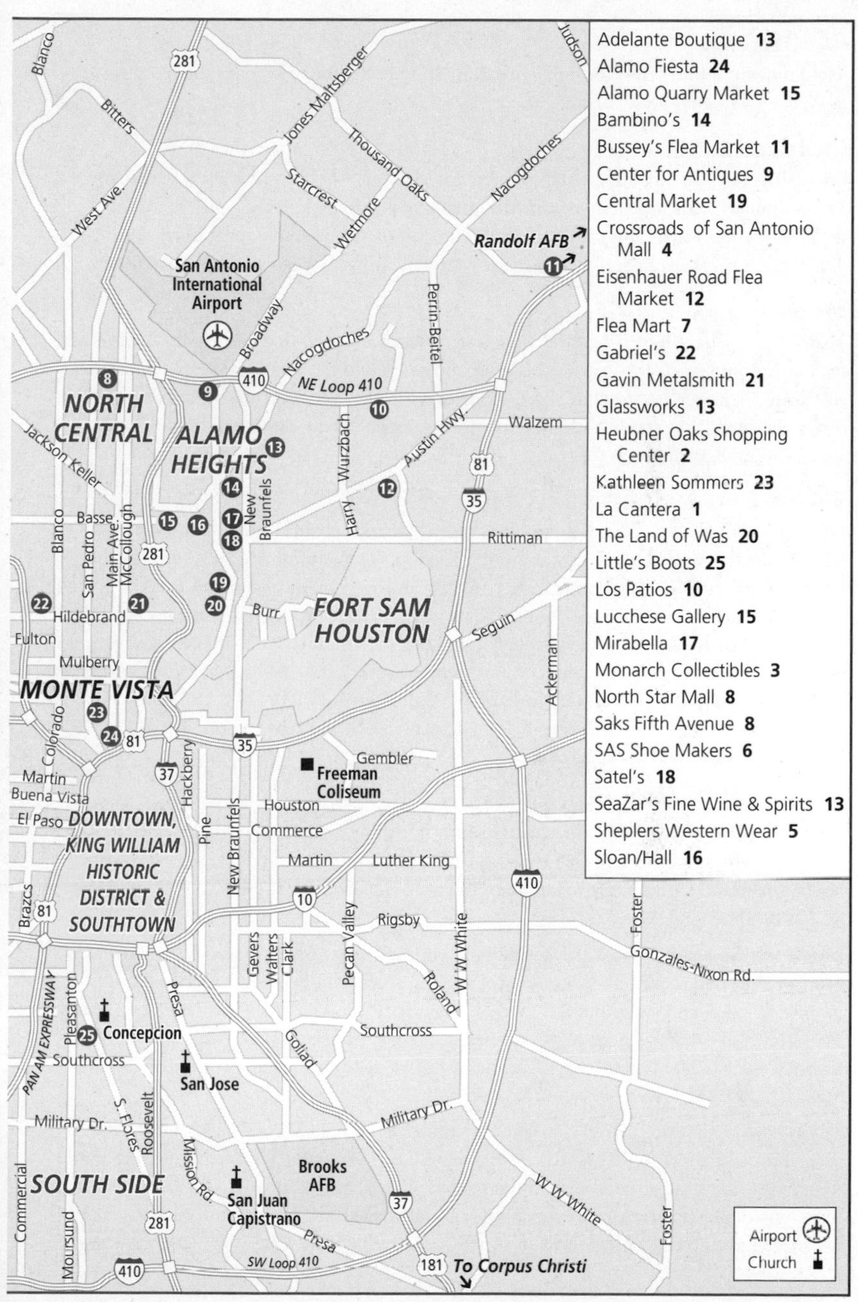
Adelante Boutique 13
Alamo Fiesta 24
Alamo Quarry Market 15
Bambino's 14
Bussey's Flea Market 11
Center for Antiques 9
Central Market 19
Crossroads of San Antonio Mall 4
Eisenhauer Road Flea Market 12
Flea Mart 7
Gabriel's 22
Gavin Metalsmith 21
Glassworks 13
Heubner Oaks Shopping Center 2
Kathleen Sommers 23
La Cantera 1
The Land of Was 20
Little's Boots 25
Los Patios 10
Lucchese Gallery 15
Mirabella 17
Monarch Collectibles 3
North Star Mall 8
Saks Fifth Avenue 8
SAS Shoe Makers 6
Satel's 18
SeaZar's Fine Wine & Spirits 13
Sheplers Western Wear 5
Sloan/Hall 16
San Antonio International Airport
NORTH CENTRAL
ALAMO HEIGHTS
FORT SAM HOUSTON
MONTE VISTA
DOWNTOWN, KING WILLIAM HISTORIC DISTRICT & SOUTHTOWN
SOUTH SIDE
Randolf AFB
Freeman Coliseum
Brooks AFB
Concepcion
San Jose
San Juan Capistrano
To Corpus Christi
NE Loop 410
SW Loop 410
PAN AM EXPRESSWAY
Blanco
Bitters
West Ave.
Jones Maltsberger
Thousand Oaks
Starcrest
Wetmore
Nacogdoches
Judson
Broadway
Perrin-Beitel
Walzem
Austin Hwy.
Wurzbach
Harry
Jackson Keller
Basse
San Pedro
Main Ave.
McCollough
New Braunfels
Rittiman
Hildebrand
Fulton
Mulberry
Burr
Seguin
Ackerman
Colorado
Gembler
Martin
Buena Vista
El Paso
Hackberry
Pine
Houston
Commerce
Martin Luther King
Brazos
Rigsby
W W White
Foster
Gonzales-Nixon Rd.
Gevers
Walters
Clark
Pecan Valley
Roland
Pleasanton
Presa
Goliad
Southcross
S. Flores
Roosevelt
Military Dr.
Mission Rd.
Commercial
Moursund
Airport
Church

from a Saks Fifth Avenue, but it also has a 40-foot-high pair of cowboy boots standing out front. 650 North Star Mall. ✆ **210/341-4111.**

FASHIONS

The following stores offer clothing in a variety of styles; if you're keen on the cowpuncher look, see "Western Wear," below.

Children's

Bambinos Whether your child goes in for the English-country look or veers more toward punk rocker, you'll find something to suit his or her (okay, your) tastes at this delightful store, which also carries a great selection of kiddie room furnishings and toys. The focus is on the younger set—infants to age 7, that is. 5934 Broadway. ✆ **210/822-9595.**

Men's

Satel's This family-run Alamo Heights store has been the place to shop for menswear in San Antonio since 1950; classic, high-quality clothing and personal service make it a standout. A newer location in the Colonnade, 9801 I-10 West (✆ **210/694-0944**), offers the same fine goods and attention to customer needs. 5100 Broadway. ✆ **210/822-3376.** www.satels.com.

Shoes

SAS Shoemakers This San Antonio footwear store is such an institution that the website for the VIA bus line lists it among the city's attractions. Men and women have been coming here to buy comfortable, sturdy, and well-made shoes and sandals since 1976. The factory store, on the south side of town, is the one to visit; you can even take one of three daily tours Monday through Thursday. Call in advance to make a reservation and to get directions. Other branches are located at Westlake Village, 1305 Loop 410 (✆ **210/673-2700**); Shoemakers Inn, 16088 San Pedro (✆ **210/494-1823**); and Garden Ridge, in Shertz, 17885 I-35 N (✆ **210/651-5312**). 101 New Laredo Hwy. ✆ **210/921-7415** or 210/924-6507 (tour reservations).

Women's

Adelante Boutique The focus here is on the ethnic and the handmade, with lots of colorful, natural fabrics and free-flowing lines. The store also offers a nice selection of leather belts and whimsical jewelry and gifts. 6414 N. New Braunfels Ave. (in Sunset Ridge). ✆ **210/826-6770.**

Kathleen Sommers ★ This small shop on the corner of Main and Woodlawn has been setting trends for San Antonio women for years. Kathleen Sommers, who works mainly in linen and other natural fabrics, designs all the clothes, which bear her label. The store also carries great jewelry, bath items, books, fun housewares, and a selection of unusual gifts, including the San Antonio–originated Soular Therapy candles. 2417 N. Main. ✆ **210/732-8437.** www.kathleensommers.com.

Mirabella Super-stylish but friendly Mirabella owner Misti Riedel buys clothes according to the credo "Girls just wanna have fun." If it's sexy, colorful, creative, and wearable, you'll find it here. Good looks never come cheap, but many of the designers represented on the racks of this cozy shop are not well-known, which means costs are by no means prohibitive either. And if you're lucky, there'll be a sale on. 5910 Broadway. ✆ **210/829-4435.**

FOOD

Central Market Free valet parking at a supermarket? On Saturday and Sunday, so many locals converge here to take advantage of the huge array of delectable samples that it's easy to understand why the store is willing to alleviate parking stress. You'll feel as though you've died and gone to food heaven as you walk amid gorgeous mounds of produce, cheeses and other dairy products, sauces, pastas, and more. If you don't want to just graze, there are freshly prepared hot and cold gourmet foods, including a soup and salad bar, and a seating area in which to enjoy them. Wine tastings and cooking classes draw crowds in the evenings. 4821 Broadway. ✆ **210/368-8600.** www.centralmarket.com.

GIFTS/SOUVENIRS

Alamo Fiesta *Finds* Head just north of downtown to this two-level store near Monte Vista for a huge selection of Mexican folk art and handicrafts—everything from tinwork to colorful masks and piñatas—at extremely reasonable prices. Less touristy than most such shops, Alamo Fiesta is geared to local Hispanic families looking to celebrate special occasions. 2025 N. Main at Ashby. ✆ **210/738-1188.** www.alamofiesta.com.

San Angel Folk Art Combing the crafts markets of Mexico might be more fun, but exploring this large store in the Blue Star Arts Complex is a pretty good substitute. Painted animals from Oaxaca, elaborate masks from the state of Guerrero—this place is chockablock with things colorful, whimsical, and well-made. Of course, prices are better south of the border, but you're saving on airfare/gas and traveling time. 1404 S. Alamo, Ste. 110, in the Blue Star Arts Complex. ✆ **210/226-6688.** www.sanangelfolkart.com.

Sloan/Hall A cross between The Body Shop, Sharper Image, and Borders, only more concentrated and more upscale, this addictive boutique carries an assortment of toiletries, gadgets, books, and those uncategorizable items that you probably don't need but may find you desperately want. 5922 Broadway. ✆ **210/828-7738.** www.sloanhall.com.

Tienda Guadalupe Folk Art & Gifts This incense-scented shop in the Southtown/King William area is brimming with Hispanic items: paintings and handicrafts from Latin America, Mexican antiques and religious items, and more. Come here to pick up a Day of the Dead T-shirt or anything else relating to the early November holiday celebrated with great fanfare in San Antonio. 1001 S. Alamo. ✆ **210/226-5873.**

JEWELRY

See also "Crafts" and "Gifts/Souvenirs," above.

Chamade Jewelers Expect the unexpected and the beautiful at this dazzling jewelry store, representing more than 30 U.S. and international artists. You'll find everything from classically designed gold rings with precious gemstones to funny sterling silver earrings encasing beans for one ear and rice for the other. Some of the pieces are crafted by local and Southwest artisans, including Native Americans; others come from as far afield as France, Italy, China, and Indonesia. 504 Villita St. (La Villita). ✆ **210/224-7753.** www.chamadejewelers.com.

Gavin Metalsmith For contemporary metal craft at its most creative, come to this small women's crafts gallery, where the exquisite original pieces range from wedding rings to salt-and-pepper shakers. The artists whose work is sold here incorporate lots of unusual stones into silver and white-gold settings. They also frequently do custom work for fair prices. 4024 McCullough Ave. ✆ **210/821-5254.**

Love Potion No. 9

Ask a proprietor of a **botanica,** "What kind of store is this?" and you'll hear anything from "a drugstore" to "a religious bookstore." But along with Christian artifacts (including glow-in-the-dark rosaries and dashboard icons), botanicas carry magic floor washes, candles designed to keep the law off your back, wolf skulls, amulets, herbal remedies, and, of course, love potions. The common theme is happiness enhancement, whether by self-improvement, prayer, or luck.

Many of San Antonio's countless small botanicas specialize in articles used by *curanderos,* traditional folk doctors or medicine men and women. Books directing laypersons in the use of medicinal herbs sit next to volumes that retell the lives of the saints. It's easy enough to figure out the use of the *santos* (saints), candles in tall glass jars to which are affixed such labels as "Peaceful Home," "Find Work," and "Bingo." *Milagros* (miracles) are small charms that represent parts of the body—or mind—that a person wishes to have healed. Don't worry that many of the labels are in Spanish, as the person behind the counter will be happy to translate.

Papa Jim's, 5630 S. Flores (✆ **210/922-6665;** www.papajimsbotanica.com), is the best known of all the botanicas (Papa Jim, who used to bless the various artifacts he sold, died a few years ago). Can't make it to the shop? Order online or get a copy of the more comprehensive print catalog by phoning or ordering through the Papa Jim's website.

MALLS/SHOPPING COMPLEXES

Alamo Quarry Market Alamo Quarry Market may be its official name, but no one ever calls this popular mall anything but "The Quarry" (from the early 1900s until 1985, the property was in fact a cement quarry). The four smokestacks, lit up dramatically at night, now signal play, not work. There are no anchoring department stores, but a series of large emporiums (Old Navy; Bed, Bath & Beyond; OfficeMax; and Borders) and smaller upscale boutiques (Laura Ashley, Aveda, and Lucchese Gallery—see "Western Wear," below) will keep you spending. A multiplex cinema and an array of refueling stations—Chili's and Starbucks, as well as the more upscale Koi Kowa, a revolving sushi bar, and Piatti's, an Italian eatery well liked by locals—complete this low-slung temple to self-indulgence. 255 E. Basse Rd. ✆ **210/824-8885.** www.quarrymarket.com.

Crossroads of San Antonio Mall Located near the South Texas Medical Center, this is San Antonio's bargain mall, featuring Burlington Coat Factory, Super Target, and Stein Mart department stores alongside smaller discount stores. Some glitzier shops and performances at the food court are part of an effort to draw San Antonians to this low-profile shopping destination. 4522 Fredericksburg Rd. (off Loop 410 and I-10). ✆ **210/735-9137.**

Huebner Oaks Shopping Center This upscale open-air mall, in the north central part of town, houses a variety of yuppie favorites, including Old Navy, The Gap, Banana Republic, Victoria's Secret, and Eddie Bauer. When your energy flags, retreat to one of several casual dining spots, such as La Madeleine, serving good fast French food, or head straight to Starbucks for a caffeine boost. 11745 I-10. ✆ **210/697-8444.**

Los Patios The self-proclaimed "other River Walk" features about a dozen upscale specialty shops in a lovely 18-acre wooded setting. You'll find shops carrying imported clothing, crafts, jewelry, and antique furniture among other offerings here. 2015 NE Loop 410, at the Starcrest exit. ✆ **210/655-6171.** www.lospatios.com.

North Star Mall Starring Saks Fifth Avenue and such upscale boutiques as Abercrombie & Fitch, J. Crew, Aveda, Sharper Image, and Williams-Sonoma, this is the crème de la crème of the San Antonio indoor malls. But there are many sensible shops here, too, including a Mervyn's department store. Food choices also climb up and down the scale, ranging from a Godiva Chocolatier to a Luby's Cafeteria. Loop 410, between McCullough and San Pedro. ✆ **210/340-6627.** www.northstarmall.com.

Rivercenter Mall There's a festive atmosphere at this bustling, light-filled mall, fostered, among other things, by its location on an extension of the San Antonio River. You can pick up a ferry from a downstairs dock or listen to bands play on a stage surrounded by water. Other entertainment options include the IMAX theater, the multiple-screen AMC, the Cyber Zone video arcade, and the Rivercenter Comedy Club. The shops—more than 130 of them, anchored by Dillard's and Foleys—run the price gamut, but tend toward upscale casual. Food picks similarly range from Dairy Queen and A&W Hot Dogs to Morton's of Chicago. This can be a great place to shop, but remember that it's thronged with teeny-boppers Friday and Saturday nights. 849 E. Commerce, btw. S. Alamo and Bowie. ✆ **210/225-0000.** www.shoprivercenter.com.

The Shops at La Cantera The newest, fanciest mall is in far northwest San Antonio, off Loop 1604, beside the Six Flags Fiesta Texas theme park. This, too, is an outdoor mall, and it's nicely designed. All the stores face a central pedestrian concourse, and the parking is kept separate, behind the stores. As was mentioned earlier, it has two of San Antonio's fanciest department stores: Neiman Marcus and Nordstrom, and several boutiques, jewelers, and cosmetics stores. 15900 La Cantera Pkwy. ✆ **210/582-6255.** www.theshopsatlacantera.com.

MARKETS

Market Square Two large indoor markets, El Mercado and the Farmers' Market—often just called, collectively, the Mexican market—occupy adjacent blocks on Market Square. Competing for your attention are more than 100 shops and pushcarts and an abundance of food stalls. The majority of the shopping booths are of the border-town sort, filled with onyx chess sets, cheap sombreros, and the like, but you can also find a few higher quality boutiques, including Galería Ortiz (see above). Come here for a bit of local color, good people-watching, and food—in addition to the sit-down Mi Tierra, detailed in chapter 6, and La Margarita, there are loads of primo places for street snacking. You'll often find yourself shopping to the beat of a mariachi band. 514 W. Commerce St. (near Dolorosa). ✆ **210/207-8600.**

FLEA MARKETS

Bussey's Flea Market Unless you're heading to New Braunfels or Austin, Bussey's is a bit out of the way. But these 20 acres of vendors selling goods from as far afield as Asia and Africa are definitely worth the drive (about a half-hour north of downtown). Crafts, jewelry, antiques, incense—besides perishables, it's hard to imagine anything you couldn't find at this market. And who could resist coming to a spot with a giant armadillo in the parking lot? 18738 I-35 N. ✆ **210/651-6830.**

Eisenhauer Road Flea Market The all-indoors, all air-conditioned Eisenhauer, complete with snack bar, is a good flea market to hit at the height of summer. You'll see lots of new stuff here—purses, jewelry, furniture, toys, shoes—and everything from houseplants to kinky leather wear. Closed Monday and Tuesday. 3903 Eisenhauer Rd. ✆ **210/653-7592.**

Flea Mart On weekends, Mexican-American families make a day of this huge market, bringing the entire family to exchange gossip, listen to live bands, and eat freshly made tacos. There are always fruits and vegetables, electronics, crafts, and new and used clothing—and you never know what else. 12280 Hwy. 16 S. (about 1 mile south of Loop 410). ✆ **210/624-2666.**

TOYS

If your child is especially hard on playthings or your cash supply is running low, consider buying used toys at **Kids Junction Resale Shop,** 2267 NW Military Hwy. (✆ **210/340-5532**), or **Too Good to Be Threw,** 7115 Blanco (✆ **210/340-2422**).

Monarch Collectibles (Kids) Welcome to doll heaven. Many of the models that fill Monarch's four rooms—about 3,000 dolls in all—are collectible and made from such delicate materials as porcelain and baked clay, but others are cute and cuddly. Some come with real hair and eyelashes, and some are one of a kind. Doll furniture is also sold here—with a 6,000-square-foot dollhouse to showcase it—along with plates and a few stuffed animals. An entire room is devoted to Barbies. (Maybe the other dolls don't want to play with them?) 2012 NW Military Hwy. ✆ **210/341-3655.** www.dollsdolls.com.

WESTERN WEAR

Boot Hill This one-stop shopping center for all duds Western, from Tony Lama boots to Stetson hats and everything in between, is one of the few left in town that's locally owned. Arnold Schwarzenegger and Ashley Judd are among the stars who have been outfitted here. Rivercenter Mall, 849 E. Commerce, Ste. 213. ✆ **210/223-6634.**

Little's Boots (Finds) Lucchese (see below) is better known, but this place—established in 1915—uses as many esoteric leathers and creates fancier footwear designs. You can get anything you like bespoke if you're willing to wait a while—possibly in line behind Reba McEntire and Tommy Lee Jones, who have had boots handcrafted here. Purchase some just so you can tell your friends back home, "Oh, Lucchese is so commercial. Little's is still the real thing." 110 Division Ave. ✆ **210/923-2221.** www.davelittleboots.com.

Lucchese Gallery The name says it all: Footwear is raised to the level of art at Lucchese. If it ever crawled, ran, hopped, or swam, these folks can probably put it on your feet. The store carries boots made of alligator, elephant, ostrich, kangaroo, stingray, and lizard. Come here for everything from executive to special-occasion boots, all handmade and expensive and all still serious Texas status symbols. Lucchese also carries jackets, belts, and sterling silver belt buckles. 255 E. Basse, Ste. 800. ✆ **210/828-9419.** www.lucchese.com.

Paris Hatters What do Pope John Paul II, Prince Charles, Jimmy Smits, and Dwight Yoakam have in common? They've all had headgear made for them by Paris Hatters, in business since 1917 and still owned by the same family. About half of the sales are special orders, but the shelves are stocked with high-quality ready-to-wear hats, including Kangol caps from Britain, Panama hats from Ecuador, Borsolina hats from Italy, and, of course, Stetson, Resistol, Dobbs, and other Western brands. A lot of them can be adjusted to your liking while you wait. Check out the pictures and newspaper articles in the back of the store to see which other famous heads have been covered here. 119 Broadway. ✆ **210/223-3453.** www.parishatters.com.

Sheplers Western Wear If you want instant (as in trying on the clothes) gratification rather than waiting to get your duds in the mail from what has turned into the world's largest online western store (www.sheplers.com), come to this Ingram Mall Super Store branch of the national chain founded in Wichita, Kansas, during the 1950s. 6201 NW Loop 410. ✆ **210/681-8230.** www.sheplers.com.

WINES

See also Central Market, under "Food," above.

Gabriel's A large, warehouse-style store, Gabriel's combines good selection with good prices. You never know what oenological bargains you'll find on any given day. The Hildebrand store is slightly north of downtown; there's also another location near the airport at 7233 Blanco (✆ **210/349-7472**). 837 Hildebrand. ✆ **210/735-8329.**

SeaZar's Fine Wine & Spirits A temperature-controlled wine cellar, a large selection of beer and spirits, a cigar humidor, and a knowledgeable staff all make this a good choice for aficionados of the various legal vices. 6422 N. New Braunfels, in the Sunset Ridge Shopping Center. ✆ **210/822-6094.**

9 San Antonio After Dark

San Antonio has its symphony and its Broadway shows, and you can see both at one of the most beautiful old movie palaces in the country. But much of what the city has to offer is not quite so mainstream. Latin influences lend spice to some of the best local nightlife. Don't forget San Antonio is America's capital for Tejano music, a unique blend of German polka and northern Mexico ranchero sounds (with a dose of pop added for good measure). You can sit on one side of the San Antonio River and watch colorful dance troupes such as **Ballet Folklórico** perform on the other. And Southtown, with its many Hispanic-oriented shops and galleries, celebrates its art scene with the monthly First Friday, a kind of extended block party.

Keep in mind, too, that the Fiesta City throws big public parties year-round: Fiestas Navideñas and Las Posadas around Christmastime, Fiesta San Antonio and Cinco de Mayo events in spring, the Texas Folklife Festival in summer, and Oktoberfest and the International Accordion Festival in autumn (see also "San Antonio Calendar of Events," in chapter 3).

For the most complete listings of what's on while you're visiting, pick up a free copy of the weekly alternative newspaper, the ***Current,*** or the Friday "Weekender" section of the ***San Antonio Express-News.*** You can also check out the website of **San Antonio Arts & Cultural Affairs:** www.sanantonio.gov/art. There's no central office in town for tickets, discounted or otherwise. You'll need to reserve seats directly through the theaters or clubs, or, for large events, through **Ticketmaster** (✆ **210/224-9600;** www.ticketmaster.com). Generally, box office hours are Monday to Friday 10am to 5pm, and 1 to 2 hours before performance time. The **Majestic** (p. 153) and **Empire** (p. 152) also have hours on Saturday from 10am to 3pm.

1 THE PERFORMING ARTS

The San Antonio Symphony is the city's only resident performing arts company of national stature, but smaller, less professional groups keep the local arts scene lively, and cultural organizations draw world-renowned artists. The city provides them with some unique venues—everything from standout historic structures such as the Majestic, Empire, Arneson, and Sunken Garden theaters to the state-of-the-art AT&T Center. Because, in some cases, the theater is the show and, in others, a single venue offers an eclectic array of performances, I've included a category called "Major Arts Venues," below.

CLASSICAL MUSIC

San Antonio Symphony The city's symphony orchestra was founded in 1939. It celebrated its 50th anniversary by moving into the Majestic Theatre, the reopening of which was planned to coincide with the event. The symphony offers two major annual series, classical and pops. The classical series showcases the talents of music director emeritus Christopher Wilkens and a variety of guest performers, while for the pops series, you might find anyone from banjo virtuoso Buddy Wachter to Tito Puente, Jr., to Three Dog Night. 222 E. Houston St. ✆ **210/554-1000** or 554-1010 (box office). www.sasymphony.org. Tickets $11–$90 classical, $11–$62 pops.

THEATER

Most of San Antonio's major shows turn up at the Majestic or Empire theaters (see "Major Art Venues," below), but several smaller theaters are of interest too. The **Actors Theater of San Antonio,** 1920 Fredericksburg Rd. (✆ **210/738-2872**), uses local talent for its productions, which tend to be in the off-Broadway tradition. Their venue is the Woodlawn Theatre, opened as a movie house in 1945. At the King William district's **Church Bistro & Theatre,** 1150 S. Alamo (✆ **210/271-7791;** www.churchbistroandtheatre.com), interactive comedies and murder mysteries take place on Friday and Saturday nights in the Green Room Dinner Theatre—the former choir rooms of a converted 1912 church—accompanied by buffet meals; upstairs, in the former sanctuary now called The Mainstage, there are lectures, concerts, musicals, comedies, and dramas, sans food. The community-based **Josephine Theatre,** 339 W. Josephine St. (✆ **210/734-4646;** www.josephinetheatre.org), puts on an average of five productions a year—mostly musicals—at the Art Deco–style theater, only 5 minutes from downtown. Whether it's an original piece by a member of the company or a work by a guest artist, anything you see at the **Jump-Start Performance Company,** 108 Blue Star Arts Complex (1400 S. Alamo; ✆ **210/227-JUMP;** www.jump-start.org), is likely to push the social and political envelope. This is the place to find such big-name performance artists as Karen Finley or Holly Hughes who tour San Antonio. The only professional family theater in town, the popular **Magik Theatre,** Beethoven Hall, 420 S. Alamo, in HemisFair Park (✆ **210/227-2751;** www.magiktheatre.org), features a daytime series with light fare for ages 3 and older, and evening performances, recommended for those 6 and older, that may include weightier plays. About half the plays are adaptations of published scripts, while the other half are originals, created especially for the theater. San Antonio's first public theater, the **San Pedro Playhouse,** 800 W. Ashby (✆ **210/733-7258;** www.sanpedroplayhouse.com), presents a wide range of plays in a neoclassical-style performance hall built in 1930. For information on other small theaters in San Antonio and links to many of those listed in this section, log on to the website of the **San Antonio Theater Coalition** at www.satheatre.com.

MAJOR ARTS VENUES

See also the "For Those Interested in Hispanic Heritage" section of chapter 7 for information on the Alameda Theater.

Arneson River Theatre If you're visiting San Antonio in the summer, be sure to see something at the Arneson. It was built by the Works Project Administration in 1939 as part of architect Robert Hugman's design for the River Walk. The stage for this unique theater sits on one bank of the river, while the audience sits in the amphitheater on the opposite bank. Most of the year, performance schedules are erratic and include everything from opera to Tejano, but the summer brings a stricter calendar: the Fandango folkloric troupe performs every Tuesday and Thursday in June and July, and the Fiesta Noche del Río takes the stage on Friday and Saturday May through July. Both offer lively music and dance with a south-of-the-border flair. La Villita. ✆ **210/207-8610.** www.lavillita.com/arneson.

Fun Facts A Theater that Lives Up to Its Name

Everyone from Jack Benny to Mae West played the **Majestic,** one of the last "atmospheric" theaters to be built in America. The stock market crashed 4 months after its June 1929 debut, and no one could afford to build such expensive showplaces afterward. Designed in baroque Moorish/Spanish revival style by John Eberson, this former vaudeville and film palace features an elaborate village above the sides of the stage and, overhead, a magnificent night sky dome, replete with twinkling stars and scudding clouds. Designated a National Historic Landmark, the Majestic affords a rare glimpse into a gilded era (yes, there's genuine gold leaf detailing).

Beethoven Halle and Garten San Antonio's German heritage is celebrated at this venue, a converted 1894 Victorian mansion in the King William area. It's open Tuesday through Saturday as a beer garden, with bands playing everything from oompah to rock. Among the regular performers are the Mannerchor (men's choir), which dates back to 1867. Lots of traditional German food, drink, and revelry make Oktoberfest an autumn high point. In December, a Kristkrindle Markt welcomes the holiday season with an old country–style arts-and-crafts fair. 422 Pereida. ✆ **210/222-1521.** www.beethovenmaennerchor.com.

Carver Community Cultural Center Located near the Alamodome on the east edge of downtown, the Carver theater was built for the city's African-American community in 1929, and hosted the likes of Ella Fitzgerald, Charlie "Bird" Parker, and Dizzy Gillespie over the years. It continues to serve the community while providing a widely popular venue for an international array of performers in a variety of genres, including drama, music, and dance. In 2004, the center completed a major renovation, so performances that had been held elsewhere, returned for the 2005 season to a newly spiffy—and structurally sound—venue. 226 N. Hackberry. ✆ **210/207-7211** or 207-2234 (box office). www.thecarver.org. Tickets $25.

The Empire Theatre Among the celebrities who trod the boards of the Empire Theatre before its motion picture prime were Roy Rogers and Trigger; Mae West put in an appearance, too. Fallen into disrepair and shuttered for 2 decades, this 1914 opera house made its grand re-debut in 1998 after a massive renovation. Smaller than its former rival the Majestic (see below), just down the block, the Empire hosts a similarly eclectic array of acts, including musical performances, lectures, and literary events. 226 N. St. Mary's St. ✆ **210/226-5700.** www.majesticempire.com.

Guadalupe Cultural Arts Center There's always something happening at the Guadalupe Center. Visiting and local directors put on six or seven plays a year; the resident Guadalupe Dance Company might collaborate with the city's symphony or invite modern masters up from Mexico City. The Xicano Music Program celebrates the popular local *conjunto* and Tejano sounds; an annual book fair brings in Spanish-language literature from around the world; and the CineFestival, running since 1977, is one of the town's major film events. And then there are always the parties thrown to celebrate new installations at the theater's art gallery and its annex. 1300 Guadalupe. ✆ **210/271-3151.** www.guadalupeculturalarts.org.

Laurie Auditorium Some pretty high-powered people turn up at the Laurie Auditorium, on the Trinity University campus in the north-central part of town. Everyone from former weapons inspector David Kay to Fox news correspondent Brit Hume has taken part in the university's Distinguished Lecture Series, subsidized by grants and open to the public free. The 2,700-seat hall also hosts major players in the popular and performing arts: Chick Corea and the Preservation Hall Jazz Band were among those who took the stage in recent years. Dance recitals, jazz concerts, and plays, many with internationally renowned artists, are held here, too. Trinity University, 715 Stadium Dr. ✆ **210/999-8117** (box office information line) or 999-8119. www.trinity.edu/departments/Laurie.

Majestic Theatre This theater introduced air-conditioning to San Antonio—the hall was billed beforehand as "an acre of cool, comfortable seats"—and society women wore fur coats to its opening, held on a warm June night in 1929. The Majestic hosts some of the best entertainment in town—the symphony, major Broadway productions, big-name solo performers—and, thanks to a wonderful restoration of this fabulous showplace, completed in 1989, coming here is still pretty cool. 230 E. Houston. ✆ **210/226-3333.** www.majesticempire.com.

Sunken Garden Theater Built by the WPA in 1936 in a natural acoustic bowl in Brackenridge Park, the Sunken Garden Theater boasts an open-air stage set against a wooded hillside; cut-limestone buildings in Greek revival style hold the wings and the dressing rooms. This appealing outdoor arena, open from March through October, offers a little bit of everything—rock, country, hip-hop, rap, jazz, Tejano, Cajun, and sometimes even the San Antonio Symphony. Annual events include Taste of New Orleans (a Fiesta event in Apr), the Margarita Pour-Off in August, and a biannual Bob Marley Reggae Festival. Brackenridge Park, 3875 N. St. Mary's St. (Mulberry Ave. entrance). ✆ **210/207-7275.**

2 THE CLUB & MUSIC SCENE

The closest San Antonio comes to having a club district is the stretch of North St. Mary's between Josephine and Magnolia—just north of downtown and south of Brackenridge Park—known as the Strip. This area was hotter about 15 years ago, but it still draws a young crowd to its restaurants and lounges on the weekend. The River Walk clubs tend to be touristy, and many of them close early because of noise restrictions. Downtown's **Sunset Station,** 1174 E. Commerce (✆ **210/474-7640;** www.sunset-station.com), a multivenue entertainment complex in the city's original train station, has yet to take off when there are no events in the nearby Alamodome. When there are, you can get down at Club Agave, where the movement has a Latin flavor. More regular action occurs on Sunday at noon, when the House of Blues lays on a gospel brunch buffet in a covered outdoor pavilion. Call the Sunset Station office or check the website for details.

In addition to the **Alamodome,** 100 Montana St. (✆ **210/207-3663;** www.sanantonio.gov/dome), the major concert venues in town include **Verizon Wireless Amphitheater,** 16765 Lookout Rd., north of San Antonio just beyond Loop 1604 (✆ **210/657-8300;** www.vwatx.com), and, when the Spurs aren't playing there, downtown's **AT&T Center,** One AT&T Center Pkwy (✆ **210/444-5000;** www.nba.com/spurs).

COUNTRY & WESTERN

Floores Country Store ★★ John T. Floore, the first manager of the Majestic Theatre and an unsuccessful candidate for mayor of San Antonio, opened up this country store in 1942. A couple of years later, he added a cafe and a dance floor—at half an acre, the largest in south Texas. And not much has changed since then. Boots, hats, and antique farm equipment hang from the ceiling of this typical Texas roadhouse, and the walls are lined with pictures of Willie Nelson; Hank Williams, Sr.; Conway Twitty; Ernest Tubb; and other country greats who have played here. There's always live music on weekends, and Dwight Yoakum, Robert Earl Keen, and Lyle Lovett have all turned up along with Willie. The cafe still serves homemade bread, homemade tamales, old-fashioned sausage, and cold Texas beer. 14464 Old Bandera Rd./Hwy. 16, Helotes (2 miles north of Loop 1604). ✆ **210/695-8827.** www.liveatfloores.com. Cover $5–$35.

Leon Springs Dancehall This lively 1880s-style dance hall can—and often does—pack some 1,200 people into its 18,000 square feet. Lots of people come with their kids when the place opens at 7pm, though the crowd turns older (but not much) as the evening wears on. Some of the best local country-and-western talent is showcased here on Friday and Saturday nights, the only two nights the dance hall is open. Get a group of more than 10 together and you can order barbecue from the original Rudy's, just down the road. 24135 I-10 (Boerne Stage Rd. exit). ✆ **210/698-7072.** www.leonspringsdancehall.com. Cover usually $5, kids under 12 free.

ROCK

White Rabbit One of the few alternative rock venues on the Strip—and one of the only ones large enough to have a raised stage—the Rabbit attracts a mostly young crowd to its black-lit recesses. Those 18 to 20 years old are allowed in for a higher cover. 2410 N. St. Mary's St. ✆ **210/737-2221.** www.sawhiterabbit.com. Cover $6.

ECLECTIC

Casbeers at the Church Casbeers, has recently moved from its original location on Blanco Road, in the Monte Vista district, to a larger venue in the popular Southtown area. It still showcases the same artists, performing a mix of roots rock, blues, country, and folk. It still serves the same food, featuring popular burgers and hearty Tex-Mex. But the new venue—an old abandoned Methodist church that in recent years was restored and converted into a restaurant—is a radical departure from the old setting. With the new venue comes a full bar and two different stages for performances: a cafe where local acts play for no cover charge, and the church nave where headliners perform, and cover charges run between $10 and $15. 1150 South Alamo. ✆ **210/271-7791.** www.casbeers.com. No cover in cafe, cover for some shows $10-$15.

Kingston Tycoon Flats (Kids) This friendly music garden is a fun place to kick back and listen to blues, rock, acoustic, reggae, or jazz. The burgers and such Caribbean specialties as jerk chicken are good, too. Bring the kids—an outdoor sandbox is larger than the dance floor. There's rarely any cover for the almost nightly live music. 2926 N. St. Mary's St. ✆ **210/731-9838.** Cover $5 or less when there is one.

JAZZ & BLUES

The Landing ★★ You might have heard cornetist Jim Cullum on the airwaves. His American Public Radio program, *Riverwalk, Live from the Landing,* is now broadcast on more than 160 stations nationwide, and his band has backed some of the finest jazz players of our time. This is the best traditional jazz club in Texas, and if you like big bands and Dixieland, there's no better place to listen to this music. The Landing Cafe features a fairly basic steak and seafood menu, with a few Mexican/Southwest touches.

Conjunto: An American Classic

Cruise a San Antonio radio dial or go to any major city festival, and you'll most likely hear the happy, boisterous sound of conjunto. Never heard of it? Don't worry, you're not alone. Although conjunto is one of our country's original contributions to world music, for a long time few Americans outside Texas knew much about it.

Conjunto evolved at the end of the 19th century, when South Texas was swept by a wave of German immigrants who brought with them popular polkas and waltzes. These sounds were easily incorporated into—and transformed by—Mexican folk music. The newcomer accordion, cheap and able to mimic several instruments, was happily adopted, too. With the addition at the turn of the century of the *bajo sexto,* a 12-string guitarlike instrument used for rhythmic bass accompaniment, conjunto was born.

Tejano (Spanish for "Texan") is the 20th-century offspring of conjunto. The two most prominent instruments in Tejano remain the accordion and the *bajo sexto,* but the music incorporates more modern forms, including pop, jazz, and country-and-western, into the traditional conjunto repertoire. At clubs not exclusively devoted to Latino sounds, what you're likely to hear is Tejano.

Long ignored by the mainstream, conjunto and Tejano were brought into America's consciousness by the murder of Hispanic superstar **Selena.** Before she was killed, Selena had already been slotted for crossover success—she had done the title song and put in a cameo appearance in the film *Don Juan de Marco* with Johnny Depp—and the movie based on her life boosted awareness of her music even further.

San Antonio is to conjunto music what Nashville is to country. The most famous *bajo sextos,* used nationally by everyone who is anyone in conjunto and Tejano music, were created in San Antonio by the Macías family—the late Martín and now his son, Alberto. The undisputed king of conjunto, **Flaco Jiménez**—a mild-mannered triple-Grammy winner who has recorded with the Rolling Stones, Bob Dylan, and Willie Nelson, among others—lives in the city. And San Antonio's **Tejano Conjunto Festival,** held each May (see the "San Antonio Calendar of Events," in chapter 2), is the largest of its kind, drawing aficionados from around the world—there's even a conjunto band from Japan.

Most of the places to hear conjunto and Tejano are off the beaten tourist path, and they come and go fairly quickly. Those that have been around for a while—and are visitor-friendly—include **Arturo's Sports Bar & Grill,** 3310 S. Zarzamora St. (✆ **210/923-0177**), and **Cool Arrows,** 1025 Nogalitos St. (✆ **210/227-5130**). For live music schedules, check the Tejano/Conjunto section under "Entertainment" and "Music" of www.mysanantonio.com, the website of the *San Antonio-Express News.* You can also phone **Salute!** (see below) to find out which night of the week they're featuring a Tejano or conjunto band. Best yet, just attend one of San Antonio's many festivals—you're bound to hear these rousing sounds.

 Hyatt Regency Hotel, River Walk. ✆ **210/223-7266.** www.landing.com. Cover $5 Mon–Sat, free Sun (outdoor stage only, when other bands entertain).

Salute! Like the crowd, the music at this red-lit little wonder is eclectic, to say the least. The live jazz at this tiny club tends to have a Latin flavor, but you never know what you're going to hear—anything from synthesized '70s sounds to conjunto. There is not set cover, but some nights it can be as much as $10 to get in the door. So, call ahead or pocket a tenspot, just in case. 2801 N. St. Mary's St. ✆ **210/732-5307.** www.saluteinternational bar.com.

COMEDY

Rivercenter Comedy Club This club books such big names in stand-up as Dennis Miller and Garry Shandling, but it also takes advantage of local talent on Mondays (Comedy Potpourri nights) and Fridays (open-mic night in the Ha!Lapeno Lounge 5–7:30pm; no cover). The late, late (12:20am) adult-oriented shows on Friday nights are also free. 849 E. Commerce St. (Rivercenter Mall, third level). ✆ **210/229-1420.** www.rivercenter comedyclub.com. Cover $8 Mon–Tues, $10 Wed–Thurs, $13 Fri–Sun.

THE GAY SCENE

In addition to the Bonham (see below), Main Street just north of downtown has three gay men's clubs in close proximity (it's been nicknamed the "gay bar mall"). **Pegasus,** 1402 N. Main (✆ **210/299-4222**), is your basic cruise bar. **The Silver Dollar,** 1418 N. Main (✆ **210/227-2623**), does the country-and-western thing. And **The Saint,** 1430 N. Main (✆ **210/225-7330**), caters to dancing fools. Covers are low to nonexistent at all three. Popular lesbian bars include **Bermuda Triangle** (119 El Mio; ✆ **210/342-2276**) and **Petticoat Junction** (1812 N. Main; ✆ **210/737-2344**).

Bonham Exchange Tina Turner, Deborah Harry (aka Blondie), and LaToya Jackson—the real ones—have all played this high-tech dance club near the Alamo. While you may find an occasional cross-dressing show here, the mixed crowd of gays and straights, young and old, come mainly to move to the beat under wildly flashing lights. All the action—five bars, three dance floors, three levels—takes place in a restored German-style building dating back to the 1880s. Roll over, Beethoven. 411 Bonham. ✆ **210/271-3811** or 224-9219. www.bonhamexchange.net. No cover for ages 21 and older before 10pm, then $5 Fri–Sat, $3 Sun.

3 THE BAR SCENE

Most bars close at 2am, although some alternative spots stay open until 3 or 4am. Some of the hottest bars in town are also in restaurants: see Acenar and Azuca in chapter 6.

Blue Star Brewing Company Restaurant & Bar Preppies and gallery types don't often mingle, but the popularity of this brewpub in the Blue Star Arts Complex with college kids demonstrates the transcendent power of good beer. (The pale ale is especially fine.) And if a few folks who wouldn't know a Picasso from a piccolo happen to wander in and see some art after dinner, then the owners have performed a useful public service. The food's good, too. 1414 S. Alamo, #105 (Blue Star Arts Complex). ✆ **210/212-5506.** www. bluestarbrewing.com.

Cadillac Bar & Restaurant During the week, lawyers and judges come to unwind at the Cadillac Bar, set in a historic stucco building near the Bexar County Courthouse and City Hall. On the weekends, singles take over the joint. A DJ spins on Saturday nights, but on Thursdays and Fridays, the sounds are live and local—anything from '70s disco to classic rock to pop. Full dinners are served on a patio out back. 212 S. Flores. ✆ **210/223-5533.**

Cappyccino's Although it's by no means deficient in the caffeine department, don't mistake Cappyccino's for a coffee bar: The name derives from neighboring Cappy's restaurant (p. 105), of which it's an offshoot. The forte here is yuppie hard stuff, including classic cocktails, tequilas, and single-malt scotches. A skinny but high-ceilinged lightwood dining room and a plant-filled patio create a relaxed setting for drinking and dining off the stylish Southwest bistro menu. 5003 Broadway. ✆ **210/828-6860.** www.cappyccinos.com.

Durty Nellie's Irish Pub Chug a lager and lime, toss your peanut shells on the floor, and sing along with the piano player at this wonderfully corny version of an Irish pub. You've forgotten the words to "Danny Boy"? Not to worry—18 old-time favorites are printed on the back of the menu. After a couple of Guinnesses, you'll be bellowing "H-A-double-R-I-G-A-N spells Harrigan!" as loud as the rest of 'em. 715 River Walk (Hilton Palacio del Rio Hotel). ✆ **210/222-1400.**

Howl at the Moon Saloon It's hard to avoid having a good time at this rowdy River Walk bar; if you're shy, one of the dueling piano players will inevitably embarrass you into joining the crowd belting out off-key oldies from the '60s, '70s, and '80s. Don't worry. You're probably never going to see most of these people again. Ages 21 and older only. 111 W. Crockett St. ✆ **210/212-4695.** www.howlatthemoon.com. Cover $5 Sun–Thurs, $7 Fri–Sat until 10pm, $10 after 10pm.

Menger Bar More than 100 years ago, Teddy Roosevelt recruited men for his Rough Riders unit at this dark, wooded bar (they were outfitted for the Spanish-American War at nearby Fort Sam Houston). Constructed in 1859 on the site of William Menger's earlier successful brewery and saloon, the bar was moved from its original location in the Victorian hotel lobby in 1956, but 90% of its historic furnishings remain intact. Spanish Civil War uniforms hang on the walls. It's still one of the prime spots in town to toss back a few. Menger Hotel, 204 Alamo Plaza. ✆ **210/223-4361.**

Stone Werks Cafe and Bar At this offbeat venue—a 1920s building that used to be the Alamo Cement Company's office—a 30-something crowd moves to local cover bands from Wednesday through Saturday. A fence, hand-sculpted from cement by Mexican artist Dionicio Rodríguez, surrounds an oak-shaded patio. 7300 Jones-Maltsberger. ✆ **210/828-3508.**

Swig Martini Bar Craving a chocolate martini? Belly up to the bar at the River Walk's nod to retro chic. Single-barrel bourbon, single-malt scotch, and a wide selection of beer and wines fill out the drink menu, but James Bond's preferred poison is always the top seller. Nightly live jazz adds to the pizzazz. The big cigars are the catch (or draw) here. This place was so popular it spurred a national chain. 111 W. Crockett, #205. ✆ **210/476-0005.** www.swigmartini.com.

Tex's Grill If you want to hang with the Spurs, come to Tex's, regularly voted San Antonio's best sports bar in the *Current* readers' polls. Three satellite dishes, 2 large-screen TVs, and 17 smaller sets keep the bleachers happy, as do the killer margaritas and giant burgers. Among Tex's major collection of exclusively Texas sports memorabilia are a signed Nolan Ryan jersey, a football used by the Dallas Cowboys in their 1977 Super

Finds Mission Accomplished

When it premiered in 1947, the screen of the **Mission Drive-In,** 3100 Roosevelt Ave. (✆ **210/532-3259** or 210/496-2221), was framed with a neon outline of nearby Mission San Jose, replete with moving bell, burro, and cacti. San Antonio's last remaining open-air movie house, refurbished and reopened in 2001, now has four screens and features first-run films. It's as much fun to come here for a family filmfest or romantic under-the-stars evening as it ever was.

Bowl victory, and one of George Gervin's basketball shoes (the other is at the newer Tex's on the River, at the Hilton Palacio del Rio). San Antonio Airport Hilton and Conference Center, 611 NW Loop 410. ✆ **210/340-6060.**

Zinc This chic wine bar, open until 2am nightly, is perfect for a romantic after-hours glass of champagne. Hardwood floors, brick walls, and a cozy library make the indoor space appealing, but on temperate nights, head for the pretty back patio. 209 N. Presa St. ✆ **210/224-2900.** www.zincwine.com.

4 MOVIES

The alternative cinemas in San Antonio are not in the most trafficked tourist areas, but if you're willing to go out of your way for an indie fix you can get one at the **Regal Fiesta Stadium 16,** 12631 Vance Jackson (✆ **210/641-6906**). The city also boasts a cinema that not only screens off-beat films, but also allows you to munch on more than popcorn and licorice while viewing them. At the homegrown **Bijou at Crossroads: A CaféCinema,** 4522 Fredericksburg, Crossroads Mall (✆ **210/737-0291** [show times] or 496-1300, ext 0; www.santikos.com/bijou.htm), you can dine on deli sandwiches, burgers, or pizzas, accompanied by a cold one (or glass of wine) at bistro-style tables in the lobby or at your seat in the theater. An Austin import (its name notwithstanding), the **Alamo Drafthouse Westlakes,** 1255 SW Loop 410 (✆ **210/677-8500;** www.originalalamo.com), shows mostly first-run films but accompanies them with seat-side food service.

The **Guadalupe Cultural Arts Center** (see "Major Arts Venues," earlier in this chapter) and the **McNay** and **Witte museums** (see chapter 7) often have interesting film series; and the **Esperanza Center,** 922 San Pedro (✆ **210/228-0201;** www.esperanza center.org), usually offers an annual gay and lesbian cinema festival. In addition to *Alamo, the Price of Freedom,* the **San Antonio IMAX Theater Rivercenter,** 217 Alamo Plaza (✆ **210/225-4629;** www.imax-sa.com), shows such high-action films as *Spider-Man* or *Into the Deep* suited to the big, big screen.

Side Trips from San Antonio

Besides the Hill Country, there are other options for places to visit in the vicinity of San Antonio. It all depends on what you want to do and how much time you have.

1 NEW BRAUNFELS & GRUENE

Only 35 miles northeast of San Antonio, on I-35, is the old German town of **New Braunfels,** which sits at the junction of the Comal and Guadalupe rivers. German settlers established the town in 1845, under the leadership of Prince Carl of Solms-Braunfels, who was the commissioner general of the Society for the Protection of German Immigrants in Texas, the same group that later founded Fredericksburg (see chapter 18). As enterprising as the prince was, he could not persuade his fiancée to give up Germany for Texas, so he returned to settle down in his homeland. But the colony he left behind prospered. By the 1850s, New Braunfels was the fourth-largest city in Texas after Houston, San Antonio, and Galveston.

Although you have to look a little to find its quainter side today, this is an enjoyable town that still reflects some of its German heritage. The town's main street is a pleasant mix of new and old, with a number of old-fashioned stores. There's plenty of water to play around in, including the largest water park in Texas, **Schlitterbahn,** as well as tubing on the river—a favorite Texas pastime. There is also an impressive cavern in the vicinity.

Fifteen miles farther up I-35, in the direction of Austin, is San Marcos (see chapter 17), which doesn't have the attractions of New Braunfels but does have major shopping at two large outlet malls.

WHAT TO SEE & DO

At the **New Braunfels Chamber of Commerce,** 390 S. Seguin, New Braunfels, TX 78130 (✆ **800/572-2626** or 830/625-2385; www.nbjumpin.com), open weekdays 8am to 5pm, you can pick up a pamphlet detailing the 40-point historic walking tour of midtown. Highlights include the Romanesque-Gothic **Comal County Courthouse** (1898) on Main Plaza; the nearby **Jacob Schmidt Building** (193 W. San Antonio), built on the site where William Gebhardt, of canned chili fame, perfected his formula for chili powder in 1896; and the 1928 **Faust Hotel** (240 S. Seguin), believed by some to be haunted by its owner. These days, drafts pulled from the microbrewery on the Faust's premises help allay even the most haunting anxieties. **Henne Hardware,** 246 W. San Antonio (✆ **830/606-6707**), established in 1857, sells modern bits and bobs, but maintains its original tin-roof ceiling, rings for hanging buggy whips, and an old pulley system for transporting cash and paperwork through the back business office. It's said to be the oldest hardware store in Texas. **Naeglin's,** 129 S. Seguin Ave. (✆ **830/625-5722**), opened in 1868, stakes its claim as the state's longest-running bakery. It's the place to try some kolaches—Czech pastries filled with cheese, fruit, poppy seeds, sausage, or ham, among other delicious fillings.

Several small museums are worth a visit. Prince Carl never did build a planned castle for his sweetheart, Sophia, on the elevated spot where the **Sophienburg Museum,** 401 W. Coll St. (✆ **830/629-1572;** www.sophienburg.org), now stands, but it's nevertheless an excellent place to learn about the history of New Braunfels and other Hill Country settlements. It's open Tuesday to Saturday 10am to 4pm; admission is $5 adults and $1 for students younger than 18. The **Museum of Texas Handmade Furniture ★**, 1370 Church Hill Dr. (✆ **830/629-6504;** www.nbheritagevillage.com), also sheds light on local domestic life of the 19th century with its beautiful examples of Texas Biedermeier by master craftsman Johan Michael Jahn. They're displayed at the gracious 1858 Breustedt-Dillon Haus. The 11-acre **Heritage Village** complex also includes an 1848 log cabin and a barn that houses a reproduction cabinetmaker's workshop. The museum is open Tuesday through Sunday from 1 to 4pm from February 1 through November 30, closed December and January. The last tour begins at 3:30pm. Admission costs $5 for adults, $4 for seniors, $1 for children ages 6 to 12.

You can tour other historic structures, including the original 1870 schoolhouse and such transported shops as a tiny music studio, at the nearby **Conservation Plaza,** 1300 Church Hill Dr. (✆ **830/629-2943**), centered around a gazebo and garden with more than 50 varieties of antique roses. Guided tours (included in admission) are offered every day except Monday. It's open Tuesday to Friday, 10am to 2:30pm, and Saturday and Sunday, 2 to 5pm; adult admission costs $2.50, while children 6 to 17 pay 50¢. Also owned by the New Braunfels Conservation Society, the 1852 **Lindheimer Home ★**, 491 Comal Ave. (✆ **830/608-1512**), is probably the best example of an early *fachwerk* house still standing in New Braunfels. Ferdinand J. Lindheimer, one of the town's first settlers—he scouted out the site for Prince Solms—was an internationally recognized botanist and editor of the town's German-language newspaper. Museum hours are Tuesday to Friday from 10am to 2:30pm, and Saturday and Sunday from 2 to 5pm. You can wander the lovely grounds planted with Texas natives (38 species of plant were named for Lindheimer) even if you can't get in to see the house.

Historic Gruene ★★

You can get a more concentrated glimpse of the past at **Gruene** (pronounced "green"), 4 miles northwest of downtown New Braunfels. First settled by German farmers in the 1840s, Gruene was virtually abandoned during the Depression in the 1930s. It remained a ghost town until the mid-1970s, when two investors realized the value of its intact historic buildings and sold them to businesses rather than raze them. These days, tiny Gruene is crowded with day-trippers browsing the specialty shops in the wonderfully restored structures, which include a smoked-meat shop, lots of cutesy gift boutiques, and several antiques shops.

The **New Braunfels Museum of Art & Music ★**, 1259 Gruene Rd., on the river behind Gruene Mansion (✆ **800/456-4866** or 830/625-5636), focuses on popular arts in the West and South (as opposed to, say, high culture and the classics). Subjects of recent exhibits, which change quarterly and combine music and art components, have included Texas accordion music, central Texas dance halls, and cowboy art and poetry. Live music throughout the year includes an open mic on Sunday afternoons, and the recording of New Braunfels Live radio show of roots music on Thursday evenings. The museum is open Wednesday through Sunday from noon to 6pm from September 1 through April 30 and Monday through Thursday from 10am to 6pm, Friday and Saturday from 10am to 8pm, Sunday noon to 8pm the rest of the year. No admission; donations gratefully accepted (and you can contribute by shopping at the museum's excellent gift shop).

A brochure detailing the town's retailers, restaurants, and accommodations is available from the New Braunfels Chamber of Commerce (see above) or at most of Gruene's shops.

Watersports

Gruene also figures among the New Braunfels area's impressive array of places to get wet, most of them open only in summer. Outfitters who can help you ride the Guadalupe River rapids on raft, tube, canoe, or inflatable kayak include **Rockin' R River Rides** (✆ **800/553-5628** or 830/629-9999; www.rockinr.com) and **Gruene River Company** (✆ **888/705-2800** or 830/625-2800; www.toobing.com), both on Gruene Road just south of the Gruene bridge.

You can go tubing, too, at **Schlitterbahn ★**, Texas's largest water park and one of the best in the country, 305 W. Austin St., in New Braunfels (✆ **830/625-2351;** www.schlitterbahn.com). If there's a way to get wet 'n' wild, this place has got it. Six separate areas feature gigantic slides, pools, and rides, including Master Blaster, one of the world's steepest uphill water coasters. The combination of a natural river-and-woods setting and high-tech attractions make this splashy 65-acre playland a standout. The park usually opens inlate April and closes in mid-September; call or check the website for the exact dates. All-day passes cost $40 for adults, $32 for children 3 to 11; children under 3 enter free.

Those who like their water play a bit more low-key might try downtown **New Braunfels's Landa Park** (✆ **830/608-2160**), where you can either swim in the largest spring-fed pool in Texas or calmly float in an inner tube down the Comal River—at 2½ miles the "largest shortest" river in the world, according to Ripley's Believe It or Not. There's also an Olympic-size swimming pool, and you can rent paddle boats, canoes, and water cycles. Even if you're not prepared to immerse yourself, you might take the lovely 22-mile drive along the Guadalupe River from downtown's Cypress Bend Park to Canyon Lake, whose clarity makes it perfect for scuba diving.

For more details about all the places where camping, food, and water toys are available along the Guadalupe River, pick up the Water Recreation Guide pamphlet at the New Braunfels Visitors Center.

Perhaps you want to buy your own toys—and learn how to use them. The 70-acre **Texas Ski Ranch,** 6700 I-35 N. (✆ **830/627-2843;** www.texasskiranch.com), is paradise for those interested in wake, skate, and motor sports. Features of this expanding complex include a cable lake, boat lake, skate park, and motor track—at all of which you can test the equipment you want to purchase or rent (you can also bring your own), and show off the latest athletic clothing, sold here, too. Training clinics and private lessons for a variety of sports are offered. It costs $5 (free for over 65 and under 6) to enter the recreation areas plus a variable amount for use of facilities and classes. The complex is open Tuesday through Thursday from 10am to 8pm, Friday and Saturday 10am to 9pm, Sunday 10am to 6pm.

Nearby Caverns & Animals

Natural Bridge Caverns, 26495 Natural Bridge Caverns Rd. (✆ **210/651-6101;** www.naturalbridgecaverns.com), 12 miles west of New Braunfels, is named for the 60-foot limestone arch spanning its entryway. More than a mile of huge rooms and passages is filled with stunning, multihued formations—still being formed, as the dripping water attests. The daring—and physically fit—can opt to join one of the Adventure Tours, which involve crawling and, in some cases, rappelling, in an unlighted cave not open to the general public ($100 for 3–4 hours), while those who prefer their adventures outdoors can opt for the new Watchtower Challenge, a 40-foot climbing tower with a zipline (prices vary, subject to weather and availability). The caverns are open 9am to 7pm June through Labor Day, 9am to 4pm the rest of the year; closed Thanksgiving Day, Christmas Day, and New Year's Day; two different tours cost the same $18 adults, $10 ages 3 to 11. The Discovery Tour explores a half mile of the cavern, viewing many formations of all types. The Illuminations Tour focuses on two chambers with lots of delicate formations, which are dramatically lit.

Just down the road, the **Natural Bridge Wildlife Ranch,** 26515 Natural Bridge Caverns Rd. (✆ **830/438-7400;** www.nbwildliferanchtx.com), lets you get up close and personal—from the safety of your car—with some 50 threatened and endangered species from around the world; there's also a shorter (and equally safe) walking safari. Packets of food sold at the entryway inspire even some generally shy types to amble over to your vehicle. It is open daily 9am to 5pm, with extended summer hours until 6:30pm; admission costs $17 adults, $16 seniors 65 and older, $8.50 ages 3 to 11.

WHERE TO STAY IN NEW BRAUNFELS & GRUENE

The **Prince Solms Inn,** 295 E. San Antonio St., New Braunfels, TX 78130 (✆ **800/625-9169** or 830/625-9169; www.princesolmsinn.com), has been in continuous operation since it opened its doors to travelers in 1898. A prime downtown location, tree-shaded courtyard, downstairs piano bar, and gorgeously florid, High Victorian–style sleeping quarters have put accommodations at this charming bed-and-breakfast in great demand. Three Western-themed rooms in a converted 1860 feed store next door are ideal for families, and there's an ultraromantic separate cabin in the back of the main house. Rates range from $125 to $175.

For history with a river view, consider the **Gruene Mansion Inn,** 1275 Gruene Rd., New Braunfels, TX 78130 (✆ **830/629-2641;** www.gruenemansioninn.com). The barns that once belonged to the opulent 1875 plantation house were converted to rustic elegant cottages with decks; some also offer cozy lofts (if you don't like stairs, request a single-level room). Accommodations for two go from $170 to $240 per night, including breakfast served in the plantation house. Two separate lodges, suitable for families, are available, too ($260–$340).

The nearby **Gruene Apple Bed and Breakfast,** 1235 Gruene Rd. (✆ **830/643-1234;** www.grueneapple.com), set on a bluff overlooking the Guadalupe River, is less historic, more upscale. This opulent limestone mansion, built expressly to serve as an inn, hosts 14 luxurious theme rooms, from "Wild West" and "Shady Lady" to the more decorous "1776"; many look out on the river from private balconies. On-site recreation includes a natural stone swimming pool, hot tub, pool table, player piano—even a small movie theater. Doubles range from $175 to $235; midweek discounts available.

If you're planning to come to town during the Wurstfest sausage festival (late Oct–early Nov), be sure to book well in advance, no matter where you stay—that is high season here.

WHERE TO DINE IN NEW BRAUNFELS & GRUENE

The **New Braunfels Smokehouse,** 1090 N. Business 35 (✆ **830/625-2416;** www.nbsmokehouse.com), opened in 1951 as a tasting room for the meats it started hickory smoking in 1943. Savor it in platters or on sandwiches, or have some shipped home as a savory souvenir. It's open daily for breakfast, lunch, and dinner; prices are moderate. The far newer **Huisache Grill,** 303 W. San Antonio St. (✆ **830/620-9001;** www.huisache.com), has an updated American menu that draws foodies from as far as San Antonio. The pecan-crusted pork-chop catfish and Yucatan chicken are among the excellent entrees. Lunch and dinner are served daily; prices are moderate to expensive. An even more recent arrival on downtown's fine dining scene, **Myron's,** 136 Castell Rd. (✆ **830/624-1024;** www.myronsprimesteakhouse.com), serves perfectly prepared Chicago prime steak in a retro swank dining room (a converted 1920s movie palace). Prices are big-city expensive (all the sides are extra, for example), but the outstanding food and service, combined with the atmosphere, make any meal here a special occasion. Myron's is open for dinner nightly. Reservations are recommended for dinner at both the Huisache Grill and Myron's.

In Gruene, the **Gristmill River Restaurant & Bar,** 1287 Gruene Rd. (✆ **830/625-0684;** www.gristmillrestaurant.com), a converted 100-year-old cotton gin, includes burgers and chicken-fried steak as well as healthful salads on its Texas-casual menu. Kick back on one of its multiple decks and gaze out at the Guadalupe River. Lunch and dinner daily; prices are moderate.

NEW BRAUNFELS & GRUENE AFTER DARK

At the **Brauntex Performing Arts Theatre,** 290 W. San Antonio (✆ **830/627-0808;** www.brauntex.org), a restored 1942 movie theater in midtown New Braunfels, you can expect to see anything from Frula, an eastern European folk-dancing extravaganza that played Carnegie Hall, to such local acts as the Flying J. Wranglers.

Lyle Lovett and Garth Brooks are just a few of the big names who have played **Gruene Hall ★★**, Gruene Road, corner of Hunter Road (✆ **830/629-7077;** www.gruenehall.com), the oldest country-and-western dance hall in Texas and still one of the state's most outstanding spots for live music. Some of the scenes in *Michael,* starring John Travolta, were shot here. By itself, the hall is worth a detour; when in town, if there's live music playing, it is an absolute must—just remember to wear your cowboy boots and hat.

2 SMALL-TOWN TEXAS

If you want to get out of San Antonio and away from the crowds, and you want to see a part of Texas that is less touristy, then consider this day trip to a few of the old towns to the east of San Antonio. The trip includes a smattering of things: a little history, a little antique shopping, a tour of Texas's last independent brewery, cactus shopping, some award-winning barbecue, plus a good amount of local color. It's best to go on a weekday, when the brewery is open for tours. This is a relaxing trip—the roads are good, the traffic is light, and the driving is easy. There won't be any crowds, which is especially important during wildflower season in the spring. Visitors show a strong preference for the Hill Country, but the wildflowers do not.

GONZALES

Start by heading out of San Antonio East on Highway I-10 to Hwy. 183 (60 miles), then south to the town of **Gonzales** (12 miles). One of the original Anglo settlements made under agreement with the Mexican government, Gonzales was a hot bed for Texas independence and saw the first hostilities of the war. While driving around the town, you're sure to see signs and banners with the words "Come and take it" below an image of a canon. This was the battle cry of the local settlers when, in October of 1835, a regiment of Mexican cavalry came to collect a small cannon that had been lent to the settlement to fend off the Comanche. What followed was more of a skirmish than a battle, but it set Texas on the road to independence. A few months later, the town was burned to the ground by orders of General Sam Houston when the Texan army retreated eastwards, during what is called the Runaway Scrape.

In the oldest part of Gonzales (pop. 7,000), the streets are still named after saints, following the original layout proposed by the Mexican government. There's a relatively large business sector with old brick storefronts, which tells of past prosperity. Occupying a few of these (and a couple of warehouses, too) is **Discovery Architectural Antiques** (✆ **830/672-2428;** www.discoverys.com) at 409 St. Francis St. It sells all manner of old building materials and details, including original lumber, doors, windows, and hardware, stained glass, and small details, such as doorknobs, for instance.

The **town courthouse** is one of the prettiest in Texas. It was built in 1898 in Richardsonian Romanesque (a style named after the architect who built Trinity Church in Boston). It was designed by J. Riely Gordan, who also designed Bexar County Courthouse in San Antonio and the Comal County Courthouse in New Braunfels. This is the best of the three and is one of the best-preserved courthouses in the state, having retained its clock tower and original roof. The interior is well preserved, too. It contains a few paintings, one of which depicts the town circa 1925. The **old jailhouse,** which sits at the opposite corner of the square (facing St. Lawrence St.), is home of the chamber of commerce and visitor center. It dates from 1887 and is open to visitors. It must have been a grim sight for prisoners, to judge by the way the cells were built and the gallows room, which was used for executions until the 1920s, when capital punishment was brought under state control. Gonzalez did have a criminal element, and its most famous member was John Wesley Harden (son of a Methodist preacher). He killed several men in the Sutton-Taylor feud, which raged throughout several counties in this part of Texas during 1870s. For a while he was jailed in Gonzales (in an earlier jailhouse) but managed to escape.

Gonzales has several large houses in the old part of town, as well as a **Pioneer Village** (✆ **830/672-2157;** www.gonzalespioneervillage.com), which is at the north end of town, on 2122 N. St. Joseph St. It holds a collection of 19th-century buildings brought here from different parts of the county and restored, including a ranch house, a cabin, and a saloon. It's open from 10am to 2pm Tuesday to Saturday. Admission is $3.50 per adult. It's probably a good idea to call ahead to make sure someone is there. You also need to be mindful of the time because you'll want to get to the next town, Shiner, before either 11:30am or 1pm, when the brewery tours start. It's 20 minutes away.

SHINER

Shiner (pop. 2,000) is home to the **Spoetzl brewery,** the makers of Shiner beer. This is the last independent brewery in Texas, and in 2009 will be celebrating its 100th anniversary. Take Hwy. 90 East for 18 miles. When you drive into Shiner, the brewery will be on your left. It's the highest structure in town.

Shiner Bock beer, sold in brown longnecks, is now available in various parts of the country, but, as late as the 1970s it was available only seasonally and only in central and southeast Texas. But it soon shot up in popularity until it is now the default beer in Austin, San Antonio, and most other parts of central Texas.

Free tours are offered Monday to Friday, at 11:30am and 1pm, and take about 30 minutes, with beer tastings before and after in the hospitality room. It's an impressive tour. All the Shiner beer sold is made at this small brewery; no production is contracted out to other plants.

FLATONIA

After immersion into the German/Czech beer culture, it's time to move on. From the brewery, take a left on Hwy. 95 North and drive 18 miles to **Flatonia** (pop. 1,000). This is a small agricultural town and railroad depot. Really, the main reason to come here is that firstly, it's on the way to the next destination; and secondly, so that you can tell your friends back home that you were in Flatonia, Texas. (The name doesn't actually refer to its lack of topography, but you don't have to mention that.) If you want to know more about the town, you will pass right by the **town archives and museum** (on your right). It's occasionally open, and you can stretch your legs while examining a few antiques.

LULING

From Flatonia, head back west on either Hwy. 90 or I-10. I enjoy the slower Hwy. 90. Your destination is **Luling** (pop. 5,000), but before you get there, you'll pass a couple possible stops, depending on your interests. The first is **Kactus Korral** (**© 830/540-4521;** www.kactus.com), at the intersection of Hwy. 290 and Hwy. 304, about 20 miles from Flatonia. It sells cactus and aloe vera wholesale and retail and offers a lot of variety. Passersby are welcome; you might want to call first. The other interesting business on this route is **Tiny Texas Houses** (**© 830/875-2500;** www.tinytexashouses.com). The owner, who also owns Discovery Architectural Antiques in Gonzales, builds small, fully functional, energy-efficient houses, using recycled lumber and hardware. Examples of his houses are on view for anyone who stops by. They're beautiful and distinctive, and are small enough to transport by truck. The business is on the southeast corner of the intersection of I-10 and Hwy. 80 (exit 628).

Luling has some of the best barbecue in the state. The town is divided down the middle by the railroad tracks. Where the highway crosses the tracks, look for **City Market** (**© 830/875-9019**) on the left, a few doors down at 633 E. Davis St. (It's reviewed, and its barbecue is discussed, in the first section of chapter 17.) It's open Monday through Saturday until 6pm. Luling is also known for watermelon, and they have a festival the last week of June called the **Watermelon Thump.** If you arrive during the festival, you will have a hard time scoring some barbecue, as the town gets crowded.

In the 1920s and '30s, Luling was at the center of a central Texas oil boom. After you finish your barbecue, you can stroll down Davis Street to no. 421, where you'll find the **Central Texas Oil Patch Museum** (**© 830/875-1922;** www.oilmuseum.org). Inside, you'll find a very large space, filled with artifacts of the early days of oil extraction and of the city of Luling. It's an interesting exhibit, and the building itself, with its old-time tin ceiling, is a pleasure to see. While you are there, you can pick up a brochure and map for the **Pumpjack Tour.** Within the city are several pumpjacks (those rocking-horse-like machines that bob up and down in oil fields). Denizens of Luling started dressing up the pumpjacks for fun, and then the local chamber of commerce commissioned Texas sign artist, George Kalesik, to decorate some. The pumpjacks are located close enough together that you can see the majority on foot.

After your visit to Luling, you can return to San Antonio or head to San Marcos or New Braunfels.

3 CORPUS CHRISTI & BEYOND

If you're in San Antonio, you're only 2½ hours from the ocean and some of the best stretches of Texas coastline. The communities around **Corpus Christi** and **Copano Bays** have a lot going for them. In the summer, you can do some kayaking, windsurfing, fishing, and other watersports. And, with Texas's mild weather, you can do the better part of these activities in other seasons. In spring and fall, birders flock to this area for the migrations, when birds rest up before and after hopping the Gulf of Mexico. Another attraction in the region is the Aransas National Wildlife Refuge, the winter home of the whooping crane, the largest bird in North America, and the rarest, too. For a more detailed view of this region, search "Gulf Coast Texas" at frommers.com.

HOW TO GET THERE

Take I-37 straight to Corpus Christi. The town of Rockport is north of the city. From I-37, take Hwy. 181 over the Bay Causeway, then continue on TX 35. To get to the beach town of Port Aransas, follow the signs for Aransas Pass, and from there take the causeway that leads to the Port Aransas ferry. Another nice beach is on Mustang Island. As you approach central Corpus Christi on I-37, look for signs reading TX 358 or "S.P.I.D." (South Padre Island Drive).

WHAT TO DO

Corpus Christi's top two attractions are on the north side of the tall bridge that spans the Nueces River: The **Texas State Aquarium** (✆ **800/477-4853;** www.texasstateaquarium.org), at 2710 N. Shoreline Blvd., and the **USS** ***Lexington*** (✆ **800/523-9539;** www.usslexington.com), an old aircraft carrier docked at 2914 N. Shoreline Blvd.

Admission to the Texas State Aquarium is $16 adult, $14 seniors, and $11 for children 3 to 12. It has several large tanks displaying different saltwater and freshwater habitats. You can see and participate in dolphin training, and chat with some of the staff. Each day there's a schedule of presentations. Check it when you first arrive. To see the *Lexington* costs a little less: $13 adults, $11 seniors, and $8 for children 4 to 12. Touring the boat requires a good bit of stair climbing. This aircraft carrier saw service in the Pacific during WWII. It shows its age, which conveys to a great degree the difficulty and risk of being a crewman or a pilot back in those days. Part of the hangar deck has been converted into a large-format film theater, which offers shows, not necessarily about the ship. Both the aquarium and the *Lexington* are open daily, with slightly longer hours during the summer season.

If you're in Corpus Christi during baseball season, you might want to check out the local minor league baseball team, called the **Corpus Christi Hooks** (✆ **361/866-TEAM** [866-8326]; www.cchooks.com). They are a AA farm club for the Houston Astros and play in the Texas League. Their ballpark, **Whataburger Field,** is the most attractive farm-club ballpark you'll ever see. It's at the water's edge, at the foot of the tall bridge, but on the south side (the same side as central Corpus Christi). Tickets run from $5 to $12. (Whataburger is a chain of fast-food restaurants, which began in Corpus and still keeps its corporate offices here.)

Outdoor Activities

Most visitors come to this area either for some relaxing beach time or for one of the many activities offered here, or both.

DOLPHIN AND WHOOPING CRANE CRUISES These tours are done in large shallow-draft boats that go out for 3 to 4 hours. Tours to see the whooping cranes run from November through March. Boats depart from the Fulton Harbor, which is in the Rockport area. Fulton is a township next to Rockport and it's difficult to tell where one town ends and the other begins. There are a number of small outfits, and they usually charge about $40 per person. The best thing to do is go down to the piers and inquire about which company might have a boat departing imminently.

FISHING Most visitors interested in fishing go to Port Aransas. There are several outfits and many guides. Go to **Woody's Sports Center** (✆ **361/749-5271;** www.gulfcoastfishing.com) at 136 W. Cotter, on the main pier of Port Aransas.

SEA KAYAKING There are several good places to explore by kayak in the bays surrounding Corpus Christi, and most are in the vicinity of Rockport. You might want to try **Rockport Kayak Outfitters** (✆ **361/729-1505**) at 106 S. Austin St. It offers rentals and tours. Tours require a minimum of four people, but you might be able to hook up with another group or do a self-guided tour on your own with a map provided by the store. The staff can haul you and your kayaks to a drop-off spot and pick you up later.

SURFING For surfing, you have to be on the barrier islands. Your easiest path is to go to **Pat Magee's Surf Shop** (✆ **361/749-4177**) at 124 Ave. G, in Port Aransas. Here you can rent a board and find out where the surfers go. The shop has vintage surfboards and old Hawaiian shirts for sale, too.

WINDSURFING The best place to learn windsurfing or hone your skills is in the sheltered water of the Laguna Madre, on North Padre Island, which is south of Mustang Island. Inside the Padre Island National Seashore, you'll find a small but well-known concessionaire called **Worldwinds Windsurfing** (✆ **361/949-7472;** www.worldwinds.net), which sells and rents windsurfing equipment and wet suits, and in summer, offers windsurfing lessons.

WHERE TO STAY

If you're staying in Corpus Christi and want a hotel with a view, inquire about a room in the Bayfront Tower of the **Omni Corpus Christi Hotel** (✆ **800/843-6664;** www.omnihotels.com) at 900 N. Shoreline Blvd. Rates run from $160 to $220 for a double, depending on the season and the day of the week.

Corpus Christi has a lovely bed and breakfast called the **George Blucher House** (✆ **866/884-4884;** www.georgeblucherhouse.com), at 211 N. Carrizo, in an old residential area close by the city's downtown. The location is good, and the rooms and the house in general have lots of character. Rates run from $120 to $190.

If you're looking for an inexpensive motel, there is a concentration of them in the vicinity of the Texas State Aquarium and USS *Lexington.* This is not a bad location for visitors. One inexpensive independent motel among the chain properties is the **Sea Shell Inn** (✆ **361/888-5291**) at 202 Kleberg Place, with rates for a double from $50 to $125.

In Rockport, the nicest full-service hotel is **The Lighthouse Inn** (✆ **866/790-8439;** www.lighthousetexas.com) at 200 S. Fulton Beach Rd. Rates run from $140 to $220 depending upon the season. A good bed and breakfast is **Hoope's House** (✆ **800/924-1008;** www.hoopeshouse.com), at 417 N. Broadway, where rates are $160 for a double.

In Port Aransas and all the barrier islands in this area, the predominant form of lodging is condo towers. These almost always rent by the week and advertise heavily on the

Internet. If you want hotel lodging, there's a great old hotel called **The Tarpon Inn** (✆ **800/365-6784;** www.thetarponinn.com) in Port Aransas at 200 E. Cotter. As this is an old place, the double rooms are awfully small but economical, at $69 to $99. The premium rooms are a substantial upgrade ($110–$130) and worth the extra money, but the suites ($145–$250), especially the FDR suite, have the style and size to warrant the extra money and are one of a kind.

For roomy, inexpensive lodging, try the **Balinese Flats** (✆ **888/951-6381;** www.balineseflats.com), at 121 Cut-off Rd., in Port Aransas. It offers 2-bedroom apartments for $75 in winter, $95 in spring and fall, and $155 in summer.

WHERE TO DINE

In downtown Corpus Christi, you can't go wrong with **Water Street Seafood Company** (✆ **361/882-8683**) at 309 N. Water St. It's easy to find and is very popular, but it's big enough that you usually don't have to wait long for a table. Good and cheap Tex-Mex can be had at **La Playa** (✆ **361/853-4282**), at 4201 S.P.I.D., which isn't as easy to find but is worth the extra trouble.

For Tex-Mex in Rockport, try **Los Comales** (✆ **361/729-3952**) at 431 Hwy. 35. It offers several kinds of enchiladas, which are all good. It also offers a few dishes from central Mexico, which is a bit surprising for being a small-town restaurant on the Texas coast. For sandwiches and pizzas in Rockport, head to **Tony Legner's Culinary Productions** (✆ **361/729-6395**), at 1003 E. Concho, in the middle of Rockport.

Port Aransas has plenty of good restaurants, and a favorite is **La Playa Mexican Grille** (✆ **361/749-0022**), at 222 Beach St., which has no connection with La Playa Restaurant in Corpus Christi. For something of a surprise for Port Aransas, there's **Venetian Hot Plate** (✆ **361/749-7617**), just down the way at 232 Beach St. The Italian owners care about food and care about wine. The menu has some wonderful northern Italian dishes.

Suggested Austin Itineraries

There is an old joke that circulates among Austinites about what to do with family and friends who come to town wanting to see the sights. Anytime someone mentions visitors, anyone present is supposed to ask "So when are you taking them to San Antonio?

It's not that Austin doesn't have places of interest; it just that most of these aren't sights in the traditional sense. A trip here is more about absorbing the atmosphere than it is about sight-seeing. Don't get me wrong, there are places to see, such as the State Capitol and the LBJ Library. And there are plenty of local activities to indulge in, such as swimming in Barton Springs and watching the bats take flight from the Congress Avenue Bridge, though both of those can usually only be enjoyed seasonally. The following itineraries should allow visitors to both take in the attractions and experience the laid-back Austin vibe. Day 1 hits all the biggest sights. Day 2 is more an exploration of city life—a day in the life of bohemian Austin, taken to its utopian extreme. During it, you'll hit some of the important centers of local culture. Day 3 gets you out of Austin to see some nearby towns, where you can enjoy a variety of activities.

But first, I'll describe the principal parts of town, where you'll find these attractions. For more information about navigating the city, see the "Getting Around" section of chapter 3.

NEIGHBORHOODS IN BRIEF

Although Austin, designed to be the capital of the independent Republic of Texas, has a planned, grand city center similar to that of Washington, D.C., the city has spread out far beyond those original boundaries. These days, with a few exceptions, detailed below, locals tend to speak in terms of landmarks (the University of Texas) or geographical areas (East Austin) rather than neighborhoods.

Downtown The original city, laid out by Edwin Waller in 1839, runs roughly north from the Colorado River. The river has been dammed in several places, forming a series of lakes. By downtown, it is called Lady Bird Lake. The first street on the north shore of Town Lake used to be called First Street, now it's called **Cesar Chavez Street.** Downtown extends north up to 11th Street, where the capitol building is. The main north–south street is **Congress Avenue.** It runs from the river to the capitol. Downtown's eastward limit is the I-35 freeway, and its westward limit is Lamar Boulevard. This is a prime sightseeing area (it includes the capitol and several historic districts), and a hotel area, with music clubs, restaurants, shops, and galleries. There are a lot of clubs on and around **Sixth Street,** just east of Congress, in the **Warehouse District,** centered on Third and Fourth streets just west of Congress, and in the **Red River District,** on (where else?) Red River, between 6th and 10th streets.

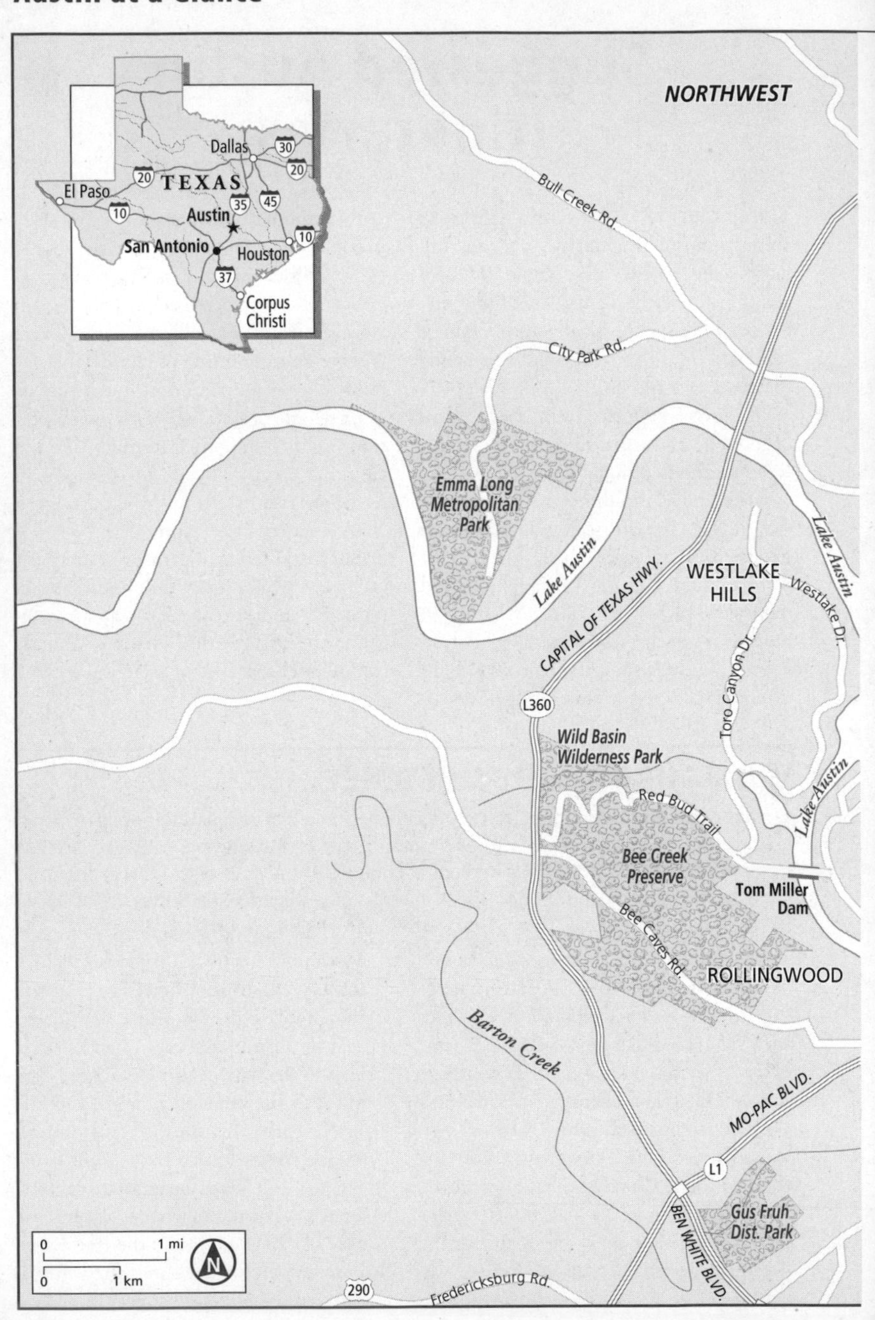
NORTHWEST
Dallas
30
20
20
TEXAS
El Paso
10
35
45
Austin
10
San Antonio
Houston
37
Corpus Christi
Bull Creek Rd.
City Park Rd.
Emma Long Metropolitan Park
Lake Austin
CAPITAL OF TEXAS HWY.
WESTLAKE HILLS
Westlake Dr.
Lake Austin
Toro Canyon Dr.
L360
Wild Basin Wilderness Park
Red Bud Trail
Lake Austin
Bee Creek Preserve
Tom Miller Dam
Bee Caves Rd.
ROLLINGWOOD
Barton Creek
MO-PAC BLVD.
L1
BEN WHITE BLVD.
Gus Fruh Dist. Park
0
1 mi
0
1 km
N
290
Fredericksburg Rd.

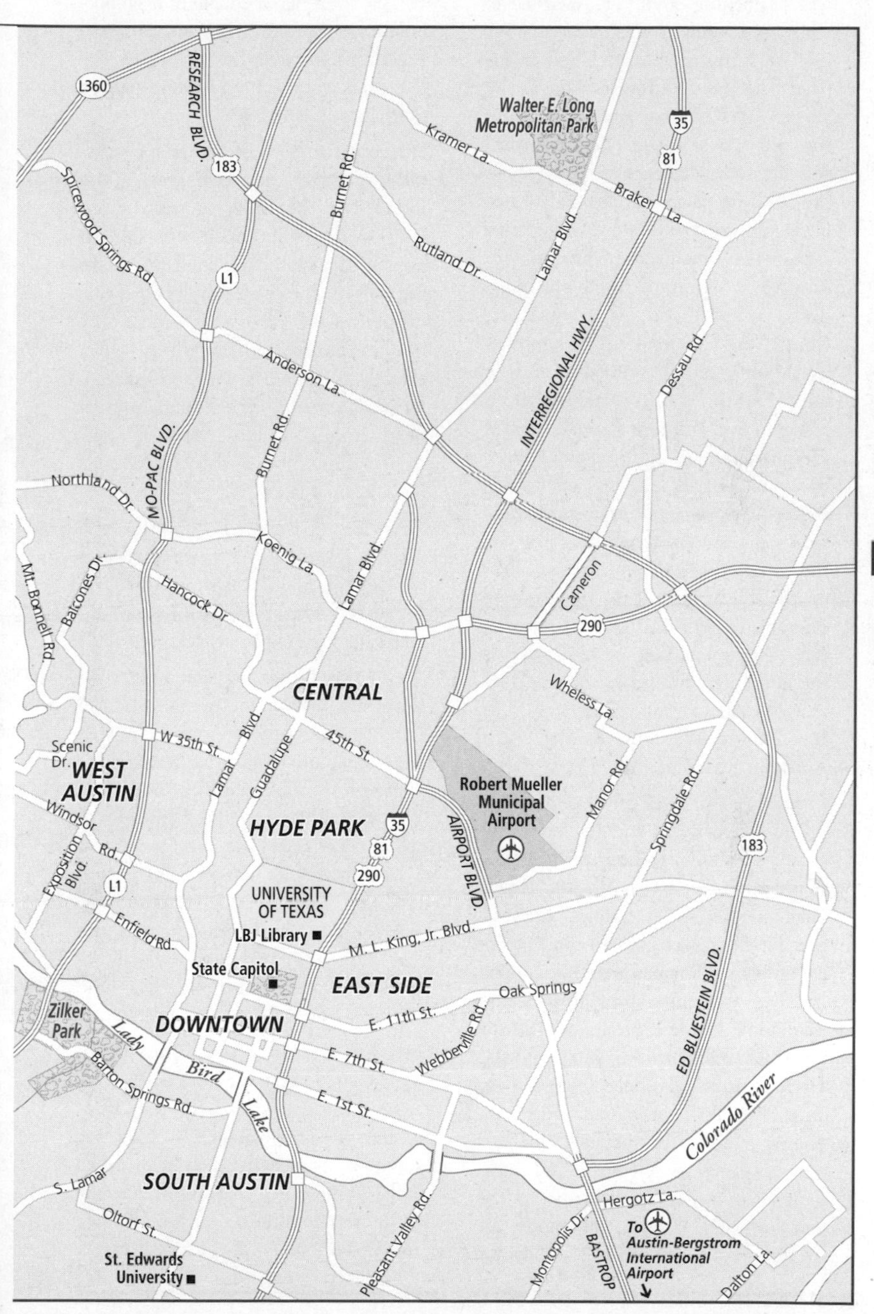

Walter E. Long Metropolitan Park
RESEARCH BLVD.
Kramer La.
Braker La.
Spicewood Springs Rd.
Burnet Rd.
Rutland Dr.
Lamar Blvd.
INTERREGIONAL HWY.
Dessau Rd.
Anderson La.
MO-PAC BLVD.
Northland Dr.
Koenig La.
Mt. Bonnell Rd.
Balcones Dr.
Hancock Dr.
Cameron
Wheless La.
CENTRAL
W 35th St.
45th St.
Scenic Dr.
WEST AUSTIN
Windsor Rd.
Lamar Blvd.
Guadalupe
Robert Mueller Municipal Airport
Manor Rd.
Springdale Rd.
HYDE PARK
AIRPORT BLVD.
Exposition Blvd.
UNIVERSITY OF TEXAS
LBJ Library
Enfield Rd.
M. L. King, Jr. Blvd.
State Capitol
EAST SIDE
Oak Springs
Zilker Park
DOWNTOWN
E. 11th St.
Webberville Rd.
Lady Bird Lake
E. 7th St.
Barton Springs Rd.
E. 1st St.
ED BLUESTEIN BLVD.
Colorado River
S. Lamar
SOUTH AUSTIN
Oltorf St.
Pleasant Valley Rd.
Hergotz La.
Montopolis Dr.
BASTROP
To Austin-Bergstrom International Airport
St. Edwards University
Dalton La.

South Austin For a long time, not a lot was happening south of Town Lake. This was largely a residential area—a mix of working class and bohemians lived here. **South Congress,** the sleepy stretch of Congress Avenue running through the middle of South Austin, was lined with cheap motels. Then, in the 1980s, it started taking off. The area became attractive to store and restaurant owners who liked the proximity to downtown without the high rents. Trendy shops moved into the old storefronts. Yuppies started buying houses in the adjoining neighborhoods. And now South Austin is one of the preferred places to live. **Fairview Park** and **Travis Heights,** adjoining neighborhoods between Congress and I-35, are perhaps the most popular. They were Austin's first settlements south of the river. At the end of the 19th century, the bluffs on the south shore of the river became desirable as Austin residents realized they were not as likely to be flooded as the lower areas on the north bank. Farther south and west, toward the Lady Bird Johnson Wildflower Center, south Austin begins to reassert its rural roots.

Central Austin This is a larger area that includes downtown and the university campus. It's not a precisely defined area. If you were to travel north from Town Lake through the downtown area and past the capitol, you would come across a complex of state government office buildings (btw. 15th and 19th sts.). Past that would be the UT campus (19th to 26th sts.). Farther north, you get to the **Hyde Park** neighborhood (35th to 51st sts.). Hyde Park got its start in 1891 as one of Austin's first planned suburbs; renovation of its Victorian and early Craftsman houses began in the 1970s, and now there's a real neighborhood feel to this pretty, tree-lined area. Beyond Hyde Park, numbered streets disappear. You pass through a couple of neighborhoods, and eventually you come to Research Boulevard. For a lot of Austinites, this is where central Austin ends and north Austin begins.

West Austin West of Lamar is **Clarksville,** formerly a black community founded in the 1870s by freed slaves. It's now a neighborhood of small, old houses that command high prices. To the west of Clarksville, on the other side of the Mo-Pac Freeway, is a more tony neighborhood called **Tarrytown,** which extends as far as Lake Austin (upstream from downtown, the Colorado river bends around in a more northerly direction, where another dam creates this long, narrow lake).

East Side East of I-35 are several neighborhoods, which are predominantly Hispanic and African American. Because it has a central location, this area is gentrifying at a quick pace.

West Lake The name denotes the townships that are on the opposite side of Lake Austin from West Austin. This is an affluent suburban area that includes the communities of **Rollingwood** and **Westlake Hills.** If you head upstream to the next dam, you come to Lake Travis, a large lake with lots of marinas and lakeside communities, such as **Lakeway.** But you don't have to live here to play here: This is also where those who live in Central Austin come to splash around and kick back on nice weekends.

Northwest This is where most of the high-tech industry is located. It is largely suburban. It includes the Arboretum, a large mall and surrounding shopping area, and a new mall called The Domain. Farther north are the bedroom communities of Round Rock and Cedar Park.

1 THE BEST OF AUSTIN IN 1 DAY

Between March and November, the bats will be in town. If you're here at the cusp of one of those months, call the Bat Hotline to check and to get the estimated time that they take flight. See p. 220. ***Note:*** This itinerary requires a car.

❶ LBJ Library and Museum ★

If you're in town for just a short time, visiting the LBJ Library may afford you the best view of campus that you'll get. From the stone platform, you can see the campus to the west of you sloping down the hill and then rising up on the next one. There's no mistaking the well-known University Tower. Inside the library, you'll find all the former president's papers bound neatly in red cordovan leather. But it's the museum you'll really want to head toward. Be sure not to miss the animatronic version of LBJ. See p. 225.

❷ Blanton Museum of Art ★

The new Blanton has a gracious interior and a good bit of space to show its works. Of its holdings, the Latin American art is probably the most fun, and the Renaissance collection is probably the most important. There might also be a visiting show. See p. 219.

❸ Bob Bullock Texas State History Museum ★

This museum was built more with Texans in mind than out-of-staters. Outsiders are welcome, but the museum does delve into some Texas history minutiae that might not be so interesting to others. The exhibits are beautifully done, and some have a sense of humor. There are a lot of choices to consider at the ticket booth: exhibits, IMAX, the Texas Spirit Theater. You might have time to do all of them if you haven't lollygagged at the earlier stops. The combo ticket package includes a decent discount, and the Texas Spirit Theater, with its multiculturalist message, doesn't take long to see. See p. 219.

South of the Bob Bullock Museum, and so obvious that you can't miss it, is the:

❹ State Capitol ★★

This is fun for everyone. The biggest capitol building in the 50 states has seen a lot of shenanigans. Take the guided tour, which is free and is more interesting than the self-guided tour. See p. 224.

TAKE A BREAK

Step into this delightful Congress Avenue restaurant, **The Roaring Fork,** on the ground floor of the old Stephen F. Austin Hotel (now the InterContinental). Lunches are hearty and reasonably priced. 701 Congress Ave. ✆ **512/583-0000.** See p. 200.

❺ Lady Bird Johnson Wildflower Center ★★★

You can end up spending a lot more time here than you planned, especially if you come in the spring when most of the wildflowers are in bloom. Watch the clock to ensure that you're back in town in time to catch the next (and last) stop on this itinerary. There are some attractions indoors worth your attention, and don't miss the gift shop. See p. 225.

❻ Evening Bat Flight

When the largest urban bat colony in North America takes wing out from under downtown's Congress Avenue Bridge, it's an impressive act of nature. Call the Bat Hotline (✆ **512/416-5700,** ext. 3636) for the daily estimated flight time. If you arrive early, get a space on the east side of the bridge close by the southern bank of Town Lake. You should also check out the information module set up by Bat Conservation International; it explains something about the habits and life of a bat colony. See p. 220.

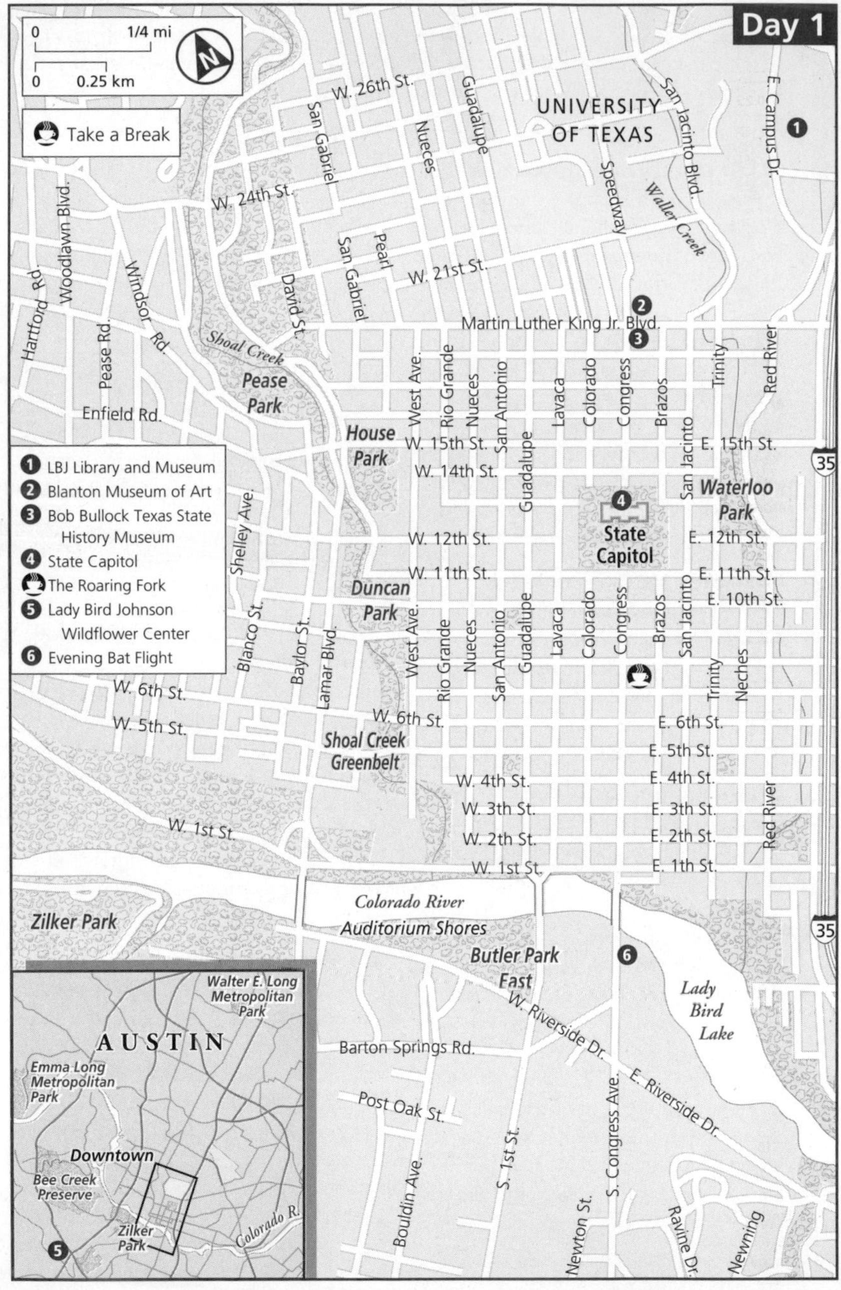
Day 1
0 1/4 mi
0 0.25 km
N
Take a Break
1 LBJ Library and Museum
2 Blanton Museum of Art
3 Bob Bullock Texas State History Museum
4 State Capitol
The Roaring Fork
5 Lady Bird Johnson Wildflower Center
6 Evening Bat Flight
UNIVERSITY OF TEXAS
W. 26th St.
W. 24th St.
W. 21st St.
Martin Luther King Jr. Blvd.
San Gabriel
Nueces
Guadalupe
Pearl
Speedway
San Jacinto Blvd.
E. Campus Dr.
Waller Creek
Woodlawn Blvd.
Hartford Rd.
Windsor Rd.
Pease Rd.
David St.
Shoal Creek
Pease Park
Enfield Rd.
House Park
W. 15th St.
W. 14th St.
West Ave.
Rio Grande
San Antonio
Lavaca
Colorado
Congress
Brazos
San Jacinto
Trinity
Red River
E. 15th St.
Waterloo Park
State Capitol
W. 12th St.
W. 11th St.
E. 12th St.
E. 11th St.
E. 10th St.
Shelley Ave.
Duncan Park
Blanco St.
Baylor St.
Lamar Blvd.
Neches
W. 6th St.
W. 5th St.
E. 6th St.
E. 5th St.
E. 4th St.
E. 3th St.
E. 2th St.
E. 1th St.
Shoal Creek Greenbelt
W. 4th St.
W. 3th St.
W. 2th St.
W. 1st St.
35
Colorado River
Zilker Park
Auditorium Shores
Butler Park East
W. Riverside Dr.
E. Riverside Dr.
Lady Bird Lake
Barton Springs Rd.
Post Oak St.
Bouldin Ave.
S. 1st St.
S. Congress Ave.
Newton St.
Ravine Dr.
Newning
AUSTIN
Walter E. Long Metropolitan Park
Emma Long Metropolitan Park
Downtown
Bee Creek Preserve
Zilker Park
Colorado R.

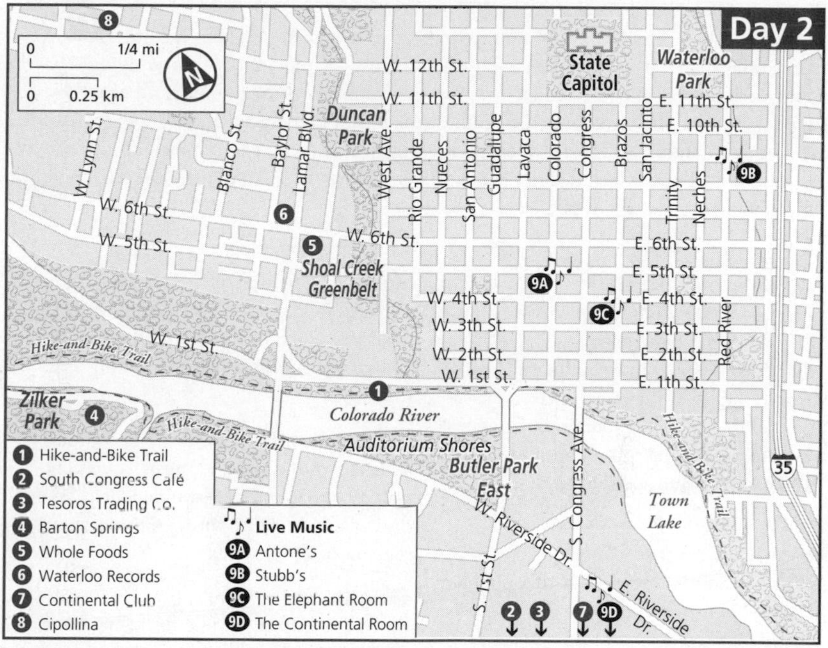
Day 2
0 1/4 mi
0 0.25 km
N
W. 12th St.
W. 11th St.
State Capitol
Waterloo Park
E. 11th St.
E. 10th St.
Duncan Park
W. Lynn St.
Blanco St.
Baylor St.
Lamar Blvd.
West Ave.
Rio Grande
Nueces
San Antonio
Guadalupe
Lavaca
Colorado
Congress
Brazos
San Jacinto
Trinity
Neches
W. 6th St.
W. 5th St.
W. 6th St.
Shoal Creek Greenbelt
E. 6th St.
E. 5th St.
W. 4th St.
E. 4th St.
W. 3th St.
E. 3th St.
W. 2th St.
E. 2th St.
W. 1st St.
E. 1th St.
Red River
W. 1st St.
Hike-and-Bike Trail
Zilker Park
Colorado River
Hike-and-Bike Trail
Auditorium Shores
Butler Park East
S. Congress Ave.
Hike-and-Bike Trail
Town Lake
35
W. Riverside Dr.
S. 1st St.
E. Riverside Dr.
1 Hike-and-Bike Trail
2 South Congress Café
3 Tesoros Trading Co.
4 Barton Springs
5 Whole Foods
6 Waterloo Records
7 Continental Club
8 Cipollina
Live Music
9A Antone's
9B Stubb's
9C The Elephant Room
9D The Continental Room

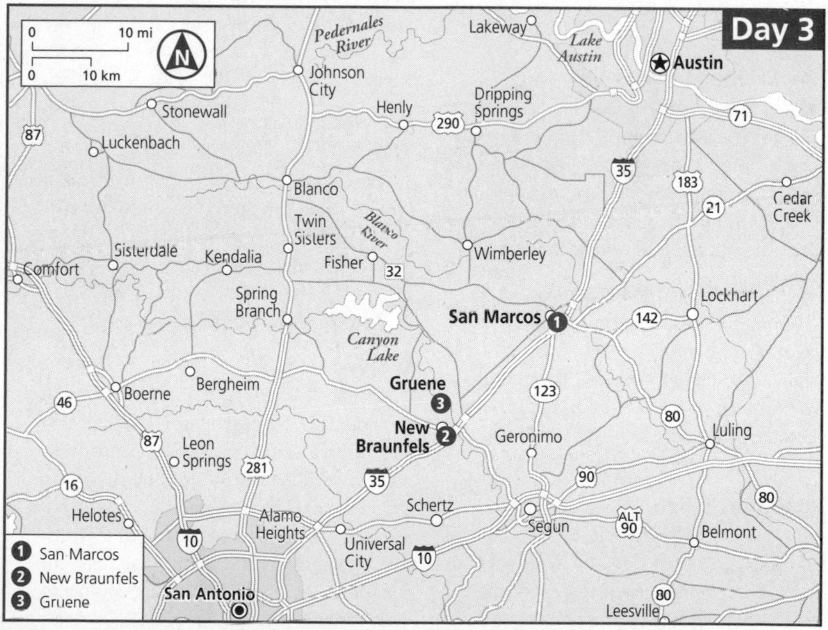
Day 3
0 10 mi
0 10 km
N
Pedernales River
Lakeway
Lake Austin
Austin
Johnson City
Stonewall
Henly
290
Dripping Springs
71
87
Luckenbach
35
183
Blanco
21
Cedar Creek
Twin Sisters
Blanco River
Sisterdale
Kendalia
Fisher
32
Wimberley
Comfort
Spring Branch
Lockhart
San Marcos
142
Canyon Lake
Gruene
123
46
Boerne
Bergheim
80
New Braunfels
Geronimo
Luling
87
Leon Springs
281
35
90
16
Schertz
80
Helotes
Alamo Heights
Segun
ALT 90
Belmont
10
Universal City
10
San Antonio
80
Leesville
1 San Marcos
2 New Braunfels
3 Gruene

2 THE BEST OF AUSTIN IN 2 DAYS

Think of this itinerary as a cultural exploration. The idea is less about accomplishing a set of tasks than it is about blending into Austin's easy-going culture. This trip should be done in midweek, otherwise you'll have to work your way through the crowd of workaday wage slaves who only come out on the weekends. I've included a lot of stops to give you options. Should you linger at one place longer than most, you can pick up the trail as you see fit. I've not included any places to take a break because, in practice, this whole day amounts to taking a break.

❶ Hike-and-Bike Trail

The first activity is a leisurely stroll along the hike-and-bike trail (unless you're a late riser, in which case move on to the second activity). One of the most interesting sections of the path is the loop from Congress Avenue west to the pedestrian bridge next to the Lamar Bridge. See p. 244.

Walk up South Congress a few blocks to:

❷ South Congress Cafe

Walk up South Congress to this popular brunch spot, where you can enjoy a local favorite—*migas*—or try something out of the ordinary, such as the wild boar *pozole*. See p. 208.

Stroll back a block towards downtown to:

❸ Tesoros Trading Co.

Tesoros is a large import business that carries a huge variety of things large and small. You don't have to buy anything; just enjoy the showroom's unique mix of ethno-crafts and ethno-kitsch. See p. 257.

❹ Barton Springs Pool

By now, if it's gotten warm enough, it's time to relax at Barton Springs. A lot of folks show up at night in summer to cool off for free, but why not enjoy it during the hottest hours of the day? Catch some rays, cool off in the water, repeat. See p. 224.

❺ Whole Foods

Explore the flagship store of the chain of natural and organic foods. Whole Foods sells a lot besides food. It's also a great place to have a light lunch, as you can browse through all the steam tables and prepared food counters and pick up exactly what you want in just the right amount. There's a pretty little outdoor seating area, too. See p. 258.

❻ Waterloo Records

This is Austin's favorite music store. The staff is knowledgeable and can help you find what you didn't know you were missing. See p. 261.

❼ Continental Club

By now it should be time for happy hour, and if reading the entertainment section of the paper didn't provide any guidance, make the Continental Club your default choice. Sometimes you get really lucky. See p. 272.

❽ Cipollina

This little neighborhood bistro in the Clarksville area buys all it can from local growers and producers. It even does its own butchering and curing. The pasta, too, is all made in-house. If you don't want a formal dinner, try one of their small pizzas, with unusual toppings. See p. 210.

❾ Live Music

This stop is where your morning research should really be paying off. The clubs to pay special attention to are Antone's, Stubb's, the Elephant Room, and the Saxon Pub. Alternatively, you can decide to stroll through the downtown entertainment districts looking for the music that fits your taste. The entire area is compact enough to walk through it easily. See p. 269.

3 THE BEST OF AUSTIN IN 3 DAYS

The three towns on the following itinerary provide opportunities for any number of activities—strolling a town square, canoeing, shopping for discounts at outlet malls, visiting a water park, and even tubing on the Guadalupe River. If tubing strikes your fancy, the day trip is usually best done in the late spring to early summer when the water in the lower Guadalupe is flowing fast and deep enough so you don't have to paddle and you won't scrape your backside on the rocks. If you have kids, they will enjoy Schlitterbahn, an extremely large water park that counts many faithful among central Texas's youth. ***Start:*** Head south from Austin on I-35.

❶ San Marcos

Thirty miles south of Austin is San Marcos, a college town that some are calling the new Austin. San Marcos has a nicely restored courthouse and town square, making it a nice stop for stretching your legs. If you're looking for a more active endeavor, San Marcos is a great place for canoeing. Ask at the Aquarena Center (1 Aquarena Springs Dr.; ✆ **512/245-7575;** www.aquarena.txstate.edu) for outfitters renting canoes. Just past San Marcos on the Interstate are two outlet malls, Prime Outlets (✆ **800/628-9465** or 512/396-2200) and Tanger Factory Outlet Center (✆ **800/408-8424** or 512/396-7446), which boast hundreds of name brand stores and attract a lot of visitors. See p. 281.

Continue south on I-35 to reach:

❷ New Braunfels

When you get to New Braunfels, drive through the center of town. It still has a good deal of small-town feel about it, despite the town having grown considerably in the last few years. New Braunfels is home to the Schlitterbahn water park, a great destination for families looking to get wet. If you'd rather do your cooling off in a less hectic environment, head to nearby Gruene (now practically a suburb of New Braunfels), the next (and last) stop on the itinerary. See p. 159.

❸ Gruene

Gruene (pronounced *green*) is upstream from New Braunfels and is the lower end of the long stretch of the Guadalupe River. For many locals, it's a favorite spot for tubing. Drive up River Road, and you'll see one outfitter after another renting inner tubes. Rent one, and then plunk down into the refreshing Guadalupe. You'll see what all the fuss is about. See p. 160.

TAKE A BREAK

After tubing and changing clothes, you can grab a bite to eat at the traditional Texas **Gristmill River Restaurant & Bar,** 1287 Gruene Rd. (✆ **830/625-0684**). See p. 163.

12 Where to Stay in Austin

Unlike San Antonio, Austin doesn't have a large stock of downtown hotel rooms dependent on large conventions, so it can sometimes be difficult to find a discounted room downtown. In slack times, the properties at the margins of the city feel the pinch; but the central properties don't, because normal business and leisure travel can fill most of their rooms. When you look on the Internet for bargains, you're more often than not pointed toward properties in the southeast corner of the city, near the intersection of I-35 and Hwy. 71, where a large number of hotels sit. This location is not a good choice for exploring the city because traffic is often heavy in that area, but the difference in rates may be too good to pass up.

Of course, in this sort of situation the market is supposed to add to the supply of downtown hotel rooms. And, in 2007, there were, in fact, eight new hotels in the works; but with the credit crisis continuing beyond 2008 and into 2009, all but one have been stalled. That one, a W hotel and residence property, has slowed down construction.

In looking for discounts, keep in mind the calendars of the state legislature and the University of Texas. Lawmakers and lobbyists converge on the capital from January through May of odd-numbered years, so you can expect tighter bookings. The beginning of fall term, graduation week, and football weekends—UT's football stadium now seats 98,000—draw thousands of out-of-towners.

The busiest season, however, is the month of March, when the South by Southwest (SXSW) music festival fills entire hotels. It is designed to coincide with UT's spring break, usually the third week of the month. SXSW is the largest gathering of the year for the music industry. It attracts more than a hundred bands from all over the world trying to get record deals, thousands of music fans, and lots of producers and music company execs. And now there's a film and media festival the week before the music begins. To make matters worse, Austin often hosts regional playoffs for NCAA basketball, and the university likes to take advantage of spring break by hosting academic conferences. So, especially try to avoid a perfect storm of booking nightmares: the March of an odd-numbered year when UT's basketball team is in the regionals. Of course, there are a few other spots in the calendar when the city is busier than usual, such as in late September for the Austin City Limits Music Festival. This festival has caught on in a big way and attracts thousands now.

You'll get a far better feel for what makes Austin special if you stay somewhere in central Austin. The verdant Town Lake area includes both downtown, near the capitol, and the resurgent South Congress area. The areas near the University of Texas, including west campus and the Hyde Park neighborhood, are ideal for those willing to trade some modern perks for hominess and character. Those with a penchant for playing on the water or putting around should consider holing up near the lakes and golf courses to the west.

Austin has some glitzy high-rises but only a few historic hotels; so if it's character you're after, you should opt for a B&B. For an Austin B&B that belongs to Hospitality Accommodations of Texas, check the website at www.hat.org or contact the organization at P.O. Box 139, Fredericksburg, TX 78624 (✆ **800/HAT-0368**).

Most hotels catering to business travelers offer weekend discounts and, of course, corporate discounts. In the last couple of years, weekend discounts have not been common for the downtown hotels, but that might change with the slowdown in discretionary travel. You'll find lots of Austin room deals on the Internet (see chapter 3), but don't stop there. Be sure to phone and ask about packages—which might include such extras as breakfast or champagne—and reduced rates for senior citizens, families, active-duty military personnel . . . whatever you can think of. Call the toll-free number and the hotel itself, because sometimes the central reservation agent doesn't know about local deals. Sure, calling is not as impersonal as the Internet, but don't be afraid of being a pain if the deal is worth it.

Speaking of which, please note that rates listed below do not include the city's 15% hotel sales tax.

Wherever you bunk in Austin, it is safe to expect air-conditioning and Internet connections. Even B&B rooms offer high-speed wireless Internet connections these days, and many hotels also offer WebTV, enabling you to retrieve e-mail and cruise the Internet via the tube.

1 BEST AUSTIN HOTEL BETS

- **Best for Conducting Business:** Located near a lot of the high-tech companies in northwest Austin, the **Renaissance Austin Hotel,** 9721 Arboretum Blvd. (✆ **800/HOTELS-1** [468-3571] or 512/343-2626), has top-notch meeting and schmoozing spaces, not to mention fine close-the-deal-and-party spots. See p. 189.
- **Best Place to Play Cattle Baron:** If you want to imagine you've acquired your fortune in an earlier era, bed down at **The Driskill,** 604 Brazos St. (✆ **800/252-9367** or 512/474-5911), where big meat mogul Jesse Driskill still surveys (via stone image) the opulent 1886 hotel that bears his name. See p. 180.
- **Hippest Budget Hotel:** Look for the classic neon sign for the **Austin Motel,** 1220 S. Congress St. (✆ **512/441-1157**), in Austin's cool SoCo district. The rooms have been individually furnished, many in fun and funky styles, but the place retains its 1950s character and its retro prices. See p. 186.
- **Best New Arrival: Hotel Saint Cecilia,** 112 Academy Dr. (✆ **512/852-2400**), is a small one-of-a-kind hotel in the heart of SoCo. It has beautiful rooms, beautiful grounds, and amenities like no hotel in Austin, including mattresses as if made by Swedish elves. See p. 185.
- **Best View of Town Lake:** Lots of downtown properties have nice water views, but the **Hyatt Regency's** location, 208 Barton Springs Rd. (✆ **800/233-1234** or 512/477-1234), on the lake's south shore gives it the edge. You get a panoramic spread of the city with the capitol as a backdrop. See p. 182.
- **Best Place to Tee Off:** Austin isn't a major destination for duffers, but you'd never know it if you stay at **Barton Creek Resort,** 8212 Barton Club Dr. (✆ **800/336-6158** or 512/329-4000), featuring courses designed by a pantheon of golf greats—two by Tom Fazio, one by Ben Crenshaw, and one by Arnold Palmer—plus a golf school run by Austinite Chuck Cook. See p. 192.
- **Greenest Hotel:** Several hotels in Austin take ecoconsciousness beyond the old "we won't wash your towels" option, but no one takes it nearly as far as **Habitat Suites,** 500 E. Highland Mall Blvd. (✆ **800/535-4663** or 512/467-6000). Almost everything here is ecofriendly. See p. 188.

- **Best for Forgetting Your Troubles:** Stress? That's a dirty word at the **Lake Austin Spa Resort,** 1705 S. Quinlan Park Rd. (✆ **800/847-5637** or 512/372-7300). After a few days at this lovely, ultrarelaxing spot, you'll be ready to face the world again, even if you don't especially want to. See p. 193.

2 DOWNTOWN

VERY EXPENSIVE

The Driskill ★★★ Opened in 1886, the Driskill is Austin's original grand hotel. This national historic landmark has seen its share of history. Lyndon Johnson both managed the final days of his presidential campaign and received the election results here. The Daughters of the Republic of Texas, the saviors of the Alamo, met here to agree on their plan of action. It was here, too, that the Texas Rangers plotted their ambush on Bonnie and Clyde. Indeed, all kinds of plots have been hatched here.

Over time, the hotel has weathered ups and downs. Right now it's living a golden age. A hugely expensive renovation project put the "grand" back into the hotel. All the public areas have been refurbished to give them an impressive old-and-expensive look. Off the lobby, you'll find the **1886 Café;** the **Driskill Grill,** for fine dining (see review, p. 199); and a cushy piano bar (p. 276); plus a small but well-equipped spa.

The Driskill offers guests a choice between rooms in the original 1886 building (labeled "historic") or in the 1928 addition ("traditional"); the latter are the better deal, especially those on the 12th floor, which have higher ceilings. Rooms are well lit, distinctively decorated, and furnished with period pieces. Bathrooms in many rooms are on the small side but are sleek and attractive and come with several amenities, including plush bathrobes. This hotel is on Austin's lively Sixth Street, and some of the "historic" rooms with balconies can catch street noise. Also, some of the "traditional" king rooms are small. In 2008, the Driskill spent $4 million to refurnish the rooms, including replacing all mattresses and installing flatscreen televisions. In this same year, it was awarded the Five Dog Bone Award for pet-friendliness by the readers of *Animal Fair* magazine. The hotel has only a handful of smoking rooms.

604 Brazos St. (at E. Sixth St.), Austin, TX 78701. ✆ **800/252-9367** or 512/474-5911. Fax 512/474-2214. www.driskillhotel.com. 188 units. $250–$340 double; suites from $465. AE, DC, DISC, MC, V. Valet parking $25. Pets under 25 lb. accepted with $50 fee per pet per stay. **Amenities:** 2 restaurants; bar; health club; spa; concierge; business center; 24-hr. room service; laundry service; dry cleaning. *In room:* A/C, TV w/pay movies, free Wi-Fi, hair dryer, safe.

Four Seasons Austin ★★★ (Kids This member of the well-known luxury chain has an ideal location on the north shore of Town Lake, with great views and close proximity to all the downtown hot spots. Large, comfortable rooms; an excellent spa; beautifully manicured grounds; and direct access to Austin's Hike and Bike Trail are just a few reasons for staying here. And, of course, there's the famous Four Seasons service, which sets this hotel apart from all others. No place in Austin can make life easier.

The look of the place is part modern, part traditional, and part Texas. Polished stone floors, with plush area rugs, deep easy chairs and sofas, and a smattering of Western art form a seamless blend in muted tones. It's a look that has much in common with many other luxury hotels I've seen. These hotels obviously know the tastes of their clientele, but to my eye, the interiors lacks character. The guest rooms have the same plush and

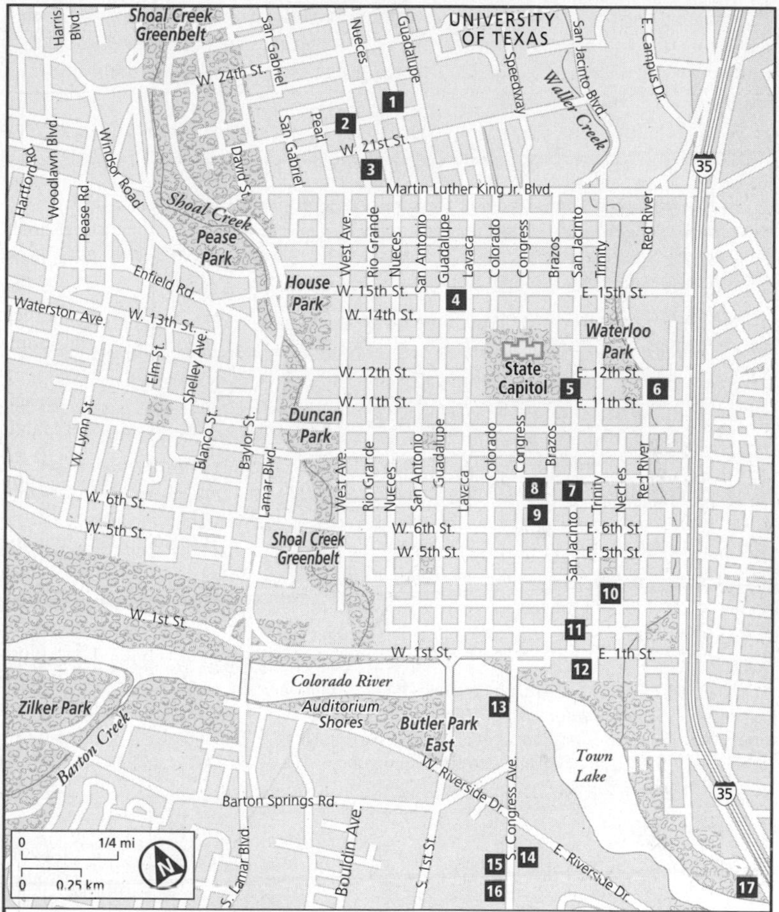

- Austin Folk House **1**
- Austin Motel **15**
- Doubletree Guest Suites Austin **4**
- The Driskill **9**
- Four Seasons Austin **12**
- Hampton Inn & Suites Austin-Downtown **11**
- Hilton Austin **10**
- Holiday Inn Austin Town Lake **17**
- Hotel Saint Cecilia **14**
- Hotel San José **16**
- Hyatt Regency Austin on Town Lake **13**
- InterContinental Stephen F. Austin **8**
- La Quinta Inn-Capitol **5**
- Mansion at Judges Hill **3**
- Omni Austin **7**
- Sheraton Austin **6**
- Star of Texas Inn **2**

conservative feel. The city views are fine, but the ones of the lake are finer still. You can choose between rooms with balconies and rooms without.

If you're traveling with toddlers, the staff can provide such necessary gear as strollers and baby seats; and there are plenty of weekend activities. Older kids can enjoy complimentary treats, such as popcorn and soda or milk and cookies, if you notify the hotel when you make your reservations.

98 San Jacinto Blvd. (at First/Cesar Chavez St.), Austin, TX 78701. ✆ **800/332-3442** or 512/478-4500. Fax 512/478-3117. www.fourseasons.com/austin. 291 units. $320–$480 double; suites from $570. Lower rates Sat–Sun; spa packages available. AE, DC, DISC, MC, V. Valet parking $25. Pets no taller than 12–15 inches accepted; advance notice to reservations department required. **Amenities:** Restaurant; bar; outdoor heated saltwater pool; health club; spa; concierge; tours; car-rental desk; town car; business center; 24-hr. room service; in-room massage; laundry service; dry cleaning. *In room:* A/C, TV/DVD player w/pay movies, Wi-Fi, minibar, coffeemaker, hair dryer, iron, safe.

Hyatt Regency Austin on Town Lake ★★ Austin's Hyatt Regency brings the outdoors indoors, with its signature atrium lobby anchored by a Hill Country tableau of a limestone-banked flowing stream, waterfalls, and oak trees. It's impressive. The hotel sits on Town Lake's south shore (strictly speaking, this is South Austin, but its size and feel are downtown traits). The north-facing rooms have lake vistas with the downtown skyscrapers as a backdrop. The wealth of outdoor recreation opportunities makes this hotel a good choice. Bat tours and other Town Lake excursions depart from a private dock, where you can also rent paddle boats and canoes. In addition, guests can rent mountain bikes to ride on the hike-and-bike trail outside the door. Rooms have recently been remodeled. They have good beds and a comfortable, modern-functional look that seems geared more to the business traveler. Rooms on higher floors facing Town Lake are the most coveted.

208 Barton Springs Rd. (at S. Congress), Austin, TX 78704. ✆ **800/233-1234** or 512/477-1234. Fax 512/480-2069. http://austin.hyatt.com. 446 units. $199–$314 double; $450–$650 suite. Sat–Sun specials, corporate, and government rates available. AE, DC, DISC, MC, V. Self-parking $12; valet parking $18. **Amenities:** Restaurant; bar; outdoor pool; health club; Jacuzzi; bike rentals; business center; room service; laundry service; dry cleaning; club-level rooms. *In room:* A/C, TV, Wi-Fi and high-speed Internet access, coffeemaker, hair dryer, iron.

EXPENSIVE

Doubletree Guest Suites Austin ★ Value Kids If you're not going to be by the lake, you might as well be by the capitol. This hotel is one of the most comfortable places to stay in the downtown area and a favorite with lobbyists and state contractors. Standard one-bedroom suites are oversize and a great bargain for the price. Many come with balconies. The two-bedroom suites all have balconies and are only $80 dollars more. Many rooms have a capitol view. Full-sized appliances with all the requisite cookware allow guests to prepare meals in comfort. And, unlike kitchens in many all-suite hotels, the ones here are separate—you don't have to stare at dirty dishes after you eat. (The housekeepers wash them every day, regardless.) These suites with kitchens appeal to families with mouths to feed; the sturdy and practical way the rooms are furnished and decorated seems particularly apt for people with younger kids.

303 W. 15th St. (at Guadalupe), Austin, TX 78701. ✆ **800/222-TREE** [222-8733] or 512/478-7000. Fax 512/478-3562. www.doubletree.com. 189 units. 1-bedroom suite $179–$229; 2-bedroom suite $239–$319. Corporate, extended-stay, Internet, and other discounts available. Children under age 18 stay free in parent's room. AE, DC, DISC, MC, V. Self-parking $12; valet parking $18. Pets less than 25 lb. accepted for $25 per day. **Amenities:** Restaurant; outdoor pool; health club; Jacuzzi; sauna; concierge; business

center; secretarial services; Wi-Fi in public areas; room service; laundry service; dry cleaning; coin-op laundry. *In room:* A/C, TV w/pay movies, Wi-Fi, full-size kitchen, hair dryer, iron.

Hampton Inn & Suites Austin-Downtown Value Opened in 2003, this conventioneer hotel is definitely a cut above cookie-cutter. The attractive and comfortable rooms are done in clean-lined Western style with wood headboards, polished stone floors, and wrought-iron curtain rods. The generous hot-breakfast buffet is included in the room rate. And how many hotels, even upscale ones, offer room service from P.F. Chang's and Fleming's? Other perks include free local phone calls and no surcharge for using a calling card, as well as a coin-op laundry. The location, a block from the convention center and close to all of downtown's sights, restaurants, and nightlife, is hard to beat.

200 San Jacinto Blvd. (at Second St.), Austin, TX 78701. ✆ **800/560-7809** or 512/472-1500. Fax 512/472-8900. www.hamptoninn.com. 209 units. $179–$249 double. Corporate, AAA discounts available. Children under 18 stay free in parent's room; rates include breakfast buffet and happy hour (Mon–Thurs). AE, DC, DISC, MC, V. Valet (only) parking $14. **Amenities:** Heated outdoor pool; fitness room; business center; room service; coin-op laundry. *In room:* AC, TV, Wi-Fi, minifridge, coffeemaker, hair dryer, iron.

Hilton Austin This recently built hotel directly across from the convention center fills up with conventiongoers when a convention is in town but gives discounts when this is not the case. Despite being relatively new, the hotel is already refreshing the rooms with new paint jobs and carpets—a good sign that the property is being kept up. The new paint and carpeting also add a bit of character to what is admittedly fairly bland decor. Regular rooms are a tad small. Bathrooms are okay for the price category and offer plenty of amenities. When considering this hotel, remember that it's a convention hotel 1 block off of Sixth Street, which means that you might hear some partying going on in the room next door or out on the street. There is a $10 charge for using the hotel's health club and about as much again for high-speed Internet access (a common charge in a lot of business hotels).

500 E. Fourth St., Austin, TX 78701. ✆ **800/HILTONS** or 512/482-8000. Fax 512/486-0078. www.hilton.com. 447 units. $189–$384 double; suites from $550. Weekend and online specials. AE, DC, DISC, MC, V. Valet parking $25, self-parking $16. **Amenities:** 2 restaurants; bar; coffee shop; heated outdoor pool; health club; business center; room service; laundry service; dry cleaning. *In room*: A/C, TV w/pay movies, Wi-Fi and high-speed Internet access, minibar, coffeemaker, hair dryer, iron, safe.

InterContinental Stephen F. Austin ★ Built in 1924 to compete with the Driskill (see above) a block away, the Stephen F. Austin was another favorite power center for state legislators, along with such celebrities as Babe Ruth and Frank Sinatra. Closed in 1987 and reopened in 2000 after being gutted and rebuilt from the ground up, the hotel is once again welcoming movers and shakers. Most of its clientele are business travelers, and the InterContinental offers a lot of amenities aimed at this market.

The public areas are elegant, if not quite as grand as those in the Driskill. The guest rooms are simply furnished but comfortable. Reserve a deluxe room as the standards are small. Luxe amenities include down duvets, alarm clock/CD players, in-room safes large enough to fit a laptop, and every type of in-room business perk that you could want, including ergonomic chairs. Corner suites are large and not much more pricey than deluxe rooms. Two other assets: **Stephen F's Bar and Terrace,** with great views of Congress Avenue and the capitol, and the excellent **Roaring Fork** restaurant (p. 200).

701 Congress Ave. (at E. Seventh St.), Austin, TX 78701. ✆ **800/327-0200** or 512/457-8800. Fax 512/457-8896. www.intercontinental.com. 189 units. $169–$329; suites from $399. Weekend and Internet discounts. AE, DC, DISC, MC, V. Valet (only) parking $27. **Amenities:** 2 restaurants; bar; indoor pool; health club; spa; concierge; business center; 24-hr. room service; dry cleaning; club-level rooms. *In room:* A/C, TV w/pay movies, Wi-Fi and high-speed Internet access, minibar, hair dryer, iron, safe.

Omni Austin Part of the posh Austin Center office and retail complex, the Omni's 200-foot rise of sun-struck glass and steel leaves you feeling simultaneously dwarfed and exhilarated. Rooms are far less overwhelming; they're not especially large, and ceilings tend to be low. But they're comfortable enough and well equipped. If you need to hole up for a while and your company is footing the bill, your best bet is one of the condominium rooms—studio efficiencies with full kitchens, walk-in closets, and jetted tubs. I especially like the Omni's rooftop pool, sun deck, and Jacuzzi (with terrific city views), which are a big part of the hotel's attraction. The hotel's Get Fit program gives you incentive to exercise, offering free fitness kits and healthy snacks; for $25, a treadmill will be brought to your room (inducement to leave or stay? Only you can say . . .).

700 San Jacinto Blvd. (at E. Eighth St.), Austin, TX 78701. ✆ **800/THE-OMNI** [843-6664] or 512/476-3700. Fax 512/320-5882. www.omnihotels.com. 375 units. $239–$279 double; $299–$389 suite. AE, DC, DISC, MC, V. Self-parking $16; valet parking $25. Pets up to 50 lb. accepted with $50 nonrefundable deposit (pet menu available). **Amenities:** Restaurant; bar; heated outdoor pool; health club; Jacuzzi; sauna; car-rental desk; business center; secretarial services; Wi-Fi in public areas; shopping arcade; salon; room service; dry cleaning; club-level rooms. *In room:* A/C, TV w/pay movies, Wi-Fi, minibar, hair dryer, iron.

Sheraton Austin For those who want to be downtown but within easy walking distance of the University of Texas, this is a good pick. Just 4 blocks from the capitol, the hotel mainly targets business travelers. In addition to business amenities, it offers a relaxed, comfortable atmosphere with some attractive common areas, especially the outdoor terrace area and a well-designed indoor/outdoor pool complex. The glass walls of the atrium give the hotel's public areas good light and an open, airy feel. The guest rooms, though without much character, are large and attractive. If you can, get a room with a view of the capitol building. This hotel has nonsmoking rooms.

701 E. 11th St. (at Red River), Austin, TX 78701. ✆ **800/325-3535** or 512/478-1111. Fax 512/478-3700. www.starwoodhotels.com. 365 units. $199–$289 double; suites from $350. Weekend discounts, holiday rates. AE, DC, DISC, MC, V. Self-parking $15; valet parking $24. **Amenities:** Restaurant; bar; indoor pool; outdoor pool; exercise room; Jacuzzi; sauna; concierge; business center; secretarial services; Wi-Fi in public areas; 24-hr. room service; babysitting; dry cleaning; coin-op laundry; concierge-level rooms. *In room:* A/C, TV w/pay movies, Wi-Fi, coffeemaker, hair dryer, iron.

MODERATE

Holiday Inn Austin Town Lake (Kids) The most upscale Holiday Inn in Austin, this high-rise hotel is situated on the north shore of Lady Bird Lake, at the edge of downtown, and just off I-35. Many of the units have sofa sleepers, which can work for families, especially because kids stay free (and if they're under 12, they eat free at the hotel restaurant, too). Other amenities include a rooftop pool large enough for swimming laps, happy-hour specials, and a big-screen TV in the lounge. The hotel underwent a thorough renovation in 2007. Furniture and appliances were changed out in the guestrooms, and the fitness center was re-equipped. This is a nonsmoking hotel.

20 N. I-35 (exit 233, Riverside Dr./Town Lake), Austin, TX 78701. ✆ **800/HOLIDAY** [465-4329] or 512/472-8211. Fax 512/472-4636. www.holiday-inn.com/austintownlake. 320 units. $129–$199 double. Weekend and holiday rates, corporate discounts. Children under age 18 stay free. AE, DC, DISC, MC, V. Valet parking $12. **Amenities:** Restaurant; bar; outdoor pool; exercise room; unstaffed business center; secretarial services; Wi-Fi in public areas; room service; laundry service; dry cleaning; coin-op laundry; executive floors. *In room:* AC, TV w/pay movies, Wi-Fi, coffeemaker, hair dryer, iron.

La Quinta Inn–Capitol (Value) (Finds) Practically on the grounds of the state capitol, this is a great bargain for both business and leisure travelers. Rooms are more attractive than those in your typical motel: TVs are large, the rich-toned furnishings are far from cheesy, and perks such as free local phone calls (on dataport phones with voice mail), free high-speed Internet access, and free continental breakfasts keep annoying extras off your bill. The sole drawback is the lack of a restaurant on the premises. But there's a 'Dillo stop on 11th Street, a half-block from the hotel; and an increasing number of area restaurants are staying open on the weekends, so getting in a car is less necessary than it once was.

300 E. 11th St. (at San Jacinto), Austin, TX 78701. ✆ **800/NU-ROOMS** or 512/476-1166. Fax 512/476-6044. www.lq.com. 150 units. $119–$175 double; $185–$210 suite. Rates include continental breakfast. Children under 18 stay free in parent's room. AE, DC, DISC, MC, V. Valet parking $13. Pets accepted (no deposit or extra fee). **Amenities:** Outdoor pool. *In room:* A/C, TV w/pay movie, high-speed Internet access, coffeemaker, hair dryer, iron.

3 SOUTH AUSTIN

VERY EXPENSIVE

Hotel Saint Cecilia ★★★ (Finds This small hotel is my new favorite place to stay in Austin (if I only had the money). At the time of this writing, it was at the point of opening for business. Earlier, this was the site of a traditional bed-and-breakfast, which sat on nearly an acre of land in the heart of the SoCo District. The new owner, Liz Lambert, of the Hotel San José, added a few bungalows at the low end of the property beside a pool. Each has an upstairs and a downstairs suite. Another building beside the original house holds the breakfast and bar area and three guest rooms. A gorgeous landscaped yard, set off by large old oak trees, separates it from the street. The original house (1888) is at the opposite side of the property from the bungalows. From the outside it looks the same, but the floor plan was tweaked to create five large suites. These vary greatly, and each has a different emphasis (the bathroom in one, the bedroom in another, the garden in a third).

All the hotel's rooms are oversized but one (which has a panoramic view of the Austin skyline as recompense). Designed with clean lines and attractive spaces, each room has its own outdoor porch, patio, or garden. Each comes with a minibar stocked with expensive delicacies and most offer a wet bar (aka separate sink and counter space for your ice bucket). Bathroom minibars are stocked with pampering lotions and bath salts. A turntable in each room is connected to a Geneva sound system (with vintage vinyl collection at the reception). But the real capper is that each comes with a Swedish-made Hastens mattress, which costs a fortune, is made of all-natural materials, and feels like nothing I've ever experienced.

After spending the night on one of these, you can go down to the indoor/outdoor lounge area and order your breakfast crepe, gaze out at the old oak trees, and ponder what you could possibly do to make your life any better.

112 Academy Dr.(a block east of S. Congress Ave.), Austin, TX 78704. ✆ **512/852-2400.** Fax 512/852-2401. www.hotelsaintcecilia.com. 14 units. $300–$540 double. Rates include full breakfast. AE, DC, DISC, MC, V. Free secure off-street parking. Pets under 25 lb. accepted with $25 fee per pet per stay. **Amenities:** Bar; outdoor pool; concierge; laundry service; dry cleaning. *In room:* A/C, TV/DVD player, free Wi-Fi and high-speed Internet access, minibar, fridge, hair dryer, iron upon request, sound system.

EXPENSIVE

Hotel San José ★★ This revamped 1930s motor court gets a lot of attention from the national press for a design that weds beauty to simplicity. The San Jose is a good choice for design enthusiasts and hipsters, who enjoy both the nonconformist vibe and

It Pays to Stay

If you're planning to settle in for a spell, two downtown accommodations at prime locations will save you major bucks. Rooms at **Extended Stay America Downtown,** 600 Guadalupe (at Sixth St.), Austin, TX 78701 (✆ **800/EXT-STAY** [398-7829] or 512/457-9994; www.extstay.com), within easy walking distance of both the Warehouse District and the Lamar and Sixth shops; and at **Homestead Studio Suites Austin–Downtown/Town Lake,** 507 S. First St. (at Barton Springs), Austin, TX 78704 (✆ **888/782-9473** or 512/476-1818; www.homesteadhotels.com), near the Barton Springs restaurant row and the hike-and-bike trail, will run you from $400 to $500 per week. Full kitchens and coin-op laundries at both bring your costs down even more.

the social scene in South Austin. Other travelers may think that the minimalist rooms are overpriced. Even if you don't stay here, you might enjoy coming here in the late afternoon/early evening to enjoy the comfortable surroundings of the hotel's popular beer and wine bar. The rooms are indeed spare and come furnished with beds and chairs made from Texas pine, but they also come with amenities such as CD players. Most rooms have pleasant small outdoor sitting areas. The design achieves a certain serenity that evaporates the moment you step out on to South Congress Avenue's lively street scene. Right across the way is the famous Continental Club, a great place for happy hour. Book a room in the back to avoid the Congress Avenue traffic noise.

1316 S. Congress Ave. (south of Nelly, about 1/2 mile south of Riverside), Austin, TX 78704. ✆ **800/574-8897** or 512/444-7322. Fax 512/444-7362. www.sanjosehotel.com. 40 units. $100–$110 double w/shared bathroom; $180–$280 double w/private bathroom; $300–$400 suite. AE, DISC, MC, V. Free parking. Dogs accepted for $10 per dog per day. **Amenities:** Bar/lounge; coffee shop; outdoor pool; bike rentals; breakfast-only room service; laundry service; dry cleaning. *In room:* AC, TV/DVD player, free Wi-Fi, hair dryer, CD player.

INEXPENSIVE

Austin Motel ★ Value This establishment, the best lodging bargain on South Congress, is one of the old motels that was built when this was the main road to San Antonio. Built in 1938, it has been in the hands of the same family since the 1950s. A convenient (but not quiet) location in the heart of SoCo and great rates makes this place very popular. It has a classic kidney-shaped pool, a great neon sign, free HBO, free coffee in the lobby, and a certain quirkiness that's part of the local charm. It also has one of those rarities: real single rooms, so those traveling on their own don't have to pay for a bed they're not sleeping in. All rooms are different, many decorated with murals. For instance, room 257 has a cactus mural. You can check out pictures of the rooms before you make a reservation by going to the website.

1220 S. Congress St., Austin, TX 78704. ✆ **512/441-1157.** Fax 512/441-1157. www.austinmotel.com. 41 units. $70–$96 single; $87–$96 double; $110–$119 poolside and deluxe; $146 suite. AE, DC, DISC, MC, V. Free parking. Limited number of rooms for pets; one-time $15 fee. **Amenities:** Outdoor pool; coin-op laundry. *In room:* A/C, TV, Wi-Fi, fridge (in some rooms), hair dryer, iron, safe (in some rooms).

Hostelling International–Austin Value Youth-, nature-, and Internet-oriented Austin goes all out for its hostellers at this winning facility, located on the hike-and-bike trail and boasting views of Town Lake that many would pay through the nose to get. Amenities not only include the standard laundry room and kitchen, but also a high-speed Internet kiosk (with a meager $1 fee per stay), not to mention the fact that the grounds are Wi-Fi, too. The former boathouse is solar paneled, and other ecofriendly features include low-flow shower heads. The entire hostel shares one bathroom and shower area.

2200 S. Lakeshore Blvd. (east of I-35, on the southern shore of Town Lake), Austin, TX 78741. ✆ **800/725-2331** or 512/444-2294. Fax 512/444-2309. www.hiaustin.org. 39 beds in 4 dorms, all w/shared bathrooms. $17 for AYH members, $3 additional for nonmembers, half-price for those under age 14. AE, MC, V. Free parking. **Amenities:** Kayak rentals; bike rentals; Internet kiosk; Wi-Fi in public areas; coin-op laundry; kitchen. *In room:* A/C, no phone.

4 CENTRAL

EXPENSIVE

Mansion at Judges Hill ★★ All the rooms in this boutique hotel are furnished and decorated with much more character than you'll find at any of the local chain hotels. This is as true of the rooms in the modern building at the rear of the property as it is for the ones in the original mansion. The second-story signature rooms are the most fun; they all open onto a sweeping upstairs porch and have tall ceilings and large bathrooms with special amenities (including L'Occitane toiletries and bathrobes). Beds have particularly good mattresses and linens. The third-floor rooms are a little smaller, but lovely and with a real feel of the old house. The ground floor holds the bar and the restaurant.

The modern building is called the North Wing. Built in 1983 in the rear of the property, it offers rooms far from the traffic sounds coming from MLK. The rooms vary quite a bit. Most come without tubs. The deluxe king rooms are the nicest (particularly room 212). All rooms are nonsmoking. The West Campus location is convenient to the university and to downtown.

1900 Rio Grande (at MLK, Jr. Blvd./19th St.), Austin, TX 78705. ✆ **800/311-1619** or 512/495-1800. www.judgeshill.com. 48 units. $169–$229 North Wing; $189–$299 Mansion. Rates go higher for special events. AE, DC, DISC, MC, V. Free off-street parking. Pets accepted with restrictions. **Amenities:** Restaurant; bar; limited room service; in-room massage; babysitting; limited laundry service. *In room:* A/C, TV, Wi-Fi, coffeemaker, hair dryer, iron, CD player.

MODERATE

Austin Folk House ★★ Value You get the best of both worlds at this appealing B&B that combines old-time charm with new plumbing. When it was transformed from a tired apartment complex at the beginning of the new millennium, this 1880s house near the University of Texas got a complete interior overhaul, but it maintained such integral traditional assets as the comfy front porch. The sunny rooms have cheerfully painted walls and the wiring to accommodate megachannel cable TVs, private phone lines, broadband cable access, and radio/alarms with white noise machines. At the same time, nice antiques and such amenities as fancy bedding and towels, candles, robes, expensive lotions, and soaps make you feel like you're in a small luxury inn. The lavish breakfast buffet, served in a dining room decorated with the folk art for which the B&B

is named, does nothing to dispel that idea. Prices are reasonable for all this, while the free off-street parking, near the heart of UT, puts this place at a premium all by itself. Local phone calls are gratis.

506 W. 22nd St. (at Nueces), Austin, TX 78705. ✆ **866/472-6700** or 512/472-6700. www.austinfolkhouse.com. 9 units. $110–$225 double; Internet specials sometimes available. Rates include full breakfast. AE, DISC, MC, V. Free off-street parking. **Amenities:** Wi-Fi in public areas; video library. *In room:* A/C, TV/VCR, Wi-Fi and high-speed Internet access, hair dryer, iron.

Doubletree Hotel Austin Two miles north of the university, just off the I-35 freeway, is this hacienda-style hotel. The reception area has polished Mexican-tile floors and carved-wood ceiling beams; in keeping with the hacienda theme, rooms are arranged around a landscaped courtyard, dotted with umbrella-shaded tables. Guest quarters are airy and spacious, if a bit dull. If you're driving around the city, this is a good choice for its convenient location and easy access to your vehicle. All the sleeping floors have direct access, via room key, to the parking garage. The hotel is located near the intersection with Hwy. 2222, which is one of the few convenient east–west corridors in the city, and is close by Highland Mall.

6505 N. I-35 (btw. Hwy. 290 E. and St. Johns Ave.), Austin, TX 78751. ✆ **800/222-TREE** [222-8733] or 512/454-3737. Fax 512/454-6915. www.austin.doubletree.com. 350 units. $169–$199 double; suites from $199–$219. Corporate, weekend rates available. AE, DC, DISC, MC, V. Self-parking $8; valet parking $14. Pets under 25 lb. accepted with $50 refundable deposit. **Amenities:** Restaurant; bar; outdoor pool; health club; Jacuzzi; concierge; business center; room service; babysitting; concierge-level rooms. *In room:* A/C, TV, dataport, high-speed Internet access, coffeemaker, hair dryer, iron.

Habitat Suites ★★ Kids Finds This hotel just might represent the future of green businesses. At present, it is but an island of ecological awareness in a sea of mainstream commercialism, as it is located in one of the satellite buildings of Highland Mall. This improbable location was the result of historical accident. The hotel was taken over in 1991 by the same people who are behind the Casa de Luz macrobiotic restaurant (see dining chapter). They strive to do all that a truly green hotel can: use natural materials and cleaning products over synthetics and chemicals; save, and even generate, electricity; recycle materials; conserve water; grow organic foods; and act in a socially conscious manner.

For the guests, it means never running the risk of getting a room that reeks of chemicals. In fact, this is the ideal lodging for anyone with chemical sensitivities. It also means friendly service—the hotel staff has bought into the green concept and even enjoy a profit-sharing arrangement; consequently, the staff retention rate is way above the industry norm. Staying here also means healthful food choices for breakfast (but not to the exclusion of regular fare); and if you decide to cook for yourself, you can make use of some of the organically grown vegetables, if available. All of these green activities are performed without fanfare, though the hotel quietly piles up awards for its ecoconsciousness. To the casual observer, the hotel looks like a standard three-story residential hotel. The rooms are oversize and come with complete kitchens. Sheets and towels are of natural materials. Paints are water-based. The furniture, though not of the latest style, is comfortable (pieces are refinished or reupholstered to avoid adding to the waste stream). Each room has a small separate outdoor area with chairs.

The location is central, just 2 miles north of the university campus. It's not noisy, and the hotel institutes quiet hours between 9pm and 9am. It gets a lot of repeat business from frequent visitors to Austin and is one of the best-kept secrets in Austin's lodging scene.

500 E. Highland Mall Blvd. (take exit 222 off I-35 to Airport Blvd., take a right to Highland Mall Blvd.), Austin, TX 78752. ✆ **800/535-4663** or 512/467-6000. Fax 512/467-6000. www.habitatsuites.com.

96 units. $147 1-bedroom suite; $207 2-bedroom suite. Extended-stay rates available. Rates include full breakfast and (Mon–Fri) afternoon wine and snacks. AE, DC, DISC, MC, V. Free parking. **Amenities:** Outdoor pool; Jacuzzi; Wi-Fi in public areas; environmentally sound dry-cleaning; coin-op laundry. *In room:* A/C, TV, Wi-Fi and some with high-speed Internet access, kitchen, fridge, coffeemaker, hair dryer, iron.

Star of Texas Inn ★ Longtime visitors to Austin might remember this as the Governor's Inn, a converted 1897 neoclassical residence. Bought and refurbished by the young owners of the Austin Folk House, Sylvia and Chris (see above), this B&B is a bit more traditional than its sister property a block away but still has friendly perks for the business traveler as well as upscale amenities. It also has more porch and deck space. Rooms vary quite a bit in size and layout, but most are a little larger than at the Folk house. The Star of Texas also harbors that hard-to-find gem, a real single bedroom that's small but not claustrophobic. Three rooms open directly onto a very appealing covered porch, and the others have access to it. All offer lovely antiques but don't have any of the fustiness you sometimes find in B&Bs—and B&B owners—that take their furniture way too seriously.

611 W. 22nd St. (at Rio Grande), Austin, TX 78705. ✆ **866-472-6700** or 512/472-6700. www.staroftexasinn.com. 10 units. $110–$225 double. Internet specials sometimes available. Rates include full breakfast. AE, DISC, MC, V. Free off-street parking. **Amenities:** Bike rentals; Wi-Fi in public areas; video library. *In room:* A/C, TV/VCR, Wi-Fi, hair dryer, iron.

INEXPENSIVE

The Adams House *Value* *Finds* Monroe Shipe, the developer of Hyde Park, designed his homes to be both attractive and affordable to the middle class. This B&B honors Shipe's egalitarian spirit. Built as a single-story bungalow and expanded into a two-story colonial revival in 1931, is was restored in the 1990s by a preservation architect. The house is beautifully furnished and has a friendly, open feel—in part because of its 12-foot ceilings and in part because of the hospitable Sydney Lock, who owns and runs it with her cocker spaniel, Dulce. All the rooms are lovely, but the nicest is the suite with a king-size four-poster bed and a sun porch with a foldout couch. A separate house out back doesn't have as much character, but compensates with a TV/VCR and Jacuzzi. The house's location in leafy Hyde Park is not only attractive and restful, but is quite practical, as it is just a block away from a small neighborhood center that includes a small grocery, coffee bar, Laundromat ("washateria" in Texas), and a few superb local restaurants

4300 Ave. G (at 43rd St.), Austin, TX 85751. ✆ **512/453-7696.** Fax 512/453-2616. www.theadamshouse.com. 5 units. $99–$110 double; $149 suite and bungalow. Monthly rates available. Rates include breakfast. MC, V. Free off-street parking. No children under 12. *In room:* A/C, TV (in 1 room).

5 NORTHWEST

EXPENSIVE

Renaissance Austin Hotel Anchoring the upscale Arboretum mall on Austin's northwest side, the Renaissance caters to executives visiting nearby high-tech firms. But on weekends, when rates are slashed, even underlings can afford to take advantage of the hotel's many amenities, including an excellent health club, a nightclub, and direct access to the myriad allures of the mall (movie theaters among them). Guests buzz around the eateries, elevator banks, and lounges in the nine-story-high atrium lobby, but the space is sufficiently large to avoid any sense of crowding.

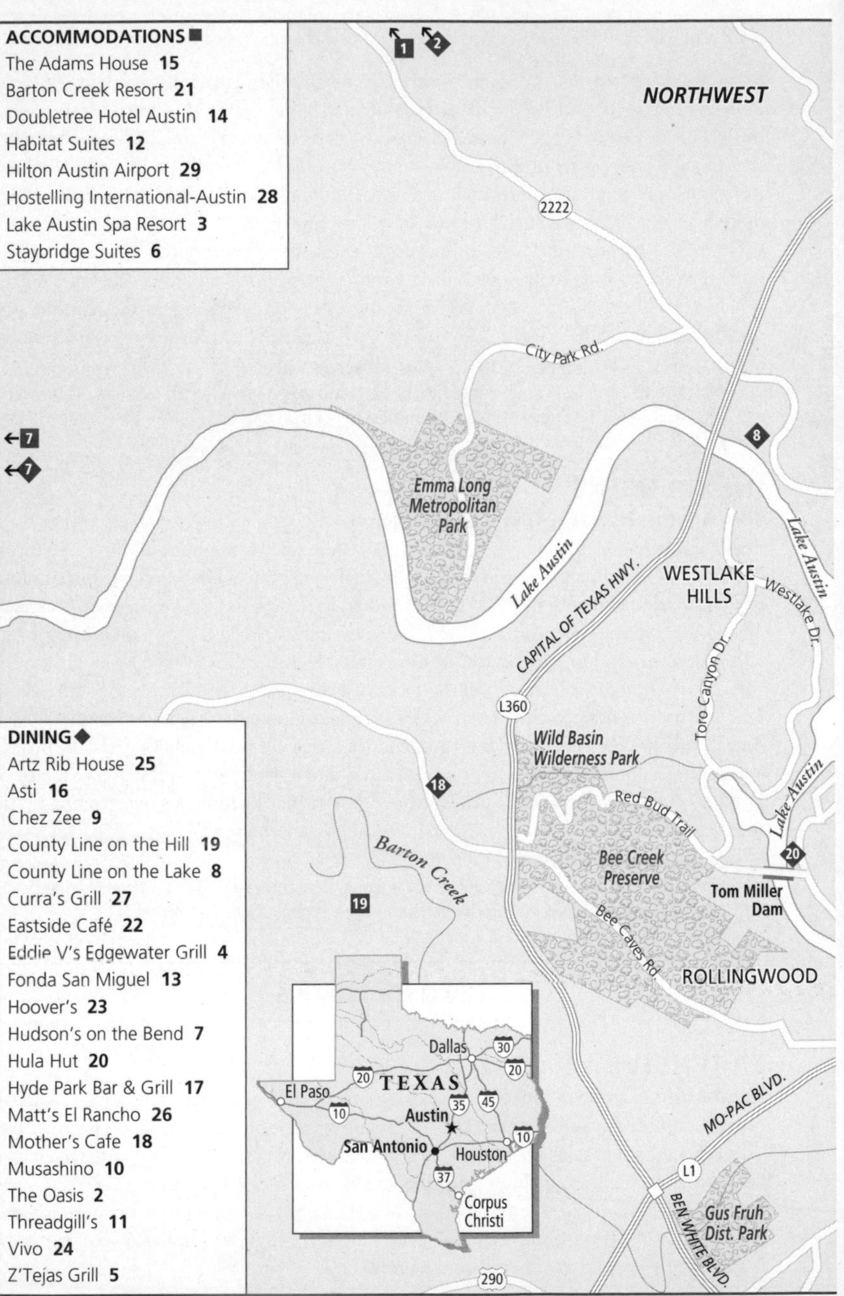

ACCOMMODATIONS ■
The Adams House 15
Barton Creek Resort 21
Doubletree Hotel Austin 14
Habitat Suites 12
Hilton Austin Airport 29
Hostelling International-Austin 28
Lake Austin Spa Resort 3
Staybridge Suites 6
DINING ◆
Artz Rib House 25
Asti 16
Chez Zee 9
County Line on the Hill 19
County Line on the Lake 8
Curra's Grill 27
Eastside Café 22
Eddie V's Edgewater Grill 4
Fonda San Miguel 13
Hoover's 23
Hudson's on the Bend 7
Hula Hut 20
Hyde Park Bar & Grill 17
Matt's El Rancho 26
Mother's Cafe 18
Musashino 10
The Oasis 2
Threadgill's 11
Vivo 24
Z'Tejas Grill 5
NORTHWEST
2222
City Park Rd.
Emma Long Metropolitan Park
Lake Austin
CAPITAL OF TEXAS HWY.
WESTLAKE HILLS
Westlake Dr.
Toro Canyon Dr.
L360
Wild Basin Wilderness Park
Red Bud Trail
Barton Creek
Bee Creek Preserve
Tom Miller Dam
Bee Caves Rd.
ROLLINGWOOD
MO-PAC BLVD.
L1
BEN WHITE BLVD.
Gus Fruh Dist. Park
290
TEXAS
Dallas
El Paso
Austin
San Antonio
Houston
Corpus Christi

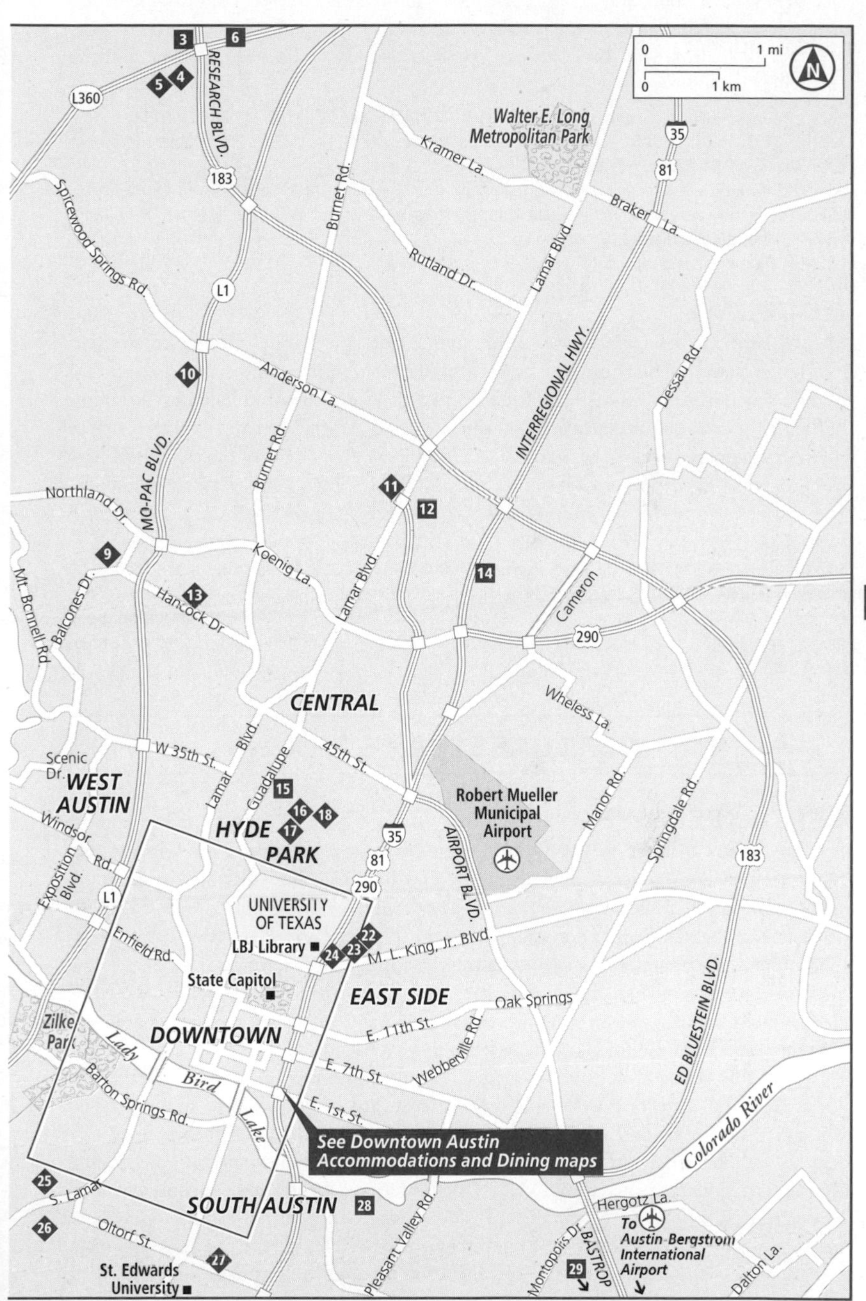

Walter E. Long Metropolitan Park
Kramer La.
Braker La.
Rutland Dr.
Lamar Blvd.
Burnet Rd.
RESEARCH BLVD.
Spicewood Springs Rd.
Anderson La.
INTERREGIONAL HWY.
Dessau Rd.
MO-PAC BLVD.
Northland Dr.
Koenig La.
Hancock Dr
Balcones Dr.
Mt. Bonnell Rd
Cameron
Wheless La.
CENTRAL
W 35th St.
45th St.
Scenic Dr.
WEST AUSTIN
Windsor Rd.
Exposition Blvd.
Guadalupe
HYDE PARK
Robert Mueller Municipal Airport
AIRPORT BLVD.
Manor Rd.
Springdale Rd.
UNIVERSITY OF TEXAS
LBJ Library
Enfield Rd.
M. L. King, Jr. Blvd.
State Capitol
EAST SIDE
Oak Springs
ED BLUESTEIN BLVD.
Zilker Park
DOWNTOWN
E. 11th St.
Webberville Rd.
Lady Bird Lake
E. 7th St.
Barton Springs Rd.
E. 1st St.
See Downtown Austin Accommodations and Dining maps
Colorado River
S. Lamar
SOUTH AUSTIN
Oltorf St.
St. Edwards University
Pleasant Valley Rd.
Montopolis Dr.
BASTROP
Hergotz La.
To Austin-Bergstrom International Airport
Dalton La.
0 1 mi
0 1 km

Guest rooms, decorated in a contemporary Hill Country look—warm russets, browns, and greens, dark wood, and leather chairs—are all oversize and offer comfortable sitting areas. Suites include extras such as wet bars and electric shoe buffers. Another perk is the pet-friendly environment: Not only can you check in with Fido free of charge, but the chef whips up some mean dog biscuits.

9721 Arboretum Blvd. (off Loop 360, near Research Blvd.), Austin, TX 78759. ✆ **800/HOTELS-1** [468-3571] or 512/343-2626. Fax 512/346-7945. www.marriott.com. 478 units. $229–$269 double; suites from $289. Weekend packages available. AE, DC, DISC, MC, V. Free self-parking; valet parking $14. Pets accepted. **Amenities:** 3 restaurants; bar; nightclub; indoor pool; outdoor pool; health club; Jacuzzi; sauna; concierge; car-rental desk; business center; secretarial services; Wi-Fi in public areas; 24-hr. room service; babysitting; same-day laundry and dry cleaning; club-level rooms. *In room:* A/C, TV w/pay movies, Wi-Fi, fridge (in some rooms), coffeemaker, hair dryer, iron.

MODERATE

Staybridge Suites (Kids) (Value) Although it's designed with business travelers in mind, this cheery Holiday Inn property is also ideal for families, who can take advantage of the kitchen in every suite, the multiple TVs (with VCR), the complimentary breakfast buffet, the pool in a leafy courtyard, and the free laundry facilities that adjoin the exercise room (the latter is small but has good cardio machines). Both types of travelers appreciate the proximity to the Arboretum and other upscale shopping complexes, as well as the many restaurants in this burgeoning area.

10201 Stonelake Blvd. (btw. Great Hills Trail and Braker Lane), Austin, TX 78759. ✆ **800/238-8000** or 512/349-0888. Fax 512/349-0809. www.staybridge.com. 121 units. $165–$195 studio suite; $179–$209 1-bedroom suite; $205–$235 2-bedroom suite. Rates include breakfast. Extended-stay and Sat–Sun discounts. AE, DC, DISC, MC, V. Free parking. Pets accepted; $20 fee per night. **Amenities:** Outdoor pool; tennis court; health club; business center. *In room:* A/C, TV/VCR w/pay movies, Wi-Fi, kitchen, coffeemaker, hair dryer, iron.

6 WESTLAKE/LAKE TRAVIS

VERY EXPENSIVE

Barton Creek Resort ★★★ (Kids) Austin's only real full-service resort—one that caters to business travelers, couples, singles, and families alike—Barton Creek would stand out even in more resort-rich cities. The facilities are top-notch, including four 18-hole championship golf courses and the Chuck Cook Golf Academy, tennis courts and a tennis clinic, and an excellent health club with an indoor track. Members of the affiliated country club, which shares the recreational facilities, include such local celebrities as überbiker Lance Armstrong, Sandra Bullock, and Michael Dell. You might even see tennis star Andy Roddick playing a few sets with friends.

With 4,000 gently rolling and wooded acres and relative proximity to Lake Travis, the resort feels rural, but it's close enough to central Austin (about 15 min. away) that you can easily sightsee or party there. Rooms are spacious in both the main buildings, one resembling a European château and the other a nine-story tower connecting the spa and the conference center. The custom-made Drexel Heritage furnishings are complemented by such Texas touches as cowhide chairs and work by local artists. Some rooms have balconies, and those in the back offer superb views of the Texas Hill Country. The main restaurant of the resort does a great job with contemporary American cuisine, including some great steaks and seafood.

 Family-Friendly Hotels

Barton Creek Resort (p. 192) In addition to the great recreational activities here (including a basketball court), this resort also has an activity room for ages 6 months to 8 years, open from morning 'til evening. It's $10 per hour to drop your kids off here for a maximum of 4½ hours, with additional fees for longer periods.

Doubletree Guest Suites (p. 182), **Habitat Suites** (p. 188), and **Staybridge Suites** (p. 192) That "suites" in the name of these properties says it all. These guest quarters all offer spacious, common-sense living quarters, plus the convenience (and economy) of kitchen facilities, so you don't have to eat out all the time.

Four Seasons Austin (p. 180) Tell the reservations clerk that you're traveling with kids, and you'll be automatically enrolled in the free amenities program, which offers age-appropriate snacks—cookies and milk for children under 10, popcorn and soda for those older—along with various toys and games that will be waiting for you when you arrive. And you don't have to travel with all your gear, because the hotel will provide such items as a car seat, stroller, playpen, bedrails, disposable pacifiers, a baby bathtub, shampoo, powder and lotions, bib, bottle warmers, and disposable diapers.

Hollday Inn Austin Town Lake (p. 184) You're near lots of the outdoor play areas at Town Lake, and kids stay and (under 12) eat free. It's hard to beat that!

Lakeway Inn (p. 194) There's plenty for kids to do here, and this property offers a Family Playdays Package, which includes a $100 credit toward recreational activities (such as boat rentals and tennis), plus a free meal and dessert for children 12 and under, with the purchase of adult entree. Prices vary depending on the time of year.

8212 Barton Club Dr. (1 mile west of the intersection of Loop 360 and R.R. 2244), Austin, TX 78735. ✆ **800/336-6158** or 512/329-4000. Fax 512/329-4597. www.bartoncreek.com. 300 units. $260–$380 double; suites from $500. Big discounts in off season (winter). Spa and golf packages available. AE, DC, DISC, MC, V. Free self-parking; valet parking $25. **Amenities:** 2 restaurants; bar; indoor pool; outdoor pool; 4 golf courses; 11 tennis courts; health club; spa; children's center and programs; business center; salon; room service; babysitting; laundry service; dry cleaning. *In room:* A/C, TV, dataport, Wi-Fi, minibar, hair dryer, iron.

Lake Austin Spa Resort ★★★ If you had to create the quintessential Austin spa, it would be laid-back, located on a serene body of water, offer lots of outdoor activities, and feature super-healthy food that lives up to high culinary standards. You can check off every item of that wish list here. The spa takes advantage of its proximity to the Highland Lakes and the Hill Country by offering such activities as combination canoe/hiking trips and excursions to view the wildflowers. The aromatic ingredients for soothing spa treatments, such as a honey-mango scrub, are grown in the resort's garden, also the source for the herbs used at mealtimes. Guest rooms, many in cottages with private gardens, fireplaces, and hot tubs, are casually elegant, with all-natural fabrics and locally crafted furniture.

This resort is a destination spa. In 2008, the readers of *Condé Nast* gave it the top spot on their favorite spa list, and the editors of *Travel + Leisure* perennially include it in their list of the world's top spas. If you go, you'll see why. It's simply an incredibly relaxing experience, with a winning combination of beauty; a welcoming, knowledgeable staff; and delicious, healthful food.

1705 S. Quinlan Park Rd. (5 miles south of Hwy. 620), Austin, TX 78732. ✆ **800/847-5637** or 512/372-7300. Fax 512/266-1572. www.lakeaustin.com. 40 units. 3-day packages available for $1,550 per person (double occupancy). Rates include all meals, classes, and activities. Spa treatments/personal trainers are extra. AE, DC, DISC, MC, V. Free parking. Dogs accepted in Garden Cottage rooms; $250 pet guest fee. Children 14 and up only. **Amenities:** Restaurant; indoor pool; 2 outdoor pools; health club; spa; kayaks; canoes; hydrobikes; room service; laundry service. *In room:* A/C, TV/DVD player, dataport, Wi-Fi, hair dryer, CD player.

EXPENSIVE

Lakeway Inn Value Kids Not as glitzy as Barton Creek, nor as picture-perfect as the Lake Austin Spa, this conference resort in a planned community on Lake Travis is for those seeking traditional recreation at prices that won't require a second mortgage.

There's something for everyone in the family. At the resort's marina, you can rent pontoons, ski boats, sculls, sailboats, water-skis, WaveRunners, fishing gear and guides—just about everything but fish that promise to bite. Lakeway's excellent 32-court tennis complex, designed for indoor, outdoor, day, and night games, has a pro shop with trainers and even a racket-shaped swimming pool. Duffers can tee off from 36 holes of golf on the property, get privileges at other courses nearby, or brush up on their game at the Jack Nicklaus–designed Academy of Golf. All rooms are nonsmoking.

The main lodge of this older property was razed and rebuilt at the end of the 1990s, but, oddly, the rooms were reincarnated with a rather dark and staid 1970s look. Still, they're spacious and comfortable, with all the requisite conference attendee business amenities and, in many cases, lake views.

101 Lakeway Dr., Austin, TX 78734. ✆ **800/LAKEWAY** [525-3929] or 512/261-6600. Fax 512/261-7322. www.lakewayinn.com. 239 units. $169–$289 double. Romance, golf, spa, B&B, and family packages available. AE, DC, DISC, MC, V. Free self-parking; valet parking $15. **Amenities:** Restaurant; bar; 2 outdoor pools; health club; spa; watersports rentals; concierge; business center; room service. *In room:* A/C, TV w/ pay movies, dataport, high-speed Internet access in most rooms, coffeemaker, hair dryer, iron.

7 AT THE AIRPORT

MODERATE

Hilton Austin Airport ★ This Hilton's circular shape gives Austin's only full-service airport hotel, formerly the headquarters of Bergstrom Air Force Base, a distinctively modern look. Although the hotel retains few of the features that made it one of three bunkers where the President of the United States might be spirited in the event of a nuclear attack, the building remains rock-solid—and blissfully soundproof. (If you stay here, ask for a sheet that details the fascinating history of "The Donut," which also served as a strategic air command center during the Vietnam War, the Persian Gulf War, and Desert Storm.) These days, the dome serves as a skylight for a bright and airy lobby. The theme throughout is Texas Hill Country, with lots of limestone and wood and plenty of live plants for good measure. Large, comfortable rooms are equipped with all the amenities.

9515 New Airport Dr. (1/2 mile from the airport, 2 miles east of the intersection of Hwy. 183 and Hwy. 71), Austin, TX 78719. ✆ **800/445-8667** or 512/385-6767. Fax 512/385-6763. www.hilton.com. 263 units. $139–$199 double; suites from $190. Sat–Sun, online, and parking discounts. AE, DC, DISC, MC, V. Self-parking $11; valet parking $15. **Amenities:** Restaurant; lounge; outdoor pool; health club; business center; 24-hr. room service; laundry service; dry cleaning; club-level rooms. *In room:* A/C, TV w/pay movies, dataport, high-speed Internet access, minibar, coffeemaker, hair dryer, iron.

13 Where to Dine in Austin

Austin has many one-of-a-kind establishments that serve regional cooking, international cuisine, or their own style of cooking. It also has restaurants, such as Sullivan's, Fleming's, Ruth's Chris, P.F. Chang's, and Roy's, which you're probably familiar with and need not be reviewed here. Instead, I'll list mainly local establishments.

Many restaurants are concentrated in and around downtown and the area immediately south of Lady Bird Lake. In other parts of the city they tend to set up along the major commercial corridors, but in some old neighborhoods a few restaurants will be tucked away in small clusters on fairly quiet streets. These are some of the most interesting of local restaurants. In the Hyde Park neighborhood (north of the university campus), one such cluster is at Duval Street and 43rd, where you'll find Asti, Hyde Park Bar & Grill, and Mother's Café & Garden; in the Clarksville neighborhood (west of downtown) is another cluster at West Lynn and 12th Street (Jeffrey's, Cipollina, and Zocalo); and in central East Austin, on the boundary between French Place and Blackland neighborhoods, is yet another cluster on Manor Road (Eastside Cafe, Hoover's, and Vivo). As neighborhood restaurants, these places are comfortable and welcoming, and reflect the tastes of the local community.

Also, a concentration of restaurants is located on Guadalupe Street, by the university campus. These cater to students and don't have to be good; they just have to be cheap. I would avoid them.

To locate restaurants outside of downtown, see the map on p. 205. Wherever you eat, think casual. There isn't a restaurant in Austin that requires men to put on a tie and jacket, and many upscale dining rooms are far better turned out than their rich tech-industry clientele.

Dining out can be a competitive sport in Austin. Make reservations wherever you can or dine at off hours. If you turn up at some of the most popular spots at around 7:30pm, you might wait an hour or more. Austin restaurants tend to be noisier than those of other cities. The locals seem to be okay with this, but, in my opinion, it's yet another reason to dine at off hours.

Finally, Austin has a large population of vegetarians and vegans, so local restaurants offer lots of vegetarian options, and there are a number of purely vegetarian restaurants.

(See p. 91 for an explanation of culinary categories.)

1 BEST AUSTIN DINING BETS

- **The Best Dining-as-Happening Scene: Uchi,** 801 S. Lamar Blvd. (✆ **512/916-4808**), has drama, action, and a beautiful *mise en scène.* It's a great restaurant with creative cooking that transcends its humble roots. See p. 205.
- **Most Impressive Vegetarian Cuisine:** Given all the dietary strictures of macrobiotics and veganism, it amazes me that **Casa de Luz,** 1701 Toomey Rd. (✆ **512/476-2535**), can produce the delicious meals that it does. Vegetarians of all stripes leave here completely sated. See p. 207.

- **Best Quintessentially Austin:** Its laid-back Texas menu, huge outdoor patio, and "unplugged" music series all make **Shady Grove** (1624 Barton Springs Rd.; ✆ **512/474-9991**) the ideal of *the* Austin restaurant. See p. 209.
- **Best Brunch:** It's a tie between the Sunday buffet at **Green Pastures,** 811 W. Live Oak Rd. (✆ **512/444-4747**), where Austinites have been imbibing milk punch—liberally dosed with bourbon, rum, brandy, ice cream, and nutmeg—seemingly forever; and the one at **Fonda San Miguel,** 2330 W. North Loop (✆ **512/459-4121**), where the spread runs deliciously toward Mexico. See p. 204 and 211.
- **Best Melding of Old and New Worlds:** The **Driskill Grill,** 604 Brazos St. (✆ **512/391-7162**), has the grace and tone that befits the historic hotel it serves, but there's nothing dated about the New American cuisine that dazzles this era's gastronomically demanding guests. See p. 199.
- **Best if You're Game for Game:** It's a bit of a drive and more than a bit of a wallet bite, but if you want to see how tasty venison or bison can be, you can't beat **Hudson's on the Bend,** 3509 Hwy. 620 N. (✆ **512/266-1369**). See p. 216.
- **Best View:** The easy winner is **The Oasis,** 6550 Comanche Trail, near Lake Travis (✆ **512/266-2442**), which has multiple decks that afford stunning views of Lake Travis and the Texas Hill Country. See p. 216.
- **Sweetest Contribution to the Dining Scene:** For years, **Amy's** has been Austin's favorite ice cream stop. College-age servers put on a show for the customers, tossing scoops of ice cream about and crushing toppings into it with rhythmic glee. The ice cream is rich and the flavorings are natural and distinctive. There are 10 locations in Austin, including the airport. Central locations include 1012 W. Sixth St. (at Lamar; ✆ **512/480-0673**); one in SoCo, 1301 S. Congress Ave. (by the Continental Club; ✆ **512/440-7488**); and one just north of the UT campus, 3500 Guadalupe (✆ **512/458-6895**). See p. 206.

2 RESTAURANTS BY CUISINE

American
Eastside Cafe (East Side, $$, p. 213)
Hoover's (East Side, $, p. 214)
Hula Hut (West Austin, $$, p. 210)
Hut's Hamburgers (Downtown, $, p. 204)
Hyde Park Bar & Grill ★ (Central and South Austin, $$, p. 212)
The Oasis (Lake Travis, $$, p. 216)
Shady Grove ★ (South Austin, $, p. 209)
Threadgill's ★ (Central and South Austin, $, p. 212)

Asian/Fusion
Thai Tara ★ (Downtown, $, p. 204)
Uchi ★★★ (South Austin, $$$, p. 205)

Barbecue
Artz Rib House ★ (South Austin, $$, p. 206)
County Line on the Hill ★ (Westlake/Lake Travis, $$, p. 216)
The Iron Works ★ (Downtown, $, p. 204)

Cajun/Creole
Gumbo's ★ (Downtown, $$$, p. 199)

French

Aquarelle ★★ (Downtown, $$$$, p. 199)
Chez Nous ★ (Downtown, $$$, p. 199)

Indian

Clay Pit ★ (Downtown, $$, p. 202)

Italian

Asti ★ (Central, $$, p. 211)
Cipollina ★★ (West Austin, $$, p. 210)
Enoteca Vespaio ★ (South Austin, $$$, p. 206)
Frank & Angie's (Downtown, $, p. 203)
La Traviata ★★ (Downtown, $$$, p. 200)
Vespaio ★ (South Austin, $$$, p. 206)

Japanese

Musashino ★ (Northwest, $$, p. 215)
Uchi ★★★ (South Austin, $$$, p. 205)
Zen (South Austin, Central, $, p. 209)

Mexican

Curra's Grill ★★ (South Austin, $$, p. 207)
Fonda San Miguel ★ (Central, $$$, p. 211)
Manuel's ★ (Downtown and Northwest, $$, p. 202)
Zocalo (West Austin, $, p. 210)

New American

Chez Zee ★ (Northwest, $$, p. 215)
Driskill Grill ★★ (Downtown, $$$$, p. 199)
Green Pastures ★ (South Austin, $$$, p. 204)
Hudson's on the Bend ★★ (Lake Travis, $$$$, p. 216)
Jeffrey's ★★ (West Austin, $$$$, p. 209)
Shoreline Grill ★★ (Downtown, $$$, p. 200)
Wink ★★ (Central, $$$, p. 211)

Pizza

Frank & Angie's (Downtown, $, p. 203)

Seafood

Eddie V's Edgewater Grille ★ (Downtown and Northwest, $$$$, p. 214)
Shoreline Grill ★★ (Downtown, $$$, p. 200)

Southern

Hoover's (East Side, $, p. 214)
Threadgill's ★ (Central and South Austin, $, p. 212)

Southwest

Roaring Fork ★★ (Downtown, $$$, p. 200)
Ranch 616 ★ (Downtown, $$, p. 203)
South Congress Cafe ★ (South Austin, $$, p. 208)
Z'Tejas Southwestern Grill ★ (Downtown and Northwest, $$, p. 215)

Steaks

Eddie V's Edgewater Grille ★ (Northwest, $$$$, p. 214)

Tex-Mex

Chuy's (South Austin and Northwest, $, p. 207)
Güero's ★ (South Austin, $$, p. 208)
Hula Hut (West Austin, $$, p. 210)
Matt's El Rancho (South Austin, $$, p. 208)
The Oasis (Lake Travis, $$, p. 216)
Vivo ★ (East Side, $, p. 214)

Thai

Thai Tara ★ (Downtown, $, p. 204)

Vegetarian

Casa de Luz ★ (South Austin, $, p. 207)
Mother's Café & Garden (Central Austin, $, p. 212)

3 DOWNTOWN

VERY EXPENSIVE

Aquarelle ★★ FRENCH A converted neoclassical house with gilded mirrors, fresh flowers, tiny candle lamps flickering on the tables, strains of "La Vie en Rose" floating in the background—you get the picture. Aquarelle is a haven for French tradition. The food stays largely traditional, too, as Jacques Richard, the chef, doesn't believe in messing with success. The prix-fixe menus are always a good bet, but such dishes as the warm duck foie gras with red cherry-onion compote or *loup de mer*—Mediterranean sea bass with sautéed squash and eggplant—are worth going a la carte. Prepare to make an evening of dinner here in classic French fashion; you're likely to spend at least 3 hours slowly savoring the experience. Cap the night off with a chocolate soufflé cake with a molten center, and you're likely to keep savoring the memory days later.

606 Rio Grande. ✆ **512/479-8117.** www.aquarellerestaurant.com. Reservations highly recommended. Main courses $27–$45; prix fixe: "Rapide" $40 or $55 with wine, "gourmand" $80 or $115 with wine. AE, DISC, MC, V. Tues–Thurs 6–9pm; Fri–Sat 6–10pm.

Driskill Grill ★★ NEW AMERICAN The dining room, softly lit and reminiscent of a prosperous *fin de siecle,* amounts to a calming and inviting escape from the trying times of the present. And it makes the perfect setting for enjoying a leisurely, sumptuous dinner. The cooking here doesn't shy away from rich ingredients as some other versions of New American cooking do. The menu changes seasonally, but representative dishes include the following: prawns with bits of grilled chorizo, charred tomatoes, corn butter, and coriander; charred beef tenderloin with jumbo shrimp and black truffle potato puree; and a cinnamon-dusted duck breast with whipped artichokes and Savoy cabbage. As might be expected from the restaurant's name, there are always offerings from the grill—venison, pork, beef, and seafood. At the end you'll want to linger a little longer with a snifter of cognac, especially if you've come to town with an expense account.

604 Brazos St., in The Driskill. ✆ **512/391-7162.** www.driskillgrill.com. Reservations recommended. Main courses $35–$48; 3-course prix fixe $55 per person; 5-course tasting menu $85, $135 with wine pairings. AE, DC, DISC, MC, V. Tues–Sat 5–9:30pm.

EXPENSIVE

Chez Nous ★ Value FRENCH With its lace curtains, fresh flowers in anisette bottles, and Folies Bergère posters, this intimate bistro feels closer to Paris, France, than to Paris, Texas. The French owners have maintained consistency and quality throughout the years. The most popular choice here is the prix-fixe dinner with a choice of soup, salad, or pâté; one of three designated entrees; and crème caramel, chocolate mousse, or brie for dessert. The main courses might include a *poisson poivre vert* (fresh fish of the day with a green-peppercorn sauce) or a simple but delicious roast chicken. Everything from the pâtés to the profiteroles is made on the premises.

510 Neches St. ✆ **512/473-2413.** www.cheznousaustin.com. Reservations accepted for parties of 6 or more only. Main courses $20–$28; menu du jour $26. AE, DC, DISC, MC, V. Tues–Fri 11:45am–2pm; Tues–Sun 6–10:30pm.

Gumbo's ★ CAJUN/CREOLE People forget that Texas shares a border with Louisiana. During the oil boom years of the first half of the last century, many from southern Louisiana settled in Texas to make their fortune. They brought their cooking with them, and over the years Texans have developed quite a taste for such Creole dishes as blackened fish, spicy jambalaya, and rich crawfish étoufée. These and other dishes from the broader Gulf Coast region are on the menu at Gumbo's. The mainstay is seafood, but beef, duck, and chicken are also included. If you go for lunch you can enjoy a New Orleans–style oyster po' boy. The dining room, with high ceilings and a black-and-white tiled floor, re-creates the atmosphere of a Louisiana cafe. The restaurant is in the renovated Art Deco Brown Building (1938), where LBJ used to have an office.

701 Colorado. ✆ **512/480-8053.** www.gumbosaustin.com. Reservations recommended on weekends. Main courses $18–$32. AE, DC, DISC, MC, V. Mon–Thurs 11am–2pm and 5:30–10pm; Fri 11am–2pm and 5:30–11pm; Sat 5:30–11pm.

La Traviata ★★ ITALIAN If you're tired of Italian restaurant clichés, you'll love this cozy, Euro-chic trattoria, with textured limestone walls complementing the hardwood floors, sleek bar, and sunny yellow walls. The food is just as unfussy and fresh. All the ingredients used by chef/owner Marion Gilchrist are of the highest quality, and the sauces are delicious without being overwhelming. You'll remember why such classics as chicken Parmesan or spaghetti Bolognese became popular in the first place and be dazzled by such creative dishes as scallops with couscous or crispy polenta with Gorgonzola cheese. Don't miss the tiramisu, wonderfully light with toasted hazelnuts and a dusting of espresso. The narrow room bustles with energy, especially on weekend pretheater evenings, but the staff never seems overwhelmed. Service is both knowledgeable and friendly.

314 Congress Ave. ✆ **512/479-8131.** www.latraviata.net. Reservations highly recommended Sat–Sun. Pasta $14–$16; main courses $16–$26. AE, DISC, MC, V. Mon–Fri 11:30am–2pm; Mon–Sat 5:30–10pm.

Roaring Fork ★★ SOUTHWEST The interpretation of Western cooking found at this restaurant leans heavily on cooking with wood fires. The dishes don't get too fancy but are executed with flair. Favorites include a hearty green chili pork, an extra large hamburger, spit-roasted chicken, and some lovely steaks. The menu changes seasonally, but you'll always find these selections or something comparable, as well as at least one item flavored with green chili. Seafood is always available as well.

On a recent visit, delicate crab cakes dusted in blue cornmeal, the aforementioned green chili pork stew, and a rich tortilla soup were on the menu. They were all delicious. Portions are generous; you can save money by going for lunch, which costs about half what dinner does. The dining room is comfortable, softly lit, and quieter than your average Austin restaurant. As might be expected, it's decorated in a Western theme that, while subdued, is still a bit clichéd. The desserts are impressive, but leave room for the margaritas.

701 Congress Ave. (in the InterContinental Stephen F. Austin). ✆ **512/583-0000.** www.roaringfork.com. Reservations recommended. Main courses $15–$30. AE, DC, DISC, MC, V. Mon–Fri 11:30am–10pm; Sat 5–11pm; Sun 5–9pm.

Shoreline Grill ★★ SEAFOOD/NEW AMERICAN Fish is the prime lure at this tony grill, which looks out over Town Lake and the Congress Avenue Bridge from beside the Four Seasons hotel. From late spring through early fall, many patrons come to catch a view of the bats taking flight from beneath the bridge. Thousands of Mexican free-tailed bats emerge in unison at dusk, and patio tables for viewing the phenomenon are at a premium.

When they're not admiring the view, diners focus on such starters as semolina-crusted oysters or venison chorizo quesadillas. Drum, or redfish, is a delicate, meaty fish from the Gulf and is worth trying if it's on the menu. And you can't go wrong with the salmon

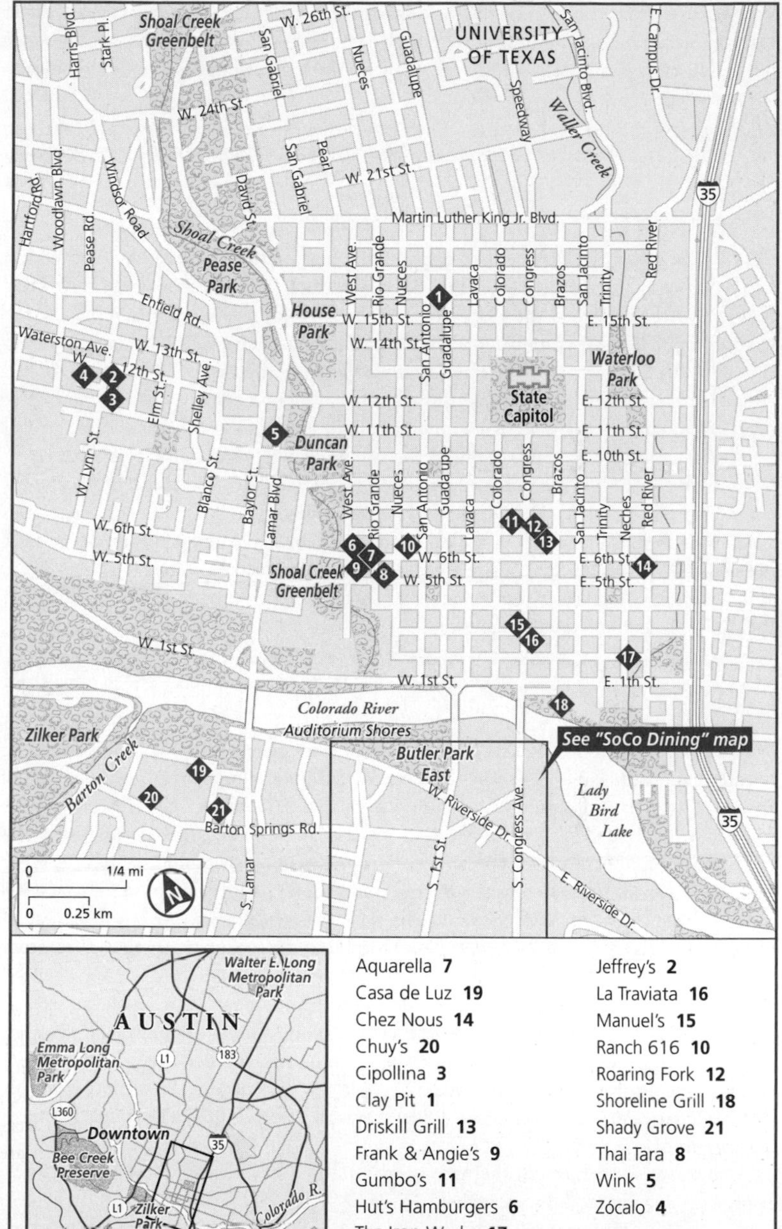
UNIVERSITY OF TEXAS
Shoal Creek Greenbelt
Pease Park
House Park
Duncan Park
State Capitol
Waterloo Park
Colorado River
Auditorium Shores
Zilker Park
Butler Park East
Lady Bird Lake
Barton Creek
Waller Creek
Shoal Creek
W. 26th St.
W. 24th St.
W. 21st St.
Martin Luther King Jr. Blvd.
W. 15th St.
W. 14th St.
W. 13th St.
W. 12th St.
W. 11th St.
W. 6th St.
W. 5th St.
W. 1st St.
E. 15th St.
E. 12th St.
E. 11th St.
E. 10th St.
E. 6th St.
E. 5th St.
E. 1th St.
Enfield Rd.
Waterston Ave.
Windsor Road
Barton Springs Rd.
W. Riverside Dr.
E. Riverside Dr.
S. Congress Ave.
S. 1st St.
S. Lamar
See "SoCo Dining" map
0 1/4 mi
0 0.25 km
N
Walter E. Long Metropolitan Park
AUSTIN
Emma Long Metropolitan Park
Downtown
Bee Creek Preserve
Zilker Park
Colorado R.
Aquarella 7
Casa de Luz 19
Chez Nous 14
Chuy's 20
Cipollina 3
Clay Pit 1
Driskill Grill 13
Frank & Angie's 9
Gumbo's 11
Hut's Hamburgers 6
The Iron Works 17
Jeffrey's 2
La Traviata 16
Manuel's 15
Ranch 616 10
Roaring Fork 12
Shoreline Grill 18
Shady Grove 21
Thai Tara 8
Wink 5
Zócalo 4

roasted on a plank of alder wood and served with a cilantro beurre blanc. Non-seafood dishes include Parmesan-crusted chicken with penne pasta and prime rib with horseradish potatoes. This restaurant has been in existence for 20 years and attracts a crowd of regulars, including many old Austin-establishment types. The no-nonsense dining room has comfortable furniture and white tablecloths. The high ceilings and tall windows give it an airy feel.

98 San Jacinto Blvd. ✆ **512/477-3300.** www.shorelinegrill.com. Reservations recommended (patio seating can't be guaranteed, but requests are taken). Main courses $16–$39. AE, DC, DISC, MC, V. Mon–Fri 11am–10pm; Sat–Sun 5–10pm.

MODERATE

Clay Pit ★ (Value INDIAN The old building that houses this restaurant had been a saloon for many years, as far back as the 1870s. The thick limestone walls and rough wood floors show their age, and the proportions of the large room still bring to mind the old saloon. But oh how the custom and wares have changed! The Clay Pit is known for Indian cooking with a bit of a twist. A good example would be the starter of perfectly cooked coriander calamari served with a piquant cilantro aioli. For an entree, consider *khuroos-e-tursh,* baked chicken breast stuffed with nuts, mushrooms, and onions, and smothered in a cashew-almond cream sauce; or one of the many dazzling vegetarian dishes.

At night, the dining room is softly lit, creating an attractive and romantic setting for dates or special occasions. During the day, it's something quite different—a place to grab a quick lunch from the buffet of typical Indian standards. The restaurant is located near the courthouse and the state office buildings just north of the capitol, so it gets a fare amount of office workers. Keep this in mind should you get hungry while touring either the capitol or the university campus.

1601 Guadalupe St. ✆ **512/322-5131.** www.claypit.com. Reservations recommended. $6.95 lunch buffet; main courses $10–$16. AE, DC, DISC, MC, V. Mon–Fri 11am–2pm and 5–10pm (till 11pm on Fri); Sat noon–3pm and 5–11pm.

Manuel's ★ MEXICAN This is one of the few moderately priced holdouts still to be found in a downtown dining scene that's been steadily heading uptown. Although there are some Tex-Mex dishes on the menu, most of the menu items are interior Mexican. You can get well-prepared versions of Mexican standards and some tweaked versions of the more common dishes, but Manuel's also offers hard-to-find specialties such as the *chiles rellenos en nogada* (chilies stuffed with pork and topped with walnut-cream sauce). A more common dish would be the *enchiladas banderas,* which are arrayed in the colors of the Mexican flag: a green *tomatillo verde* sauce, a white cream *suiza* sauce, and a red sauce.

In the evenings, Manuel's gets a lot of young professionals. The small bar area is crowded, and on weekends the wait for a table is about normal for Austin restaurants. The decor is assertively modern to draw a contrast with the building's original brick walls. There's a lively happy hour (daily 4–7pm), with half-price hors d'oeuvres, discounted drinks, and salsa music (see "Only in Austin," later in this chapter, for the musical Sun brunch).

A northwest branch is near the Arboretum, 10201 Jollyville Rd. (✆ **512/345-1042**). It presents live music Thursday nights.

310 Congress Ave. ✆ **512/472-7555.** www.manuels.com. Reservations accepted for 5 or more only. Main courses $9–$23. AE, DISC, MC, V. Mon–Thurs 11am–10pm; Fri–Sat 11am–midnight; Sun 10am–10pm.

Grocery Store Dining

Austinites have a fondness for dining in grocery stores, and I'm not talking about grazing the produce aisle. Indeed, the city's two grocery palaces, **Central Market** and **Whole Foods,** have large dining areas. Austinites like the casual feel of a grocery store and the convenience of mixing dining with the opportunity to pick up a couple of things forgotten on the last shopping trip. But for visitors, it's a good choice, too. Both of these stores are popular sightseeing destinations, so you can grab a bite and explore Austin's utopian vision of fine grocery shopping. The food is good, quick, and wholesome, and you control the portions. The prices are moderate and compare favorably to sitting down in a full-service restaurant. In both stores, indoor and outdoor seating are available, sometimes with live music. Whole Foods probably has more variety, though it's more self-serve and can be a little confusing. Food at both places is available during regular store hours. For more information see "Grocery Stores" in chapter 15.

Ranch 616 ★ SOUTHWEST The huge snake logo on the outside of an otherwise nondescript building—created by Bob "Daddy-O" Wade, best known for the oversize boots that front San Antonio's North Star Mall—is your first hint that this place might be a bit, well, different. Inside, cowboy kitsch, 1950s diner decor, and Mexican folk art mingle, as do workers from the nearby county offices, local movers and shakers, and anyone else looking for terrific food that, like the decor, defies easy categorization.

Call it South Texas gourmet. You can really taste the chipotle chilies in the tartar sauce that comes with some of the best crispy oysters this side of the Mason-Dixon Line, and the Gulf fish tacos are gussied up with chili lime aioli and Tabasco jalapeño onions. You get the idea—lots of spicy dishes. More soothing and delicious are such desserts as the banana shortbread tart and any of the fried pies. In case you hadn't guessed from the description of the decor, this place is a hoot. On Tuesdays and Thursdays, the diners are serenaded with live country music, usually good, but often too loud for conversation.

616 Nueces St. ✆ **512/479-7616.** http://ranch616.ypguides.net. Reservations recommended. Lunch $7–$10; dinner $14–$22. AE, DC, DISC, MC, V. Mon–Thurs 11am–2:30pm and 5:30–10pm; Fri–Sat 11am–2:30pm and 5:30–11pm.

INEXPENSIVE

Frank & Angie's Kids ITALIAN/PIZZA This unpretentious pizza joint offers some of the best thin-crust pizza in Austin. It's just west of the downtown area, right behind local landmark Hut's Hamburgers (see below). There's a full Italian menu, but pizza, the sandwiches, and calzone are what they do best here—especially the pizza, which comes with a crispy crust and is available by the slice. Prices are reasonable, service is fast and friendly, and the homey decor, with its half-hearted homage to Frank Sinatra, is enjoyable.

508 West Ave. (btw. Fifth and Sixth sts., near Lamar). ✆ **512/472-3534.** Sandwiches and calzones $6–$8; 18-in. pizzas $14–$18. AE, DISC, MC, V. Mon–Sat 11am–10pm; Sun 5–10pm.

Hut's Hamburgers Value AMERICAN This classic burger shack is very Austin. It opened its doors as Sammie's Drive-In in 1939, serving the traditional-style Texas burger with lettuce and onions. Now it offers 19 types of burgers, including a vegetarian garden burger (which is very Austin, too). As you might expect, you can also get fries and shakes, the usual burger complements; but for those who enjoy onion rings, this place is a special treat. Also on the menu are blue-plate specials of meatloaf, chicken-fried steak, and fried catfish. The decor is sports pennants and '50s memorabilia.

807 W. Sixth St. ✆ **512/472-0693.** Sandwiches and burgers $5–$8; plates $8–$9. AE, DISC, MC, V. Daily 11am–10pm.

The Iron Works ★ BARBECUE Some of the best barbecue in Austin is served in one of the most unusual settings. Until 1977, this building housed the ironworks of the Weigl family, who came over from Germany in 1913. You can see their ornamental craft all around town, including at the state capitol. Cattle brands created for Jack Benny ("Lasting 39"), Lucille Ball, and Bob Hope are displayed in front of the restaurant. The beef ribs are the most popular order, with the brisket running a close second. Lean turkey breast and juicy chicken are also smoked to perfection.

100 Red River (at E. First St.). ✆ **800/669-3602** or 512/478-4855. www.ironworksbbq.com. Reservations accepted for large parties only. Sandwiches $3–$5; plates $6–$12; meat by the lb. $5–$11. AE, DC, MC, V. Mon–Sat 11am–9pm.

Thai Tara ★ ASIAN/THAI This restaurant is nothing fancy, but it offers some of the best Thai food in Austin at the right price, and it's well positioned for visitors to the downtown area. The lunch specials are a good deal during the week, but my favorite time to go is in the evening after the temperatures have come down. The green curry is very aromatic. Also delicious is the Pad Kee Mao, with lots of fresh basil. The Pad Thai is good, too. The tree-shaded patio, with nice views of the Austin skyline, is a lovely spot for dinner.

601 W. Sixth St. ✆ **512/236-0856.** Reservations not accepted. Lunch specials $6–$8; main courses $8.50–$14. MC, V. Mon–Fri 11am–3pm and 5–10pm; Sat noon–11pm; Sun noon–10pm.

4 SOUTH AUSTIN

EXPENSIVE

Green Pastures ★ NEW AMERICAN Peacocks strut their stuff among wooded grounds surrounding this 1894 mansion, which was converted into a restaurant in 1945. The Southern graciousness and impeccable service have been a constant over the years, but the new millennium brought a new chef, who gently nudged the menu away from its staid moorings toward a brasher, more inventive cuisine.

With its peaceful grounds and calm, attractive dining spaces, this is a comfortable place to have an elegant and delicious meal. But it's definitely not one of the talked-about places. The menu changes seasonally, but you might find something like the following: pumpkin seed–seared salmon with poached prawns served with grilled cactus, garlic butter, hibiscus reduction, and cilantro oil; smoked prime rib-eye with crab, avocado, and cured tomatoes; and seared duck breast with Swiss chard, bacon, roasted garlic, and apple-rhubarb chutney. The presentation and combinations of tastes are excellent. You'll

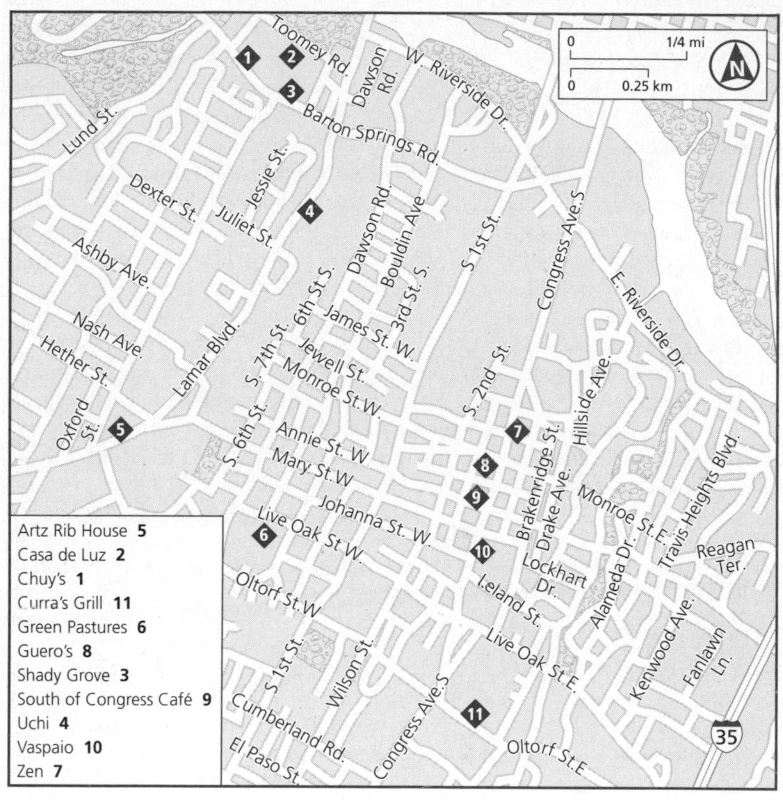

need to exercise the most restraint at dessert when offered such treats as Texas Pecan Ball (vanilla ice cream rolled in nuts and dripping fudge) and Bananas Foster.

811 W. Live Oak Rd. ✆ **512/444-4747.** www.greenpasturesrestaurant.com. Reservations recommended. Main courses $19–$35; Sunday brunch $30. AE, DC, DISC, MC, V. Daily 11am–2pm and 6–10pm (Sun brunch buffet 11am–2pm).

Uchi ★★★ ASIAN/JAPANESE Chef/owner Tyson Cole is getting lots of recognition for his inventive Japanese food. Three years ago he was named one of America's best new chefs by *Food & Wine* magazine. He loves to play with ingredients Texans are familiar with to create Asian dishes that are beautifully presented and exciting to Austin's tastes. His Uchiviche—citrus-marinated whitefish and salmon mixed with tomato, peppers, cilantro, and chilies—will make a believer out of you. It's not only the seafood that gets the culinary crossover treatment: Brie, pumpkin, shiitake mushrooms, and asparagus are among the food items that you can order tempura-style. And the skewered kobe beef should satisfy those who eschew vegetables and fish. Choose from a long list of cold sakes—especially the rare upmarket brands—for the perfect complement. The space, a converted 1930s bungalow done up in Asian reds and blacks, is at once dramatic and spare.

 801 S. Lamar Blvd. ✆ **512/916-4808.** www.uchiaustin.com. Reservations accepted (and strongly recommended) for Mon–Thurs 5:30–9pm and Fri–Sat 5:30–6:30pm. Main courses $15–$30; sushi (per piece) $3–$5; sashimi, hot and cold plates $5–$25. AE, DISC, MC, V. Mon–Thurs 5–10pm; Fri–Sat 5–11pm.

Vespaio & Enoteca Vespaio ★ ITALIAN Austin isn't really known for its Italian food, but when Austinites want Italian, this is their preferred destination. Vespaio's swanked-up old storefront with lots of exposed brick and glass is an elegant setting, and the food is worth waiting for, but you can drop quite a bit of dough on expensive wines while you're doing so. Your best bet is to get an order of the crispy calamari (they're huge) while you're waiting for a table. The spaghetti alla carbonara is super, as is the veal scallopini with mushrooms. Many come for the pizza. Try the *boscaiola,* topped with wild boar sausage and Cambozola cheese. Among the 10 chalkboard specials offered nightly, the mixed meat and seafood grills are usually top-notch. It's important to note that reservations are limited to off-peak hours and days (see below).

Next door is the Enoteca, which is more informal, a bit less expensive, and offers lighter fare. It's open for lunch and dinner. The dining room is a little more cramped but is a very attractive space, perfect for an afternoon coffee, a panini, or a glass of wine. There's a small outdoor patio, too. One of the starters served here is a plate of crispy fried risotto balls filled with fontina. There's a small cold case filled with Italian delicacies for those interested in taking something back to the hotel room.

1610 S. Congress Ave. ✆ **512/441-6100.** www.austinvespaio.com. Reservations accepted for Sun–Thurs 5:30–6:30pm only. Pizzas and pastas $14–$21; main courses $17–$28. AE, DISC, MC, V. Daily 5:30–10:30pm (bar 5pm–midnight). **Enoteca Vespaio** ✆ **512/441-7672.** No reservations. Pizzas and pastas $12–$16. AE, DISC, MC, V. Mon–Sat 10am–10pm; Sun 9am–3pm.

MODERATE

Artz Rib House ★ Kids BARBECUE If you want to be really efficient in your visit to Austin, you can get your fill of live music and BBQ all in one convenient stop. Artz gets some talented local musicians playing bluegrass and country music from 7:30 to 9:30pm just about every night (except Sunday, when they play from 6:30–8:30pm). The

Tips Sweet Tooth

Amy's, Austin's homegrown brand of ice cream, is wonderfully rich and creamy. But eating it is only half the fun. Watching the colorfully clad servers juggling the scoops is a kick. Amy's has nine Austin locations, including one on the west side of downtown, 1012 W. Sixth St., at Lamar Boulevard (✆ **512/480-0673**); one in SoCo, 1301 S. Congress Ave. (✆ **512/440-7488**); and one at the Arboretum, 10000 Research Blvd. (✆ **512/345-1006**). And if you don't have a chance to try it in town, you can catch this tasty treat at the airport.

Another place to keep in mind is **Hey Cupcake!** (no phone), which sells oversize cupcakes from an Airstream trailer parked on the 1600 block of South Congress at Milton Street. It opens Tuesday to Saturday at noon and Sunday at 1pm, and it closes when the cupcakes run out. The place is so popular that when the land on which the trailer sits was sold recently, the new owners assured the public that Hey Cupcake! would remain. The most popular flavors are the red velvet and the "Michael Jackson."

food merits a visit even if a band isn't playing. The country-style pork ribs are indeed the standout, but the brisket and sausage aren't far behind. The good news is that you don't have to choose between them; just tell the waiter you want a plate with all three. For lovers of white meat, Artz offers turkey and chicken. The plates come with a choice of the traditional sides, of which the cole slaw and the potato salad are my favorites. The decor is homey, and the staff is easy-going yet efficient.

2330 South Lamar. ✆ **512/442-8283.** www.artzribhouse.com. Reservations not accepted. Sandwiches $5–$7; plates $9–$18. No credit cards. Mon–Sat 11am–10pm; Sun noon–9pm.

Casa de Luz ★ Value VEGAN/MACROBIOTIC Austin has a large vegetarian community, and this is one of its favorite restaurants. The dining experience here is easy and relaxed. The restaurant is part of a larger project to be more environmentally sound and nurturing (but not preachy). From the Parkside Montessori school at the front of the property, a shaded walkway leads to the dining room in back, past a book/gift shop, massage rooms, and a yoga studio. The dining room is a large, attractive space with lots of windows shaded with bamboo. Lunch and dinner consist of a set menu of soup, salad, and entree for a fixed price. (Check the website or call to find out what's cooking.) All the food is organic, vegan, macrobiotic, and gluten-free. Those with a sweet tooth can grab a piece of pie or cake at the dessert bar. There is no waitstaff and no tipping, as guests are expected to bus their own dishes.

1701 Toomey Rd. ✆ **512/476-2335,** ext. 3 (ext. 2 for menu). www.casadeluz.org. No reservations. Breakfast $7, lunch or dinner $12. MC, V. Daily 7–10am, 11:30am–2pm, and 6–8:30pm.

Chuy's Kids TEX-MEX In the row of low-priced, friendly restaurants that line Barton Springs Road just east of Zilker Park, Chuy's stands out for its determinedly wacky decor—hubcaps lining the ceiling, Elvis memorabilia galore—and its sauce-smothered Tex-Mex food. You're not likely to leave hungry after specials such as Chuy's special enchiladas, piled high with smoked chicken and cheese and topped with sour cream, or one of the "big as yo' face" burritos, stuffed with ground sirloin, say, and cheese and beans.

This has been a local landmark since long before presidential daughter Jenna Bush got busted here for underage drinking. It's difficult to blame her. Chuy's is popular and doesn't take reservations; most people wait for a table by grabbing a seat in the bar area and ordering appetizers and "Mexican martinis" (like margaritas, but bigger and with olives). Try to stay away from the free nacho bar or you'll ruin your appetite. Other locations have sprouted up: in the north on 10520 N. Lamar Blvd. (✆ **512/836-3218**), in the northwest at 11680 N. Research Blvd. (✆ **512/342-0011**), and far south at 4301 William Cannon (✆ **512/899-2489**).

1728 Barton Springs Rd. ✆ **512/474-4452.** www.chuys.com. Reservations not accepted. Main courses $8–$12. AE, DISC, MC, V. Sun–Thurs 11am–10pm; Fri–Sat 11am–11pm.

Curra's Grill ★★ Kids MEXICAN This plain, unassuming restaurant has a strong local following for its large menu of interior Mexican dishes and moderate prices. The tortillas are handmade. The Mexican tamales (not the kind usually served in Texas) come in several flavors and are quite good, with moist, spongy *masa.* You can build your own enchiladas from a selection of sauces and fillings—I like the *mole* and the *chile pasilla.* The Yucatecan *cochinita pibil* (pork baked in a marinade of achiote, sour orange, and herbs and spices) is tender and complex. The *pescado veracruzano* is fish baked in a sauce of tomatoes, onions, olives, and capers. It's a bit different from the dish as it is served in its home of Veracruz, but great nonetheless. There are also a lot of Tex-Mex options as well, such as the tostadas, piled high with lettuce and crumbled fresh cheese. For dessert, the flan can't be beat.

614 E. Oltorf. ✆ **512/444-0012.** Reservations recommended for large parties. Main courses $8–$17. AE, DISC, MC, V. Daily 7am–10pm.

Güero's ★ Kids TEX-MEX This is one of the main hangouts on South Congress. It occupies an old feed store that dates from the time when South Austin was a low-rent area at the margins of the city. The restaurant has retained as much of the old feed store as it could, capturing the feel of homey informality that Austinites love. Floors of worn wood and stained cement; brick walls coated in old, faded paint; tall ceilings; tin roof; cheap tables and chairs—it's welcoming and friendly. It's also popular, and noisy when crowded. I like it best during off-hours. The restaurant makes its own tortillas by hand for dishes such as tacos (and the tacos *al pastor,* served Mexican style on small tortillas, folded around deliciously seasoned, grilled pork with pineapple, onion, and cilantro, are one of the dishes this place is known for). Lots of people come for the queso. I like the chicken breast marinated in achiote and Mexican oregano, which can be served on a salad, in enchiladas, or in tacos. If you're trying to get your vegetables, the spinach enchiladas will work. Otherwise, go with some of the Tex-Mex combo plates. None of the food is particularly spicy.

1412 S. Congress. ✆ **512/447-7688.** www.guerostacobar.com. Reservations not accepted. Main courses $7–$19. AE, DC, DISC, MC, V. Mon–Fri 11am–11pm; Sat–Sun 8am–11pm.

Matt's El Rancho TEX-MEX This old South Austin standby is avoided by the young, hip crowd, in favor of some of the seedier, "more authentic" Tex-Mex dives. To them the place lacks character. But the rest of Austin comes here to chow down on dependable old-school Tex-Mex dishes such as enchiladas in chili gravy, flautas, or fajitas. The *chiles rellenos* and shrimp a la Mexicana (smothered with peppers, onions, tomato, ranchero sauce, and Jack cheese) are perennial favorites. Or you can go for a bit of everything by ordering one of the combo plates.

The original restaurant was opened downtown in 1952 by Matt Martinez, a former prizefighter. In 1986, he moved to the present location in South Austin, and now his son, Matt, Jr., manages it. The restaurant is large with lots of parking. It gets crowded on weekend nights, especially if there's a university event, and you might have to wait up to an hour. As luck would have it, there's a bar area and terrace where you can sip a fresh-lime margarita until your table is ready. Unless Matt's is really packed, noise isn't an issue. There are several dining rooms, and the tables aren't bunched together. Service is great.

2613 S. Lamar Blvd. ✆ **512/462-9333.** www.mattselrancho.com. Reservations not accepted after 6pm on Sat Sun, except for large groups. Dinners $8.50–$18. AE, DC, DISC, MC, V. Sun–Mon and Wed–Thurs 11am–10pm; Fri–Sat 11am–11pm.

South Congress Cafe ★ SOUTHWEST A small, modern establishment in the heart of SoCo that caters mostly to South Austin's leisure crowd, the cafe opens for brunch and dinner. For brunch, order the *migas* (Austin's favorite breakfast—eggs scrambled with strips of tortillas, tomatoes, onions, and chilies), which are some of the best; avoid the omelets, which are rubbery. For something hearty, try the wild boar red *pozole* (a Mexican-style soup served as a main course) for either brunch or dinner. It's a great mix of flavors and textures—succulent bits of pork, dark red chili sauce, and spongy grains of hominy, garnished with finely shredded cabbage and minced onion. For dinner, the crab cakes, the tomato-stilton soup, and the beef tenderloin are all recommendable. The menu changes seasonally, but these dishes are always offered. The dining room is a bit cramped but has a high ceiling and tall windows facing South Congress that give it a light and airy feel. At the height of the dinner hour it can get noisy.

1600 S. Congress. ✆ **512/447-3905.** www.southcongresscafe.com. Reservations not accepted. Main courses $9–$22. AE, DC, MC, V. Mon–Fri 10am–4pm, 5–10pm; Sat–Sun 9am–4pm, 5–10pm.

INEXPENSIVE

Shady Grove ★ AMERICAN Also on Barton Springs Rd. is this ironic salute to Americana. The restaurant captures a bit of the feel of David Lynch's vision of small town "Twin Peaks," including the corny touches. Stonework and yellow pine planks make up a good bit of the dining room's interior. Deep booths lining the walls and windows covered by old-fashioned Venetian blinds complete the picture. And the menu adds to the ambience with such classics as Freddie's Airstream chili, meatloaf, and fried catfish. Shady Grove is known for its burgers made with ground sirloin. A popular choice is the green chili cheeseburger. Also, the hippie sandwich (grilled eggplant, veggies, and cheese with pesto mayonnaise) is a good bet.

When the weather is agreeable most patrons sit out on the very large patio shaded by trees. On Thursdays during spring and summer this is the site of a free concert series called Shady Grove Unplugged. It features popular local artists and runs from 7 to 10pm.

1624 Barton Springs Rd. ✆ **512/474-9991.** www.theshadygrove.com. Reservations not accepted. Main courses $8–$11. AE, DC, DISC, MC, V. Sun–Thurs 11am–10pm; Fri–Sat 11am–11pm.

Zen Value Kids JAPANESE The food is flavorful, healthy, and inexpensive, the pared-down room is light and welcoming—if you're looking for a nice, quick bite, it's hard to beat Zen. The poultry in such dishes as chicken teriyaki and veggies, for example, is organic; 25¢ gets you brown instead of white rice with your order; and the menu has so many heart-healthy symbols on it that it resembles a Valentine's card. Most of the food is typically Japanese—sushi, udon noodles, rice bowls, and teriyaki dishes—except, for some reason, for the Madison Mac & Cheese. No doubt it's a tongue-in-cheek touch, like the light fixtures that look like Chia pet doormats. You order at the counter, and the food is brought to your table (generally) very quickly.

Two newer locations are at 2900 W. Anderson Lane, Ste. 250 (✆ **512/451-4811**), and 3423 N. Guadalupe (✆ **512/300-2633**).

1303 S. Congress Ave. ✆ **512/444-8081.** www.eatzen.com. Reservations not accepted. $4.25–$8. DISC, MC, V. Daily 11am–10pm.

5 WEST AUSTIN

VERY EXPENSIVE

Jeffrey's ★★ NEW AMERICAN This little bistro in the old Clarksville neighborhood west of downtown has been a destination for food lovers for over 25 years. Some locals feel that its arrival marked the first steps of the city's march towards a food and dining culture. In keeping with the tone set by the surrounding neighborhood, the bistro is cozy, comfortable, and informal. The furniture and lighting are handled nicely, and you relax from the moment you ease into a dining chair.

Making your way through the menu, you'll find several appetizers. Most of these rotate with seasons, but one in particular, a signature dish of Jeffrey's, will always be there:

the crispy oysters on yucca chips topped with habanero honey aioli. Indeed, it alone brings many people to dine here. You might also find the duck spring rolls with a jicama-mango slaw. Main courses tend to have so many flavors inserted into a dish that the diner is sometimes left wondering whether the composition will hold together at all. Examples of these combinations are beef tenderloin with vanilla potatoes and smoked chili crab sauce, or duck and shrimp with black lentils and an orange-ginger glaze. In my experience, Jeffrey's pulls it off, but I'm still left wondering about the dishes I didn't order. If you want comfort food, try some other establishment.

1204 W. Lynn. ✆ **512/477-5584.** www.jeffreysofaustin.com. Reservations strongly recommended. Main courses $19–$44; tasting menu $76, with wines $112. AE, DC, DISC, MC, V. Mon–Thurs 6–10pm; Fri–Sat 5:30–10:30pm; Sun 6–9:30pm.

MODERATE

Cipollina ★★ (Finds) ITALIAN This former deli and sandwich shop has recently shifted gears and become an excellent neighborhood bistro. The new chefs are detail-oriented control freaks who do their own butchering and curing and insist on buying from local organic farmers and ranchers. The pizzas and the sandwiches that Cipollina was known for are still on the menu and even better. Try the bacon and gorgonzola pizza. On the third Wednesday of every month, patrons enjoy a food and wine pairing menu (6 courses and 3 wines) for $30; and on the first Wednesday, the owners plan to begin serving a "farm dinner" that features the produce of a particular local farm. Simple elegance is the hallmark of the dining room, with comfortable furniture and lots of space. Prices are good for the kind of cooking you get here, but I suspect they might climb a bit now that this bistro is attracting a loyal following. The menu changes seasonally. To finish off your meal, walk a block south to Caffe Medici for some of the best espresso in Austin.

1213 W. Lynn. ✆ **512/477-5211.** www.cipollina-austin.com. Reservations not accepted. Pizzas $7–$15; sandwiches $6–$8; main courses $10–$19. AE, MC, V. Daily 11am–10pm.

Hula Hut (Finds) TEX-MEX/AMERICAN This place scores a big hit with my out-of-town friends. Of course, they're in vacation mode when they come here. They want to enjoy some Tex-Mex in a festive setting, and this restaurant strikes the right note. The Hula Hut brings a slightly cheesy Hawaiian theme to Tex-Mex cooking. Nothing is taken seriously. Brash and colorful, the main dining room invites good cheer, but the best thing about this place is the outdoor dining on the pier extending out into Lake Austin, with a view of the hills across the way. The fajita plates are especially good, and the other Tex-Mex dishes are irreproachable. For a sampler, try the Pu pu platter (nachos, flautas, tacos, and queso). This place is popular, and parking is sometimes a problem, so go early or late if you can.

3826 Lake Austin Blvd. ✆ **512/476-4852.** www.hulahut.com. Reservations not accepted. Main courses $9–$15. AE, MC, V. Sun–Thurs 11am–10pm; Fri–Sat 11am–11pm.

INEXPENSIVE

Zocalo (Value) MEXICAN This fast-food Mexican cafe in the Clarksville neighborhood offers light, healthy fare for reasonable prices. You place your order at the counter, and the staff bring it to your table. The food is fresh, and the tortillas are made in-house. The soft tacos, which come three to the order, accompanied by rice and beans, make for just the right amount to satisfy an appetite without overeating. The fillings vary between vegetables, fish, fowl, and fajitas. Unlike Tex-Mex, they don't come topped with cheese. Specialties include the Zocalo plate, which is another name for what Mexicans call *chilaquiles con pollo*—tortilla bits, cooked with chicken in a green sauce and topped with crumbled fresh cheese and sour cream. The popular "tostada salad" comes with black beans, avocado, cilantro, roasted jalapeños, and a lime dressing. There's also a good choice of soups. The dining area is flooded by natural light from tall windows, and an outdoor area is available when the weather is agreeable.

1110 West Lynn St. ✆ **512/472-8226.** www.zocalocafe.com. Plates $6–$9. AE, DISC, MC, V. Mon–Fri 11am–10pm; Sat–Sun 10am–10pm.

6 CENTRAL

EXPENSIVE

Fonda San Miguel ★ MEXICAN This was one of the first restaurants to introduce fine dining a la Mexicana to Texas, and it's a landmark restaurant. But as of late, it has been in a holding pattern, keeping the quality up but not showing much imagination. You can get classic dishes such as *mole poblano* and *cochinita pibil* that are nicely prepared, but the dinner menu doesn't have much that's new. Fonda enjoys a faithful clientele that is locked in. These customers seek the dishes that they know, and the dining experience, when taken as a whole, is thoroughly enjoyable. There's something about the graceful rooms, the rich colors, and the attractive lighting that makes for a charming evening. For the pleasure of this experience, you pay quite a bit more than at other Mexican restaurants, but for a special evening it's worth it.

Sunday brunch is a big deal at Fonda, with a more interesting selection of dishes (such as fruit gazpacho and *chilaquiles*). If money were no object . . .

2330 W. North Loop. ✆ **512/459-4121** or 459-3401. www.fondasanmiguel.com. Reservations recommended. Main courses $18–$31; Sunday brunch $50. AE, DC, DISC, MC, V. Mon–Thurs 5:30–9:30pm; Fri–Sat 5:30–10:30pm (bar opens 30 min. earlier); Sun brunch 11am–2pm.

Wink ★★ (Finds) NEW AMERICAN This small and slightly cramped restaurant should be a prime destination for serious gourmets. Chef/owners Stewart Scruggs and Mark Paul are fresh-ingredient fanatics and have a top-notch staff. Your server should be able to fill you in on every detail of the menu, down to the organic farm where the arugula and fennel in your rabbit confit salad came from. The menu changes daily, so check the listings on the restaurant's website. The cooking aims at just the right combination of tastes and is directed by a less-is-more philosophy, as exemplified by such dishes as seared scallop on pancetta with baby sweet potatoes and more adventurous dishes such as braised boar belly with apple cider sauce. Portions are small, so you might be better of going for the tasting menu, which often includes some off-menu surprises.

1014 N. Lamar Blvd. ✆ **512/482-8868.** www.winkrestaurant.com. Reservations strongly recommended. Main courses $16–$30; 5-course tasting menu $65, $95 with wine; 7-course tasting menu $85, $125 with wines. AE, DC, DISC, MC, V. Mon–Thurs 6–11pm; Fri–Sat 5: 30–11pm.

MODERATE

Asti ★ (Value) ITALIAN This is the Italian place everyone wants in their neighborhood: casual, consistently good, and reasonably priced. An open kitchen and retro Formica-topped tables create a hip, upbeat atmosphere. The designer pizzas make a nice light meal, and northern Italian specialties such as the Calabrese-style trout and the pan-seared halibut with green beans are winners. Save room for such desserts as the creamy espresso sorbet or the amazing bittersweet chocolate cannoli. For a little restaurant, Asti has an unexpectedly large and well-selected wine list (mostly Italian and Californian bottles). The beer list is smaller, but it's good to have one at all.

408C E. 43rd St. ✆ **512/451-1218.** www.astiaustin.com. Reservations recommended Thurs–Sat. Pizzas, pastas $8–$13; main courses $10–$20. AE, DISC, MC, V. Mon–Thurs 11am–10pm; Fri 11am–11pm; Sat 5–11pm.

Hyde Park Bar & Grill ★ Value AMERICAN In the Hyde Park neighborhood's little enclave of restaurants along Duval Street is the Hyde Park Bar & Grill, easy to spot owing to the giant fork out front. Not only is it easy to find, it's easy to get to, it's easy to park your car, and, at least during off hours, it's easy to get a table here. If you do have to wait, then it's easy to have a drink at the bar. On weekends, this place is popular, especially when there are events at the university. In addition to the chicken-fried steak (and more healthful options, such as the roast chicken or any one of the various salads), people come here for the battered French fries, which are perennially voted best fries in Austin. The atmosphere at Hyde Park—a one-story former home now divided into different dining rooms—is cozy, and the service is quick and unobtrusive. There's now a south location at 4521 West Gate Blvd. (✆ **512/899-2700**), which is at the West Gate Shopping Center, on the southeast corner of the intersection of South Lamar and Ben White Blvd. (Hwy. 71).

4206 Duval St. ✆ **512/458-3168.** Reservations not accepted. Salads and sandwiches $6–$9; main courses $10–$16. AE, DC, DISC, MC, V. Daily 11am–midnight.

INEXPENSIVE

Mother's Café & Garden Value VEGETARIAN/VEGAN This neighborhood vegetarian restaurant is attractive, spacious, and softly lit. The dining rooms are understated modern with touches of hominess. They conjure up Austin's laid-back mood in much the same way as the old place did before it was gutted by fire in 2007 (caused, in an ironic twist, by a homeless man who late one night was cooking some meat behind the restaurant). Vegetarians are among the mellowest of Austin's latent hippie culture, making this place welcome relief from some of the more frenetic eateries in town. If there's a signature dish, it might be the artichoke enchiladas with mushrooms and black olives. Many prefer the zingier barbecued tofu. Aside from these and other regionally inspired dishes, there are vegetarian standards such as spinach lasagna, a vegetable stir fry, and a popular veggie burger. If you order a salad, check out the cashew-tamari dressing, which is very popular. Desserts are quite good, and you might consider ordering two—after such a healthful entree, you can afford a small indulgence.

4215 Duval St. ✆ **512/451-3994.** www.motherscafeaustin.com. Reservations not accepted. Main courses $8–$10. DISC, MC, V. Mon–Fri 11:15am–10pm; Sat–Sun 10am–10pm.

Threadgill's ★ Kids AMERICAN/SOUTHERN If you want a hit of music history along with heaping plates of down-home food at good prices, this Austin institution is for you. When Kenneth Threadgill obtained Travis County's first legal liquor license after the repeal of prohibition in 1933, he turned his Gulf gas station into a club. His Wednesday-night shows were legendary in the 1960s, with performers such as Janis Joplin turning up regularly. In turn, the Southern-style diner that was added on in 1980 became renowned for its huge chicken-fried steaks, as well as its vegetables. You can get fried okra, broccoli-rice casserole, garlic-cheese grits, black-eyed peas, and the like in combination plates or as sides.

Family-Friendly Restaurants

Curra's (p. 207), **Güero's** (p. 208), **Hoover's** (p. 214), **Threadgill's** (p. 212), and **Zen** (p. 209) all have special menus for ages 12 and under, not to mention casual, kid-friendly atmospheres and food inexpensive enough to feed everyone without taking out a second mortgage. **Chuy's** (p. 207) is great for teens and aspiring teens, who love the cool T-shirts, Elvis kitsch, and green iguanas crawling up the walls. And it provides a cautionary tale about underage drinking (or at least the perils of being related to the president). **Frank & Angie's** (p. 203) has delicious thin-crust pizza, and kids love the festive atmosphere. At the **County Line on the Hill** (p. 216), all-you-can-eat platters of meat (beef ribs, brisket, and sausage), and generous bowls of potato salad, coleslaw, and beans are just $5.95 for children under 12.

Eddie Wilson, the current owner of Threadgill's, was the founder of the now-defunct Armadillo World Headquarters, Austin's most famous music venue (the South Austin branch, 301 W. Riverside [✆ **512/472-9304**], is called Threadgill's World Headquarters). Across the street from the old Armadillo, it's filled with music memorabilia from the club and a state-of-the-art sound system. Unlike the original location, it lays on a Sunday brunch buffet and a "howdy" hour during the week. Both branches still double as live-music venues.

6416 N. Lamar Blvd. ✆ **512/451-5440.** www.threadgills.com. Reservations not accepted. Sandwiches and burgers $8–$9; main courses $9–$17. DISC, MC, V. Mon–Sat 11am–10pm; Sun 11am–9pm.

7 EAST SIDE

MODERATE

Eastside Cafe AMERICAN This was one of the earliest eateries to open in this rapidly changing area just east of the university, on the other side of the I-35 freeway. Eastside Cafe remains popular with student herbivores and congressional carnivores alike. Diners enjoy eating on a tree-shaded patio or in one of a series of small, homey rooms in a classic turn-of-the-century bungalow.

This restaurant gears its menu to all appetites. You can get half orders of such pasta dishes as the pesto ravioli, of the mixed field green salad topped with warm goat cheese, and of entrees like the sesame-breaded catfish. Many of the main courses have a Southern comfort orientation—pork tenderloin with cornbread stuffing, say—and all come with soup or salad and a vegetable. Each morning, the gardener informs the head chef which of the vegetables in the restaurant's large organic garden are ready for active duty. An adjoining store carries gardening tools, cookware, and the cafe's salad dressings.

2113 Manor Rd. ✆ **512/476-5858.** www.eastsidecafeaustin.com. Reservations recommended. Pastas $14–$18; main courses $10–$22. AE, DC, DISC, MC, V. Mon–Thurs 11:15am–9:30pm; Fri 11:15am–10pm; Sat 10am–10pm; Sun 10am–9:30pm (brunch Sat–Sun 10am–3pm).

INEXPENSIVE

Hoover's Finds Kids AMERICAN/SOUTHERN This is down-home comfort food at its best. When native Austinite Alexander Hoover, long a presence on the local restaurant scene, opened up his own place near the neighborhood where he grew up, he looked to his mother's recipes and added a smidge of Cajun and Tex-Mex for inspiration. Fried catfish, meatloaf, and gravy-smothered pork chops, with sides of mac and cheese or jalapeño-creamed spinach, come to the table in generous-sized portions. For a sandwich, try the muffaletta. And if you haven't yet tried that Texas standard, the chicken-fried steak, this is a great place to do so. Check the chalkboard for daily specials, seasonal side dishes, and available desserts. If coconut cream pie is on the list, making a decision is much easier. The crowd is a mix of the East Side African-American community, UT students, and food lovers from all around town.

2002 Manor Rd. ✆ **512/479-5006.** www.hooverscooking.com. Reservations not accepted. Sandwiches (with 1 side) $8–$9; plates (with 2 sides) $10–$15. DC, DISC, MC, V. Daily 8am–10pm.

Vivo ★ TEX-MEX Vivo bills its food as "healthful Tex-Mex" and has brown rice and tofu on the menu. I'm not sure how healthful it really is, but I can vouch for the taste. The first thing the diner is presented with—a smoky, garlicky salsa made with blackened serrano chilies—is superb. The tortilla soup is hearty and filled with crunchy bits of tortilla contrasting with smooth chunks of avocado. The puffy tacos—handmade tortillas that puff up when fried (in canola oil, of course)—are messy to eat, but are a little-known Tex-Mex classic. They come filled with spiced beef or chicken, lettuce, tomato, and cheese. The *enchiladas verdes,* stuffed with chicken and topped with a nicely spiked *tomatillo* sauce, are quite good. The sauce is plentiful, as it should be (often not the case in other restaurants). The service is good, and the margarita menu is complete. If you're looking for something different, try a paloma, made with tequila, lots of lime juice, and grapefruit soda—a popular Mexican drink perfect for hot weather.

Vivo is a date place and gets crowded on Friday and Saturday nights. Reservations aren't accepted, so if you mind waiting (even when having a drink in hand) go on another night. Indoors, the walls are painted bright yellow, purple, and red, and hung with vibrant Mexican art, including a fun version of the usual mounted head of a longhorn bull. Outside, you can dine on a deck decorated with tropical plants and a gurgling fountain.

2015 Manor Rd. ✆ **512/482-0300.** Reservations not accepted. Main courses and combination plates $10–$16. AE, DC, DISC, MC, V. Mon–Thurs 11am–10pm; Fri–Sat 11am–10:30pm; Sun 5–9pm.

8 NORTHWEST

VERY EXPENSIVE

Eddie V's Edgewater Grille ★ SEAFOOD/STEAK This swanky restaurant in the Arboretum mall is one of the hottest dinner spots in the northwest. The supper club atmosphere—white tablecloths, lots of black accents—should be credited in part, but the main hook is the top-notch seafood. The crispy calamari appetizer and lump crab cake make great starters, but you might be better off going for the less-filling oysters-on-the-half-shell. This place doesn't stint on portion sizes, and Parmesan-crusted lemon sole or smoked salmon with horseradish butter might not cut it as breakfast the next day. Besides, you want to leave room for the hot bread pudding soufflé, large enough for a table (as long as you're not dining with an entourage). The downtown Eddie V's, 301 E. Fifth St. (✆ **512/472-1860**), has the same menu, the same decor, and the same "see and be seen" cachet, but it doesn't have this room's Hill Country views at sunset. Both offer good happy hours (4:30–7pm), with half-price appetizers and $1 off wines and cocktails.

9400-B Arboretum Blvd. ✆ **512/342-2642.** www.eddiev.com. Reservations recommended. Main courses $20–$39. AE, DC, DISC, MC, V. Sun–Thurs 4:30–10pm; Fri–Sat 4:30–11pm.

MODERATE

Chez Zee ★ Finds NEW AMERICAN This is a charming neighborhood bakery/bistro noted for its incredible desserts and weekend brunches. You should consider it for lunch or dinner if you find yourself anywhere near the Mo-Pac freeway. Simply take it to the Northland (2222) exit and go 1 block west, turning left on to Balcones. The dining room, with its whimsical artwork, its many windows, and enclosed front patio, is light and cheerful. And it would be tough to bring someone here who couldn't find something to like on the eclectic menu—crunchy, fried dill pickles, perhaps, or tasty tequila-lime grilled chicken. In fact, it's hard to find a culinary category in which Chez Zee doesn't shine. It topped the "Best American," "Best Dessert," and "Best Soup" categories in the *Austin Chronicle* readers' poll. The desserts are rich and varied. It's tempting to go for something chocolaty (there's plenty to choose from), but if you're in the mood for something different, request a slice of their lemon rosemary cake—it's a poorly kept secret.

5406 Balcones. ✆ **512/454-2666.** www.chez-zee.com. Main courses $14–$19. AE, DC, DISC, MC, V. Mon–Thurs 11am–10:30pm; Fri 11am–midnight; Sat 9am–midnight; Sun 9am–10pm.

Musashino ★ JAPANESE This place has the freshest, best-prepared sushi in town, and every Austin aficionado knows it—which is why, in spite of its inauspicious location (on the southbound access road of Mo-Pac in northwest Austin) and less-than-stunning setting (beneath a Chinese restaurant called Chinatown), it's always jammed. A combination of Musashino's local star status and its policy of not accepting reservations means you're likely to have to wait awhile for a table, especially on Friday and Saturday nights. The cozy upstairs area, which has a sushi bar and table service but a shorter menu, is a good substitute. Be sure to ask your server what's special before you order; delicacies not listed on the regular menu are often flown in.

3407 Greystone Dr. ✆ **512/795-8593.** www.musashinosushi.com. Reservations not accepted. Sushi $2–$12 (including maki); main courses $14–$27. AE, DC, DISC, MC, V. Mon–Fri 11:30am–2pm; Tues–Thurs and Sun 5:30–10pm; Fri–Sat 5:30–10:30pm.

Z'Tejas Southwestern Grill ★ Value SOUTHWEST An offshoot of a popular downtown eatery (and the second link in what became a small chain), this Arboretum restaurant is notable not only for its zippy Southwestern cuisine but also for its attractive dining space, featuring floor-to-ceiling windows, a soaring ceiling, Santa Fe–style decor, and, in cool weather, a roaring fireplace. Grilled shrimp and guacamole tostada bites make a great starter, and if you see it on a specials menu, go for the smoked *chile rellenos* made with apricots and goat cheese. Entrees include a delicious horseradish-crusted salmon and a pork tenderloin stuffed with chorizo, cheese, onions, and poblano chilies. Even if you think you can't eat another bite, order a piece of ancho chili fudge pie.

If you're staying downtown, try the original—and smaller—Z'Tejas at 1110 W. Sixth St. (✆ **512/478-5355**).

9400-A Arboretum Blvd. ✆ **512/346-3506.** www.ztejas.com. Reservations recommended. Main courses $11–$20. AE, DC, DISC, MC, V. Mon–Thurs 11am–10pm; Fri 11am–11pm; Sat–Sun 10am–11pm.

9 WESTLAKE/LAKE TRAVIS

VERY EXPENSIVE

Hudson's on the Bend ★★ NEW AMERICAN If you're game for game, served in a very civilized setting, come to Hudson's. Soft candlelight, fresh flowers, fine china, and attentive service combine with outstanding and out-of-the-ordinary cuisine to make this worth a special-occasion splurge. Sparkling lights draped over a cluster of oak trees draw you into a series of romantic dining rooms, set in an old house some 1$^{1}/_{2}$ miles southwest of the Mansfield Dam, near Lake Travis. The chipotle cream sauce was spicy enough, I couldn't tell whether the diamondback rattlesnake cakes tasted like chicken. But they were very good, as were the duck confit *gordita* (thick corn tortilla) and wild game tamale starters. Pecan-smoked duck breast and a mixed grill of venison, rabbit, quail, and buffalo are among the excellent entrees I've sampled; there's also a superb trout served with tangy mango-habanero butter.

Hudson's indoor dining rooms can be noisy on weekends. Opt for the terrace if the weather permits.

3509 Hwy. 620 N. ✆ **512/266-1369.** www.hudsonsonthebend.com. Reservations recommended, essential Sat–Sun. Main courses $26–$48. AE, DC, DISC, MC, V. Sun–Mon 6–9pm; Tues–Thurs 6–10pm; Fri–Sat 5:30–10pm.

MODERATE

County Line on the Hill ★ (Kids) BARBECUE Opened in 1975, this scenic hillside BBQ restaurant is the original of the County Line chain. The original business on this site, dating from the 1920s, was a speakeasy, positioned strategically on the "county line" between a dry county and a wet one. But these days people come for the BBQ. Some critics deride these restaurants as "suburban" barbecue, but that doesn't stop crowds from packing in here nightly. This restaurant is now a little less packed since it started opening for lunch; but if you don't get here before 6pm for dinner, you can wait as long as an hour to eat. Should this happen, sit out on the deck and soak in the views of the Hill Country. County Line is known for its big beef ribs, but I like the pork ribs better. The brisket is lean unless you specify "moist," which I also recommend. Sausage and chicken are also good bets. The slow-cooking method employed here makes for consistently good BBQ. The sides, beans, slaw, and potato salad aren't just afterthoughts, and the bread is baked in-house. The atmosphere is rustic country house with such nostalgic accents as old signs and photos. County Line on the Lake (northwest), 5204 FM 2222 (✆ **512/346-3664**), offers the same menu, and is also open for lunch and dinner.

6500 W. Bee Cave Rd. ✆ **512/327-1742.** Reservations not accepted. Plates $11–$20; all-you-can-eat platters $19–$27 ($6–$8 for children under 12). AE, MC, V. Mon–Thurs 11:30am–2pm and 5–9pm; Fri 11:30am–2pm and 5–10pm; Sat 11:30am–10pm; Sun 11:30am–9:30pm (closing times are a half-hour earlier in winter).

The Oasis AMERICAN/TEX-MEX This is the required spot for Austinites to take out-of-town guests at sunset. From the multilevel decks nestled into the hillside hundreds of feet above Lake Travis, visitors and locals alike cheer—with toasts and applause—as the fiery orb descends behind the hills on the opposite shores. No one ever leaves unimpressed. The food is another matter entirely: It can be erratic. Keep it simple—nachos, burgers—and you'll be okay. Then add a margarita, and kick back. It doesn't get much mellower than this.

In 2005, lightning struck the restaurant and burned most of the decking that extended across a good portion of the hillside, causing more than a million dollars in damage. Two days later the restaurant was back open, and after a year's worth of restoration, it was returned to its former glory. Those who have been there before will recognize that some of the decks have been reconfigured in an effort to improve the overall arrangement. But everything else is the same.

6550 Comanche Trail, near Lake Travis. ✆ **512/266-2442.** www.oasis-austin.com. Reservations not accepted. Main courses $12–$20. AE, DC, DISC, MC, V. Mon–Thurs 11:30am–10pm; Fri 11:30am–11pm; Sat 11am–11pm; Sun 11am–10pm (brunch 11am–2pm); closing an hour earlier in fall/winter.

10 ONLY IN (OR AROUND) AUSTIN

For information on Austin's funky, original cafe scene, see "Late-Night Bites" in chapter 16.

WORLD FAMOUS BARBECUE

Austin is at the center of an area rich in classic barbecue joints. Head out of town in just about any direction, and you'll come upon small towns that are home to famous institutions. A list of the most famous of these would have to include Lockhart, 30 miles south, which might be considered the BBQ capital of Texas. It's home to such landmarks as **Kreuz Market, Black's,** and **Smitty's Market.** Southwest of Austin, in the town of Driftwood (25 miles), is **The Salt Lick,** where friends go on weekends with ice chests full of beer to sit at the picnic tables and wait their turn for some brisket served up right out of the pit. For some context, more description, and greater detail, see the BBQ section in chapter 17.

A BAT'S-EYE VIEW

From late March through mid-November, the most coveted seats in town are the ones with a view of the thousands of bats that fly out from under the Congress Avenue Bridge in search of a hearty bug dinner at dusk. The **Shoreline Grill** (see earlier in this chapter) is the toniest spot for observing this astounding phenomenon. **TGIF's** at the Radisson Hotel on Town Lake, 11 E. First St. (✆ **512/478-9611**), and **SWB** at the Hyatt Regency Austin on Town Lake, 208 Barton Springs Rd. (✆ **512/477-1234**), offer more casual, collegial roosts.

MUSICAL BRUNCHES

For a spiritual experience on Sunday morning, check out the gospel brunch at **Stubb's Bar-B-Q,** 801 Red River St. (✆ **512/480-8341**). The singing is heavenly, the pork ribs divine. **South Congress Cafe** (see earlier this chapter) has a popular soul brunch that also mixes in a little gospel. At **Threadgill's World Headquarters** (p. 212), you can graze at a Southern-style buffet while listening to live inspirational sounds; find out who's playing at www.threadgills.com. If you're more in the mood for jazz, check out the brunches at both locations of **Manuel's** (p. 202), where you can enjoy eggs with venison chorizo, or corn gorditas with garlic and cilantro, while listening to smokin' traditional or Latin jazz. Log on to www.manuels.com to find out who's going to be sizzling while you're visiting.

COFFEEHOUSES

Coffeehouse culture, students, and the Internet seem to go together naturally. Austin has seen a steady growth of independent coffeehouses, each with its own feel, refreshingly different from the corporate designs of the national chains. All the following are wireless Internet hot spots.

In the downtown area, you can find **Little City** at 916 Congress Ave. (✆ **512/476-2489**). It's close to the capitol and other downtown tourist sights. In south Austin, at 1300 S. Congress, is **Jo's** (✆ **512/444-3800**), which is the meeting place for SoCo's coffee set at any time of day. In the mornings, they sell pastries and an old Austin standard, breakfast tacos. In the afternoon, simple sandwiches go with the coffee, which is quite good. You're apt to encounter one of Austin's several local characters here, including Leslie, the bearded transvestite and former mayoral candidate who can be seen around town wearing revealing garb. Also in South Austin, in the Zilker Park area, is **Flipnotics,** 1601 Barton Springs Rd. (✆ **512/322-9750**), a two-story, indoor/outdoor "coffee space," where you can sip great caffeine drinks or beer while listening to acoustic singer/songwriters most nights. In West Austin, in the Clarksville neighborhood is **Caffé Medici** at 1101 West Lynn (✆ **512/524-5049**). It serves excellent espresso drinks, perhaps the best in town. Farther west is **Mozart's,** 3825 Lake Austin Blvd. (✆ **512/477-2900**). It enjoys a beautiful location on the shores of Lake Austin; on a pretty day, the views are lovely from the deck. Here you can get great white-chocolate-almond croissants. In central Austin, across from the University of Texas campus, is a second branch of **Caffé Medici** (✆ **512/474-5730**) at 2222-B Guadalupe. Just north of campus, and just off Guadalupe, is an atmospheric coffee bar called **Spider House,** 2908 Fruth St. (✆ **512/480-9562**). It's frequented by a mix of students and artists. Besides coffee, it sells tempeh chili, Frito pies, smoothies, all-natural fruit sangrias, and beer. Farther north, in the homey Hyde Park neighborhood, is the **Flightpath** coffeehouse (✆ **512/458-4472**) at 5011 Duval St. It's furnished '50s mod style.

Exploring Austin

I have two pieces of advice for visitors to Austin. First, don't hesitate to ask locals for directions or advice. Austinites are friendly and approachable. It's common practice here for complete strangers to engage in conversation. Indeed, one of the great things about Austin is how welcoming the city is. And second, take full advantage of the city's Visitor Information Center at 209 E. Sixth Street. It offers free walking tours, has pamphlets for self-guided tours, and is the point of departure for the motorized city tours. The office will know if one of the daily tours is cancelled for whatever reason.

What sets Austin apart from other Texas cities and what puts it on all those "most livable" lists is the amount of green space and outdoor activities available to its denizens, whose attitude towards the outdoors borders on nature worship. From bats and birds to Barton Springs, from the Highland Lakes to the hike-and-bike trails, Austin lays out the green carpet for its visitors. You'd be hard-pressed to find a city that has more to offer fresh-air enthusiasts.

1 THE TOP ATTRACTIONS

DOWNTOWN

Blanton Museum of Art ★ Located on the University of Texas campus (across the street from the Bob Bullock Museum), this museum was built a couple of years ago to hold the university's art collection, which is ranked among the top university art collections in the United States. Most notable is the Suida-Manning Collection, a gathering of Renaissance works by such masters as Veronese, Rubens, and Tiepolo that was sought after by the Metropolitan museum, among others. Other permanent holdings include the Mari and James Michener collection of 20th-century American masters, a large collection of Latin American art, and a collection of 19th-century plaster casts of monumental Greek and Roman sculpture.

The museum has been a big success in its first few years, attracting large crowds. The directors are working hard to increase public involvement through a variety of events. On the first Friday of every month, it hosts a little happening called "B scene," which mixes art with live music, wine, finger foods, and socializing. It costs $10, runs from 6 to 11pm, and is fun. Check the website for their other events that mix things such as yoga with the arts. The Blanton opened a second building in early fall of 2008, which holds a cafe for visitors, in addition to administration offices and lecture halls.

Martin Luther King, at Congress. ✆ **512/471-7324.** www.blantonmuseum.org. $5 adults, $4 seniors (65 and over), $3 youth (13–25), free for children 12 and under. Admission is free on Thurs. Parking is $3 with validation. Tues–Sat 10am–5pm (until 8pm Thurs); Sun 1–4pm. Closed university holidays. Bus: UT Shuttle.

The Bob Bullock Texas State History Museum ★ Value Kids You'll get a quick course in Texas 101 at this museum, opened near the state capitol in 2001 and designed to echo some of its elements. Three floors of exhibits are arrayed around a rotunda set off

Going Batty

Austin has the largest urban bat population in North America. Some visitors are dubious at first, but it's difficult to be unimpressed by the sight of 1.5 million of the creatures, who emerge from under the Congress Avenue Bridge shortly before dusk and flitter through the air in a long winding ribbon floating above the river on the east side of the bridge.

Each March, free-tailed bats migrate from central Mexico to various roost sites in the Southwest. In 1980, when a deck reconstruction of Austin's bridge created an ideal environment for raising bat pups, some 750,000 pregnant females began settling in every year. Each bat gives birth to a single pup, and by August these offspring take part in nightly forays for bugs, usually around dusk. Depending on the size of the group, they might consume anywhere from 10,000 to 30,000 pounds of insects a night—one of the things that makes them so popular with Austinites. By November, these youngsters are old enough to hitch rides back south with their group on the winds of an early cold front.

While the bats are in town, an educational kiosk designed to dispel some of the more prevalent myths about them is set up each evening on the south bank of the river, just east of the bridge. You'll learn, for example, that bats are not rodents, they're not blind, and they're not in the least interested in getting in your hair. **Bat Conservation International** (© **512/327-9721;** www.batcon.org), based in Austin, has lots of information, as well as bat-related items for sale. Log on to the website or phone © **800/538-BATS** (538-2287) for a catalog. To find out what time the bats are going to emerge from the bridge, call the *Austin American-Statesman* **Bat Hot Line** (© **512/416-5700,** category 3636). A lot of people don't know this, but sometimes the bats don't leave all at once. If you can still hear bats chattering from beneath the bridge, sit tight; you may have an encore presentation.

by a 50-foot, polished granite map of Texas. It's an impressive building, and the permanent displays—everything from Stephen F. Austin's diary to Neil Armstrong's spacesuit—and rotating exhibits are interesting enough. Still, for all the interactive video clips and engaging designs (lots of different rooms to duck into, varied floor surfaces), the presentations didn't strike me as dramatically different from those in other history museums. The real treat is the multimedia, special effects Spirit Theater, the only one of its kind in Texas, where you can experience the high-speed whoosh of the great Galveston hurricane and feel your seats rattle as an East Texas oil well hits a gusher. Austin's only IMAX Theater with 3-D capabilities is pretty dazzling too, though the films don't necessarily have a direct relation to Texas history. If you do everything, plan to spend at least 2½ to 3 hours here.

1800 N. Congress Ave. © **512/936-8746.** www.thestoryoftexas.com. Exhibit areas: $7 adults, $6 seniors 65 and over, $4 youth 5–18 (youth), free for children 4 and under. IMAX Theater: $7 adults, $6 seniors, $5 youth. Texas Spirit Theater: $5 adults, $4 seniors, $4 youth. Combination tickets for admission to exhibits and one or both theaters are available. Parking $8 (IMAX parking free after 6pm). Mon–Sat 9am–6pm; Sun noon–6pm. Phone or check website for additional IMAX evening hours. Closed Jan 1, Easter, Thanksgiving, and Dec 24–25. Bus: UT Shuttle.

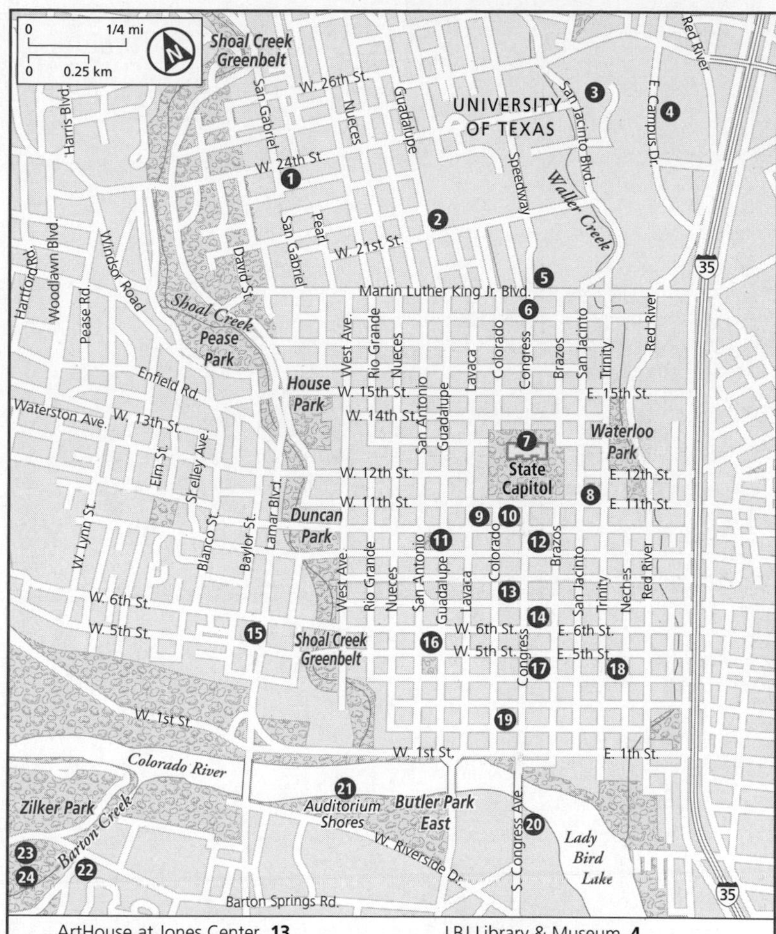

ArtHouse at Jones Center **13**
Austin Children's Museum **19**
Austin History Center **11**
Austin Museum of Art–Downtown **12**
Barton Springs Pool **23**
Bats **20**
Blanton Museum of Art **5**
Bob Bullock Texas State History Museum **6**
The Bremond Block **16**
Capitol Visitors Center **8**
Driskill Hotel **14**
Governor's Mansion **9**
Harry Ransom Humanities Research Center **2**
LBJ Library & Museum **4**
MEXIC-ARTE Museum **17**
Neill-Cochran Museum House **1**
O. Henry Museum **18**
Old Bakery & Emporium **10**
Philosopher's Rock **23**
Splash **23**
State Capitol **7**
Stevie Ray Vaughn Statue **21**
Texas Memorial Museum **3**
Treaty Oak **15**
Umlauf Sculpture Garden & Museum **22**
Zilker Zephyr Miniature Train **24**

Greater Austin Attractions

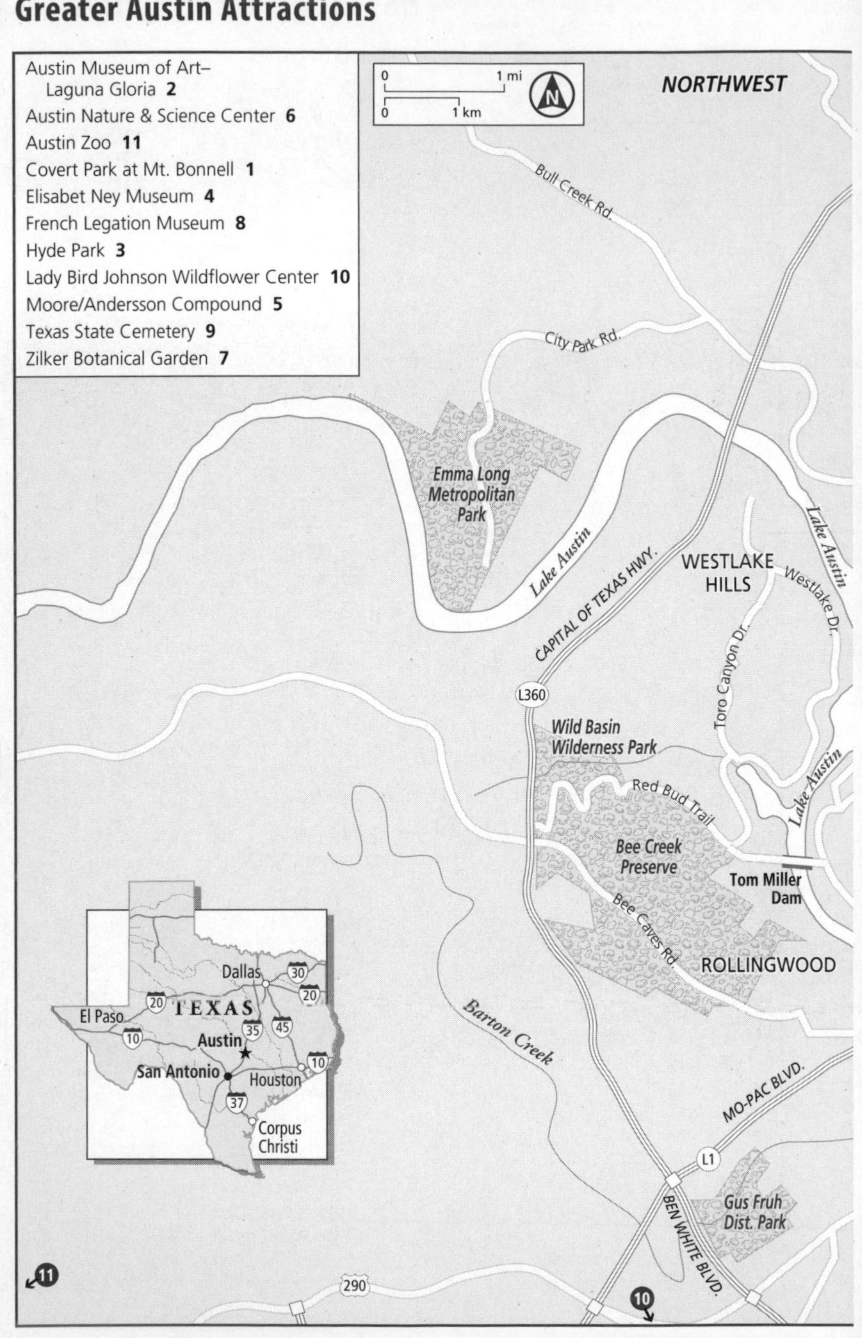

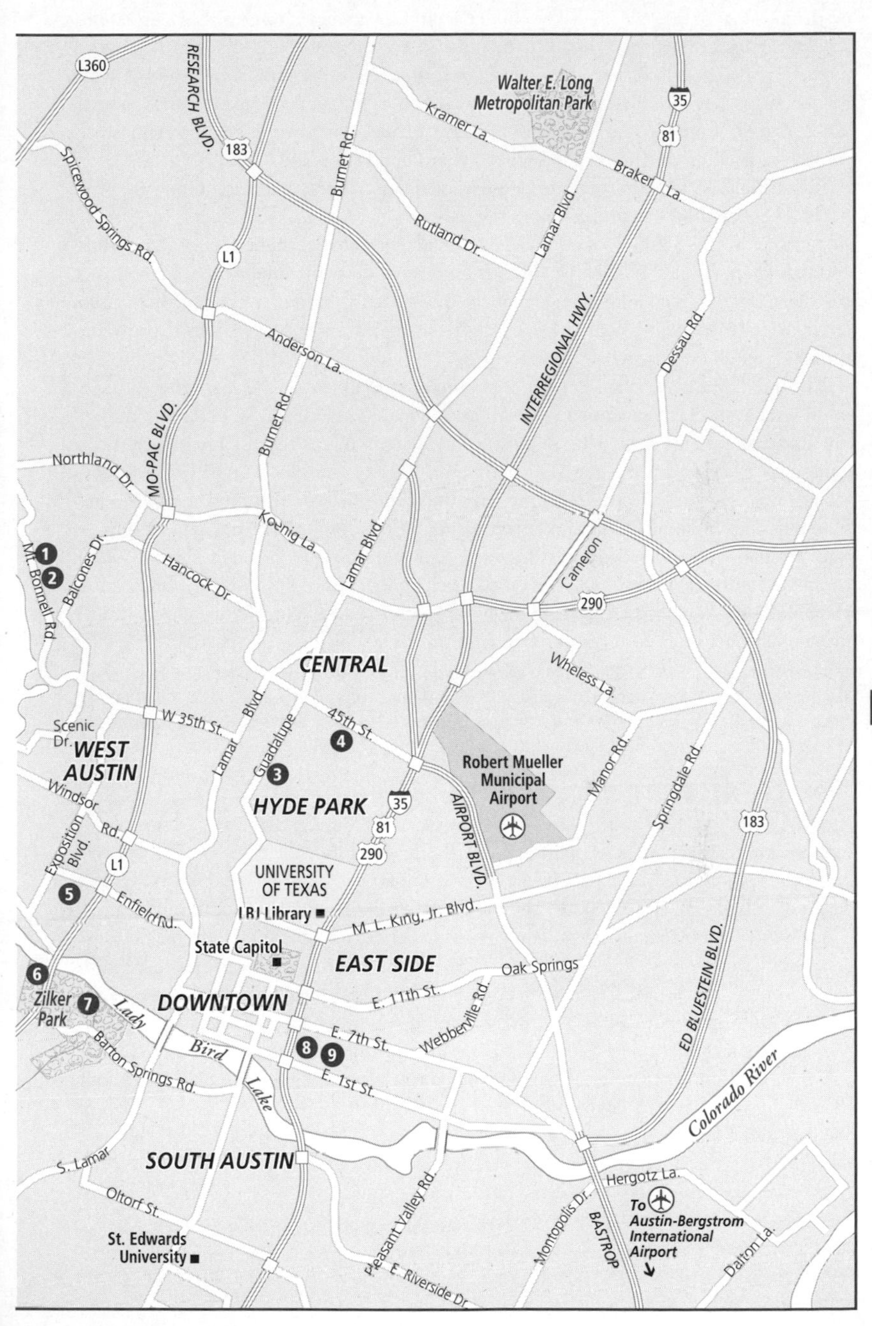
Walter E. Long
Metropolitan Park
Kramer La.
Braker La.
Rutland Dr.
Lamar Blvd.
Burnet Rd.
RESEARCH BLVD.
Spicewood Springs Rd.
Anderson La.
INTERREGIONAL HWY.
Dessau Rd.
MO-PAC BLVD.
Northland Dr.
Koenig La.
Hancock Dr.
Balcones Dr.
Mt. Bonnell Rd.
Cameron
CENTRAL
Wheless La.
W 35th St.
45th St.
Guadalupe
Scenic Dr.
WEST AUSTIN
Windsor Rd.
HYDE PARK
Robert Mueller
Municipal
Airport
AIRPORT BLVD.
Manor Rd.
Springdale Rd.
Exposition Blvd.
UNIVERSITY
OF TEXAS
LBJ Library
Enfield Rd.
M. L. King, Jr. Blvd.
State Capitol
EAST SIDE
Oak Springs
ED BLUESTEIN BLVD.
Zilker
Park
DOWNTOWN
E. 11th St.
Webberville Rd.
E. 7th St.
Lady Bird Lake
Barton Springs Rd.
E. 1st St.
Colorado River
SOUTH AUSTIN
S. Lamar
Oltorf St.
St. Edwards
University
Pleasant Valley Rd.
E. Riverside Dr.
Montopolis Dr.
BASTROP
Hergotz La.
To
Austin-Bergstrom
International
Airport
Dalton La.

State Capitol ★★ (Value) The history of Texas's legislative center is as turbulent and dramatic as that of the state itself. The current capitol, erected in 1888, replaced a limestone statehouse that burned down in 1881. A land-rich but otherwise impecunious Texas government traded 3 million acres of public lands to finance its construction. Gleaming pink granite was donated to the cause, but a railroad had to be built to transport the material some 75 miles from Granite Mountain, near the present-day town of Marble Falls. Texas convicts labored on the project alongside 62 stonecutters brought in from Scotland.

It is the largest state capitol in the country, covering 3 acres, and is second in size only to the U.S. capitol—but still, in typical Texas style, measuring 7 feet taller. The cornerstone alone weighs 16,000 pounds, and the total length of the wooden wainscoting runs approximately 7 miles. A splendid rotunda and dome lie at the intersection of the main corridors. The House and Senate chambers are located at opposite ends of the second level. Go up to the third-floor visitors' gallery during the legislative sessions if you want see how politics are conducted Texas-style.

The building had become dingy and its offices warrenlike over the past century, but a massive renovation and expansion in the 1990s restored its grandeur. The expansion project was fascinating in its own right: Almost 700,000 tons of rock were chiseled from the ground to create an underground annex (often called the "inside-out, upside-down capitol"). It was constructed with similar materials and connected to the capitol and four other state buildings by tunnels. You can either opt for a 30- to 45-minute free guided tour or walk around on your own using self-guided tour pamphlets (you might want to use a pamphlet for the capitol grounds, but do take the guided tour of the building). Include the Capitol Visitors Center (see "More Attractions," below), and figure on spending a minimum of 2 hours here. Wear comfortable shoes; you'll be doing a lot of walking.

11th and Congress sts. ✆ **512/463-0063.** www.tspb.state.tx.us. Free admission. Mon–Fri 7am–10pm; Sat–Sun 9am–8pm; hours extended during legislative sessions (held in odd years, starting in Jan, for 140 straight calendar days). Closed all major holidays. Free guided tours Mon–Fri 8:30am–4:30pm; Sat 9:30am–3:30pm; Sun noon–3:30. Bus: Multiple bus lines; Congress 'Dillo.

SOUTH AUSTIN

Barton Springs Pool ★★ (Kids) If the University of Texas is the seat of Austin's intellect, and the state capitol is its political pulse, Barton Springs is the city's soul. The Native Americans who settled near here believed these waters had spiritual powers, and today's residents still place their faith in the abilities of the spring-fed pool to soothe and cool.

Each day, approximately 32 million gallons of water from the underground Edwards Aquifer bubble to the surface here, and at one time, this force powered several Austin mills. Although the original limestone bottom remains, concrete was added to the banks to form uniform sides to what is now a swimming pool of about 1,000 feet by 125 feet. Maintaining a constant 68°F (20°C) temperature, the amazingly clear water actually feels colder in the summer than in the winter, when a few brave souls unwilling to do without their daily swim have the large pool all to themselves. Lifeguards are on duty for most of the day, and a large bathhouse operated by the Parks and Recreation Department offers changing facilities and a gift shop. For details about the Splash! environmental information center, see "Especially for Kids," later in this chapter.

Zilker Park, 2201 Barton Springs Rd. ✆ **512/476-9044.** www.ci.austin.tx.us/parks/bartonsprings.htm. Admission $3 adults, $2 ages 12–17, $1 seniors and children 11 and younger (admission charged only after 9am Mar 13–Oct; free for early birds). Daily 5am–10pm except during pool maintenance (Thurs 9am–7pm). Splash! Tues–Fri noon–6pm; Sat–Sun 10am–6pm. Bus: 30 (Barton Creek Sq.).

Lady Bird Johnson Wildflower Center ★★★ If you know anything about Lady Bird Johnson, then you've heard that her big cause was the preservation of wildflowers and native plants. She insisted that natural habitats and native species were beautiful in their own right, that they are part of what defines regional identity, and that they could even be economically beneficial. She was right, you know. And her efforts have had an enormous impact on the way gardeners practice their craft in central Texas. She also prevailed upon the state highway agency to seed the roadsides with wildflowers, which have flourished throughout the state but especially in central Texas where fields of bluebonnets, Indian paintbrush, evening primrose, and other wildflowers paint the landscape in rich colors, attracting visitors from far and wide.

To further the cause, Mrs. Johnson founded the Wildflower Center to research native species and habitat and educate the public on the benefits of gardening with these plants and wildflowers. The center has a large staff and scores of volunteers, 279 acres of land, large greenhouses, and an elaborate rainwater collection system. The facility's research library is the largest in the United States for the study of native plants. For visitors, the main attractions are the 12 acres of beautiful gardens displaying 650 species of native plants (most of which are labeled) in varying habitats, 2 miles of trails, and an observation tower. There is also a large and colorful gift shop and a cafe serving soups and sandwiches. Free lectures and guided walks are usually offered on the weekends—it's best to phone or check the website for current programs.

Once you get on Mo-Pac freeway, it's a 20-minute ride from west Austin. If you're really interested in gardening or botany, you can spend the better part of a day here.

4801 La Crosse Ave. ✆ **512/292-4200.** www.wildflower.org. Admission $7 adults, $6 students and seniors 60 and older, $3 ages 5–12, free for children under age 5. Tues–Sat 9am–5:30pm; Sun noon–5pm. (Mar–Apr rates go up to $7/$5 and grounds are open Mon.) Take Loop 1 (Mo-Pac) south to La Crosse Ave. and turn left.

CENTRAL

LBJ Library and Museum ★ Value A presidential library may sound like a big yawn, but this one's almost as interesting as the 36th president to whom it's devoted. Lyndon Baines Johnson's popularity in Texas and his many successes in Washington are often forgotten in the wake of his actions regarding the Vietnam War. The story of Johnson's long political career, starting with his early days as a state representative and continuing through to the Kennedy assassination and the groundbreaking Great Society legislation, is told through a variety of documents, mementos, and photographs. Johnson loved political cartoons, even when he was the object of their satire, and examples from his large collection are among the museum's most interesting rotating exhibits. Other exhibits might include anything from photographs from the American Civil Rights era to a display of presidential holiday cards. Adults and kids alike are riveted by the animatronic version of LBJ. Dressed in his clothes and speaking with a tape recording of his voice, the life-size, gesticulating figure seems eerily alive from afar. From 1971, when it was dedicated, until his death in 1973, Johnson himself kept an office in this building, which commands an impressive campus view. A large, free parking lot next to the library makes it one of the few UT campus sights that's easy to drive up to.

University of Texas, 2313 Red River. ✆ **512/721-0200.** www.lbjlib.utexas.edu. Free admission. Daily 9am–5pm. Closed Dec 25. Bus: 15; UT shuttle.

2 MORE ATTRACTIONS

DOWNTOWN

Arthouse at Jones Center The Jones Center is home to Arthouse, also known as Texas Fine Arts Association, an organization whose purpose is to promote all forms of contemporary art in Texas. The building was once a movie theater and in the 1950s was a popular department store. Most of the space inside is dedicated to the exhibition of a wide variety of visual art forms, and it doesn't cost anything to walk in and see what's cooking. Arthouse is in the middle of a fundraising drive to renovate and enlarge the space, while keeping intact many of the architectural elements of the structure. It has hired New York architecture firm Lewis, Tsurumaki, Lewis to design the project.

700 Congress Ave. ✆ **512/453-5312.** www.arthousetexas.org. Free admission. Tues–Wed and Fri 11am–7pm; Thurs 11am–9pm; Sat 10am–5pm; Sun 1–5pm. Bus: Congress or Sixth St. 'Dillo.

Austin History Center/Austin Public Library Built in 1933, this Renaissance revival–style public library not only embodies some of the finest architecture, ironwork, and stone carving of its era, but also serves as the best resource for information about Austin from before the city's founding in 1839 to the present. The center often hosts exhibitions drawn from its vast archives of historical photographs and sketches. And, of course, it's full of books and photos.

810 Guadalupe St. ✆ **512/974-7480.** www.ci.austin.tx.us/library. Free admission. Mon–Wed 10am–9pm; Sat 10am–6pm; Sun noon–6pm. Closed Thurs–Fri, and most holidays. Bus: 171.

Austin Museum of Art–Downtown This has become the main gallery space for Austin's local art association. It represents a sizable expansion from the association's other location in the Laguna Gloria mansion in West Austin. The downtown gallery hosts some interesting, often highly original, exhibits. It's not formal at all and can be visited as an afterthought if you're downtown with some time on your hands. And you can always check what's currently on display by going to their Web page.

823 Congress Ave. (at Ninth St.). ✆ **512/495-9224.** www.amoa.org. Admission $5 adults, $4 seniors 55 and over and students, $1 for everyone on Tues, free for children under 12. Tues–Wed and Fri–Sat 10am–6pm; Thurs 10am–8pm; Sun noon–5pm. Bus: Congress 'Dillo.

Bremond Block ★ "The family that builds together, bonds together" might have been the slogan of Eugene Bremond, an early Austin banker who established a mini-real-estate monopoly for his own kin in the downtown area. In the mid-1860s, he started investing in land on what was once Block 80 of the original city plan. In 1874, he moved into a Greek revival home made by master builder Abner Cook. By the time he was through, he had created a family compound, purchasing and enlarging homes for himself, two sisters, a daughter, a son, and a brother-in-law. Some were destroyed, but those that remain on what is now known as the Bremond Block are exquisite examples of elaborate late-19th-century homes.

Between Seventh and Eighth, San Antonio and Guadalupe sts. Bus: Sixth St. 'Dillo.

Capitol Visitors Center ★ Tucked away at the southeast corner of the extensive capitol grounds is Texas's oldest state office building, the 1857 General Land Office building. It's a squat, three-story limestone structure built in a Romanesque medieval-revival style with crenellated walls. The short story writer O. Henry worked here as a draftsman from 1887 to 1891 and based two stories on his experiences. Now the building houses the visitor center for the Capitol. It benefited from a thorough remodeling in the 1990s.

A Walter Cronkite–narrated video tells the history of the complex, and changing exhibits on the first floor highlight the Capitol Preservation Project, while upstairs the displays focus on the Land Office and other aspects of Texas's past. A good gift shop carries lots of historical books and souvenirs.

112 E. 11th St. (southeast corner of Capitol grounds). ✆ **512/305-8400.** www.texascapitolvisitorscenter.com. Free admission. Mon–Sat 9am–5pm; Sun noon–5pm. Bus: Congress 'Dillo.

The Driskill Col. Jesse Driskill was not a modest man. When he opened a hotel in 1886, he named it after himself, put busts of himself and his two sons over the entrances, and installed bas-relief sculptures of longhorn steers to remind folks how he had made his fortune. Nor did he build a modest property. The ornate four-story structure, which originally boasted a sky-lit rotunda, has the largest arched doorway in Texas over its east entrance. It was so posh that the state legislature met here while the 1888 capitol was being built. The hotel has had its ups and downs over the years, but it was restored to its former glory in the late 1990s. You can pick up a history of the hotel at the front desk, and if the concierge has time, he'll be happy to help orient you. For a full hotel review, see p. 180.

604 Brazos St. ✆ **512/474-5911.** Bus: Congress or Sixth St. 'Dillo.

Governor's Mansion ★ This venerable public building suffered serious damage when it was targeted by arsonists on the night of June 8, 2008. That night the mansion was closed and unoccupied, owing to some renovation work. The officers of the Department. of Public Safety who were charged with guarding the building and grounds did not detect the intruders, and some of the closed-circuit cameras were not working. All of this will make it extremely difficult to catch the vandals. At present there is no date set for reopening. Workers managed to stabilize the structure and protect it from the elements, but extensive restoration is necessary and none can say how long the work will take.

In ordinary times, this mansion is the governor's residence. State law requires that the governor live here whenever he or she is in Austin. The house was originally built by Abner Cook in 1856. Originally it had no indoor toilets (there are now seven). The nation's first female governor, Miriam "Ma" Ferguson, entertained her friend Will Rogers in the mansion, and Gov. John Connally recuperated here from gunshot wounds received when he accompanied John F. Kennedy on his fatal motorcade through Dallas. Among the many historical artifacts on display are a desk belonging to Stephen F. Austin and portraits of Davy Crockett and Sam Houston.

Tip: Only a limited number of visitors are allowed to tour the mansion, so make your required advance reservations as soon as you know when you're planning to visit—and at least 1 business day ahead of time.

1010 Colorado St. ✆ **512/463-5516** (recorded information) or 512/463-5518 (tour reservations). www.txfgm.org. Free admission. Tours generally offered every 20 min. Mon–Thurs 10am–noon (last tour starts 11:40am). Closed Fri–Sun, some holidays, and at the discretion of the governor; call the 24-hr. information line to see if tours are offered the day you want to visit. Bus: Congress 'Dillo.

MEXIC-ARTE Museum The first organization in Austin to promote multicultural contemporary art when it was formed in 1983, MEXIC-ARTE has a small permanent collection of 20th-century Mexican art, including photographs from the Mexican revolution and a fascinating array of masks from the state of Guerrero. It's supplemented by visiting shows—including some from Mexico, such as a recent survey of south-of-the-border contemporary art—and a back gallery of works of local Latino artists.

419 Congress Ave. ✆ **512/480-9373.** www.mexic-artemuseum.org. Admission $5 adults, $4 seniors and students, $1 children under 12. Mon–Thurs 10am–6pm; Fri–Sat 10am–5pm; Sun noon–5pm. Bus: Congress 'Dillo.

O. Henry Museum When William Sidney Porter, better known as O. Henry, lived in Austin (1884–98), he published a popular satirical newspaper called *Rolling Stone.* He also held down a string of odd jobs, including a stint as a teller at the First National Bank of Austin, where he was later accused of embezzling funds. It was while he was serving time for this crime that he wrote the 13 short stories that established his literary reputation. The modest Victorian cottage in which O. Henry lived with his wife and daughter from 1893 to 1895 showcases the family's bedroom furniture, silverware, and china, as well as the desk at which the author wrote copy for his failed publication. Temporary exhibits, which change throughout the year, include displays of O. Henry letters. Visitors are asked to wear flat, soft-soled shoes to prevent damage to the original pine floors.

409 E. Fifth St. ✆ **512/472-1903.** www.ci.austin.tx.us/parks/ohenry.htm. Free admission. Wed–Sun noon–5pm. Closed Thanksgiving, Dec 25, and Jan 1. Bus: Sixth St. 'Dillo.

Old Bakery and Emporium On the National Register of Historic Landmarks, the Old Bakery was built in 1876 by Charles Lundberg, a Swedish master baker, and continuously operated until 1936. You can still see the giant oven and wooden baker's spade inside. Rescued from demolition by the Austin Heritage Society and now owned and operated by Austin's Parks and Recreation Department, the brick-and-limestone building is one of the few unaltered structures on Congress Avenue. It houses a gift shop selling crafts handmade by seniors, a reasonably priced lunchroom (Mon–Fri 11am–1:30pm), and a hospitality desk with visitors' brochures.

1006 Congress Ave. ✆ **512/477-5961.** www.ci.austin.tx.us/parks/bakery1.htm. Free admission. Mon–Fri 9am–4pm; first 3 Sat in Dec 10am–2pm. Closed most holidays. Bus: Congress 'Dillo.

Sixth Street Formerly known as Pecan Street—all the east–west thoroughfares in Austin were originally named for trees—Sixth Street was once the main connecting road to the older settlements east of Austin. During the Reconstruction boom of the 1870s, the wooden wagon yards and saloons of the 1850s and 1860s began to be replaced by the more solid masonry structures you see today. After the new state capitol was built in 1888, the center of commercial activity began shifting toward Congress Avenue, and by the middle of the next century, Sixth Street had become a skid row.

Restoration of the 9 blocks designated as a Historic District by the National Register of Historic Places began in the late 1960s. In the 1970s, the street started thriving as a

Fun Facts Old-Fashioned Moonlight

Austin is the only city in the world to preserve its first public electric lights—17 of the original 31 "moonlight towers" from 1894 are still operating around thecity. A special moonlight tower was erected for scenes in the movie *Dazed and Confused,* when it was filmed in Austin by one of the state's native sons, Richard Linklater.

live-music center. Austin's former main street is now lined with restaurants, galleries, bars, and shops. Despite the makeover, East Sixth still retains an air of decadence that reminds many of Bourbon Street. (West Sixth is much more sanitized.) On any night, you'll find a mostly young crowd walking the sidewalks looking for just the right bar.

Between Lavaca Ave. and I-35. Bus: Sixth St. 'Dillo.

Treaty Oak Legend has it that Stephen F. Austin signed the first boundary treaty with the Comanche under the spreading branches of this 500-year-old live oak, which once served as the symbolic border between Anglo and Indian territory. Whatever the case, this is the sole remaining tree in what was once a grove of Council Oaks—which made the well-publicized attempt on its life in the late 1980s especially shocking. But almost as dramatic as the story of the tree's deliberate poisoning by an attention-seeking Austinite is the tale of its rescue by an international team of foresters. The dried wood from major limbs that they removed was allocated to local artists, whose works were auctioned off for the tree's 500th anniversary in 1993. Now such items as pen sets, gavels, and clocks made out of the tree's severed limbs are for sale, with proceeds going to plant additional trees throughout public areas of Austin.

503 Baylor St., btw. W. Fifth and Sixth sts. ✆ **512/440-5194.** www.ci.austin.tx.us/treatyoak. Bus: Sixth St. 'Dillo.

SOUTH AUSTIN

Umlauf Sculpture Garden & Museum This is a great museum for people who don't enjoy being cooped up in a stuffy, hushed space. An art instructor at the University of Texas for 40 years, Charles Umlauf donated his home, studio, and more than 250 pieces of artwork to the city of Austin, which maintains the lovely native garden where much of the sculpture is displayed. Umlauf, whose pieces reside in such places as the Smithsonian Institution and New York's Metropolitan Museum, worked in many media and styles. Though he used several models, the one you're likely to recognize is Farrah Fawcett, Umlauf's most famous UT student. The museum video is captioned for those who are hearing-impaired, and, with advance notice, "touch tours" can be arranged for those who are blind or visually impaired.

605 Robert E. Lee Rd. ✆ **512/445-5582.** www.umlaufsculpture.org. Admission $3.50 adults, $2.50 seniors, $1 students, free for children under 6. Wed–Fri 10am–4:30pm; Sat–Sun 1–4:30pm. Closed major holidays. Bus: 29 or 30.

WEST AUSTIN

Austin Museum of Art–Laguna Gloria ★ This is the old home of Austin's fine art's community. It made for a small museum that hosted modest shows. Since the creation of the downtown gallery space (see above), the mansion houses a small arts school for kids and some exhibits focusing on the historic aspects of the mansion and grounds. It is a Mediterranean-style villa built in 1916 by Austin newspaper publisher Hal Sevier and his wife, Clara Driscoll, best known for her successful crusade to save the Alamo from commercial development. The villa sits on 12½ wooded acres bordering Lake Austin. There is a small well-tended, attractive garden.

Tip: If the weather's nice, bring along a picnic lunch to enjoy by the lake. It's one of the prettiest spots in the city and, during the week, one of the most peaceful.

3809 W. 35th St. ✆ **512/458-8191.** www.amoa.org. At the end of West 35th St., before it arrives at the lake.

Moore/Andersson Compound Those interested in architecture might enjoy checking out the compound where Charles Moore spent the last decade of his life. The peripatetic American architect, who kept a low profile but had a great influence on post-modernism, built five homes, but this one, which he designed with Arthur Andersson, perfectly demonstrates his combination of controlled freedom, whimsical imagination, and connection to the environment. The wildly colorful rooms are filled with folk art from around the world, while odd angles, bunks, and dividers render every inch of space fascinating. The compound now functions as a conference and lecture center. Tours are by appointment only, and no children under 12 are permitted.

2102 Quarry Rd. ✆ **512/220-7923.** www.charlesmoore.org. Tours by appointment only $25 adults, $10 students.

CENTRAL

Elisabet Ney Museum ★ Elisabet Ney was a celebrated German sculptor who was accustomed to carving the likenesses of philosophers, statesmen, and kings (Schopenhauer, Garibaldi, Bismarck, Ludwig II, among others). She was also a woman of ideas and was part of a circle of intellectuals in Munich. She and her scientist husband were on the outs with the Prussians and had to flee Germany just before the war of 1870, first to Georgia, then to Texas. Strong-willed and independent, she moved to Austin by herself in 1891 because she was bored with life on the family farm near Hempstead, Texas. She constructed the studio that is now part of the museum and got busy creating sculptures of Texas leaders, including Stephen F. Austin and Sam Houston. She also had an immediate impact on Austin society, entertaining all the local intelligentsia, politicians, and visiting celebrities, such as William Jennings Bryan and Enrico Caruso. After her death in 1907, her friends claimed the studio-residence for a museum dedicated to this fascinating woman. It's a great way to spend an hour, if you have the chance.

304 E. 44th St. ✆ **512/458-2255.** www.elisabetney.org. Free admission. Wed–Sat 10am–5pm; Sun noon–5pm. Bus: 1 or 5.

Harry Ransom Humanities Research Center ★ The special collections of the Harry Ransom Center (HRC) contain approximately 1 million rare books (including a Gutenberg Bible, one of only five complete copies in the U.S.); 30 million literary manuscripts (including those by James Joyce, Ernest Hemingway, and Tennessee Williams); 5 million photographs, including the world's first; and more than 100,000 works of art, with several pieces by Diego Rivera and Frida Kahlo. Most of this wealth remains the domain of scholars, although anyone can request a look at it; but since new gallery space was opened in 2003, visitors are treated to select portions of it in excellent rotating exhibitions. Recent exhibits have examined the Beat generation, the American '20s, and the technology of the written word. Check the website for the various lectures, plays, and poetry readings held here, too, and for displays at the affiliated Leeds Gallery.

University of Texas, Harry Ransom Center, 21st and Guadalupe sts. ✆ **512/471-8944.** www.hrc.utexas.edu. Free admission. Galleries Tues–Wed and Fri 10am–5pm; Thurs 10am–7pm; Sat–Sun noon–5pm; call for reading-room hours. Closed university holidays. Bus: UT shuttle.

Hyde Park Developer Monroe Martin Shipe laid out this neighborhood of graceful houses and tree-lined streets in the 1890s, in what was at that time the northern edge of Austin. Part of the land had been home to the state fair until that was moved to Dallas in 1875. Connecting Hyde Park to downtown was a streetcar that passed through the university campus. It stopped operating in the 1940s, and with the rising availability of cars, the neighborhood entered a slow decline. By the 1960s, many of the houses served as rental properties for students. But in the next 10 years, young professionals started moving here, charmed by the central location and the quiet, shady streets. Today Hyde Park is one of the most popular neighborhoods in Austin. This is a good place to take a relaxing walk. Most of the houses you'll see are cottages that express a sweet and simple domesticity, while a few lean more towards grandeur. Shipe's own architecturally eclectic home can be seen at 3816 Ave. G.

Btw. E. 38th and E. 45th, Duval and Guadalupe sts. Bus: 1 or 7.

Neill-Cochran Museum House Abner Cook, the architect-contractor responsible for the governor's mansion and many of the city's other Greek Revival mansions, built this home in 1855. It bears his trademark portico with six Doric columns and a balustrade designed with crossed sheaves of wheat. Almost all its doors, windows, shutters, and hinges are original, which is rather astonishing when you consider the structure's history: The house was used as the city's first Blind Institute in 1856 and then as a hospital for Union prisoners near the end of the Civil War. The well-maintained furnishings, dating from the18th and 19th centuries, are eye-catching, but many people come just to see the painting of bluebonnets that helped convince legislators to designate these native blooms as the state flower.

2310 San Gabriel St. ✆ **512/478-2335.** Admission $5 adults, free for children under 10. Tues–Sat 2–5pm; free 20-min. tours given (with admission). Bus: UT shuttle.

Texas Memorial Museum Kids This museum, opened in 1936 to guard the natural and cultural treasures of the state, is now devoted to the natural sciences alone. Despite a major revamp in the early 2000s, it still seems oddly old-fashioned in parts, especially the lifeless dioramas and weird stuff in jars on the fourth floor. But kids will like first-floor Hall of Geology, with its huge Texas Pterosaur—the largest flying creature ever found—suspended from the ceiling. The admission price is right, and the gift shop carries lots of good science toys.

University of Texas, 2400 Trinity St. ✆ **512/471-1604.** www.texasmemorialmuseum.org. Free admission (donations appreciated). Mon–Fri 9am–5pm; Sat 10am–5pm; Sun 1–5pm. Closed major holidays. Bus: UT shuttle.

University of Texas at Austin In 1883, the 221 students and eight teachers who made up the newly established University of Texas in Austin had to meet in makeshift classrooms in the town's temporary capitol. At the time, the 2 million acres of dry west Texas land that the higher educational system had been granted barely brought in 40¢ an acre for grazing. Now, nearly 50,000 students occupy 120 buildings on UT's main campus alone, and that arid West Texas land, which blew a gusher in 1923, has raked in more than $4 billion in oil money—two-thirds of it directed to the UT school system.

The Texas Union Information Center, at 24th and Guadalupe (✆ **512/475-6636**), is the best place to get information about the campus; it's open Monday through Friday from 7am to 3am (really), Saturday from 10am to 3am, and Sunday from noon to 3am. In addition, you can pick up campus maps and other UT Austin–related materials at the ground floor of the Main building/UT Tower (near 24th and Whitis), which is also the point of departure for free campus tours—they're designed for prospective students and their families, but anyone can come. These leave weekdays at 11am and 2pm (only at 2pm in Dec and May) and Saturday at 2pm. Call ✆ **512/475-7399,** option 2, for recorded details. It's a lot tougher to get on the free Moonlight Prowl Tours, packed with amusing anecdotes of student life and campus lore, because they're held only a few evenings a month and they fill up quickly; but if you want to give it a try, log on to www.utexas.edu/tours/prowl and fill out the registration form.

See also "The Top Attractions," earlier in this chapter, for more on the LBJ Library and Museum; listings above in this section for the Harry Ransom Humanities Research Center, Blanton Museum of Art, and Texas Memorial Museum; the Walking Tour of university sights section, later; and information on visiting the UT Tower in the "Organized Tours" section, later in this chapter.

Guadalupe and I-35, Martin Luther King, Jr. Blvd. and 26th St. Ⓒ **512/471-3434.** www.utexas.edu. Bus: UT shuttle.

EAST SIDE

French Legation Museum The oldest residence still standing in Austin was built in 1841 for Count Alphonse Dubois de Saligny, France's representative to the fledgling Republic of Texas. Although his home was extravagant for the then-primitive capital, the flamboyant de Saligny didn't stay around to enjoy it for very long; he left town in a huff after his servant was beaten in retaliation for making bacon out of some pigs that had dined on the diplomat's linens. The house sits on a hill above downtown Austin and is considered one of the best examples of French colonial architecture outside Louisiana. Behind the house, in a separate structure, is a reconstruction of the original Creole kitchen.

802 San Marcos. Ⓒ **512/472-8180.** www.frenchlegationmuseum.org. Admission $4 adults, $3 seniors, $2 students/teachers, free for children 5 and under. Tours Tues–Sun 1–4:30pm. Bus: 4 and 18 stop nearby (at San Marcos and Seventh sts.). Go east on Seventh St., then turn left on San Marcos St.; the parking lot is behind the museum on Embassy and Ninth sts.

Texas State Cemetery ★ The city's namesake, Stephen F. Austin, is the best-known resident of this East Side cemetery, established by the state in 1851. Judge Edwin Waller, who laid out the grid plan for Austin's streets and later served as the city's mayor, also rests here, as do eight former Texas governors, various fighters in Texas's battles for independence, and Barbara Jordan, the first black woman from the South elected to the U.S. Congress (in 1996, she became the first African American to gain admittance to these grounds). Perhaps the most striking monument is one sculpted by Elisabet Ney (see "Central," above), for the tomb of Confederate general Albert Sidney Johnston, who died at the Battle of Shiloh.

The narrow drive that runs through the cemetery is actually a state highway. In the 1990s, the cemetery grounds were refurbished and extensively landscaped. This was the pet project of Lt. Gov. Bob Bullock, a politician who was nothing if not resourceful. Thwarted in getting funding passed by the state legislature, Bullock got the driveway designated as a highway so he could allocate funds from the Texas Department of Transportation. When you pay a visit, you can see the highway signs at the entrances. And you can check out a rather fancy tomb with Mr. Bullock's name on it. There are two self-guided-tour pamphlets at the visitor center/museum, which is designed to suggest the long barracks at the Alamo.

909 Navasota St. Ⓒ **512/463-0605.** www.cemetery.state.tx.us. Free admission. Grounds daily 8am–5pm; visitor center Mon–Fri 8am–5pm. Bus: 4 and 18 stop nearby.

AUSTIN OUTDOORS

Lakes

Highland Lakes The six dams built by the Lower Colorado River Authority in the late 1930s through the early 1950s not only controlled the flooding that had plagued the areas surrounding Texas's Colorado River (not to be confused with the river of the same name that flows through the Grand Canyon), but also transformed the waterway into a sparkling chain of lakes, stretching some 150 miles northwest of Austin. The narrowest of them, Lady Bird Lake, is also the closest to downtown. The heart of urban recreation in Austin, its banks are lined by trails and a shoreline park. Lake Austin, just upstream, divides West Austin from Westlake Hills. On its banks is Emma Long Park (see "Parks & Gardens," below). Next in the series is Lake Travis, the longest lake in the chain. It offers the most possibilities for boating and general recreation. Together with the other Highland Lakes—Marble Falls, LBJ, Inks, and Buchanan, some of which are discussed in chapter 17—these compose the largest concentration of freshwater lakes in Texas. See also "Staying Active," later in this chapter, for activity and equipment-rental suggestions.

Mountains

Covert Park at Mount Bonnell ★ For the best views of the city, Lake Austin, and some of the Hill Country stretching out westward, take a drive up to this hilltop park. It's 785 feet tall and the highest point in Austin. The oldest tourist attraction in town, it has also long been a favorite spot for romantic trysts, and rumor has it that any couple who climbed the 106 stone steps to the top together would fall in love (an emotion often confused with exhaustion). The peak was named for George W. Bonnell, Sam Houston's commissioner of Indian affairs in 1836, while the far-from-secret park at the summit gets its moniker from Frank M. Covert, Jr., who donated the land to the city in 1939.

3800 Mt. Bonnell Rd. No phone. Free admission. Daily 5am–10pm. Take Mt. Bonnell Rd. 1 mile past the west end of W. 35th St.

Nature Preserves

For information on **Wild Basin Wilderness Preserve,** see "Organized Tours," later in this chapter.

City of Austin Nature Preserves Highlights of the remarkably diverse group of natural habitats Austin boasts in its city-run nature preserves include **Blunn Creek** (1100 block of St. Edward's Dr.), 40 acres of upland woods and meadows traversed by a spring-fed creek. One of the two lookout areas is made of compacted volcanic ash. Spelunkers will like **Goat Cave** (3900 Deer Lane), which is honeycombed with limestone caves and sinkholes. You can arrange for cave tours by phoning the **Austin Nature Center** (✆ **512/327-8181**). Lovely **Mayfield Park** (3505 W. 35th St.) directly abuts the Barrow Brook Cove of Lake Austin. Peacocks and hens roam freely around lily ponds, and trails cross over bridges in oak and juniper woods. Visitors to the rock-walled ramada (a shaded shelter) at the **Zilker Preserve** (Barton Springs Rd. and Loop 1), with its meadows, streams, and cliff, can look out over downtown Austin. All the preserves are maintained in a primitive state with natural surface trails and no restrooms. The preserves are free and open daily from dawn to dusk. For additional information, including directions, phone ✆ **512/327-7723,** or log on to www.ci.austin.tx.us/preserves.

Westcave Preserve If you don't like the weather in one part of Westcave Preserve, you might like it better in another: Up to a 25° difference in temperature has been recorded between the highest area of this beautiful natural habitat, an arid Hill Country scrub, and the lowest, a lush woodland spread across a canyon floor. Because the ecosystem here is so delicate, the 30 acres on the Pedernales River may be entered only by guided tour. Reservations are taken for weekday visits, while on weekends, the first 30 people to show up at the allotted times are allowed in.

Star Rte. 1, Dripping Springs. ✆ **830/825-3442.** www.westcave.org. Sat–Sun for tours at 10am, noon, 2, and 4pm (weather permitting). $5 adults, $2 children under 12, or $15 per family. Take Hwy. 71 to Ranch Rd. 3238. Follow the signs 15 miles to Hamilton Pool, across the Pedernales River Bridge from the preserve.

Outdoor Art

Philosophers' Rock Glenna Goodacre's bronze sculpture of three of Austin's most recognized personalities from midcentury—naturalist Roy Bedichek, raconteur J. Frank Dobie, and historian Walter Prescott Webb—captures the essence of the three friends who used to schmooze together at Barton Springs Pool. No heroic posing here: Two of the three are wearing bathing trunks, which reveal potbellies, wrinkles, and sagging muscles, and all three are sitting down in mid-discussion. The casual friendliness of the pose and the intelligence of the men's expressions have made this piece, installed in 1994, an Austin favorite.

Zilker Park, 2201 Barton Springs Rd., just outside the entrance to Barton Springs Pool.

Stevie Ray Vaughan Statue In contrast to the Philosophers' Rock (see above), Ralph Roehming's bronze tribute to Austin singer/songwriter Stevie Ray Vaughan is artificial and awkward. Although he's wearing his habitual flat-brimmed hat and poncho, the stiffly posed Stevie Ray looks more like a frontiersman with a gun than a rock star with a guitar. But his devoted fans don't seem to mind, as evidenced by the flowers and devotions that almost always can be found at the foot of the statue.

South side of Town Lake, adjacent to Auditorium Shores.

Parks & Gardens

Emma Long Metropolitan Park More than 1,100 acres of woodland and a mile of shore along Lake Austin make Emma Long Park—named after the first woman to sit on Austin's city council—a most appealing space. Water activities revolve around two boat ramps, a fishing dock, and a protected swimming area, guarded by lifeguards on summer weekends. This is the only city park to offer camping, with permits ($6 for open camping, $15 utility camping in addition to entry fee) available on a first-come, first-served basis. If you hike through the stands of oak, ash, and juniper to an elevation of 1,000 feet, you'll get a view of the city spread out before you. Note that the park closes whenever its maximum capacity is reached.

1706 City Park Rd. ✆ **512/346-1831** or 512/346-3807. Admission $5 per vehicle Mon–Thurs; $8 Fri–Sun and holidays. Daily 7am–10pm. Exit I-35 at 290W, then go west (street names will change to Koenig, Allendale, Northland, and FM 2222) to City Park Rd. (near Loop 360). Turn south (left) and drive 6¼ miles to park entrance.

Zilker Botanical Garden ★ Kids There's bound to be something blooming at the Zilker Botanical Garden from March to October, but no matter what time of year you visit, you'll find this a soothing outdoor oasis in which to spend some time. The Oriental Garden, created by the landscape architect Isamu Taniguchi when he was 70 years old, is particularly peaceful. Be sure to ask someone at the garden center to point out how Taniguchi landscaped the word "Austin" into a series of ponds in the design. A butterfly garden attracts gorgeous winged visitors during April and October migrations, and you can poke and prod the many plants in the herb garden to get them to yield their fragrances. One hundred million–year-old dinosaur tracks, discovered on the grounds in the early 1990s, are part of the 1.5-acre Hartman Prehistoric Garden, which includes plants from the Cretaceous Period and a 13-foot bronze sculpture of an Ornithomimus dinosaur.

2220 Barton Springs Rd. ✆ **512/477-8672.** www.zilkergarden.org. Free admission. Grounds dawn–dusk. Garden center Mon–Fri 8:30am–4pm; Sat 10am–5pm (Jan–Feb 1–5pm); Sun 1–5pm (sometimes open earlier Sat–Sun for special garden shows; phone ahead). Bus: 30.

Zilker Park ★ Kids Comprising 347 acres, the first 40 of which were donated to the city by the wealthy German immigrant for whom the park is named, this is Austin's favorite public playground. Its centerpiece is Barton Springs Pool (see "The Top Attractions," earlier in this chapter), but visitors and locals also flock to the Zilker Botanical Garden, the Austin Nature Preserves, and the Umlauf Sculpture Garden and Museum, all described in this chapter. See also the "Especially for Kids" and "Staying Active" sections for details about the Austin Nature and Science Center, the Zilker Zephyr Miniature Train, and Town Lake canoe rentals. In addition to its athletic fields (nine for soccer, one for rugby, and two multiuse), the park hosts a 9-hole disk (Frisbee) golf course and a sand volleyball court.

2201 Barton Springs Rd. ✆ **512/476-9044.** www.ci.austin.tx.us/zilker. Free admission. Daily 5am–10pm. Bus: 30.

3 ESPECIALLY FOR KIDS

The Bob Bullock Texas State History Museum and the **Texas Memorial Museum,** both described in earlier sections, are child-friendly, but outdoor attractions are still Austin's biggest draw for children. There's lots of room for children to splash around at **Barton Springs,** and even youngsters who thought bats were creepy are likely to be converted on further acquaintance with the critters. In addition, the following attractions are especially geared toward children.

Austin Children's Museum ★ Located in a large, state-of-the-art facility, this excellent children's museum has something for people of all ages. Tots enjoy the low-tech but creative playscapes, tweens take on a variety of "creation stations," and grown-up environments such as a studio sound stage (part of "Austin Kiddie Limits") please even incipient adolescents. Parents will get a kick out of the replica Austin city landscapes, including the recently introduced Rising Star Ranch, where a Hill Country pond is stocked with wooden musical frogs.

Dell Discovery Center, 201 Colorado St. ✆ **512/472-2499.** www.austinkids.org. Admission $5.50 adults, $3.50 for children 12–23 months, free for children under 12 months. Tues–Sat 10am–5pm; Sun noon–5pm; donations only Wed 5–8pm, free Sun 4–5pm. Closed Mon and some holidays. Bus: 10, 12, 15, 16, or 64.

Austin Nature and Science Center ★ Bats, bees, and crystal caverns are among the subjects of the Discovery Lab at this museum in the 80-acre Nature Center, which features lots of interactive exhibits. The tortoises, lizards, porcupine, and vultures in the Animal Exhibits—among more than 90 orphaned or injured creatures brought here from the wild—also hold kids' attention. An Eco-Detective trail highlights pond-life awareness. The Dino Pit, with its replicas of Texas fossils and dinosaur tracks, is a lure for budding paleontologists. A variety of specialty camps, focusing on everything from caving to astronomy, are offered from late May through August.

Zilker Park, 301 Nature Center Dr. ✆ **512/327-8181.** www.ci.austin.tx.us/ansc. Donations requested; occasional special exhibits charge separately. Mon–Sat 9am–5pm; Sun noon–5pm. Closed July 4th, Thanksgiving, and Dec 25. Bus: 30.

Austin Zoo This small zoo, some 14 miles southwest of downtown, may not feature the state-of-the-jungle habitats of larger facilities, but it's easy to get up close and personal with the critters here. Most of the animal residents, who range from turkeys and potbellied pigs to marmosets and tigers, were mistreated, abandoned, or illegally imported before they found a home here. It costs $2.25 to board the 1½-mile miniature train for a scenic Hill Country ride, which lets you peer at some of the shyer animals. There are no food concessions here, just plenty of picnic tables.

10807 Rawhide Trail. ✆ **512/288-1490.** www.austinzoo.org. Admission $8 adults, $6 seniors, $5 children ages 2–12, free for children under age 2. Daily 10am–6pm. Closed Thanksgiving and Dec 25. Take Hwy. 290W to Circle Dr., turn right, go 1½ miles to Rawhide Trail, and turn right.

Splash! Into the Edwards Aquifer The Edwards Aquifer, Austin's main source of water, is fed by a variety of underground creeks filtered through a large layer of limestone. You'll feel as though you're entering one of this vast ecosystem's sinkholes when you walk into the dimly lit enclosure—formerly the bathhouse at Barton Springs pool—where a variety of interactive displays grab kids' attention. Young visitors can make it rain on the city, identify water bugs, or peer through a periscope at swimmers. Although the focus is on the evils of pollution, the agenda is by no means heavy-handed.

Zilker Park, 2201 Barton Springs Rd. ✆ **512/481-1466.** www.ci.austin.tx.us/splash. Free admission. Tues–Sat 10am–5pm; Sun noon–5pm. Bus: 30 (Barton Creek Sq.).

Zilker Zephyr Miniature Train Take a scenic 25-minute ride through Zilker Park on a narrow-gauge, light-rail miniature train, which takes you at a leisurely pace along Barton Creek and Town Lake. The train departs approximately every hour on the hour during the week and every half-hour on the weekend, weather permitting.

Zilker Park, 2100 Barton Springs Rd. (just across from the Barton Springs Pool). ✆ **512/478-8286.** Admission $2.75 adults, $1.75 under 12 and seniors, free for infants (under 1) on guardian's lap. Mon–Fri 10am–5pm; Sat–Sun 10am–7pm. Bus: 30.

4 SPECIAL-INTEREST SIGHTSEEING

AFRICAN-AMERICAN HERITAGE

The many contributions of Austin's African-American community are highlighted at **George Washington Carver Museum and Cultural Center,** 1165 Angelina St. (✆ **512/472-4809;** www.ci.austin.tx.us/carver), the first in Texas devoted to black history. Rotating exhibits of contemporary artwork share the space with photographs, videos, oral histories, and other artifacts from the community's past. A number of other sites on the East Side are worth visiting, too. Less than 2 blocks from the Carver, on the corner of Hackberry and San Bernard streets, stands the **Wesley United Methodist Church.** Established at the end of the Civil War, it was one of the leading black churches in Texas. Diagonally across the street, the **Zeta Phi Beta Sorority,** Austin's first black Greek letter house, occupies the Thompson House, built in 1877, which is also the archival center for the Texas chapter of the sorority. Nearby, at the **State Cemetery** (see "More Attractions," earlier in this chapter), you can visit the gravesite of congresswoman and civil rights leader Barbara Jordan, the first African American to be buried here.

In 1863, during the time of the Civil War, a black freeman, of which there were few in Texas, settled down on the east side of Austin and built a small cabin for himself and his family. He built it near the present-day intersection of I-35 and East 11th Street. His name was Henry Green Madison, and during Reconstruction, he became Austin's first African-American city councilmember. The cabin he built was preserved more by accident than by design and, in 1973, was donated to the city, which moved it to its present site in nearby Rosewood Park at 2300 Rosewood Ave. (✆ **512/472-6838**). There you can see the **Henry G. Madison** cabin and how simple and small it must have been for his family of eight. A contemporary of Madison was Charles Clark, a slave who was emancipated after the Civil War and in 1871 founded a small utopian community of freed blacks just to the west of Austin around what is now West 10th Street. It was called Clarksville and is now a mostly white neighborhood still known by that name.

For a more up-to-date look at the Austin scene, visit **Mitchie's Fine Art & Gift Gallery,** 6406 I-35 (Lincoln Village Shopping Center), Suite 2800 (✆ **512/323-6901;** www.mitchie.com).

5 STROLLING THE UNIVERSITY OF TEXAS

No ivory tower, the University of Texas is fully integrated into Austin's economic and cultural life. To explore the vast main campus is to glimpse the city's future as well as its past. Here, state-of-the-art structures—including information kiosks that can play the school's team songs—sit cheek by jowl with elegant examples of 19th-century architecture. The following tour points out many of the most interesting spots on campus. You'll probably want to drive or take a bus between some of the first seven sights. (Parking limitations were taken into account in this initial portion of the circuit.) For a walking-only tour, begin at stop 8; also note that stops 2, 5, 6, 12, and 20 are discussed earlier in this chapter, and stop 9 is detailed in the "Organized Tours" section, below.

WALKING TOUR UT AUSTIN

START: **The Arno Nowotny Building.**

FINISH: **The Littlefield Fountain.**

TIME: **1 hour, not including food breaks or museum visits.**

BEST TIMES: **On the weekends, when the campus is less crowded, more parking is available, and the Tower is open.**

WORST TIMES: **Morning and midday during the week when classes are in session and parking is impossible to find. (*Beware:* Those tow-away zone signs mean business.)**

In 1839, the Congress of the Republic of Texas ordered a site set aside for the establishment of a "university of the first class" in Austin. Some 40 years later, when the flagship of the new University of Texas system opened, its first two buildings went up on that original 40-acre plot, dubbed College Hill. Although there were attempts to establish master-design plans for the university from the turn of the century onward, they were only carried out in bits and pieces until 1930, when money from an earlier oil strike on UT land allowed the school to begin building in earnest. Between 1930 and 1945, consulting architect Paul Cret put his mark on 19 university buildings, most showing the influence of his education at Paris's Ecole des Beaux-Arts. If the entire 357-acre campus will never achieve stylistic unity, its earliest section has a grace and cohesion that make it a delight to stroll through.

Though it begins at the oldest building owned by the university, this tour commences far from the original campus. At the frontage road of I-35 and the corner of Martin Luther King, Jr. Boulevard, pull into the parking lot of:

❶ The Arno Nowotny Building

In the 1850s, several state-run asylums for the mentally ill and the physically handicapped arose on the outskirts of Austin. One of these was the State Asylum for the Blind, built by Abner Cook around 1856. The ornate Italianate-style structure soon became better known as the headquarters and barracks of General Custer, who had been sent to Austin in 1865 to reestablish order after the Civil War. Incorporated into the university and restored for its centennial celebration, the building is now used for administration.

Take Martin Luther King, Jr. Boulevard to Red River, then drive north to the:

❷ LBJ Library and Museum

This library and museum offers another rare on-campus parking lot. (You'll want to leave your car here while you see sights 3–6.) The first presidential library to be built on a university campus, the huge travertine marble structure oversees a beautifully landscaped 14-acre complex. Among the museum's exhibits is a seven-eighths-scale replica of the Oval Office as it looked when the Johnsons occupied the White House. In the adjoining Sid Richardson Hall are the Lyndon B. Johnson School of Public Affairs and the Barker Texas History Center, housing the world's most extensive collection of Texas memorabilia.

Stroll down the library steps across East Campus Drive to 23rd Street, where, next to the large Burleson bells on your right, you'll see the university's $41-million:

❸ Performing Arts Center

This arts center includes the 3,000-seat Bass Concert Hall, the 700-seat Bates Recital Hall, and other College of the Fine Arts auditoriums. The state-of-the-art acoustics at the Bass Concert Hall enhance the sounds of the largest tracker organ in the United States. Linking contemporary computer technology with a design that goes back some 2,000 years, it has 5,315 pipes—some of them 16 feet tall—and weighs 48,000 pounds.

From the same vantage point to the left looms the huge:

❹ Darrell K. Royal/Texas Memorial Stadium

The first of the annual UT–Texas A&M Thanksgiving Day games was played here in 1924. The upper deck directly facing you was added in 1972. In a drive to finance the original stadium, female students sold their hair, male students sold their blood, and UT alum Lutcher Stark matched every $10,000 they raised with $1,000 of his own funds. The stadium's mid-1990s name change to honor legendary Longhorns football coach Darrell K. Royal angered some who wanted the stadium to remain a memorial to Texas veterans, and confused others who wondered if Royal is still alive (he is).

Continue west on 23rd; at the corner of San Jacinto, a long staircase marks the entrance to the:

❺ Art Building

This used to be the home of the Blanton Museum (see "Top Attractions," earlier in this chapter); now it is used for classes and to exhibit student art shows.

Walk a short distance north on San Jacinto. A stampeding group of bronze mustangs will herald your arrival at the:

❻ Texas Memorial Museum

This monumental art moderne building was designed by Paul Cret, and ground was broken for the institution by Franklin Roosevelt in 1936. Once home to the capitol's original zinc goddess of liberty, which was moved to the Bob Bullock Texas State History Museum along with other historic treasures, this museum now focuses solely on the natural sciences.

1 Arno Nowotny Building
2 LBJ Library and Museum
3 Performing Arts Center
4 Darrell K. Royal/Texas Memorial Stadium
5 Art Building
6 Texas Memorial Museum
7 Santa Rita No. 1
8 Littlefield Memorial Fountain
9 Main Building and Tower
10 Garrison Hall
11 Battle Hall
12 Flawn Academic Center
13 Hogg Auditorium
14 Battle Oaks
15 Littlefield Home
16 The Drag
17 Texas Union Building
18 Goldsmith Hall
19 Sutton Hall
20 Harry Ransom Humanities Research Center

Exit the building and take Trinity, which, curving into 25th Street, will bring you back to the parking lot of the LBJ Library and your car. Retrace your original route along Red River until you reach Martin Luther King, Jr. Boulevard. Drive west, and at the corner of San Jacinto, you'll see:

7 Santa Rita No. 1

No. 1 is an oil rig transported here from West Texas, where black gold first spewed forth from it on land belonging to the university in 1923. The money was distributed between the University of Texas system, which got the heftier two-thirds, and the Texas A&M system. Although not its main source of income, this windfall has helped make UT the second richest university in the country, after Harvard.

Continue on to University Avenue and turn left. There are public parking spaces around 21st Street and University, where you'll begin your walking tour at the:

8 Littlefield Memorial Fountain

This fountain was built in 1933. Pompeo Coppini, sculptor of the magnificent bronze centerpiece, believed that the rallying together of the nation during World War I marked the final healing of the wounds caused by the Civil War. He depicted the winged goddess Columbia riding on the bow of a battleship sailing across the ocean—represented by three rearing sea horses—to aid the Allies. The two figures on the deck represent the Army and the Navy. This three-tiered fountain graces the most dramatic entrance to the university's original 40 acres. Behind you stands the state capitol.

Directly ahead of you, across an oak-shaded mall lined with statues, is the:

9 Main Building and Tower

The university's first academic building was built here in 1884. The 307-foot-high structure that now rises above the university was created by Paul Cret in 1937. It's a fine example of the Beaux Arts style, particularly stunning when lit to celebrate a Longhorn victory. Sadly, the clock tower's many notable features—the small classical temple on top, say, or the 56-bell carillon, the largest in Texas—will probably always be dogged by the shadow of the carnage committed by Charles Whitman, who, in August 1966, shot and killed 16 people and wounded 31 more from the tower before he was gunned down by a sharpshooter. Closed off to the public in 1975 after a series of suicide leaps from its observation deck, the tower reopened for supervised ascensions in 1999 (see "Organized Tours," below). If you climb the staircase on the east (right) side of the tower to the stone balustrade, you can see the dramatic sweep of the entire eastern section of campus, including the LBJ Library.

The first building in your direct line of vision is:

10 Garrison Hall

Garrison Hall is named for one of the earliest members of the UT faculty and home to the department of history. Important names from Texas's past—Austin, Travis, Houston, and Lamar—are set here in stone. The walls just under the building's eaves are decorated with cattle brands; look for the carved cow skulls and cactuses on the balcony window on the north side.

If you retrace your steps to the western (left) side of the Main Building, you'll see:

11 Battle Hall

This building is regarded by many as the campus's most beautiful building. Designed in 1911 by Cass Gilbert, architect of the U.S. Supreme Court building, the hall was the first to be done in the Spanish Renaissance style that came to characterize so many of the structures on this section of campus (note the terra-cotta–tiled roof and broadly arched windows). On the second floor, you can see the grand reading room of what is now the Architecture and Planning Library.

Exit Battle Hall and walk left to the northern door, which faces the much newer:

12 Flawn Academic Center

An undergraduate library shares space here with exhibits from the archives of the

Humanities Research Center (see stop 20, below). Among the permanent displays in the Academic Center's Leeds Gallery is a cabin furnished with the effects of Erle Stanley Gardner, Perry Mason's creator. In front of the building, Charles Umlauf's *The Torch Bearers* symbolizes the passing of knowledge from one generation to the next.

Continue along the eastern side of the Academic Center, where you'll pass:

⓭ The Hogg Auditorium

This auditorium is another Paul Cret building, designed in the same monumental art moderne mode as his earlier Texas Memorial Museum.

A few steps farther along, you'll come to the trees known as the:

⓮ Battle Oaks

The three oldest members of this small grove are said to predate the city of Austin itself. They survived the destruction of most of the grove to build a Civil War fortress and a later attempt to displace them with a new Biology Building. It was this last, near-fatal skirmish that earned them their name. Legend has it that Dr. W. J. Battle, a professor of classics and an early university president, holed up in the largest oak with a rifle to protect the three ancient trees.

Look across the street. At the corner of 24th and Whitis, you'll see the:

⓯ Littlefield Home

This home was built in high Victorian style in 1894. Major George W. Littlefield, a wealthy developer, cattle rancher, and banker, bequeathed more than $1 million to the university on the condition that its campus not be moved to land that his rival, George W. Brackenridge, had donated. During the week, when the UT Development Office is open, you can enter through the east carriage driveway to see the house's gorgeous gold-and-white parlors, griffin-decorated fireplace, and other ornate details. On the weekend, just ogle the architecture and the shaggy, 35-foot-high deodar cedar, which Littlefield had shipped over from its native Himalayas.

> **TAKE A BREAK**
>
> **O's Campus Cafe,** in the A.C.E.S. building on 24th Street and Speedway (✆ **512/232-9060;** www.oscampuscafe.com), is brought to you by the same folks who created Jeffrey's and Cipollina (see chapter 13 for both), so you know it's going to be a notch up from standard campus fare. Its gourmet sandwiches, pizzas, and muffins don't disappoint. If you haven't stopped here en route to the central campus from stop 7, head east to Speedway along 24th Street. O's has various to-go outlets and an additional sit-down location at the McCombs School of Business. See website for details.

Backtrack to stop 15 and walk west about a block to Guadalupe to reach:

⓰ The Drag

As its name suggests, the Drag is Austin's main off-campus pedestrian strip. Bookstores, fast-food restaurants, and shops line the thoroughfare, which is usually crammed with students trying to grab a bite or a book between classes. On weekends, the pedestrian mall set aside for the 23rd Street Renaissance Market overflows with crafts vendors.

To get back to the university, cross Guadalupe at the traffic light in front of the huge Co-op, between 24th and 22nd streets. You'll now be facing the west mall.

On your left is the:

⓱ Texas Union Building

UT's student union building is yet another Paul Cret creation. A beautifully tiled staircase leads up to the second level, where, through the massive carved wooden doors, you'll see the Cactus Cafe, a popular coffeehouse and music venue (see chapter 16). This bustling student center hosts everything from a bowling alley to a formal ballroom.

Immediately across the mall to the right stands:

⑱ Goldsmith Hall

This is one of two adjacent buildings where architecture classes are held. Also designed by Paul Cret, this hall has beautifully worn slate floors and a palm tree–dotted central courtyard.

Walk through the courtyard and go down a few steps. To your right is:

⑲ Sutton Hall

This hall was designed by Cass Gilbert in 1918 and is part of the School of Architecture. Like his Battle Hall, it is gracefully Mediterranean, with terra-cotta moldings, a red-tile roof, and large Palladian windows.

Enter Sutton Hall through double doors at the front and exit straight through the back. You are now facing the:

⑳ Harry Ransom Center

The Humanities Research Center (HRC) is housed here. The satirical portrait of a rich American literary archive in A. S. Byatt's best-selling novel *Possession* is widely acknowledged to be based on HRC. On the first floor of this building, you can view the center's extremely rare Gutenberg Bible, one of just five complete copies in the U.S., as well as the world's first photograph, created by Joseph Nicèphore Nièpce in 1826.

Exit the building to 21st Street and the fountain where the tour began.

6 ORGANIZED TOURS

See also chapter 16 for details on touring the *Austin City Limits* studio.

AN AMPHIBIOUS TOUR

Austin Duck Adventures It's a hoot—or should I say a quack? Whether or not you opt to use the duck call whistle included in the tour price to blow at the folks you pass in the street, you'll get a kick out of this combination land and sea tour. You'll be transported in a six-wheel-drive amphibious vehicle (originally created for British troops during the Cold War) through Austin's historic downtown and the scenic west side before splashing into Lake Austin. Comedy writers helped devise the script for this 1½-hour tour, so it's funny as well as informative.

Boarding in front of the Austin Convention and Visitors Bureau, 209 E. Sixth St. ✆ **512/4-SPLASH** (477-5274). www.austinducks.com. Tours $26 adults, $24 seniors and students, $16 ages 3–12. Daily tours; times change seasonally; call to check schedule.

BOAT TOURS

Capital Cruises From March through October, Capital Cruises plies Town Lake with electric-powered boats heading out on a number of popular tours. The bat cruises are especially big in summer, when warm nights are perfect for the enjoyable and educational hour-long excursions. The high point is seeing thousands of bats stream out from under their Congress Avenue Bridge roost. Dinner cruises, featuring fajitas from the Hyatt Regency's La Vista restaurant, are also fun on a balmy evening, and the afternoon sightseeing tours are a nice way to while away an hour on the weekend.

Hyatt Regency Town Lake boat dock. ✆ **512/480-9264.** www.capitalcruises.com. Bat and sightseeing cruises $8 adults, $6 seniors, $5 children 5–12; dinner cruises (including tax and tip) $27–$81 depending on options. Bat cruise daily ½ hour before sunset (call ahead for exact time), weather permitting; sightseeing cruise Sat–Sun at 1pm; dinner cruise Fri–Sun at 6pm. Reservations required for dinner cruises; for bat and sightseeing cruises, show up at the dock a minimum of 30 min. in advance.

Lone Star Riverboat You'll set out against a backdrop of Austin's skyline and the state capitol on this riverboat cruise and move upstream past Barton Creek and Zilker Park. Along the way, you'll glimpse 100-foot-high cliffs and million-dollar estates. These scenic tours, accompanied by knowledgeable narrators, last 1½ hours. Slightly shorter bat-watching tours leave around half an hour before sunset, so call ahead to check.

South shore of Town Lake, btw. the Congress Ave. and S. First St. bridges, just next to the Hyatt. ✆ **512/327-1388.** www.lonestarriverboat.com. Scenic and bat tours $10 adults, $8 seniors, $7 children 4–12. Scenic tours Sat–Sun 1pm Mar–Oct only. Bat tours nightly Apr–Oct only; call for exact times.

VAN TOUR

Austin Overtures This 90-minute tour of the city takes you to the south and west sides of town and through the heart of central Austin. You can check departure times (there are a couple per day), make reservations, and buy tickets at the visitor center. Or you can make a reservation on the company's website. This tour is a little lighter on the comedy than the Duck tours, it covers more ground, and it gives more history.

Boarding in front of the Austin Convention and Visitors Bureau, 209 E. Sixth St. ✆ **512/659-9478.** www.austinovertures.com. Tours $25 adults, $21 seniors and military, $17 ages 12 and under. Daily tours; call to check schedule.

WALKING TOURS

Austin Ghost Tours If you favor activities that are likely to keep you from sleeping, these tours are for you. Not only are the various outings held in the evening, but they're all concerned with ghouls. **The Ghosts of Austin Downtown Walking Tour** explores the stories of those that even death couldn't separate from downtown, while the tavern-crawl **Haunted Sixth Street Tour** capitalizes on the spirits that liked their spirits (and visitors who like both the spectral and the alcoholic manifestations). Austin Ghost Tours has also teamed up with the Austin Museum of Art for a special 90-minute **Haunted History Walking Tour,** featuring the museum exhibit "The Disembodied Spirit," the Wooten building, the Old Miller Opera House, and the Capitol. A variety of other tours are available as well, so be sure to check the website, and then call ahead to make the required reservations.

Tour departure points vary; check ahead. ✆ **512/853-9826.** www.austinghosttours.com. 90-min. Ghosts of Austin and 2-hr. Haunted Sixth Street tours $15. Tour schedules vary; call or check the website.

University of Texas Tower Observation Deck Tour Off-limits to the public for nearly a quarter of a century, the infamous observation deck of the UT Tower (see "Strolling Around the University of Texas," earlier in this chapter)—where crazed gunman Charles Whitman went on a deadly shooting spree in 1966—was remodeled with a webbed dome and reopened in 1999. Billed as tours, these excursions to the top of the tower are really supervised visits, although a guide gives a short, informative spiel and stays on hand to answer questions. Frankly, it would probably be better if these visits—now about 30 minutes long—were half as short and half as expensive (I saw lots of people looking bored after about 10 minutes).

Deck tours are available by reservation only. Check the website or phone the numbers listed below on Monday to Friday 8am to 5pm to pin down the schedule and to find out how to get your tickets.

Note: You are permitted to bring along a camera, binoculars, or a camcorder to take advantage of the observation deck's spectacular, 360-degree view of the city and environs, but you must leave behind everything else, including purses, camera bags, tripods, strollers, and so forth. (Lockers are available at the Texas Union for $1.)

UT Campus, Texas Union Building. ✆ **877/475-6633** (outside Austin) or 512/475-6633. www.utexas.edu/tower. Tours $5. Tours are offered Sat–Sun on the hour—starting as early as 11am and lasting until as late as 8pm—most of the year. Schedules vary according to the academic schedule; late May–late Aug, tours may be offered on Thurs and Fri evenings, and Sun tours eliminated.

Wild Basin Wilderness Preserve The varied menu of guided tours at this preserve on a lovely 227-acre peninsula will keep nature and wildlife lovers happy, night and day. Native plants, birds, arrowheads, and snakes are among the topics covered (though not at the same time) during daylight walks. After dark, there are either moonlight tours (coinciding with the full moon) or stargazing tours 3 or 4 days after the new moon. Call ahead or check the website for exact dates.

805 N. Capital of Texas Hwy. ✆ **512/327-7622.** www.wildbasin.org. Preserve admission $3 adults, $2 seniors and ages 5–12; 2-hour tours $4 adults, $2 ages 5–12, free for children under 5. Preserve daily dawn–dusk; office daily 9am–5pm, Sat–Sun 8am–3pm. Hiking tours every weekend, weather permitting, stargazing tours twice monthly, weather permitting, generally 8 or 8:30pm to 9:30 or 10pm.

SELF-GUIDED TOURS

In addition to the guided walking tours offered by the **Austin Convention and Visitors Bureau** (see below), the ACVB sells mp3 audio tours for $15. These come with a map to guide you and include mellow background music as you navigate from one stop to the next. One tour covers the main attractions of Austin's downtown. The other tour takes you around the most popular live-performance venues in the downtown area.

The visitor center also offers seven self-guided tour booklets, which are free. Five tours (Bremond Block, Hyde Park, Congress Ave. and E. Sixth St., Texas State Cemetery, and Oakwood Cemetery) require foot power alone. The other two (West Austin and O. Henry Trail) combine walking and driving. They make for interesting reading even if you don't have time to follow the routes.

GUIDED WALKS

Enjoyable guided walking **tours ★★** are offered free of charge by the **Austin Convention and Visitors Bureau (ACVB;** ✆ **866/GO-AUSTIN** [462-8784] or 512/478-0098; www.austintexas.org). There are two tours to choose from. Both are downtown; both last approximately 90 minutes; and both depart punctually from the south entrance of the capitol, weather permitting. The tour of the historic Bremond Block takes place on Saturday and Sunday at 11am. The tour of Congress Avenue and East Sixth Street takes place on Thursday, Friday, and Saturday at 9am, and on Sunday at 2pm. Make reservations for the tours at least 24 hours in advance. You can do so by calling the visitor center or by going to the website.

7 STAYING ACTIVE

BIKING A city that has a "bicycle coordinator" on its payroll must take biking seriously. Austin publishes a map of city bike routes for the benefit of local bike commuters and those visitors who want to pedal around town. You can download a PDF version of the map or order a hard copy by going to this website: www.ci.austin.tx.us/bicycle/bikemap.htm.

If you want to ride on trails, you have your choice of the mellow hike-and-bike trail around Lady Bird Lake (10 miles), or the more challenging Barton Creek Greenbelt (7.8 miles). Contact **Austin Parks and Recreation,** 200 S. Lamar Blvd. (✆ **512/974-6700;** www.ci.austin.tx.us/parks), for more information on these and other bike trails. There is also a paved **Veloway,** a 3.1-mile paved loop in Slaughter Creek Metropolitan Park in far south Austin. It is devoted exclusively to bicyclists and in-line skaters.

You can rent bikes and get maps and other information from **University Cyclery,** 2901 N. Lamar Blvd. (✆ **512/474-6696;** www.universitycyclery.com). A number of downtown hotels rent or provide free bicycles to their guests. For information on weekly road rides, contact the **Austin Cycling Association,** P.O. Box 5993, Austin, TX 78763 (✆ **512/282-7413;** www.austincycling.org), which also publishes a monthly newsletter, *Southwest Cycling News,* though only local calls or e-mails are returned. For rougher mountain-bike routes, try the **Austin Ridge Riders.** Their website, www.austinridge riders.com, has the latest contact information.

BIRD-WATCHING Endangered golden-cheeked warblers and black-capped vireos are among the many species you might spot around Austin. The **Travis Audubon Society** (✆ **512/926-8751;** www.travisaudubon.org) organizes regular birding trips and even has a rare-bird hot line.

Texas Parks and Wildlife publishes *The Guide to Austin-Area Birding Sites,* which points you to the best urban perches. You should be able to pick up a copy at the Austin Visitor Center or at the offices of any of Austin's parks and preserves (see "More Attractions," earlier in this chapter). Avid birders should also enjoy ***Adventures with a Texas Naturalist,*** by Roy Bedichek. The author is one of the three friends depicted on the Philosophers' Rock, also listed in the "More Attractions" section, p. 234.

CANOEING You can rent canoes at **Zilker Park,** 2000 Barton Springs Rd. (✆**512/478-3852;** www.fastair.com/zilker), for $10 an hour or $40 all day (daily from Apr–Sept; only weekends, holidays, weather permitting, from Oct–Mar). **Capital Cruises,** Hyatt Regency boat dock (✆ **512/480-9264;** www.capitalcruises.com), also offers hourly rentals on Town Lake. If your paddling skills are a bit rusty, check out the instructional courses of UT's **Recreational Sports Outdoor Program** (✆ **512/471-3116**).

FISHING **Git Bit** (✆ **512/773-7401;** www.gitbitfishing.com) provides guide service for half- or full-day bass-fishing trips on Lake Travis.

GOLF For information about Austin's five municipal golf courses and to set up tee times, log on to www.ci.austin.tx.us/parks/golf.htm. All but the 9-hole Hancock course offer pro shops and equipment rental, and their greens fees are reasonable. The **Hancock** course was built in 1899 and is the oldest course in Texas. The **Lions** course is where Tom Kite and Ben Crenshaw played college golf for the University of Texas.

HIKING Austin's parks and preserves abound in nature trails; see "Austin Outdoors" in the "More Attractions," section earlier in this chapter for additional information. Contact the **Sierra Club** (✆ **512/472-1767;** www.texas.sierraclub.org/austin), if you're interested in organized hikes. **Wild Basin Wilderness Preserve** (see "Organized Tours," above) is another source for guided treks, offering periodic "Haunted Trails" tours along with its more typical hikes.

ROCK CLIMBING Those with the urge to hang out on cliffs can call **Mountain Madness** (✆ **512/329-0309;** www.mtmadness.com), which holds weekend rock-climbing courses at Enchanted Rock, a stunning granite outcropping in the Hill Country. **Austin**

Rock Gym (✆ **512/416-9299;** www.austinrockgym.com) offers two family-friendly indoor climbing facilities, as well as a variety of classes and guided outdoor trips.

SAILING Lake Travis is the perfect place to let the wind drive your sails; among the operators offering sailboat rentals in the Austin area are **Commander's Point Yacht Basin** (✆ **512/266-2333**) and **Texas Sailing Academy** (✆ **512/261-6193;** www.texassailing.com). Both offer instruction.

SCUBA DIVING The clarity of the waters of Lake Travis varies a good bit. On some days it's quite good for diving. You can spot boat wrecks and metal sculptures that have been planted on the lake bottom of the private (paying) portion of **Windy Point Park** (✆ **512/266-3337;** www.windypointpark.com); and Mother Nature has provided the park's advanced divers with an unusual underwater grove of pecan trees. Equipment rentals and lessons are available nearby from **Dive World** (✆ **512/219-1220;** www.diveworldaustin.com), located at 12129 R.R. 620, #440.

SPELUNKING The limestone country in the Austin area is rife with dark places in which to poke around. In the city, two wild caves you can crawl into with the proper training are **Airman's Cave,** on the Barton Creek Greenbelt, and **Goat Cave Preserve,** in southwest Austin. Check the website of the Texas Speleological Association, www.cavetexas.org, and that of the University Speleological Society, www.utgrotto.org (you don't have to be a student to join), for links to statewide underground attractions. See also chapter 18 for other caves in nearby Hill Country.

SWIMMING The best known of Austin's natural swimming holes is **Barton Springs Pool** (see "The Top Attractions," earlier in this chapter), but it's by no means the only one. Other scenic outdoor spots to take the plunge include **Deep Eddy Pool,** 401 Deep Eddy Ave., at Lake Austin Boulevard (✆ **512/472-8546**), and **Hamilton Pool Preserve,** 27 miles west of Austin, off Texas 71, on FM 3238 (✆ **512/264-2740**).

For lakeshore swimming, consider **Hippie Hollow** (www.co.travis.tx.us/tnr/parks/hippie_hollow.asp) on Lake Travis, 2½ miles off FM 620, where you can let it all hang out in a series of clothing-optional coves, or **Emma Long Metropolitan Park** on Lake Austin (see "More Attractions," earlier in this chapter).

You can also get into the swim at a number of **free neighborhood pools;** contact the City Aquatics Department (✆ **512/476-4521;** www.ci.austin.tx.us/parks/aquatics.htm) for more information.

TENNIS The very reasonably priced **Austin High School Tennis Center,** 2001 W. Cesar Chavez St. (✆ **512/477-7802**); **Caswell Tennis Center,** 2312 Shoal Creek Blvd. (✆ **512/478-6268**); and **Pharr Tennis Center,** 4201 Brookview Dr. (✆ **512/477-7773**), all have enough courts to give you a good shot at getting one to play on. To find out about additional public courts, contact the **Tennis Administration** office (✆**512/480-3020;** www.ci.austin.tx.us/parks/tennis.htm).

8 SPECTATOR SPORTS

College sports are very big, particularly when the **University of Texas (UT) Longhorns** are playing. The most comprehensive source of information on the various teams is www.texassports.com, but you can phone the **UT Athletics Ticket Office** (✆ **512/471-3333**) to find out about schedules and **UTTM Charge-A-Ticket** (✆ **512/477-6060**) to order tickets.

BASEBALL The **University of Texas** baseball team goes to bat February through May at Disch-Falk Field (just east of I-35, at the corner of Martin Luther King, Jr. Blvd. and Comal). Many players from this former NCAA championship squad have gone on to the big time, including two-time Cy Young award winner Roger Clemens.

Baseball Hall-of-Famer Nolan Ryan's **Round Rock Express,** a Houston Astros farm club, won the Texas League championship in 1999, their first year in existence (they now compete in the Pacific Coast League). See them play at the Dell Diamond, 3400 E. Palm Valley Rd., in Round Rock (✆ **512/255-BALL** or 512/244-4209; www.roundrock express.com), an 8,688-seat stadium where you can choose from box seats or stadium seating; an additional 3,000 fans can sit on a grassy berm in the outfield. Tickets range from about $6 to $12.

BASKETBALL The **University of Texas** Longhorns and Lady Longhorns basketball teams, both former Southwest Conference champions, play in the Frank C. Erwin, Jr. Special Events Center (just west of I-35 on Red River, btw. Martin Luther King, Jr. Blvd. and 15th St.) November through March.

FOOTBALL It's hard to tell which is more central to the success of an Austin Thanksgiving: the turkey or the UT–Texas A&M game. Part of the Big 12 Conference, the **University of Texas** football team often fills the huge Darrell K. Royal/Texas Memorial Stadium (just west of I-35, btw. 23rd and 21st sts., E. Campus Dr., and San Jacinto Blvd.) during home games, played August through November.

GOLF The **Triton Financial Classic** (✆ **512/732-2666;** www.tritonclassic.com), previously called the FedEx Kinko's Classic, continues to be played at the Hills Country Club at Lakeway Resort the first week of June. This Austin stop on the PGA's Champions Tour began back in 2003 and has boasted a $1.6 million purse.

HOCKEY The **Austin Ice Bats** hockey team (✆ **512/927-PUCK** [927-7825]; www.icebats.com) has been getting anything but an icy reception from its Austin fans. This typically rowdy team plays at the Travis County Exposition Center, 7311 Decker Lane (about 15 min. east of UT). Tickets, which run from $10 to $35, are available at any UTTM outlet or from **Star Tickets** (✆ **888/597-STAR** [597-7827] or 512/469-SHOW [469-7469]; www.startickets.com). The team generally plays on weekends, mid-October through late March; a phone call will get you the exact dates and times.

HORSE RACING Pick your ponies at **Manor Downs,** 8 miles east of I-35 on U.S. 290 East (✆ **512/272-5581;** www.manordowns.com), Texas's oldest parimutuel horse racetrack. The track is open for quarter horse and thoroughbred live racing on Saturday and Sunday, mid-February through May (general admission $2; main grandstand general seating $3; box seats or entrance to Turf Club restaurant/bar $5). The rest of the year, you can see simulcasts. Call or check the website for the current schedule.

ROLLER DERBY In 2001, some local women with a taste for mayhem and too much time on their hands formed an amateur women's roller derby league. For those of you who don't remember roller derby (or don't care to), it was a defunct late-night television sport of the '70s, which was celebrated in celluloid by Raquel Welch in that immortal film classic, *Kansas City Bombers.* Two teams in old-style roller skates (not in-line skates) circle a banked track, pushing and elbowing and colliding with each other a lot. Scoring points doesn't really matter all that much. As a sport, it has all the low-brow panache of wrestling, but with less of the good-versus-evil script, and just more pure anything-but-wholesome fun. Attending roller derby bouts quickly became a hip thing to do in Austin, and the league attracted more recruits until it can now field five teams. All the women get in character for their competition and ham it up with as much poor taste as possible. You have the Holy Rollers, the Hellcats, the Cherry Bombs, and so on. The skyrocketing popularity has led to the formation of leagues in other cities. Whether they are as fun as what goes on in Austin, I can't say. The season lasts from January to October. There are usually two bouts per month, which usually take place on Sundays at the Austin Convention Center. If you want to see some Austin quirkiness and celebrate low-brow culture in a tongue-in-cheek fashion, you will appreciate these events. To see their schedule, check out the **Lonestar Rollergirls** website www.txrd.com. There is now also a flat-track league that is just as fun to watch called the **Texas Rollergirls** (www.txrollergirls.com). Their season lasts from March through August, with bouts taking place at the Playland Skate Center at 8822 McCann Blvd., close to the intersection of Hwy. 183 and Burnet Road.

SOCCER From August through November, you can find the University of Texas women's soccer team competing against the other NCAA teams. In 2008, the team made it into the second round of the NCAA playoffs, losing to Portland 2-0. Home games are played either Friday or Sunday at the Mike A. Myers Stadium and Soccer Field, just northeast of the UT football stadium at Robert Dedman Drive and Mike Myers Drive.

Shopping in Austin

Visitors to Austin don't really come for the shopping, but the opportunistic shopper can be rewarded with some wonderful discoveries. Folk art, arts and crafts, music, books—these are the areas where Austin excels. And it's got the rest of the material world pretty well covered, too. As for the shopping experience, I think most will enjoy the helpfulness and lack of artifice shown by salespersons here.

1 THE SHOPPING SCENE

What follows is a brief description of where the most "Austintatious" shopping can be found. Specialty shops in Austin tend to open around 9 or 10am, Monday through Saturday, and close at about 5:30 or 6pm, and many have Sunday hours from noon to 6pm. Malls tend to keep the same Sunday schedule, but Monday through Saturday they don't close their doors until 9pm. Sales tax in Austin is 8.25%.

DOWNTOWN Most shops are located along several blocks of East Sixth, along Congress Ave., and along West Second, 1 block off Congress in a nascent shopping area that extends for just 2 or 3 blocks. If the weather is agreeable, this is an easy area to cover on foot and a good spot for window shopping. Specialty stores include apparel, interior design, music paraphernalia, hot sauce, and folk art.

SOUTH CONGRESS Just across the river from downtown begins the SoCo shopping area. Most of the shops are on South Congress, and the majority of these are located up the hill, in a stretch running from the 1400 block to the 2500 block. On the first Thursday of every month, the SoCo merchants sponsor a street festival with music and other forms of entertainment (see sidebar, below). Shops include art galleries, boutiques, bargain antiques stores, and clothing and folk art shops. There are also shops scattered along South Lamar, but they are not concentrated enough to allow for window shopping, and South Lamar isn't as interesting to navigate as South Congress.

NORTH LAMAR Just west of downtown (you could almost call it downtown but not quite), in the vicinity of where Fifth and Sixth streets cross Lamar Boulevard, you have a high concentration of one-of-a-kind shops extending for 1 or 2 blocks in any direction. The shops continue, scattered along both sides of Lamar northwards up to 12th street. You'll find music, books, clothing, food—all the necessities, plus a lot of extravagance, too. It's a mixture of chic, quirky, folksy, and artsy. Also located here is Whole Foods' flagship store.

NORTH LAMAR AND 38TH STREET Within a few blocks of this intersection, heading either north on Lamar or west on 38th Street (where it curves south and becomes 35th Street), there is serious shopping. On Lamar you'll find the shopping center where Central Market's flagship food store is located, surrounded by specialty shops selling cameras, paper goods, cosmetics, and pottery. West on 38th are two small shopping centers that host boutiques and specialty stores: 26 Doors and Jefferson Square.

First Thursdays

As if there weren't already enough street theater in Austin, the merchants on South Congress Avenue decided a few years back to start hosting a monthly street festival. They began keeping their doors open late and providing food, drinks, and entertainment on the first Thursday of every month. Soon impromptu open-air markets sprang up, and jugglers, drum circles, and of course live bands performed indoors, outdoors, and in between.

First Thursdays have become quite popular for their mix of shopping, entertainment, people-watching, and the surprise factor—you never know what you're going to meet up with. It's also a way for locals to celebrate the approach of the weekend. The street festival occupies about 8 blocks along both sides of South Congress. Traffic along the avenue is not cordoned off, but everyone drives slowly because of the crowds crisscrossing the avenue. It starts around 6pm and runs until about 10pm. To find out more, check www.firstthursday.info.

THE DRAG Bordering the university on Guadalupe Street is a stretch of stores selling mostly hip apparel to students: boutiques, beads, books, and an open-air area where hippies sell jewelry, tie-dyed shirts, and such, which for some reason has always had the name Renaissance Market.

NORTHWEST There's no lack of malls in Austin. In the northwest, three upscale shopping centers, **The Arboretum, The Arboretum Market,** and **The Gateway complex** (consisting of the Gateway Courtyard, the Gateway Market, and Gateway Square) have earned the area the nickname "South Dallas." A bit farther north off of Mo-Pac, where it intersects Burnet Road, lies the city's newest mall, called **The Domain.**

SOUTH OF AUSTIN Bargain hunters go farther afield to the huge collections of factory outlet stores in San Marcos; see chapter 17 for details.

2 SHOPPING A TO Z

ANTIQUES

In addition to the one-stop antiques markets listed below, a number of smaller shops line Burnet Road north of 45th Street. See also the **Travis County Farmers' Market** under "Food," below.

Antique Marketplace For people who like antiques but don't enjoy speaking in hushed tones, the Antique Marketplace offers bargains and treasures in a friendly, relaxed atmosphere. You'll find a little bit of everything under the roof of this large warehouse-type building in central Austin: Czech glass, funky collectibles, and expensive furnishings. 5350 Burnet Rd. ✆ **512/452-1000.**

Austin Antique Mall You can spend anywhere from five bucks to thousands of dollars in this huge collection of antiques stores. More than 100 dealers occupying a

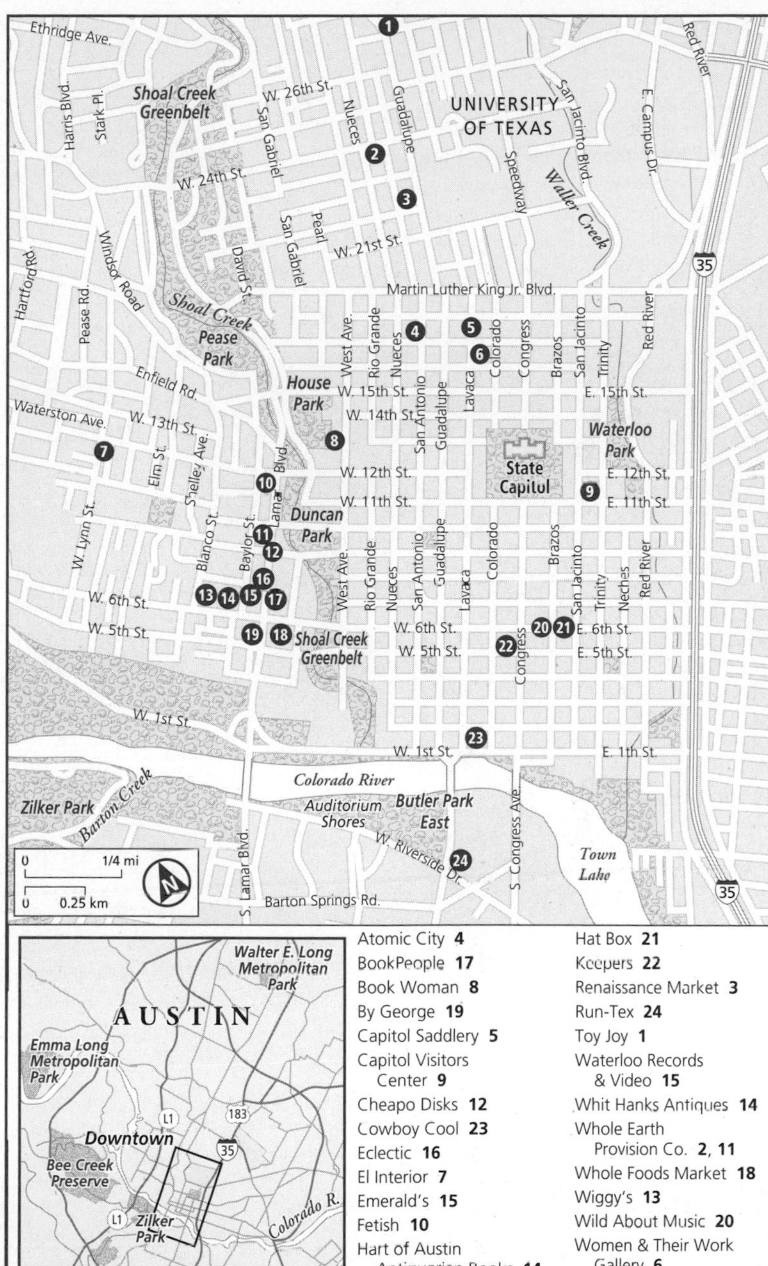
Ethridge Ave.
Shoal Creek Greenbelt
W. 26th St.
Harris Blvd.
Stark Pl.
San Gabriel
Nueces
Guadalupe
UNIVERSITY OF TEXAS
San Jacinto Blvd.
Red River
E. Campus Dr.
W. 24th St.
Speedway
Waller Creek
Pearl
W. 21st St.
Hartford Rd.
Pease Rd.
Windsor Road
David St.
Martin Luther King Jr. Blvd.
Shoal Creek
Pease Park
West Ave.
Rio Grande
Colorado
Congress
Brazos
San Jacinto
Trinity
Enfield Rd.
House Park
W. 15th St.
San Antonio
Lavaca
E. 15th St.
Waterston Ave.
W. 13th St.
W. 14th St.
Waterloo Park
Elm St.
Shelley Ave.
Lamar Blvd.
W. 12th St.
State Capitol
E. 12th St.
W. 11th St.
E. 11th St.
W. Lynn St.
Blanco St.
Baylor St.
Duncan Park
Neches
W. 6th St.
W. 5th St.
Shoal Creek Greenbelt
E. 6th St.
E. 5th St.
W. 1st St.
E. 1th St.
Colorado River
Zilker Park
Barton Creek
Auditorium Shores
Butler Park East
W. Riverside Dr.
S. Congress Ave.
Town Lake
S. Lamar Blvd.
Barton Springs Rd.
35
0 1/4 mi
0 0.25 km
N
Walter E. Long Metropolitan Park
AUSTIN
Emma Long Metropolitan Park
L1
183
Downtown
Bee Creek Preserve
35
Zilker Park
Colorado R.
Atomic City 4
BookPeople 17
Book Woman 8
By George 19
Capitol Saddlery 5
Capitol Visitors Center 9
Cheapo Disks 12
Cowboy Cool 23
Eclectic 16
El Interior 7
Emerald's 15
Fetish 10
Hart of Austin Antiquarian Books 14
Hat Box 21
Keepers 22
Renaissance Market 3
Run-Tex 24
Toy Joy 1
Waterloo Records & Video 15
Whit Hanks Antiques 14
Whole Earth Provision Co. 2, 11
Whole Foods Market 18
Wiggy's 13
Wild About Music 20
Women & Their Work Gallery 6

Greater Austin Shopping

Allen's Boots **28**
Antique Marketplace **10**
The Arboretum **2**
Austin Antique Mall **5**
Austin Country Flea Market **9**
Barton Creek Square **32**
Breed & Co. Hardware **19**
Capra & Cavelli **16**
Central Market **18**
Clarksville Pottery **18**
Dillard's **11**
The Domain **3**
Eco-Wise **22**
Electric Ladyland **23**
El Taller Gallery **8**
Gallery Shoal Creek **15**
The Gateway Shopping Centers **4**
Grape Vine Market **6**
Highland Mall **11**
Hill Country Weavers **28**
Hog Wild **14**
Lakeline Mall **1**
Neiman Marcus **3**
Neiman Marcus Last Call **31**
Nordstrom **32**
Russell Korman **17**
Sabia Botanicals **30**
Saks **4**
Shelpers **12**
Spec's Liquor Warehouse **13**
Ten Thousand Villages **26**
Terra Toys **7**
Tesoros Trading Co. **25**
Therapy **21**
Toy Joy **20**
Whip in Beer & Wine **27**
Yard Dog **24**

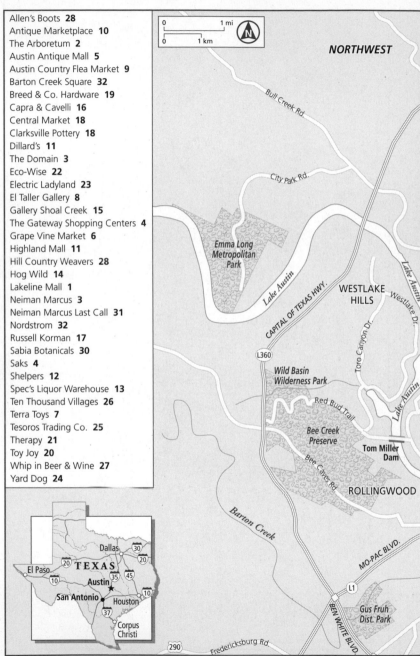

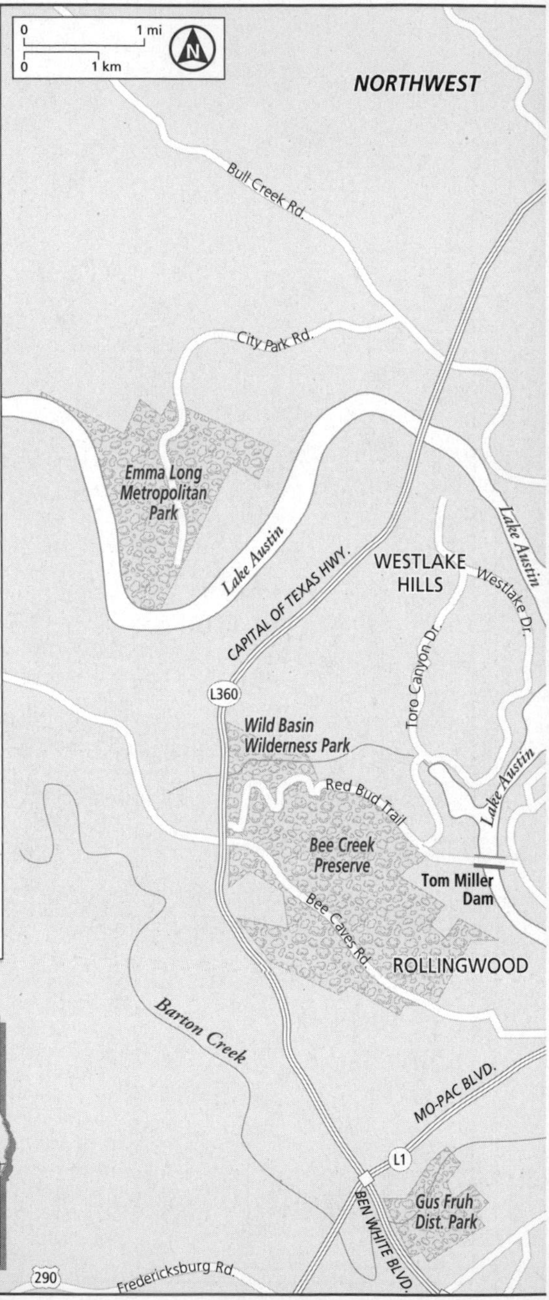

0 1 mi
0 1 km
N
NORTHWEST
Bull Creek Rd.
City Park Rd.
Emma Long Metropolitan Park
Lake Austin
CAPITAL OF TEXAS HWY.
WESTLAKE HILLS
Westlake Dr.
Toro Canyon Dr.
L360
Wild Basin Wilderness Park
Red Bud Trail
Bee Creek Preserve
Tom Miller Dam
Bee Caves Rd.
ROLLINGWOOD
Barton Creek
MO-PAC BLVD.
L1
BEN WHITE BLVD.
Gus Fruh Dist. Park
290
Fredericksburg Rd.

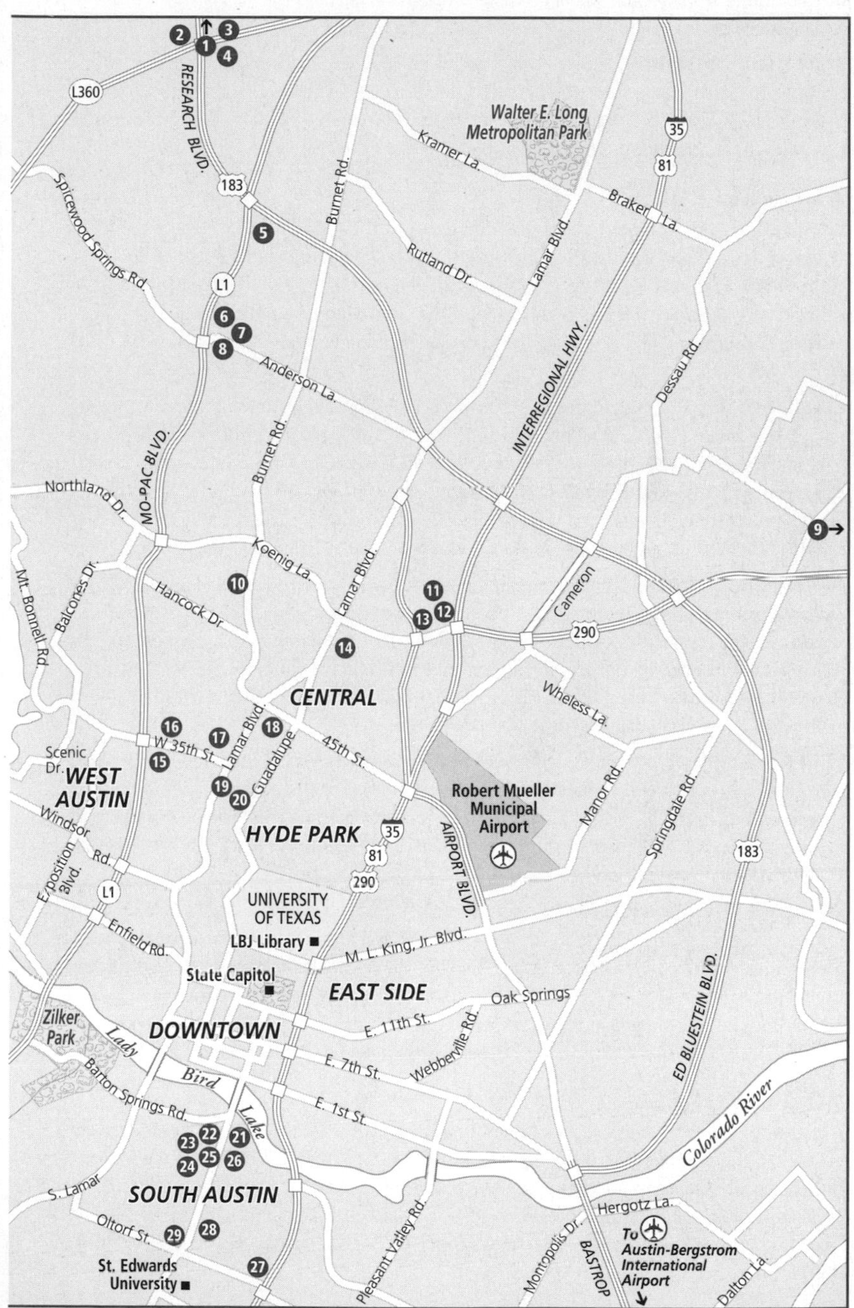
Walter E. Long
Metropolitan Park
Kramer La.
Braker La.
Rutland Dr.
Lamar Blvd.
INTERREGIONAL HWY.
Dessau Rd.
RESEARCH BLVD.
Spicewood Springs Rd.
Burnet Rd.
Anderson La.
MO-PAC BLVD.
Northland Dr.
Koenig La.
Hancock Dr.
Balcones Dr.
Mt. Bonnell Rd.
Cameron
Wheless La.
CENTRAL
W 35th St.
Guadalupe
45th St.
Scenic Dr.
WEST AUSTIN
Windsor Rd.
Exposition Blvd.
HYDE PARK
AIRPORT BLVD.
Robert Mueller
Municipal
Airport
Manor Rd.
Springdale Rd.
UNIVERSITY
OF TEXAS
LBJ Library
Enfield Rd.
M. L. King, Jr. Blvd.
State Capitol
EAST SIDE
Oak Springs
ED BLUESTEIN BLVD.
Zilker Park
Lady Bird Lake
DOWNTOWN
E. 11th St.
E. 7th St.
Webberville Rd.
Barton Springs Rd.
E. 1st St.
Colorado River
S. Lamar
SOUTH AUSTIN
Oltorf St.
St. Edwards
University
Pleasant Valley Rd.
Montopolis Dr.
BASTROP
Hergotz La.
To
Austin-Bergstrom
International
Airport
Dalton La.

 30,000-square-foot indoor space offer Roseville pottery, Fiesta dishes, Victorian furniture, costume jewelry, and much, much more. 8822 McCann Dr. © **512/459-5900.** www.antiquetexas.com.

Whit Hanks Antiques More than a dozen independent dealers gather at tony Whit Hanks, just across the street from Treaty Oak. This is Austin's premier outlet for fine antiques. Even if you can't afford to buy anything, it's fun to ogle items from fine crystal and vases to Chinese cabinets and neoclassical columns. 1009 W. Sixth St. © **512/478-2101.**

ART GALLERIES

It's not exactly SoHo, but the area just northwest of the Capitol and south of the University of Texas—specifically, the block bounded by Guadalupe and Lavaca to the west and east and 17th and 18th streets to the south and north—has a large concentration of galleries. They include the group clustered in the **Guadalupe Arts Building,** 1705 Guadalupe; **D. Berman,** next door at 1701 Guadalupe; and Women & Their Work Gallery (see below).

El Taller Gallery Located just east of Mo-Pac, this appealing showcase for Southwestern art sells Santa Fe pieces at Austin prices. Amado Peña, Jr., who once owned the gallery, is represented here, and you'll also find work by R. C. Gorman and other Native American artists, as well as whimsical Western paintings by Darryl Willison. Handmade Pueblo pottery and vintage Southwestern jewelry are among the gallery's other interesting offerings. 2438 W. Anderson Lane. © **800/234-7362** or 512/302-0100. www.eltallergallery.com.

Gallery Shoal Creek Since it opened in 1965, Shoal Creek has moved away from an exclusive emphasis on Western art to encompass work from a wide range of American regions. The focus is on contemporary painting in representational or Impressionist styles—for example, Jerry Ruthven's Southwest landscapes or Nancy McGowan's naturalist watercolors. Like El Taller, this is an Austin outlet for many artists who also have galleries in Santa Fe. 1500 W. 34th St. © **512/454-6671.**

Wild About Music Austin's commitment to music makes it a perfect location for this gallery and shop, strictly devoted to items with a musical theme. Some of the pieces are expensive, but nearly all of them are fun. Items run the gamut from books, posters, and musician-designed T-shirts to musical instruments and furniture. 115 E Sixth St. © **512/708-1700.** www.wildaboutmusic.com.

Women & Their Work Gallery Founded in 1978, this nonprofit gallery is devoted to more than visual art—it also promotes and showcases women in dance, music, theater, film, and literature. Regularly changing exhibits have little in common except innovation. This art space often gets the nod for "Best Gallery" from the readers of the *Austin Chronicle.* The gift shop has a great selection of unusual crafts and jewelry created by female artists. 1710 Lavaca St. © **512/477-1064.** www.womenandtheirwork.org.

BOOKSTORES

As might be expected, there are a couple of bookstores in the University of Texas area, on the Drag. The **University Co-Op,** 2244 Guadalupe St. (© **512/476-7211;** www.coopbookstore.com), opened in 1896, has many volumes of general interest, along with the requisite burnt-orange-and-white Longhorn T-shirts, mugs, and other UT souvenirs. Also on the Drag is **Follett's Intellectual Property** at 2402 Guadalupe St. (© **512/478-0007;** www.intellectualpropertyaustin.com).

For a good selection of used and remaindered books, check out **Half-Price Books** at 5555 N. Lamar Blvd. (✆ **512/451-4463;** www.halfpricebooks.com; four other locations); it also carries CDs, cassettes, DVDs, and videos.

BookPeople This is one of the largest and best independent bookstores you're likely to find these days. Expanded in the mid-1990s from its New Age roots, but remaining stubbornly quirky and independent, this BookPeople stocks more than 250,000 titles ranging over a wide variety of subjects. It also sells technical videos, books on tape, and gift items (the KEEP AUSTIN WEIRD T-shirt is their bestseller). Lots of intimate sitting areas and an espresso bar prevent this huge store—the largest in Texas—from feeling overwhelming. More than 200 author signings and special events are held here every year. 603 N. Lamar Blvd. ✆ **800/853-9757** or 512/472-5050. www.bookpeople.com.

BookWoman Offering the largest selection of books by and about women in Texas, this store is also one of the best feminist resource centers, the place to find out about women's organizations and events statewide. Readings and discussion groups are regularly held here, too. BookWoman also carries a great selection of T-shirts, cards, posters, and music. 918 W. 12th St. ✆ **512/472-2785.** www.ebookwoman.com.

Hart of Austin Antiquarian Books You'll have to enter the Whit Hanks complex (see Antiques, above) to locate this excellent repository of rare books, maps, and prints, many of them devoted to Texas subjects—no outside sign alerts you to its presence (perhaps a side effect of focusing on the past?). 1009 W. Sixth St. ✆ **512/477-7755.**

DEPARTMENT STORES

Dillard's This Little Rock–based chain, spread throughout the Southwest, carries a nice variety of mid- to high-range merchandise. In Highland Mall, there are two separate outlets, one focusing on home furnishings and women's clothing, the other devoted to men's and children's wear. All the stores have western wear shops with good selections of styles. Two other locations are at the Barton Creek Square Mall (✆ **512/327-6100**) and the Lakeline Mall (✆ **512/257-8740**). Highland Mall. ✆ **512/452-9393.** www.dillards.com.

Neiman Marcus Neiman Marcus, a Texas-based chain of department stores long associated with conspicuous consumption, recently opened its first full-fledged store in the Austin area, at The Domain shopping center. The store always has items for sale that are uniquely Texan in a nonstereotypical way. This is high-end retail; if you're seeking bargains, shop at their Last Call store (see below). The Domain Shopping Center, 3400 Palm Way, north of Braker Lane, btw. Mo-Pac and Burnet Rd. ✆ **512/719-1200.** www.neimanmarcus.com.

Nordstrom Now that Nordstrom has come, fashion- and status-conscious Austin shoppers—the segment of the city not devoted to keeping Austin weird—have much ground to cover with the 144,000 square feet of floor space that this store fills with merchandise. It's located in the Barton Creek Square Mall. 2901 S. Capital of Texas Hwy. ✆ **512/691-3500.** www.nordstrom.com.

Saks Although smaller than many of the other Saks stores, it still offers the high-tone fashions and accouterments you'd expect, as well as a personal shopper service. 9722 Great Hills Trail. ✆ **512/231-3700.** www.saksfifthavenue.com.

DISCOUNT SHOPPING

Neiman Marcus Last Call ★ Fans of Texas-grown Neiman Marcus will want to take advantage of Last Call, which consolidates fashions from 27 of the chain's department stores and sells them here at prices 50% to 75% off retail. New merchandise shipments arrive every week, and not only can you find great bargains, but you needn't sacrifice the attention for which Neiman Marcus is famous because the staff here is as helpful as at any other branch, and a personal shopper service is available as well. Brodie Oaks Shopping Center, 4115 S. Capital of Texas Hwy., at S. Lamar. ✆ **512/447-0701.** www.neimanmarcus.com.

ECOWARES

Eco-wise It's hard to typecast a shop that sells everything from greeting cards, natural insect repellent, and hand-woven purses to building materials and home decorating supplies. The common denominator? Everything you'll find here is created with an eye toward the environment—that is, it's recycled, made from natural fabrics, and/or chemical free. Staff is knowledgeable and helpful, and customers are passionately loyal. The store offers baby and wedding-shower registries for Earth-friendly brides and grooms or moms and dads. 110 W. Elizabeth. ✆ **512/326-4474.** www.ecowise.com.

ESSENTIAL OILS

Sabia Botanicals All those soothing oils and lotions in their pretty bottles on the shelves seem to whisper, "Buy me, I'll make you feel better." This is aromatherapy central, but along with New Age products, the store also carries old-time herbal lines, such as Kiehl's. 1100 South First St. ✆ **512/469-0447.** www.sabia.com.

FASHIONS

For children's clothing, see **Terra Toys** under "Toys," p. 262.

Men's

See also **By George** under "Women," below, and **Cowboy Cool** under "Western Wear," below.

Capra & Cavelli Funny radio ads—not to mention hip and classic fashions—draw image-conscious guys (and gals) into this west Austin store. And talk about service: C&C will bring items to your home or office for your perusing pleasure. 3500 Jefferson, Ste. 110. ✆ **512/450-1919.** www.capracavelli.com.

Keepers Austinites seeking to make the transition from geek to fashion chic turn to this locally owned men's specialty store for friendly but expert advice and the latest in men's clothing. You'll find an "image consultant" and expert tailors on the premises. 515 Congress Ave., Ste. 140 ✆ **512/473-2512.** www.keepersclothing.com.

Women's

See also **The Cadeau,** listed under "Gifts/Souvenirs," below; **Capra & Cavelli,** under "Men," above; and **Cowboy Cool,** under "Western Wear," below.

By George These two boutique shops offer an uncommon assortment of designer clothes. The main store, across from Whole Foods, is larger and offers more in the way of cocktail dresses and high heels. The South Congress shop (1400 S. Congress; ✆ **512/441-8600**) offers more designer denim and party wear. 524 N. Lamar Blvd. ✆ **512/472-5951.**

Emeralds It's young, it's hip, it's got Carrie Bradshaw shoes by the dozens, plus racks of outrageous party dresses to wear them with. You can also buy cards, candles, aromatherapy bath salts, and funky jewelry here. 624 N. Lamar Blvd. ✆ **512/476-3660.**

Fetish At this shoe-fashionista heaven, featuring footwear from the classical to the fanciful, you can also find plenty of trendy and elegant stuff to wear from the ankles up—dresses, tops, skirts, pants, lingerie, jewelry, and more. 1112 N. Lamar Blvd. ✆ **512/457-1007.**

Therapy Many of Austin's top singer/songwriters come to this hip SoCo boutique. A small and constantly updated inventory of creative styles by local designers—everything from purses and casual halters to flowing skirts and evening gowns—is sold at prices that fall well below what you'd find at the large national stores. Feeling better yet? 1113 S. Congress Ave. ✆ **877/326-2331** or 512/326-2331. www.therapyclothing.com.

Vintage

Electric Ladyland/Lucy in Disguise Feather boas, tutus, flapper dresses, angel wings, and the occasional gorilla suit overflow the narrow aisles of Austin's best-known costume and vintage clothing outlet. The owner, who really *does* dress like that all the time, is a walking advertisement for her fascinating store. You'll find floral-print dresses and bold-striped shirts, lots of costume jewelry, outrageous Western belt buckles, and the most bodacious selection of sunglasses you've ever seen. 1506 S. Congress Ave. ✆ **512/444-2002.**

FOLK ART & CRAFTS

Eclectic A dazzling panoply of hand-painted furniture, pottery, and art—new and old—from around the world is beautifully presented in this large store (with a bonus parking lot in back). An outstanding jewelry section includes pieces from Mexico, Africa, Indonesia, Afghanistan, and other exotic places. 700 N. Lamar Blvd. ✆ **512/477-1816.**

El Interior Nestled in the small cluster of restaurants in the middle of the Clarksville neighborhood is this small, but fun, import shop. The merchandise is collected from the countries of Mexico and Guatemala. Though there are crafts of several varieties, there's an emphasis on textiles and clothing. 1009 West Lynn St. ✆ **512/474-8780.** www.elinterior.com.

Ten Thousand Villages This is the local retail outlet for the national nonprofit organization dedicated to fair trade with folk artists, craftsmen, and small farmers from developing nations. This store sells all kinds of merchandise: jewelry, toys, decorative objects, coffee, and chocolate, among many other things. 1317 S. Congress Ave. ✆ **512/440-0440.** http://austin.tenthousandvillages.com.

Tesoros Trading Co. Now in its new location on trendy South Congress, this folk art store has an incredible variety of objects both large and small from around the world: bronze figurines from Indonesia, *milagro* charms from Mexico, wood cuts from Brazil, talismans from Turkey. You can walk in, intending to spend 15 minutes here, but then get sucked in for a couple of hours. The variety is impressive. The owners operate a wholesale imports business and sell around the country, which allows them to stock their own store with one-of-a-kind pieces they find on their trips. 1500 South Congress Ave. ✆ **512/447-7500.** www.tesoros.com.

Yard Dog Folk Art "Outsider" art, created in the deep, rural South, usually by the poor and sometimes by the incarcerated, is not for everyone, but for those interested in contemporary American folk art, this gallery is not to be missed. 1510 S. Congress Ave. ✆ **512/912-1613.** www.yarddog.com.

FOOD

Through no more cause than historical accident, Austin has become the new frontier of grocery shopping—grocery shopping as aesthetic experience. And the two entities that are busy at work pushing the envelope are Whole Foods (headquartered in Austin) and Central Market. Both were born in Austin, and both have a vision of ravishing displays of fresh produce, gourmet foods, wines, and delicacies from around the world. I am told by the tourism office that both of these stores are among the most popular tourist attractions in the city.

But for sheer ease of use, and for its being a countercultural artifact, there's Austin's own community grocery store, **Wheatsville Food Co-op** at 3101 Guadalupe St. (✆ **512/478-2667**). It's owned and operated by its members, but anyone can shop there. They make the maximum use of their limited floor space, including a good selection of beer and wine and a deli, and have excellent service. Unlike the stores of the future, you're in and out of this one in two shakes of a lamb's tail. Starting in 2008, the store undertook major renovation that increased the floor space considerably. Work should be completed by the summer of 2009.

A handy store for visitors when they are in South Austin is **Cissi's Market** at 1400 South Congress (✆ **512/225-0521**). It's a small gourmet and deli market where you can pick up a bottle of wine, a copy of the *New York Times,* a toothbrush, and pastries (made on the premises). It, too, is having a renovation and will soon sport a wine bar open in the evenings.

Austin also has an abundance of farmers' markets. Perhaps the most notable of them, **Austin Farmers' Market,** held downtown at Republic Square Park, Fourth Street at Guadalupe, every Saturday from 9am to 1pm March through November (✆ **512/236-0074**), not only features food products but also live music, cooking demonstrations, kids' activities, and workshops on everything from organic gardening to aromatherapy.

South Congress Organic Farmers' Market, held Saturday from 8am to 1pm in the parking lot of El Gallo Restaurant, 2910 S. Congress Ave. (✆ **512/281-4712**), is smaller, but you've got the guarantee that all the goods are locally grown without chemicals.

In north central Austin you'll find **Travis County Farmers' Market,** 6701 Burnet Rd. (✆ **512/454-1002**), which hosts monthly festivals honoring particular crops and/or growing seasons. It keeps long hours; open from 8am to 6pm daily.

Central Market ★★ Ah, foodie heaven! Not only can you buy every imaginable edible item at these gourmet megamarkets—fresh or frozen, local or imported—but you also can enjoy quality vittles in the restaurant section, which features cowboy, bistro, Italian, vegetarian—you name it—cuisines. Moreover, prices are surprisingly reasonable. A monthly newsletter announces what's fresh in the produce department, which jazz musicians are entertaining on the weekend, and which gourmet chef is holding forth at the market's cooking school. The newer Westgate Shopping Center branch, 4477 S. Lamar Blvd. (✆ **512/899-4300**), in South Austin, is as impressive as its history-making sibling north of UT. 4001 N. Lamar Blvd. ✆ **512/206-1000.** www.centralmarket.com.

Whole Foods Market The first link in what is now the world's largest organic and natural foods supermarket chain celebrated its 25th birthday by opening an 80,000-square-foot store near its original downtown location (as well as an adjacent office tower to serve as corporate headquarters). From chemical-free cosmetics to frozen tofu burgers, Whole Foods has long covered the entire spectrum of natural products, and now it's looking to compete with Central Market (see above) in the food-entertainment arena by creating a 600-seat amphitheater, a playscape, gardens, on-site massages, a cooking school, and more. The northwest store in Gateway Market, 9607 Research Blvd. (✆ **512/345-5003**), is a simpler version of the main store. 525 N. Lamar Blvd. ✆ **512/476-1206.** www.wholefoods.com.

GIFTS/SOUVENIRS

See also **Wild About Music,** listed under "Art Galleries," p. 254; and **Emeralds,** listed under the "Women" subsection of the "Fashions" section, above.

Capitol Visitors Center Over the years, visitors have admired—sometimes excessively—the intricately designed door hinges of the capitol. The gift shop at the visitor center sells brass bookends made from the original models used, during the capitol's renovation, to cast replacements for hinges that were cadged over the years. Other Texas memorabilia includes paperweights made from reproductions of the capitol's Texas seal doorknobs and local food products. There are also a variety of educational toys and an excellent selection of historical books. 112 E. 11th St. (southeast corner of capitol grounds). ✆ **512/305-8400.** www.texascapitolvisitorscenter.com.

GLASS & POTTERY

Clarksville Pottery & Galleries This pottery emporium, filled with lovely pieces created by local artisans, has long been transplanted from its namesake location in the artsy section of town to a prime spot near Central Market (see "Food," above). You'll find everything ceramic, from candleholders to bird feeders, as well as hand-blown glass, woodcarvings, and contemporary jewelry in a variety of media; there's a unique selection of Judaica, too. An additional outlet, in the Arboretum Market, 9828 Great Hills Trail, Ste. 110 (✆ **512/794-8580**), carries equally impressive stock. 4001 N. Lamar Blvd., Ste. 200. ✆ **512/454-9079.** www.clarksvillepottery.com.

HARDWARE & MORE

Breed & Co. Hardware You don't have to be a power-drill freak to visit Breed & Co. How many hardware stores, after all, have bridal registries where you can sign up for Waterford crystal? This darling of Austin DIY has everything from nails to tropical plants, organic fertilizer, gardening book and cookbooks, pâté molds, and cherry pitters. There's also a branch in the prosperous Westlake Hills area, 3663 Bee Cave Rd. (✆ **512/328-3960**). 718 W. 29th St. ✆ **512/474-6679.** www.breedandco.com.

JEWELRY

See also **Eclectic** and **Tesoros,** under "Crafts," above; and **Clarksville Pottery,** under "Glass & Pottery," above.

Russell Korman You'd never know it from his current elegant digs, but Russell Korman got his start in Austin's jewelry trade by selling beads on the Drag. Although he's moved on to fine 14-karat gold, platinum, and diamond pieces, along with fine pens and watches—there's an experienced watchmaker on the premises—his store still has a considerable collection of more casual sterling silver from Mexico. Prices are very competitive, even for the most formal baubles. 3806 N. Lamar Blvd. ✆ **512/451-9292.** www.russellkormanjewelry.com.

MALLS/SHOPPING CENTERS

The Arboretum The retail anchor of the far northwest part of town is a shopping center so chic that it calls itself a market, not a mall. This two-level collection of outdoor boutiques doesn't include any department stores, but it does have a Barnes & Noble Superstore and a huge Pottery Barn. You'll find your basic selection of yuppie shops—everything from upscale clothing stores to a cigar humidor. The second floor features art galleries, a custom jeweler, and crafts shops. Dining options, including a Cheesecake

Factory, a T.G.I. Friday's, and an outlet for Amy's—Austin's local favorite ice cream—tend to be on the casual side, but there's also a good local steakhouse, Dan McKlusky's. 10000 Research Blvd. (Hwy. 183 and Loop 360). ✆ **512/338-4437.** www.shopsimon.com.

Barton Creek Square Set on a bluff with a view of downtown, Barton Creek tends to be frequented by upscale Westsiders; the wide-ranging collection of more than 180 shops is anchored by Nordstrom, Dillard's, Foley's, Sears, and JCPenney. One of the newest malls in Austin, it's refined and low-key, but the presence of Frederick's of Hollywood and Victoria's Secret lingerie boutiques makes one wonder if the daytime soaps might not be onto something about the bored rich. At least they've got a sense of humor: There's also a jewelry store called Filthy Rich of Austin. 2901 S. Capital of Texas Hwy. ✆ **512/327-7040.** www.bartoncreeksquare.com.

The Domain The newest shopping center in town, this one didn't open for business without stirring up a hornets nest of controversy from some rather generous tax rebates that the city council unwisely bestowed on the developers. This mall brings a lot of upmarket stores to town, including Tiffany, Burberry, Louis Vuitton, and Calypso. The mall is anchored by Macy's and Neiman Marcus. It's located in north Austin, off Mo-Pac, between Braker Lane and Burnet Road. 11410 Century Oaks Terrace. ✆ **512/795-4320.** www.simon.com.

Gateway Shopping Centers Comprising three not-so-distinct shopping areas, the Gateway Courtyard, the Gateway Market, and Gateway Square, this large, open complex includes mainly national chains such as Crate & Barrel, REI, Old Navy, and CompUSA. There are also branches of Austin-based stores, including Run-Tex and Whole Foods Market, discussed individually in this chapter. 9607 Research Blvd. at Hwy. 183 and Capital of Texas Hwy. ✆ **512/338-4755.** www.simon.com.

Highland Mall Austin's first mall, built in the 1970s, is still one of the city's most popular places to shop. Its central location is handy for visitors, and the shopping crowds are lighter than at the suburban malls. It lies between I-35 and Airport Boulevard, about 3 miles north from downtown. Reasonably priced casual-clothing stores, such as Gap and Express, vie with higher-end shops such as Ann Taylor. Dillard's (two of 'em!), Foley's, and JCPenney department stores coexist with specialty such stores as Papyrus and the Warner Bros. Studio Store. 6001 Airport Blvd. ✆ **512/454-9656.** www.highlandmall.com.

Lakeline Mall This mall serves a suburban public in a far northwest location. It's notable for an attention-grabbing design, featuring lots of colorful murals and detailed reliefs of the city. The shops, including Foley's, Dillard's, Mervyn's, Sears, JCPenney, Brookstone, the Bombay Company, and Best Buy, are not nearly so unusual, but there are some interesting smaller shops, from Dollar Tree, where everything costs a buck, to the Stockpot, with state-of-the art cookware. 11200 Lakeline Mall Dr., Cedar Park. ✆ **512/257-SHOP.** www.lakelinemall.com.

MARKETS

Austin Country Flea Market Every Saturday and Sunday year-round, more than 550 covered spaces are filled with merchants selling all the usual flea market goods and then some—new and used clothing, fresh herbs and produce, electronics, antiques. This is the largest flea market in central Texas, covering more than 130 paved acres. There's live music every weekend—generally a spirited Latino band—to step up the shopping pace. 9500 Hwy. 290 E. (4 miles east of I-35). ✆ **512/928-2795** or 928-4711.

Renaissance Market Flash back or be introduced to tie-dye days at this hippie crafts market, where vendors are licensed by the City of Austin (read: no commercial schlock). Billed as the only continuously operated, open-air crafts market in the United States, it's theoretically open daily 8am to 10pm, but most of the merchants turn up only on the weekends. You'll find everything from silver jewelry and hand-carved flutes to batik T-shirts. Many of the artisans come in from small towns in the nearby Hill Country. W. 23rd St. and Guadalupe St. (the Drag). ✆ **512/397-1456.**

MUSIC

Cheapo Discs In spite of being an import, Cheapo has carved out a niche in the hearts of Austin music lovers. It's *the* place to buy, sell, and trade new and used CDs, and thanks to the knowledgeable (if often surly) staff, there are always treasures to be found in its half-acre of bins. 914 N. Lamar Blvd. ✆ **512/477-4499.** www.cheapotexas.com.

Waterloo Records and Video Carrying a huge selection of sounds, Waterloo is always the first in town to get the new releases. If they don't have something on hand, they'll order it for you promptly. They love looking for arcane stuff. The store has a popular preview listening section, offers compilation tapes of Austin groups, and sells tickets to all major-label shows around town. It also hosts frequent in-store CD-release performances by local bands. The staff is knowledgeable and helpful. There's a video annex just west of the record store (✆ **512/474-2525**) and, for purists, a vinyl section. 600A N. Lamar Blvd. ✆ **512/474-2500.** www.waterloorecords.com.

OUTDOOR GEAR

Run-Tex Owned by the footwear editor for *Runner's World* magazine—and serving as the official wear test center for that publication—this store not only has a huge inventory of shoes and other running gear, but also does everything it can to promote healthful jogging practices, even offering free running classes and a free injury-evaluation clinic. The staff will make sure any footwear you buy is a perfect fit for your feet and running style. There's a larger Run-Tex in Gateway Market, 9901 Capital of Texas Hwy. (✆ **512/343-1164**); a location at 2201 Lake Austin Blvd. (✆ **512/477-9464**); and a related WalkTex at 4001 N. Lamar Blvd. (✆ **512/454-WALK** [454-9255]). But this downtown store is best: It's near that runner's mecca, Town Lake. 422 W. Riverside Dr. ✆ **512/472-3254.** www.runtex.com.

The Whole Earth Provision Co. Austin's large population of outdoor enthusiasts flocks to this store to be outfitted in the latest gear and Earth-friendly fashions. If you wouldn't think of hiking without a two-way radio or a Magellan positioning navigator, you can find them here. The Austin-based chain also carries gifts, housewares, educational toys, and travel books. There are additional locations at 1014 N. Lamar Blvd. (✆ **512/476-1414**) and Westgate Shopping Center, 4477 S. Lamar Blvd. (✆ **512/899-0992**). 2410 San Antonio St. ✆ **512/478-1577.** www.wholeearthprovision.com.

TEXTILE ARTS

Hill Country Weavers This store has the largest selection of yarns in Texas. Also basket supplies, dyes, spinning wheels, and felting supplies, but it's really the selection and variety of yarns, many made by independents, that cause lots of visitors to Austin to seek out this store. The de facto center of the local weaving and knitting community, this store is often the scene of some kind of social gathering. 1701 S. Congress Ave. ✆ **512/707-7396.** www.hillcountryweavers.com.

TOYS

Atomic City Playthings—including a sizable collection of vintage metal wind-up toys—are just one component of the merchandise at this funky, eclectic store in a deceptively prim-looking house near the University of Texas. You'll also find a sizable collection of cult classic film and TV memorabilia and, in the back, hundreds of styles of shoes and boots for the ultrahip rockabilly crowd. It's all a bit surreal—but in a good way. 1700 San Antonio St. ✆ **512/477-0293.**

Hog Wild Always regretted throwing out that Howdy Doody lunch box? You can get it back—for a few more bucks, of course—at this nostalgia-inducing little toyshop on the edge of Hyde Park. Photos of celebrity customers such as Quentin Tarantino and Mira Sorvino hang on the wall. 100A E. North Loop Blvd. ✆ **512/467-9453.**

Terra Toys Steiff teddy bears, the plastic Playmobil world, and other high-quality imported toys are among the kiddie delights at Terra, which, along with its children's-apparel component, **Dragonsnaps** (✆ **512/445-4497**), is located in north central Austin, off Lamar Boulevard. The store also carries a variety of miniatures, train sets, books, and kites. 2438 W. Anderson Lane. ✆ **800/247-TOYS** (247-8697) or 512/445-4489. www.terratoys.com.

Toy Joy The name says it all! The only question is whether kids or grown-ups will have more Toy Joy here. Ambi and Sailor Moon are among the appealing children's lines sold in the large back room. Out front, such things as lava lamps, yo-yos, and cartoon-character watches keep Gen Xers and boomers alike fascinated. Amazingly, it's open until midnight on Friday and Saturday. 2900 Guadalupe St. ✆ **512/320-0090.**

WESTERN WEAR

Allen's Boots Name notwithstanding, Allen's sells a lot more than just footwear. Come here too for hats, belts, jewelry, and other boot-scootin' accouterments, and bring the young 'uns too. This store, in now trendy SoCo—which explains the appearance of tie-dyed KEEP AUSTIN WEIRD T-shirts with the Allen's logo—has been around since 1970. Its staying power through the area's sleazy years is a testament to its quality and fair prices. 1522 S. Congress St. ✆ **512/447-1413.**

Capitol Saddlery The custom-made boots of this classic three-level Western store near the capitol were immortalized in a song by Jerry Jeff Walker. Run by the same family for 7 decades, this place is a bit chaotic, but it's worth poking around to see the hand-tooled saddles, belts, tack, and altogether functional cowboy gear. 1614 Lavaca St. ✆ **512/478-9309.** www.capitolsaddlery.com.

Cowboy Cool Western wear with an edge is what you'll find at this boutique in the new downtown shopping district on Second Street. Belts, boots, jewelry, clothing—the designs here are meant to shake up the staid world of Western wear a little. 217 W. Second. ✆ **512/708-9000.**

Hat Box Though this place sells hats of various styles, from pork pie to bowlers, its specialty is cowboy hats—custom shaped, painted, and even "dirt" hats. These last are the stiff canvas light-weight hats that are a common sight, but these have been darkened with dirt and charcoal and then sealed. These are popular items. Walking around Austin, you'll see quite a few of them, especially among the night prowlers. 115 E. Sixth St. ✆ **512/476-1203.**

Sheplers Adjacent to Highland Mall, the huge Austin branch of this chain of Western-wear department stores has everything the well-dressed urban cowboy or cowgirl might require. If you're already back home and you get a sudden urge for a concho belt or bolo tie, the mail-order and online business can see you through any cowpoke-fashion crisis. 6001 Middle Fiskville Rd. ✆ **512/454-3000** or 800/835-4004 (mail order). www.sheplers.com.

WINE & BEER

See also **Central Market** and **Whole Foods Market** in "Food," p. 258.

Grape Vine Market This warehouse-size wine store, with an expert staff, a huge selection of bottles at good prices, and a large menu of wine tastings and classes, is yet another sign that Austin is coming of yuppie age. If you're seeking a unique wine gift, this is definitely the place to come. There's a good selection of brews and spirits here, too. 7938 Great Northern Blvd. ✆ **512/323-5900.** www.grapevinemarket.com.

Spec's Liquor Warehouse A recent arrival to Austin, this store is a member of a Houston chain of liquor stores, noted for discounted prices. The selection of wines and beers is large. Cigars are available, too, at low prices. There's also a selection of gourmet and deli foods from around the world, but these aren't quite so economical. One satellite location is in southwest Austin, in the Sunset Valley area, at 4960 West Hwy. 290. (✆ **512/366-8260**). Another is in northwest Austin, near the Arboretum mall, at 10515 N. Mo-Pac Expressway (✆ **512/342-6893**). The central location is near the Highland Mall shopping center. 5775 Airport Blvd. #100 ✆ **512/366-8300.**

Whip In Beer and Wine (Finds) Beginning life as a convenience store just off the freeway, this place doesn't have much in the way of atmosphere. What it does have is an amazing selection of beer: At a conservative estimate, Whip In has almost 400 different types of brews at any given time, and even more come Oktoberfest or other special beer-producing seasons. In 2003, one of the members of the family that owns Whip In opened **Travis Heights Beverage World,** which features a terrific selection of wines and spirits of all varieties, weekly wine and spirit tastings, and fine cigars. It's right next door to Whip In at 1948 S. I-35 (✆ **512/440-7778;** www.travisheightsbevworld.com). 1950 S. I-35, Woodland Avenue exit on southbound service road. ✆ **512/442-5337.** www.whipin.com.

Wiggy's If liquor and tobacco are among your vices, Wiggy's can help you indulge in high style. In addition to its extensive selection of wines (more than 1,500 in stock) and single-malt scotches, this friendly West End store also carries a huge array of imported smokes, including humidified cigars. Prices are reasonable, and the staff is very knowledgeable. The newer location at 1104 N. Lamar Blvd. (✆ **512/479-0045**) is smaller and doesn't have the congenial neighborhood feel of the downtown branch. 1130 W. Sixth St. ✆ **512/474-WINE.**

16

Austin After Dark

Entertainment in Austin starts with live music. In fact, you might get your first taste of it before you even pick up your bags at the airport. The city offers 11 concerts per week there to serenade travelers. Live music is what this city is mostly known for. A lot of musicians live here, and you can run into them anywhere. Austin's music scene is fluid; there's a lot of mixing of styles and genres, some well known, such as country and rock hybrids, others more incongruous, such as punk and bluegrass. It all makes the music scene here really rich and worth exploring. The level of virtuosity is impressive. Many famous musicians, such as the Dixie Chicks and Shawn Colvin, call Austin home and frequently perform here. But there is also a large number of lesser known but great performers, who for one reason or another are content to stay in Austin and enjoy a comfortable and modest level of success, which they supplement occasionally, by going on tour, just to pay the bills.

Another aspect of the live music scene here is that it's inexpensive. Some really good bands play for tips on weekdays and for starving-artist pay at other times. This has been true for years, and it makes you feel that the city is getting a lot more from this arrangement than it's having to put out. Not that Austin doesn't try to support its local musicians. Social groups organize benefit concerts, and the city and some companies offer lots of free concerts to promote the local talent.

Keep an eye out for performances by checking out the ***Austin Chronicle*** and ***XLent,*** the entertainment supplement of the *Austin-American Statesman.* Both are available in hundreds of outlets every Thursday.

But, for major shows, the quickest way to check out what's happening is to go to the website of **Austin Circle of Theaters:** www.acotonline.org. This is funded by the city and works with many venues. Click on "Now Playing Austin" for a well organized calendar of events. To buy tickets, there's a further link to another department: The **Austix Box Office** (✆ **512/474-8497;** www.austix.com). You can buy your tickets online and pick them up at the event, or you can go by the Austix office, located in the city's Visitor Center at 301 Congress Ave. Austix offers discount tickets and sometimes half-priced, last-minute tickets.

Front Gate Tickets (✆ **512/389-0315;** www.frontgatetickets.com), is another option. It handles Austin City Limits Festival tickets as well as those for some of the shows at larger clubs such as Stubb's, Antone's, La Zona Rosa, the Parish, and Emo's.

In March of 2008, the city inaugurated its new concert hall, **The Long Center for Performing Arts,** which is the new venue for symphony concerts, operas, and the ballet (see below).

The University of Texas brings many touring performances to town, too, and also hosts local concerts and productions. Go to the website of Texas Box Office at www.texasboxoffice.com and click on "Performing Arts Center" to access a calendar of events. You can buy tickets online or by phone at ✆ **512/477-6060.**

Smaller venues that book well known performers include La Zona Rosa, One World Theatre, Austin Music Hall, and the Paramount Theatre.

Austin City Limits

PBS's longest-running television program (it first aired in 1975), ***Austin City Limits*** has showcased such major talent as Lyle Lovett, Willie Nelson, Garth Brooks, Mary Chapin Carpenter, the Dixie Chicks, and Phish. Originally pure country, it has evolved to embrace blues, zydeco, Cajun, Tejano—you name it. The show is taped live, from August through February, at the KLRU-TV studio, 2504B Whitis St. (near Dean Keeton, 1 block in from Guadalupe), but the schedule is very fluid, so you have to be vigilant to nab the free tickets, which are distributed on a first-come, first-served basis on the day of the taping. Log on to **www.pbs.org/klru/austin** for details of how to get tickets, or phone the show's hot line at ✆ **512/475-9077.**

You don't have to plan in advance to get a free tour of the recording studio, where you can watch an interesting video clip of the show's highlights, stroll through the control room, and get up on the studio stage and play air guitar. Tours are offered at the KLRU studio at 10:30am every Friday except holidays (call ✆ **512/471-4811** to verify the schedule around holidays).

You do, however, have to plan ahead if you want to attend the **Austin City Limits Music Festival,** a 3-day outdoor event with multiple stages and many, many performers representing a mix of established artists and up-and-coming talent. The concert festival debuted in September 2002 and has been extremely popular since its inception. Each year it becomes more of a happening, with acts arriving early to make surprise appearances in clubs around town. In 2008, the festival sold out quickly at $135 per ticket. There were more than 100 bands playing on eight stages. Performers included Beck, Foo Fighters, Manu Chao, John Fogerty, Robert Plant, and Alison Krauss, among many others. The festival is held in late September. It's usually still warm, though not hot, at that time of year. Many festivalgoers complained about the dust raised by the crowd, so festival organizers have given money to the city to resurface the park land where the festival is held. If you go to the festival, be sure to take a dust mask or a bandana just in case the city's efforts don't bear fruit. This event is beginning to resemble South by Southwest (SXSW; see the "Label It Successful" box, below), but without the stuffy conference part. For information on past and future festivals, log on to **www.aclfestival.com**.

1 THE PERFORMING ARTS

With completion of the **Long Center for the Performing Arts** (✆ **512/457-5500;** www.thelongcenter.org), Austin now has a new venue for its symphony orchestra, opera, and ballet performances and for visiting performances, as well. The new hall, set on the south shore of Lady Bird Lake, was designed to take advantage of its location. A raised terrace framed by a circular colonnade looks out over the lake, to the downtown skyline. The grand concert hall, named after Michael and Susan Dell, seats 2,400 people and is grand indeed. It is a modern version of the classic concert hall, using vertical space to accommodate seating. Seats are positioned relatively close to the stage, and multitiered balconies wrap around the walls. A studio theater hosts small performances.

The University of Texas's **Performing Arts Center (PAC; ✆ 512/471-2787;** www.utpac.org) still attracts major shows, including Broadway musicals, pop singers, and classical music ensembles. It has six theaters, the largest of which, Bass Hall, is just finishing major renovation. It also is the venue for some performances by university theater and dance groups.

OPERA & CLASSICAL MUSIC

Austin Chamber Music Center The Austin Chamber Music Center is a local organization, which includes members of the symphony orchestra and the university music school, who are interested in performing a wide range of compositions in small ensembles, usually quartets. Concerts usually take place in churches or at private residences to small audiences. Performances may include works by anyone from a classical composer such as Mozart to a modern composer such as Glen Gould to a tango composer such as Astor Piazzolla. The best way to find the concerts is to check the center's website (www.austinchambermusic.org). 3814 Medical Parkway. ✆ **512/454-7562** or 512/454-0026.

Austin Lyric Opera This small, professional opera company, founded in 1985, presents three productions a year. These performances are held at the Long Performing Arts Center. For the 2009–2010 season, the company will perform Puccini's *La Boheme,* Chabrier's *The Star,* and Humperdink's *Hansel & Gretel.* ✆ **512/472-5992.** www.austinlyricopera.org.

Austin Symphony In existence since 1911, the symphony orchestra performs a range of classic and modern works. The season runs from September to May. It also has a Pops series in the fall and winter. Most of these performances are held at the Long Center; a few are held at another auditorium called the Riverbend Centre (**✆ 512/327-9416;** www.riverbendcentre.com). It's located in Westlake Hills at 4214 N. Capital of Texas Hwy. In June and July, every Wednesday from 9:30am to about 11:30am, kids can try out various orchestral instruments in the symphony's version of a petting zoo. This is held at Symphony Square, where the organization's offices are located. Symphony Square is a grouping of historic buildings at the intersection of Red River and 11th Street. These are situated around an outdoor amphitheater built of limestone. The buildings date from 1871 to 1877. Waller Creek runs between the seats and the stage of the amphitheater. The box office is open Monday to Friday 9am to 5pm; concert days noon to 5pm. 1101 Red River St. ✆ **888/4-MAESTRO** or 512/476-6064. www.austinsymphony.org. Tickets $19–$48.

THEATER

Founded in 1932, the **Zachary Scott Theatre Center** (**✆ 512/476-0541** [box office] or 512/476-0594; www.zachtheatre.org) is one of the oldest arts organizations in Austin. It produces plays for its two theaters in South Austin; just off of Lamar Boulevard is the John E. Whisenhunt Arena at 1510 Toomey Rd., and directly behind it is the theater-in-the-round Kleburg at 1421 W. Riverside Dr.

Other theaters in town tend toward the smaller and, in some cases, more offbeat. Top players include the intimate **Hyde Park Theatre,** 511 W. 43rd St. (**✆ 512/479-PLAY** [479-7529; box office] or 512/479-7530; www.hydeparktheatre.org), focused on Austin writers, actors, and designers. It's the venue for the Short Fringe performances at the

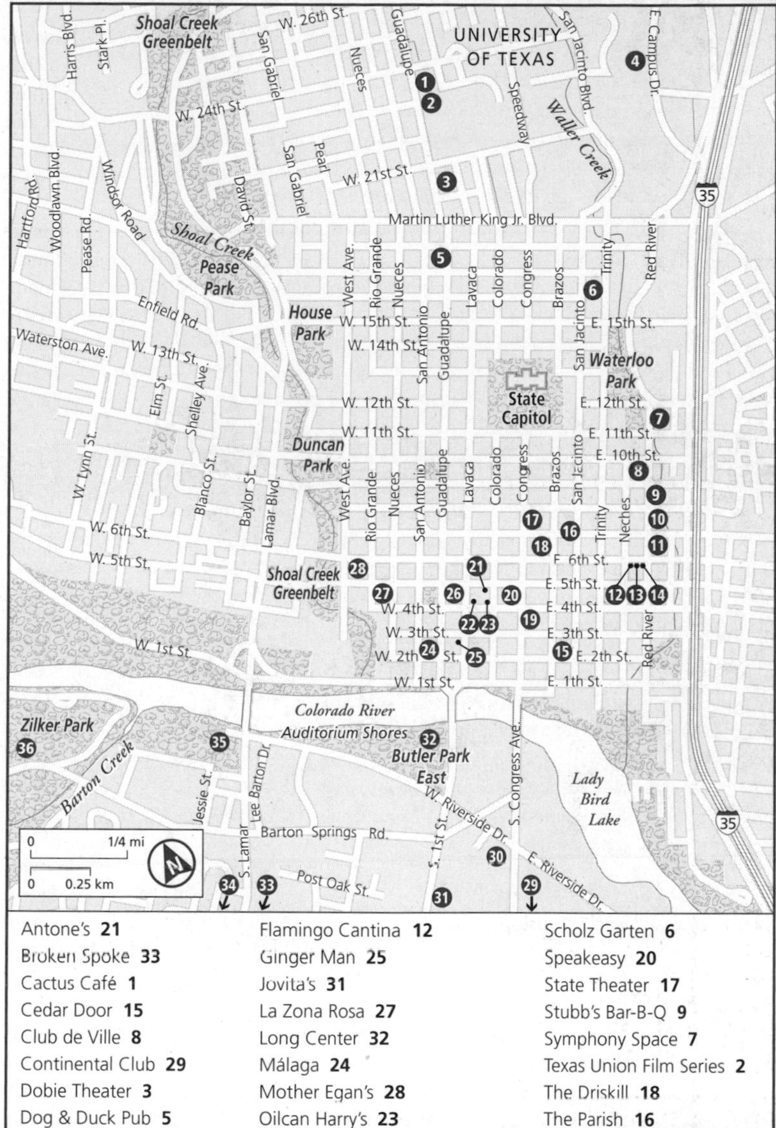

Antone's **21**
Broken Spoke **33**
Cactus Café **1**
Cedar Door **15**
Club de Ville **8**
Continental Club **29**
Dobie Theater **3**
Dog & Duck Pub **5**
Ego's **30**
Elephant Room **19**
Emo's **11**
Esther's Follies **13**
Fado **22**
Flamingo Cantina **12**
Ginger Man **25**
Jovita's **31**
La Zona Rosa **27**
Long Center **32**
Málaga **24**
Mother Egan's **28**
Oilcan Harry's **23**
Paramount Theater **17**
Performing Arts Center and Bass Concert Hall **4**
Rainbow Cattle Company **26**
Saxon Pub **34**
Scholz Garten **6**
Speakeasy **20**
State Theater **17**
Stubb's Bar-B-Q **9**
Symphony Space **7**
Texas Union Film Series **2**
The Driskill **18**
The Parish **16**
The Red Eyed Fly **10**
Velveeta Room **14**
Zachary Scott Theater Center **35**
Zilker Hillside Theater **36**

Kids A Venerable Venue

The Marx Brothers, Sarah Bernhardt, Helen Hayes, and Katherine Hepburn all entertained at the **Paramount Theatre,** 713 Congress Ave. (✆ **512/472-5470** [box office] or 512/472-2901; www.austintheatre.org), a former vaudeville house, which opened as the Majestic Theatre in 1915 and functioned as a movie palace for 50 years. Now restored to its original glory, the Paramount hosts a diverse roster of nationally touring plays, visiting celebrity performers and lecturers, film festivals and series, and local dance and theatrical productions.

annual 5-week-long FronteraFest, the largest fringe theater/performance art festival in the Southwest. At the thriving theater department at St. Edward's University, the **Mary Moody Northern Theatre,** 3001 S. Congress Ave. (✆ **512/448-8484** [box office] or 512/448-8483; www.stedwards.edu/hum/thtr/mmnt.html), gets support for its performances from a variety of professional directors and guest actors.

East Austin is the home of many experimental performance and film venues. The most established is **The Vortex,** 2307 Manor Rd. (✆ **512/478-LAVA;** www.vortexrep.org), home to the Vortex Repertory Company. You can tell by the titles alone—*The Dark Poet's Binge,* say, or *St. Enid and the Black Hand*—that you're well into the fringe. Others to look out for are **The Off Center,** 2211 Hidalgo St. (✆ **512/567-7833;** www.rudemechs.com), and **The Blue Theater,** 916 Springdale Rd. (✆ **512/927-1118;** www.bluetheater.org). The latter hosts such annual events as the full-length FronteraFest performances and Flicker Fest film screenings.

DANCE

The two dozen professional dancers of **Ballet Austin** (✆ **512/476-2163** [box office] or 512/476-9051; www.balletaustin.org), leap and bound in such classics as *The Nutcracker* and *Swan Lake,* as well as in the more avant-garde pieces of the trendsetting *Director's Choice* series, which pairs the work of various contemporary choreographers with the music of popular local Latin musicians and singer-songwriters. When in town, the troupe performs at the Long Center.

FREE ENTERTAINMENT

The amount of free live music offered here is almost absurd. There are several free concert series. One such is **Live from the Plaza,** which is sponsored by the city to showcase local musicians. Performances are most Fridays at noon, in front of City Hall, at 301 W. Second St. Other concert series take place only in the summer, such as the **Ensemble Concerts,** which are held every Sunday from June through August at 7:30pm on the grounds of the Long Center. The ensembles are formed of members of the symphony orchestra and play classical and jazz pieces. In May and June, there are free **Wednesday night concerts** at Waterloo Park, at 15th and Trinity streets. These begin at 7:30pm. Bands range from rock and reggae to Latin and country-and-western. Every other Wednesday night from June through August, **Blues on the Green** is held at Zilker Park Rock Island, 2100 Barton Springs Rd., sponsored by radio station KGSR (www.kgsr.com). This series can attract some major bands. Check the website or the local paper for who's playing. Shady Grove, one of the restaurants on Barton Springs Road (see chapter 13), offers a series of free outdoor concerts called **Shady Grove Unplugged.** They take place in the restaurant's large shaded patio every Thursday in the spring and summer at 7pm. Acts include popular local and touring bands, such as James McMurtry, the Derailers, Jimmy LaFave, the South Austin Jug Band, Ruthie Foster, and Ray Wilie Hubbard. Check the restaurant's website: www.theshadygrove.com.

Other places to hear free music include Central Market (www.centralmarket.com/Stores/Austin-Central.aspx), which has live music three times a week at both its central and south locations. Whole Foods Market (www.wholefoodsmarket.com), at Fifth Street and Lamar, has the Music at the Market series taking place on Thursdays from 6 to 7:30pm. Also, bands are always playing at First Thursdays on South Congress (see Whole Foods review in chapter 15).

From mid-July through late August, the **Beverly F. Sheffield Zilker Hillside Theater,** across from Barton Springs Pool, hosts a summer musical (Zilker Theater Productions; **© 512/479-9491;** www.zilker.org). Started in the late 1950s, this is the longest-running series of its type in the United States. The summer **Austin Shakespeare Festival** is often held at the theater, too; for up-to-date information, call **© 512/454-BARD** (454-2273) or log on to www.austinshakespeare.org. More than 5,000 people can perch on the theater's grassy knoll to watch performances. If you can, take something to sit on, such as a blanket or a lawn chair.

2 THE CLUB & MUSIC SCENE

Music was always important to life in Austin, but it became a big deal in the early '70's with the advent of "progressive country" (aka redneck rock). Local boy Willie Nelson became its principal proponent, along with several other Austin musicians. And the Armadillo World Headquarters, a music hall known for hosting all the '60s rock bands, became the center of events and symbolized the marriage of country with counterculture. The city has since become an incubator for a wonderfully vital, crossbred alternative sound that mixes rock, country, folk, blues, punk, and Tejano. Although the Armadillo is now gone, live music in Austin continues to thrive in bars all across central Austin.

While **Sixth Street** is well known to many outsiders and is home to some good bars, just as popular but less famous is the **Warehouse District** with more glitz than grunge. And for those wanting exposure to more of the local sound, there are cheap dives just off Sixth, on **Red River Street** (see sidebar below for a short guide for downtown barhopping). And then there are the many venues that don't fall inside these districts, like the Continental Club and the Saxon Pub. All in all, there's a lot to explore. Have fun and poke around. You might come across the next Janis Joplin, Stevie Ray Vaughan, or Jimmie Dale Gilmore, to name just a few who were playing local gigs here before they hit the big time. All of this applies to Austin in its more or less normal state. When gatherings occur, such as SXSW (see box, below; Mar), the Republic of Texas Biker Rally (June), or the Custom Car and Hot Rod Show (Jan), things get a little crazy and bar hopping becomes impossible, but walking Sixth Street becomes highly entertaining.

A couple of years ago, a smoking ban at all bars was instituted after a voter-referendum narrowly passed. This ban was successfully challenged in federal court but won on appeal and is now enforced. Smoking is still permitted in the outdoor areas of some bars.

Note: Categories of clubs in a city known for crossover are often very rough approximations, so those that completely defy typecasting are dubbed "eclectic." Cover charges range from $5 to $15 for well-liked local bands. Note, too, that in addition to the clubs detailed below, several of the restaurants discussed in chapter 13, including **Threadgill's** (p. 212) and **Artz Rib House** (p. 206), offer live music regularly.

FOLK & COUNTRY

Broken Spoke ★★ This is one of the great country music dance halls. It dates back to 1964 when this level of South Lamar was the edge of town. People would come out here to two-step across the large wood-plank floor. It hasn't changed much, except for the occasional busload of tourists that stops by. It's a lot of fun and well worth the effort of dragging your potential dance partner out of the cozy hotel room. This is Austin, so you don't have to be all duded up for dancing here. Granted, boot scootin' is nice to do with real boots, but lots of people show up in sneakers and Hawaiian shirts. Photos of Hank Williams, Tex Ritter, and other country greats line the walls of the club's "museum." You can eat in a large, open room out front (the chicken-fried steak can't be beat), or bring your long necks back to a table overlooking the dance floor. 3201 S. Lamar Blvd. ✆ **512/442-6189.** www.brokenspokeaustintx.com. Cover $5–$15.

Jovita's Jovita's is part Mexican restaurant, part nightclub, part Mexican-American cultural center. The food is okay, not great, but it's quite the place to sip a margarita while watching some of the best acts in town—mostly country but also some Latin groups. 1619 S. First St. ✆ **512/447-7825.** www.jovitas.com. Cover $5–$10.

JAZZ & BLUES

Antone's ★ Although Willie Nelson and crossover country-and-western bands such as the Austin Lounge Lizards have been known to turn up at Clifford Antone's place, the club owner's name has always been synonymous with the blues. Stevie Ray Vaughan used to be a regular, and when such major blues artists as Buddy Guy, Etta James, or Edgar Winter venture down this way, you can be sure they'll either be playing Antone's or stopping by for a surprise set. Clifford Antone died recently, and the response by the blues community was a large outpouring of performances to honor the man. Look for the club to continue the same trajectory set out by its former owner. 213 W. Fifth St. ✆ **512/320-8424.** www.antones.net. Cover $8–$35 (depending on performer).

Elephant Room This downtown bar is a great setting for listening to jazz—a cozy, softly lit chamber in the basement of one of Congress Avenue's old buildings. You have to be purposeful to get here because the Elephant Room entrance is a small door with a tiny sign, and the club isn't on Sixth or in the Warehouse District. The club lines up first-class acts, mostly contemporary jazz. The best night to go is on a weeknight when the bar is less crowded. 315 Congress Ave. ✆ **512/473-2279.** www.elephantroom.com. Cover $5–$15.

LATIN & REGGAE

Flamingo Cantina The Flamingo attracts local and touring acts in all subgenres of reggae—dancehall, ska, rocksteady, and dub—as well as a range of local Latin bands and DJs. Lounge around one of several bars and open-air decks when you're not sitting on the comfy carpeted bleachers listening to the performers. 515 E. Sixth St. ✆ **512/494-9336.** www.flamingocantina.com. Cover $5–$20.

ROCK

Emo's This is one of Austin's best known clubs with a reputation for signing up bands that are on their way up. The music tends to be alternative forms of rock, pop, hip-hop,

Navigating Austin's Downtown Bar Scene

Austin's downtown bars are concentrated in three areas called Sixth Street, the Warehouse District, and Red River. When people talk of **Sixth Street,** they are referring to a 5-block portion of East Sixth, from Congress Avenue to Red River. This strip has all kinds of bars, from noisy saloons that cater to college students and offer $1 beer nights, such as **The Aquarium** and **The Library,** to a piano bar **(Pete's Dueling Pianos),** where the crowd is older and the volume of the music much lower. The best thing you can do is just walk the street and see what you like. You're apt to hear cover bands, Irish folk music, hip-hop, and Latin, to name just a few of the sounds.

Red River Street, between Sixth and 10th streets, is for those seeking out the local, underground music scene. You'll pass by a collection of bars that are less commercial and, frankly, don't look like much, but are where Austinites and music aficionados, mostly in their 20s and 30s, go to hear local bands of various stripes. Bars such as **The Red Eyed Fly** (see listing below) will mix blues, country, and metal bands; **Beerland** will usually have something "indie-garagey-punky;" **Room 710** something hard, metal, or punk. Farther down the street are **Club de Ville** and **Mohawk,** which might have just about anything, including lounge music. All these clubs have low cover charges in the range of $3 to $10, depending on the night. The one exception is **Stubb's** (see listing below), which is a large venue that signs name touring acts as well as some of the most popular local bands, and their cover charges are correspondingly higher.

The Warehouse District is west of Congress Avenue and extends from Second to Fifth streets, and from Congress Avenue to Guadalupe, encompassing 9 square blocks. It's more of a social scene with less emphasis on live music. It will work for those who want to have a drink and perhaps some food in attractive surroundings. Again, the best thing to do would be to stroll around until you see something that fits your mood. For the beer drinker, there are bars, such as the **Ginger Man** (currently at 304 W. Fourth St., but will probably relocate around the corner to 301 Lavaca), a bar with an astonishing array of beers from around the world. On the tony side would be a new cocktail bar called **Qua** (213 W. Fourth St.). **Malaga,** a tapas bar listed below, would be in the same category.

and anything that seems to be different and original. Lots of bands covet a gig here. About 75% are touring bands. It's all about the music here, not the decor. There's an urban-jungle feel to the place, much of which is outdoors, and the public seems to like it that way. There are two stages, each with its own entrance (one on Sixth, the other on Red River). Both areas connect to a biergarten of sorts in the middle of the block. Emo's attracts a mostly young crowd and many off-duty musicians. 603 Red River St. ✆ **512/477-EMOS** (477-3667). www.emosaustin.com. Cover $5–$12.

The Red Eyed Fly A good representative of the clubs along Red River, the Fly signs up about 90% local bands of all kinds. There's nothing fancy about the club. The first part is a lounge with a pool table, a bar, a jukebox, and some furniture in varying degrees of decay; the back is where the bands perform and where you pay a cover charge to see them. It's an outdoor stage bordering Waller Creek. The crowd is mostly young and stands around with beers in hand or dances to the music in a way that's hard to describe—other than to say that it's very Austin. 715 Red River St. ✆ **512/474-1084.** www.redeyedfly.com. Cover $5–$10.

SINGER-SONGWRITER

Cactus Cafe ★ A small, dark cavern with great acoustics and a fully stocked bar, UT's Cactus Cafe is home-away-from-home for a lot of singer-songwriters. There's a crowd of regulars who come here to see the likes of solo artists such as Alison Krauss and Suzanne Vega, along with well-known acoustic combos. The adjacent **Texas Union Ballroom** (✆ **512/475-6645**) draws larger crowds with such big names as the Dixie Chicks. Texas Union, University of Texas campus (24th and Guadalupe sts.). ✆ **512/475-6515.** www.utexas.edu/student/txunion/ae/cactus. Cover $10–$35.

Ego's Part of the charm of this place is its unlikely location, underground in the parking garage of an apartment building on South Congress at Riverside. It's dark, seedy, and different. About every other night a singer-songwriter performs for a few hours, and then the place is turned over to the practitioners of karaoke. A couple of run-down pool tables and video games add to the funky scene. 510 S. Congress Ave. ✆ **512/474-7091.** No cover.

ECLECTIC

Carousel Lounge In spite of (or maybe because of) its out-of-the-way location and bizarre circus theme—complete with elephant and lion-tamer murals and an actual carousel behind the bar—the Carousel Lounge is a highly popular local watering hole. You never know what will turn up onstage—this place has hosted everything from smaller musical acts to belly dancers. 1110 E. 52nd St. ✆ **512/452-6790.** Cover up to $5.

Continental Club ★ This Austin institution showcases rock, rockabilly, country, Latino, and new wave sounds. So many local acts have played here on their way to fame, and so many already famous acts will occasionally return, that it's worth your while to check out this small, dark club on South Congress. With high stools and a pool table in the back room, it feels much more like a neighborhood bar than a major venue, which is the lure of the place. It's got the best happy hour music in town. The club also operates a gallery club in the upstairs of the building next door. It features smaller acts and often has no cover. 1315 S. Congress Ave. ✆ **512/441-2444.** www.continentalclub.com. Cover $5–$20.

La Zona Rosa ★★ Another Austin classic, LZR has departed from its funky roots a bit to go upmarket, featuring bigger names and bigger covers than in the past. But the

Girl Power

The Austin sound may have long been dominated by such names as Willie, Stevie Ray, and Jerry Jeff (Janis was a too-brief blip on the all-male radar screen), but that's changing. Austin is now becoming known as the home of such prominent female performers as Sara Hickman, Shawn Colvin, Patrice Pike, Kelly Willis, Eliza Gilkyson, and the Dixie Chicks.

Label it Successful—Austin's SXSW

Started in 1987 as a way to showcase unsigned Texas bands, SXSW soon became *the* place for fledgling musicians from around the world to come to schmooze music-industry bigwigs. In the mid-1990s, film and interactive (high-tech and Internet) components were added to the event, and now they're almost as important as the original musical showcases. A list of festival participants could easily be mistaken for a *Rolling Stone* or *People* magazine table of contents.

Even if you're not looking to make it in the music, film, or Internet industries, this is still the hottest conference ticket around. Programs might include as many as 60 panels and workshops and 900 musical appearances at more than 40 venues around town. Prices for 2009 range from $150 (if you register early for the film or interactive aspects alone) to $810 for the walk-up Platinum rate, which affords access to all conference and music events.

The **South by Southwest (SXSW) Music and Media Conference & Festival** (its full name) is held during UT's spring break, usually the third week of March. For current schedules and speakers/performers, check the website at **www.sxsw.com** or call ✆ **512/467-7979.**

venue has remained the same—a renovated garage brightly painted with monsters and filled with kitschy memorabilia—and this is still a fun place to listen to good bands, from the Gourds to Mose Allison to Greg Allman and Friends. 612 W. Fourth St. ✆ **512/263-4146;** 888/597-STAR (597-7827) or 512/469-SHOW (469-7469) for tickets. www.lazonarosa.com. Tickets $8–$12 local acts, $20–$50 national acts.

The Parish Formerly called "The Mercury," this upstairs club on Sixth Street is known locally as a great place to hear live music in a range of genres—hip-hop, rock, funk, reggae, Latin, and electronic. 214 E. Sixth. ✆ **512/478-6372.** www.theparishroom.com. Tickets $5–$12 local acts, $13–$20 national acts.

Saxon Pub Look for the oversize knight in suit of armor on South Lamar Boulevard to find this iconic club that gets country, rock, and blues performers, big and small. The crowd is older and more laid back, and the volume is lower than at most of the Sixth Street bars. Check the calendar on the club's website, and you'll find performers who rarely play in such a small venue. This is a very comfortable place to catch great bands performing. 1320 S. Lamar Blvd. ✆ **512/448-2552.** www.thesaxonpub.com. Cover $5–$15.

Speakeasy The walk down a dark alley in the warehouse district to reach this multilevel club is all part of the 1920s Prohibition theme, which, mercifully, is not taken to an obnoxious extreme. Lots of dark wood and red velvet drapes help create a swanky atmosphere. Walk up two flights of narrow stairs to enjoy a drink or dance on the romantic Evergreen terrace. Lately the club has been signing some good Latin bands, mellow rock bands, and the occasional funk band. 412 Congress Ave. ✆ **512/476-8086.** www.speakeasyaustin.com. Cover $5–$15.

Late-Night Bites

If it's 3am and you have a hankering for a huge stack of pancakes to soak up the excess alcohol you shouldn't have downed, Austin has you covered. Austin's all-night cafes offer funky atmosphere and large quantities of hippie food. In addition to the usual cafe offerings, you can get local favorites, including Tex-Mex items such as *migas,* breakfast tacos, vegetarian versions of traditional Texas fare, and large creative salads.

One of the earliest on the scene and still hugely popular is **Kerbey Lane,** 3704 Kerbey Lane (✆ **512/451-1436;** www.kerbeylanecafe.com). Sunday mornings, locals spill out on the porch of the comfortable old house, waiting for a table so they can order the signature "pancakes as big as your head." Musicians finishing up late-night gigs at the Continental Club usually head over to the **Magnolia Cafe South,** 1920 S. Congress Ave. (✆ **512/445-0000;** www.cafemagnolia.com). On nice nights, enjoy the Love Veggies sautéed in garlic butter or the Deep Eddy burrito on an outdoor deck. Both cafes are open 24 hours daily. Kerbey Lane has three other locations, and Magnolia Cafe has one clone; but the originals are far more interesting.

Stubb's Bar-B-Q Within the rough limestone walls of a renovated historic building you'll find great barbecue and country Texas fare and three friendly bars—plus terrific music, ranging from singer-songwriter solos to hip-hop open mics to all-out country jams. Out back, the Waller Amphitheater hosts some of the bigger acts that come to Austin. See chapter 13 also for Stubb's Sunday gospel brunches. 801 Red River St. ✆ **512/480-8341.** www.stubbsaustin.com. Cover $6–$25.

COMEDY CLUBS

Cap City Comedy Top ranked on the stand-up circuit, Cap City books nationally recognized comedians such as Dave Chapell, Carlos Mencia, and Bobcat Goldthwait. The cream of the crop turn up on Friday and Saturday, of course, but you'll find plenty to laugh at (including lower cover charges) the rest of the week. Performances are nightly at 8pm with additional performances Friday and Saturday at 10:30pm. 8120 Research Blvd., Ste. 100. ✆ **512/467-2333.** www.capcitycomedy.com. Tickets $4.50–$25.

Esther's Follies You might miss a couple of the punch lines if you're not in on the latest twists and turns of local politics, but the no-holds-barred Esther's Follies doesn't spare Washington, either. It's satirical, irreverent, and very Austin. Performances are Thursday, at 8pm; Friday through Saturday, 8 and 10pm. 525 E. Sixth St. ✆ **512/320-0553.** www.esthersfollies.com. Tickets $18–$23; $2 off for students and seniors.

Velveeta Room For one-stop comedy consumption, go straight from Esther's to the Velveeta Room next door, a deliberately cheesy club serving more generic stand-up, local and national, as well as an open mic. Open-mic night is Thursday at 10pm; performances Friday and Saturday are 9:30 and 11pm. 521 E. Sixth St. ✆ **512/469-9116.** www.thevelveetaroom.com. Tickets $5–$10.

3 THE BAR SCENE

BRITISH & IRISH PUBS

Dog & Duck Pub This drinking spot captures the comfy, worn-in feel of pubs in the U.K. A lot of regulars and a lot of happy faces are to be seen here, drinking pints of their favorite brews, several of which are imported from the mother country. Sit outside at the outdoor picnic tables or roam indoors past the dart boards and the bar area, to find some of the cozier nooks and crannies. Though the Dog & Duck goes out of its way to evoke the feel of a British public house, it can't escape its Austin roots; something can be said for the authentic taste of the bangers and mash, but that's not necessarily a good thing. 406 W. 17th St. ✆ **512/479-0598.** www.dogandduckpub.com.

Fado This Irish pub in the Warehouse District looks surprisingly like the genuine article. The regulars can even be seen following soccer matches from the old country on large television screens. On weekend nights, local bands play on the small outdoor stage. The food, however, is a New World departure from Irish pub grub—something international, with burgers, quesadillas, and the like. 214 W. Fourth St. ✆ **512/457-0172.** www.fadoirishpub.com.

Mother Egan's The weekday happy hour is animated by lively, friendly banter and a general atmosphere of bonhomie, while on the weekends, the bar welcomes patrons from the open-air artists' market next door. There's no shortage of classic pub entertainment, either, with a mix of TV football, live music in the singer-songwriter vein, and tournaments for trivia. The Irish classics (corned beef and cabbage, shepherd's pie, and so on) and American pub grub are crowd pleasers, too. 715 W. Sixth St. ✆ **512/478-7747.** www.motheregansirishpub.com.

GAY BARS

Oilcan Harry's Its name notwithstanding—it's known locally as The Can—this slick warehouse-district bar attracts a clean-cut, upscale, mostly male crowd. Consistently voted Austin's Best Gay Club by readers of the *Austin Chronicle,* this is the place to go if you're looking for a buttoned-down, Brooks Brothers kind of guy. There's dancing, but not with the same frenzy as at many of the other clubs. 211 W. Fourth St. ✆ **512/320-8823.** www.oilcanharrys.com.

Rainbow Cattle Co. This is Austin's prime gay country-western dance hall. It's about 75% male, but also attracts a fair share of lesbian two-steppers, especially on Thursday, which is Ladies Night. 305 W. Fifth St. ✆ **512/472-5288.** www.rainbowcattleco.com.

A HISTORIC BAR

Scholz Garten ★ Since 1866, when councilman August Scholz first opened his tavern near the state capitol, every Texas governor has visited it at least once (and many quite a few more times). In recent years, Texas's oldest operating bar was sold to the owners of the popular Green Mesquite BBQ, giving it new life. The extensive menu now combines barbecue with German favorites, such as bratwurst and sauerkraut, and jagerschnitzel. This place is packed during Longhorn football games or when some other special university event is happening; otherwise it's generally a quiet spot to drink a beer out in the biergarten. On Thursdays in the spring and fall, when the weather holds, a

Impressions

There is a very remarkable number of drinking and gambling shops [in Austin], but not one book store.

—Frederick Law Olmsted,
A Journey Through Texas, 1853

group of talented amateurs get together to play old-style brass band songs for the crowd—a Scholz's tradition. All in all, a great place to drink in some Austin history. 1607 San Jacinto Blvd. ✆ **512/474-1958.**

LOCAL FAVORITE

Cedar Door Think "Cheers" with a redwood deck in downtown Austin. In spite of the fact that it keeps changing location—it's moved four times in its 26-year history—the Cedar Door remains Austin's favorite dumpy bar, drawing a group of regulars ranging from hippies to journalists and politicos. The beer's cold and the drinks are strong. The signature cocktail is the Mexican martini. If you're smart, you'll limit yourself to one. 201 Brazos. ✆ **512/473-3712.** www.cedardooraustin.com.

A PIANO BAR

The Driskill Sink into one of the plush chairs arrayed around a grand piano and enjoy everything from blues to show tunes in the upper-lobby bar of this newly opulent historic hotel. A pianist accompanies the happy hour hors d'oeuvres (nightly 5–7pm), but the ivory thumping gets going around 8pm Tuesday through Saturday. 604 Brazos St. ✆**512/391-7162.** www.driskillgrill.com/bar.html.

A WINE & TAPAS BAR

Málaga Come to this sleek, sophisticated spot to sip fine wines at good prices—50 selections by the glass—and nibble Spanish appetizers (the swordfish bites are especially tasty). 440 W. Second St. ✆ **512/236-8020.**

4 FILMS

Not surprisingly, you can see more foreign films in Austin than anywhere else in the state. Nearly every cinema in town devotes at least one screen to something off Hollywood's beaten track. In the university area, the largest concentration of art films can be found at the **Dobie Theatre,** 2025 Guadalupe St., on the Drag (✆ **512/472-FILM** [472-3456]), and at the two venues of the **Texas Union Film Series,** UT campus, Texas Union Building and Hogg Auditorium (✆ **512/475-6656**). **Alamo Drafthouse,** 1120 S. Lamar Blvd. (✆ **512/707-8262;** www.originalalamo.com) is an Austin original that combines "dinner and a movie" into a one-stop affair. The owners have taken over old movie theaters and refitted the seating in order to add counter space for patrons. They provide a menu of basic food and drink, including beer and wine, ordered and delivered straight to your seat. Seeing movies here can be fun. The staff make custom film shorts before the

Celluloid Austin

Austin has long had an undercover Hollywood presence. During the past 3 decades, more than 90 films were shot in the city and its vicinity. But you'd be hard-pressed to identify Texas's capital in any of them. Because it has such a wide range of landscapes, Austin has filled in for locations as far-flung as Canada and Vietnam.

The city has less of an identity crisis behind the camera. It first earned its credentials as an indie director–friendly place in 1982, when the Coen brothers shot *Blood Simple* here. And when University of Texas graduate Richard Linklater captured some of the loopier members of Austin's denizens in *Slackers*—adding a word to the national vocabulary in the process—Austin arrived on the *cinéaste* scene. Linklater is often spotted around town with Robert Rodriguez, who shot all or part of several of his films (*Alienated, The Faculty,* and the *Spy Kids* series) in Austin, and with Quentin Tarantino, who owns property in town. Mike Judge, of *Beavis and Butthead* and *King of the Hill* fame, lives in Austin, too.

Of the many cinematic events held in town, October's **Austin Film Festival** is among the more interesting. Held in tandem with the Heart of Films Screenwriters Conference, it focuses on movies with great scripts. For current information, contact the Austin Film Festival, 1604 Nueces, Austin, TX 78701 (✆ **800/310-FEST** [310-3378] or 512/478-4795; fax 512/478-6205; www.austinfilmfestival.com). And the come-lately film component of SXSW (see sidebar earlier in this chapter) gets larger every year. Panelists have included Linklater and John Sayles, whose film *Lone Star* had its world premiere here.

See also chapter 3 for information on the Austin Gay and Lesbian International Film Festival.

feature presentation. Other locations include Alamo Village, 2700 W. Anderson Lane (north central), and Alamo Lake Creek, 13729 Research Blvd. (far north). There is a downtown location, in the old Ritz Theater on Sixth Street, but it shows only a few films, and usually hosts live acts.

17 Side Trips from Austin

If you're looking for a quick day trip out of town, or if you're arriving to Austin by car from Dallas, Houston, or San Antonio, there are a few amusements you should know. With just a short drive or detour, or perhaps no detour at all, you can, for instance, find one-of-a-kind world-famous barbecue, see a bit of small-town Texas that's not the least bit touristy, canoe on a clear river under tall cypress trees, hike in a pine forest, or shop in a Texas-size outlet mall.

1 SMALL TOWNS & TEXAS BARBECUE

More so than chili con carne or chicken-fried steak, barbecue can justly lay claim to being the quintessential Texas food. Not only is it a highly prized food in all corners of the state, barbecue is also the recipient of contributions from just about every major culture and ethnic group that came to Texas. Everyone lent a hand in its creation—cowboys and Indians, Mexicans and Germans, Anglos and African Americans. And it took every one of those contributions to perfect the technique of combining meat, fire, and smoke into a rare sensory delight. All of this created a rich lore surrounding barbecue, lots of traditions, and, of course, endless debate over such important matters as wet or dry, direct or indirect heat, and sauce or no sauce.

CITY VS. COUNTRY

Before we tackle such complex and weighty issues, it's important to note that Austin is at the center of a constellation of small towns famous for their barbecue. Here you'll find the real deal. Much can be said for city barbecue, and, if you can't manage the time to get out to the small towns, then you can comfort yourself with excellent barbecue from such Austin joints as the Iron Works or County Line. But if you can leave the city, in just about any direction you will find small-town barbecue, where the slower rhythms of life and the importance of tradition apply to the cooking of barbecue.

Another advantage small towns have is the lack of clean-air ordinances, because to create old-time barbecue you need lots of smoke. City barbecue is leaning more and more on the use of commercial cookers, which have improved over the years, and can make good barbecue. But they still can't match the character of barbecue cooked in a proper "pit."

In central Texas, a barbecue pit is a large brick or stone oven with a wood fire at one end and a flue at the other. On its way out the flue, the smoke wafts through racks of meats, doing its job. Wood is the fuel of choice, not charcoal, because charcoal burns too cleanly. The moisture and sap in the wood create the smoke that gives the meat its flavor. If you want visual proof, look at a slice of barbecued brisket. You'll see a pink line running just below the surface of the meat. This line is produced when nitrogen dioxide in the smoke reacts with the myoglobin in the meat. If the brisket has been cooked with a wood fire in a proper pit, the line will be redder, extend deeper, and be better defined than brisket cooked in a commercial smoker. And, of course, a taste of the meat will confirm the difference.

Experiencing Texas Barbecue

Barbecue joints in central Texas will cook a variety of meats, but there are three constants: brisket, spareribs, and sausage. All other meats, such as beef ribs, pork chops, turkey, and chicken might be offered, but are not considered essential. Another hallmark of Texas barbecue is the sauce—a sweet and spicy tomato-based concoction. There is a debate in Texas as to whether good barbecue needs sauce or not. There is no definitive answer here, as it is entirely a matter of personal taste. But, at least, it offers a good conversation topic. Almost all barbecue joints will offer sauce, and the customers are free to use it or not.

In Texas, barbecue is always served with plain white bread (anything else would be too highfalutin'), onions, and pickles. Popular side dishes include chili beans, potato salad, and coleslaw. Often the barbecue is served on butcher paper (as plates would also be too highfalutin').

It's important to note that barbecue is traditionally eaten early, to allow ample time for digestion. Many small town barbecue joints will close by 6 or 7pm. And one more thing to remember when heading to these small towns for barbecue: bring cash. Credit cards are often not accepted.

LOCKHART

This little town 30 miles south of Austin is the most famous town in Texas for barbecue. If you have but one shot to try real barbecue, this is the place you should go. From Austin, take Hwy. 183 south. Try to leave before 4pm to avoid traffic (many working families have moved out here for the inexpensive housing). If you're headed to Austin from San Antonio, you can make a little detour at San Marcos. Follow Hwy. 80 E. to Martindale, then Hwy. 142 to Lockhart.

Lockhart has three important barbecue joints, perhaps the most famous (and a personal favorite) is **Kreuz Market** (pronounced krites). It's located at 619 N. Colorado St. (✆ **512/398-2361**). Hours are Monday to Saturday 10:30am to 8pm. As you enter Lockhart on Hwy. 183, you'll come to a flyover. Take the last right before the flyover and you'll practically be in the parking lot.

Once you walk through the doors, head to the pit room in back. A sign on the wall reads like an edict: "No salad. No sauce. No credit cards." This is one of the few places that refuses to provide sauce. A lot of barbecuers agree with this position in theory but aren't about to chase off those customers who like sauce. The guys here just don't care. Once you buy your barbecue, head to the large dining room where you can buy drinks and what few side dishes are available. The sides are few and not very good, but the meat is amazing. With one bite of the brisket or the ribs, you'll understand what Texas barbecue is all about. The sausage is spicy and coarsely ground. For some it's too fatty, but I love it.

If you want sauce with your barbecue, head to **Black's Barbecue** (✆ **512/398-2712**), at 215 N. Main St. It's located 3 blocks north of the town square. You'll see signs pointing the way as you enter Lockhart. In addition to excellent barbecue and a tangy sauce, Black's also offers well-prepared side dishes. Food is served daily from 10am to 8pm.

Your third option is **Smitty's Market** (© **512/398-9344**), at 208 South Commerce, a half block south of the town square. It's open Monday to Saturday from 7am to 6pm. Even if you eat elsewhere, make a point of strolling into Smitty's just to see the smoke-caked pit room. This is the original location of Kreuz Market. The family had a parting of ways. One side kept the original location while the other side kept the name. The recipes are about the same in both places, but I think the quality of the meat is a little better at the new place. While you're walking off your meal, take a spin around the town square and county courthouse, which was renovated in 2000. It's a distinctive building with mansard roofs on the corners and strangely shaped decorative towers in the center and on the north and south sides. The businesses that front the main square are indicative of the state of the local economy. Barbecue may be the town's economic engine.

LULING

This town is 16 miles south of Lockhart. It's actually a bit closer to San Antonio than Austin. And, if you're traveling between Houston and San Antonio, it's but a short detour off I-10. The place to go is **Luling City Market** (© **830/875-9019**), at 633 E. Davis, where Hwy. 183 crosses the railroad tracks. As with other barbecue joints, first you buy your barbecue in the pit room, before getting your sauce, drinks, and side dishes in the dining room. Only beans and potato salad are available. In my opinion the ribs and the brisket are the best of the offerings. The dry rub on the ribs gives them a slightly crispy texture, and the brisket melts in your mouth. Luling City Market is open Monday to Saturday 7am to 6pm. You can walk off your meal by strolling down Davis Street to the Oil Museum. Both the museum and the town are described in greater detail in chapter 10.

DRIFTWOOD

Seventeen miles southwest of Austin is the tiny town of Driftwood and its famous barbecue joint, **The Salt Lick** (© **512/858-4959**). Take Hwy. 290 west. As you pass through Oak Hill, keep to your left when the highway forks. After you pass the fork, make a left on to FM 1826 at the third traffic light. Drive 13 miles to the Salt Lick. It will be on your right, and Camp Ben McCulloch will be on your left. The address is 18001 FM 1826, but that's not going to help you much, and it's not important, because you can't miss the place. If you're in the vicinity of San Marcos, continue north on I-35 and exit Kyle, taking Hwy. 150 W. Stay on 150 until you get to FM 1826, then turn right.

The Salt Lick is open daily 11am to 10pm. It can get crowded on weekends when Austinites come down with their ice chests full of beer, which they drink while waiting for a table. The restaurant can't sell beer because Hays County is dry. The Salt Lick cooks its barbecue a little differently from the places mentioned above. It uses an open stone pit and direct heat. With this technique, the pit boss has to be careful to control the heat and not overcook. The food gets a good smoke flavor, but leans more heavily on the rub and the sauce for flavor. The sauce is rich and tangy and a favorite with the locals. The setting is charming and rustic, in a long rambling building filled with picnic tables. There's a screened porch area, which is pleasant when the weather is mild. Food is served all-you-can-eat family style (with platters of meat and side dishes). All the sides are good, as are the desserts.

LLANO

Llano is 75 miles northwest of Austin, which is too far to go just to get some barbecue, when there are great places closer by. But if you're already up in the Highland Lakes area,

> **Finds** **For Hard Core Only**
>
> In the town of Lexington, which is 20 miles north of Giddings, there is a barbecue joint that *Texas Monthly* magazine calls the best barbecue in Texas in its 2008 barbecue issue. Unfortunately, it's open only Saturday mornings from 8am until noon. So, if you're serious about eating in all the great central Texas barbecue joints, and you have confidence in the opinion of *Texas Monthly's* food editors, you'll need to pay a visit to **Snow's Barbecue** (✆ **979-542-8189**), at 516 Main. I can't give my opinion because I haven't tried it yet.

in the vicinity of Lake Buchanan, you can take advantage of your proximity and enjoy some barbecue at **Cooper's** (✆ **325/247-5713**). It's located at 604 W. Young (Hwy. 29). Like the Salt Lick, Cooper's uses the direct-heat method, and the same comments apply. The brisket is the star of the show. Cooper's opens daily between 10:30am to 8pm.

TAYLOR

Northeast of Austin is the town of Taylor. It's about a 35-mile trip. Take I-35 north to Round Rock, then Hwy. 79 E. This is the home of a famous barbecue joint called **Louie Mueller's** (✆ **512/352-6206**), at 206 W. Second St., open Monday through Saturday from 10am to 6pm. If you're on your way to Austin from either Dallas or Houston (via Hwy. 290), it's only a 16-mile detour. Barbecue is cooked with the indirect heat method in an impressive pit. The rub uses a lot of black pepper, and combined with the smoke, makes a wonderful black crust on the brisket. The restaurant is large and old-fashioned and smells of smoke that's been wafting through here for 50 years.

GIDDINGS

If you're coming from Houston on Hwy. 290, you won't have to make any detour whatsoever to have some excellent barbecue at **City Meat Market** (✆ **979/542-2740**). It's located at the corner of Austin Street and the highway, in an old-fashioned brick storefront. You can't miss it. This place continues to be a market selling fresh meat, unlike the other places mentioned above, despite the fact that it's also been selling barbecue for about 50 years. It's open Monday to Friday from 7:30am to 5:30pm and Saturdays from 7:30am to 4pm. The sausage is extremely good here. Giddings is 55 miles east of Austin.

2 SAN MARCOS

Some 26 miles south of Austin via I-35, San Marcos was first settled by Native Americans around 12,000 years ago. Some scholars claim it is the oldest continuously inhabited site in the Western Hemisphere. Temporary home to two Spanish missions in the late 1700s, as well as to the Comanche and Apaches (which explains the "temporary" part), this site at the headwaters of the San Marcos River was permanently settled by Anglos in the middle of the 19th century. Now host to Texas State University–San Marcos (formerly Southwest Texas State University), the alma mater of LBJ, and the only university in the state to graduate a future president—San Marcos has the laid-back feel of a college town. It's also fast becoming a bedroom community of Austin, only half an hour away.

Just 15 miles farther south, towards San Antonio, is the town of New Braunfels, which has several attractions for visitors, including caverns, a large water park, tubing on a river, and a classic country dance hall (in Gruene). New Braunfels is described in chapter 10.

WHAT TO SEE & DO

In the center of town—and, clearly, the reason for its existence—more than 1,000 springs well up from the Balcones Fault to form Spring Lake; its astonishingly clear waters maintain a constant temperature of 72°F (22°C). On the lake's shore sits the **Aquarena Center ★★**, 1 Aquarena Springs Dr. (✆ **512/245-7575;** www.aquarena.txstate.edu), an exemplar of tourist trends. The first theme park to be opened in Texas, and once home to Ralph the Swimming Pig, it was purchased in the mid-1990s by Texas State University, which then spent $16 million to convert it into an environmental research center. Glass-bottom boat tours, which allow you to view the lake's rare flora and fauna, cost $8 for adults, $7 for seniors 55 and older, and $6 for children ages 4 to 15. In addition, there are environmental tours (2 weeks advance arrangement required), an endangered species exhibit, a natural aquarium, hikes, and a boardwalk over the wetlands, where more than 100 species of birds have been spotted. You can also visit the log home of Gen. Edward Burleson, who built the dam that created Spring Lake to power his gristmill.

The **San Marcos River,** which begins at Spring Lake, is also getting (somewhat) eco-conscious. Log on to www.sanmarcosriver.org to find out about conservation measures taken by the San Marcos River Foundation. Not-so-rare species on the river include canoeists and rafters: Between May and September, the local Lions Club (✆ **512/396-LION** [396-5466]; www.centuryinter.net/smlc/tuberental.html) rents inner tubes and operates a river shuttle at City Park; check the website for a schedule and rates.

When the Balcones Fault was active some 30 million years ago, an earthquake created the cave at the center of **Wonder World,** 1000 Prospect St., off Bishop (✆ **877/492-4657** or 512/392-3760; www.wonderworldpark.com). You might not want to visit this much-hyped attraction. The petting farm, for example, is essentially a tram ride through an enclosure of depressed-looking deer. A tour of the cave eventually takes you to the so-called Anti-Gravity House, where you can see water flowing upward. The cave ($14 adults, $11 children ages 5–12, $5 children under 5) is okay, but there are better ones such as Natural Bridge Caverns (discussed in chapter 10). And the Anti-Gravity House is just tacky. This attraction is open daily from June through August from 8am to 8pm; Monday through Friday from 9am to 5pm, Saturday and Sunday from 9am to 6pm the rest of the year; it is closed Christmas Eve and Christmas.

San Marcos's entire downtown area is listed in the National Register of Historic Places. Its hub is **Courthouse Square,** where several turn-of-the-century buildings are being restored. The **State Bank and Trust Building,** dating back to the late 1800s, was robbed by the Newton Gang in 1924 and (most likely) by Machine Gun Kelly in 1933; *The Getaway,* starring Steve McQueen and Ali McGraw, was shot here in 1972. See "Where to Stay & Dine," below, for the building's latest incarnation.

To get an inside look at one of the town's two tree-lined residential districts, make an appointment to view the **Millie Seaton Collection of Dolls and Toys,** 1104 W. Hopkins (✆ **512/396-1944**), housed in the opulent 1908 Augusta Hofheinz mansion. Thousands of tiny eyes peer at you from the three stories crammed with figurines that

Mrs. Seaton has been collecting since 1965, including some rare historical specimens. You're likely to recognize a few of them from your childhood. Admission is free.

Texas State University's Albert B. Alkek Library isn't old, but it's home to some of the state's most important literary artifacts, as well as to a good gallery specializing in photographs. The **Southwestern Writers Collection ★**, on the seventh floor of the library, at 601 University Dr. (✆ **512/245-3861;** www.library.txstate.edu/swwc), showcases materials donated by the region's leading filmmakers, musicians, and wordsmiths. You might see anything from a 1555 printing of the journey of Spanish adventurer Cabeza de Vaca to a songbook created by an 11-year-old Willie Nelson to the costumes worn by Tommy Lee Jones and Robert Duvall in *Lonesome Dove.* (The collection was founded by screenwriter Bill Wittliff, who wrote the script for that TV miniseries as well as for *Legends of the Fall* and *A Perfect Storm.*) The collection is generally open to the public Monday, Tuesday, and Friday 8am to 5pm, Wednesday and Thursday 8am to 7pm, Saturday 9am to 5pm, Sunday 2 to 6pm, but hours change with university holidays and breaks; phone ahead or check the website. The **Wittliff Gallery of Southwestern & Mexican Photography ★** (✆ **512/245-2313**) exhibits not only works from an excellent permanent collection, but also temporary shows by other renowned photographers. Call ahead for directions to the building and parking garage; hours are the same as for the Southwestern Writers Collection.

Outlet Shopping

Lots of people bypass San Marcos altogether and head straight for the two factory outlet malls a few miles south of downtown—the biggest discount shopfest in Texas. Take exit 200 from I-35 for both the **Tanger Factory Outlet Center** (✆ **800/408-8424** or 512/396-7446; www.tangeroutlet.com) and the larger and tonier **Prime Outlets** (✆ **800/628-9465** or 512/396-2200; www.primeoutlets.com) right next door. Among the almost 150 stores, you'll find everything from Dana Buchman, Anne Klein, and Brooks Brothers to Coach, Samsonite, and Waterford/Wedgwood. There's also a Saks Fifth Avenue outlet.

The **San Marcos Convention and Visitors Bureau,** 202 N. C. M. Allen Pkwy., San Marcos, TX 78666 (✆ **888/200-5620** or 512/393-5900; www.sanmarcoscharms.com), can provide you with information on mall bus transportation, as well as a complete list of places to eat and stay in town.

Shopping in Buda

On the Interstate between San Marcos and Austin is the tiny town of Buda (pronounced *Byou*-duh). Not a lot happens here, but if you take the Buda exit (exit 220) you'll see **Texas Hatters** (✆ **800/421-HATS** [421-4287] or 512/295-4287; www.texashatters.com) on the access road on the east side of the highway. In business for more than 50 years, this Western hatter has had an unlikely mix of famous customers, from Tip O'Neill, George Bush, and the king of Sweden to Al Hirt, Willie Nelson, Chuck Norris, and Arnold Schwarzenegger—to name just a few. You can pick out a hat, have it shaped, and have a custom band put on in no time.

Also in Buda, along the highway feeder road (this time on the west side) is Cabela's store (✆ **512/295-1100;** www.cabelas.com) selling outdoor gear. This is one of those destination stores that are said to have everything you could possibly want for hunting, fishing, and camping. You'll see signs marking the exit (#220), and you can see the store from the highway.

WHERE TO STAY & DINE

The **Crystal River Inn,** 326 W. Hopkins, San Marcos, TX 78666 (© **888/396-3739** or 512/396-3739; www.crystalriverinn.com), offers something for everyone. Nine rooms and three suites, beautifully decorated with antiques, occupy a large 1883 Victorian main house and two smaller historic structures behind it. There's also a fully furnished executive apartment across the street. Rates, which range from a low of $105 for a room during the week to a high of $175 for a two-bedroom suite on the weekend, include a full breakfast. The elaborately scripted (and enthusiastically acted) murder-mystery weekends are popular.

The prettiest place to have a meal in town is the courtyard at **Palmer's,** 216 W. Moore (© **512/353-3500;** www.palmerstexas.com), where you can sit among lovely native plants and trees and enjoy dishes ranging from penne pasta Alfredo with artichoke hearts and sun-dried tomatoes or charbroiled ahi tuna to a hefty Kansas City strip steak. Save room for the delicious Key lime or chocolate satin pies. The restaurant is open for lunch and dinner daily, and meals are moderate to expensive.

For a bit of history with your meal, you can't beat the **Hill Country Grill,** 100 W. Hopkins St. (© **512/396-6100;** www.hillcountrygrill.com), in the old State Bank and Trust Building. Dine on such well-prepared standards as grilled salmon or rib-eye in a couple of the former vaults—they're windowless, so the claustrophobic might opt for the airy exterior dining room—or sip such cocktails as Getaway Gold at a bar that incorporates the bank counter. The restaurant is open for lunch and dinner Monday through Saturday; prices are moderate to expensive.

NEARBY WIMBERLEY

A river resort town some 15 miles northwest of San Marcos, Wimberley attracts Austinites with a slew of bed-and-breakfasts—it's a favorite setting for family reunions—and a concentration of resident artists. From April through December, the first Saturday of each month is **Market Day,** a huge crafts gathering on Lion's Field; check www.visitwimberly.com/marketdays for additional information.

If you like artsy-craftsy (and, especially, country cutesy) stuff, you could spend all day browsing the shops and boutiques on and near the town square. But one of the most interesting places to visit is 1½ miles south of the town center: **Wimberley Glass Works,** Spoke Hill Road (© **512/847-9348;** www.wgw.com), stands out for its rainbowlike array of blown glassware. The jewelry, made with shards of broken glass, is outstanding. You can watch owner/artist Tim de Jong at work much of the time (except Tues, when the furnaces are refilled).

A Literary Aside

Pulitzer Prize–winning author Katherine Anne Porter, best known for her novel *Ship of Fools,* spent most of her childhood just a few miles south of Buda, in the town of Kyle. In 2001, the **1880 Katherine Anne Porter House,** 508 W. Center St. (© **512/268-6637;** www.english.txstate.edu/kap), was dedicated and opened to the public, as well as to a visiting writer chosen by the Texas State University–San Marcos. The house, which was restored and furnished with period antiques, hosts Porter's works and a collection of her photographs. There's no admission charge, but you need to call ahead for an appointment.

Lost Pines

Thirty miles southeast of Austin lies an ecological anomaly—a pine forest surrounded on all sides by prairie. It is the last remnant of an extensive pine forest that once extended all the way from Piney Woods of East Texas. This one patch of forest has survived because the soils in this one area are rich in iron, which favors the growth of pine trees over the grasses of the surrounding prairie. It is very hilly, which also marks a difference with the surrounding land. Located within the forest is **Bastrop State Park** (✆ **512/321-2101;** www.tpwd.state.tx.us/spdest/findadest/parks/bastrop), which offers plenty of hiking trails, a golf course, a swimming pool, campsites, and cabins (which must be reserved by phone well in advance: ✆ **512/389-8900**). Mountain biking is not permitted, but the park road, which extends to a nearby park, is one of the most popular bike rides in Texas. This park is situated just off Hwy. 71, which is one of the main roads between Austin and Houston. Also located in this pine forest is **Hyatt Regency Lost Pines Resort and Spa** (✆ **512/308-1234;** www.lostpines.hyatt.com), which is a family-oriented resort in the same style as the Hyatt Regency Hill Country Resort on the outskirts of San Antonio (see chapter 5). It's located on the banks of the Colorado River and offers such activities as kayaking and canoeing, as well as horseback riding. Rates for a standard room run from $249 to $329, depending on the day of week and time of year. Promotional rates and packages are often available.

Right next door is another great reason to come to Wimberley. The **Blair House,** 100 Spoke Hill Rd., Wimberley, TX 78676 (✆ **877/549-5450** or 512/847-8828; www.blairhouseinn.com), is a luxury property on 85 Hill Country acres, offering eight beautifully decorated rooms and two separate cottages in a Texas limestone ranch complex. What with a cooking school on the premises, you know the breakfasts—and dinners, offered to outsiders as well as guests every Saturday night—are going to be good. Rates run $150 to $209 for double rooms, $244 to $285 for the cottages. The cooking classes and dinners are popular with Austinites (and others), so book in advance if you want to attend.

For information about other places to stay, eat, or shop in Wimberley, contact the **Chamber of Commerce,** 14100 R.R. 12, just north of the town square (✆ **512/847-2201;** www.wimberley.org). Another resource for accommodations is **All Wimberley Lodging,** 400 River Rd. (✆ **800/460-3909** or 512/847-3909; www.texashillcountrylodging.com).

18

Touring the Texas Hill Country

A rising and falling land of rivers, lakes, springs, and caverns, the Hill Country is one of Texas's prettiest regions—especially in early spring, when wildflowers daub it with every pigment in nature's palette. Dotted with old dance halls, country stores, quaint Teutonic towns—more than 30,000 Germans emigrated to Texas during the great land-grant years of the Republic—and birthplace to one of the U.S.'s most colorful presidents, the region also lays out an appealing mosaic of the state's history.

San Antonio lies at the southern edge of the Hill Country; Austin at its eastern edge. Interstate highway I-35, which connects the two cities, parallels the Balcones Escarpment, a narrow line of steep hills separating the Edwards Plateau from the coastal prairie. The Edwards Plateau is an ancient seabed that was pushed upwards by volcanic activity, uplifting about 1,200 feet above the coastal plains. This plateau extends for hundreds of miles north and west of San Antonio and Austin; the part closest to these cities is called the Hill Country. The extra elevation makes the climate a little drier and milder in summer.

The uplifting produced fissures in the limestone substrate. Water on the plateau seeps into these cracks and pours back out in the lower elevations in the form of natural springs, which are numerous in the area. In coursing through the stone, the water has also carved out dramatic caverns, several of which are open to the public.

In the 19th century, these features attracted many German and Czech settlers who were fleeing the social upheavals in Europe. They established small towns that now dot the area and add a little contrast to the prevailing cowboy culture. The mild climate, rolling hills, and abundant springs continue to attract visitors to this part of the state, with summer camps, guest ranches, and resorts serving a public that comes here to enjoy the outdoors.

The state government sells maps of different regions of the state for wildlife enthusiasts. The one for the Hill Country is called **Heart of Texas–Wildlife Trail West.** It details loop routes covering a variety of the region's natural attractions and is available at several Hill Country town visitor centers. You can also order the map in advance for $4 by logging on to **www.tcebookstore.org** or by calling **✆ 888/900-2577.**

1 BOERNE ★

If you're starting from San Antonio, the quickest route to the Hill Country is to take I-10 northwest to Boerne (rhymes with "journey"). Boerne's a good base for travelers, as it's near both a big city (just 30 miles from San Antonio) and the more rural areas to the north and west. A popular health resort in the 1880s, the little (2¼-mile-long) town near Cibolo Creek was first settled 30 years earlier by freedom-seeking German intellectuals, including firebrand journalist Ludwig Börne, for whom it was named. A gazebo with a Victorian cupola in the center of the main plaza often hosts concerts by the Boerne Village Band, the oldest continuously operating German band in the world outside Germany (it first tuned up in 1860). A number of the town's 19th-century limestone buildings house small historical museums, boutiques, and restaurants, and old-fashioned lampposts and German street signs add atmosphere. But Boerne's biggest draw are the crafts and antiques shops lining the *Hauptstrasse,* or main street. For details, stop in at the **Boerne Visitors Center,** 1407 S. Main (south corner of the Wal-Mart parking lot), Boerne, TX 78006 (© **888/842-8080** or 830/249-7277; www.visitboerne.org).

WHAT TO SEE & DO

Those who want to spend their time outdoors can explore four distinct ecosystems—grassland, marshland, woodland, and river bottom—via short treks on the **Cibolo Nature Center,** City Park Road, off Hwy. 46 E. next to the Kendall County Fairgrounds (© **830/249-4616;** www.cibolo.org). Dinosaur tracks trace the route of *Acrocanthosaurus atokensis* and friends, whose fossilized footprints were uncovered when the area was flooded in 1997. If you like your strolls to include sand traps, the top-rated **Tapatio Springs Golf Course,** Johns Road exit off I-10 West (© **800/999-3299** or 830/537-4611; www.tapatio.com), is your place.

One of the most popular nearby attractions is **Cascade Caverns** (© **830/755-8080;** www.cascadecaverns.com); drive about 3 miles south of Boerne on I-10, take Exit 543, and drive a little over 2 1/5 miles east. This active cave boasts huge chambers, a 100-foot underground waterfall, and comfortable walking trails; guides provide 45-minute to 1-hour interpretive tours every 30 minutes. It's open Memorial Day through mid-August daily 9am to 5pm; off season Monday through Friday 10am to 4pm, Saturday and Sunday 9am to 4pm. Admission is $11 adults, $7 children. Another popular underground attraction is the stalactite- and stalagmite-filled **Cave Without a Name,** 325 Kreutzberg Rd., 12 miles northeast of Boerne (© **830/537-4212;** www.cavewithoutaname.com). Hour-long tours of the six chambers are offered throughout the day. The chambers are well lit and display plenty of features and living rock. Open Memorial Day through Labor Day daily 9am to 6pm; off season daily 10am to 5pm. Admission $14 adults, $7 children.

Rafters and canoeists like **Guadalupe River State Park,** some 13 miles east of Boerne, off Hwy. 46 on P.R. 31 (© **830/438-2656;** www.tpwd.state.tx.us/park/guadalup), comprising more than 1,900 acres surrounding a lovely cypress-edged river. Keep an eye out and you might spot white-tailed deer, coyotes, armadillos, or even a rare golden-cheeked warbler. The river makes for enjoyable swimming. Camping is available (make reservations using the website). Often the park rangers offer a 2-hour interpretive tour of a nearby natural area (inquire ahead of time). The park is open daily from 8am to 10pm, and the entrance fee is $6, kids age 12 and under are free.

WHERE TO STAY

Now an appealing B&B in the heart of town, **Ye Kendall Inn,** 128 W. Blanco, Boerne, TX 78006 (© **800/364-2138** or 830/249-2138; www.yekendallinn.com), opened as a stagecoach lodge in 1859. The rooms ($110–$130) and suites ($140–$160) are individually—and attractively—decorated, some with Victorian antiques, others with American rustic pieces. Historic cabins ($160–$180) transported to the grounds are available, too.

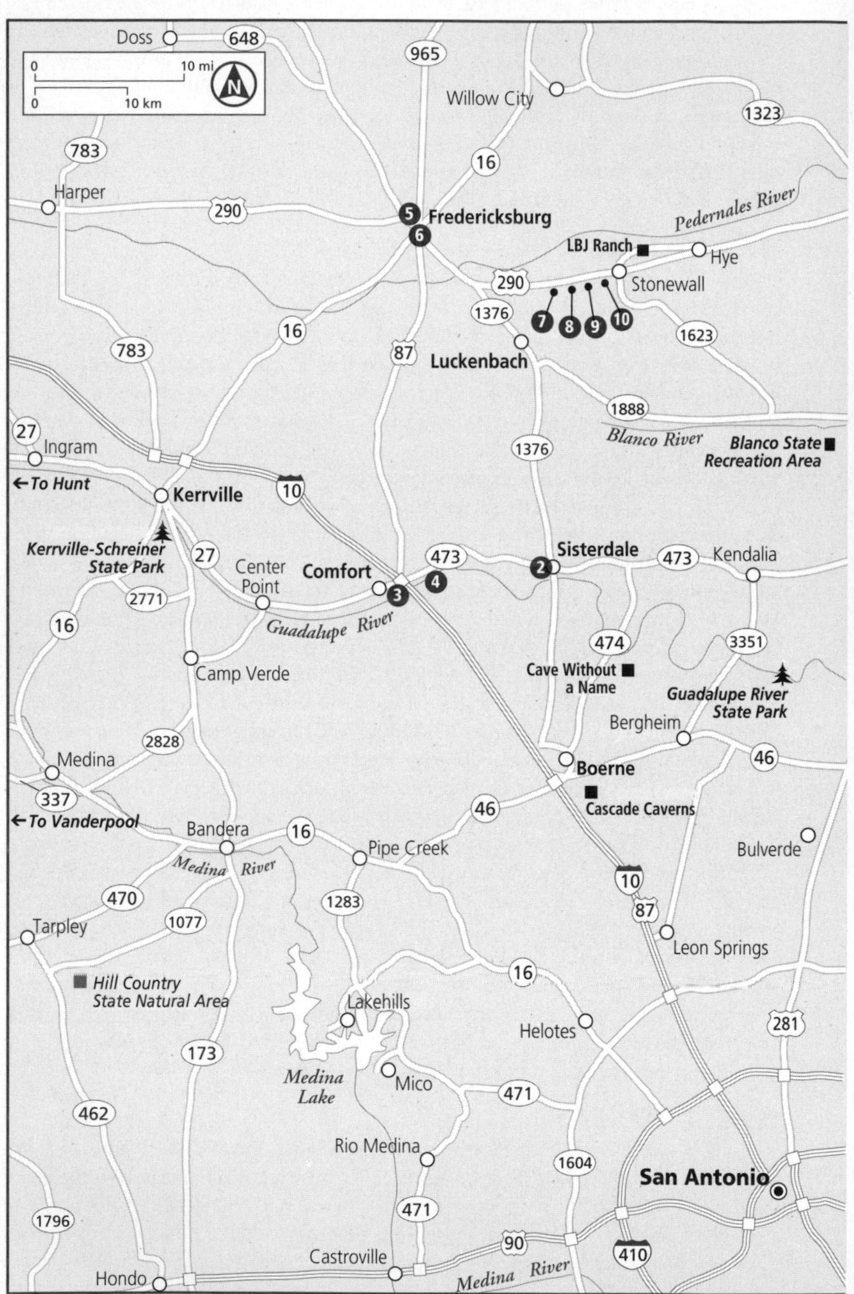

Doss
648
965
0
10 mi
0
10 km
N
Willow City
1323
783
16
Harper
290
5
Fredericksburg
6
Pedernales River
LBJ Ranch
Hye
290
Stonewall
1376
7
8
9
10
16
1623
783
87
Luckenbach
1888
Blanco River
Blanco State Recreation Area
27
Ingram
1376
← To Hunt
Kerrville
10
Kerrville-Schreiner State Park
27
Center Point
Comfort
473
4
2
Sisterdale
473
Kendalia
3
2771
16
Guadalupe River
474
3351
Camp Verde
Cave Without a Name
Guadalupe River State Park
Bergheim
2828
Medina
Boerne
46
337
46
Cascade Caverns
← To Vanderpool
Bandera
16
Pipe Creek
Bulverde
Medina River
10
470
1283
87
Tarpley
1077
Leon Springs
16
Hill Country State Natural Area
Lakehills
Helotes
281
173
Medina Lake
Mico
471
462
Rio Medina
1604
San Antonio
471
1796
90
410
Castroville
Hondo
Medina River

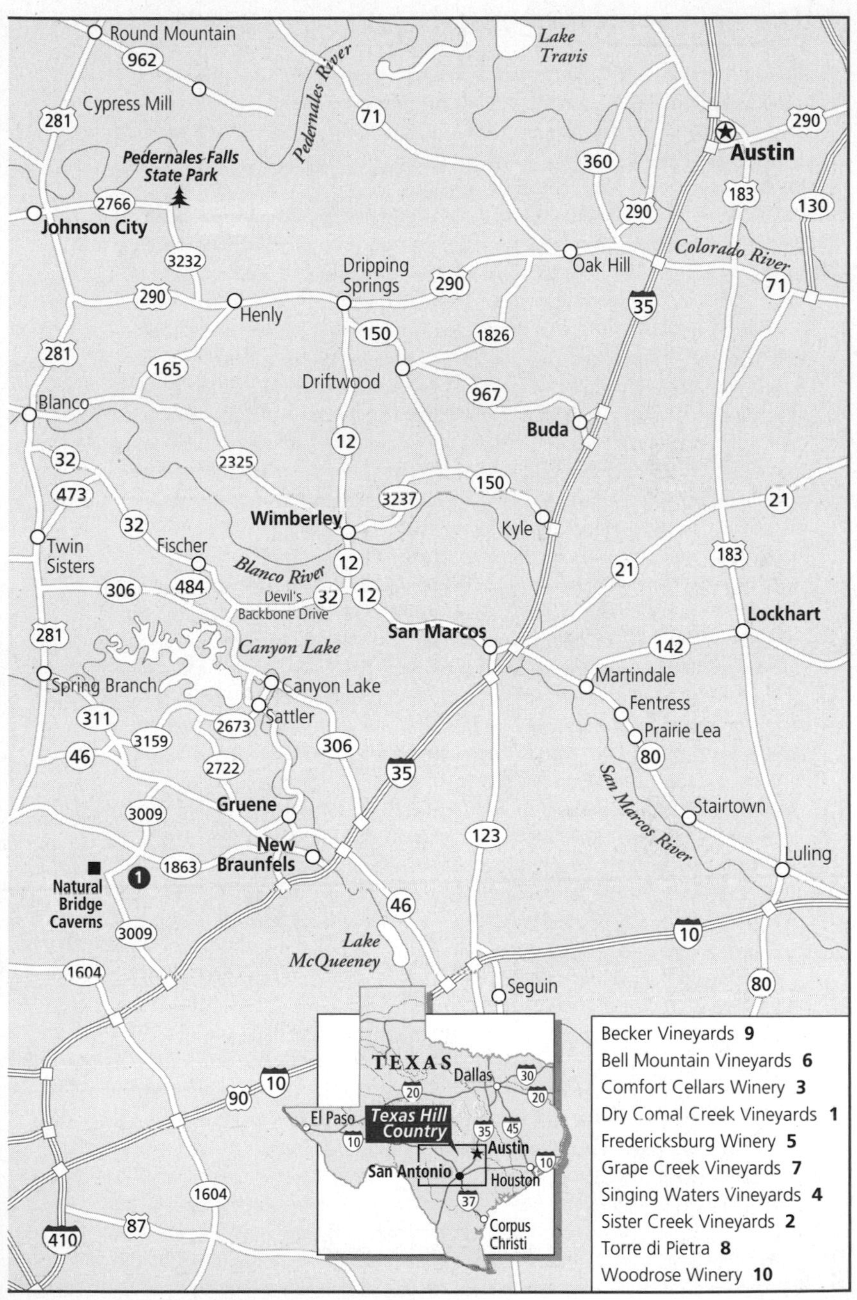
Round Mountain
Cypress Mill
Pedernales River
Lake Travis
Pedernales Falls State Park
Johnson City
Austin
Colorado River
Oak Hill
Dripping Springs
Henly
Driftwood
Blanco
Buda
Wimberley
Kyle
Twin Sisters
Fischer
Blanco River
Devil's Backbone Drive
San Marcos
Lockhart
Canyon Lake
Spring Branch
Canyon Lake
Sattler
Martindale
Fentress
Prairie Lea
San Marcos River
Stairtown
Gruene
New Braunfels
Luling
Natural Bridge Caverns
Lake McQueeney
Seguin
TEXAS
Dallas
El Paso
Texas Hill Country
Austin
San Antonio
Houston
Corpus Christi
Becker Vineyards 9
Bell Mountain Vineyards 6
Comfort Cellars Winery 3
Dry Comal Creek Vineyards 1
Fredericksburg Winery 5
Grape Creek Vineyards 7
Singing Waters Vineyards 4
Sister Creek Vineyards 2
Torre di Pietra 8
Woodrose Winery 10

The Hill Country Wine Trail

One of the most popular activities for visitors to the Hill Country is taking a wine-tasting tour. Though most people don't know it, Texas has an old connection to winemaking and grape growing. Domesticated grapes first came to Texas in the late 16th century when Franciscan Friars brought them from Mexico for cultivation at the Spanish missions.

Viticulture in Texas would surely have kept developing had it not been for Prohibition, which was disastrous in a way no plague could have been, because it destroyed the market for local growers. A few vineyards remained in business, selling their grapes to consumers, but all the others collapsed.

It wasn't until the 1970s that grape growing was able to reestablish itself. At first it grew in fits and starts, but then took off in the 1990s. In the Hill Country, it has taken the form of small wineries. These now number more than 30, with that number growing each year. These wineries can be visited at any time of year, but spring and fall are perhaps the best time. There are several wineries in and around Fredericksburg that are open to the public throughout the week, but the rest open their tasting rooms only on weekends. For more information about Hill Country Wineries, see www.texaswinetrail.com.

Between New Braunfels and Boerne, you will find:

- **Dry Comal Creek Vineyards** (✆ **830/855-4076;** www.drycomalcreek.com), at 1471 Herbelin Rd., is just off Hwy. 46 between New Braunfels and Bulverde. It's known for being one of the first wineries to highlight a local varietal called Black Spanish and make it the predominant grape in wines. This grape is a descendant of the cuttings brought from Mexico long ago by Franciscan friars. Available are red and white wines made with this grape and a wonderful port. Also of note is the bone-dry French Colombard.

Between Boerne and Fredericksburg:

- **Sister Creek Vineyards** (✆ **830/324-6704;** www.sistercreekvineyards.com), in Sisterdale, close to the intersection of RR 473 and FM 1376, is in a gloriously rough-hewn old cotton gin that dates from 1885. You can stroll through some of the fermentation rooms and see the large vats and oak barrels used in the production of the wine. The winery employs traditional French techniques but is as down-home as the building it occupies.
- **Comfort Cellars Winery** (✆ **830/995-3274;** www.comfortcellars.com), at 723 Front St., in the town of Comfort, has a full range of wines from dry to sweet, but the latter are what sells the most, including an intriguing orange Chardonnay and what the owner calls sweet rojo (red).
- **Singing Water Vineyards** (✆ **830/995-2246;** www.singingwatervineyards.com) is located 2 miles east of Comfort at 316 Mill Dam Rd. The winery is best known for its Sauvignon Blanc and a Merlot/Cabernet blend.

In the Fredericksburg area:

- **Fredericksburg Winery** (✆ **830/990-8747;** www.fbgwinery.com) is on Fredericksburg's Main Street. It's run by three brothers who are rebels in the winemaking business. Visitors will always find something out of the ordinary, and the wines available for tasting are always changing.

- **Bell Mountain Vineyards** (✆ **830/685-3297;** www.bellmountainwine.com) is located 14 miles north of Fredericksburg off Hwy. 16. The tasting room at the vineyard is open only on Saturday. A trip there can be combined with an outing to Enchanted Rock. But the vineyard has opened a tasting room on Fredericksburg's Main Street, above the Rathskeller Restaurant.
- **Grape Creek Vineyard** (✆ **820/644-2710;** www.grapecreek.com). Ten miles east of town on Hwy. 290, in the direction of Stonewall, are four beautiful vineyards loosely bunched together. Grape Creek is on a hilltop with a panoramic vista that you can enjoy from beneath a copse of old oak trees. Try the Cabs and the Fumé blanc.
- **Torre di Pietra** (✆ **830/744-2829;** www.texashillcountrywine.com) is another impressive winery with an inviting terrace. The Cab/Syrah/Sangiovese blends are what most people go for.
- **Becker Vineyards** (✆ **830/644-2681;** www.beckervineyards.com) in the spring offers a field of blooming lavender for the enjoyment of the visitor. The tasting room is within an old-style stone barn, and the old bar was taken from a saloon in San Antonio. This is probably the Hill Country's most famous vineyard. It grows classic French varietals with which it makes some skillfully produced Cabernet and Viognier, among many others.
- **Woodrose Winery** (✆ **830/644-2539;** www.woodrosewinery.com) has another beautiful outdoor setting for sampling the wines. The Cabernet Sauvignon is popular.

In the Northern Hill Country and Lakes:

- **Flat Creek Vineyards** (✆ **512/267-6310;** www.flatcreekestate.com) is on the north side of upper Lake Travis. From Austin take Hwy. 183 (avoid getting on the toll road) to Cedar Park and go west on RM 1431 for 14 miles, then left on Singleton Bend Road (there's a sign). This is one of the grandest of Hill Country vineyards, with a large tasting room offering wide vistas of rolling terrain. Only a few of the wines here use locally grown grapes. The Muscato is very popular.
- **Pillar Bluff Vineyards** (✆ **512/556-4078;** www.pillarbluff.com) is the treasure for those who stay on Hwy. 183 all the way to Lampasas (66 miles from Austin), and then take FM 1478 west, to these two small wineries owned by twin brothers Gill and Bill Bledsoe. Gill Bledsoe produces an interesting white Merlot, a full-flavored Cabernet, and a medium dry port, among other wines.
- **Texas Legato** (✆ **512/556-9600;** www.texaslegato.com), within sight of Pillar Bluff, this winery, owned by Bill Bledsoe, produces Merlot and Malbec wines.
- **Alamosa Wine Cellars** (✆ **325/628-3313;** www.alamosawinecellars.com) is 25 miles west of Lampasas, near the tiny town of Bend. The owners have been careful to select varietals that they believe have the best chance of producing outstanding wines when grown in Texas. Try the Tempranillo, which is bottled under the label "El Guapo," the Viognier, and a fruity Grenache.

WHERE TO DINE

The Limestone Grille, in Ye Kendall Inn (see above), 128 W. Blanco (© **830/249-9954**), sets an elegant tone for its eclectic Southwestern/American menu. It's open for lunch Monday through Saturday, dinner Tuesday to Saturday, brunch only Sunday; entrees are moderate to expensive. An adjoining wine bar made the scene in late 2004. The more casual **Bear Moon Bakery,** 401 S. Main St. (© **830/816-BEAR** [816-2327]), is ideal for a hearty breakfast or light lunch. Organic ingredients and locally grown produce enhance the flavor of the inventive soups, salads, sandwiches, and wonderful desserts. It's open Tuesday to Saturday 6am to 5pm, Sunday 8am to 4pm, and is inexpensively priced. At the **Dodging Duck Brewhaus** (© **830/248-DUCK** [248-3825]), at 402 River Rd., the food is mix and match—a variety of portion sizes and ethnic origins—and somewhat hit-and-miss, but you can't beat the views of Cibolo Creek from the front deck, and the beer, handcrafted on the premises, is top-notch. It's open daily for lunch and dinner. Prices are moderate.

2 BANDERA

Established as a lumber camp in 1853, this popular guest-ranch center still has the feel of the frontier. Not only are many of its historic buildings intact, but people are as genuinely friendly as any you might imagine from America's small-town past. True, the roads are getting more crowded each year, but once you hunker down, you're unlikely to need to do much driving around.

WHAT TO SEE & DO

Interested in delving into the town's roots? Pick up a self-guided tour brochure of historic sites—including **St. Stanislaus** (1855), the country's second-oldest Polish parish—at the **Bandera County Convention and Visitors Bureau,** 1206 Hackberry St., Bandera, TX 78003 (© **800/364-3833** or 830/796-3045; www.banderacowboycapital.com), open weekdays 9am to 5pm, Saturday 9am to 2pm. Or explore the town's living traditions by strolling along Main Street, where a variety of crafters work in the careful, hand-hewn style of yesteryear. Shops include **Kline Saddlery** (© **830/522-0335**), featuring belts, purses, briefcases, and flask covers as well as horse wear; the **Stampede** (© **830/796-7650**), a good spot for Western collectibles; and the huge **Love's Antique Mall** (© **830/796-3838**), a one-stop shopping center for current local crafts as well as things retro. Off the main drag, buy beautiful customized belt buckles, spurs, and jewelry at **Hy O Silver,** 715 13th St. (© **830/796-7961**). Naturally, plenty of places in town, such as **The Cowboy Store,** 302 Main St. (© **830/796-8176**), can outfit you in Western duds.

If you want to break those clothes in, the Convention and Visitors Bureau can direct you to the outfitter who can match you with the perfect mount; most of the guest ranches (see "Staying at a Guest Ranch," below) offer rides for day-trippers. Check the CVB, too, to find out if any rodeos or roping exhibitions are in the area. (They occur often in summer and less regularly in fall.)

The Great Outdoors

You don't have to go farther than **Bandera Park** (© **830/796-3765**), a 77-acre green space within the city limits, to enjoy nature, whether you want to stroll along the River

A Taste of Alsace in Texas

Just 20 miles west of San Antonio (via U.S. 90 W.), Castroville has become something of a bedroom community for San Antonio, but the center of town retains its heritage as an old Alsatian community. Henri Castro, a Portuguese-born Jewish Frenchman, received a 1.25-million-acre land grant from the Republic of Texas in exchange for his commitment to colonize the land. He founded it on a scenic bend of the Medina River in 1842. Second only to Stephen F. Austin in the number of settlers he brought over, Castro recruited most of his 2,134 immigrants from the Rhine Valley, especially from the French province of Alsace. A few of the oldest citizens still can speak Alsatian, a dialect of German, though the language is likely to die out in the area when they do.

Get some insight into the town's history at the **Landmark Inn State Historic Site,** 402 E. Florence St., Castroville, TX 78009 (✆ **830/931-2133;** www.tpwd.state.tx.us/park/landmark), which also counts a nature trail, an old gristmill, and a stone dam among its attractions. The park's centerpiece, the **Landmark Inn,** offers eight simple rooms decorated with early Texas pieces dating up until the 1940s.

For a delicious taste of the past, visit **Haby's Alsatian Bakery,** 207 U.S. 90 E. (✆ **830/931-2118**), owned by the Tschirhart family since 1974 and featuring apple fritters, strudels, stollens, breads, and coffeecakes. Open Monday to Saturday 5am to 7pm.

For additional information, contact the **Castroville Chamber of Commerce,** 802 London St., P.O. Box 572, Castroville, TX 78009 (✆ **800/778-6775** or 830/538-3142; www.castroville.com), where you can pick up a walking-tour booklet of the town's historical buildings, as well as a map that details the local boutiques and antiques shops (they're not concentrated in a single area). It's open 9am to noon and 1 to 3pm Monday through Friday.

Note: Downtown Castroville tends to close down on Monday and Tuesday, and some places are shuttered on Wednesday and Sunday as well. If you want to find everything open, come on Thursday, Friday, or Saturday.

Bend Native Plant Trail or picnic by the Medina River. Or you can canter through the **Hill Country State Natural Area,** 10 miles southwest of Bandera (✆ **830/796-4413;** www.tpwd.state.tx.us/park/hillcoun), the largest state park in Texas allowing horseback riding. It has about 40 miles of trails for the use of riders, hikers, and mountain bikers. A few adjacent ranches can provide mounts. You should inquire at the Bandera Visitors Bureau. Be sure to take water along because none is available at the park. Primitive camping sites are available.

A visit to the nonprofit **Brighter Days Horse Refuge,** 682 Krause Rd., Pipe Creek, about 9 miles northeast of Bandera (✆ **830/510-6607;** www.brighterdayshorserefuge.org), will warm any animal lover's heart. The price of admission to this rehabilitation center for abandoned and neglected horses is a bag of carrots or apples; donations are also very welcome.

About 20 miles southeast of town (take Hwy. 16 to R.R. 1283), **Bandera County Park at Medina Lake** (✆ **800/364-3833;** www.wildtexas.com/parks/medinalk.php) is the place to hook crappie, white or black bass, and especially huge yellow catfish; the public boat ramp is on the north side of the lake, at the end of P.R. 37. Outfitters for those who want to kayak, canoe, or tube the Medina River include **Bandera Beach Club Kayak & Tube Rental** (1106 Cherry St.; ✆ **830/796-7555**) and **Bandera Kayak & Tube** (1006 Main St.; ✆ **830/796-3861**), in the True Value Hardware store.

Lost Maples State Natural Area, about 40 miles west of Bandera, near Vanderpool (✆ **830/966-3413;** www.tpwd.state.tx.us/park/lostmap), is a popular destination in autumn, when the leaves put on a brilliant show. But birders come in winter to look at bald eagles, hikers like the wildflower array in spring, and anglers try to reduce the Guadalupe bass population of the Sabinal River in summer.

STAYING AT A GUEST RANCH

Accommodations in this area range from rustic cabins to upscale B&Bs, but for the full flavor of the region, plan to stay at one of Bandera's many guest ranches (you'll find a full listing of them, as well as of other lodgings, on the Bandera website). Note that most of them have a 2-night (or more) minimum stay. You wouldn't want to spend less time at a dude ranch, anyway; it'll take at least half a day to start to unwind. Expect to encounter lots of European visitors. These places are great for cultural exchange, and you'll learn about all the best beers in Texas—and Germany.

Rates at each of the following are based on double occupancy and include three meals, two trail rides, and most other activities.

At the **Dixie Dude Ranch,** P.O. Box 548, Bandera, TX 78003 (✆ **800/375-YALL** [375-9255] or 830/796-7771; www.dixieduderanch.com), a longtime favorite retreat, you're likely to see white-tailed deer or wild turkeys as you trot on horseback through a 725-acre spread. The down-home, friendly atmosphere keeps folks coming back year after year. Rates are $135 per adult per night.

Tubing on the Medina River and soaking in a hot tub are among the many activities at the **Mayan Ranch,** P.O. Box 577, Bandera, TX 78003 (✆ **830/796-3312** or 460-3036; www.mayanranch.com), another well-established family-run place ($150 per adult); corporate groups often come for a bit of loosening up. The ranch provides plenty of additional Western fun for its guests during high season—things like two-step lessons, cookouts, hayrides, singing cowboys, or trick-roping exhibitions.

The owner of **Silver Spur Guest Ranch,** 9266 Bandera Creek Rd., Bandera, TX 78003 (✆ **830/796-3037** or 460-3639; www.ssranch.com), used to be a bull rider, so the equestrian expertise of the staff is especially high ($130 per adult). So is the comfort level. The rooms in the main ranch house and the separate cabins are individually decorated, with styles ranging from Victorian pretty to country rustic. The ranch, which abuts the Hill Country State Natural Area, also boasts the region's largest swimming pool, some roaming buffalo, and a great kids' play area.

WHERE TO DINE

Those not chowing down at a guest ranch might want to put on the feed bag on Main Street's **O.S.T.** (✆ **830/796-3836**), named for the Old Spanish Trail that used to run through Bandera. Serving up down-home Texas and Tex-Mex victuals since 1921, this cafe has a room dedicated to The Duke and other cowboy film stars. It's open daily for breakfast, lunch, and dinner; entrees are inexpensive to moderate.

Brick's River Cafe, 1105 Main St. (✆ **830/460-3200**), lays on huge platters of down-home country standards such as chicken-fried steak or fried catfish for seriously hungry diners. Less health-defying dishes such as green salads and plenty of vegetable side dishes are available here, too. An open deck and huge windows afford excellent Medina River vistas. It's open daily for lunch and dinner; meals are moderately priced.

It's not easy to find a seat inside **Mac and Ernie's,** a quirky, semigourmet eatery in a shack some 12 miles west of Bandera in Tarpley (✆ **830/562-3250**). But that's okay, because the picnic tables out back are the perfect setting for the outstanding steaks, catfish, and specials such as quail in ancho honey, served on paper plates with plastic utensils. Hours are very limited (lunch Wed, lunch and dinner Fri–Sat), and prices are moderate.

SOME LOCAL HONKY-TONKS

Don't miss **Arkey Blue & The Silver Dollar Bar** ★★ (✆ **830/796-8826**), a genuine spit-and-sawdust cowboy honky-tonk on Main Street usually called Arkey's. When there's no live music, plug a quarter in the old jukebox and play a country ballad by the owner. And look for the table where Hank Williams, Sr., carved his name.

No one who tends toward the P.C. should enter the tiny **11th Street Cowboy Bar,** 307 11th St. (✆ **830/796-4849**), what with all the bras hanging off the rafters. But you can always retreat to the spacious deck out back, and listen to Cajun and country bands.

At the **Bandera Saloon,** 401 Main St. (✆ **830/796-3699**), the deck is out front and overlooks the town's main drag, but the boot scootin' to live rockabilly and country music takes place inside the large barnlike structure.

EN ROUTE TO KERRVILLE

Each of the roads from Bandera to Kerrville has its distinct allure. The longer Hwy. 16 route—37 miles compared to 26—is one of the most gorgeous in the region, its scenic switchbacks snaking through new-growth forest, river-bottom lands, and rolling ranch land. The road is curvy but not precipitous, and you're at river level most of the time. Go this way and you'll also pass through Medina. You won't doubt the little town's self-proclaimed status as Apple Capital of Texas when you come to **Love Creek Orchards Cider Mill and Country Store** (✆ **800/449-0882** or 830/589-2588; www.lovecreekorchards.com) on the main street. Along with apple pies and other fresh-baked goods, you can buy apple cider, apple syrup, apple butter, apple jam, and apple ice cream—you can even have an apple sapling shipped back home. Not feeling fruity? The restaurant out back serves some of the best burgers in the area.

Military buffs and souvenir seekers might want to take the more direct but also scenic Hwy. 173, which passes through **Camp Verde,** the former headquarters (1856–69) of the short-lived U.S. Army camel cavalry. Widespread ignorance of the animals' habits and the onset of the Civil War led to the abandonment of the attempt to introduce "ships of the desert" into dry Southwest terrain, but the commander of the post had great respect for his humpbacked recruits. There's little left of the fortress itself, but you can tour the **1877 General Store and Post Office** (✆ **830/634-7722**), purveying camel memorabilia and artifacts as well as country-cute contemporary crafts. The store also sells fixings for picnics at the pleasant roadside park nearby.

3 KERRVILLE

With a population of close to 25,000, Kerrville is larger than the other Hill Country towns described here. It's a popular retirement and tourist area without either the cowboy aura of Bandera or the quaintness of Fredericksburg. Most of the available activities center around the upper Guadalupe River, parts of which are very scenic and lined with large cypress trees. The town was founded in the 1840s by Joshua Brown, from Gonzales, Texas, who was attracted to the region by these cypress trees, which he hoped to mill into roof shingles. (Before the arrival of industry, all Central Texas rivers were lined by cypress trees. The wood was in high demand because it resists rot.) Brown was a friend of Maj. James Kerr, who first established Gonzales, and was one of the founding fathers of Texas independence. (He died in 1850 and never actually saw the town and county named after him.) A rough-and-tumble camp, which contrasted with the more civilized German settlements, Kerrville soon became a ranching center for longhorn cattle and, more unusually, for Angora goats, eventually turning out the most mohair in the United States. After it was lauded in the 1920s for its healthful climate, Kerrville began to draw youth camps, sanitariums, and artists. The area surrounding the town has, in the last 20 years, seen a construction boom of weekend houses for people living as far away as Houston or Dallas. Kerrville has not been able to keep up with the increase in traffic created by these visitors, so traffic jams sometimes occur. Try to plan your trip such that you arrive in Kerrville during the week.

WHAT TO SEE & DO

It's a good idea to make your first stop the **Kerrville Convention and Visitors Bureau,** 2108 Sidney Baker, Kerrville, TX 78028 (© **800/221-7958** or 830/792-3535; www.kerrvilletexascvb.com), where you can get a map of the area as well as of the historic downtown district. Open weekdays 8:30am to 5pm, Saturday 9am to 3pm, Sunday 10am to 3pm.

Tip: If you're planning to come to Kerrville around Memorial Day weekend, when the huge, 18-day **Kerrville Folk Festival** kicks off and the **Official Texas State Arts and Crafts Fair** is held, book far in advance.

For your second stop, head to the restored downtown, flanked by the Guadalupe River and a pleasant park. Its historic buildings, most of them concentrated on Earl Garrett and Water streets, host a variety of restaurants and shops, many selling antiques and/or country cutesy knickknacks. Among the most impressive structures is the mansion built of native stone by Alfred Giles for pioneer rancher and banker Capt. Charles Schreiner. It's now home to the **Hill Country Museum,** 226 Earl Garrett St. (© **830/896-8633**), open Monday to Saturday 11:30am to 3:30pm; admission is $5 adults, $2 students. Highlights include a collection of antique ball gowns. Those interested in updating their own wardrobe of party clothes might consider visiting **Schreiner's,** 736 Water St. (© **830/896-1212**), established in 1869 and continuously operating since then as a general merchandise store. The 1935 post office now hosts the **Kerr Arts & Cultural Center,** 228 Earl Garrett St. (© **830/895-2911;** www.kacckerrville.com), where local artists and artisans strut—and sell—their stuff.

You'll need to drive about 3½ miles north of town to visit the headquarters of **James Avery Craftsman,** Harper Road (© **830/895-1122**), where you can watch artisans work on silver and gold jewelry designs, many of which incorporate Christian symbols. Naturally, there's an adjoining retail shop.

Old England Finds the Old West

Several attractions, some endearingly offbeat, plus beautiful vistas along the Guadalupe River, warrant a detour west of Kerrville. Drive 5 miles from the center of town on Hwy. 27 W. to reach tiny **Ingram.** Take Hwy. 39 W. to the second traffic light downtown. After about a quarter mile, you'll see a sign for the Historic Old Ingram Loop, once a cowboy cattle driving route and now home to rows of **antiques shops, crafts boutiques,** and **art galleries** and **studios.** Back on Hwy. 39, continue another few blocks to the **Hill Country Arts Foundation** (✆ **800/459-4223** or 830/367-5121; www.hcaf.com), a complex comprising two theaters, an art gallery, and studios where arts-and-crafts classes are held. Every summer since 1948, a series of musicals has been offered on the outdoor stage. Continue 7 miles west on Hwy. 39 to the junction of FM 1340, where you'll find **Hunt,** which pretty much consists of a combination general store, bar, and restaurant that would look right at home in any Western. Now head west on FM 1340 for about a quarter mile. ***Surprise:*** There's a replica of **Stonehenge** sitting out in the middle of a field. It's not as large as the original, but this being Texas, it's not exactly diminutive, either. A couple of reproduction Easter Island heads fill out the ancient mystery sculpture group commissioned by Al Shepherd, a wealthy eccentric who died in the mid-1990s.

Whether or not you think you like Western art, the **Museum of Western Art** (formerly the Cowboy Artists of America Museum), 1550 Bandera Hwy. (✆ **830/896-2553;** www.museumofwesternart.org), is not to be missed. Lying just outside the main part of town, the high-quality collection is housed in a striking Southwestern structure. Open Monday to Saturday 9am to 5pm, Sunday 1 to 5pm from Memorial Day through Labor Day; closed Monday the rest of the year; $7 adults, $6 seniors, $5 children ages 9 to 17, free for 8 and under. Outdoor enthusiasts will enjoy the nearby **Kerrville-Schreiner Park,** 2385 Bandera Hwy. (✆ **830/257-5392;** www.kerrville.org/index.asp?NID=318), a 500-acre green space boasting 7 miles of hiking trails, as well as swimming and boating on the Guadalupe River. Camp sites and small cabins are available for guests. Call the number for more information or to make reservations.

A NEARBY RANCH

You'll need a reservation to visit the **Y.O. Ranch,** 32 miles from Kerrville, off Hwy. 41, Mt. Home, TX 78058 (✆ **800/YO-RANCH** [967-2624] or 830/640-3222; www.yoranch.com). Originally comprising 550,000 acres purchased by Charles Schreiner in 1880, the Y.O. Ranch is now a 40,000-acre working ranch known for its exotic wildlife (1½- to 2-hr. tours cost $33 per person) and Texas longhorn cattle. A variety of overnight accommodations are available, too, but you should know that this ranch isn't the same as a guest ranch. Many of the activities here revolve around hunting, and there are fewer of the activities normally associated with guest ranches.

WHERE TO STAY

The **Y.O. Ranch Resort Hotel and Conference Center,** 2033 Sidney Baker, Kerrville, TX 78028 (✆ **877/YO-RESORT** [967-3767] or 830/257-4440; www.yoresort.com)—not near the Y.O. Ranch (see above), but in Kerrville itself—offers large and attractive Western-style quarters. Its Branding Iron dining room features big steaks as well as continental fare, and the gift shop has a terrific selection of creative Western-theme goods. Double rooms range from $79 to $119, depending on the season.

Inn of the Hills Resort, 1001 Junction Hwy., Kerrville, TX 78028 (✆ **800/292-5690** or 830/895-5000; www.innofthehills.com), looks like a motel from the outside, but it has the best facilities in town, including tennis courts, three swimming pools, a putting green, two restaurants, a popular pub, and free access to the excellent health club next door. Rates for double rooms range seasonally from $100 to $135.

The **Sunset Inn and Studio,** 124 Oehler Road St. (off FM 479), Mountain Home, TX 78058 (✆ **877/739-1214** or 830/866-3336; www.sunsetinn-studio.com), offers two rooms for guests with full breakfasts. The inn and artist studio are a mile off Hwy. I-10, 3 miles east of "downtown" Mountain Home and 14 miles from Kerrville. This is a great place to relax. The property has longhorn cattle and miniature donkeys that the guests can feed and pet. At dusk, the owners offer a retreat time to sit out and enjoy the evening with some refreshments. Dinner can be had if you reserve ahead of time. Room rates are $130.

WHERE TO DINE

The setting—a beautifully restored 1915 depot with a lovely patio out back—is not the only thing outstanding about **Rails,** 615 Schreiner (✆ **830/257-3877**), which serves some of the best food in the Hill Country. Everything, from the creative salads and Italian panini sandwiches to a small selection of hearty entrees, is made with the freshest ingredients, many produced locally. The restaurant is open for lunch and dinner Monday through Saturday, and prices are moderate. In warm weather, there's live classic jazz on the patio from Thursday to Saturday.

The name is Italian, but the menu is eclectic, with lots of nods toward Mexico, at **Francisco's,** 201 Earl Garrett St. (✆ **830/257-2995**), housed in the 1890s Weston building. A downtown business crowd samples soup and salad combos at lunchtime; many return on weekend evenings for such mix-it-up entrees as cilantro lime shrimp or teriyaki chipotle chicken. Francisco's is open for lunch Monday through Saturday, dinner Thursday through Saturday. Prices range from moderate to expensive.

TAKING TIME OUT FOR COMFORT

The direct route from Kerrville to Fredericksburg (25 miles) is Hwy. 16 N., but if you're not in a hurry, you could take a detour of 18 miles by taking Hwy. 27 east to Comfort, a small German town. It has been said that the freethinking German immigrants who founded the town in 1852 were originally going to call it Gemütlichkeit—a more difficult-to-pronounce native version of its current name—when they arrived at this welcoming spot after an arduous journey from New Braunfels. The story is apocryphal, but it's an appealing explanation of the name, especially as no one is quite sure what the truth is.

The rough-hewn limestone buildings in the center of Comfort may contain the most complete 19th-century business district in Texas. Architect Alfred Giles, who also left his distinctive mark on San Antonio's streets, designed some of the offices. These days, most

Bats & Ostriches Along a Back Road to Fredericksburg

If you missed the bats in Austin, you've got a second chance to see some in an abandoned railroad tunnel supervised by the Texas Parks and Wildlife Department. From Comfort, take Hwy. 473 N. for 5 miles. When the road winds to the right toward Sisterdale, keep going straight on Old Hwy. 9. After another 8 or 9 miles, you'll spot a parking lot and a mound of large rocks on top of a hill. During migration season (May–Oct), you can watch as many as 3 million Mexican free-tailed bats set off on a food foray around dusk. There's no charge to witness the phenomenon from the Upper Viewing Area, near the parking lot; it's open daily. If you want a closer view and an educational presentation lasting about 30 minutes to an hour, come to the Lower Viewing Area, open from Thursday through Sunday ($5 adults, $3 seniors, $2 children 6–16). There are 60 seats, filled on a first-come, first-served basis. Contact the **Old Tunnel Wildlife Management Area** (✆ **830/990-2659;** www.tpwd.state.tx.us/wma/find_a_wma/list/?id=17) to find out when its occupants are likely to flee the bat cave, as well as other information.

Even if you don't stop for the bats, this is a wonderfully scenic route to Fredericksburg. You won't see any road signs, but have faith—this really will take you to town, eventually. You're likely to spot grazing goats and cows and even some strutting ostriches.

of these structures, and especially those on High Street, host high-quality (and high-priced) antiques shops. More than 30 dealers gather at the **Comfort Antique Mall,** 734 High St. (✆ **830/995-4678**). The nearby complex of antiques shops known as **Comfort Common,** 717 High St. (✆ **830/995-3030**), also doubles as a bed-and-breakfast. If you're in town Thursday to Sunday from 11am to 3:30pm, combine shopping and noshing at **Arlene's Café and Gift Shop,** 426 Seventh St., just off High Street (✆ **830/995-3330**). The tasty soups, sandwiches, and desserts are freshly made on the premises.

The **Comfort Chamber of Commerce,** on Seventh and High streets (✆ **830/995-3131**), has very limited hours, but who knows—you might be lucky enough to arrive when it's open. Alternatively, try the **Ingenhuett Store,** 830–834 High St. (✆ **830/995-2149**), owned and operated by the same German-American family since 1867. Along with groceries, outdoor gear, and sundries, the store carries maps and other sources of tourist information.

4 FREDERICKSBURG

Fredericksburg is a town of 10,000 inhabitants located just about 75 miles from either San Antonio or Austin. (All the towns mentioned until now are closer to San Antonio.) Fredericksburg is a town noted for its picturesque main street—old-time storefronts with sidewalk canopies, in the tradition of small-town Texas. It's also known for its German heritage, serving as the center of a large German farming community in the past. These days, the farmers are known for the peaches they grow (available at orchards and roadside stands May–July), and more recently, their vineyards. Fredericksburg is the hub of the Hill Country wineries. See the Wine Trail sidebar, earlier in this chapter.

The town serves as a weekend escape for city dwellers in San Antonio and Austin. It has lots of bed-and-breakfasts and guest houses, as well as hotels and motels. Many visitors come for the shopping and to relax, and perhaps taste some wine. Others come to explore the surrounding countryside, including nearby Enchanted Rock, the Hill Country's most famous geological feature.

Though Fredericksburg has become fairly touristy, it also remains devoted to its European past. Baron Ottfried Hans von Meusebach was 1 of 10 nobles who formed a society designed to help Germans resettle in Texas, where they would be safe from political persecution and economic hardship. In 1846, he took 120 settlers in ox-drawn carts from the relative safety of New Braunfels to this site in the wild lands of the frontier. He named the settlement for Prince Frederick of Prussia. Meusebach negotiated a peace treaty with the Comanche in 1847, claiming to be the only one in the United States that was so honored. The settlement prospered during the California Gold Rush, as it was the last place travelers could get supplies on the southern route, until the town of Santa Fe, New Mexico. Fredericksburg is the seat of Gillespie County.

WHAT TO SEE & DO

In Town

For a virtual preview, go to **www.fredericksburg-texas.com**. Once you're in town, the **Visitor Information Center,** 302 E. Austin St., Fredericksburg, TX 78624 (✆ **888/997-3600** or 830/997-6523), can direct you to the many points of interest in the town's historic district. It's open weekdays 8:30am to 5pm, Saturday 9am to noon and 1 to 5pm, Sunday noon to 4pm.

While walking around town, you're likely to see some very small frame houses (usually having only two rooms). Called **Sunday Houses,** they were built by German farmers in the 19th century, whose farms were too far from Fredericksburg to allow them to live in town. These simple dwellings were meant to be a humble *pied-à-terre* for use on market days, Sundays, and holidays. You'll also notice many homes built in the Hill Country version of the German *fachwerk* design, made out of limestone with diagonal wood supports.

On the town's main square, called Market Square, is an unusual octagonal **Vereins Kirche (Society Church).** It's actually a replica (built in 1935) of the original 1847 building. The original was the first public building in Fredericksburg. It was built to be a church where both Lutheran and Catholic Germans could hold services, and as such, was a symbol of unity for the early pioneers. It originally stood on Main Street until the 1890s, when it had decayed to the point where it had to be torn down. The replica shows how primitive the original construction had been. Inside is a historical exhibit of the town, which can be viewed in a half hour. It's open 10am to 4pm Monday to Saturday, 1 to 4pm Sunday. The Vereins Kirche is operated by the Historical Society, which also maintains the **Pioneer Museum Complex,** 309 W. Main St. Admission to either museum is valid for the other. The cost is $5 for adults, $3 for students 6 to 17 years old, and free for younger children. The Pioneer Museum consists of the 1849 Kammlah House (which was a family residence and general store until the 1920s), as well as the barn and the smokehouse. Later, other historical structures were moved onto the site.

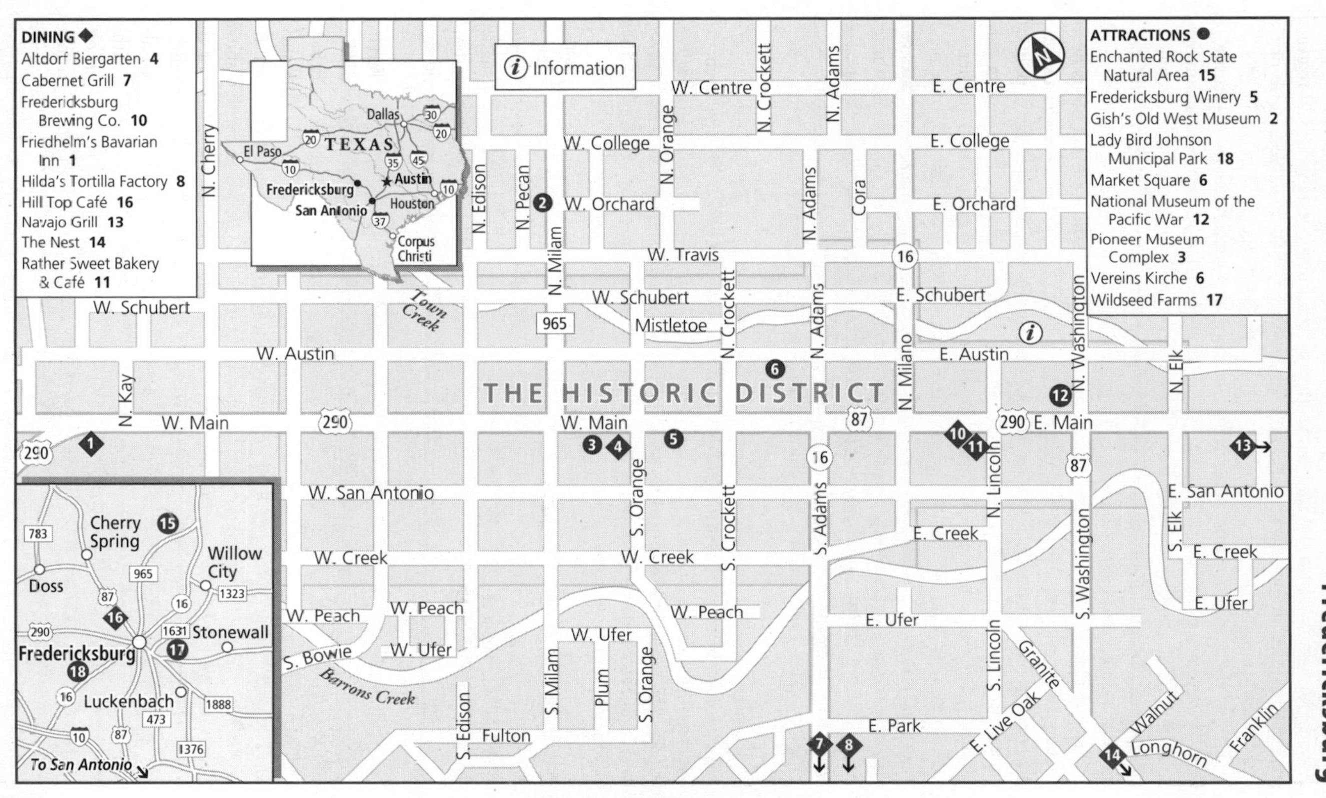

DINING ◆
Altdorf Biergarten 4
Cabernet Grill 7
Fredericksburg Brewing Co. 10
Friedhelm's Bavarian Inn 1
Hilda's Tortilla Factory 8
Hill Top Café 16
Navajo Grill 13
The Nest 14
Rather Sweet Bakery & Café 11
ATTRACTIONS ●
Enchanted Rock State Natural Area 15
Fredericksburg Winery 5
Gish's Old West Museum 2
Lady Bird Johnson Municipal Park 18
Market Square 6
National Museum of the Pacific War 12
Pioneer Museum Complex 3
Vereins Kirche 6
Wildseed Farms 17
Information
THE HISTORIC DISTRICT
Town Creek
Barrons Creek
TEXAS
Dallas
Austin
Houston
San Antonio
Corpus Christi
El Paso
Fredericksburg
Cherry Spring
Willow City
Stonewall
Doss
Luckenbach
To San Antonio
W. Centre
E. Centre
W. College
E. College
W. Orchard
E. Orchard
W. Travis
W. Schubert
E. Schubert
Mistletoe
W. Austin
E. Austin
W. Main
E. Main
W. San Antonio
E. San Antonio
W. Creek
E. Creek
W. Peach
W. Ufer
E. Ufer
E. Park
S. Bowie
Fulton
Granite
E. Live Oak
Walnut
Longhorn
Franklin
Cora
N. Cherry
N. Kay
N. Edison
N. Pecan
N. Milam
N. Orange
N. Crockett
N. Adams
N. Milano
N. Lincoln
N. Washington
N. Elk
S. Edison
S. Milam
Plum
S. Orange
S. Crockett
S. Adams
S. Lincoln
S. Washington
S. Elk

These include a one-room schoolhouse and a blacksmith's forge. The complex is open Monday to Saturday 10am to 5pm, Sunday 1 to 5pm. For information on both places and on the other historical structures in town, phone ✆ **830/997-2835** or log on to www.pioneermuseum.com.

The 1852 Steamboat Hotel, originally owned by the grandfather of World War II naval hero Chester A. Nimitz, is now part of the **National Museum of the Pacific War ★★**, 311 E. Austin St. (✆ **830/997-4379;** www.nimitz-museum.org), a 9-acre Texas State Historical Park and the world's only museum focusing solely on the Pacific theater. It just keeps expanding and getting better. In addition to the exhibits in the steamboat-shaped hotel devoted to Nimitz and his comrades, there are also the Japanese Garden of Peace, a gift from the people of Japan; the Memorial Wall, the equivalent of the Vietnam wall for Pacific War veterans; the life-size Pacific Combat Zone (2$^1/_2$ blocks east of the museum), which replicates a World War II battle scene; and the George Bush Gallery, where you can see a captured Japanese midget submarine and a multimedia simulation of a bombing raid on Guadalcanal. The Center for Pacific War Studies, a major research facility, is slated to open by the end of the decade as part of an expansion that will double the exhibition area of the George Bush Gallery. Until then, limited access to the library archives can be arranged by special request. Indoor exhibits are open daily from 9am to 5pm but are closed Thanksgiving and Christmas. Adult admission is $7; seniors, military, and veterans $6; students pay $4; and children younger than 6 enter free.

If you're interested in saddles, chaps, spurs, sheriffs' badges, and other cowboy-bilia, visit **Gish's Old West Museum,** 502 N. Milam St. (✆ **830/997-2794**). A successful illustrator for Sears & Roebuck, Joe Gish started buying Western props to help him with his art. After more than 40 years of trading and buying with the best, he has gathered a very impressive collection. Joe opens the museum when he's around (he generally is), but if you don't want to take a chance, phone ahead to make an appointment.

Nearby

One of the many attractions in the Fredericksburg vicinity is **Lady Bird Johnson Municipal Park,** 2 miles southwest of town off Hwy. 16 (✆ **830/997-4202;** www.fbgtx.org/departments/ladybirdpark.htm). It features an 18-hole golf course; a baseball field; basketball, volleyball, and tennis courts; an Olympic-size swimming pool (open summer only); a lake for fishing; and a wilderness trail.

A visit to the **Wildseed Farms ★**, 7 miles east on Hwy. 290 (✆ **830/990-1393;** www.wildseedfarms.com), will disabuse you of any naive notions you may have had that wildflowers grew wild. At this working wildflower farm, from April through July, beautiful fields of blossoms are harvested for seeds that are sold throughout the world. During the growing season, for $5 you can grab a bucket and pick bluebonnets, poppies, or whatever's blooming when you visit. There are a gift shop and the Brew-Bonnet beer garden, which sells light snacks. Entry to the grounds, open 9:30am to 6pm daily, is free, but you'll have to pay ($4 adults, $3.50 seniors and ages 4–12) to visit the latest addition, the Butterfly Haus, featuring pretty flitters native to Texas.

North of town is **Enchanted Rock State Natural Area ★★** (✆ **325/247-3903;** www.tpwd.state.tx.us/park/enchantd), a 640-acre site with a dome of solid pink granite that was pushed up to the surface by volcanic uplifting. Take FM 965 north for 18 miles. You'll know when you get there. It's a stark sight that shares nothing in common with the surrounding hills. The dome is almost 600 feet high. To hike up and down on the trail takes about an hour. The creaking noises that emanate from it at night—likely caused by the cooling of the rock's outer surface—led the area's Native American tribes to believe that evil spirits inhabited the rock. Though the park is fairly large, the parking lot is not, and as soon as it fills, no more visitors are admitted. On weekends, if you get there by 10am, you shouldn't have a problem. The park is open daily 8am to 10pm; day-use entrance fees are $6 adults and free for children 12 and under.

Shopping

In town, there are more than 100 specialty shops, many of them in mid-19th-century houses, which feature work by Hill Country artisans. You'll find candles, lace coverlets, cuckoo clocks, hand-woven rugs, even dulcimers. At **Homestead,** 230 E. Main St. (✆ **830/997-5551;** www.homesteadstores.com), a fashionable, three-story home furnishings emporium, European rural retro (chain-distressed wrought-iron beds from France, for example) meets contemporary natural fabrics. Pooch people will go barking mad over **Dogologie,** 148b W. Main St. (✆ **830/997-5855;** www.dogologie.com), carrying everything the fashionable canine might need. For something less effete, check out **Texas Jack's,** 117 N. Adams St. (✆ **830/997-3213;** www.texasjacks.com), which has outfitted actors for Western films and TV shows, including *Lonesome Dove, Tombstone,* and *Gunsmoke.* This is the place to stock up on red long johns. **Chocolat,** 330 W. Main St. (✆ **800/842-3382** or 830/990-9382; www.chocolat-tx.us), is like no other chocolate shop you've visited. The owner, Lecia Duke, is an architect by training but later found out that she got more satisfaction working with chocolate. She has mastered an Old World technique for encasing any alcohol in chocolate by manipulating the sugar in the liquor to form a thin cocoon around the liquid. This method is practiced nowhere else in the U.S. and by only a handful of small chocolate makers in Europe. In her store you'll find a wide variety of chocolates, with and without spirits.

Becoming increasingly well-known via its mail-order business is the **Fredericksburg Herb Farm,** 405 Whitney St. (✆ **800/259-HERB** [259-4372] or 830/997-8615; www.fredericksburgherbfarm.com), just a bit south of town. You can visit the flower beds that produce salad dressings, teas, fragrances, and air fresheners (including lavender, one of the area's major crops these days), and then sample some of them in the on-site restaurant (lunch only; moderate), B&B, and day spa.

WHERE TO STAY

Fredericksburg is well known for having more than 300 bed-and-breakfasts and *gastehauses* (guest cottages). If you choose one of the latter, you can spend the night in anything from an 1865 homestead with its own wishing well to a bedroom above an old bakery or a limestone Sunday House. Most *gastehauses* are romantic havens complete with robes, fireplaces, and even spas. And, unlike the typical B&B, these places ensure privacy because either breakfast is provided the night before—the perishables are left in a refrigerator—or guests are given coupons to enjoy breakfast at a local restaurant. *Gastehauses* run anywhere from $120 to $200. Most visitors reserve lodgings through one of the main booking services: **First Class Bed & Breakfast Reservation Service,** 909 E. Main (✆ **888/991-6749** or 830/997-0443; www.fredericksburg-lodging.com); **Gästehaus Schmidt,** 231 W. Main St. (✆ **866/427-8374** or 830/997-5612; www.fbglodging.com); **Absolute Charm,** 709 W. Main St. (✆ **866/244-7897** or 830/997-2749; www.absolutecharm.com); and **Main Street B&B Reservation Service,** 337 E. Main (✆ **888/559-8555** or 830/997-0153; www.travelmainstreet.com). Specializing in the more familiar type of B&B is **Fredericksburg Traditional Bed & Breakfast Inns** (✆ **800/494-4678;** www.fredericksburgtrad.com). For something less traditional, consider the

Roadrunner Inn (✆ **830/997-1844;** www.theroadrunnerinn.com), a modern B&B at 306 E. Main St., above a boutique. It has very large, uncluttered rooms furnished with a mix of mod and industrial. Rates start at $150.

If you would rather stay in a hotel, the **Hangar Hotel,** 155 Airport Rd., Fredericksburg, TX 78624 (✆ **830/997-9990;** www.hangarhotel.com), has large, comfortable rooms. It banks on nostalgia for the World War II flyboy era. Located at the town's tiny private airport, as its name suggests, this hotel hearkens back to the 1940s with its clean-lined art moderne–style rooms, as well as an officer's club (democratically open to all) and retro diner. The re-creation isn't taken too far: Rooms have all the mod-cons. Rates—which include one $5 "food ration," good at the diner, per night—run from $120 on weekdays to $170 on weekends. For bargain rates, the old **Frederick Motel** (✆ **800/996-6050;** www.frederick-motel.com), at 1308 East Main St., offers rates from $40 to $100 and, on weekends, includes full breakfast.

See also Rose Hill Manor, in the nearby town of Stonewall, reviewed in the "Lyndon B. Johnson Country" section, below.

WHERE TO DINE

Fredericksburg's dining scene is diverse, catering to the traditional and the trendy alike. For breakfast or lunch, a jewel of a place is **Rather Sweet Bakery & Cafe,** 249 E. Main St. (✆ **830/990-0498**). Rebecca Rather, the owner, is a noted cookbook author, who makes everything from scratch using the freshest ingredients, including home-grown herbs and vegetables. The bakery is open Monday through Saturday until 5pm, but the cafe stops serving lunch at 2pm. For breakfast takeout, you should try **Hilda's Tortilla Factory** (✆ **830/997-6105**) at 149 Tivydale Rd. (at S. Adams St.). This place serves good tacos on fresh-made flour tortillas. "El Especial" has poblano, eggs, beans, bacon, and tomatoes. Be sure to ask for a couple of packs of green sauce. Often there's a line stretching out the door, but it moves quickly.

If you don't mind driving 10 miles, a great place to go for dinner (or for lunch on the weekend) is the **Hill Top Café** (✆ **830/997-8922;** www.hilltopcafe.com), right on Hwy. 87 to Mason. This was an old country gas station that was converted into a restaurant by John and Brenda Nichols. John used to be a member of a legendary Austin band called Asleep at the Wheel. He usually plays music on Friday and Saturday evenings. Brenda runs the kitchen, and the food is well-prepared—American with a smattering of Greek and Cajun dishes. Reservations are highly recommended.

If you've come to Fredericksburg for German food, you can try **Altdorf Biergarten,** 301 W. Main St. (✆ **830/997-7865**), open Wednesday to Monday for lunch and dinner, Sunday for brunch; and **Friedhelm's Bavarian Inn,** 905 W. Main St. (✆ **830/997-6300**), open Tuesday to Sunday for lunch and dinner, both featuring moderately priced, hearty schnitzels, dumplings, and sauerbraten, and large selections of German beer.

Also on main, the **Fredericksburg Brewing Co.,** 245 E. Main St. (✆ **830/997-1646**), offers typical pub food with a few lighter selections. The beer is quite good. Try the Pioneer Porter or the Peace Pipe Pale Ale, both of which have won awards. It's open daily for lunch and dinner; prices are moderate.

Local foodies like to roost in **The Nest,** 607 S. Washington St. (✆ **830/990-8383**), which features updated American cuisine in a lovely old house Thursday through Monday evenings; meals are expensive. Equally popular and a bit more cutting edge, the contemporary-chic **Navajo Grill,** 803 E. Main St. (✆ **830/990-8289**), offers food inspired by New Orleans, the Southwest, and occasionally the Caribbean. It's open nightly for dinner and on Sunday for brunch, and meals are expensive.

Going Back (in Time) to Luckenbach

About 11 miles southeast of Fredericksburg on R.R. 1376, but light-years away in spirit, the town of **Luckenbach** (pop. 25) was immortalized in song by Waylon Jennings and Willie Nelson. The town pretty much consists of a dance hall and a post office/general store/bar. But it's a very mellow place to hang out. Someone's almost always strumming a guitar, and on weekend afternoons and evenings, Jerry Jeff Walker or Robert Earl Keen might be among the names who turn up at the dance hall. Tying the knot? You can rent the dance hall—or even the entire town. Call ✆ **830/997-3224** for details. And to get a feel for the town, log on to www.luckenbachtexas.com.

Whenever you visit, lots of beer is likely to be involved, so consider staying at the **Full Moon Inn,** 3234 Luckenbach Rd., Fredericksburg, TX 78624 (✆ **800/997-1124** or 830/997-2205; www.luckenbachtx.com), just half a mile from the action on a rise overlooking the wildflower-dotted countryside. The best of the accommodations, which range in price from $125 to $200, is the 1800s log cabin, large enough to sleep four. Rooter Boy, the resident pot-bellied pig, is usually around to greet guests.

Another popular dinner spot is the **Cabernet Grill,** 2805 S. Hwy. 16 (✆ **830/990-5734**), which focuses on Texas wines and local produce from area ranches and farms, such as quail and striped bass. Dinner is served Monday through Saturday. Entrees range from moderate to expensive. During the week it offers a lunch buffet that runs $10.

NIGHTLIFE

Yes, Fredericksburg's got nightlife, or at least what passes for it in the Hill Country. Some of the live music action takes place a bit outside of the center of town. On Fridays and Saturdays at the Hill Top Café, John Nichols jams with friends starting at about 7pm. Luckenbach (see above) also hosts lots of good bands.

And lately, Fredericksburg's main (and side) streets have also come alive with the sound of music—everything from rockabilly and jazz to oompah—especially from Thursday through Saturday nights. An offshoot of The Luckenbach Dancehall, **Hondo's on Main,** 312 W. Main St. (✆ **830/997-1633**), also tends to feature Texas roots bands. Check with the Visitor Information Center for a complete weekly listing.

5 LYNDON B. JOHNSON COUNTRY

Fifty miles west of Austin is Johnson City, where the forebears of the 36th president settled almost 150 years ago. Even before he attained the country's highest office, Lyndon Baines Johnson was a local hero whose successful fight for funding a series of dams provided the region with inexpensive water and power. A visit to LBJ's boyhood home (in Johnson City) and the sprawling ranch that became known as the Texas White House (14 miles farther west, near Stonewall), and other attractions can take a whole day. Even if you're not usually drawn to the past, you're likely to be intrigued by the picture of LBJ and his origins that these sites depict.

LBJ NATIONAL HISTORICAL PARK

From Austin, take U.S. 290 west to **Johnson City,** a pleasant agricultural town named for founder James Polk Johnson, LBJ's first cousin once removed. The **Boyhood Home ★**—the house on Elm Street, where Lyndon was raised after age 5—is the centerpiece of this unit of the **Lyndon B. Johnson National Historical Park.** The modest white clapboard structure the family occupied from 1913 was a hub of intellectual and political activity: LBJ's father, Sam Ealy Johnson, Jr., was a state legislator, and his mother, Rebekah, was one of the few college-educated women in the country at the beginning of the 20th century. From here, you can walk over to the **Johnson Settlement,** where LBJ's grandfather, Sam Ealy Johnson, Sr., and his great-uncle, Jessie, engaged in successful cattle speculation in the 1860s. The rustic dogtrot cabin out of which they ran their business is still intact. Before exploring the two sites, stop at the park headquarters and **visitor center** (✆ **830/868-7128**)—from U.S. 290, which turns into Main Street, take F Street to Lady Bird Lane, and you'll see the signs—where a number of interactive displays and two half-hour-long films (one about Johnson's presidency, and the other about Lady Bird) provide background for the buildings you'll see.

The Boyhood Home, visitor center, and Johnson Settlement are all open 8:45am to 5pm daily except Christmas, Thanksgiving, and New Year's Day. Admission is free. The Boyhood Home can be visited only by tours, offered every half-hour, from 9 to 11:30am and 1 to 4:30pm.

STATE PARK & LBJ RANCH

Continue west on Hwy. 290 for 15 miles, and just east of the town of Stonewall you'll see signs for **Lyndon B. Johnson State Park** and the **LBJ Ranch ★**. The first is operated by the Texas Parks and Wildlife Department (✆ **830/644-2252;** www.tpwd.state.tx.us/park/lbj) and the ranch by the National Park Service (✆ **830/868-7128;** www.nps.gov/lyjo). You need to go to the state park visitor center first, so that you can get a free visitor's permit to visit the LBJ Ranch. The visitor center displays interesting memorabilia from Johnson's boyhood, to the still-operating Johnson Ranch. Lady Bird Johnson spent about a third of her time at the Ranch before her death in 2008.

Crossing over the Pedernales River and through fields of phlox, Indian paintbrush, and other wildflowers, you can see why Johnson used the ranch as a second White House, and why, discouraged from running for a second presidential term, he came back here to find solace and, eventually, to die. A reconstruction of the former president's modest birthplace lies close to his (also modest) final resting place, shared with five generations of Johnsons.

On the side of the river from where you started out, period-costumed "occupants" of the **Sauer-Beckmann Living History Farm** give visitors a look at typical Texas-German farm life at the turn of the century. Chickens, pigs, turkeys, and other farm animals roam freely or in large pens, while the farmers go about their chores, which might include churning butter, baking, or feeding the animals. The midwife who attended LBJ's birth grew up here. Interesting in the same way as Colonial Williamsburg, but much less known (and thus not as well funded), this is a terrific place to come with kids. Nearby are nature trails, a swimming pool (open only in summer), and lots of covered picnic spots. The park also keeps a small number of bison for visitor's to view.

All state park buildings, including the visitor center, are open daily 8am to 5pm; the Sauer-Beckmann Living History Farm is open daily 8am to 4:30pm. The Nature Trail, grounds, and picnic areas are open until dark every day. All facilities in both sections of the park are closed Thanksgiving, Christmas, and New Year's Day.

BEYOND LBJ

Johnson City has attractions that have little to do with the 36th president or history, although, perhaps with a little rationalization, you can claim that shopping for antiques is also a history-oriented activity. Several low-key antiques shops dot Main Street; perhaps the best is the **Old Lumber Yard,** 209 E. Main St. (✆ **830/868-2381**), selling reasonably priced items from a variety of eras, including the present one. One of the highlights of the complex is the **Silver K Café** (✆ **830/868-2911**), where soups, salads, and sandwiches are served at lunchtime from Monday to Saturday. From Thursday through Saturday evenings, you might dine on Gulf Coast cioppino, perhaps, or pan-grilled top sirloin with mustard sauce. Prices range from moderate to expensive. If you prefer your meats more portable, visit **Whittington's,** 602 Hwy. 281 S. (✆ **877/868-5501**), renowned around Texas for its beef and turkey jerky (just drop in for a sample; fresh jerky bears little resemblance to the convenience store kind).

The area's top place to dine—and to bed down—isn't in Johnson City, however, but about 16 miles to the west. You'll drive down a rural back road to reach **Rose Hill Manor,** 2614 Upper Albert Rd., Stonewall, TX 78671 (✆ **877/ROSEHIL** [767-3445] or 830/644-2247; www.rose-hill.com), a reconstructed southern manse. Light and airy accommodations—four in the main house, and six in separate cottages—are beautifully but comfortably furnished with antiques. All offer porches or patios and great Hill Country views. Rates run from $155 to $179 on weekdays, and $199 to $249 on weekends. The inn's New American cuisine, served Wednesday through Sunday evenings in an ultraromantic dining room, is outstanding. Reservations are essential; prices are expensive.

The **Johnson Chamber of Commerce and Tourism Bureau,** 604 Hwy. 281 S., Johnson City, TX 78636 (✆ **830/868-7684;** www.johnsoncity-texas.com), can provide information about other local dining, lodging, and shopping options.

If you're heading on to Austin, take a short detour from U.S. 290 to **Pedernales Falls State Park,** 8 miles east of Johnson City on F.R. 2766 (✆ **830/868-7304;** www.tpwd.state.tx.us/park/pedernal). When the flow of the Pedernales River is high, the stepped waterfalls that give the 4,860-acre park its name are quite impressive.

6 THE NORTHERN LAKES

One of the nice things about touring these lakes is that you have to take it slow: The roads that wind around the lakes force you to meander along rural roads rather than drive directly to your destination. And, of course, engaging with that water—whether submerging in it or just gazing at it—is the reason most people come here. For additional information about where to kayak, sail, swim, or fish, check with the chambers of commerce and visitor centers listed in this section.

From Austin, it's 48 miles northwest on Hwy. 71 to the town of **Marble Falls,** known for two natural features, only one of which still exists. The cascades for which the town was named once descended some 20 feet along a series of marble ledges, but they were

Viewing Bluebonnets & Other Wildflowers

Of its many names—*lupinus subcarnosus, lupinus texensis,* buffalo clover, wolf flower, even *el conejo*—bluebonnet is the most descriptive. And when the official state flower of Texas puts in an appearance, starting in March and peaking in April, hordes of people descend on the Hill Country to ogle and photograph the fields of flowers (think East Coast leaf-watching in autumn, only in a more concentrated area and time frame).

To enjoy the bluebonnets and other wildflowers you must be flexible. When the conditions are perfect, they can be blooming everywhere, but sometimes the rains don't fall where they should. In 2008, the northern Hill Country had few wildflowers for lack of rain. Greater numbers were seen in the southern parts, and even more were blooming in the coastal prairies south and east of Austin and San Antonio.

For up-to-date info on where to find the best views of wildflowers in central Texas, contact the **Wildflower Hotline** (aka the National Wildflower Research Center in Austin; see chapter 16) at ✆ **512/929-3600.**

submerged when the Max Starcke Dam, which created Lake Marble Falls, was completed in 1951. (You can occasionally get a peek at the falls when the Lower Colorado River Authority lowers the water level to repair the dam.) The town's other natural claim to fame is the still very visible Granite Mountain, from which the pink granite used to create the state capitol in Austin was quarried.

The main reason most people come to Marble Falls these days is its three parks and two lakes (Lake LBJ lies a little upstream), but it's also pleasant to wander around the center of town, where there are a number of historic homes, antiques shops, and the (new) Old Oak shopping complex, featuring such whimsical gift boutiques as It's All About Me.

One of the town's other attractions is also the place to get details on what to see and do in the area: The **Marble Falls/Lake LBJ Visitor Center,** 801 Hwy. 281 (✆ **800/759-8178** or 830/693-4449; www.marblefalls.org), is located in the Historic Depot Building, built to serve the railroad spur used to transport granite to Austin. The visitor center is open Monday to Friday from 8am to 5pm.

Trains no longer make it to Marble Falls, but they do go to **Burnet,** some 14 miles to the north. The Austin Steam Train Association restored the five historic coaches and the 1916 locomotive that you can board for the **Hill Country Flyer Steam Train Excursion** (✆ **512/477-8468;** www.austinsteamtrain.org), a leisurely 33-mile ride from Cedar Park, a northwest suburb of Austin. The train runs Saturday and Sunday March through May, Saturday only June to November, and selected December evenings. Fares are $28 adults, $25 seniors, and $18 for children in coach with no heat or A/C; or $33, $30, and $23 with heat or A/C; and $43, $39, and $27 for a lounge car ticket. (On some days the train only goes half the distance and is called the Bertram Flyer, and the tickets are correspondingly cheaper.)

The train makes a 3-hour layover on Burnet's historic town square, which, with its impressive courthouse—not to mention its collectibles shops and cafes—is also a good spot for visitors who drive into town to explore. (***Beware:*** A gunfight is staged at 2:30pm on most Saturdays when the train comes in.) Burnet grew up around a U.S. Army post established in 1849, and you can still visit the **Fort Croghan Grounds and Museum,** 703 Buchanan Dr. (Hwy. 29 W.; ✆ **512/756-8281;** www.fortcroghan.org), home to several historic outbuildings and more than 1,200 historic artifacts from around the county. Admission is free; the museum is open April through August, Thursday through Saturday, from 10am to 5pm. In the same complex (but not in a historic building and open year-round) is the **Burnet Chamber of Commerce** (✆ **512/756-4297;** www.burnetchamber.org). Here, among other things, you can find out why Burnet calls itself the Bluebonnet Capital of Texas—and when you should come to see if it lives up to that claim. The chamber is open 8:30am to 5:30pm Monday through Friday.

Some 11 miles southwest of Burnet, **Longhorn Cavern State Park,** Park Road 4, 6 miles off U.S. 281 (✆ **877/441-CAVE** [441-2283] or 830/598-CAVE [598-2283]; www.longhorncaverns.com), has as its centerpiece one of the few river-formed caverns in Texas. Its past visitors include Ice Age animals, Comanche Indians, Confederate soldiers, and members of the Civilian Conservation Corps, who, in the 1930s, built the stairs that descend into the main room. The cave's natural and human history is detailed on narrated tours—the only way you can visit—that last about an hour and a half; they're offered from Labor Day to Memorial Day Monday to Thursday at 11am, 1pm, and 3pm, Friday to Sunday from 10am to 4pm every hour on the hour. In summer, tours run every day on the hour from 10am to 4pm. Admission is $13 adults, $12 for seniors and teens, and $8 ages 2 to 12.

Continue north on Park Road 4, beyond where it intersects with R.R. 2342, and you'll reach **Inks Lake State Park,** 3630 Park Road 4 W. (✆ **512/793-2223;** www.tpwd.state.tx.us/park/inks), offering some 1,200 acres of recreational facilities on and adjacent to the lake for which it's named: hiking trails, canoe and paddle-boat rentals, swimming, fishing—even golf on an 18-hole course. Don't miss Devil's Waterhole, flanked by pink granite boulders and a waterfall. You can canoe through it, hike to it, or just view it from a scenic overlook on Park Road 4.

Those with limited time might want to skip Inks Lake in favor of the oldest, most remote, and largest of the Highland Lakes, the 32-mile-long Lake Buchanan. The best way to see it—and the highlight of any trip to this area—is the **Vanishing Texas River Cruise ★★** (✆ **800/4-RIVER-4** [474-8374] or 512/756-6986; www.vtrc.com), which departs from the Canyon of the Eagles Lodge & Nature Park (see "Where to Stay & Dine," below), at the end of R.R. 2341 on the lake's north shore (call for directions, or check the website). The lake's banks are still startlingly pristine (though private development may soon make the "vanishing" part of the cruise's name too true), and no matter what time of year you come, you're bound to see some wildlife. From November through March, bald eagles troll the skies, while the rest of the year wild turkeys and deer abound. These expertly narrated tours, which offer a lot of historical as well as natural information, vary season by season; prices range from about $20 for adults for the basic $2^1/_2$-hour naturalist tours to $33 for sunset dinner cruises ($30 for children). Reservations are recommended

If you want to get more up close and personal with the water, book one of the kayaking tours run by **Lake Buchanan Adventures** (✆ **512/756-9911;** www.lakebuchananadventures.com), which depart from the same north Lake Buchanan dock as the river

Speaking the Local Lingo

Want to talk like a local?

1. For Buchanan, lake or dam, say "*Buck*-anon," not "*Byou*-kanon." The body of water was named after congressman James Buchanan, who got federal funds to complete the dam in the 1930s, not after the U.S. president.
2. The town of Tow rhymes with "now."
3. Llano is pronounced "*lay*-no."
4. Burnet, town and county, is pronounced "*burn*-it" (as in "Durn it, can't you learn it?").

cruises. A 4-hour trip, which includes a deli lunch at the scenic Fall Creek waterfalls, and all equipment, gear, and experienced guides, runs $95 for adults. Hiking and kayaking trips, overnight camping trips, and boat rentals are available too. Reservations are essential.

WHERE TO STAY & DINE

Rustic lakeside cabins and small motels dot this entire area, but two lodgings stand out. If you head 15 miles east of Marble Falls on FM 1431, you'll reach the town (such as it is) of Kingsland and **The Antlers,** 1001 King St., Kingsland, TX 78639 (✆ **800/383-0007** or 916/388-4411; www.theantlers.com), a restored turn-of-the-century resort occupying 15 acres on Lake LBJ. You've got a choice of bedding down in one of six antiques-filled suites in the 1901 railroad hotel, as President William McKinley did ($120–$140); in one of three colorful converted train cabooses ($120) or a converted railroad coach ($130–$150), parked on a piece of original track; or in one of seven appealing cabins scattered around the grounds ($140–$220). Some of the accommodations sleep four or six people comfortably, and one of the lodges accommodates up to eight. Activities include strolling several nature trails, boating or fishing on the lake, or browsing the antiques shop in the main hotel building. For fortification, cross the road to the Kingsland Old Town Grill, a good place for steak, regular or chicken-fried. Look eerily familiar? This 1890s Victorian house served as the film set for the original *Texas Chainsaw Massacre.*

Opened in 1999 on 940 acres owned by the Lower Colorado River Authority—most of it still wilderness preserve—the **Canyon of the Eagles Lodge & Nature Park,** 16942 R.R. 2341, Burnet, TX 78611 (✆ **800/977-0081** or 512/756-8787; www.canyonofthe eagles.com), is ideal for those seeking serious escape. You can indulge in the Lake Buchanan excursions or adventures described in the previous section, hike the property's trails, stargaze at the lodge's observatory, or just kick back on your porch and watch birds flitting by. The Canyon Room restaurant offers everything from Fredericksburg bratwurst to pecan-crusted trout. Rates for the rooms, which are country-style rustic but feature such conveniences as phones with dataports (in case your escape is not *that* serious) and, in the Cottage Rooms, minifridges and microwaves, range from $130 to $170. A minimum of 2 nights is required for popular weekends, but you wouldn't want to stay less time than that anyway.

In addition to the Kingsland Old Town Grill and the Canyon Room—the latter has the advantage of being BYOB and the disadvantage of being far from most everywhere if you're not staying at the lodge—I'd recommend another place in Marble Falls, which fall at the opposite ends of the history (and sophistication) spectrum. **Blue Bonnet Cafe,** 211 Hwy. 281 (✆ 830/693-2344; www.bluebonnetcafe.net), first opened its doors in 1929 and has received accolades for its down-home country food—chicken-fried steak, pot roast, fried okra. It's open every day for breakfast and lunch, and serves dinner every day except Sunday. Prices are inexpensive to moderate.

If you're in the mood for barbecue and you're in the vicinity of Llano, you can stop by a well-known joint called Cooper's, where the Wootan family has been smoking big meat in a big pit forever, at 505 W. Dallas St. (✆ **325-247-5713;** www.coopersbbq.com). For more information on Texas barbecue and Cooper's, see the barbecue section in the chapter 17. Coopers is open daily 10:30am to 8pm. Prices are inexpensive to moderate.

Fast Facts, Toll-Free Numbers & Websites

1 FAST FACTS: SAN ANTONIO

AMERICAN EXPRESS The Alamo Travel Group, Inc., 9000 Wurzbach Rd. (✆ **210/593-0084**), is open Monday to Friday 9am to 5pm.

AREA CODE The telephone area code in San Antonio is **210.**

AUTOMOBILE ORGANIZATIONS Auto clubs will supply maps, suggested routes, guidebooks, accident and bail-bond insurance, and emergency road service. The **American Automobile Association (AAA)** is the major auto club in the United States. If you belong to an auto club in your home country, inquire about AAA reciprocity before you leave. You may be able to join AAA even if you're not a member of a reciprocal club; to inquire, call AAA (✆ **800/222-4357**). AAA is actually an organization of regional auto clubs, so look under "AAA Automobile Club" in the White Pages of the telephone directory. AAA has a nationwide emergency road service telephone number (✆ **800/AAA-HELP** [222-4357]).

BUSINESS HOURS Banks are usually open Monday to Friday 9am to 4pm, Saturday 9am to 1pm. Drive-up windows are open 7am to 6pm Monday to Friday, and 9am to noon on Saturday. Office hours are generally weekdays from 9am to 5pm. Shops tend to be open from 9 or 10am until 5:30 or 6pm Monday to Saturday, with shorter hours on Sunday. Most malls are open Monday to Saturday from 10am to 9pm, Sunday from noon to 6pm.

CAR RENTALS See "By Car," under the "Getting Around" section of chapter 3.

CLIMATE See "When to Go," in chapter 3.

CURRENCY The most common bills are the $1 (a "buck"), $5, $10, and $20 denominations. There are also $2 bills (seldom encountered), $50 bills, and $100 bills (the last two are usually not welcome as payment for small purchases).

Coins come in seven denominations: 1¢ (1 cent, or a penny); 5¢ (5 cents, or a nickel); 10¢ (10 cents, or a dime); 25¢ (25 cents, or a quarter); 50¢ (50 cents, or a half dollar); the gold-colored Sacagawea coin, worth $1; and the rare silver dollar.

For additional information see "Money," in chapter 3.

DENTIST To find a dentist near you in town, contact the San Antonio District Dental Society, 3355 Cherry Ridge, Ste. 214 (✆ **210/732-1264**).

DOCTOR For a referral, contact the Bexar County Medical Society at 6243 W. IH 10, Ste. 600 (✆ **210/301-4368;** www.bcms.org), Monday through Friday from 8am to 5pm.

DRIVING RULES See "Getting Around," chapter 3.

DRUGSTORES Most branches of CVS (formerly Eckerd) and Walgreens, the major chain pharmacies in San Antonio, are open late Monday through Saturday. There's a CVS downtown at 211 Losoya/

River Walk (✆ **210/224-9293**). Call ✆ **800/925-4733** to find the Walgreens nearest you; punch in the area code and the first three digits of the number you're phoning from and you'll be directed to the closest branch.

ELECTRICITY Like Canada, the United States uses 110 to 120 volts AC (60 cycles), compared to 220 to 240 volts AC (50 cycles) in most of Europe, Australia, and New Zealand. If your small appliances use 220 to 240 volts, you'll need a 110-volt transformer and a plug adapter with two flat parallel pins to operate them here. Downward converters that change 220 to 240 volts to 110 to 120 volts are difficult to find in the United States, so bring one with you.

EMBASSIES/CONSULATES All embassies are located in the nation's capital, Washington, D.C. Some consulates are located in major U.S. cities, and most nations have a mission to the United Nations in New York City. If your country isn't listed below, call for directory information in Washington, D.C. (✆ **202/555-1212**), or log on to **www.embassy.org/embassies**.

The embassy of **Australia** is at 1601 Massachusetts Ave. NW, Washington, DC 20036 (✆ **202/797-3000;** www.austemb.org). There are consulates in New York, Honolulu, Houston, Los Angeles, and San Francisco.

The embassy of **Canada** is at 501 Pennsylvania Ave. NW, Washington, DC 20001 (✆ **202/682-1740;** www.canadianembassy.org). Other Canadian consulates are in Buffalo (New York), Detroit, Los Angeles, New York, and Seattle.

The embassy of **Ireland** is at 2234 Massachusetts Ave. NW, Washington, DC 20008 (✆ **202/462-3939;** www.irelandemb.org). Irish consulates are in Boston, Chicago, New York, San Francisco, and other cities. See their website for a complete listing.

The embassy of **New Zealand** is at 37 Observatory Circle NW, Washington, DC 20008 (✆ **202/328-4800;** www.nzemb.org). New Zealand consulates are in Los Angeles, Salt Lake City, San Francisco, and Seattle.

The embassy of the **United Kingdom** is at 3100 Massachusetts Ave. NW, Washington, DC 20008 (✆ **202/588-7800;** www.britainusa.com). Other British consulates are in Atlanta, Boston, Chicago, Cleveland, Houston, Los Angeles, New York, San Francisco, and Seattle.

EMERGENCIES For police, fire, or medical emergencies, dial ✆ **911.**

GASOLINE (PETROL) Petrol is known as gasoline (or simply "gas") in the United States, and petrol stations are known as both gas stations and service stations. Gasoline costs about half as much here as it does in Europe (about $2 per gallon at press time), and taxes are already included in the printed price. One U.S. gallon equals 3.8 liters or .85 imperial gallons.

HOLIDAYS Banks, government offices, post offices, and many stores, restaurants, and museums are closed on the following legal national holidays: January 1 (New Year's Day), the third Monday in January (Martin Luther King, Jr., Day), the third Monday in February (Presidents' Day), the last Monday in May (Memorial Day), July 4th (Independence Day), the first Monday in September (Labor Day), the second Monday in October (Columbus Day), November 11 (Veterans' Day/Armistice Day), the fourth Thursday in November (Thanksgiving Day), and December 25 (Christmas). Also, the Tuesday following the first Monday in November is Election Day and is a federal government holiday in presidential-election years (held every 4 years, and next in 2012).

HOSPITALS The main downtown hospital is Baptist Medical Center, 111 Dallas St. (✆ **210/297-7000**). Christus Santa Rosa Health Care Corp., 333 N. Santa

Rosa St. (✆ **210/704-2011**), is also downtown. Contact the San Antonio Medical Foundation (✆ **210/614-3724**) for information about other medical facilities in the city.

HOT LINES Contact the National Youth Crisis Hot Line at ✆ **800/448-4663;** Rape Crisis Hot Line at ✆ **210/349-7273;** Child Abuse Hot Line at ✆ **800/252-5400;** Mental Illness Crisis Hot Line at ✆ **210/227-4357;** Bexar County Adult Abuse Hot Line at ✆ **800/252-5400;** and Poison Control Center at ✆ **800/764-7661.**

INFORMATION See "Visitor Information," below.

INTERNET See the "Staying Connected" section in chapter 3.

LEGAL AID If you are "pulled over" for a minor infraction (such as speeding), never attempt to pay the fine directly to a police officer; this could be construed as attempted bribery, a much more serious crime. Pay fines by mail, or directly into the hands of the clerk of the court. If accused of a more serious offense, say and do nothing before consulting a lawyer. Here the burden is on the state to prove a person's guilt beyond a reasonable doubt, and everyone has the right to remain silent, whether he or she is suspected of a crime or actually arrested. Once arrested, a person can make one telephone call to a party of his or her choice. Call your embassy or consulate.

LIBRARIES San Antonio's magnificent main library is located downtown at 600 Soledad Plaza (✆ **210/207-2500**). See "More Attractions," in chapter 7 for details.

LIQUOR LAWS The legal drinking age in Texas is 21. Under-age drinkers can legally imbibe as long as they stay within sight of their legal-age parents or spouses, but they need to be prepared to show proof of the relationship. Open containers are prohibited in public and in vehicles. Liquor laws are strictly enforced; if you're concerned, check www.tabc.state.tx.us for the entire Texas alcoholic beverage code. Bars close at 2am.

LOST PROPERTY Be sure to tell all of your credit card companies the minute you discover your wallet has been lost or stolen and file a report at the nearest police precinct. Your credit card company or insurer may require a police report number or record of the loss. Most credit card companies have an emergency toll-free number to call if your card is lost or stolen; they may be able to wire you a cash advance immediately or deliver an emergency credit card in a day or two. Visa's U.S. emergency number is ✆ **800/847-2911** or 410/581-9994. American Express cardholders and traveler's check holders should call ✆ **800/221-7282.** MasterCard holders should call ✆ **800/307-7309** or 636/722-7111. For other credit cards, call the toll-free number directory at ✆ **800/555-1212.**

If you need emergency cash over the weekend when all banks and American Express offices are closed, you can have money wired to you via **Western Union** (✆ **800/325-6000;** www.westernunion.com).

MAIL At press time, domestic postage rates were 27¢ for a postcard and 42¢ for a letter. For international mail, a first-class letter of up to 1 ounce costs 94¢ (72¢ to Canada and Mexico); a first-class postcard costs 90¢ (69¢ to Canada and Mexico). For more information, go to **www.usps.com** and click on "Calculate Postage."

If you aren't sure what your address will be in the United States, mail can be sent to you in your name, c/o General Delivery, at the main post office of the city or region where you expect to be. (Call ✆ **800/275-8777** for information on the nearest post office.) The addressee must pick up mail in person and must produce proof of identity (driver's license, passport, and so on). Most post offices will hold your mail for up to 1 month, and are open Monday to Friday from 8am to 6pm, and Saturday from 9am to 3pm.

Generally found at intersections, mailboxes are blue with a red-and-white stripe and carry the inscription U.S. MAIL. If your mail is addressed to a U.S. destination, don't forget to add the five-digit postal code (or zip code), after the two-letter abbreviation of the state to which the mail is addressed. This is essential for prompt delivery.

NEWSPAPERS & MAGAZINES The *San Antonio Express-News* is the only mainstream source of news in town. See "Visitor Information," in chapter 3 for more publications.

PASSPORTS **For Residents of Australia:** You can pick up an application from your local post office or any branch of Passports Australia, but you must schedule an interview at the passport office to present your application materials. Call the **Australian Passport Information Service** at ✆ **131-232,** or visit the government website at www.passports.gov.au.

For Residents of Canada: Passport applications are available at travel agencies throughout Canada or from the central **Passport Office,** Department of Foreign Affairs and International Trade, Ottawa, ON K1A 0G3 (✆ **800/567-6868;** www.ppt.gc.ca). ***Note:*** Canadian children who travel must have their own passport. However, if you hold a valid Canadian passport issued before December 11, 2001, that bears the name of your child, the passport remains valid for you and your child until it expires.

For Residents of Ireland: You can apply for a 10-year passport at the **Passport Office,** Setanta Centre, Molesworth Street, Dublin 2 (✆ **01/671-1633;** www.irlgov.ie/iveagh). Those under age 18 and over age 65 must apply for a 3-year passport. You can also apply at 1A South Mall, Cork (✆ **021/272-525**) or at most main post offices.

For Residents of New Zealand: You can pick up a passport application at any New Zealand Passports Office or download it from their website. Contact the **Passports Office** at ✆ **0800/225-050** in New Zealand or 04/474-8100, or log on to www.passports.govt.nz.

For Residents of the United Kingdom: To pick up an application for a standard 10-year passport (5-yr. passport for children under age 16), visit your nearest passport office, major post office, or travel agency or contact the **United Kingdom Passport Service** at ✆ **0870/521-0410** or search its website at www.ukpa.gov.uk.

POLICE Call ✆ **911** in an emergency. For non-emergency calls, dial ✆ **311.**

POST OFFICE The city's most convenient post office for visitors is at 615 Houston St., at North Alamo Street, in the San Antonio Federal Building.

SAFETY The crime rate in San Antonio has gone down in recent years, and there's a strong police presence downtown (in fact, both the transit authority and the police department have bicycle patrols); as a result, muggings, pickpocketings, and purse snatchings in the area are rare. Still, use common sense as you would anywhere else: Walk only in well-lit, well-populated streets. Also, it's generally not a good idea to stroll south of Durango Avenue after dark.

SMOKING Smoking is prohibited in all public buildings and common public areas (that includes hotel lobbies, museums, enclosed malls, and so on). It's permitted in bars or enclosed bar areas of restaurants, on designated restaurant patios, and in smoking sections of restaurants that comply with city codes.

TAXES The sales tax here is 8.25%, and the city surcharge on hotel rooms increases to a whopping 16.75%.

TAXIS Call Yellow-Checker Cab (✆ **210/222-2222**).

TIME ZONE San Antonio and Austin (and all of the rest of Texas except for the El Paso area) are in the Central Time zone. The continental United States is divided into **four time zones:** Eastern Standard Time (EST), Central Standard Time (CST), Mountain Standard Time (MST), and Pacific Standard Time (PST). Alaska and Hawaii have their own zones. For example, noon in New York City (EST) is 11am in Chicago (CST), 10am in Denver (MST), 9am in Los Angeles (PST), 8am in Anchorage (AST), and 7am in Honolulu (HST).

Daylight saving time is in effect from 2am on the second Sunday in March through 2am on the first Sunday in November, except in Arizona, Hawaii, the U.S. Virgin Islands, and Puerto Rico. Daylight saving time moves the clock 1 hour ahead of standard time.

TIPPING Tips are a very important part of certain workers' income, and gratuities are the standard way of showing appreciation for services provided. (Tipping is certainly not compulsory if the service is poor!) In hotels, tip **bellhops** at least $1 per bag ($2–$3 per bag if you have a lot of luggage) and tip the **chamber staff** $1 to $2 per day (more if you've left a disaster area for him or her to clean up). Tip the **doorman** or **concierge** only if he or she has provided you with some specific service (for example, calling a cab for you or obtaining difficult-to-get theater tickets). Tip the **valet-parking attendant** $1 every time you get your car.

In restaurants, bars, and nightclubs, tip **service staff** 15% to 20% of the check, tip **bartenders** 10% to 15%, tip **checkroom attendants** $1 per garment, and tip **valet-parking attendants** $1 per vehicle.

As for other service personnel, tip **cab drivers** 15% of the fare; tip **skycaps** at airports at least $1 per bag ($2–$3 per bag if you have a lot of luggage); and tip **hairdressers** and **barbers** 15% to 20%.

TOILETS You won't find public toilets or "restrooms" on the streets in most U.S. cities, but they can be found in hotel lobbies, bars, restaurants, museums, department stores, railway and bus stations, and service stations. Large hotels and fast-food restaurants are probably the best bet for good, clean facilities. If possible, avoid the toilets at parks and beaches, which tend to be dirty; some may be unsafe. Restaurants and bars in resorts or heavily visited areas may reserve their restrooms for patrons. Some establishments display a notice indicating this. You can ignore this sign or, better yet, avoid arguments by paying for a cup of coffee or a soft drink, which will qualify you as a patron.

USEFUL PHONE NUMBERS For transit information, call ✆ **210/362-2020;** call ✆ **210/226-3232** for time and temperature.

VISAS For information about U.S. Visas go to **http://travel.state.gov** and click on "Visas." Or go to one of the following websites:

Australian citizens can obtain up-to-date visa information from the **U.S. Embassy Canberra,** Moonah Place, Yarralumla, ACT 2600 (✆ **02/6214-5600**) or by checking the U.S. Diplomatic Mission's website at **http://usembassy-australia.state.gov/consular**.

British subjects can obtain up-to-date visa information by calling the **U.S. Embassy Visa Information Line** (✆ **0891/200-290**) or by visiting the "Visas to the U.S." section of the American Embassy London's website at **www.usembassy.org.uk**.

Irish citizens can obtain up-to-date visa information through the **Embassy of the USA Dublin,** 42 Elgin Rd., Dublin 4, Ireland (✆ **353/1-668-8777**), or by checking the "Consular Services" section of the website at **http://dublin.usembassy.gov**.

Citizens of **New Zealand** can obtain up-to-date visa information by contacting the **U.S. Embassy New Zealand,** 29 Fitzherbert Terrace, Thorndon, Wellington (© **644/472-2068**), or get the information directly from the "For New Zealanders" section of the website at **http://wellington.usembassy.gov**.

VISITOR INFORMATION San Antonio Visitor Information Center (© **210/207-6748**) is at 317 Alamo Plaza, across from the Alamo.

2 FAST FACTS: AUSTIN

AMERICAN EXPRESS The branch at 10710 Research Blvd., Ste. 328 (© **512/452-8166;** www.americanexpress.com), is open Monday to Friday 9am to 5:30pm, Saturday 10am to 2pm.

AREA CODE The telephone area code in Austin is **512.**

BUSINESS HOURS Banks are usually open Monday to Friday 9am to 4pm, Saturday 9am to 1pm. Drive-up windows are open 7am to 6pm Monday to Friday, and 9am to noon on Saturday. Office hours are generally weekdays from 9am to 5pm. Shops tend to be open from 9 or 10am until 5:30 or 6pm Monday to Saturday, with shorter hours on Sunday. Most malls are open Monday to Saturday from 10am to 9pm, Sunday from noon to 6pm.

CAR RENTALS See "By Car," under the "Getting Around" section of chapter 3.

CLIMATE See "When to Go," in chapter 3.

DENTIST Call the Dental Referral Service at © **800/917-6453.**

DOCTOR The Medical Exchange (© **512/458-1121**) and Seton Hospital (© **512/324-4450**) both have physician referral services.

DRIVING RULES See "Getting Around," chapter 3.

DRUGSTORES You'll find many Walgreens, Eckerd, and Randalls drugstores around the city; most H-E-B grocery stores also have pharmacies. Several Walgreens are open 24 hours. Have your zip code ready and call © **800/925-4733** to find the Walgreens branch nearest you.

EMBASSIES/CONSULATES See above.

EMERGENCIES Call © **911** if you need the police, the fire department, or an ambulance.

HOSPITALS Brackenridge, 601 E. 15th St. (© **512/324-7000**); St. David's, 919 E. 32nd St., at I-35 (© **512/397-4240**); and Seton Medical Center, 1201 W. 38th St. (© **512/324-1000**), have good and convenient emergency-care facilities.

HOT LINES Crisis Hot Line (© **512/472-4357**); Poison Center (© **800/764-7661**); Domestic Violence Crisis Hot Line (© **512/928-9070**); Sexual Assault Crisis Hot Line (© **512/440-7273**).

INTERNET See the "Staying Connected" section in chapter 3.

LIBRARIES Downtown's Faulk Central Library, 800 Guadalupe St. (© **512/974-7400**), and adjoining Austin History Center, 810 Guadalupe St. (© **512/974-7480**), are excellent information resources. To find the closest local branch, log on to **www.ci.austin.tx.us/library**.

LIQUOR LAWS The legal drinking age in Texas is 21. Under-age drinkers can legally imbibe as long as they stay within sight of their legal-age parents or spouses, but they need to be prepared to show proof of the relationship. Open containers are prohibited in public and in vehicles. Liquor laws are strictly enforced; if you're concerned, check www.tabc.state.tx.us for the entire Texas alcoholic beverage code. Bars close at 2am.

LOST PROPERTY Be sure to tell all of your credit card companies the minute you discover your wallet has been lost or stolen and file a report at the nearest police precinct. Your credit card company or insurer may require a police report number or record of the loss. Most credit card companies have an emergency toll-free number to call if your card is lost or stolen; they may be able to wire you a cash advance immediately or deliver an emergency credit card in a day or two. Visa's U.S. emergency number is © **800/847-2911** or 410/581-9994. American Express cardholders and traveler's check holders should call © **800/221-7282.** MasterCard holders should call © **800/307-7309** or 636/722-7111. For other credit cards, call the toll-free number directory at © **800/555-1212.**

If you need emergency cash over the weekend when all banks and American Express offices are closed, you can have money wired to you via **Western Union** (© **800/325-6000;** www.westernunion.com).

NEWSPAPERS/MAGAZINES The daily *Austin American-Statesman* (www.austin360.com) is the only large-circulation, mainstream newspaper in town. The *Austin Chronicle* (www.auschron.com), a free alternative weekly, focuses on the arts, entertainment, and politics. Monday through Friday, the University of Texas publishes the surprisingly sophisticated *Daily Texan* (www.dailytexanonline.com) newspaper, covering everything from on-campus news to international events.

POLICE Call © **911** in an emergency. The non-emergency number for the Austin Police Department is © **311.**

POST OFFICE The city's main post office is located at 8225 Cross Park Dr. (© **512/342-1252**); more convenient for visitors are the Capitol Station, 111 E. 17th St., in the LBJ Building; and the Downtown Station, 510 Guadalupe St. For information on other locations, phone © **800/275-8777.**

SAFETY Austin has been ranked one of the five safest cities in the United States, but that doesn't mean you can throw common sense to the wind. It's never a good idea to walk down dark streets alone at night, and major tourist areas always attract pickpockets, so keep your purse or wallet in a safe place. Although Sixth Street itself tends to be busy, use caution on the side streets in the area.

SMOKING Smoking is prohibited in all public buildings and common public areas (that includes hotel lobbies, museums, enclosed malls, and so on). It's also prohibited in enclosed bars or enclosed bar areas of restaurants. But it is permitted in open-air bar areas.

TAXES The tax on hotel rooms is 15%. Sales tax, added to restaurant bills as well as to other purchases, is 8.25%.

TAXIS Call American Yellow Checker Cab (© **512/452-9999**).

TRANSIT INFORMATION Call Capital Metro Transit (© **800/474-1201,** or 512/474-1200 from local pay phones; TTY 512/385-5872).

USEFUL TELEPHONE NUMBERS Get the time and temperature by dialing © **512/476-7744.**

VISITOR INFORMATION The Austin Visitor Center (© **866/GO-AUSTIN** [462-8784]) is at 209 E. Sixth St.

3 TOLL-FREE NUMBERS & WEBSITES

MAJOR U.S. AIRLINES

(*flies internationally as well)

American Airlines*
✆ 800/433-7300 (in U.S. or Canada)
✆ 020/7365-0777 (in U.K.)
www.aa.com

Continental Airlines*
✆ 800/523-3273 (in U.S. or Canada)
✆ 084/5607-6760 (in U.K.)
www.continental.com

Delta Air Lines*
✆ 800/221-1212 (in U.S. or Canada)
✆ 084/5600-0950 (in U.K.)
www.delta.com

Northwest Airlines
✆ 800/225-2525 (in U.S.)
✆ 870/0507-4074 (in U.K.)
www.flynaa.com

United Airlines*
✆ 800/864-8331 (in U.S. and Canada)
✆ 084/5844-4777 (in U.K.)
www.united.com

US Airways*
✆ 800/428-4322 (in U.S. and Canada)
✆ 084/5600-3300 (in U.K.)
www.usairways.com

MAJOR INTERNATIONAL AIRLINES

Aeroméxico
✆ 800/237-6639 (in U.S.)
✆ 020/7801-6234 (in U.K., information only)
www.aeromexico.com

Air France
✆ 800/237-2747 (in U.S.)
✆ 800/375-8723 (in U.S. and Canada)
✆ 087/0142-4343 (in U.K.)
www.airfrance.com

Air India
✆ 212/407-1371 (in U.S.)
✆ 91 22 2279 6666 (in India)
✆ 020/8745-1000 (in U.K.)
www.airindia.com

Alitalia
✆ 800/223-5730 (in U.S.)
✆ 800/361-8336 (in Canada)
✆ 087/0608-6003 (in U.K.)
www.alitalia.com

American Airlines
✆ 800/433-7300 (in U.S. and Canada)
✆ 020/7365-0777 (in U.K.)
www.aa.com

British Airways
✆ 800/247-9297 (in U.S. and Canada)
✆ 087/0850-9850 (in U.K.)
www.british-airways.com

China Airlines
✆ 800/227-5118 (in U.S.)
✆ 022/715-1212 (in Taiwan)
www.china-airlines.com

Continental Airlines
✆ 800/523-3273 (in U.S. and Canada)
✆ 084/5607-6760 (in U.K.)
www.continental.com

Delta Air Lines
✆ 800/221-1212 (in U.S. and Canada)
✆ 084/5600-0950 (in U.K.)
www.delta.com

EgyptAir
✆ 212/581-5600 (in U.S.)
✆ 09/007-0000 (in Egypt)
✆ 020/7734-2343 (in U.K.)
www.egyptair.com

El Al Airlines
✆ 972/3977-1111 (outside Israel)
✆ *2250 (from any phone in Israel)
www.elal.com

Finnair
✆ 800/950-5000 (in U.S. and Canada)
✆ 087/0241-4411 (in U.K.)
www.finnair.com

Iberia Airlines
✆ 800/722-4642 (in U.S. and Canada)
✆ 087/0609-0500 (in U.K.)
www.iberia.com

Japan Airlines
✆ 012/025-5931 (international)
www.jal.com

Lufthansa
✆ 800/399-5838 (in U.S.)
✆ 800/563-5954 (in Canada)
✆ 087/0837-7747 (in U.K.)
www.lufthansa.com

Olympic Airlines
✆ 800/223-1226 (in U.S.)
✆ 514/878-9691 (in Canada)
✆ 087/0606-0460 (in U.K.)
www.olympicairlines.com

Qantas Airways
✆ 800/223-1226 (in U.S.)
✆ 084/5774-7767 (in Canada or U.K.)
✆ 13 13 13 (in Australia)
www.quantas.com

Swiss Air
✆ 877/359-7947 (in U.S. and Canada)
✆ 084/5601-0956 (in U.K.)
www.swiss.com

Turkish Airlines
✆ 90 212 444 0 849
www.thy.com

United Airlines*
✆ 800/864-8331 (in U.S. and Canada)
✆ 084/5844-4777 (in U.K.)
www.united.com

US Airways*
✆ 800/428-4322 (in U.S. and Canada)
✆ 084/5600-3300 (in U.K.)
www.usairways.com

BUDGET AIRLINES

Air Berlin
✆ 087/1500-0737 (in U.K.)
✆ 018/0573-7800 (in Germany)
✆ 180/573-7800 (all others)
www.airberlin.com

CAR-RENTAL AGENCIES

Auto Europe
✆ 888/223-5555 (in U.S. and Canada)
✆ 0800/2235-5555 (in U.K.)
www.autoeurope.com

Avis
✆ 800/331-1212 (in U.S. and Canada)
✆ 084/4581-8181 (in U.K.)
www.avis.com

Budget
✆ 800/527-0700 (in U.S.)
✆ 800/268-8900 (in Canada)
✆ 087/0156-5656 (in U.K.)
www.budget.com

Dollar
✆ 800/800-4000 (in U.S.)
✆ 800/848-8268 (in Canada)
✆ 080/8234-7524 (in U.K.)
www.dollar.com

Enterprise
✆ 800/261-7331 (in U.S.)
✆ 514/355-4028 (in Canada)
✆ 012/9360-9090 (in U.K.)
www.enterprise.com

Hertz
✆ 800/645-3131 (in U.S.)
✆ 800/654-3001 (international)
www.hertz.com

Kemwel (KHA)
✆ 877/820-0668 (international)
www.kemwel.com

MAJOR HOTEL & MOTEL CHAINS

Best Western International
✆ 800/780-7234 (in U.S. and Canada)
✆ 0800/393-130 (in U.K.)
www.bestwestern.com

Crowne Plaza Hotels
✆ 888/303-1746 (international)
www.ichotelsgroup.com/crowneplaza

Four Seasons
✆ 800/819-5053 (in U.S. and Canada)
✆ 0800/6488-6488 (in U.K.)
www.fourseasons.com

Hilton Hotels
✆ 800/HILTONS (800/445-8667; in U.S. and Canada)
✆ 087/0590-9090 (in U.K.)
www.hilton.com

Holiday Inn
✆ 800/315-2621 (in U.S. and Canada)
✆ 0800/405-060 (in U.K.)
www.holidayinn.com

Hyatt
✆ 888/591-1234 (in U.S. and Canada)
✆ 084/5888-1234 (in U.K.)
www.hyatt.com

InterContinental Hotels & Resorts
✆ 800/424-6835 (in U.S. and Canada)
✆ 0800/1800-1800 (in U.K.)
www.ichotelsgroup.com

Marriott
✆ 877/236-2427 (in U.S. and Canada)
✆ 0800/221-222 (in U.K.)
www.marriott.com

Radisson Hotels & Resorts
✆ 888/201-1718 (in U.S. and Canada)
✆ 0800/374-411 (in U.K.)
www.radisson.com

Ramada Worldwide
✆ 888/2-RAMADA (888/272-6232; in U.S. and Canada)
✆ 080/8100-0783 (in U.K.)
www.ramada.com

Sheraton Hotels & Resorts
✆ 800/325-3535 (in U.S.)
✆ 800/543-4300 (in Canada)
✆ 0800/3253-5353 (in U.K.)
www.starwoodhotels.com/sheraton

Westin Hotels & Resorts
✆ 800-937-8461 (in U.S. and Canada)
✆ 0800/3259-5959 (in U.K.)
www.starwoodhotels.com/westin

INDEX

See also Accommodations and Restaurant indexes, below.

Accommodations—San Antonio and Environs

Accommodations—Austin and Environs

Accommodations—the Hill Country

Restaurants—San Antonio and Environs

Restaurants—Austin and Environs

Restaurants—The Hill Country

A Guide for Every Type of Traveler

Frommer's Complete Guides
For those who value complete coverage, candid advice, and lots of choices in all price ranges.

Pauline Frommer's Guides
For those who want to experience a culture, meet locals, and save money along the way.

MTV Guides
For hip, youthful travelers who want a fresh perspective on today's hottest cities and destinations.

Day by Day Guides
For leisure or business travelers who want to organize their time to get the most out of a trip.

Frommer's With Kids Guides
For families traveling with children ages 2 to 14 seeking kid-friendly hotels, restaurants, and activities.

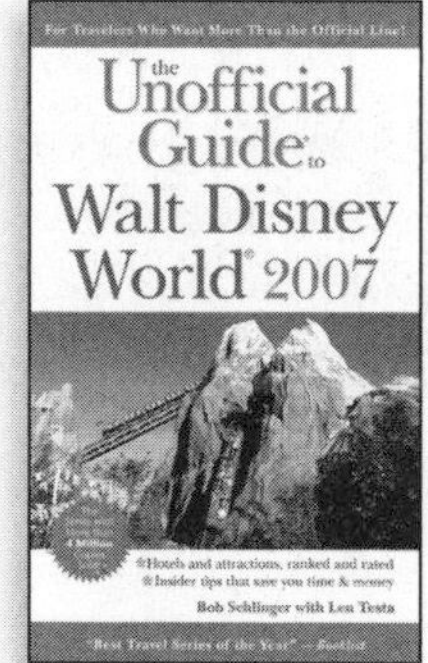

Unofficial Guides
For honeymooners, families, business travelers, and others who value no-nonsense, *Consumer Reports*–style advice.

For Dummies Travel Guides
For curious, independent travelers looking for a fun and easy way to plan a trip.

Visit Frommers.com

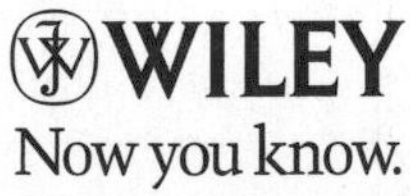

Frommer's® Complete Travel Guides

Alaska
Amalfi Coast
American Southwest
Amsterdam
Argentina
Arizona
Atlanta
Australia
Austria
Bahamas
Barcelona
Beijing
Belgium, Holland & Luxembourg
Belize
Bermuda
Boston
Brazil
British Columbia & the Canadian Rockies
Brussels & Bruges
Budapest & the Best of Hungary
Buenos Aires
Calgary
California
Canada
Cancún, Cozumel & the Yucatán
Cape Cod, Nantucket & Martha's Vineyard
Caribbean
Caribbean Ports of Call
Carolinas & Georgia
Chicago
Chile & Easter Island
China
Colorado
Costa Rica
Croatia
Cuba
Denmark
Denver, Boulder & Colorado Springs
Eastern Europe
Ecuador & the Galapagos Islands
Edinburgh & Glasgow
England
Europe
Europe by Rail
Florence, Tuscany & Umbria
Florida
France
Germany
Greece
Greek Islands
Guatemala
Hawaii
Hong Kong
Honolulu, Waikiki & Oahu
India
Ireland
Israel
Italy
Jamaica
Japan
Kauai
Las Vegas
London
Los Angeles
Los Cabos & Baja
Madrid
Maine Coast
Maryland & Delaware
Maui
Mexico
Montana & Wyoming
Montréal & Québec City
Morocco
Moscow & St. Petersburg
Munich & the Bavarian Alps
Nashville & Memphis
New England
Newfoundland & Labrador
New Mexico
New Orleans
New York City
New York State
New Zealand
Northern Italy
Norway
Nova Scotia, New Brunswick & Prince Edward Island
Oregon
Paris
Peru
Philadelphia & the Amish Country
Portugal
Prague & the Best of the Czech Republic
Provence & the Riviera
Puerto Rico
Rome
San Antonio & Austin
San Diego
San Francisco
Santa Fe, Taos & Albuquerque
Scandinavia
Scotland
Seattle
Seville, Granada & the Best of Andalusia
Shanghai
Sicily
Singapore & Malaysia
South Africa
South America
South Florida
South Korea
South Pacific
Southeast Asia
Spain
Sweden
Switzerland
Tahiti & French Polynesia
Texas
Thailand
Tokyo
Toronto
Turkey
USA
Utah
Vancouver & Victoria
Vermont, New Hampshire & Maine
Vienna & the Danube Valley
Vietnam
Virgin Islands
Virginia
Walt Disney World® & Orlando
Washington, D.C.
Washington State

Frommer's® Day by Day Guides

Amsterdam
Barcelona
Beijing
Boston
Cancun & the Yucatan
Chicago
Florence & Tuscany
Hong Kong
Honolulu & Oahu
London
Maui
Montréal
Napa & Sonoma
New York City
Paris
Provence & the Riviera
Rome
San Francisco
Venice
Washington D.C.

Pauline Frommer's Guides: See More. Spend Less.

Alaska
Hawaii
Italy
Las Vegas
London
New York City
Paris
Walt Disney World®
Washington D.C.

Frommer's® Portable Guides

Acapulco, Ixtapa & Zihuatanejo
Amsterdam
Aruba, Bonaire & Curacao
Australia's Great Barrier Reef
Bahamas
Big Island of Hawaii
Boston
California Wine Country
Cancún
Cayman Islands
Charleston
Chicago
Dominican Republic
Florence
Las Vegas
Las Vegas for Non-Gamblers
London
Maui
Nantucket & Martha's Vineyard
New Orleans
New York City
Paris
Portland
Puerto Rico
Puerto Vallarta, Manzanillo & Guadalajara
Rio de Janeiro
San Diego
San Francisco
Savannah
St. Martin, Sint Maarten, Anguila & St. Bart's
Turks & Caicos
Vancouver
Venice
Virgin Islands
Washington, D.C.
Whistler

Frommer's® Cruise Guides

Alaska Cruises & Ports of Call
Cruises & Ports of Call
European Cruises & Ports of Call

Frommer's® National Park Guides

Algonquin Provincial Park
Banff & Jasper
Grand Canyon
National Parks of the American West
Rocky Mountain
Yellowstone & Grand Teton
Yosemite and Sequoia & Kings Canyon
Zion & Bryce Canyon

Frommer's® With Kids Guides

Chicago
Hawaii
Las Vegas
London
National Parks
New York City
San Francisco
Toronto
Walt Disney World® & Orlando
Washington, D.C.

Frommer's® PhraseFinder Dictionary Guides

Chinese
French
German
Italian
Japanese
Spanish

Suzy Gershman's Born to Shop Guides

France
Hong Kong, Shanghai & Beijing
Italy
London
New York
Paris
San Francisco
Where to Buy the Best of Everything.

Frommer's® Best-Loved Driving Tours

Britain
California
France
Germany
Ireland
Italy
New England
Northern Italy
Scotland
Spain
Tuscany & Umbria

The Unofficial Guides®

Adventure Travel in Alaska
Beyond Disney
California with Kids
Central Italy
Chicago
Cruises
Disneyland®
England
Hawaii
Ireland
Las Vegas
London
Maui
Mexico's Best Beach Resorts
Mini Mickey
New Orleans
New York City
Paris
San Francisco
South Florida including Miami & the Keys
Walt Disney World®
Walt Disney World® for Grown-ups
Walt Disney World® with Kids
Washington, D.C.

Special-Interest Titles

Athens Past & Present
Best Places to Raise Your Family
Cities Ranked & Rated
500 Places to Take Your Kids Before They Grow Up
Frommer's Best Day Trips from London
Frommer's Best RV & Tent Campgrounds in the U.S.A.
Frommer's Exploring America by RV
Frommer's NYC Free & Dirt Cheap
Frommer's Road Atlas Europe
Frommer's Road Atlas Ireland
Retirement Places Rated